PERCEPTUAL DEVELOPMENT

Perceptual development: Visual, auditory, and speech perception in infancy

edited by

Alan Slater *University of Exeter, UK*

Psychology Press
a member of the Taylor & Francis group

Psychology Press Ltd., Publishers
27 Church Road
Hove
East Sussex, BN3 2FA
UK

British Library Cataloguing in Publication Data

A catalogue record for this book is available from the British Library.

   ISBN 0–86377–850–X (Hbk)
   ISBN 0–86377–851–8 (Pbk)

Phototypeset by Intype London Ltd
Printed and bound in the UK by Biddles Ltd, Guildford and King's Lynn

Contents

List of Contributors

Geoffrey Amsel, Department of Psychology, University of Texas at Austin, TX 78712, USA.

Marianella Casasola, Department of Psychology, University of Texas at Austin, TX 78712, USA.

Leslie B. Cohen, Department of Psychology, University of Texas at Austin, TX 78712, USA.

Michelle de Haan, MRC Cognitive Development Unit, 4 Taviton Street, London, WC1H 0BT, UK.

Renee Desjardins, Department of Psychology, University of British Columbia, Vancouver, BC, Canada V6T 1Z4.

Alistair R. Fielder, Academic Unit of Ophthalmology, The Western Eye Hospital, Imperial College School of Medicine, Marylebone Road, London NW1 5YE, UK.

Mara Goodman, Department of Psychology, State University of New York at Buffalo, Buffalo, NY 14260, USA.

Ian Gordon, Department of Psychology, University of Exeter, Washington Singer Laboratories, Exeter EX4 4QG, UK.

Louise Hainline, Infant Study Center, Brooklyn College of the City University of New York, 2900 Bedford Avenue, Brooklyn, NY 11210–2899, USA.

Derek Houston, Department of Psychology, Johns Hopkins University, Baltimore, 21218, USA.

Scott P. Johnson, Department of Psychology, Texas A&M University, College Station, Texas 77843, USA.

Peter W. Jusczyk, Department of Psychology, Ames Hall, 3400 N. Charles Street, Johns Hopkins University, Baltimore, 21218–2686, USA.

Jean-Pierre Lecanuet, Université René Descartes (Paris V), Institut de Psychologie, 28, rue Serpente, F-75006 Paris, France.

Merrick J. Moseley, Academic Unit of Ophthalmology, The Western Eye Hospital, Imperial College School of Medicine, Marylebone Road, London NW1 5YE, UK.

Darwin W. Muir, Department of Psychology, Queen's University, Kingston, Ontario, Canada K7L 3N6.

Jacqueline Nadel, Laboratoire de Psycho-Biologie du Développement, EPHE-CNRS, 41, rue Gay-Lussac, 75005 Paris, France.

Charles A. Nelson, University of Minnesota, Twin Cities Campus, Institute of Child Development, 51 East River Road, Minneapolis, MN 55455–0345, USA.

Meir Neufeld, Academic Unit of Ophthalmology, The Western Eye Hospital, Imperial College School of Medicine, Marylebone Road, London NW1 5YE, UK.

Michelle Patterson, Department of Psychology, University of British Columbia, Vancouver, BC, Canada V6T 1Z4.

Judith E. Pegg, BC Research Institute for Child and Family Health, Centre for Community Child Health Research, Vancouver, BC, Canada.

Linda Polka, School of Communication Sciences & Disorders, McGill University, 1266 Pine Avenue West, Montreal, QC Canada H3G 1A8.

Paul C. Quinn, Department of Psychology, Washington and Jefferson College, Washington, PA 15301, USA.

Melissa A. Redford, Department of Psychology, University of Texas at Austin, TX 78712, USA.

Rushen Shi, Department of Psychology, University of British Columbia, Vancouver, BC, Canada V6T 1Z4.

Alan Slater, Department of Psychology, University of Exeter, Washington Singer Laboratories, Exeter EX4 4QG, UK.

Janet Werker, Department of Psychology, University of British Columbia, 2136 West Mall, Vancouver, BC, Canada V6T 1Z4.

Preface

Developments in infancy are some of the most exciting and important to be found in human development, and have been the subject of intense speculations and theorising. A major aspect of this development is sensory and perceptual abilities, and research in this area has progressed at a rapidly increasing pace over the past 35 years: the aim of this book is both to reflect current knowledge and to point to some of the many questions that remain unanswered.

The book is organised into four sections. In Part I the development of basic visual functions is considered, together with abnormal development. In Part II, from sensation to cognition, the five chapters consider theoretical views about visual perception, the functioning of the visual system at birth, the role of learning in visual development, and the important areas of development concerning infants' ability to categorise what is seen, their growing ability to comprehend cause and effect, and their growing awareness of the world of object. Part III considers social perception, the ways in which infants interact with people, and how they come to understand different facial expressions. Part IV has three chapters that discuss infants' responsiveness to, and growing comprehension of, speech, from auditory abilities in the foetus to the segmentation of words. The final chapter discusses some of the methodologies that have developed to allow researchers to study speech perception in infants.

I am grateful to the Series Editor, Charles Hulme, for the opportunity to edit this book, but particularly to the authors for their contributions:

these contributions come from many of the world's leading researchers and teams worldwide working in the areas of visual, auditory, and speech perception in infancy. From reading the chapters it becomes apparent both that we have an increasingly detailed understanding of infant perceptual competence, and that the study of perceptual development is now a sophisticated science. The majority of the chapters also tell a fascinating detective story: the way in which 30 years of research are uncovering the ways in which infants perceive and understand the world as they develop.

Each of the four major sections is prefaced by introductory comments, and the hope is that the book will be useful for advanced undergraduates, postgraduates, researchers and other professionals who have an interest in early perceptual development and in infancy in general.

Alan Slater

PART I

How the visual system develops: Normal and abnormal development

Introduction

In order to begin to make sense of the visual world the infant has to see it! Some 40 years ago it was often assumed that infants were born blind, despite having their eyes open: that is, visual acuity is zero at birth and sight in any meaningful sense begins only some weeks after birth. This long-standing view persisted, and a belief still commonly held, even among professionals who care for babies, is that they are born blind. We now know that this view is wrong, although of course considerable development takes place throughout infancy in almost all aspects of visual functioning. In Chapter 1 Hainline takes us through this period of rapid development, describing in detail the information picked up and transmitted by the visual system. The basic visual functions she discusses include acuity and contrast sensitivity, colour vision, accommodation and vergence, binocular vision, and the development of the oculomotor system that allows the infant both to point the fovea at objects of interest and to maintain fixation on these objects.

A number of important themes run through Hainline's chapter. One is that although infant vision is poor – infants simply do not see as well as adults do – it is sufficient for their role as infants. Their vision, even at birth, is good enough to gain an understanding and accurate perception of the visual world that is close to them. Infants do not need the fine acuity of the adult, and Hainline suggests that higher levels of visual functioning might even make for problems for the infant if they add to the visual "noise" that needs to be filtered out in order for infants to attend

3

to the most relevant information. A second theme is that the methods used to test infant vision will often underestimate their true abilities because one does not have the ability to instruct an infant to attend: naive and uninstructed adults also perform below their "best" functioning.

David Hubel and Torsten Weisel, in the 1960s, were among the first to demonstrate that in order for mammalian vision to develop properly a normal visual environment, with binocular visual input, is essential: animals who are visually deprived when young will often fail to develop normal visual functions. Infants also are at risk, and Moseley, Neufeld, and Fielder in Chapter 2 consider some of the causes and consequences of abnormal visual development. In the early part of the chapter they focus on one particular condition, amblyopia. The term amblyopia is from the Greek meaning "blunt sight", and its defining characteristic is a loss of vision, usually in one eye, although on ophthalmic examination the eye appears normal: they give a delightful quote from Von Graefe (1888) – "amblyopia is the condition in which the examiner sees nothing and the patient very little". Amblyopia can easily be induced in experimental animals by unilateral eye closure, squint, or otherwise preventing binocular vision.

Amblyopia is the most common visual disorder of childhood, afflicting between 2% and 5% of the world's population. There is a critical period during which the developing visual system is most at risk: although "amblyogenic" factors may arise at any point during a lifetime, only during visual development is there a risk of permanent visual loss. Moseley et al. discuss the various factors which are thought to cause, or are associated with, amblyopia. They describe the nature of the visual loss: while spatial resolution is reduced, other visual functions may also be affected. They also describe the range of treatments that have been attempted, the most common of which is occlusion ("patching") of the better eye in the hope of promoting the use of the amblyopic eye.

In the second part of their chapter Moseley et al. discuss other, less common, paediatric disorders. The list of possible problems affecting the visual system is large, but fortunately these problems are rare except in populations that are particularly at risk.

CHAPTER ONE

The development of basic visual abilities

Louise Hainline
Brooklyn College of the City University of New York, USA

INTRODUCTION

Our sensory systems serve as a kind of filter between us and the world. Information from the environment must cause a detectable response in one or more of the body's sensory systems before the brain can make any use of the information. Different species have evolved to rely more heavily on some sensory systems than others. Primates, and in particular, human primates have evolved to depend heavily on vision. In the adult human, it has been estimated that more than half of the brain deals in some way with the processing of visual information (e.g. Sereno, et al., 1995). To understand the world of the human infant, then, it is critical to understand how the visual system develops, as visual abilities form a vital link between the infants and objects and events around them.

Vision clearly undergoes substantial development from infancy to adulthood. Infants simply do not see as well as adults do, a fact that has been well-documented over the last 25 years. Acuity, colour vision, binocular vision, and other basic visual processes all are substantially poorer compared with adults, during the first year and even beyond. On the basis of this body of research, one might legitimately conclude that infants' poor vision would make them significantly visually handicapped.

It is therefore surprising when one observes young infants interacting with people and things around them. These interactions are often complex and impressively nuanced, with little indication that young infants are handicapped by their purported primitive visual abilities. The limitations in their behaviours seems more related to attentional and cognitive factors than to the lack of well-developed visual abilities. Indeed, infants faced with complex real-world stimuli appear to fare rather better than the typical laboratory study might lead one to think. Research in the Gibsonian tradition (e.g. Kellman, 1988, 1993; Spelke, 1988) demonstrates that infants actually are fairly competent when faced with visual stimuli that are more complex and regular than the isolated patches of light or sine wave gratings favoured by researchers working in the tradition of experimental sensory psychophysics. This paradox is one of the more interesting issues in the study of infant vision. Although infants may not, indeed, see as well as adults do, they normally see well enough to function effectively in their roles as infants. Vision does not limit an infant's development, although for an infant with abnormal vision, it may be another matter.

But, in this chapter, the task is to try to give an account of how infants experience their visual world. The attempt to define what infants see evokes deep philosophical questions about the nature of our personal sensory experiences that have been pondered by philosophers and scientists for centuries. The critical question, of course, is how we can know how *anyone* else experiences events in the world. With verbally competent individuals, one has, at least, a social communication system that can help, but ultimately, we have to admit to the validity of solipsistic concerns about the nature of personal experience even for an observer who speaks our language. The problem is amplified when one is interested in the experiences of nonverbal organisms we would like to understand better, like infants and our pets.

Scientific experimentation offers some help, at least part of the way. The process of vision is usefully conceived of as a series of processing stages, with the results of early stages feeding into the processing of higher and generally more complex later stages. Using a kind of bottom-up logic, it is generally safe to assume if visual information does not get transferred from input to output at a lower level of processing, that information is not available for processing at higher stages. In other words, infants can see no better than their basic neural structures allow; for various reasons we will discuss, their effective vision could be worse if higher centres do not use the visual information provided by lower centres efficiently, but this issue can be addressed by appropriate research strategies to detect a mismatch between basic visual abilities and perceptual performance. The first stage of translation (or "transduction") of information about environmental stimuli, in the case of vision, of physical dimensions of light energy into neural energy, is termed "sensation". After the transduction stage, one may study the organisation of these sensory inputs, the processes of perception, and the interpretation and analysis of perceptual information by higher mental processes, generically typically termed "cognition". The nature of these processes in infants will be dealt with in other chapters in this book. The purpose of this chapter is to describe the visual sensory abilities of infants as understood today, as a preliminary answer to the question of what things look like to a baby.

A CONTEXT FOR ASSESSING INFANT VISION

Excellent recent reviews of the research on infant vision can be found in Aslin (1987), Atkinson and Braddick (1989), Van Sluyters et al. (1990), and various chapters in Simons (1993) and Vital-Durand, Atkinson, and Braddick (1996). In most cases, individual visual abilities have been treated separately, with visual abilities summarised one by one (e.g. acuity, binocular vision, colour vision, etc.). Although one can understand the temptation to segment the processes of vision thus for expository reasons, this focus on separate visual abilities can be misleading, because effective use of visual information requires coordination among different functions and abilities. The image of the visually deficient infant may stem in part from the failure to consider the infant as an ensemble of mutually supporting functions, a system in which the whole is greater than the sum of the parts.

To take just one instance, it is unlikely that we can understand what the visual experiences of young infants are like without taking both sensory and motor behaviours into account. Adults are capable of acute vision because they are able to localise with rapid (saccadic) eye movements objects that are detected but not clearly seen in the periphery; adults see more clearly with the central portions of their retina (the sheet of neural tissue at the back of the eye, containing the photoreceptors, specialised cells that transduce light into neural signals; for humans the central portion of the retina, the fovea, is responsible for the highest-acuity vision). As a result, to inspect objects closely, they need to point their foveae at them directly. Once an adult is foveating an object, the two eyes' foveae must be made to point at similar targets in the world, which is accomplished by a system of eye movements called "vergence"; we converge our eyes to look at closer targets, diverge to look at objects further away to maintain a single percept. Once we have positioned an object in corresponding locations on the two eyes, we need either to keep the eyes steady, "fixate", so that the brain can analyse the detailed properties of a stationary object, such as form, colour and fine detail, or to follow a moving object with our eyes (through an eye movement termed "pursuit" – with either smooth movements, or a series of rapid, saccadic episodes) to keep the object of interest on our foveae. Development of vision requires a coordination of both the sensory aspects of vision (detection of form, motion, colour, pattern, etc.) with accurate eye movements. A good sensory apparatus without good oculomotor control will have its vision severely compromised, and good oculomotor control cannot be achieved without adequate visual feedback from sensory levels. So, "seeing" for infants necessarily involves the development of well-balanced sensorimotor interactions.

Another point of discussion will be whether we should accept uncritically reports of reduced vision in young infants. Although there is no question that infants see more poorly than adults, the situation may not be as bad as it has been portrayed. Inherent in many of the methods in the tool kit used to test infants is the tendency to under- rather than overestimate infants' capacities. Most of the paradigms that are currently used to study vision in infants depend on some level of interest and attentiveness toward the test stimuli. A legitimate concern with maintaining a desirable level of experimental control has meant that stimuli have been physically well-specified, but rather simple, varied along one dimension of interest at a time. Despite the merit of this rationale for designing stimuli, certain of the early "deficiencies" in vision may actually be reflections of infants' disinterest in the austere stimuli chosen by researchers.

Even if we acknowledge that current methods yield underestimates, infant vision is still obviously inferior compared to adult vision. But which adults? In many aspects, everyday adult vision may also be far less acute and precise than we imagine, probably because many of the daily tasks requiring vision can be done with less than full attention and the recruitment of less than the highest levels of performance. Indeed, in our own studies, we regularly find that adults, if they are naive and uninstructed, also perform at a level considerably below that commonly reported in the published literature for the practised adult subjects who are measured in most psychophysical experiments. Although an interesting observation about vision in its own right, this fact must change our perspective on the visual performance of infants, who necessarily are unpractised and uninstructed. Comparing infant performance to that of "world-class" adult subjects can give a misleading impression of infant vision; not all adults are equal.

Further, infants might not have much use for better, more adult-like vision, were it available to them. To put infant vision in some perspective, it is useful to ask what infants use their vision for. Adopting a functionalist stance, it could be said that the sensory "deficits" of early infancy may not really make much difference in the infant's daily life. The most acute levels of adult vision depend on anatomical structures that are immature in young infants; but these structures support visual functions that are not of great use early in life (for example, extremely fine acuity for detecting and hunting distant prey, and its modern analogue, reading, or exquisitely fine stereoscopic discriminations of depth). Young babies simply do not need to be good hunters or be able to read the fine print in a contract.

What this amounts to is the suggestion that visually normal infants have the level of visual functioning that is required for the things that infants need to do. Despite documented immaturities, infants' vision is good enough to derive an accurate impression of the world in their immediate vicinity and to stimulate further visual, cognitive, and social developments. Even with their poor vision, it would be a mistake to see infants as "handicapped" functionally, given the functions appropriate for their age. We might even posit that higher levels of visual functioning could actually interfere with these tasks, if they add to the visual "noise" that needs to be filtered out in order for infants to attend to the most relevant information (Hainline & Abramov, 1992; Turkewitz & Kenny, 1982).

THE NEED FOR ASSESSMENT OF INFANT VISION

The observation that infants might not benefit from more acute vision does not detract from the need to study the development of visual abilities. On the contrary, it is important to understand visual development in early infancy and to evaluate infants' vision earlier and on a much wider basis than has been customary. Visual development does not follow a fixed blueprint, and irregularities in the normal developmental sequence can have permanent effects on the final level of visual functioning. A well-documented fact about mammalian vision is that the development of the visual system depends greatly on the nature of the visual stimulation early in life; in other words, visual development is characterised by a series of sensitive periods for different visual functions, with the developmental process shaped by the nature of the inputs the system receives. Animals that are visually deprived when young often fail to develop a full range of visual abilities as they age (Atkinson & Braddick, 1988; Mitchell, 1988; Movshon & Van Sluyters, 1981), and humans appear to show similar developmental plasticity as vision develops during infancy (e.g. Archer, 1993; Atkinson, 1993; Held, 1981; Levi & Carkeet, 1993; Tychsen, 1993). The issue here is to delineate the normal sequence of some important visual milestones. Clinical assessment of vision and visual disabilities in infants is dealt with more extensively in Chapter 2, by Moseley et al.

DEVELOPMENT OF VISUAL STRUCTURES

The visual system consists of a sequence of stages for the translation of light energy in the world into neural impulses, which are processed at a series of higher and increasingly more complex levels in the nervous system. At the earliest stage, the relevant parts of the visual system are optical (cornea, lens, etc.); these structures form an adjustable optical system to bring images into focus on the retina at the back of the eye. Actually, as we have two eyes, at this stage the system consists of two separate optical systems, forming separate images on each of the eyes' retinas. Thus, the quality of vision depends, first of all, on the ability to change the lens's focus appropriately (accommodation), and to rotate the eyes to point at a specific target location (vergence). Failure of accommodation results in blurred images. Failure of convergence results in the perception of double images (diplopia), or the suppression of information from one of the eyes. The brain is responsible for fusing the two retinal images into one coherent image; in most cases, the brain also uses the information from the two eyes to allow fine depth discriminations through stereopsis.

Because humans' eyes move to allow inspection of the details of the world, visual functioning depends critically on how well an individual is able to fixate and to make saccades and pursuit movements. In normal life, the head is not stabilised by laboratory artifices, such as chin rests or bite bars; rather, some form of compensation is needed for movements of both head and body in order for vision to remain stable. The vestibulo-ocular reflex serves to stabilise vision during self-produced motion, while smooth pursuit and optokinetic nystagmus assist in nulling the motion of the retinal image that results both from self-produced motion and from movement of objects past a stationary viewer. Problems or immaturities in any of these abilities can significantly compromise basic sensory as well as "higher" aspects of vision and visual information processing.

The image formed on the retina by the eye's optics consists of a pattern of energy that contains information about the colours and spatial arrangements of objects in the world. It is the job, first, of the cells in the retina, and, later, of cells at subsequent neural processing sites in the visual pathway to transduce and encode this pattern of energy into one that the brain can interpret. The visual system, in other words, is also a complex neural network for coding the spatial, temporal, and chromatic characteristics of successive visual images; it serves as an important "front end" for higher mental processing. In turn, both perceptual and higher cognitive processes modify the way in which basic optical, oculomotor, and sensory functioning proceeds (e.g. see Neisser, 1976). In the final analysis, seeing is not only a sensorimotor but also a cognitive process.

Infant retina

The visual system of the human infant is structurally immature compared to the level of development seen in older children and adults. This immaturity begins at the retina, particularly in its area of highest acuity, the fovea (Abramov et al., 1982; Hendrickson & Yuodelis, 1984; Yuodelis & Hendrickson, 1986). Figure 1.1A is a photograph through a light microscope of a section from a region just outside the fovea of an adult retina;

Fig. 1.1B is a stylised drawing (based partly on electron microscopy) of the cell types and interconnections shown in panel A. In these figures, the front of the eye is in the direction of the top of the page, so that light passes, as indicated, through three layers of cells before reaching the outer segments of the receptors; the outer segments contain the photopigments that absorb and transduce the incident light in the image formed by the eye's optics. It is clear from Fig. 1.1B that there is considerable neural interaction and processing of the responses of the receptors before the information is transmitted to the brain by the axons of the ganglion cells, which together form the optic nerve. Figure 1.1C is a section through an adult fovea, which shows some of the features that are unique to the fovea. First, the receptors are more slender and are more densely packed together. Second, the inner nuclear and ganglion cell layers are much *less* dense and even absent from the very centre, which creates the pit-like appearance of the fovea. However, this apparent reduction in cell density is misleading: the ganglion and inner nuclear cells associated with the foveal receptors are in fact more numerous than in peripheral regions – the bodies of these cells have simply migrated to the edges of the fovea so that light does not have to pass through them, which would reduce the sharpness of the image on the fovea.

Figures 1.1D and 1.1E show sections from the retina of a human neonate. Figure 1.1D is from a region just outside the fovea, which is just beyond the range of this photograph on the right. The left-hand portion of this section appears to be much like the adult peripheral retina in Fig. 1.1A, and only on the right, as the fovea is approached, are any marked immaturities encountered: the density of receptor cells decreases, the available space for the outer segments of the receptors becomes progressively narrower, and there are other signs of immaturity, particularly in the fovea. Figure 1.1E shows the neonate's fovea, in which the above abnormalities are even more pronounced. In particularly, the morphology of the receptors is very different, with the outer segments of the cones quite short and thick, rather than elongated and slender as in the normal adult and the infant periphery. In addition, the cells in the inner nuclear and ganglion cell layers have not yet migrated to the edges of the foveal pit. At this point we know that these neonatal immaturities have mostly disappeared by the end of the first year, but we still lack detailed information of the time course of many of the changes, especially during the first two to three months from birth when visual performance is changing very rapidly. The structural immaturity of the fovea is mirrored at successive levels in the visual pathway (e.g. Garey & De Courten, 1983; Hendrickson, 1993; Hickey, 1977; Huttenlocher, 1979; see Daw, 1995, for a particularly complete and clear discussion of visual neural development in humans)

Given the striking state of the anatomy at birth, it has not been difficult

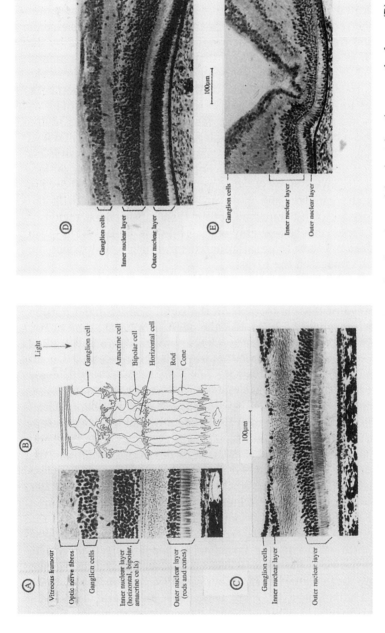

FIG. 1.1. Anatomy of the human retina. (A) Photomicrograph of a section through an adult primate's retina, near the fovea. (B) Schematic representation of the cells and connections in the preceding photograph. (C) Photomicrograph of an adult retina in the foveal region. (D) Section through a newborn human infant's peripheral retina, near the fovea, which is off to the right of this view. (E) Section through the fovea of the same infant as in the preceding panel. Note the decrease in number of receptors in fovea. (Panels A, B, C modified from Abramov & Gordon, 1973. Panels D, E modified from Abramov et al., 1982.)

to assimilate data purportedly showing that young infants are unskilled or inept at behaviours such as accommodation and convergence (e.g. Aslin, 1977; Banks, 1980; Haynes, White, & Held, 1965), eye movements (Aslin, 1981; Aslin & Salapatek, 1975), or the detection of spatially distributed patterns (Atkinson, Braddick, & Moar, 1977; Banks & Salapatek, 1981). But attribution of functional immaturities to anatomical immaturities must be done cautiously. We rarely know the degree to which changes in structure will be reflected in differences in function. However, there have been some detailed attempts to relate structure and function, based largely on the still incomplete data on changes in retinal anatomy during the first year (Banks & Bennett, 1988; Banks & Crowell, 1993; Banks & Shannon, 1993; Brown, Dobson, & Maier, 1987; Wilson, 1988, 1993); clearly there is much that remains to be learned about the relationship between structural development and functional vision in infancy, but with ready access to foveal structural immaturity as an explanation of infants' assessed incompetence, it is easy to lose sight of other characteristics of infants that can be as influential for performance on standard laboratory tasks, namely vagaries of infant attentional state, inherent attentional preferences, and habituation.

DEVELOPMENT OF SPATIAL VISION

Spatial contrast sensitivity

Discrimination among objects in the world depends on spatial vision, that is, the ability to resolve the components of the image on the retina. According to Linear Systems Analysis, based on Fourier's theorem, any such image can be mathematically described by a linear summation of a specific set of basis functions (see Levine & Shefner, 1990, for an introductory treatment; also, De Valois & De Valois, 1988, and Graham, 1989). It is common to use sine waves as the basis functions; each sinusoidal component of the particular set is described by its spatial frequency (measured as cycles per degree of visual angle), phase (starting point relative to the other sinusoids), and amplitude (power); in most cases the results of the analysis are given as a power spectrum, which plots the amplitude of each sinusoidal component versus spatial frequency.

Like all optical systems, the visual system selectively filters different spatial frequencies due to imperfections in its optical structures. These factors are most obvious at the acuity limit, which is a measure of the finest pattern (i.e. highest spatial frequency) that the eye can resolve when the pattern consists of extreme dark/light transitions (i.e. high contrast). However, as the retinal image also contains many lower-frequency components, measures of only acuity provide incomplete descriptions of visual performance. A more complete measure of spatial vision is the spatial contrast sensitivity function (CSF), on which acuity is only one high-frequency point.

The stimuli typically used to measure the spatial contrast sensitivity function (CSF) are gratings with alternating lighter and darker bars, each pair of light and dark bars constituting one cycle of the grating. Starting with the edge of a light bar, the luminance of the pattern gradually increases, then gradually decreases, and so on across the grating, to produce a luminance profile that varies sinusoidally across the grating (Fig. 1.2a). Although sine waves are not *per se* "ecologically valid" stimuli, quantitative approaches to vision argue that detection and recognition of objects (at least while stationary) can be predicted from the functions measured with such stimuli; this is discussed further later. In an experiment to measure the spatial CSF, the spatial frequency of the grating (number of grating cycles per degree of visual angle) is varied systematically, and for each grating, the contrast needed for threshold detection is found. The normal CSF has a characteristic inverted U-shape when contrast sensitivity (i.e. reciprocal of threshold contrast) is plotted as a function of spatial frequency (see Fig. 1.2b). At higher spatial frequencies, as the acuity limit is approached, optical factors impose a fundamental limit: the eye's optics simply cannot form an image of an extremely fine grating – the light and dark bars are so blurred that the image is a spatially uniform field. However, the drop in sensitivity at lower spatial frequencies cannot be optical in origin in a human eye and is caused, in all likelihood, by neural factors such as lateral inhibition, that is, a type of neural interaction in which stimulation of one area reduces responses to stimulation of a neighbouring area (e.g. Ratliff, 1965). The exact location of the spatial CSF with respect to the spatial frequency and contrast sensitivity axes depends greatly on the conditions under which the function is measured. For example, changes in the mean luminance shift the absolute location of the curve, with higher luminances increasing sensitivity particularly at high spatial frequencies. The method used to measure the function also influences the form and location of the curve (Graham, 1989).

Infant spatial CSF

The early studies of spatial resolution in infants concentrated on acuity (see Dobson, 1993; Dobson & Teller, 1978), which develops rapidly over the first year of life. Although very important, these studies cannot provide all the information inherent in measures of complete spatial CSFs. The methods that have been used to obtain CSFs from infants include forced-choice preferential looking (FPL), visual evoked potentials (VEP), and a method we have developed that is based on recordings of subjects' eye movements, which we term eye movement-voting (EMV). FPL is derived

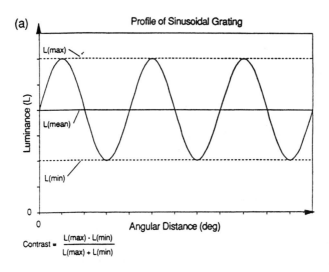

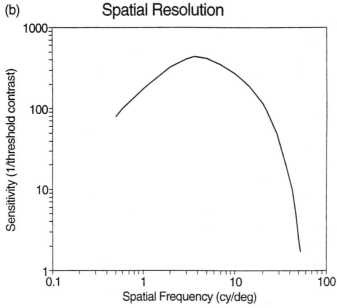

FIG. 1.2. (a) Contrast sensitivity is typically measured by presenting patterns whose lumin-ance profile across the stimulus increases and decreases according to a sine function, as illus-trated in this example. Contrast is a measure describing the difference between the highest and lowest luminances compared to the mean. (b) An example of an adult spatial contrast sensitivity function (CSF), based on data presented by Van Nes and Bouman (1967). Spatial frequency, on the abscissa, is a measure of the fineness of the pattern; high spatial frequencies have many cycles of light-to-dark transitions in the same spatial extent for which a low-frequency grating has only a few such transitions. Contrast sensitivity is the reciprocal of the contrast at threshold, that is, the minimum contrast required for the detection of that spatial frequency; high contrast sensitivity implies that a low contrast is enough for detection, where-as low contrast sensitivity implies that a high level of contrast is needed to detect the pattern. (From Hainline & Abramov, 1992.)

from Fantz' (1956) preferential looking paradigm, with the variant that the dependent measure is not seconds of looking but a judgement by a person observing the infant about the position of a stimulus being viewed by the infant (Teller, 1979). Visibility and position of the stimuli are manipulated across trials to derive a threshold estimate. VEP methods use electrodes attached to the scalp to record the EEG during presentation of the stimulus. Because the visually evoked response is very small and the record very noisy, stimuli are presented in some repetitive fashion and successive responses are averaged. Usually this is done by alternating between two versions of the grating stimulus such that a pattern is always present, but the bright bars of one replace the dark bars of the other; this counterphase reversal of the pattern is at some fixed temporal rate and the responses to each cycle of the temporal alternation are averaged. The studies we will describe later use a specific form of VEP, the sweep-VEP. In this variant, one of the stimulus parameters is "swept" through a series of values to find the value at which some criterion response level is reached; for the spatial CSF, the contrast of each grating is varied, in a series of small steps from high to low, to find the contrast at which the averaged response falls within the EEG signal's noise (Norcia, 1993; Norcia, Clarke, & Tyler, 1985; Tyler, Apkarian, Levi, & Nakayama, 1979). In EMV (Abramov et al., 1984; Hainline, Camenzuli, Abramov, Rawlick, & Lemerise, 1986; Hainline, De Bie, Abramov, & Camenzuli, 1987; Hainline & Abramov, 1997), detailed records of eye movements are made while the infant views a moving pattern of stripes with different levels of visibility. As with FPL, an observer blind to the characteristics of the stimulus "votes" on each trial on which way the stimulus is moving, using the infant's eye movements. Using standard psychophysical methods, one can determine a CSF from the pattern of correct and incorrect responses of the observer, as a function of stimulus contrast and spatial frequency.

There are several sets of data on the development of the spatial CSF for human infants, including but not limited to: Atkinson et al. (1977), Banks and Salapatek (1978), Hainline et al., 1986; Norcia, Tyler, and Allen (1986), and Norcia, Tyler, and Hamer (1990); some of these are shown in Fig. 1.3. Although these studies differ in the absolute sensitivities that are found, they agree in finding a gradual improvement in both absolute contrast sensitivity and in the range of spatial frequencies to which the system is sensitive; that is, with increasing age over the first year, the CSF (plotted as in Fig. 1.2b) shifts laterally to higher frequencies and upward to higher sensitivities. There is also evidence that sensitivity to low and middle frequencies approaches the adult asymptote at an earlier age than does the sensitivity to high spatial frequencies close to the acuity limit (Norcia et al., 1990). There is general agreement that these changes in spatial contrast sensitivity largely reflect retinal immaturities, with lesser contributions from neural processing contributed by higher centres (Banks & Crowell, 1993; Banks & Shannon, 1993).

Although showing the same general developmental pattern across age, the absolute sensitivities obviously differ as a function of the method used, with FPL producing the lowest estimates of sensitivities, VEP about 10 times higher, and EMV intermediate. It is possible that some of these differences come from differences in the specific stimuli used in the different studies cited; for adults, factors such as luminance and field size influence sensitivities (Kelly, 1961; Robson & Graham, 1981; Van Nes & Bouman, 1967). FPL is, of course, dependent on detecting infants' relatively gross attentional discriminations between more and less visible stimuli; it has been assumed that these attentionally driven responses are voluntary and thus dependent on "higher" neural centres, although the method may also be tapping reflexive orienting to salient peripheral stimuli. A VEP depicts an average of the composite neural activity to repeated presentations of a stimulus, after processing at many different levels in the visual system. Except for the need for a minimal level of alertness, it does not depend on voluntary behaviours of the infant. VEP is generally believed to reflect the spatial sensitivity of central retina. Our EMV method is based on following eye movements elicited by moving gratings. Such eye movements are a behavioural response to moving stimuli; some kinds of following eye movements have been described as reflexive, although in practice it is not easy to discriminate between reflexive and voluntary following eye movements. Although it is a behavioural method, EMV may be more similar to VEP than FPL: in both cases, stimuli are presented directly in front of the subject and so the thresholds are more likely to represent those of central, rather than peripheral, retina.

Another major difference among methods is how long it takes to get an estimate of the CSF. The methods clearly demand different degrees of cooperation from the infant. FPL is time-consuming. With FPL, derivation of a full CSF extends over several lengthy sessions, with the risk of significant habituation to the stimuli and to the testing situation itself, as well as the possibility of centrally caused reductions in alertness. Compared with FPL, VEP is a rapid method; in some sweep-VEP procedures, a complete spatial CSF can be obtained in as little as 10–15 minutes. The EMV method takes about the same time as the sweep-VEP to derive a CSF.

Thus there are many reasons why one would not expect identical spatial CSF from the different methods – indeed, the similarities in results are all the more striking in the face of these methodological variations. It is likely that postnatal development of infant contrast sensitivity reflects predominantly the development of the fovea and central visual field, although in infant monkeys who have been used as a model of infant human visual development there is also evidence of peripheral

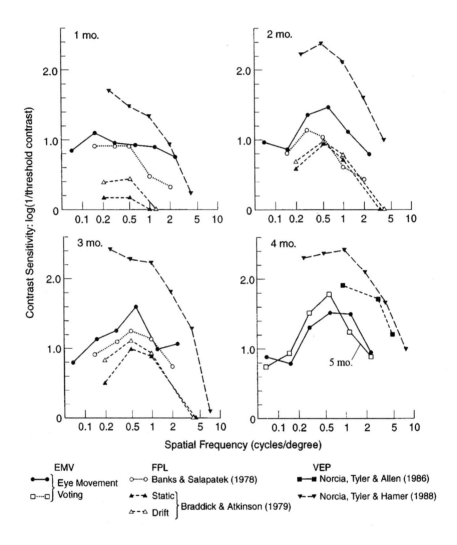

FIG. 1.3. Examples of infant spatial CSFs obtained from the three methods that have been used to derive infant CSFs: FPL, VEP, and EMV. Note the differences in absolute sensitivities, but the general similarity of the shapes of the curves, in most cases. (Adapted from Hainline & Abramov, 1992.)

development (Kiorpes, 1996). It is important to underscore, however, that the level of spatial vision that young infants possess is normally adequate to make many of the visual discriminations that infants need to make to respond adaptively to events around them.

Spatiotemporal interactions

Visual stimuli vary simultaneously in both space and time, and the visual system's sensitivities to these dimensions are inextricably linked. The particular relevance in the case of infants is the possibility that, as a result of poorer eye movement control, infants cannot keep patterns stable on their retinas. The visibility (i.e. contrast at threshold) of a grating of any given spatial frequency depends on the temporal parameters of the stimulus; that is, a CSF is best expressed as a particular section through a three-dimensional spatiotemporal solid (Kelly, 1979a,b). Rather than there being one CSF, there is an infinite family of spatiotemporal CSFs that describe an entire spatiotemporal contrast sensitivity surface. Moreover, the details of any such surface also depend on a host of other stimulus parameters such as luminance, spatial extent, and so on. An example of a spatiotemporal surface we have obtained from adults is shown in Fig. 1.4. The figure shows the smooth surface fitted over the separate CSFs obtained for different rates of pattern movement. The exact ordinate values for such a surface will depend, of course, on stimulus details. For example, Fig. 1.4 shows that we did not use gratings of very high spatial frequencies, and hence the front corner of the solid is truncated; the reason was simply that the mean luminance of our display was relatively low and under these conditions, very high frequencies were not visible. Spatiotemporal surfaces have, however, general properties that hold over a range of experimental conditions.

Consider the changes in the shape of the spatial CSF that would result from changes in the temporal rate. Such curves can be obtained by slicing the solid parallel to the spatial frequency abscissa. At very low temporal rates, overall sensitivity of the spatial CSF is depressed and the peak is shifted towards higher spatial frequencies. As temporal rate is increased, the peak shifts to lower spatial frequencies and sensitivity to those frequencies increases. However, because of the shift of the function towards lower spatial frequencies, there is a *loss* in sensitivity at the highest frequencies (i.e. the acuity limit is shifted to lower values), and a *gain* in sensitivity at low frequencies; indeed, the usual drop in sensitivity at low spatial frequencies may no longer be evident at very high temporal rates. This is the reason why the infant VEP CSFs in Fig. 1.3 fail to "turn down" at lower spatial frequencies: in order to obtain a VEP, it is necessary to use a time-varying stimulus, which increases sensitivity at lower spatial frequencies compared to a static stimulus.

The eyes of even highly motivated adult observers fixating static targets can drift at rates of the order of 0.5 to 1deg/sec, unless subjects' heads are rigidly stabilised (Skavenski, Hansen, Steinman, & Winterson, 1979), and this can be demonstrated to produce changes in threshold. Except in the few cases when the effects of eye movements have been nullified (e.g. Kelly, 1979b), unknown temporal variations influence measures of the spatial CSF, even for stimuli that the experimenter intends to be "static". How much this affects the resulting CSF is an empirical question and depends on many factors. It is likely that similar effects occur for infants.

Besides this sensory effect of spatiotemporal interactions, motion of the stimulus has attentional implications for infants. A fact established fairly early about infant preferences is that even for simple stimuli, infants prefer moving and time-varying stimuli over the equivalent static stimulus (e.g. Carpenter, 1974; Volkman & Dobson, 1976), possibly because movement

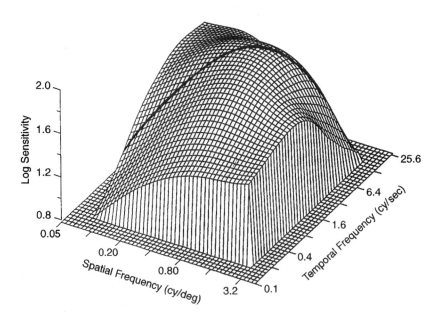

FIG. 1.4. An example of a spatiotemporal CSF. The smooth surface was fitted to EMV data from adults (data from Hainline et al., 1987). Stimuli were sinusoidal gratings at a low photopic luminance, but the gratings were drifting at various velocities. The smooth surface was fitted across the data points, but following the usual convention, we have plotted contrast sensitivity versus spatial and temporal frequency, rather than velocity. The dark line traces a single CSF at a retinal velocity of 7deg/sec. (From Hainline & Abramov, 1992.)

is an important characteristic of the stimuli infants naturally attend to; it is likely that infants find the stimuli in VEP studies and in our EMV studies more interesting than in many FPL versions and this may influence measured thresholds. Gibsonians and neo-Gibsonians would of course argue that motion is not interesting because of its influence on sensory thresholds, but because much information about objects and our relationship to objects is revealed by motion (e.g. Gibson, 1979). Indeed, it can be argued that for very young infants, the components of the world that are perceived as relating to "objects" are those components that move as a coherent unit (Kellman, 1993; Kellman & Spelke, 1983); this motion could either be due to real motion of the object relative to the background or to motion of the infant (Kellman, Gleitman, & Spelke, 1987). The ability to detect both the degree and direction of movement has been studied developmentally (see Braddick, 1993; Braddick, Atkinson & Hood, 1996, and Wattam-Bell, 1996) and appears to change with age during infancy in a way that reflects higher levels of processing, particularly for faster-moving stimuli. However, the current data support the notion that even the young infant has the rudiments to attend to, process, and deal with moderate movement in visual stimuli.

Functional consequences of the infant CSF

A subject's CSF can be regarded as a selective filter for the spatial frequencies represented by the Fourier power spectrum of a given stimulus; this is the central assumption of "linear systems" approaches in vision (see e.g. De Valois & De Valois, 1988; Ginsberg, 1986). Although it is clear that above threshold vision is in many respects nonlinear, the linear systems approach has been successful in describing many aspects of visual performance. Some studies, for example, suggest that object recognition depends heavily on information at lower spatial frequencies (Ginsberg, Evans, Sekuler, & Harp, 1982); low frequencies communicate information about an object's broad features. Discrimination among similar objects may depend, however, much more on high-frequency information; this is clearly seen in letter discrimination tasks like the traditional Snellen test, in which reductions in high spatial frequency vision (i.e. acuity), often due to optical blur, severely impair visual performance (e.g. Thorn & Schwartz, 1990). At this point we must add that it is a serious oversimplification to consider only the power spectrum of a stimulus: the phase spectrum (i.e. the starting point on its cycle of each sinusoidal component of the stimulus) is also very important; if a stimulus is recreated using its original power spectrum but with a random phase spectrum, the object may no longer be recognised (Piotrowski & Campbell, 1982).

The ability of the visual system to recognise and discriminate among patterns will depend both on the individual viewer's CSF and on the Fourier spectra of the particular stimuli involved. The assumptions of linear systems analysis allow us to simulate what various objects might look like to a young infant: in essence, to substitute their visual system for our own in a limited way. Because faces are such an important part of the infant's visual world, we have used them to illustrate some of these points. In Fig. 1.5a we start with a sharply focused image of a face, which we will filter so that when it is viewed by an adult with normal vision it will appear as if the adult's visual system had been replaced by that of a 2-month-old infant. In Fig. 1.5b we show the CSFs for a normal adult and a typical 6- to 8-week-old infant that will be used in the filtering process. These particular curves are in fact examples of Kelly's (1979b) model of spatial CSFs that we have generated for a specific set of viewing conditions, as follows: a moderate photopic luminance level (e.g. equivalent to viewing the figure under a good reading light), and a temporal parameter value approximating a normal, casual, nonlaboratory degree of fixational stability (1deg/sec). The original image of the face was analysed to obtain its two-dimensional Fourier spectrum; the power at each spatial frequency was then rescaled according to the infant's sensitivity to each frequency to produce an *effective* (or filtered) power spectrum of the image. (Strictly speaking, the CSF, or filter, in Fig. 1.5b is for a one-dimensional stimulus, and a two-dimensional filter had to be derived from it for the filtering operation.) This filtered spectrum could have been used to resynthesise a filtered image of the face. But had we done so, the resulting image would have been quite misleading. The reason is that when adults look at such a filtered image, they are imposing a second stage of filtering – that due to their own visual systems. The problems raised by this are best appreciated by considering some low spatial frequency to which the adult and the infant are approximately equally sensitive; at that frequency the double filtering would be equivalent to squaring the infant's filter, which would lead to overfiltering at these frequencies. To compensate for this, we have rescaled the infant-filtered power spectrum by the inverse of the adult's CSF before resynthesising the image. Thus, assuming that the viewer's CSF is like the adult CSF in Fig. 1.5b, the inverse filtering according to that function is negated by the filtering imposed by the viewer's own CSF, and the viewer should see the face as if the viewer's visual system had been replaced by that of the infant. Because the spatial frequency content of a face necessarily changes with viewing distance, we have repeated the operations for two viewing distances of 30cm and 150cm. The resulting images are shown in Fig. 1.5c,d. At the near distance, the stimulus is clearly still recognisable as a face, although at the further distance, this becomes a questionable identification. In all of these manipulations, the original phase relationships have been maintained, otherwise the image would have been "scrambled". In short, at the distances at which infants are called on to recognise faces (arm's length), even the visual system of a young infant is probably adequate to discern a face's critical features.

The linear systems approach to visual discrimination has already been applied to normal infant preference data with some success: simply by using an age-appropriate CSF to filter stimuli, it is possible to predict infants' visual preferences (Atkinson, 1977; Banks & Salapatek, 1981; Gayl, Roberts, & Werner, 1983; Slater, Earle, Morison, & Rose, 1985). A lot of the work on stimulus recognition and discrimination has dealt with faces, probably because of the high "ecological validity" of such stimuli. There have recently been some attempts to examine the relative import-ance of phase and power spectra for recognition of faces by infants. As already noted, for adults the phase spectrum of a stimulus is a much more important determinant of recognition than is the power spectrum. Thus, in the recent developmental studies, "face-like" stimuli were analysed into their Fourier components and then recombined using different phase relations, but preserving the original power spectra (Dannemiller & Stephens, 1988; Kleiner, 1987; Kleiner & Banks, 1987). The results have been interpreted as showing that infants younger than 2 months are responding in their preferences on the basis of total power, irrespective of the phase relations among the components. That is, they do not always prefer the stimuli seen as face-like by adults. However, these interpre-tations must be treated cautiously: for example, Kleiner (1987) compared newborns' preferences for a schematic face versus a lattice made up of squares on a blank background; comparisons also pitted preferences for stimuli created from the phase spectrum of one and the power spectrum of the other. Kleiner's conclusions focus on the fact that newborns, unlike 2-month-olds (Kleiner & Banks, 1987), do not prefer the lattice stimulus with the face's phase relations (which looks like a slightly distorted face to adults). However, the data also show that newborns, like 2-month-olds, prefer the original schematic face to the stimulus with the face's power spectrum but the lattice's phase spectrum, which shows that they are not phase-insensitive and that the face's phase structure may be inherently attractive, even to newborns (Morton, Johnson, & Maurer, 1990).

Beyond the problems described, there is a more general question of whether such studies are indeed examining the perception of "faceness". The designation of these schematic and simplified stimuli as "face-like" is based on adults' categorisations. It is not clear that infants categorise such stimuli equivalently (Cohen, 1988). Before concluding that young infants respond to faces primarily on the basis of some low-level sensory signal (such as the total effective power in a stimulus as derived from a linear systems analysis), the studies need to be repeated using real faces.

Although powerful quantitatively, linear systems analysis may not tell

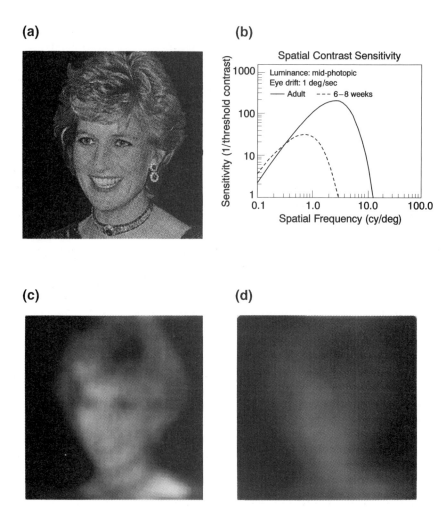

FIG. 1.5. The effect of the infant CSF on visibility of an "ecologically valid" stimulus. (a) A photograph of a prominent British subject. (b) Hypothetical CSFs for a normal 6-to 8-week-old infant and an adult under conditions of good photopic luminance and moderate fixational stability. These are used to filter the image in (a), as described in the text. (c) The same face as it might be seen by a 2-month-old viewing from a distance of 30cm. More correctly, when the figure is viewed by an adult with a normal CSF, it will be seen as if the adult's visual system had been replaced by one with the CSF of the infant in (b). (d) A similarly filtered image of our subject, but at a distance of 150cm. Image processing was done by Shuai Chen. This figure is published as a tribute to Princess Diana.

us all that we need to know about stimulus appearance. Strictly, linear systems approaches to stimulus discriminations can predict performance only when responses vary linearly with intensity. When contrasts are close to threshold, it is probably safe to assume that the visual system is behaving linearly. However, when contrasts are well above threshold, as in normal viewing conditions, the system may become nonlinear. Furthermore, the nonlinearities may be associated more strongly with certain regions of the spatial frequency spectrum. Finally, different tasks may be biased towards particular frequency ranges; for example, reading may depend more on higher spatial frequencies, but categorising something as this or that object may be more affected by sensitivity to lower frequencies. These factors make it difficult to predict exactly how a given CSF will affect visibility of real objects above threshold.

Most of the studies of the effects of the CSF on perception have dealt with static "snapshots" of the stimulus. Gibsonian theory reminds us, however, that stimulus recognition may be more crucially dependent on invariant features of *dynamic* displays extended in time (e.g. Arterberry, Craton, & Yonas, 1993; Bertenthal, Proffitt, Spetner, & Thomas, 1985; Kellman, 1993; Kellman & Spelke, 1983; Ruff, 1982). Until recently, motion of the stimulus or of the subject with respect to the stimulus have been regarded as nuisance variables rather than as a necessary dimension of study. As we saw in the discussion of spatiotemporal interactions, it is far from trivial to deal with both spatial and temporal dimensions in a controlled fashion, and the visibility of a target in motion may be different from that of an object at rest. These problems notwithstanding, linear systems analysis of the capacities of the developing visual system offers a powerful means to understand the implications of neural immaturity, to predict what visual information is available to the infant for other developmental functions, and to evaluate early visual system dysfunction. Comparisons of results from different methods can serve as the source of converging information to give a perspective on the development of spatial vision not accessible from any single method of data collection.

DEVELOPMENT OF COLOUR VISION

The ability to see light with different physical wavelengths as having different colours necessarily requires an interaction of mechanisms at the retina. Normal humans have two classes of photoreceptors, rods, which are maximally sensitive in low light levels, and cones, which are sensitive at higher light levels. There are three different cone types in the normal human (most forms of "colour blindness" result from genetic anomalies leading to abnormalities or absence of one of these cone types). The rods and cones of the retina contain different photosensitive chemicals, the photopigments, which differ from one another in what wavelengths they react to (absorb) maximally. To tell that a light is of a different hue than another (rather than just more or less intense) requires a comparison of the outputs of at least two receptors with different photopigments. The photoreceptors whose output is being compared could be two (or more) types of cones, or a rod and a cone. How sensitive to light a given photoreceptor is depends on how much opportunity the incoming light has to interact with the photopigment in a particular photoreceptor; this is directly related to the shape of the photoreceptor outer segment. Long, slender outer segments will have a better chance of responding to light, on average, than short, stumpy outer segments. This is probably why absolute sensitivity to light increases over the first months of infancy, as the receptors mature, more for the rods than the cones (Brown, 1993; Fulton, Hansen, Dorn & Hendrickson, 1996; Teller & Lindsey, 1993a), which is consistent with what we know about the structural development of photoreceptors in the infant retina. The difficulties in studying colour vision in young infants have made definitive conclusions about the nature of infant colour vision difficult to obtain. The data justify the straight-forward conclusion that colour vision develops rapidly in the first quarter-year. One-month-olds have often been reported to fail to make some colour discriminations (e.g. green vs. yellow) that one would expect they should be able to make if they had all 4 functional photoreceptors (rods plus 3 cone types), but by 2 months, evidence suggests that normal infants can make most discriminations, particularly if stimuli are large and differences between stimuli are marked (Clavadetscher, Brown, Ankrum, & Teller, 1988). One hypothesis (e.g. Brown, 1990) is that in the earliest months, at least one cone mechanism is not contributing, but rods are playing a role important to chromatic discriminations among stimuli. Another interpretation of the data is that there is an overall loss of sensitivity of all chromatic and luminance mechanisms, possibly due to the developmental differences in the morphology of the photoreceptors, with the least sensitive cone type undetectable because of both weaker neural signals and greater noise in the neural signals, i.e. a lower signal-to-noise ratio (Banks & Bennett, 1988; Banks & Shannon, 1993; Brown, 1993). VEP methods, which in tests of spatial vision appear to have greater sensitivity than behavioural methods like FPL, yield data pointing to the existence of the normal complement of colour mechanisms, albeit with weaker outputs, during early infancy (e.g. Allen, Banks, Norcia & Shannon, 1993; Burr, Marrone, & Fiorentini, 1996; Knoblauch, Bieber, & Werner, 1996; Vol-brecht & Werner, 1987).

Even if young infants have all three cone types, and all are functioning, the data do not unequivocally tell us about the salience of colour to infants. The problem is that the outputs of the different types of cones are combined in two fundamentally different ways, one of which communicates information about hue and the other brightness. In one neural pathway, the responses of the different cones are subtracted from each other to yield what is called "spectrally opponent" or "chromatic" mechanisms that communicate hue. In the other pathway, cone outputs are combined additively to yield "achromatic" luminance-detecting visual mechanisms. The colour (or strictly, the hue) of a stimulus is determined by the spectrally opponent mechanism, but the strength or salience of the colour (strictly "saturation") depends on a comparison of the relative strengths of the chromatic to achromatic responses (see Teller & Lindsey, 1993b). There is evidence that young infants are less sensitive to chromatic than luminance differences. Stimulus size and chromatic differences must be large for infants to display the chromatic discriminations that their spectrally opponent mechanisms seem capable of communicating, so, as we have seen before, aspects of the stimulus other than its wavelength will affect how an infant responds to it.

It is difficult to know for certain, but it is probably safe to say that even young infants have a form of colour vision and it is probably largely like that of adults. As a result of the lower responsiveness of their cones and related chromatic mechanisms, colours probably appear less intense than the same colours would to an older infant or an adult. If required to make discriminations among colours, infants would not be able to distinguish as many colour differences, although outside of the laboratory this is not likely to be a task often posed to young infants. Their colour vision should be enough, however, to be able to use commonality of surface colour to distinguish the boundaries of many objects as those objects move across the infant's field of view, which is an important use of colour in the viewing of natural scenes. [None of the data allow us to know whether infants (or dogs or cats) dream in colour – a question that for some reason I am frequently asked when people learn that I study infant vision. Sorry!]

DEVELOPMENT OF ACCOMMODATION AND VERGENCE

In our discussions of spatial resolution and the CSF, we assumed implicitly that changes in the eyes' optical properties had been controlled or optimised. However, in order to produce a good image on the retina, one that preserves high spatial frequencies, the eye must be appropriately focused; also, to see a single image of an object, both eyes must rotate correctly to point at the object. The abilities to do these things change with age and must be considered when evaluating infants' visual performance.

Accommodation

Accommodation refers to the process of changing the curvature of the crystalline lens to vary the eye's refractive power. Refraction is a measure of the bending of light rays by an optical system, expressed in diopters (D), a unit defined as the reciprocal of the focal length of the lens in metres (and also of viewing distance, given correct accommodation). For example, 1D corresponds to a 1 metre distance, 2D to $\frac{1}{2}$ metre, 4D to $\frac{1}{4}$ metre, etc. Less accommodation is needed to focus far objects, more to focus near objects. Emmetropia refers to the condition when an individual completely relaxes accommodation and the resulting plane of focus is very far (optical infinity, effectively about 6 metres); by increasing accommodation, it is possible to focus nearer objects. In near-sightedness or myopia, when accommodation is relaxed, the eye is focused at a relatively close distance and therefore distant objects will appear blurred. In contrast, in far-sightedness or hyperopia, the plane of focus when accommodation is relaxed is beyond optical infinity and all objects appear blurred; hyperopes must accommodate to see clearly targets at any distance. If they start with completely relaxed accommodation, all three of the described types of individual can, in principle, focus nearer objects. Hyperopes must accommodate to some degree for all distances, including very distant ones. Near-sighted or myopic individuals must accommodate for objects closer than their relaxed plane of focus. Note, however, that myopes cannot use accommodation to focus on objects beyond their plane of relaxed accommodation, which is why for myopes without optical correction, far objects appear blurred. Also, because the ability to accommodate declines steadily with age, the range of focusable distances ultimately declines for all individuals, particularly after age 40 (e.g. Millodot, 1982).

Vergence

Functional vision depends not only on the clarity of the image for each eye but also on how the eyes are jointly positioned. Vergence refers to the rotation of the eyes so that their viewing axes intersect, ideally on a plane for which the eyes are accommodated. The angle of rotation is measured in prism diopters (a prism of one diopter shifts the image by 1cm at a distance of 1m). The primary function of vergence is to reduce the disparity of the two retinal images and to bring the target into single binocular registration. In most adults, the accommodative and vergence systems are synergistically linked so that each system influences the other's performance (see Schor & Ciuffreda, 1983). Thus, there is another component of vergence caused by a change in accommodation (accommodative vergence); similarly, an important component of the accommodative response is accommodation caused by a change in vergence (vergence accommodation). As each eye looks at objects from slightly different angles, there is a disparity between the images in the two eyes that is inversely related to viewing distance. The images of an object on the plane to which the eyes are converged fall on corresponding retinal regions and are normally fused and seen as a single object. There is also a region, known as Panum's fusion area, which extends in front and back of the binocular fixation plane, within which all points are fused and seen as single objects, even though they do not fall on strictly corresponding points; these targets also are seen at difference distances in front of or behind the convergence plane. For adults, vergence driven by disparity is much more precise than accommodative vergence, and so fusional vergence is more likely to be seen under normal conditions (Schor, 1979). As fixation disparity increases, a point is reached at which Panum's region is exceeded and the fusion breaks down, resulting in double vision or diplopia. Stereoscopic information about an object's depth also depends on disparity, although it appears to be a higher function than fusion; one can have single vision, that is, fusion, without achieving stereoscopic depth perception. It is likely that these skills depend on the development of different cortical centres.

For both accommodation and vergence, the spatial frequency content of the stimulus and the observer's spatial contrast sensitivity (or, more correctly, spatiotemporal contrast sensitivity) interact with response. From a developmental standpoint, we would expect to see some correspondence between developments of the spatial CSF and the accommodation/vergence system. With cooperative, instructable subjects, the most common method to measure refractive status is retinoscopy, in which a practitioner evaluates the refractive error by determining the power of lenses that need to be substituted externally to null the amount of refraction of a test light by the various optical elements of the eye. Retinoscopy with infants requires considerable practice. In order to facilitate the evaluation of infant refractive status, several photographic methods have also been devised; among these are orthogonal, isotropic, and paraxial photorefraction (Atkinson et al., 1981; Bobier & Braddick, 1985; Howland & Howland, 1974; Norcia, Zadnik, & Day, 1986). The methods differ in the exact optical principles employed, but all provide an instantaneous photographic sample of refractive state from an uninstructed subject. Vergence is measured by monitoring changes in the eyes' angle of rotation. A common method is to measure changes in the position within each pupil of the image of a fixed reference light source reflected from the eye's cornea. The position of this corneal reflection and its shift with a given degree of eye rotation depend on a number of physical features of the eye, including corneal curvature, the location of the fovea and the separation of the eyes, all of which are known to change developmentally.

One of the widely used methods for infant refraction is paraxial photo-refraction, also called eccentric photorefraction, photoretinoscopy, and static photographic skiascopy (Abramov, Hainline, & Duckman, 1990; Bobier & Braddick, 1985; Howland, 1985). First developed by Kaakinen (1979), the method takes advantage of a problem encountered by amateur photographers: snapshots of people taken with inexpensive cameras often show an effect known as "red-eye", caused by the reflection of light from the flash back from the retina into the lens of the camera. With appropriate optics one can measure the degree of misaccommodation by measuring the size and position of a crescent of light. A system we use in our laboratory, with small lighted dolls at different distances as targets, is illustrated in Fig. 1.6a.

Figure 1.6b presents a series of pictures from an adult and an infant, both with normal refractive status. As the subject accommodates on the progressively closer targets, the crescents that are photographed through the eyes' pupils grow in size. The crescents are all across the top of the pupil, which indicates myopia in our system, because the targets are all closer than the camera distance: a subject who accommodates correctly for any of these targets will appear myopic with respect to the camera. To relate the size of a crescent to accommodation, in diopters, when calibrated, yields a sensitive estimate of plane of focus on each picture. Vergence is measurable from evaluation of the reflections of the flash source in the two pupils simultaneously. The method works effectively both to delineate the normal developmental progress of accommodation and to screen for infants with problems of vergence and/or accommodation.

Developmental studies of accommodation and vergence

Accommodation   Young infants have been reported to accommodate poorly, if at all. The earliest study of infant accommodation by Haynes et al. (1965) used dynamic retinoscopy. They reported that infants under 1 month had essentially frozen accommodation; however, refractive power changed when the subjects fell asleep, and thus the findings from the subjects when awake could not have been caused by factors such as inherent inelasticity of the lens. Not until 4 months did infants accommodate competently to targets at different distances. Subsequent research (e.g. Banks, 1980; Braddick, Atkinson, French, & Howland, 1979; Brookman, 1983) using different methods and stimuli, lowered the age of acceptable accommodation closer to 2 months, but still concluded that before 2 months, infants were poor accommodators. Assuming that accommodation was driven primarily by the need to keep high spatial frequencies

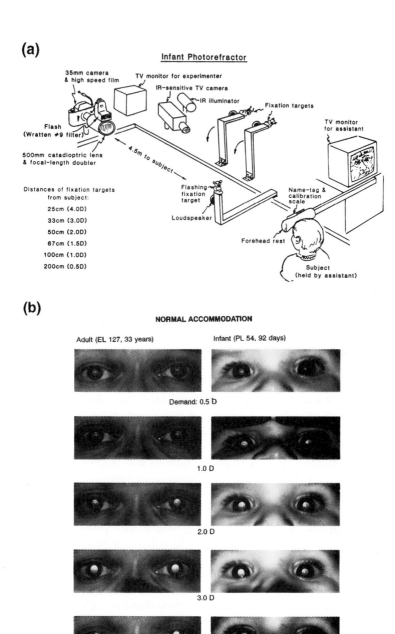

(a)

Infant Photorefractor

35mm camera & high speed film

TV monitor for experimenter

IR-sensitive TV camera

IR illuminator

Fixation targets

TV monitor for assistant

Flash (Wratten #9 filter)

500mm catadioptric lens & focal-length doubler

4.5m to subject

Distances of fixation targets from subject:

25cm (4.0D)

33cm (3.0D)

50cm (2.0D)

67cm (1.5D)

100cm (1.0D)

200cm (0.5D)

Flashing fixation target

Loudspeaker

Name-tag & calibration scale

Forehead rest

Subject (held by assistant)

(b)

NORMAL ACCOMMODATION

Adult (EL 127, 33 years)   Infant (PL 54, 92 days)

Demand: 0.5 D

1.0 D

2.0 D

3.0 D

4.0 D

FIG. 1.6. Paraxial photorefraction of infants (from Abramov et al., 1990). (a) Schematic view of photorefractor and stimuli, showing the relationship between the camera, the flash unit and the series of accommodation targets to the subject. The infrared television equipment is used to position the subject correctly for each photograph. (b) Paraxial photorefraction pictures of a visually – normal adult and infant viewing targets at different distances (demands to accommodation). The critical aspects of the photograph are the size and the position of the bright "crescent" in each eye.

31

in focus (i.e. to reduce retinal blur), Banks (1980) proposed that young infants did not accommodate better because the small sizes of their pupils together with their low acuity created an optical system with a large depth of focus, making accommodation unnecessary and irrelevant. With small viewing apertures, a wide range of focal planes is in focus simultaneously, reducing the need to accommodate. This argument overlooks another critical factor in determining depth of focus of an optical system. Decreasing pupil diameter, like reducing the aperture in a camera, increases depth of focus, but only if the focal length of the optical system is constant. That is not the case in infants' eyes, which not only have smaller pupils, but also are shorter in axial length. The small size of the infant eye is compensated for by the greater optical power of the infant lens and cornea (Bennett & Francis, 1962; Lotmar, 1976). Relative depth of focus can be measured by the ratio of an optical system's focal length to the diameter of its pupil. When both factors are taken into account, there is no great difference in depth of focus between infant and adult eyes (Banks & Bennett, 1988), so this cannot be an explanation to account for developmental differences in accommodation.

There may also be problems with the assumption that 1-month-old infants' poor accommodation is related to their reduced acuity and the role that high spatial frequencies play in accommodation. Acuity develops continuously over the first year (see e.g. Dobson & Teller, 1978), with no sudden increase being reported between 1 and 2 months. Consequently, an explanation of poor accommodation as the result of reduced acuity would seem to require the additional assumption that good accommodation requires some as yet unspecified threshold level of acuity. Alternatively, acuity may not be the most relevant ability here. High-frequency sensitivity develops over a longer time course than sensitivity to low and middle spatial frequencies (see Fig. 1.3). If intermediate spatial frequencies are more important for infants' accommodation, the time course for the development of acuity would not be immediately relevant in predicting accommodative development. The time course for development of sensitivity to intermediate sensitivities is a closer match to the accommodation data; in the data described earlier for spatial CSF development, sensitivity to intermediate spatial frequencies changes significantly between 1 and 2 months, and then stabilises.

It is also possible that accommodative performance improves for reasons other than a change in visual ability. Studies have found that infants accommodate more accurately to near than to far targets (Banks, 1980; Braddick & Atkinson, 1979). There are also findings that an infant's attention to stationary objects is inversely related to their distance from the infant, even when retinal size is kept invariant (de Schonen, McKenzie, Maury, & Bresson, 1978; McKenzie & Day 1972). This preferential attention to near objects is not seen if the objects move, flash, or rotate, presumptively because these manipulations enhance infants' attention (McKenzie & Day, 1976). The distance of an object will be related to the spatial frequency content of the object; objects farther away have more high frequencies, which young infants may not detect unless middle spatial frequencies are enhanced by movement. Or it may simply be an issue of attention, not detection; if young infants' accommodative performance were to improve with the addition of attention-enhancing features, we might not need to seek optical factors as an explanation of earlier results.

In research done in our laboratory, we have been measuring the simultaneous accommodation and vergence responses from young infants (Hainline & Riddell, 1995, 1996). What we find is that most young infants (and the occasional older infant) who do not show evidence of varying accommodation to targets at different distances often do not show any evidence of vergence either, suggesting that, for some reason, they are simply not paying attention to the change in target distance. Although we do not have an independent measure of behavioural state, our best guess is that the infants who showed no response in our system were in the open-eyed, trance-like state often seen in young infants; Banks (1980) also reported cases of flat accommodation in drowsy infants. The incidence of attending, correctly accommodating, and verging infants increases with age over the first half-year; but even young infants behave appropriately some of the time.

Such results point up a common problem in work on sensory development; if we use the kinds of stimuli that allow maximal experimental control and that are scientifically justifiable, and indeed, required in adult studies, we may at the same time be stripping the stimulus of many of the dimensions that rouse infants' interest. Sensory psychophysics typically calls for static, silent stimuli that are hard to see because they are close to threshold. Yet research on infant attentional preferences tells us that infants would rather look at moving, flashing or otherwise changing stimuli, well above threshold contrast and rich in contours. The Gibsonian tradition demands that stimuli have "ecological validity", usually meaning that a preference is given to real objects or events. When real objects are used as stimuli, however, it easy to make the mistake that the infant is responding to the stimuli as an adult would and end up attributing too much cognitive competence to an infant who is, in actuality, responding to differences across displays on only a sensory level. The obvious answer is to test the same ability with both well-controlled and more complex realistic stimuli, but this is rarely done.

Findings such as these imply that the failure to see accommodative responses in a young infant may not require an explanation in terms of the large depth of focus of the infant eye or low acuity. Under the right circumstances, it seems that infants can accommodate reasonably well. What we do not know, at this point, is what drives the accommodation of young infants. Is there a relationship within individual infants between peak CSF sensitivity and accommodation, so that younger accommodators would be found to have "precocious" spatial vision? Or are we observing vergence-driven accommodation, executed to maintain fusion? Evidence is beginning to accumulate (Currie & Manny, 1990; Hainline & Riddell, 1996) that binocular fusional mechanisms are important in determining correct accommodation in young infants. More within-subject measures are needed to address these questions.

Vergence   There is a small number of studies of binocular convergence in infancy. They agree that convergence is relatively poor, particularly for closer targets, until around 2 months, not surprisingly the age at which accommodation is also reported to be markedly improved (Aslin, 1977; Aslin & Jackson, 1979; Slater & Findlay, 1975). Our data show that even at early ages, vergence performance on average is quite good, possibly because of the attractive value of our targets. Unfortunately, the other studies have not simultaneously measured accommodation, so that the direct link between accommodation and vergence could not be checked.

DEVELOPMENT OF SENSORY BINOCULARITY

Binocular vision refers to the interaction of vision in the two eyes. "Fusion" is the term used to describe the phenomenon when the brain merges the images from the two eyes (which are slightly different because the eyes are separated by an interpupillary distance of 1–2 inches, a parameter closely correlated with age and growth of the head). The finest cue to depth perception, stereopsis, emerges when specialised cells in the brain's visual cortex compare the inputs from the two eyes and abstract a signal that conveys very small depth differences for targets that are relatively close – within arm's length. Binocular fusion depends on having the ability to point the two eyes appropriately when looking at a single object; in our research we (Hainline & Riddell, 1995; 1996) have shown that infants show reasonably good eye alignment from an early age, in most cases. Because of their lower acuities and the probability that Panum's fusional area is broader in infants (although no one to date has measured it), it is likely that even the youngest infants, if visually normal, demonstrate the behaviours precedent to fusion from an early age. Attention can influence alignment; for example, it is common to see departures from good eye alignment when an infant is very sleepy. But most of the time, infants direct their eyes so that the image of regard falls on corresponding retinal points for both eyes. In other words, consistent eye turns are not normal, even for young infants. Sometimes, the infant may appear to an observer to be "wall-eyed", that is, with each eye turned out. This "pseudo-strabismus" comes from differences in the relationship between the size of the eyeball and the position of the fovea for infants compared with adults (Slater & Findlay, 1972). The appearance is enhanced in an infant with a wide bridge of the nose, although measured alignment is usually fine. Our hypothesis is that even though crude, some ability to align the two eyes probably is necessary early on so that as the fovea develops and creates the ability of increasingly fine acuity, the eyes can continue to be kept in alignment with a degree of precision consistent with the level of spatial vision, as a platform for the eventual development of visual functions requiring high binocular acuity such as stereopsis.

The data on stereopsis in infancy agree fairly well that initially coarse stereopsis emerges rather suddenly somewhere between 3 and 6 months of age (Birch, 1993; Birch, Gwiazda, & Held; 1982; Shea, Fox, Aslin, & Dumais, 1980; Shimojo, 1993; Shimojo, Bauer, O'Connell, & Held, 1986), followed by a rapid increase in stereoacuity (a measure of the smallest binocular disparity detectable) to near adult levels in the second half of the first year. Held (1993) has argued that the appearance of stereopsis signals the development of particular cortical structures that compare the inputs from the two eyes. We have the sense from these and other data that much of the sensory and motor development that has been measured in the first half-year is a kind of preparation for the visual refinements (including stereopsis and the ability to detect very fine stimulus offsets, termed Vernier acuity (Shimojo, Birch, Gwiazda, & Held, 1984) that emerge near the end of that time period.

OCULOMOTOR DEVELOPMENT

Human infants are motorically immature compared with other primates. Because poor control of eye movements could adversely influence functional vision, it is interesting to ask how mature their oculomotor systems are. There are many ways to record and measure eye movements, some of which are inappropriate for use with infants. The most common methods in use with infants include simple observation, the electrooculogram (EOG) reflecting changes in electrical potential across two electrodes as the eye moves, and video measurements that focus on landmarks of the eye that change as the eye moves (corneal reflection methods that typically reference the position of a stationary light source to the position of the centre of the eye's pupil during eye movements). The methods have various advantages and disadvantages, which are discussed in Shupert and Fuchs (1988), Hainline and Abramov (1992), and Hainline (1993), among other sources.

Pointing the fovea: Saccades and fixations

Saccades Saccadic eye movements, among the most rapid of all muscular responses, serve to point the fovea at targets that must be examined in some detail during a fixation. They are fast presumably to minimise visual "down time" as the eye moves from fixation to fixation. Because we know that the foveae of young infants are immature, we might expect that there should be marked immaturities in the saccadic and fixational behaviour of young infants. We have measured the details of saccades and fixations in young infants looking at a variety of targets, using corneal reflection methods. An example of such an eye movement record, and how the various episodes are extracted, is shown in Fig. 1.7.

When we analyse the properties of the saccades, we discover that the quantitative parameters of saccades, for example, the maximum velocity that the eye accelerates to in a saccade, which is related to the amplitude of the saccade, are very similar for infants and adults (Hainline, Turkel, Abramov, Lemerise, & Harris, 1984); this relationship is termed a "main sequence" (Bahill, Clark, & Stark, 1975); see Fig. 1.8.

However, we find that how "adult-like" saccades are depends on whether the stimulus material that the infant is looking at has many contours, associated with infant attention (Fig. 1.8d). With simpler stimuli, infants' saccades are slower, possibly because of reduced physiological arousal and its effects on the structures in the brain stem reticular formation, implicated in both attention and eye movements.

In terms of amplitude, when freely scanning scenes, the distribution of saccadic amplitudes for infants and adults look similar (Hainline & Abramov, 1985). Some studies report that when infants are asked to look at a new target after the current target disappears, they approach the new target with a series of equal-sized, "step-like" saccades (Aslin & Salapatek, 1975). Not all studies show this effect, however (Hainline & Abramov, 1985), and it may also be the result of low attention, as the frequency of adult step-saccades increases with fatigue and inattention (Bahill & Stark, 1975). An alternative explanation is that infants need to calibrate how much of an eye movement is necessary to reach the target (Aslin, 1993), particularly in an otherwise featureless scene. We do not regularly observe step-saccades when infants look at natural scenes, so they may be an artifact of the laboratory. In general, the saccadic system seems quite mature and ready to function to reorient the fovea at high speed, even early in life.

Fixations A saccade is usually followed by a fixation, during which the eyes are held more or less stationary and the new target is examined (Fig. 1.8a and b). In contrast to positions that have characterised young infants

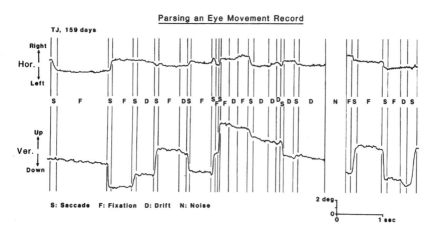

FIG. 1.7.   Parsing a typical eye movement record. Upper trace shows the horizontal component of the eye's position in time, and lower trace shows the vertical component. Vertical
lines are experimenter-determined boundaries between different types of movement.
(Reprinted from *Vision Research* **28**, Harris et al., The distribution of fixation durations in
infants and naïve adults, pp. 419–432, © 1988, with permission from Elsevier Science.)

as "captured" by visual stimuli (Stechler & Latz, 1966), we generally find
that when infants are alert and attending, their fixations are actually briefer
in many cases than those of uninstructed adults. Infant fixation duration
appears to be related to how many visual details are available to pull the
eye away from the current fixation; with many contours, fixations are
briefer than when contours are less prevalent (Hainline & Abramov, 1992;
Harris, Hainline, Abramov, Lemerise, & Camenzuli, 1988). Part of the
confusion about infant fixation may arise from an unfortunate redefinition
of the term "fixation" in the infant attention literature, where the term is
used to denote the total amount of attention directed toward a stimulus;
we would suggest that this behaviour might be better termed "looking",
leaving the term "fixation" to its traditional meaning in the oculomotor
literature (psychoanalysis obviously appropriates the term as well, but not
in a form likely to cause confusion in discussions of infant vision). It then
is not a paradox that when an infant is extremely interested in a visual
stimulus, total looking could be high, but the length of individual fixations,
as infants actively scan the interesting object, could be brief.

Another issue concerns the question of how stable the eye is during
fixation. In nonlaboratory situations, even for adults the eye actually drifts
quite a bit (e.g. Skavenski et al., 1979). Infants appear to have more
difficulty maintaining stable fixations, but seem to be sensitive to this;
higher drift rates are associated with shorter fixations, as if the visual

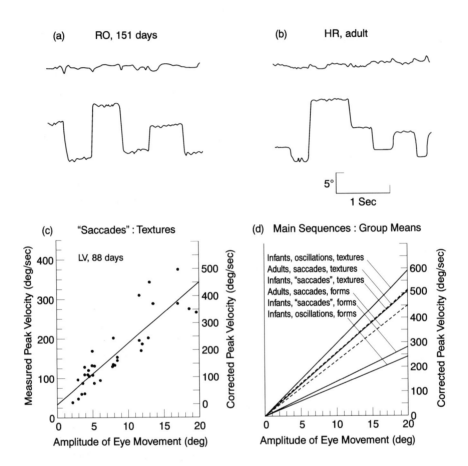

FIG. 1.8. (a), (b) Examples of saccades and fixations from an infant and an adult. Each upper trace shows the horizontal component of the eye's position in time, and the lower trace shows the vertical component. (c) Typical main sequence for peak saccadic velocity versus amplitude, with best-fitting linear regression; right ordinate shows the peak velocities corrected for the bandwidth limitations of our tracker. (d) Average main sequences for infants and adults scanning two types of stimuli. (Reprinted from *Vision Research* **24**, Hainline et al., Characterisitics of saccades in human infants, pp. 1771–1780, © 1984, with permission from Elsevier Science.)

feedback about a stimulus moving rapidly across the retina leads to a refixation (Hainline, 1993). Obviously, infants' spatiotemporal sensitivity is relevant here, because whether retinal slippage of a target elicits a saccade will depend on whether the target is above threshold or not.

A final point about fixations concerns the precision of "foveation", related to the question of whether, when a target is looked at several times (i.e. refixated), how widely scattered about the target are the successive fixations. Even highly trained adults' refixation of small targets shows some scatter, although small (with a standard deviation of about 0.1deg according to de Bie, 1986, and Snodderly, 1987). When infants refixated small targets, they showed a higher degree of refixation scatter than for trained adults (0.8deg *SD* on average), but untrained adults looking at the same targets were not substantially less variable (about 0.4 *SD*; Hainline, Harris, & Krinsky, 1990). These data suggest that infants are using some consistent small retinal area, possibly the fovea, to direct their fixations even when they are fairly young; Hainline et al.'s study did not detect age differences during infancy in the degree of refixational scatter. The present data support the contention that infants possess sufficient oculomotor control to allow deliberate inspection of static visual scenes.

Stabilising moving images: Pursuit, optokinetic nystagmus, and the vestibulo-ocular reflex

The retina is mounted in a moving eye in a moving head, on a locomoting body. The highest spatial frequencies of moving retinal images are most readily lost due to temporal factors, but as we have seen already, many aspects of visual function may continue uninterrupted based on inter-mediate spatial frequencies, to which even young infants are relatively sensitive.

Smooth pursuit Smooth pursuit is the ability to rotate the eye smoothly so as to keep the image of a moving target stable on the fovea. To stabilise a moving target the gain of the pursuit (the ratio of eye velocity to target velocity) must be close to unity. Well-trained adults can maintain such gains for velocities as high as 30–40deg/sec, although this takes extreme attention and the subject fatigues rapidly (Howard, 1982). Early data reported that young infants, whose foveae are quite immature, had poorly developed smooth pursuit (Aslin, 1981; Dayton, Jones, Steele, & Rose, 1964; Shea & Aslin, 1984). Others using targets that may have been more salient to the infant have shown evidence of smooth pursuit at slow speeds and for larger targets in young infants, including newborns (Carchon & Block 1996; Hainline, 1985; Kreminitzer, Vaughan, Kurtzberg & Dowling, 1979; Roucoux, Culee, & Roucoux, 1983; Von Hofsten & Rosander, 1996; Shea & Aslin, 1990). For faster-moving targets, infants and adults both follow the target with a mixture of saccades and smooth pursuit, which is adaptive and requires less concentration, at least for adults (Hainline, 1993).

Optokinetic nystagmus (OKN) and vestibulo-ocular reflex (VOR)   OKN and VOR are two oculomotor systems closely linked to the vestibular system and its interactions with the visual system, and are important for compensating for movement of the organism through the world and some of the associated movements of the retinal image (e.g. Cohen, 1974; Cohen, Henn, Raphan, & Dennett, 1981). OKN is a repetitive series of eye movements produced when a large portion of the visual field's retinal image slips across the retina. In response, the two eyes move as a unit with alternating phases of smooth tracking (the "slow" phase of OKN) and return saccades (OKN "fast phase"; see Fig. 1.9). As a result, the slippage of the image on the retina is minimised. OKN is a phylogenetically "old" system that developed in lateral-eyed animals who do not possess a specialised fovea or show smooth pursuit of a small target. Infants show well-developed OKN from birth, although when OKN is stimulated from one eye at a time, the behaviour shows an interesting asymmetry that disappears with age; for young infants, when targets are viewed with one eye only, OKN is elicited when the pattern moves in the direction from the temple towards the nose, but not in the opposite direction. By 4–5 months of age, the monocular response is much more symmetrical (Atkinson & Braddick, 1981; Naegele & Held, 1982), although infants with various visual problems continue to show the monocular asymmetry (e.g. van Hof-van Duin & Mohn, 1983). The most common interpretation of the "disappearance" of the monocular OKN asymmetry is the emergence of new forms of cortical control in the visual system (e.g. Hoffman, 1979; Preston & Finocchio, 1993; Schor, Narayan, & Westall, 1983), but as yet there are no hard and fast data to substantiate this hypothesis for humans.

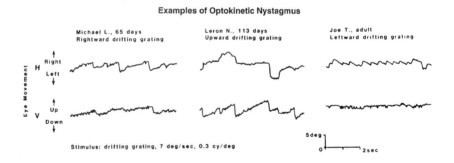

Examples of Optokinetic Nystagmus

FIG. 1.9   Examples of the alteration of fast and slow eye movements that characterise the eye movement class called optokinetic nystagmus. In the examples, the stimulus was a pattern of stripes moving in different directions at a moderate speed (7deg/sec) in front of the infant. (From Hainline & Abramov, 1985.)

Although OKN in humans may be less important for image stabilisation than the foveational systems, it may still be quite important in its intricate interactions with mechanisms for vestibular stabilisation. The OKN and VOR systems share many neuronal elements, but the VOR is designed to maintain the eye's gaze direction in spite of head rotation. It is possible that, in humans, the major role of these systems under natural conditions is to compensate for head turns; the VOR provides the initial ocular stabilisation, as it is a fast response, and OKN adds any necessary longer-duration components (Preston & Finocchio, 1993). However, both responses can be overridden when voluntarily fixating a target, and may be of less importance developmentally as fixational control and smooth pursuit improve. Some suggestive evidence comes from some recent studies of the development of the VOR. In adults, the gain of the VOR is much less than one, actually about 0.5, so that it functions relatively poorly as an overall image-stabilising system. In contrast, the gain of the VOR in infants and even in young children is close to 1.0, and so compensates better on its own for image slippage caused by head rotations or other bodily movements through space (Finocchio, Preston, & Fuchs, 1990a,b). But if adults' VOR gain is low because other systems are more suitable for keeping the fovea pointed at interesting targets, one might expect to find a close but inverse connection in the developmental rates for smooth pursuit and VOR gain. In fact, there is a fair amount of mismatch between the time courses in VOR and smooth pursuit gains; pursuit is well developed within a year, whereas VOR gain continues to drop to adult levels over at least the first 5–6 years. It is possible that, in this case, the VOR is responding to gross physical development as much as to the parameters of visual stimulation, as the VOR is also important in the maintenance of posture as the body moves. Children's gross motor coordination continues to develop well into the early school years, and so they may need a more "robust" VOR system during that time. The introduction of the physical control of the body raises another level of complexity that we do not have time to develop further here.

CONCLUSION

The study of visual development has seen significant advances in the last three decades. Real progress has been made in describing the developmental course of many visual subsystems, only some of which we have dealt with here. The major hindrance to faster progress in understanding infant vision is methodological. There is a continuing tension between making the research hew closely to the model of "good science" found in numerous elegant adult studies, and adjusting the methodologies to be sensitive to the characteristics of the organism of interest, the human infant.

It is a contrast of some interest how poorly infants often perform in laboratory studies and how well-integrated they appear to be in their natural environments. Part of this effect is probably due to the use of simple, unidimensional stimuli that are not too interesting in their own right in many laboratory studies, which suggests that our research needs to include a wider range of stimuli. We also have not always given sufficient attention to the fact that the various components of vision combine to yield a reasonably competent ensemble of abilities, including not only vision but vestibular reactions. In the main, when exercised in the rich stimulus context of the infant's everyday world, infant vision is a highly functional sense. Although single abilities may be less than fully mature, the ensemble of visual functions allows the infant to respond appropriately to relevant aspects of the environment, including the distinctive features and affordances described by Gibson (1966, 1979). When development proceeds normally, infant vision seems perfectly adequate for the things that infants need to do. There is, however, reason to be worried about the development of infants who start life with some sort of visual deficit; this will be discussed in the next chapter.

REFERENCES

Abramov I., & Gordon, J. (1973). Vision. In E. Carterette & M. Friedman (Eds.), *Handbook of perception* (Vol 3). New York: Academic Press.

Abramov, I., Gordon, J., Hendrickson, A., Hainline, L., Dobson, V., & LaBossiere, I. (1982). The retina of the newborn human infant. *Science, 217*, 265–267.

Abramov, I., Hainline, L., & Duckman, R. (1990). Screening infant visual with paraxial photorefraction. *Optometry and Vision Science, 67*, 538–545.

Abramov, I., Hainline, L., Turkel, J., Lemerise, E., Smith, H., Gordon, J., & Petry, S. (1984). Rocketship psychophysics: assessing visual functioning in young children. *Investigative Ophthalmology and Visual Science, 25*, 1307–1315.

Allen, D., Banks, M.S., Norcia, A.M., & Shannon, E. (1993). Does chromatic sensitivity develop more slowly than luminance sensitivity? *Vision Research, 33*, 2553–2562.

Archer, S.M. (1993). Detection and treatment of congenital esotropia. In K. Simons (Ed.), *Early visual development, normal and abnormal*. New York: Oxford University Press.

Arterberry, M.E., Craton, L.G., & Yonas, A. (1993). Infants' sensitivity to motion-carried information for depth and object properties. In C.E. Granrud (Ed.), *Visual perception and cognition in infancy*. Hillsdale, NJ: Erlbaum.

Aslin, R.N. (1977). Development of binocular fixation in human infants. *Journal of Experimental Child Psychology, 23*, 133–150.

Aslin, R.N. (1981). Development of smooth pursuit in human infants. In D.F. Fisher, R.A. Monty, & J.W. Senders (Eds.), *Eye movements: Cognition and visual perception*. Hillsdale, NJ: Erlbaum.

Aslin, R.N. (1987). Visual and auditory development in infancy. In J. Osofsky (Ed.), *Handbook of infant development* (2nd edn.) Hillsdale, NJ: Erlbaum.

Aslin, R.N. (1993). Perception of visual direction in human infants. In C.E. Granrud (Ed.), *Visual perception and cognition in infancy.* Hillsdale, NJ: Erlbaum.

Aslin, R.N., & Jackson, R.W. (1979). Accommodative-convergence in young infants: Development of a synergistic sensory-motor system. *Canadian Journal of Psychology,* **33,** 222–231.

Aslin, R.N., & Salapatek, P. (1975). Saccadic localization of visual targets by the very young human infant. *Perception and Psychophysics,* **17,** 293–302.

Atkinson, J. (1977). Contrast sensitivity in infants. In H. Spekreise & L.H. van der Tweel (Eds.), *Spatial contrast.* Amsterdam: North Holland.

Atkinson, J. (1993). Infant vision screening: Prediction and prevention of strabismus and amblyopia from refractive screening in the Cambridge Photorefraction Program. In K. Simons (Ed.), *Early visual development, normal and abnormal.* New York: Oxford University Press.

Atkinson, J., & Braddick, O. (1981). Development of optokinetic nystagmus in infants: An indicator of cortical binocularity? In D.F. Fisher, R.A. Monty, & J.W. Senders (Eds.), *Eye movements: Cognition and visual perception.* Hillsdale, NJ: Erlbaum.

Atkinson, J., & Braddick, O. (1988). Infant precursors of later visual disorders: correlation or causality. In A. Yonas (Ed.), *Perceptual development in infancy. The Minnesota Symposium on Child Psychology* (Vol. 20). Hillsdale, NJ: Erlbaum.

Atkinson, J., & Braddick, O. (1989). Development of basic visual functions. In A. Slater & G. Bremner (Eds), *Infant development.* Hove, UK: Lawrence Erlbaum Associates Ltd.

Atkinson, J., Braddick, O., Ayling, L., Pimm-Smith, E., Howland, H.D., & Ingram, R.M. (1981). Isotropic photorefraction: A new method for photorefractive testing of infants. *Documenta Ophthalmologica,* **30,** 217–223.

Atkinson, J., Braddick, O., & Moar, K. (1977). Development of contrast sensitivity over the first three months of life in the human infant. *Vision Research,* **17,** 1037–1044.

Bahill, A.T., Clark, M.R., & Stark, L. (1975). The main sequence: a tool for studying human eye movements. *Mathematical Biosciences,* **24,** 191–204.

Bahill, A.T., & Stark, L. (1975). Overlapping saccades and glissades are produced by fatigue in the saccadic eye movement system. *Experimental Neurology,* **48,** 95–106.

Banks, M.S., (1980). The development of visual accommodation during early infancy. *Child Development,* **51,** 646–666.

Banks, M.S., & Bennett, P.J. (1988). Optical and photoreceptor immaturities limit the spatial and chromatic vision of human neonates. *Journal of the Optical Society of America A,* **5,** 2059–2079.

Banks, M.S., & Crowell, J.A. (1993). Front-end limitations to infant spatial vision: Examination of two analyses. In K. Simons (Ed.), *Early visual development, normal and abnormal.* New York: Oxford University Press.

Banks, M.S., & Salapatek, P. (1978). Acuity and contrast sensitivity in 1-, 2-, and 3-month-old human infants. *Investigative Ophthalmology and Visual Science,* **17,** 361–365.

Banks, M.S., & Salapatek, P. (1981). Infant pattern vision: A new approach based on the contrast sensitivity function. *Journal of Experimental Child Psychology,* **40,** 1–45.

Banks, M.S., & Shannon, E. (1993). Spatial and chromatic visual efficiency in human neonates. In C.E. Granrud (Ed.), *Visual perception and cognition in infancy.* Hillsdale, NJ: Erlbaum.

Bennett, A.G., & Francis, J.L. (1962). The eye as an optical system. In H. Davison (Ed.), *The eye. Vol. 4: Visual optics and the optical space sense.* New York: Academic Press.

Bertenthal, B.I., Proffitt, D.R., Spetner, N.B., & Thomas, M.A. (1985). The development of infant sensitivity to biomechanical motions. *Child Development,* **56,** 531–543.

Birch, E.E. (1993). Stereopsis in infants and its development in relation to visual acuity. In K. Simons (Ed.), *Early visual development, normal and abnormal.* New York: Oxford University Press.

Birch, E.E., Gwiazda, J., & Held, R. (1982). Stereoacuity development for crossed and uncrossed disparities in human infants. *Vision Research, 22,* 507–513.

Bobier, W.R., & Braddick, O. (1985). Eccentric photorefraction: optical analysis and empirical measures. *American Journal of Optometry and Physiological Optics, 62,* 614–620.

Braddick, O. (1993). Orientation- and motion-sensitive mechanisms in infants. In K. Simons (Ed.), *Early visual development, normal and abnormal.* New York: Oxford University Press.

Braddick, O., & Atkinson, J. (1979). Accommodation and acuity in the human infant. In R.D. Freeman (Ed.), *Developmental neurobiology of vision.* New York: Plenum.

Braddick, O., Atkinson, J., French, J., & Howland, H.C. (1979). A photorefractive study of infant accommodation. *Vision Research, 19,* 1319–1330.

Braddick, O., Atkinson, J., & Hood, B. (1996). Striate cortex, extrastriate cortex, and colliculus: Some new approaches. In F. Vital-Durand, J. Atkinson & O. Braddick (Eds.), *Infant vision.* Oxford: Oxford University Press.

Brookman, K.E. (1983). Ocular accommodation in human infants. *American Journal of Optometry and Physiological Optics, 60,* 91–99.

Brown, A. (1990). Development of visual sensitivity to light and colour vision in human infants: A critical review. *Vision Research, 30,* 1159–1188.

Brown, A. (1993). Intrinsic noise and infant visual performance. In K. Simons (Ed.), *Early visual development, normal and abnormal.* New York: Oxford University Press.

Brown, A.M., Dobson, V., & Maier, J. (1987). Visual acuity of human infants at scotopic, mesopic and photopic luminances. *Vision Research, 27,* 1845–1858.

Burr, D.C., Marrone, C., & Fiorentini, C. (1996). Spatial and temporal properties of infant colour vision. In F. Vital-Durand, J. Atkinson & O. Braddick (Eds.), *Infant vision.* Oxford: Oxford University Press.

Carchon, I., & Bloch, H. (1996). Eye–head relations in neonates and young infants. In F. Vital-Durand, J. Atkinson & O. Braddick (Eds.), *Infant vision.* Oxford: Oxford University Press.

Carpenter, G.C. (1974). Visual regard of moving and stationary faces in early infancy. *Merrill-Palmer Quarterly, 11,* 182–193.

Clavadetscher, J.E., Brown, A.M., Ankrum, C., & Teller, D.Y. (1988). Spectral sensitivity and chromatic discriminations in 3- and 7-week-old infants. *Journal of the Optical Society of America A, 5,* 2093–2105.

Cohen, B. (1974). The vestibular-ocular reflex arc. In H.H. Kornhuber (Ed.), *Handbook of sensory physiology, VI/1, Vestibular systems, Part I: Basic mechanisms.* Berlin: Springer-Verlag.

Cohen, B., Henn, V., Raphan, T., & Dennett, D. (1981). Velocity storage, nystagmus, and visual-vestibular interactions in humans. In B. Cohen (Ed.), *Vestibular and oculomotor physiology.* New York: New York Academy of Sciences.

Cohen, L.B. (1988). An information processing approach to infant cognitive development. In L. Weiskrantz (Ed.), *Thought without language.* New York: Oxford University Press.

Currie, D.C., & Manny, R.E. (1990). Proximity as a cue for accommodation in infants. *Investigative Ophthalmology and Visual Science. 31,* (Supplement), 82.

Dannemiller, J.L., & Stephens, B.R. (1988). A critical test of infant preference models. *Child Development, 59,* 210–216.

Daw, N.W. (1995). *Visual development.* New York: Plenum.

Dayton, G.O., Jones, M.H., Steele, B., & Rose, M. (1964). Developmental study of coordinated eye movements in the human infant. II. Electrooculographic study of the fixation reflex in the newborn. *Archives of Ophthalmology, 71,* 871–875.

de Bie, J. (1986). *The control properties of small eye movements.* Dissertation, Technische Universiteit, Delft, The Netherlands.

de Schonen, S., McKenzie, B., Maury, L., & Bresson, F. (1978). Central and peripheral object distances as determinants of the effective visual field in early infancy. *Perception, 7,* 499–506.

De Valois, R.L., & De Valois, K.K. (1988). *Spatial vision.* New York: Oxford University Press.

Dobson, V. (1993). Visual acuity testing in infants: From laboratory to clinic. In K. Simons (Ed.), *Early visual development, normal and abnormal.* New York: Oxford University Press.

Dobson, V., & Teller, D.Y. (1978). Assessment of visual acuity in infants. In J.C. Armington, J. Krauskopf, & B.R. Wooten (Eds.), *Visual psychophysics and physiology.* New York: Academic Press.

Fantz, R.L. (1956). A method for studying early visual development. *Perceptual Motor Skills, 6,* 13–15.

Finocchio, D., Preston, K., & Fuchs, A. (1990a). Obtaining a quantitative measure of eye movements in human infants: A method of calibrating the electrooculogram. *Vision Research, 30,* 1119–1128.

Finocchio, D., Preston, K., & Fuchs, A. (1990b). A quantitative analysis of the development of the vestibulo-ocular reflex and visual-vestibular interactions in human infants. *Investigative Ophthalmology and Visual Science, 31,* (Supplement), 83.

Fulton, A., Hansen, R.M., Dorn, E., & Hendrickson, A. (1996). Development of primate rod structure and function. In F. Vital-Durand, J. Atkinson & O. Braddick (Eds.), *Infant vision.* Oxford: Oxford University Press.

Garey, L., & De Courten, C. (1983). Structural development of the lateral geniculate nucleus and visual cortex in monkey and man. *Behavioral Brain Research, 10,* 3–15.

Gayl, I.E., Roberts, J.A., & Werner, J.A. (1983). Linear systems analysis of infant visual pattern preferences. *Journal of Experimental Child Psychology, 35,* 159–170.

Gibson, J.A. (1966). *The senses considered as perceptual systems.* Boston: Houghton Mifflin.

Gibson, J.A. (1979). *The ecological approach to visual perception.* Boston: Houghton Mifflin.

Ginsberg, A. (1986). Spatial filtering and visual form perception. In K.K. Off, L. Kaufman & J.P. Thomas (Eds.), *Handbook of perception and human performance.* New York: Wiley.

Ginsberg, A., Evans, R., Sekuler, R., & Harp, S. (1982). Contrast sensitivity predicts pilots' performance in aircraft simulators. *American Journal of Optometry and Physiological Optics, 59,* 105–109.

Graham, N.V. (1989). *Visual pattern analyzers.* New York: Oxford University Press.

Hainline, L. (1985). Oculomotor control in human infants. In R. Groner, G.W. McConkie & C. Menz (Eds.), *Eye movements and human information processing.* Amsterdam: Elsevier-North Holland.

Hainline, L. (1993). Conjugate eye movements of infants. In K. Simons (Ed.), *Early visual development, normal and abnormal.* New York: Oxford University Press.

Hainline, L., & Abramov, I. (1985). Saccades and small-field optokinetic nystagmus in infants. *Journal of the American Optometric Association, 56,* 620–626.

Hainline, L., & Abramov, I. (1992). Assessing visual development: Is infant vision good enough? In C Rovee-Collier & L.P. Lipsitt (Eds.), *Advances in infancy research* (Vol 7). Norwood, NJ: Ablex.

Hainline, L. & Abramov, I. (1997). Eye movement-based measures of development of contrast sensitivity in infants. *Optometry and Vision Science, 74,* 790–799.

Hainline, L., Camenzuli, C., Abramov, I., Rawlick, L., & Lemerise, E. (1986). A forced-choice method for deriving infant spatial contrast sensitivity functions from optokinetic nystagmus. *Investigative Ophthalmology and Visual Science* (Supplement), *27,* 266.

Hainline, L., de Bie, J., Abramov, I., & Camenzuli, C. (1987). Eye movement voting: A new technique for deriving spatial contrast sensitivity. *Clinical Vision Sciences*, **2**, 4–9.

Hainline, L., Harris, C.M., & Krinsky, S. (1990). Variability of refixations in infants. *Infant Behavior and Development*, **13**, 321–342.

Hainline, L., & Riddell, P.M. (1995). Binocular alignment and vergence in early infancy. *Vision Research*, **35**, 3229–3236.

Hainline, L., & Riddell, P.M. (1996). Eye alignment and convergence in young infants. In F. Vital-Durand, J. Atkinson & O. Braddick (Eds.), *Infant vision*. Oxford: Oxford University Press.

Hainline, L., Turkel, J., Abramov, I., Lemerise, E., & Harris, C. (1984). Characteristics of saccades in human infants. *Vision Research*, **24**, 1771–1780.

Harris, C.M., Hainline, L., Abramov, I., Lemerise, E., & Camenzuli, C. (1988). The distribution of fixation durations in the human infant. *Vision Research*, **28**, 419–432.

Haynes, H., White, B.L., & Held, R. (1965). Visual accommodation in human infants. *Science*, **148**, 528–530.

Held, R. (1981). Development of acuity in infants with normal and anomalous visual experience. In R.N. Aslin, J.R. Alberts & M.R. Peterson (Eds.), *Development of perception: Psychobiological perspectives, Vol 2: The Visual System*. New York: Academic Press.

Held, R. (1993). Two stages in the development of binocular vision and eye alignment. In K. Simons (Ed.), *Early visual development, normal and abnormal*. New York: Oxford University Press.

Hendrickson, A.E. (1993). Morphological development of the primate retina. In K. Simons (Ed.), *Early visual development, normal and abnormal*. New York: Oxford University Press.

Hendrickson, A., & Yuodelis, C. (1984). The morphological development of the human fovea. *Ophthalmologica*, **91**, 603–612.

Hickey, T.L. (1977). Postnatal development of the human lateral geniculate nucleus: Relationship to a critical period for the visual system. *Science*, **198**, 836–838.

Hoffman, K.P. (1979). Optokinetic nystagmus and single-cell responses in the nucleus tractus opticus after early monocular deprivation in the cat. In R.D. Freeman (Ed.), *Developmental neurobiology of vision*. New York: Plenum.

Howard, I.P. (1982). *Human visual orientation*. New York: Wiley.

Howland, H.C. (1985). Optics of photoretinoscopy: Results from ray-tracing. *American Journal of Optometry and Physiological Optics*, **62**, 621–625.

Howland, H.C., & Howland, B. (1974). Photorefraction: a technique for study of refractive state at a distance. *Journal of the Optical Society of America*, **64**, 240–249.

Huttenlocher, P. (1979). Synaptic density in human frontal cortex: developmental changes and effects of aging. *Brain Research*, **163**, 195–205.

Kaakinen, K. (1979). A simple method for screening children with strabismus, anisometropia, or ametropia by simultaneous photography of the corneal and fundus reflexes. *Acta Ophthalmologica (Kbh)*, **57**, 161–171.

Kellman, P.J. (1988). Theories of perception and research in perceptual development. In A. Yonas (Ed.), *Perceptual development in infancy: The Minnesota Symposium on Child Psychology* (Vol. 20). Hillsdale, NJ: Erlbaum.

Kellman, P.J. (1993). Kinematic foundations of infant visual perception. In C.E. Granrud (Ed.), *Visual perception and cognition in infancy*. Hillsdale, NJ: Erlbaum.

Kellman, P.J., Gleitman, J., & Spelke, E. (1987). Object and observer motion in the perception of objects by infants. *Journal of Experimental Psychology: Human Perception and Performance*, **13**, 586–593.

Kellman, P.J., & Spelke, E. (1983). Perception of partly occluded objects in infancy. *Cognitive Psychology*, **15**, 483–524.

Kelly, D.H. (1961). Visual responses to time-dependent stimuli: I. Amplitude sensitivity measurements. *Journal of the Optical Society of America*, **31**, 422–429.

Kelly, D.H. (1979a). Motion and vision: I. Stabilized images of stationary gratings. *Journal of the Optical Society of America*, **69**, 1266–1274.

Kelly, D.H. (1979b). Motion and vision. II. Stabilized spatio-temporal threshold surface. *Journal of the Optical Society of America*, **69**, 1340–1349.

Kiorpes, L. (1996). Development of contrast sensitivity in normal and amblyopic monkeys. In F. Vital-Durand, J. Atkinson & O. Braddick (Eds.), *Infant vision*. Oxford: Oxford University Press.

Kleiner, K.A. (1987). Amplitude and phase spectra as indices of infants' pattern preferences. *Infant Behavior and Development*, **10**, 45–55.

Kleiner, K.A., & Banks, M.S. (1987). Stimulus energy does not account for 2-month-olds' face preferences. *Journal of Experimental Psychology: Human Performance and Perception*, **13**, 594–600.

Knoblauch, K., Bieber, M., & Werner, J.S. (1996). Assessing dimensionality in infant colour vision. In F. Vital-Durand, J. Atkinson & O. Braddick (Eds.), *Infant vision*. Oxford: Oxford University Press.

Kremenitzer, J.P., Vaughan, H.G., Kurtzberg, D., & Dowling, K. (1979). Smooth-pursuit eye movements in the newborn infant. *Child Development*, **50**, 442–448.

Levi, D.M., & Carkeet, A. (1993). Amblyopia: A consequence of abnormal visual development. In K. Simons (Ed.), *Early visual development, normal and abnormal*. New York: Oxford University Press.

Levine, M.W., & Shefner, J.M. (1990). *Fundamentals of sensation and perception*. Pacific Grove, CA: Brooks/Cole.

Lotmar, W. (1976). A theoretical model for the eye of new-born infants. *Albrecht von Graefes Archiv für Klinische und Experimentelle Ophthalmologie*, **198**, 179–185.

McKenzie, B.E., & Day, R.H. (1972). Distance as a determinant of visual fixation in early infancy. *Science*, **178**, 1108–1110.

McKenzie, B.E., & Day, R.H. (1976). Infants' attention to stationary and moving objects at different distances. *Australian Journal of Psychology*, **28**, 45–51.

Millodot, M. (1982). Accommodation and refraction of the eye. In H.B. Barlow & J.D. Mollon (Eds.), *The senses*. Cambridge: Cambridge University Press.

Mitchell, D.E. (1988). The recovery from monocular visual deprivation in kittens. In A. Yonas (Ed.), *Perceptual development in infancy. The Minnesota Symposium on Child Psychology* (Vol. 20). Hillsdale, NJ: Erlbaum.

Morton, J., Johnson, M.H., & Maurer, D. (1990). On the reasons for newborn's response to faces. *Infant Behavior and Development*, **13**, 99–103.

Movshon, J.A., & Van Sluyters, R.C. (1981). Visual neural development. *Annual Review of Psychology*, **32**, 477–522.

Naegele, J.R., & Held, R. (1982). The postnatal development of monocular optokinetic nystagmus in infants. *Vision Research*, **22**, 341–346.

Neisser, U. (1976). *Cognition and reality*. San Francisco: Freeman.

Norcia, A.M. (1993). Improving infant evoked response measurement. In K. Simons (Ed.), *Early visual development, normal and abnormal*. New York: Oxford University Press.

Norcia, A.M., Clarke, M., & Tyler, C.W. (1985). Digital filtering and robust regression techniques for estimating sensory thresholds from the evoked potential. *IEEE Engineering in Medicine and Biology*, **4**, 26–32.

Norcia, A.M., Tyler, C.W., & Allen, D. (1986). Electrophysiological assessment of contrast sensitivity in human infants. *American Journal of Optometry and Physiological Optics*, **63**, 12–15.

Norcia, A.M., Tyler, C.W., & Hamer, R. (1990). Development of contrast sensitivity in the human infant. *Vision Research*, **30**, 1475–1486.

Norcia, A.M., Zadnik, K., & Day, S.H. (1986). Photorefraction with a catadioptric lens: improvement on the method of Kaakinen. *Acta Ophthalmologica (Kbh)*, **14**, 379–385.

Piotrowski, L.N., & Campbell, F.W. (1982). A demonstration of the visual importance and flexibility of spatial-frequency amplitude and phase. *Perception*, **11**, 337–346.

Preston, K.L., & Finocchio, D.V. (1993). Development of vestibulo-ocular and optokinetic reflexes. In K. Simons (Ed.), *Early visual development, normal and abnormal*. New York: Oxford University Press.

Ratliff, F. (1965). *Mach bands: Quantitative studies on neural networks in the retina*. San Francisco: Holden-Day.

Robson, J.G., & Graham, N. (1981). Probability summation and regional variation in contrast sensitivity across the visual field. *Vision Research*, **21**, 409–418.

Roucoux, A., Culee, C., & Roucoux, M. (1983). Development of fixation and pursuit eye movements in human infants. *Behavioral Brain Research*, **10**, 133–139.

Ruff, H.A. (1982). The effect of object movement on infants' detection of object structure. *Developmental Psychology*, **18**, 462–472.

Schor, C.M. (1979). The relationship between fusional vergence eye movements and fixational disparity. *Vision Research*, **19**, 1359–1367.

Schor, C.M., & Ciuffreda, K.J. (1983). *Vergence eye movements: Basic and clinical aspects*. Boston: Butterworth.

Schor, C.M., Narayan, V., & Westall, C. (1983). Postnatal development of optokinetic after nystagmus in human infants. *Vision Research*, **23**, 1643–1647.

Sereno, M.I., Dale, A.M., Reppas, J.B., Kwong, K.K., Belliveau, J.W., Brady, T.J., Rosen, B.R., & Tootell, R.B.H. (1995). Borders of multiple visual areas in humans revealed by functional magnetic resonance imaging. *Science*, **268**, 889–893.

Shea, S.L., & Aslin, R.N. (1984). Development of horizontal and vertical pursuit in human infants. *Investigative Ophthalmology and Visual Science*, (Supplement) **25**, 263.

Shea, S.L., & Aslin, R.N. (1990). Oculomotor responses to step-ramp targets by young human infants. *Vision Research*, **30**, 1077–1092.

Shea, S., Fox, R., Aslin, R., & Dumais, S. (1980). Assessment of stereopsis in human infants. *Investigative Ophthalmology and Visual Science*, **19**, 1400–1404.

Shimojo, S. (1993). Development of interocular vision in infants. In K. Simons (Ed.), *Early visual development, normal and abnormal*. New York: Oxford University Press.

Shimojo, S., Bauer, J., O'Connell, K.M., & Held, R. (1986). Pre-stereoptic binocular vision in infants. *Vision Research*, **27**, 501–510.

Shimojo, S., Birch, E.E., Gwiazda, J., & Held, R. (1984). Development of Vernier acuity in infants. *Vision Research*, **24**, 721–728.

Shupert, C, & Fuchs, A. (1988). Development of conjugate human eye movements. *Vision Research*, **28**, 585–596.

Simons, K. (Ed.) (1993). *Early visual development, normal and abnormal*. New York: Oxford University Press.

Skavenski, A.A., Hansen, R.M., Steinman, R.M., & Winterson, B.J. (1979). Quality of retinal image stabilization during small natural and artificial body/rotations in man. *Vision Research*, **19**, 675–683.

Slater, A., Earle, D.C., Morison, V., & Rose, D. (1985). Pattern preferences at birth and their interaction with habituation-induced novelty preferences. *Journal of Experimental Child Psychology*, **39**, 37–54.

Slater, A.M., & Findlay, J.M. (1972). The measurement of fixation position in the newborn baby. *Journal of Experimental Child Psychology*, **14**, 349–364.

Slater, A.M., & Findlay, J.M. (1975). Binocular fixation in the newborn baby. *Journal of Experimental Child Psychology, 20*, 248–273.

Snodderly, M. (1987). Effects of light and dark environments on macaque and human fixational movements. *Vision Research, 27*, 401–415.

Spelke, E. (1988). Where perceiving ends and thinking begins: The apprehension of objects in infancy. In A. Yonas (Ed.), *Perceptual development in infancy: The Minnesota Symposium on Child Psychology* (Vol. 20). Hillsdale, NJ: Erlbaum.

Stechler, G., & Latz, E. (1966). Some observations on attention and arousal in the human infant. *Journal of American Academy of Child Psychiatry, 5*, 517–525.

Teller, D.Y. (1979). The forced-choice preferential looking procedure: A psychophysical technique for use with human infants. *Infant Behavior and Development, 2*, 135–153.

Teller, D.Y., & Lindsey, D.T. (1993a). Infant color vision: OKN techniques and null plane analysis. In K. Simons (Ed.), *Early visual development, normal and abnormal*. New York: Oxford University Press.

Teller, D.Y., & Lindsey, D.T. (1993b). Motion nulling techniques and infant color vision. In C.E. Granrud (Ed.), *Visual perception and cognition in infancy*. Hillsdale, NJ: Erlbaum.

Thorn, F., & Schwartz, F. (1990). Effects of dioptric blur on Snellen and grating acuity. *Optometry and Vision Science, 67*, 3–7.

Turkewitz, G., & Kenney, P. (1982). Limitations on input as a basis for neural organization and perceptual development: A preliminary theoretical statement. *Developmental Psychbiology, 15*, 357–368.

Tychsen, L. (1993). Motion sensitivity and the origins of infantile strabismus. In K. Simons (Ed.), *Early visual development, normal and abnormal*. New York: Oxford University Press.

Tyler, C.W., Apkarian, P.A., Levi, D.M., & Nakayama, K. (1979). Rapid assessment of visual function: An electronic sweep technique for the pattern VEP. *Investigative Ophthalmology and Visual Science, 18*, 703–713.

van Hof-van Duin, J., & Mohn, G. (1983). Optokinetic and spontaneous nystagmus in children with neurological disorders. *Behavioral Brain Research, 10*, 163–175.

Van Nes, F.L., & Bouman, M.A. (1967). Variation of contrast sensitivity with luminance. *Journal of the Optical Society of America., 57*, 401–406.

Van Sluyters, R.C., Atkinson, J., Banks, M.S., Held, R.M., Hoffman, K.P., & Shatz, C.J. (1990). The development of vision and visual perception. In L. Spillman & J.A. Werner (Eds.), *Visual perception: The neurological foundations*. New York: Academic Press.

Vital-Durand, F., Atkinson, J., & Braddick. O. (eds.) (1996). *Infant vision*. Oxford: Oxford University Press.

Volbrecht, V., & Werner, J. (1987). Isolation of short-wavelength-sensitive cone photoreceptors in 4-6-week-old human infants. *Vision Research, 27*, 469–478.

Volkman, F.C., & Dobson, M.V. (1976). Infant responses of ocular fixation to moving visual stimuli. *Journal of Experimental Child Psychology, 22*, 86–99.

Von Hofsten, C., & Rosander, K. (1996). The development of gaze control and predictive tracking in young infants. *Vision Research, 36*, 81–96.

Wattam-Bell, J.R.B. (1996). Development of visual motion processing. In F. Vital-Durand, J. Atkinson & O. Braddick (Eds.), *Infant vision*. Oxford: Oxford University Press.

Wilson, H.R. (1988). Development of spatiotemporal mechanisms in infant vision. *Vision Research, 28*, 611–628.

Wilson, H.R. (1993). Theories of infant visual development. In K. Simons (Ed.), *Early visual development, normal and abnormal*. New York: Oxford University Press.

Yuodelis, C., & Hendrickson, A. (1986). A qualitative and quantitative analysis of the human fovea during development. *Vision Research, 26*, 847–855.

ACKNOWLEDGEMENTS

The research reported here was supported in part by grant NIH-EY03957, NSF–IBN-9319683 and PSC-CUNY Faculty Research award programme grants 667435, 669455, 664235, and 666240. The number of people who have helped in the research reported here is too large to credit individually, but I thank all of them collectively for their assistance. I especially thank my colleague Israel Abramov for his helpful comments on this chapter, particularly in the section on colour vision.

CHAPTER TWO

Abnormal visual development

Merrick J. Moseley, Meir Neufeld, and Alistair R. Fielder
The Western Eye Hospital, Imperial College School of Medicine, London, UK

INTRODUCTION

Although visual disorders manifest during development may differ qualitatively from those of adulthood, this chapter is not an attempt to describe in detail the diagnosis and management of paediatric eye conditions.[1] Rather, we shall focus on the consequences of eye disease for visual development and the insights into normal and abnormal function that can be obtained from the study of specific conditions and associated animal models.

One particular condition features prominently in our discussions: amblyopia. Amblyopia is defined as a loss of visual acuity in an ophthalmologically normal eye. Although systematically studied for over a century, amblyopia remains of great interest to clinical scientists.[2] It is an exemplar of a truly developmental disorder; although "amblyogenic" factors may arise at any point during a lifetime, only during visual development is there a risk of a permanent visual loss. From a purely clinical perspective, amblyopia is the most prevalent (2–5%) visual disorder of childhood, providing an additional impetus for our attempts to understand this condition.

Abnormal visual development may result in an inability to process optimally one or more visual stimulus attributes, including the spatial, temporal, and chromatic. In addition, abnormal development can result in defects in visual mechanisms such as the pupillary and accommodative

51

systems. However, unless otherwise stated, we consider here only functional loss in terms of spatial resolution, i.e. visual acuity. This remains the most clinically relevant index of seeing ability and, moreover, can now be measured routinely even in the youngest infants, using a preferential looking technique such as the acuity card procedure (McDonald, Dobson, Sebris, Baitch, & Varner, 1985). In this, the infant is shown an alternating pattern of black and white stripes or grating side by side with a grey patch of equal space-average brightness. The smallest stripe width (highest spatial frequency) grating that is reliably fixated in preference to the grey provides the estimate of acuity.

VISUAL DEVELOPMENT: EFFECT OF ABNORMAL INFLUENCES

It has long been appreciated that changes in function over time can prove insightful. Worth (1903) observed that the pattern of visual loss in strabismic amblyopia was a true loss (regression) and not simply a failure of visual acuity to develop. It is only recently, however, that clinicians can routinely obtain repeated measurements of visual acuity in infants and young children that allow a quantitative analysis of natural history not previously possible.

Figure 2.1 illustrates several different patterns of visual development including the normal and those associated with a variety of visual disorders (these are deliberately schematic, and quantitative comparisons across individual sketches should not be attempted).

Normal visual development is shown in Fig. 2.1a; the sketch simply indicating that most rapid visual development occurs in early infancy, slowing in late infancy and being complete by the age of 4 to 5 years. Potentially, the severest form of maldevelopment ("regression") is shown in Fig. 2.1b and occurs as a consequence of a broad range of ocular and neurological conditions, including inherited neurodegenerative disorders, trauma, and with a generally lesser degree of severity, amblyopia. At disease onset, vision monotonically declines from its previously attained level and, if treatment is unavailable, a visual impairment will result.

Patterns of visual development reveal intriguing and sometimes counter-intuitive observations. For example, a child's acuity may appear to be developing in an age-normal manner despite the presence of a severe macular lesion visible on ocular examination ("early hidden", Fig. 2.1c). Here, parafoveal development may be unaffected by the lesion and hence development may appear to mimic normality until the limit of resolution of the unaffected retinal areas is reached, at which point the visual loss will be revealed.

A further pattern of visual development ("early delayed") is associated

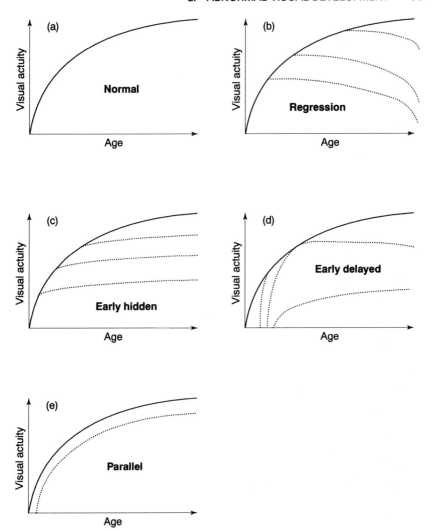

FIG. 2.1.   Patterns of visual development. (a) Normal visual development; (b) "Regression";
(c) "Early hidden"; (d) "Early delayed"; (e) "Parallel". Unbroken line: normal development
for comparison. Broken lines: abnormal visual development. Adapted from Fielder et al.
(1992).

with one specific condition: delayed visual maturation (DVM; see Tressider,
Fielder, & Nicholson, 1990). This is a heterogeneous visual disorder in
which an initially blind baby subsequently gains some or all of its visual
capacity (Fig. 2.1d). Four main types of DVM can be distinguished. In type
1 (isolated anomaly) an explosive period of visual development can occur

in a matter of days, resulting in subsequent visual development that becomes age-normal. In type 1, visual development may continue in a manner indistinguishable from normal, while in type 3 (in association with albinism or nystagmus), although age-normal acuity is similarly rapidly reached, this is not maintained and visual acuity subsequently falls away from the age norms. Where DVM occurs in association with other neurological and ocular abnormalities (types 2 and 4) slow improvement may still occur after a period of delay, although it will never attain age-normal levels, with visual loss persisting into adulthood.

So called "parallel" development is shown in Fig. 2.1e – "parallel" referring to the observation that the *rate* of visual development is on a par with normal but at any specific point in time vision is subnormal. This pattern of development is seen, for example, in aphakia (removal of the lens due to congenital cataract).

It should be stressed that the patterns of visual development described here do not encompass all ocular and neurological conditions affecting visual development. However, they do provide a useful perspective. Beyond the merely descriptive, the patterns of abnormal development can provide clues for insight into mechanisms. Take for example the rapid visual development seen in DVM (Fig. 2.1d). It has been observed that the age at which improvement occurs corresponds to the onset of certain cortical visual functions in normal infants (often around 2 months from birth: Bronson, 1974; Dubowitz, Mushin, de Vries, & Arden, 1986). Additionally, the rapidity of the onset of vision within a matter of days favours certain explanations as opposed to others – for example, a gene expression rather than a structural, maturational change such as myelination.

PRINCIPLES OF ABNORMAL VISUAL DEVELOPMENT: AMBLYOPIA

In the previous section we have highlighted the different ways in which abnormal visual development is manifested over time. In this section we consider the nature and treatment of amblyopia. This condition is the most prevalent visual disorder of childhood, generally affects only one eye, and is always present with one or more associated abnormalities (associations). The term "associations" is used judiciously here, as in some cases they may not actually be responsible for the amblyopia (see Fielder & Moseley, 1996) and their neutralisation, e.g. correction of a squint or refractive error, will generally only be preliminary (or secondary) to treatment proper.

Amblyogenesis – pathophysiology

Ciuffreda, Levi and Selenow (1991) have succinctly summarised four decades of laboratory animal research, including that of Nobel Laureates Hubel and Wiesel, into six statements. Appended to each of these we give the implication or corollary for human amblyopia.

1. *Disruption of binocular input completely disrupts the pattern of cortical excitatory binocular interaction.* This is presumed to be the nature of the visual deficit in human amblyopia where the input from each eye is "imbalanced" by refractive error, misalignment or other amblyogenic factor.
2. *Monocular deprivation has a dramatic effect on the anatomy, physiology, and function of the striate cortex.* In humans, monocular deprivation, typically by cataract or ptosis (droopy eyelid), results in the severest amblyopic deficits.
3. *Binocular deprivation has less effect than monocular deprivation.* This accords with clinical observation.
4. *The physiological consequences of deprivation are more or less confined to the striate cortex.* This corroborates the ophthalmoscopic observation of normality and suggests that the cortex should be the locus of treatment (see the section Treatment).
5. *The effects of abnormal visual experience occur only during a "sensitive" period in early life.* In humans, factors known to be highly amblyogenic remain so only for a limited period of time. There also exists a "pre-sensitive" period that lasts for only a few weeks after birth, during which amblyogenic factor(s), if present, cannot cause abnormal development.
6. *The physiological consequences of deprivation can be reversed during a "critical period" early in life.* There exists a "window of opportunity" in which treatment will be optimally effective. The challenge has been to define this period in humans and to identify and treat amblyopia at this time. While in practice treatment is not usually attempted once the teenage years have been reached, there is some evidence of persisting plasticity of the visual system, which may account for occasional reports of successful treatment in adults (Levi & Polat, 1996).

Amblyogenic factors

Normal visual development requires a correctly registered and focused image on the retina. There are many factors that may impede this process and that will result in amblyopia. We categorise these into six broad groups.

It is important to reiterate that monocular factors are more powerful in producing amblyopia than those affecting both eyes.

1. Refractive errors of all types and combinations: hypermetropia (long-sightedness), myopia (short-sightedness), anisometropia (a difference in the refractive status between the eyes), or astigmatism (differences in optical power between the meridians). Into this category also fall abnormalities of eyeball shape – too long or too short – as these can cause myopia and hypermetropia, respectively. An important cause of an enlarged eye is infantile glaucoma (Fig. 2.2). In this condition the pressure of aqueous humour within the eye is high and the still relatively malleable infant eyeball enlarges – hence the old term "buphthalmos" (ox eye). Infantile glaucoma is a potentially blinding condition but by far the most frequent resultant visual defect is amblyopia due to a refractive error. Like achromatopsia (congenital deficiency of retinal cones, see later) one of the presenting symptoms is undue sensitivity to light. Treatment is primarily surgical, but prolonged follow-up is required to correct the refractive errors and to ameliorate the amblyopia.

2. Strabismus: eye misalignment; the most common are horizontal ones, especially esotropia (convergence squint) or exotropia (divergent squint), vertical or torsional (tilt) misalignment, or any combination of these. Strabismus, like nystagmus, can be the presenting sign of a serious ophthalmic or neurological disorder.

3. Eyelid: most common are ptosis (droopy eyelid) or an eyelid swelling due to haemangioma (red vascular birthmark). The mechanism of amblyopia in ptosis can be due to occlusion of the visual axis by the drooping eyelid, but this is extreme, and more commonly the eyelid causes a distortion of the underlying cornea and hence produces a refractive error.

4. Cornea: this tissue is the major determinant of the eye's refractive state, so any deviation from normal corneal curvature can reduce vision. This is seen in microcornea (diameter <9mm) or keratoconus (central thinning of cornea). The latter condition occurs in some children with Down's syndrome. Also important are conditions that disturb corneal clarity such as scars following infection or a congenital abnormality.

5. Lens: most common is cataract (lens opacity). Less common disorders include abnormalities of the shape of the lens (e.g. lentiglobus) or a lens that is displaced from its normal position in the eye.

6. Retinal disorders: a vast number of conditions, each individually rare, and which are due to either congenital or acquired retinal pathologies. These are major causes of severe visual impairment and so

generally fall outside a discussion on amblyopia, but sometimes amblyopia is an additional factor.

In many cases ophthalmic pathology can cause amblyopia by more than one mechanism. Thus, as mentioned, a droopy eyelid can occlude the visual axis and cause deprivational amblyopia, or alter eyeball growth and cause astigmatism. Many eye conditions cause a strabismus, which is an amblyogenic factor in itself.

Over 95% of cases of amblyopia arise from the associations listed in categories 1 and 2. However, it is the rarer forms that generally result in the most severe ("deprivation") amblyopia, typically where a unilateral cataract is present (category 5).

Nature of the visual loss

Classically, the defining visual loss in amblyopia is one of spatial resolution measured clinically, age permitting, with letter charts. It is now known, however, that not only are other components of spatial vision affected, such as sensitivity to contrast, but also the ability to process temporal and

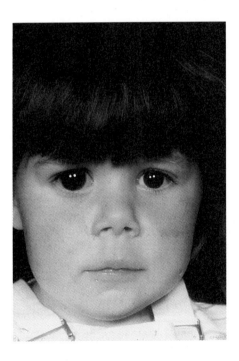

FIG. 2.2. Infantile glaucoma. Note enlargement of right eye due to raised intraocular pressure.

chromatic information, as well as defects in the accommodative, pupillary, and oculomotor systems. Indeed, it is now thought that a classification based on deficits in function may prove more insightful than one based on the already described clinical associations (McKee et al., 1992).

Treatment

Historically, amblyopia therapies have ranged across many treatment modalities including the physical, the psychological, the pharmacological, and the nutritional (see Unwin, 1991). Today, however, the mainstay of treatment remains that first proposed by De Buffon in the mid-18th century: occlusion of the better-seeing eye by an opaque patch (Fig. 2.3). This aims to eliminate the suppression of the amblyopic eye while simultaneously promoting its use. Before occlusion is prescribed it is necessary to ensure that the amblyopic eye can receive a clearly focused image by the prescription of contact lenses or spectacles where indicated.

While most clinicians would agree that occlusion offers the best hope of improving visual acuity in an amblyopic eye, this treatment has yet to be subjected to the rigorous evaluation demanded by modern evidence-based medicine. Little is known of the dose–effect relationship – how much patching is required either in terms of total duration (dose) or occlusion per day (dose-rate) – and this has led to a proliferation of pragmatically derived regimens with prescriptions of patching ranging from a few minutes each day to all waking hours. This situation has to some extent arisen out of the difficulty in knowing precisely how long children wear their patches once they have left the clinic; patching is both a physical and a psychological irritant for a child and concordance (compliance) is an acknowledged problem. Recent developments in concordance monitoring (Fielder et al., 1995) and better techniques for quantifying visual performance in children (see Moseley & Fielder, 1996) should eventually lead to optimal prescribing.

While early attempts to treat amblyopia by pharmacological means, such as by the injection of strychnine, proved fruitless, there have in the last 10 years been fresh attempts to employ pharmacological agents: principally neurotransmitter precursors and modulators such as levodopa and citicoline (see Campos, 1995). It is too early to say whether these approaches will in the long term offer a viable alternative to occlusion.

PAEDIATRIC OPHTHALMIC DISORDERS

A wide range of disorders, either acquired or hereditary, can affect the neonatal or infant eye and prevent normal vision developing. The disease can be confined to the eye itself, or it might have a systemic effect with the eye being only one of the involved organs. It is beyond the scope of

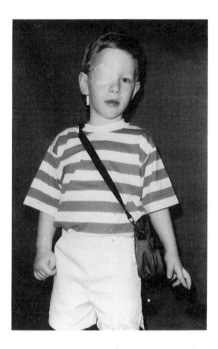

FIG. 2.3.   Occlusion therapy: an opaque patch covers the right eye. In the example shown, concordance (formally compliance) with patch wear is recorded using an occlusion dose monitor located in the shoulder bag (see text). From Fielder et al. (1995). Reprinted by permission of BMJ Publishing Group.

this chapter to deal with all of those diseases and only the more common ones will be discussed. We use the word "common" incorrectly, for in reality many of the conditions listed are quite uncommon, but for those working with visually impaired children and adults they are quite frequently encountered.

Nystagmus

Nystagmus is a rhythmic oscillation of the eyes. It is not a specific diagnosis but an important sign that can be caused by a wide range of conditions. It is a complex subject, about which only a few comments can be made here. The causes of nystagmus include reduced vision in early childhood (one important exception is cortical visual impairment, which does not cause nystagmus), and a wide range of neurological conditions – such as brain tumours, perinatal damage, cerebral malformations, infections, etc. Finally, nystagmus can develop in infancy that is not associated with any other condition. This is called infantile nystagmus, can be inherited, and persists through life. So, while nystagmus is an important sign that can signify a serious neurological or ocular disorder, as a sign *per se* it is rarely diagnostic. It follows therefore that every child with nystagmus must be fully assessed. Vision in children with nystagmus ranges from the near normal to complete blindness; so as a sign on its own it is not very informative. Children with nystagmus frequently tilt their heads as a compensatory mechanism; this reduces the oscillation and vision is improved.

Retinopathy of prematurity (ROP)

The retinal vascular system normally develops fully *in utero*, but for the baby born prematurely some development occurs after birth, and for many this is abnormal. This is known as retinopathy of prematurity (ROP): an abnormal proliferation of either retinal blood vessels (neovascularisation), or their precursors. ROP is extremely common in preterm babies; indeed, for babies with a birthweight of less than 1000 grams, more develop ROP than do not. ROP is a spectrum, and for the majority of babies it is mild and resolves spontaneously. In only a very small proportion does it progress and become sight-threatening. It becomes sight-threatening when there is florid abnormal growth of the immature blood vessels, with resultant scar tissue, which advances along the retina and into the vitreous cavity of the eye. Vision is affected by retinal distortion and in very severe cases by obstruction of the visual axis by scar tissue.

Since 1988 it has been known that treatment by cryotherapy (freezing) or by laser, which ablates large areas of the retina, improves the outcome of severe ROP if these interventions are undertaken at the correct time (usually just before full term). Treatment at a later stage to remove the abnormal vessels and scar tissue by vitrectomy is not recommended in the UK as the results are so dismal. For this reason screening for severe ROP is now important in preterm babies at risk (birthweight <1500 grams and gestational age <32 weeks) and must be undertaken at the appropriate time.

The major risk factors for ROP are the degree of immaturity – low gestational age and low birthweight. Other factors include the amount of oxygen administered in the first month or so after birth, at which time the preterm baby is susceptible to both hyperoxia and hypoxia (too much or too little oxygen). Other factors such as blood transfusions, exposure to light, and other illnesses are less well defined as ROP risk factors. Currently, despite meticulous care ROP is not entirely preventable. On the other hand, standard of care is an important issue, for there is strong evidence that if this falls short of the ideal the risk of blindness is increased. Hence, whereas ROP contributes about 5–7% of childhood blindness in the UK and USA, in less well developed countries such as those in Latin America this reaches over 25%.

As mentioned, whereas mild ROP resolves spontaneously, severe disease frequently results in high myopia, strabismus, and sometimes severe visual impairment.

Leber's congenital amaurosis and retinitis pigmentosa

Leber's amaurosis affects both rod and cone photoreceptors. It is inherited as an autosomal recessive trait. Its manifestation will be usually as nystagmus and reduced vision. Vision in affected individuals can be diminished by about a factor of ten to complete blindness. Other characteristic findings in this disease are hypermetropic refraction and sluggish pupillary response. No treatment is available. Because Leber's amaurosis, or very similar conditions, can be associated with systemic problems, a full paediatric assessment is important. Leber's amaurosis is often considered as one of the retinitis pigmentosa-like conditions that usually present in childhood or early adult life rather than infancy.

Retinitis pigmentosa is one of the major causes of severe visual impairment in children and young adults. This condition is characterised by progressive degeneration of the rod photoreceptors and is therefore characterised by night-blindness and loss of the peripheral visual field. Later, deterioration of visual acuity occurs because the retinal cones are also damaged. There are various patterns of inheritance and clinical types of retinitis pigmentosa, some of which are associated with other conditions such as deafness (Usher's syndrome), obesity, and extra digits (Bardet-Biedl syndrome). Very occasionally dietary treatment is of benefit either for the preservation of vision or prevention of another problem.

Achromatopsia

This is an inherited condition (autosomal recessive trait) in which the retinal cones are congenitally deficient. Affected children thus have complete colour blindness, reduced visual acuity, nystagmus, and undue sensitivity to light. The distance acuity of affected individuals is usually reduced by about ten-fold, but near vision can be greatly helped by low vision aids.

Albinism

This is a group of conditions with different modes of inheritance, involving defective pigmentation (melanin) of the eye and frequently the skin. There are two types of albinism that affect the skin and eye; in one the hair remains white throughout life, whereas in the other, skin and hair colour darken slightly. The latter form is clinically less severe. One type of albinism involves the eyes only and is inherited by an X-linked mode so that only males are affected. There is foveal hypoplasia (incomplete development) and a deficit of pigment in the iris and retina. The signs and symptoms the affected baby will suffer from include nystagmus, light sensitivity, high refractive error, and reduced visual acuity. Visual acuity (distance acuity) is diminished by between two to ten times that of normal, but the more important near vision is normal or near normal. No treatment is available.

Optic atrophy

Optic atrophy is simply a sign that the optic nerve has been damaged. Usually both nerves are involved, the optic disc appears pale and vision is affected to varying degrees. The causes of optic atrophy include compression of the nerve by a brain tumour or hydrocephalus (raised pressure within the brain), insults before and around the time of birth as a consequence of retinal disease, inflammation, usually during pregnancy, and inherited causes. The age at which optic atrophy develops is governed by its cause. There is no known treatment of optic atrophy *per se*, but the underlying basis may sometimes be amenable to treatment.

Optic nerve hypoplasia

This is a congenital and untreatable abnormality with underdevelopment of the optic nerve that causes visual deficits ranging from the minimal to complete blindness. Although not inherited, it can be associated with a range of neurological abnormalities, so full assessment of the baby or child is important.

Retinoblastoma

Retinoblastoma is the most commonly occurring malignant tumour affecting the eye in the paediatric age group, with an incidence of about 1 in 15,000 to 20,000. The genetic basis for this tumour is a mutation on the long arm of chromosome 13. The tumour can involve one or both eyes. The age when the tumour is first diagnosed is reducing as awareness and screening methods improve. This, along with improvement in the treatment modalities, is improving the prognosis for life and vision, with a survival rate of nearly 95%. Currently, most cases are diagnosed during the first year of life. The most common signs are leukocoria (white pupil) and strabismus (Fig. 2.4). Whereas in the past, enucleation (removal) of the eye was a common method of treatment, recently there is a trend towards local conservative treatment/management using radiation, cryotherapy or laser treatment, or chemotherapy. Vision is always affected in the involved eye; the degree of this depends on many factors such as tumour location, size, and mode of treatment. In some cases, amblyopia can be superimposed on the primary problem.

Delayed visual maturation

Delayed visual maturation (DVM) is defined as reduced vision, presumptively from birth, the severity of which cannot be explained by ophthalmoscopic findings, and which subsequently improves. It is a heterogeneous disorder, often present in association with a range of ophthalmic and neurological conditions; but it can also be an isolated anomaly. Little is known of the underlying pathophysiology, which remains intriguing due to the fact that a blind baby can literally within the space of 48 hours dramatically improve (see earlier).

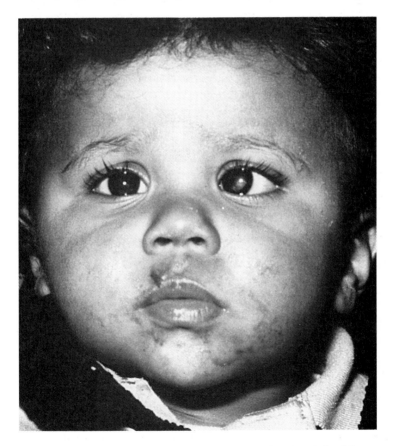

FIG. 2.4.   Retinoblastoma. Note the white pupil (leukocoria) and squinting left eye.

Cortical visual impairment

A major cause of childhood vision impairment, cortical visual impairment is due to damage to the visual cortex. Previously known as cortical blindness, the term cortical visual impairment (CVI) is now preferred as most, although not all children, exhibit some improvement. Causes of CVI include the prenatal such as infections and malformations and the perinatal such as a range of neurological insults; CVI acquired after the perinatal period is caused by, for instance, trauma, neurological infections (meningitis and encephalitis), or cardiac arrest. Not surprisingly, many children with CVI have diffuse brain damage and therefore other problems such as learning difficulty, which can range from mild, to profound and multiple. These children may have a few beats of nystagmus, but this is not a prominent feature. As mentioned, many exhibit some improvement of vision as shown in type 2 delayed visual maturation.

NOTES

1. Interested readers are referred to Taylor (1997) and to Fielder (1995) for a comprehensive text of this specialty.
2. The curious nature of this condition is adroitly encapsulated by Von Graefe's (1888) remark "that amblyopia is the condition in which the examiner sees nothing and the patient very little".

REFERENCES

Bronson, G. (1974). The postnatal growth of visual capacity. *Child Development,* **45**, 873–890.

Campos, E. (1995). Amblyopia. *Survey of Ophthalmology,* **40**, 23–39.

Ciuffreda, K.J., Levi, D.M., & Selenow, A. (1991). *Amblyopia: basic and clinical aspects.* Butterworth-Heinemann, Oxford.

Dubowitz, L.M.S., Mushin, J., de Vries, L., & Arden, G.B. (1986). Visual function in the newborn infant: is it cortically mediated? *Lancet,* **i,** 1139–1141.

Fielder, A.R. (1995). Disorders of vision. In, M.I. Levene & R.J. Lilford (Eds.), *Fetal neurology and neurosurgery* (2nd ed., pp. 565–589) Edinburgh: Churchill Livingstone.

Fielder, A.R., Dobson, V., Moseley, M.J., & Mayer, D.L. (1992). Preferential looking-clinical lessons. *Ophthalmic Paediatrics and Genetics,* **13**, 101–110.

Fielder, A.R., Irwin, M., Auld, R., Cocker, K.D., Jones, H.S., & Moseley, M.J. (1995). Compliance monitoring in amblyopia therapy: Objective monitoring of occlusion. *British Journal of Ophthalmology,* **79**, 585–589.

Fielder, A.R., & Moseley, M.J. (1996). Anisometropia and amblyopia – chicken or egg? *British Journal of Ophthalmology,* **80**, 857–858.

Levi, D.M., & Polat, U. (1996). Neural plasticity in adults with amblyopia. *Proceedings of the National Academy of Sciences of the USA,* **83**, 6830–6834.

McDonald, M., Dobson V., Sebris, S.L., Baitch, L., & Varner, D. (1985). The acuity card procedure: a rapid test of infant acuity. *Investigative Ophthalmology and Visual Science,* **26**, 1158–1162.

McKee, S.P., Schor, C.M., Steinman, S.B., et al. (1992). The classification of amblyopia on the basis of visual and oculomotor performance. *Transactions of the American Ophthalmological Society,* **90**, 123–44.

Moseley, M.J., & Fielder, A.R. (1996). Occlusion therapy for childhood amblyopia: current concepts in treatment evaluation. In F. Vital-Durand, J. Atkinson & O.J. Braddick (Eds.), *Infant Vision* (pp. 383–399). Oxford: Oxford University Press.

Taylor, D. (1997). *Paediatric ophthalmology* (2nd ed.). Oxford: Blackwell Science.

Tresidder, J., Fielder, A.R., & Nicholson, J. (1990). Delayed visual maturation: ophthalmic and neuro-developmental aspects. *Developmental Medicine and Child Neurology*, **32**, 872–881.

Unwin, B. (1991). The treatment of amblyopia – a historical review. *British Orthoptic Journal*, **48**, 28–31.

Worth, C. (1903). *Squint: its causes, pathology and treatment*. London: John Bale, Sons & Danielsson Ltd.

PART II

Visual development: From sensation to perception

Introduction

For over 300 years philosophers and visual scientists have speculated on the visual abilities of the infant and on the role of experience in visual development. Although there were few facts and little in the way of evidence, these speculations gave rise to one of the longest-running debates in psychology, concerning the question of whether perception is innate or learned. In Chapter 3 Gordon and Slater give an historical account of the debate between the Empiricist or Constructivist tradition and the contrasting position, Nativism, and a related position, Rationalism.

The debate continued for so long, and still continues in modified form, because both positions are believable, and have biological counterparts. For example, there are many different languages throughout the world, and the native language(s) we speak is dependent on experience. On the other hand, the kid of the mountain goat walks, and avoids drops, within minutes from birth, which entails considerable innate visual abilities and visuomotor coordination; the butterfly emerges from the pupa and flies effortlessly as soon as its wings are dry. By analogy, it is reasonable to argue for either of the extreme views for visual perception.

Gordon and Slater give an account of the origins of empiricism in the views of the 17th- and 18th-century philosophers Locke and Berkeley, and of nativism in the philosophers Plato, Descartes, and Kant. They then describe the views of the physiologists and psychologists Helmholtz, Hering, Hebb, and Piaget. They discuss the contributions of Gestalt theory, of ethology, and those of J.J. Gibson, Bruner, and Gregory. More recently, theorists have attempted to incorporate both innate and acquired factors into their accounts: such accounts include those of Fodor (modularity), Karmiloff-Smith ("beyond modularity"), and Aslin. Finally, Gordon and Slater discuss some of the ways in which researchers have attempted to decide between the two traditions, and conclude that the most powerful way of attempting to discover the extent to which perception is genetically determined or results from experience with the world lies in developmental studies; and such studies, of course, are the focus of this book.

In Chapter 4 Slater has an emphasis on the ways in which the visual system is prepared for visual perception at birth, and the ways in which the visual world is organised for the newborn and young infant. One emphasis in this chapter reflects the innate/acquired distinction with respect to infants' perception of the human face: is there an innate representation of the face, and in what ways does experience enhance early face perception?

However well-structured the visual world of the newborn and young infant may be, their world lacks meaning, experience, and familiarity: "they see everything, but nothing makes sense" (Gordon, 1997, p. 83). As infants develop, and indeed throughout life, their experiences change their perception of the world. In the final part of the chapter Slater discusses some of the ways in which experience changes infants' perception of the world.

Some of the most important changes to visual perception have to do with infants' gradual acquisition of knowledge about perceptual categories, about causality, and about the world of objects. These topics are the themes of Chapters 5 to 7. In Chapter 5 Quinn points out that categorisation is one of the most important human abilities: the process by which organisms recognise discriminably different objects as members of the same category based on some internalised representation of the category. Without the ability to categorise, the perceptual and cognitive world would be chaotic and disorganised: if all of the perceptual representations formed for the multitude of objects and relations encountered during a lifetime were independent of each other, the outcome would be mental disorganisation and intellectual chaos.

Quinn discusses some of the ways in which infants form categorical representations for objects ("What?"), and for spatial relations ("Where?"), and suggests how the early perceptually based categorical representations might give rise to the more conceptual, knowledge-based representations of children and adults.

In Chapter 6 Cohen, Amsel, Redford, and Casasola provide answers to the question: is the world of the infant acausal, or does the infant come predisposed to perceive or understand simple causal relations? They explore infants' reactions to different types of causal events, particularly the situation in which one inanimate object moves, hits a second inanimate object, and the latter moves on impact – what Michotte called "direct launching" – which adults uniformly perceive as a causal event. Cohen et al. evaluate several theoretical views about the origins of infants' causal perception. In particular, they give an excellent account of what a modular approach to infant causal perception would be: is there an organised, self-contained perceptual module for causality? They also make the important distinction (following Karmiloff-Smith) between the notion of "pre-speci-fied modules" and the process of "modularisation": perceptual modules may be innately provided and guide development, or they might be the product of development.

In addition to giving an account of age-related changes in causal percep-tion, they report the intriguing finding that such perception is integrally related to the nature of the objects that are shown to the infants. For example, infants who display causal perception with simple events (e.g. using moving circles) will often fail to do so if the task is made more complex. This additional complexity can be produced in at least two ways. One is to use complex objects (such as cars or trucks), and another is to familiarise infants with multiple objects (all demonstrating the same causal relations), which might transform the task to one in which object categories have to be formed. Thus, when there is an overload of information this appears to produce "regression" to a simpler level of processing. This regression causes problems for a modular view of causality perception, as such a view would predict that perception of causality should be robust against changes to stimulus events.

A number of researchers have posited some type of relationship between cognitive concepts and language acquisition: that is, that an under-standing of concepts precedes the acquisition of the language to express them. In this view, each linguistic advance shown by the infant and young child is a linguistic, but not a conceptual advance, because the speaker is expressing semantic relationships that were comprehended prior to their verbal expression: words that encode specific concepts emerge only once a child understands the concept. Cohen et al. explore this view with respect to the older infant's comprehension and learning of words that express causal relations, such as pull and push. One important message they offer is that adherence to a nativist/modular approach will often give the impression that the innate module is fully formed and therefore immune to developmental change or improvement. However, this is never the case in any area of perceptual and cognitive functioning: all areas of infant perception and cognition develop in significant ways throughout infancy.

The theme of developmental change is prominent throughout Chapter 7 on object perception. Piaget was one of the first to describe some of the ways in which infants gradually come to understand the physical world of objects, and many subsequent researchers have turned their attention to object perception. Johnson points out that object knowledge comprises several supporting skills. These include perceptual skills, such as the abilities to appreciate depth and motion, and to distinguish the boundaries, colours, luminance levels, and textures of surfaces. Cognitive skills include knowledge of objects' physical properties, such as unity, location, size, inertia, gravity, support, cohesion, and continuity across time and space.

Given the combination of these several skills it is not surprising to find that object knowledge, as Piaget suggested, develops slowly as infancy progresses. Many of the prerequisite perceptual abilities, such as size and shape constancy, are present at birth, but the newborn infant displays little in the way of true object knowledge. For instance, newborns appear to be unaware that partly occluded objects are complete, or whole, behind the occluder. This difficulty is overcome, at least in incipient form, by two months, and infants have robust knowledge of occlusion by four months. Four-month-olds are also able to represent some of the physical characteristics of occluded objects, such as their size, location, and height. By around seven months infants have some knowledge of support and gravity.

Johnson describes and evaluates a number of current theoretical models of object perception and its development. He also discusses the often hidden question of replicability of findings. In the study of object perception, as with all aspects of infancy research, some reported effects are highly replicable, whereas other are not: we are wise to maintain a sceptical attitude with respect to some of the more exotic claims that are made about infants' competences!

CHAPTER THREE

Nativism and empiricism: The history of two ideas

Ian Gordon and Alan Slater
Washington Singer Laboratories, University of Exeter, UK

INTRODUCTION

This chapter introduces a debate that has continued for centuries and that came to provoke much research in experimental psychology. This research is continuing and recent accounts of important discoveries form the basis of subsequent chapters in this book.

The question asked in this chapter is this: is perception of the world a set of innate abilities or a set of acquired skills? More formally, the debate is between the Empiricist or Constructivist tradition and the contrasting position, Nativism (or a related tradition, Rationalism).

We start this chapter by outlining the historical background to the problem. Then we show how interest in the problem among early psychologists and others led to the development of two opposed general paradigms for perception. Examples of work within each paradigm will be given, together with an account of a compromise position. Finally, we show some of the ways in which experimental psychologists have searched for evidence concerning the innate/acquired controversy. We end by asserting that of all the empirical approaches to the problem of the innate versus the acquired, the study of infant development is likely to provide the best answers, and in this manner we lead into the rest of this book.

Although we advocate a compromise between the nativist and the empiricist positions, it is worth noting that neither position is wholly absurd. For example, humans are born with functioning body parts doing complicated things: one of the main functions of the kidneys is to regulate body fluids, and part of this function is achieved by removing surplus electrolytes, particularly sodium and potassium. It takes some years of schooling before the average pupil can understand and then measure such things as sodium-ion concentration and blood pH levels. But all this chemistry is built into the kidneys during their development before birth: millions of years of evolution have seen to that. By analogy, it is not beyond comprehension that the major sense organs could be ready to deal with stimulation at birth. Indeed, in many nonhuman species they are: the herring gull does not have to learn to peck in the presence of a red mark on its mother's beak; butterflies search for food as soon as their wings are dry.

On the other hand, one distinguishing feature of humans is that much of their perceiving is associated with language. Although it has been argued that the capacity for language is innate, no one doubts that a child born in China but removed in the first weeks of life to Sweden will grow up speaking Swedish and thinking in Swedish. In this example, the role of experience is all-important: these issues are discussed in detail in Chapter 11 in the present volume. The question now is which extreme – renal functioning or language use – does visual perception most closely resemble?

At this point we should warn the reader that it has been necessary to simplify some of the historical material that follows. We do not apologise for this: whenever a discipline borrows from another this is often accompanied by some simplification, some loss of subtlety and detail. We shall be summarising philosophical traditions in which hundreds of scholars have written millions of words. No wholly accurate but brief account of these traditions exists, and it is unlikely that any ever will.

As a final remark in this section, we should add that few researchers and theorists have ever maintained an absolutely extreme position regarding innate versus acquired factors in perception. It has been obvious, even to the most casual observer, that the newborn infant is capable of responding to noxious stimuli (the age-old use of the slap to induce crying and breathing). It has also been long known that vertebrates reared in the dark experience difficulty in seeing when they are placed in a lit environment: the eye degenerates if it is not stimulated. Whether effective perception of a meaningful world is present at birth or requires a period of learning is, however, a proper question and one that has stimulated much of the research described in the rest of this book.

The remainder of this chapter is organised under the following headings.

- The historical background to empiricism and nativism
- The adoption of empiricism and nativism by early psychologists and physiologists

- Some landmarks in the development of empiricism and nativism
- The search for compromises between nativism and empiricism
- Methods of enquiry: the ways in which researchers have attempted to decide between the two traditions

THE HISTORICAL BACKGROUND TO EMPIRICISM

Much of the early research in perception was concerned with testing the empiricist assertion that our perceptual abilities develop as a result of experience. It may be helpful therefore to begin this account by outlining the important work of two empiricist philosophers whose writings had a major impact on beliefs about perceptual development: Locke and Berkeley.

The British empiricist philosophers

John Locke (1632–1704), has been described as " ... one of the most influential philosophers there has ever been" (Magee, 1978, p. 120). Locke's philosophical masterpiece, published in 1689 when he was 57, was the *Essay concerning human understanding*. The following excerpt reveals the origins of the empiricist philosophy as it concerns perceptual development:

> Let us suppose the mind to be, as we say, white paper void of all characters, without any ideas. How comes it to be furnished? Whence comes it by that vast store which the busy and boundless fancy of man has painted on it with an almost endless variety? Whence has it all the materials of reason and knowledge? To this I answer, in one word, from experience; in that all our knowledge is founded, and from that it ultimately derives itself.

It should be noted that Locke's concern was with the origins of knowledge. His use of the term "idea" refers to some sort of "mental content", including such things as sensory images, pains, emotions, and thoughts. However, all ideas have their origins in sensory information, leading to the conclusion that all our understanding and knowledge are dependent on the senses.

In Europe, the 17th and 18th centuries were periods of great interest in the philosophical problems of blindness, and in his *Essay* Locke gave prominence to what has become known as "Molyneux's question". William Molyneux was a Dublin lawyer, and a correspondent and friend of Locke (and a respected author in his own right). His question to Locke was whether a blind man, who had sight restored, would be able to name correctly a cube and a sphere that were presented to his vision. Molyneux's own answer to the question was that he would not:

... for, though he has obtained the experience of how a sphere, how a cube affects his touch, yet he has not obtained the experience that what affects his touch so and so, must affect his sight so and so.

Locke completely agreed with the reply of "this thinking gentleman, whom I am proud to call my friend", being of the view that as the sensory impressions of the senses of touch and vision are quite different we can only become aware that they occasionally give equivalent information after experiencing these correspondences. It is, however, important to stress once again that Locke's primary concern was with the origins of knowledge. In fact, both Locke and Molyneux assumed that the blind man would be able to see: the question rather was whether he would be able to *name* the sphere and the cube. However, as Morgan has pointed out:

> If Locke says that experience is necessary before we can name the cube and the sphere, it is a natural step to think that he meant we must learn to see. Of course, he thought the contrary, but what people understand by a theory is often of greater historical importance than what the theory says, and it was so in this case.
>
> (1977, p. 97)

George Berkeley (1685–1753) was greatly influenced by Locke's writings and continued the empiricist tradition in his *A new theory of vision*, published in 1709. Berkeley was born in Ireland and later developed connections with America, a country he first visited in 1728. One of the colleges at Yale University is named after him, as also is the town Berkeley in California. In 1734 he was made Bishop of Cloyne in Ireland, and he is often referred to as Bishop Berkeley.

In common with Locke, Berkeley assumed that all knowledge results from sensory input and the mind's reflections on such data. Like Locke he also felt that there can be no inherent connection between the sensory information of vision and that of touch: "That which is seen is one thing, and that which is felt is another." The association, therefore, requires practice and experience. Berkeley made various claims about distance and space perception, about the relationship between vision and touch, and about the possible experiences of a man born blind and being made to see. These issues are of continuing interest in the area of perceptual development, and it is worth outlining his views on them.

Berkeley claimed that the distance of objects, or "distance of itself", cannot be perceived directly, because the image on the retina is flat and two-dimensional. Given that the retinal image of an object changes "as you approach to, and recede from the tangible object", such that "it has no fixed or determinate greatness" (*New theory of vision*, section LV), it follows that the sense of vision provides constantly changing and ambiguous information both about distance and about an object's true size " ... the perpetual mutability and fleetingness of those immediate objects of sight" (section CLV). Therefore, the argument continues, "the judgement we make of the distance of an object, viewed with both eyes, is entirely the result of experience" (section XX). The appropriate experience is primarily given from the sense of touch, as the tangible (felt) magnitude of an object is steady and constant, and " ... fixed and immutably the same in all times and places" (section CLII). Thus, it follows that we experience by touch the ideas of space, upright, left, right, solidity, and distance, and these ideas can subsequently be connected with the ideas, or sensations, arising from vision.

The empiricist views that are often attributed to Locke and Berkeley are that our perceptual abilities develop as a result of experience, rather than being present at birth. Making sense of visual sensations and appreciating distance and direction from visual input are dependent on prior experiences with the sense of touch – thus, "touch teaches vision", and there is no innate or inevitable coordination between the senses.

These philosophers of three centuries ago laid the foundations of the empiricist views that have followed them, and raised issues that have migrated from philosophy to experimental psychology.

THE HISTORICAL BACKGROUND TO NATIVISM

We turn now to the history of the tradition that formed the great rival to empiricism: nativism. The philosophical background to nativism is complex. Plato had written about the relationship between sensation and knowledge. We can always be wrong about perception of the world based on sensations. True knowledge of things can be gained only by the process of reason. And true knowledge is always of the "essences" of the world. Thus there is no point in conducting empirical experiments: appearances can be deceptive; we may see many circles, none will be perfect, but we can conceive (through mathematics) the ideal circle – the Platonic form.

In stressing the role of reason in obtaining knowledge, Plato can be described as the first systematic rationalist; rationalism being the belief that all knowledge and truth derives from rational processes of thought – that only through reason can we attain absolute and certain knowledge. This tradition was strengthened centuries later by the widely influential writings of Descartes (1596–1650), who sought to prove that the nature of the world could be established with certainty only by reasoning – in particular, mathematical reasoning. Descartes held that there were three sources of ideas: ideas that entered the mind from experience; ideas formed by the mind's own activity; ideas created in the mind by God. (This notion of innate ideas was what inspired Locke's famous attack on Descartes: if ideas are innate, why isn't every infant born with the idea of God, or knowledge of mathematical axioms?)

For the present purpose, the most important philosopher to stress the power of a priori reason as the source of truths about the world was Immanuel Kant (1724–1804). Kant's philosophy is impossible to summarise in a few lines. However, one of his centrally important ideas, contained in his enormously influential *Critique of pure reason* (1781), may be outlined by means of a simple thought experiment described elsewhere by one of us (Gordon, 1997).

Suppose we are seeing an object that moves across our field of view. The movement takes time and occurs through space. We perceive the object and its motion, but what about the framework *within which* the object moves, namely space and time? We do not perceive space itself, as there is literally nothing to perceive, and neither do we perceive time, as it, too, is simply a framework within which events are ordered. Yet an awareness of space and time is vital to our perception of the object's movement. Kant argued that awareness of space and time are *a priori intuitions*; that is, they are "givens", and cannot be learned. Kant developed his argument to the point where he was able to claim that the world we perceive is the only one we *can* perceive: it is the way we are that determines how we are able to become aware. From this it is but a small step to believe that many aspects of perception must be the same for all humans. If so, then the origins of much of our perception must be innate. This is the start of the nativist tradition.

THE ADOPTION OF EMPIRICISM AND NATIVISM BY EARLY PSYCHOLOGISTS AND PHYSIOLOGISTS: HELMHOLTZ AND HERING

Helmholtz

Hermann Helmholtz (1821–1894) qualified as a doctor of medicine by the age of 21. When only 26 he published a paper entitled, "Über die Erhaltung der Kraft" ("On the conservation of energy"), which altered the direction of physics for decades to come and was the basis of the new science of thermodynamics. Helmholtz was one of the founders of perceptual research, and was probably the most gifted, original, and successful perceptionist to date. By mid-career, Helmholtz knew more about the human senses than anyone who had ever lived. He had produced the first major scientific account of hearing, the first quantitative theory of colour vision, the first scientific treatment of musical effects. And he had measured the speed of a nerve impulse.

As his knowledge of sensory functions developed, Helmholtz came to realise that the output from sense organs cannot form the basis of veridical perception of a stable world. For example, the image in a vertebrate eye is inverted, blurred, small, and curved. And yet, from this apparently imperfect basis, we become aware of a clear, sharply focused world. Equally significant is the fact that when objects recede from the eye their retinal images become smaller, but the objects themselves do not appear to shrink.

We can reinforce this point with another example. Helmholtz had studied touch. At that time, there was growing evidence for the punctate nature of skin receptors. That is to say, when the skin is explored with small stimuli, "warm", "cold", "pricking", and other sensations cannot be induced from every millimetre of the surface. What is found is that small regions of the skin are highly sensitive to some stimuli but not others: sensitivity is not continuous. These and other histological findings suggested the possibility that special nerve endings mediate such responses as warmth, cold, touch, and pain. And yet when we touch a cold wet surface we are conscious, not of sensations *in our skin* (although we can train ourselves to notice them), but of the surface giving rise to these sensations.

Clearly, these examples, taken together, raise formidable problems. The solution offered by Helmholtz was this. When a regular sequence of events in the world is accompanied by a corresponding regular sequences of sensations, then eventually, by a process of association, the latter will come to serve as a sign of the former. Further, as the perceiver becomes able to perceive distance, the shrinking retinal images associated with receding objects can be compensated for by a process akin to inductive reasoning. However, as all readers will agree, when objects recede from us, there is no conscious experience of anything resembling reasoning. For this reason, Helmholtz stressed that the processes that must come between the reception of incoming sense-data and the perception of a stable world must be unconscious ones.

Helmholtz thus gave enormous prestige to the empiricist or constructivist movement. If the senses alone cannot specify the world, something must be added to sensations. Thus, perception involves experience and knowledge (although the latter need not be available to consciousness). As these have to be acquired, it is inevitable that perception must be to a large extent learned. In this manner Helmholtz brought empiricism into experimental psychology.

Hering

Nativism, too, was adopted by a number of the first scientists to study perception. Among the most famous of these was the German physiologist Ewald Hering (1834–1918). It is a fact that if the image of an object lies, say, to the left of the fovea, observers will see the object as being to the right of their visual field. The earlier empiricist explanation of how positions on the retina signal positions in the world held that the patterns of eye movements required to bring such off-centre images onto the fovea give rise to muscular sensations that gradually cause each location of the retina to have its own *local sign*. Hering modified this theory by dismissing the need for learning and asserting that, on the contrary, each retinal location has a unique, innately determined, "spatial significance" relative to the angle of gaze. This was describable in terms of a three-dimensional coordinate system: above or below; left or right; and a value associated with depth – the horizontal distance of the point from the centre of the fovea. Thus as early as 1864 an important basic aspect of seeing – where things are located in space – was being accounted for by an appeal to nativism.

This introduction to the early days of perceptual research and theory has shown how two basically different ideas concerning the origins of knowledge changed to questions concerning the nature of perceptual processes themselves. In the next section we show some of the landmarks in the development of each tradition.

SOME LANDMARKS IN THE DEVELOPMENT OF EMPIRICISM AND NATIVISM

Empiricism – Hebb, Piaget, Bruner, and Gregory

Hebb   Donald Olding Hebb (1904–1985), the American psychologist, gave a theoretical account of perceptual development in *The organization of behavior* (1949) that was to strengthen, for a time, the empiricist position. His views will be presented only briefly, as they have subsequently been overtaken by advances in our understanding of neurological development; but they are of interest in that they point to possible influences of learning on the perception of very simple shapes.

Hebb argued that some aspects of visual perception are "primitive" and independent of experience. Figure–ground separation is one such organisation. We easily distinguish between the figure in our field of view and the ground against which it is perceived. Berkeley, too, was aware of figure–ground perception: "the more we fix our sight on any one object [the figure] by so much the darker and more indistinct shall the rest [the ground] appear" (section LXXXIV). A well-known illustration of figure–ground reversal is shown in Fig. 3.1: sometimes the vase is the figure, sometimes the faces. This "primitive unity" of the figure is found in all sensory modalities, for example when we attend to the voice of a speaker against the background noises of a party. In adults restored to sight after many years of blindness (following an operation to remove cataracts)

FIG. 3.1.   Figure-ground reversal – two faces or one vase?

figure–ground separation is immediately available, despite the many other visual problems they may experience.

Conceding that figure–ground perception is primitive and innate, Hebb nevertheless held that perception of even very simple shapes, such as triangles and squares, is the result of complex learning. Initially, an infant would perceive the lines and angles of such a shape as separate and unconnected; only after a long period of directing eye movements around the figure would it be seen as a unified or distinctive whole. Hebb (1949, p. 31) acknowledged that, "The idea that one has to learn to see a triangle must sound extremely improbable", but supported this proposition with evidence from animals (particularly rats and chimpanzees), and from adults who had sight restored after long periods of blindness.

Rats have very poor vision. They have great difficulty in discriminating between a circle and a square, and although they readily discriminate between an upright and an inverted triangle, it seems that they do this on the basis of attending only to parts of the figure, so that a single horizontal line may look the same as the upright triangle, presumably indicating that the bottom portion only of the shapes is used in making the discrimination. Such discrimination failures suggest that the rats' responses are determined by a part of the figure, even one as simple as a triangle. Of course, vision is not the dominant sense in rats, so we may expect their form perception to be poor; but such evidence suggests that we should not assume that what is utterly simple to us (seeing a simple shape as a whole in a single glance) is necessarily so either to other species, or to the young, or visually inexperienced, of our species or others. As an example, under normal circumstances chimpanzees have excellent vision, but if they are reared in darkness from early infancy they demonstrate an "almost complete visual incapacity" followed by considerable slowness of visual learning. Hebb gives an account of one (human) patient restored to sight who was trained to discriminate between a square and a circle over a 13-day period, but had learned so little in this time that he was only able to say which was which after counting their corners (Hebb, 1949, pp. 30–32).

This confluence of evidence, from different species, led Hebb to the apparently reasonable conclusion that, "The course of perceptual learning in man is gradual, proceeding from a dominance of colour, through a period of separate attention to each part of a figure, to a gradually arrived-at identification of the whole as a whole: an apparently simultaneous instead of a serial apprehension", and he suggested that, "It is possible then that the normal human infant goes through the same process, and that we are able to see a square as such in a single glance only as the result of complex learning" (op. cit., pp. 32–33).

Hebb argued that there are two kinds of visual learning. One is that of the normally sighted adult, which can be so rapid as to appear almost instantaneous. The other is " . . . that of the newborn infant, or the visual learning of the adult reared in darkness or with congenital cataract" (op. cit., p. 111), which is extremely inefficient and laborious. Hebb assumed that the visual world of the infant was more or less identical to that of the visually deprived adult, and used the experiences of such adults as his model for perceptual development in the normally sighted infant. As it turns out there are few parallels between the two types of development.

Piaget The empiricist approach of workers such as Hebb was also adopted by the first researcher to carry out detailed explorations of infants' perceptual and cognitive development, the Swiss psychologist Jean Piaget (1896–1981). Piaget is the most influential developmental psychologist who ever lived. In his detailed accounts and interpretations of early development he gave strong emphasis to the role of learning in developing and coordinating perception: perception becomes structured in a sequence of stages as the infant becomes able to coordinate more and more complex patterns of activity.

Piaget (1954, p. 3) said of the young infant:

The world is a world of pictures, lacking in depth or constancy, permanence or identity which disappear and reappear capriciously, in which the subject's activity is conceived as being the sole motive power.

And with respect to vision (Piaget, 1953, p. 62):

Perception of light exists from birth and consequently the reflexes which insure the adaptation of this perception (the pupillary and palpebral reflexes, both to light). All the rest (perception of forms, sizes, positions, distances, prominence, etc.) is acquired through the combination of reflex activity with higher activities.

However extreme the empiricist position one wishes to adopt, there must be some sort of initial connection to the world, however basic, if the infant is to learn at all. For Hebb, this initial connection was figure–ground organisation and the tendency to make eye movements to look around the perceived figures, coupled with the organisation of these patterns of eye movements until a whole figure is seen. For Piaget the initial connection was the behaviour patterns displayed towards lights (or sounds, etc.), such as looking towards or following objects, and these behaviours act as "a sort of reflex apprenticeship" from which later development results. Piaget argued that the sensory modalities develop separately for the first month or so, and then gradually become coordinated so that, for instance, a thing seen could be a thing grasped. The perceptual constancies, such as size and shape constancy, are not present at birth but rather are constructed by the infant, and develop from – and are a consequence of – the infant's own actions on the world: thus size constancy develops at around 6 months, after the coordination of vision and prehension – the variable retinal information about size is adjusted to the constant information that occurs with touch. Many developments during the period of infancy take place with respect to the perception and understanding of objects and their properties. For example, in early infancy babies have to learn to reconstruct or anticipate a whole object after having seen only part of it; they have to learn that when an object disappears from view it continues to exist independently of their perceptions of it. Having appreciated that hidden objects continue to exist, they gradually become aware that an object's existence and location is not magically dependent on their actions toward it. Finally, around 18 months or so, the infant is aware of being only one object in a world of countless objects.

Piaget's theorising, which extended over 60 years, is immensely complex and continues to inspire considerable research activity. With respect to perceptual development he was perhaps the last of the great empiricists.

Bruner and the New Look Experiments   The distinguished American psychologist, Jerome Bruner, is well known for a classic series of studies of thinking, in which he showed, among other things, the importance of categories in thinking. That is, until one has the categories "matches" and "fires" one can never arrive at the generalisation, "matches cause fires". In the course of this work, Bruner became interested in cognitive aspects of perceiving. He and his colleagues then carried out a series of experiments, known as The New Look Experiments. Here are some examples.

Bruner and Goodman (1947) carried out an investigation into American children's ability to judge the size of objects. It was found that size estimation was imperfect. The children tended to overestimate the sizes of valuable coins, and poor children overestimated them to a greater extent than richer children.

McGinnies (1949) performed a word-recognition experiment using tachistoscopically presented materials. Among the items presented were a number of "taboo" words. Thresholds for these taboo words were higher, that is, it took longer to recognise them. But how did the subjects know the words were taboo if they had not yet recognised them?

Lazarus and McCleary (1951) paired certain words with electric shock. These and other words were then presented tachistoscopically. Throughout the experiment the subject's Galvanic Skin Response was recorded. (The GSR is an autonomic reaction of the body during emotional changes and is not under voluntary control: it is recorded as a sweat reaction from the palms or the fingers.) Recognition thresholds were higher for the shocked words and these words (not surprisingly) induced the strongest GSR responses. Interestingly, the subjects started to show GSR responses to the shocked words *before they could say what the words were.*

From the results of these studies, the idea emerged of some sort of censor operating between the receipt of stimuli and the formation of a response. In other words, perceptual inputs interact with cognitive processes before percepts can be formed.

Each of these experiments was subsequently criticised. American coins increase in size as they increase in value: was the behaviour of the children so surprising? Similarly, taboo words are rare in printed English. And there are major theoretical problems with the idea of some sort of censor coming between perceptual inputs and consciousness: how does the censor recognise words in order to censor them?

From the point of view of the present chapter, the fact that these New Look researches were faulty matters less than the influence they had on the history of approaches to psychology. Here again is evidence to reinforce an empiricist position: to some degree perception is constructive; percepts are modified by knowledge and prior experience; thus to some extent, perception is learned.

Gregory   Richard Gregory is the most famous perception researcher in contemporary Britain. His empirical and theoretical contributions are many and varied. Some of these are summarised in an appraisal of Gregory's work by Gordon (1997).

For the present purpose, we shall emphasise one aspect of Gregory's contribution, namely his theory that Perceptions are Hypotheses. Gregory's arguments in favour of his theory form the most explicit and powerful defence of empiricism since Helmholtz.

The essence of Gregory's hypothesis theory is this. Sensory signals interact with appropriate knowledge to create psychological data. On the basis of such data, hypotheses are advanced to predict and make sense of events in the world. This chain of events is the process we call perceiving. Thus perception closely resembles problem solving and scientific inference.

Gregory cites evidence from a variety of sources to support his claim. An important fact is that we can respond to certain objects as objects – seeing them as whole or complete – even when parts of them are obscured. For example, a person walking towards one carrying, say, a tuba, does not look fractured: a top, a bottom, and a gap in the middle caused by the tuba. We see a whole person. But if the outline of the person is incomplete, as it is, we must be using knowledge of people (they don't survive as separate halves) to go beyond the sensory evidence delivered from the visual images we have of them.

Gregory claims support for his theory from the fact that perceptions can be ambiguous. Reversible figures, such as the one shown in Fig. 3.2, can be seen in two ways, as the reader will discover. Such figures are unstable. But if one physical display can induce two different percepts, then perception cannot be tied directly to stimulation.

It is also the case that highly unlikely objects tend to be mistaken for likely ones. Gregory's best-known demonstration of this is to illuminate the back of a hollow mask of a human face. Such a face is of course "inside out", with the nose forming a hollow rather than a projection, and so on. However, when the illumination is right, *the face looks normal.* How could this be possible if our *knowledge* of faces was not somehow transforming the evidence arising from the highly unusual display?

Gregory supports his theory with a much wider range of arguments and examples than we can include. However, we hope to have given enough material to demonstrate to the reader just what a powerful source of support for empiricism is contained in Gregory's writings.

After this review of some of the key developments in the history of empiricism in psychology, we turn to a discussion of nativism.

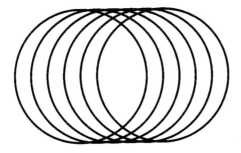

FIG. 3.2.   A reversible figure.

NATIVISM: THE GESTALT THEORY, ETHOLOGY, AND GIBSON'S CONCEPT OF THE AFFORDANCE

The Gestalt theory   During the first four decades of the present century a coherent and influential theory of perception was developed by three psychologists, Max Wertheimer (1890–1943), Kurt Koffka (1886–1941), and Wolfgang Köhler (1887–1967). Gestalt theory was inspired by a number of factors. First was a revulsion both from Behaviourism (a doctrine that maintained that observable behaviour was the only legitimate concern of psychologists) and also from Structuralism (which sought to reduce the whole of subjective experience to basic sensations). Second was the continuing European influence of Kant, which in this context emerged as a desire to focus theory and explanation on the problem of everyday, phenomenal experience. To this end Koffka asked one of the most quoted questions in the history of perception: "Why do things look as they do?" Finally, Köhler was aware of a long scientific tradition that had demonstrated that in nature, many physical and chemical systems appear to follow a basic rule – the Minimum Principle.

From this background, the Gestalt psychologists developed a theory that stressed the extent to which perceiving is an active, dynamic process. They showed how observers spontaneously organise visual scenes into figure and ground. They listed rules of perceptual organisation that describe how groups of stimuli spontaneously organise themselves into simple patterns. Some of these effects are shown in Fig 3.3. The Gestalt psychologists showed how two or more stimuli can interact to give rise to effects that cannot be predicted from knowledge of the single components acting in isolation, but that demonstrate the emergence of *Gestaltqualität* (a square can be drawn in many ways: using lines, dots, crosses, and rectangles; all versions will share the Gestalt quality of "squareness"). And a major contribution of the Gestalt psychologists was to show that what is perceived may not be tied directly to simple stimulus variables: most objects retain their true colour when illumination changes from daylight to artificial light. Nor do familiar objects appear to shrink with increased distance.

Is there a general underlying principle behind the numerous examples of organisation that the Gestalt psychologists discovered? Their belief that perception tended, wherever possible, towards simplicity, symmetry, coherence, and wholeness could be summarised by the German word *Prägnanz*. But *why* should perception show this tendency towards Prägnanz? Köhler, the leading theorist of the movement, argued as follows. Perception is the result of neural activity that, in turn, depends on electrochemical processes. But as these processes are physical, they must obey

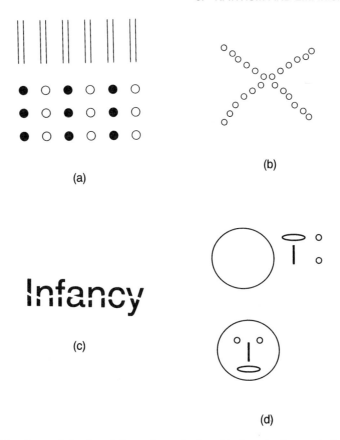

FIG. 3.3. Some of the Gestalt laws of organisation. (a) Grouping by proximity at the top and grouping by similarity at the bottom. (b) Grouping by good continuation – the figure is usually seen as an irregular cross; it could be a pair of arches. (c) The principle of closure – the word can be read effortlessly, despite the gaps. (d) This illustrates a Gestalt interaction: the stimuli in both parts are identical. At the top they are meaningless; when put together in a certain way (as at the bottom) the parts interact and a hitherto unsuspected pattern emerges.

the laws of physics. Now Köhler's knowledge of the Minimum Principle had its effect. The minimum principle emerged during the early days of mathematics, physics, and astronomy and asserted that dynamic physical systems always tend towards minimum work and minimum energy. For example, any freely suspended chain will assume a characteristic shape, known as a catenary. In this form, each link in the chain is under minimal tension. Similarly, when complex wire shapes are dipped into soap solutions, the films that form across them are surfaces in which the tension is at a minimum: a finding that has been used in the design of complicated roof structures, such as those built above sports stadiums.

It follows that if perception depends on physical (neural) systems, then it is not surprising that it tends towards Prägnanz, given that one aspect of Prägnanz is simplicity. In this manner Köhler pushed the theoretical parts of Gestalt psychology towards an extreme nativist position. (It must be acknowledged, however, that other Gestalt psychologists, particularly Koffka, did not follow Köhler in this.)

Ethology   Some biologists, from Darwin onwards, have always studied animals in the natural environment, in contrast with experimental psychologists who tended to favour laboratory studies. In the 20th century, however, two workers, Konrad Lorenz (1903–1989) and Niko Tinbergen (1907–1988) extended this tradition to the point when a new discipline emerged: Ethology. The culmination of the work of these two pioneers was the award to them of the 1973 Nobel Prize for physiology or medicine, which they shared with von Frisch – famous for his work on the dances of bees: the ways in which they signal the directions of food sources to other bees.

We shall not attempt a comprehensive review of ethological research. However, a few examples of the discoveries made in this discipline will give the flavour of the work.

Lorenz and Tinbergen (1938) and Lorenz (1953) analysed patterns of behaviour in several animal species and showed that there were "form-constant" patterns within these movements. For example, a newly hatched chicken can soon walk and quickly picks at seeds on the ground. If a hawk appears above it, it will run to its mother. A newly hatched duckling, on the other hand, will run to water, dive, and feed below the surface. What is interesting about such *fixed action patterns* is that they are unlearned. A chick reared by a duck will still show the behaviour described, as will a duckling reared by a hen. Now running away from predators, eating under water, even pecking seeds from the ground, constitute on the face of it fairly complex perceptuo-motor behaviours. It will be appreciated that the demonstration that such behaviours are unlearned (although they can sometimes be modified by experience) constituted a formidable boost to the nativist view of perception.

Ethologists discovered the existence of releasing signals. These are stimuli that can trigger apparently purposive behaviour. For example, Tinbergen and Perdeck (1950) showed in a classic study that the red spot on the beak of a herring gull releases food-begging in the chicks. There are many other examples: a female turkey's brooding behaviour is released by the cries of its young; there is some evidence that the sudden uncovering of a human face (the "peekaboo") releases smiling in infants.

However, there is a price to be paid for the innate underpinning of such behaviours, and this is rigidity. For example, the food-begging responses of young herring gulls will be made to any long rectangular object containing a red spot. The female turkey's brooding behaviour will be released by any stuffed animal, provided that it is fitted with a loudspeaker emitting the appropriate cries. Clearly, under real-life conditions this rigidity will not matter: the only red spots that herring gull chicks are likely to encounter are those on their parents' beaks; there are few stuffed animals bearing concealed loudspeakers in the wild, so the turkey will rarely brood for nothing.

The demonstrations by ethologists that such apparently automatic aspects of behaviour in some species are often associated with a rigidity of responding need not concern us further. What is very important, given the subject matter of the present chapter, it that there are many species in which perceptual competence is present at birth, even though the necessary perceiving may be only of isolated aspects of the environment. In other words, it can be done. And this is powerful support for the nativist position.

Gibson's concept of affordance   The distinguished American psychologist J.J. Gibson (1904–1979) was for many years the leading critic of the empiricist or constructivist position. The belief that perceptual inputs are necessarily distorted and impoverished emerged, according to Gibson (1950), mainly because researchers tended to investigate vision under artificially simplified conditions. If one keeps an observer's eyes and head still in a darkened room and stimulates the eyes with simple, controlled stimuli, then one is not capturing any of the complexity of perception in the real environment in which the eye evolved. In this environment, the eyes are bathed with many millions of rays of light at any moment. And within this complexity are invariant *patterns*: that is to say, despite the momentary changing flux in the input, certain abstract relationships are preserved.

As an example, consider someone approaching a textured surface. The eye receives light from this surface in the form of millions of what Gibson termed "nested solid angles". This idea should become clearer after examining Fig 3.4. As one moves, the pattern changes: there is an apparent flow of the texture away from the centre of the surface. And this flow is lawful, in that the stationary centre of the display – which expands but does not flow – is the point at which one will make contact with the surface.

Gibson defined such patterns within light as *invariants*, higher-order variables that enable observers to perceive the world effectively, *without the need for additional, constructive processes*. Thus, in Gibson's theory,

FIG. 3.4.   Gibson's demonstration of the apparent flow of textures during an approach to an airfield.

perception is not indirect, as Helmholtz and others argued, but is a direct process of resonance with information in light.

At the most abstract level, the invariants in Gibson's theory are known as *affordances* (Gibson, 1971): "Roughly, the affordances of things are what they furnish, for good or ill, that is, what they *afford* the observer."

Affordances include, for humans, surfaces that are stand-on-able or sit-on-able, objects that are graspable or throwable, objects that afford hitting, surfaces that afford supporting, substances that afford pouring. A single object may give rise to more than one affordance: an apple, for example, affords eating and grasping and throwing. Affordances will vary from one animal to another and will change across the lifespan. For example, air affords flying for birds but not humans. The surface of water affords walking for some insects (water boatmen and others) but not for larger creatures. No surface affords crawling for the pre-crawling infant, but a solid surface may afford crawling (and an undulating one not) for the older infant.

Thus affordances are the *meanings* that an environment has for an animal. As meanings, they guide behaviour: they tell the observer what is or is not possible. And they are of course *relationships* between the perceived world and possible reactions to that world.

The originality of Gibson's approach to invariants and affordances, these seemingly abstract properties of things and events, lies in his remarkable assertion that they can be perceived *directly*, without prior synthesis or analysis. Thus the properties of an object that reveal that it is graspable are there to be perceived directly from the pattern of stimulation arising from the object. This is a very bold idea and one that gives support to the nativist account of perception (a fuller account of Gibson's theory can be found in Gordon, 1997). Gibson supports this revolutionary claim by an appeal to evolution. It is accepted that environments shape eyes through evolutionary selective pressures. The variety of ways in which they have done this is the theme of one of the classic texts in vision, G.L. Walls' *The vertebrate eye and its adaptive radiation* (1942). But if evolution can shape the structure of eyes, why can it not shape their functions? Thus Gibson holds that there has in fact been learning in the perception of invariants and affordances, but that this has taken place over the course of millions of years of evolutionary history, not in the course of particular lifetimes. Gibson grants that there is a role for learning in the lifetime of an individual perceiver, but this takes the form of knowing which particular affordances to attend to.

THE SEARCH FOR COMPROMISES BETWEEN NATIVISM AND EMPIRICISM

As was asserted earlier, few theorists have maintained that perception is entirely learned or entirely innate, at least in more complex, mammalian animals. The value of the theoretical positions we have reviewed is that they have suggested experiments designed to see to which extreme perception tends. There are, however, theorists who have attempted to incorporate both innate and acquired factors into their accounts. We shall give brief accounts of two of these attempts.

Fodor and modularity

Module. A ... unit that is self-contained and has a limited task or set of tasks to perform (*Webster's Dictionary*).

Fodor's book *The modularity of mind* (1983) has exerted a powerful influence on perceptual theorists. The book comprises a sustained argument in favour of a particular view of mind and its relation to other mental capacities, including perception.

In recent years the idea of psychological faculties and (possibly) innate mental factors has re-emerged. Perhaps surprisingly, this re-emergence began during modern research into the nature of language. The pioneer of this new faculty psychology was the distinguished linguist Noam Chomsky.

In his book *Aspects of the theory of syntax* (1965), and in later publications, Chomsky put forward a view of language and its use that differed markedly from the then current empiricist/behaviourist opinion (see, for example, Skinner, 1957). Put crudely, and without recourse to his detailed and powerful analyses of syntactic structures, some relevant parts of Chomsky's views on language can be summarised as follows.

Children make original utterances that they can never have heard. For example, they say "I goed" instead of "I went"; "manses" instead of "men", and it is unlikely that these are imitations of adults' utterances. However, their utterances are structured and lawful and reveal the use of rules that the children cannot describe. When the world's languages are examined, none is truly primitive; they cannot be ranked in order of sophistication or complexity in the way that is possible when considering, say, the architectures or the music of different cultures. Even the fairly recent Pidgin English is growing rapidly in the complexity of its grammar. The ability to distinguish well-formed from ungrammatical utterances is so widespread as to make it seem impossible that this ability could have been acquired through experience alone.

Perceptual modules   Early in his book on modularity, Fodor distinguishes between perceptual or input systems and more "central" systems underlying consciousness – thought, problem solving, and so on. These central systems can be thought of as "horizontally" organised, "unencapsulated", and global in nature. An example will help flesh out this idea. A striking property of human thought is the ability to reason analogically. This appears to be particularly true in the making of scientific discoveries. Fodor shows how things get likened to other, very different, things: the solar system is suddenly seen as a model of the atom; a snake suggests the benzene ring.

However, in contrast to mind, we have the perceptual input systems. Fodor argues that the essence of these is that they are *modular*. By this is meant that they are self-contained, have limited tasks to perform, are reflexive in nature, and are cognitively impenetrable. For example, it is simply impossible to open one's eyes and *not* see a red surface as red. No amount of thought, no strongly held belief, no effort of will can alter such a basic visual response.

Modular systems are not, however, mere automatic transducers of stimulation. They have a very complicated job to do, which is to represent information about the world to the mind (brain) *in forms which it can use.* It may be here that the point of contact between nativism and empiricism can be established. If Fodor is correct, then it is entirely likely that the initial basic stages of perception are indeed innately determined: this is how they have evolved. However, in humans at least, perception is for something: it provides material on which to base our conscious awareness of the world and our responses to it. Some of these responses will naturally demand recourse to memory, habit, belief, and reasoning, and in such cases the role of experience – and hence learning – is self-evident. We can thus see how in time a possibly fruitful compromise might be reached between the age-old antagonistic views: nativism and empiricism. Another way in which this might occur is revealed in the work of Karmiloff-Smith, which we outline briefly.

Karmiloff-Smith: Beyond modularity

Annette Karmiloff-Smith, a former colleague of Piaget's, has suggested that certain versions of both nativism and empiricism may be correct. Her field is cognitive psychology and cognitive development and in her book *Beyond modularity* (1992) she analyses what she considers to be wrong with Piaget's views on the one hand, and contrasting positions – namely those of Fodor and some of the behaviourists – on the other. Karmiloff-Smith offers a model of human development that she terms "Representational Redescription". The arguments for this model are detailed and complicated and much of the material is outside the scope of the present chapter. Interested readers should read *Beyond modularity* in order to experience the force of the arguments contained therein. For now, we merely offer a brief summary of those ideas that have greatest relevance to the present chapter.

Karmiloff-Smith criticises both Piaget and Fodor for what she sees as oversimplifications in their work.

It is asserted that Piaget oversimplifies when he denies that there are any innate mental structures or domain-specific knowledge. Karmiloff-Smith argues, on the basis of available evidence, that there must be some innate predispositions associated with human development that serve to give the developing infant a "head start" in various domains of knowledge acquisition. For example, some visual stimuli are more attractive to infants (even newborns) than others. One of the most attractive is the human face. It is therefore plausible to suggest that what guarantees the particular attention newborn infants pay to faces is a representational bias taking the form of an innate instruction to attend to three blobs in the locations of eyes and mouth. The underlying evidence in support of this idea is the finding that newly born infants track such stimuli in preference to other patterns.

Fodor, too, is wrong in over-concentrating on perceptual input systems without considering what manipulations of knowledge must occur during development. It will be remembered that Fodor stresses the functional rigidity of input modules. And yet the fact is that deaf or blind children, deprived of the usual inputs, can still acquire language in other ways. There is more flexibility in the system than Fodor allows. This claim in turn is supported by the results of the effects of early brain damage: early in life the cortex shows more flexibility than an innate model of perception would predict.

One final example of Karmiloff-Smith's thinking is be given in order to help the reader appreciate the force of her ideas.

During the past 20 years or so, psychologists have become increasingly interested in connectionist networks. In contrast with classical computers, which work sequentially, use symbols and follow explicit rules, connectionist networks comprise layers of fundamental units that are highly interconnected. Typically, these units form layers: input layers, "hidden" layers, and output layers. The units interact according to weighting rules by which the strengths of their connections can change. A network can be set a problem in the form of an input pattern. A successful solution to the problem consists of a matching or otherwise acceptable output pattern. Obviously, the first "run" through the network is unlikely to yield the required match or solution; rather, only parts of the output pattern will match the input. The network can move towards the correct solution when the discrepancy between input and output is fed back into it in ways that selectively change the connections to those output units that are correct by strengthening (or reinforcing) them according to some predetermined rule. Other connections may be left unchanged or even weakened.

Described in this manner, a connectionist network resembles Locke's "tabula rasa". It also resembles behaviourist versions of empiricism, in that it lacks innate knowledge but can use experience (in the form of inputs and feedback correction) and so learn to recognise patterns. For this reason, a successful network, capable of learning to distinguish between, say, male and female faces (and some networks can do this), would seem to confirm empiricist notions as to how perception can develop strictly through experience.

Simultaneously, however, Karmiloff-Smith is able to show that the behaviour of some connectionist networks has features that would at once be described as evidence for nativism rather than empiricism. Here is a key example. It has been found that if a network is constructed in which two types of units are present, *differing only in the speed with which they operate*, then when identical inputs are fed to the two types of unit (Karmiloff-Smith, 1996):

> With time, the network progressively develops such that one set of units represents where things are in the network's environment and the other set represents what objects are present. In other words, two very specialised, differential pathways *emerge* from the slightly different parameters in the initial processing.

Many contemporary theorists believe that connectionist networks are providing us with the best model of the brain to date. If this is so, then the finding described earlier is very exciting. It shows how very slight (by analogy, "genetic") inbuilt biases in systems may, following some experience with the world, lead to the development of very different systems. Karmiloff-Smith argues that this is exactly what may happen in the development of perception in the human infant. There is no light in the womb, *but there is sound.* By the seventh month of pregnancy, the infant is hearing its mother's voice. At birth the infant then shows a preference for its mother's voice to that of a strange female voice. But during pregnancy the mother is using *language,* not simply making sounds. Her speaking follows rules. Thus when the infant is born and suddenly gains vision, it has already experienced an important set of structured stimuli. May this not be of great help in dealing with what might otherwise be a chaotic array of new types of stimuli? In other words, Piaget may have been wrong in maintaining that the newborn infant is assailed by a mass of competing, undifferentiated stimuli.

It will be seen that from this point of view the question of the innate versus the acquired in perception fades in importance. Things are more complicated than this. Just how much more complicated is the question that will continue to be asked by workers such as Karmiloff-Smith and her colleagues.

METHODS OF ENQUIRY: THE WAYS IN WHICH RESEARCHERS HAVE ATTEMPTED TO DECIDE BETWEEN THE TWO TRADITIONS

The reader should now have a grasp of the processes by which the question of the innate versus the acquired nature of perception arose within philosophy and migrated to psychology, together with some familiarity with the opposing schools of thought in contemporary psychological theory. To end this chapter, and to provide an appropriate setting for the chapters that follow, we offer a brief sketch of the ways in which psychologists and others have gone about the task of finding evidence relevant to the innate/acquired controversy in perception.

Basically, psychologists have undertaken three types of experimental investigation in the search for evidence:

1. Perceptual deprivation studies, particularly with animals.
2. Perceptual distortion studies.
3. Developmental studies.

Perceptual deprivation studies

The reasoning behind many of the deprivation studies published to date is as follows. If some aspect of perception is innately determined, then it should make little difference if an organism is prevented from using the particular sense for the first weeks or months of life. The capacity should remain intact and should be evident once the period of deprivation has ended. As we shall show, this approach ignores certain important problems; nevertheless, it has been used on many occasions, with both animal and human subjects.

Animal deprivation studies   There is a long history of these. One generalis-ation can be offered immediately, which is that in what are called "lower" species, major forms of behaviour are little affected by deprivation. To quote a single example, the red-backed shrike (a European bird that displays hawk-like behaviour) has a fixed-action pattern of impaling prey, usually small birds and insects, on thorns: the thorn bush then acts as a form of "larder". When shrikes are hand-reared and therefore deprived of relevant experience, they aim their prey at the thorns in an appropriate manner as soon as they are exposed to them. In other words, they have little difficulty in carrying out the pattern-recognition required.

Many published deprivation studies with "higher" animals such as chim-panzees have resulted in fewer clear-cut results. The problem here is that when, for example, a chimpanzee's eyes are covered with translucent goggles for a period after birth, and the goggles are then removed, what should one expect? If the animal has been adequately fed during the deprivation period, to what use is it suddenly expected to put its eyes? Further, suddenly gaining a new sense may be extremely aversive: any degradation in performance may result from motivational rather than purely perceptual factors.

There is, however, one animal deprivation study that yielded results of great interest. Melzack and Scott (1957) reared some puppies in a labora-tory environment designed as far as possible to prevent them from ever experiencing noxious stimuli. The environment contained no sharp edges, no steps, no hard surfaces. A very interesting behavioural effect was observed when the puppies were eventually exposed to a noxious stimulus in the form of a burning candle. The puppies were clearly highly curious about the flickering flame. Some sniffed it, burning their noses in the process. What was significant was at the moment of contact with the flame, a puppy would emit sounds of distress, *without immediately removing the nose from the flame*. In other words, the puppies' pain systems seemed to be delivering information about the noxious stimulus, but the puppies did not know what to *do* as a result of this novel sensory input. This finding may have an important theoretical implication, namely that to link percep-tion with action may require a degree of learning (see Held & Hein, 1963, and Campos, Bertenthal, & Kermoian, 1992, for more evidence relating to this idea).

We shall not review any more animal deprivation studies. They are described in many of the older textbooks, but have, as we have attempted to show, rather limited usefulness in the resolution of the innate–acquired controversy.

Human deprivation studies   There has long been interest in human blindness and what would happen if a blind person was restored to sight. As we discussed earlier, this was a question that attracted the attention of early philosophers such as Locke. We shall now describe two of the most famous cases of adults restored to sight.

The cases of HB and SB   Miraculous reports of restoration of vision are to be found in the Bible, although such reports may be allegorical in the sense that "blindness" may refer to lack of faith. The earliest reported operation to restore sight dates from AD 1020, and an account of all published cases (up to the 1920s) was given by von Senden in 1932 (available in English translation, 1960).

Operable cases are of two kinds: cataracts of the lenses, where the treatment consists of removing the opaque lenses and, in modern times, replacing them with clear plastic ones, and opacity of the corneas (also referred to as cataracts) where the treatment (available only in modern times) is corneal transplants.

It is worth noting that in order for an operation to have any chance of success the retina(s) must be functional, and this means that preoperative visual perception of some sort has to have been available to the patient: indeed, in almost all recorded cases the patients had useful vision at some time in the past. There are no cases of recovery from complete life-long blindness, and in this sense the philosophers' speculations about the blind man given sight can never be tested.

Two case studies will illustrate both the great differences between different patients, and also the considerable postoperative visual problems they face. Patient HB was born and lived in the Middle East, and had normal vision until the age of 3 years, at which point she contracted smallpox, which caused severe scarring of the corneas of both eyes, making her effectively blind. She had a university education and was bilingual, and at the age of 27 she received a corneal graft to her left eye. The operation was a success, but she showed little recovery of effective vision. Six months after the operation she could detect and locate conspicuous moving objects: for instance, she could see the pigeons as they alighted in London's Trafalgar Square, but curiously she said that they seemed to vanish as they came to rest. Sadly, her vision was never very useful to her, and she never learned to recognise even simple visual shapes, and she eventually reverted to the life of a blind person (Ackroyd, Humphrey, & Warrington, 1974).

Patient SB, investigated by Gregory and Wallace (1963), was born in 1906 and lost effective sight in both eyes about 10 months after birth. After 50 years as a blind person, at the age of 52, he received corneal grafts to restore his sight. In a letter to Gregory, the surgeon reported that " ... After the operation he seemed to have absolutely no difficulty with spatial perception, and he could recognise faces and ordinary objects (i.e. chairs, bed, table, etc.) immediately. He learned the names of colours very quickly, and seemed to have no difficulty in recognising cars, windows, doors, etc."

The contrast between these two patients presents a puzzle: HB had sight for 3 years and was then blind for 24 years; SB had sight for 10 months and was blind for 50 years. Yet SB's postoperative vision seemed much better than HB's: why, we do not know. The newly sighted are people who have learned to live, often very successfully, with their other senses, and what is almost invariably the case is that they have great difficulties in organising and making sense of their new visual world. Because of this, sadly, it is extremely common to find a postoperative reactive depression that can last for many years. HB eventually decided to return to the world of the blind, and SB, who as a blind man had been a cheerful, active, dominant, and often aggressive person, became dispirited and bored, and his sight was "almost entirely disappointing". He became listless, and less than two years after the operation he died (Gregory & Wallace, 1963, p. 37).

> He suffered one of the greatest handicaps, and yet he lived with energy and enthusiasm. When his handicap was apparently swept away, as by a miracle, he lost his peace and his self-respect ... SB found disappointment with what he took to be reality.

Fortunately, it is now extremely rare to find cases of early cataracts that remain untreated after the first few years of life. Cases of adults restored to sight no longer hold the promise they once seemed to for an understanding of perceptual development. In addition to the fact that there are no cases of adults who have been born completely blind having their sight restored, the adults who have been operated on successfully have had years of experience with their other senses, on which they have learned to depend, unlike the baby whose senses develop together. One important point that has become increasingly apparent since the time of Hebb is that we now know that the visual system, if it is not used, will deteriorate – "use it or lose it" is the maxim that applies to the developing system. The eyes, the eye muscles, the retina, and parts of the brain that normally respond to visual input are likely to be damaged in various ways through disuse. This deterioration almost certainly means that the newly sighted will never achieve normal vision, and is the cause of many patients' profound visual learning difficulties.

Once again, we are forced to conclude that a highly interesting and, on the face of it, valuable means of examining the innate/acquired problem in perception has serious flaws. We turn now to a brief discussion of another technique that has been used, that of perceptual distortion.

Distortion studies

The assumption in this area of research is this: if perception is innately programmed, then it should be inflexible. However, if it could be shown that important aspects of perception are easily modifiable as a result of experience, then these aspects may themselves be shaped by experience in normal development, supporting the empiricist view of perception. The reader should be warned that in this area problems of emotion and motivation are as likely to arise as they do in deprivation research.

Animal distortion studies   There have been a large number of studies in which normal stimulus inputs are rendered abnormal by experimental procedures. One generalisation can be offered immediately: the results of distortion studies reveal major intra-species differences.

Many animals can recover from mild distortion. Monkeys and other "higher" species can recover when made to wear lenses that tilt or even invert the world. With inverting lenses, the monkeys tend to sit down at first (baffled!), but soon they are moving around competently. The question is, of course, whether the monkeys' perceptual worlds have normalised, or whether they have simply learned to make appropriate motor adjustments to the inverted visual inputs?

Lower animals, however, show great rigidity after perceptual distortion. The best-known studies in this area are those carried out by Sperry (1951). In one experiment, the eyeball of an amphibian was loosened in its socket and rotated by 180°. After this, whenever a suspended fly was dangled in the amphibian's visual field the usual striking response of the tongue was observed: however, the response was always 180° wrong – and never adapted. Similar results were found when the heads of flies were rotated – no adaptation took place.

Perhaps the best-known studies in this area are those carried out by Blakemore and Cooper (1970), who reared kittens in environments that were painted with either horizontal or vertical stripes. After varying periods the discrimination abilities of the kittens were tested. It was found that rearing in, for example, a vertically striped environment severely impaired the ability to discriminate among horizontal stimuli. Equally interesting was the fact that the population of the kittens' visual cortical cells mediating responses to lines of different orientation changed as a result of exposure to a particular striped environment: relatively fewer cells showed special sensitivity to inputs from stripes in orientations other than those used during the distortion period. Blakemore and his colleagues discovered that there is a limited period during which the visual cortex shows this kind of plasticity. (The concept of the *critical period* will be discussed at length later in this book.)

Human distortion studies   Humans can recover from mild perceptual distortion. If prisms are worn in front of the eyes, coloured fringes are seen. After a few hours' exposure, these disappear. If certain lenses (known as aniesokontic lenses) are worn, these cause edges and contours in the world to appear curved. After a few days, this curvature disappears and the world appears as normal again.

Severe distortion in humans has been studied by having volunteers wear inverting lenses. The two most famous studies here are those by Stratton (1896; 1897) and Kohler (1955). Kohler certainly adapted to visual inversion, in the sense that he was eventually able to ride a bicycle while wearing the lenses. Stratton too showed considerable improvement in motor coordination after a period of time wearing the lenses.

However, close examination of reports by these workers and others suggests that perceptual adaptation may not have taken place. That is to say, one's motor behaviour can change so as to adapt to inverted visual inputs, but it is by no means clear that the perceived world also changes. The ambiguity that appears in reports in this area suggests that those who do these heroic experiments experience extreme difficulty in describing how the world appears. To experience this difficulty, the reader should invert a familiar picture on a wall and then look at the picture from between the legs. The effect of doing this is odd: in one sense the picture looks upside-down, as it is relative to the wall; but in another it looks correct, as it is relative to the eye. But the fact that this simple situation is so hard to report on suggests that inverted vision studies may continue to tell us something about the flexibility of human behaviour, but little about the flexibility or rigidity of human perception.

Developmental studies

This is the major topic to be discussed in the rest of this book. The most powerful way of attempting to discover the extent to which perception is genetically determined or results from experience with the world lies in developmental studies. It will become obvious from the material described in subsequent chapters in this book that research conducted from the 1960s onwards fails to support either an extreme nativist or empiricist

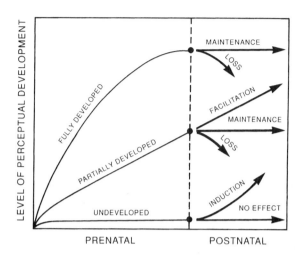

FIG. 3.5. Aslin's (1981) model of perceptual development. (See text for details.)

position. The reason for this is that there are many aspects of vision, ranging from visual acuity to form and object recognition. A useful model that avoids the extremes and the oversimplification of nativism and empiricism is that described by Aslin and Pisoni (1980; see also Aslin, 1981) and shown in Fig 3.5.

In primates the onset of visual experience (the vertical dotted line in Fig. 3.5) coincides with birth, at which time a particular visual ability may be fully developed, partially developed, or undeveloped. Perceptual experience can play different roles, in part dependent on the specific ability and its state of development at birth. For example, saccadic eye movements reveal adult-like maturity at birth, so that postnatal experience may act both to maintain their functioning and to improve their latency and accuracy (see Chapter 1 in this volume). It is also the case that shape and size constancy are present at birth (see Chapters 4 and 7 in this volume) so that postnatal experience may be relatively unimportant.

As examples of abilities that are only partially developed at birth, we know that visual acuity and contrast sensitivity are much poorer in the newborn than in the adult and that visual experience, which can be thought of as serving a facilitating function, is necessary for their postnatal development.

Finally, many visual abilities are undeveloped at birth. These include binocular vision and stereopsis, which first appear between 3 and 5 months after birth and continue to improve thereafter. Similarly, infants know very little about the world of objects, about causality, or about perceptual categories. For these abilities experience is clearly vital for their development.

REFERENCES

Ackroyd, N.K., Humphrey, N., & Warrington, E.K. (1974). Lasting effects of early blindness: a case study. *Quarterly Journal of Experimental Psychology.* **26**, 114–124.

Aslin, R.N. (1981). Experiential influences and sensitive periods in perceptual development. In R.N. Aslin, J.R. Alberts, & M.R. Peterson (Eds.), *Development of perception: psychobiological perspectives. Vol. 2. The visual system.* New York: Academic Press.

Aslin, R.N., & Pisoni, D.B. (1980). Some developmental processes in speech perception. In G.H. Yeni-Komshian, J. Kavanagh, & C.A. Ferguson (Eds.), *Child phonology. Vol.2. Perception.* New York: Academic Press.

Blakemore, C., & Cooper, G.F. (1970). Development of the brain depends on visual environment. *Science,* **228**, 477–478.

Bruner, J.S., & Goodman, C.C. (1947). Value and need as organizing factors in perception. *Journal of Abnormal and Social Psychology,* **42**, 33–44.

Campos, J.J., Bertenthal, B.I., & Kermoian, R. (1992). Early experience and emotional development: the emergence of wariness of heights. *Psychological Science,* **3**, 61–64.

Chomsky, N. (1965). *Aspects of the theory of syntax.* Cambridge, MA: MIT Press.

Fodor, J.A. (1983). *The modularity of mind.* Cambridge, MA: MIT Press.

Gibson, J.J. (1950). *The perception of the visual world.* Boston: Houghton Mifflin.

Gibson, J.J. (1971). A preliminary description and classification of Affordances. Unpublished manuscript reproduced in E. Reed & R. Jones (Eds.) (1982), *Reasons for realism.* Hillsdale, NJ: Erlbaum.

Gordon, I.E. (1997). *Theories of visual perception.* (2nd edn.). Chichester, UK: Wiley.

Gregory, R.L., & Wallace, J.G. (1963). Recovery from early blindness: a case study. *Experimental Psychology Society Monograph,* Number 2. Cambridge, UK: W. Heffer and Son.

Hebb, D.O. (1949). *The organization of behaviour.* New York: Wiley.

Held, R., & Hein, A. (1963). Movement produced stimulation in the development of visually guided behavior. *Journal of Comparative and Physiological Psychology,* **56**, 872–876.

Karmiloff-Smith, A. (1992). *Beyond modularity.* Cambridge, MA: MIT Press.

Karmiloff-Smith, A. (1996). The connectionist infant: Would Piaget turn in his grave? *SRCD Newsletter* (A publication of the Society for Research in Child Development.) Fall edition.

Kohler, I. (1955). Experiments with prolonged optical distortion. *Acta Psychologica,* **11**, 176–178.

Lazarus, R.S., & McCleary, R.A. (1951). Autonomic discrimination without awareness: a study in subception. *Psychological Review,* **58**, 113–122.

Lorenz, K. (1953). Die Entwicklung der vergleichenden Verhaltensforschung in den letzten 12 Jahren. *Zoologischer Anzeiger,* **16**, (Supplement) 36–58.

Lorenz, K. & Tinbergen, N. (1938). Taxis und Instinkthandlung in der Eirollbewegung der Graugans. *Zeitschrift für Tierpsychologie,* **2**, 1–29.

Magee, B. (1978). *Men of ideas: Some creators of contemporary philosophy.* London: British Broadcasting Corporation.

McGinnies, E. (1949). Emotionality and perceptual defense. *Psychological Review,* **56**, 244–251.

Melzack, R., & Scott, T.H. (1957). The effects of early experience on the response to pain. *Journal of Comparative and Physiological Psychology,* **50**, 155–161.

Morgan, M.J. (1977). *Molyneux's question: vision, touch and the philosophy of perception.* Cambridge: Cambridge University Press.

Piaget, J. (1953). *The origins of intelligence in the child.* London: Routledge & Kegan Paul.

Piaget, J. (1954). *The construction of reality in the child.* London: Routledge & Kegan Paul.

Skinner, B.F. (1957). *Verbal behavior.* New York: Appleton-Century-Crofts.

Sperry, R.W. (1951). Mechanisms of neural maturation. In S.S. Stevens (Ed.), *Handbook of Experimental Psychology.* New York: Wiley.

Stratton, G. (1896). Some preliminary experiments on vision without inversion of the retinal image. *Psychological Review,* **3**, 611–617.

Stratton, G. (1897). Vision without inversion of the retinal image. *Psychological Review,* **4**, 341–360.

Tinbergen, N., & Perdeck, A.C. (1950). On the stimulus situation releasing the begging response in the newly hatched herring gull chick (*Larus argentatus*). *Behaviour,* **3**, 1–38.

Von Senden, M. (1960). *Space and sight.* London: Methuen.

Walls, G.L. (1942). *The vertebrate eye and its adaptive radiation.* Birmingham, MI: Cranbrook Institute of Science.

CHAPTER FOUR

The competent infant: Innate organisation and early learning in infant visual perception

Alan Slater
Washington Singer Laboratories, University of Exeter, UK

INTRODUCTION

The study of perceptual development has its origins in the classic nature/ nurture debate (discussed in Chapter 3). Perhaps because the young infant appears to be so helpless, early theories emphasised an empiricist view of perceptual development, that perception is extremely impoverished at birth and develops as a consequence of experience and learning. However, research carried out over the last 30 years has changed the traditional view of the young infant's perceptual world from one of "incompetence" to one of "competence". Although experience is of great importance, infants display considerable perceptual competence at an early age, and even the newborn baby perceives an organised and structured world. This chapter reviews some of the evidence leading to the conceptualisation of "the competent infant" in the next four sections: *preparedness for visual perception, visual organisation soon after birth, innate representations and early learning,* and *visual organisation in the early months.* Clearly, however visually competent young infants may be they have an immense amount to learn about the visual world. The role of learning and experience in contributing to visual development is illustrated in the fifth section on *the roles of experience.*

PREPAREDNESS FOR VISUAL PERCEPTION

The first patterned input to the visual system begins at birth, and for newborns, lacking visual experience, it would seem sensible for evolution to have equipped them with innate endogenous mechanisms that guide their initial confrontation with the visual world. Haith (1980) reports a number of studies in which newborn infants' eye movements and eye fixations were recorded (using infrared recording procedures) either in complete darkness (rule 2) or in the presence of a simple stimulus such as an edge (rules 3 and 4). He described a number of dispositions or "rules" that guide newborns' spontaneous visual exploration of the world. The first four of these "rules" are (Haith, 1980, p. 96):

Rule 1: If awake and alert and light not too bright, open eyes
Rule 2: If in darkness, maintain a controlled, detailed search
Rule 3: If in light with no form, search for edges by relatively broad, jerky sweeps of the (visual) field
Rule 4: If an edge is found, terminate the broad scan and stay in the general vicinity of that edge.

Newborn infants are also "prepared" for visual perception in the sense that they will attend to some types of visual stimuli when these are shown paired side-by-side with others. Preferential-looking studies have found at least nine "natural" preferences in newborn infants ("natural" in that they are found without prior visual experience). Newborns will prefer to look at: (1) patterned rather than unpatterned stimuli; (2) horizontal rather than vertical gratings (stripes); (3) moving rather than stationary stimuli; (4) three-dimensional rather than two-dimensional stimuli; (5) curvilinear in preference to rectilinear patterns; (6) objects in the fronto-parallel plane rather than those at an angle; (7) high-contrast rather than low-contrast stimuli; (8) objects at an optimal size (where this is usually the larger of two objects); (9) face-like in preference to non-face-like stimuli (this last is discussed later in this chapter).

This list of newborn preferences (which is discussed in detail by Slater, 1995) is large and no doubt as experimentation increases, the number of dimensions will increase. The underlying mechanisms that cause some of these preferences are not understood, although for some of them a reasonable guess can be made. In the natural world, it is moving and three-dimensional stimuli that are likely to provide the most information about objects and events. High-contrast stimuli are more readily detected, and seen more clearly, by the immature visual system. The human face is one of the most important visual stimuli for the infant. Hence it is not surprising that these stimuli should be especially attention-getting and attention-holding.

The baby is born usually with the eyes wide open, and actively searching for information. As discussed earlier, some of this visual search can be described in terms of a few simple rules, and it is affected by changes to a number of stimulus variables, such as pattern detectability, movement, three-dimensionality, contrast, size, and approximation to a human face. These attentional proclivities serve to ensure that newborn infants actively scan their newly encountered visual world.

VISUAL ORGANISATION SOON AFTER BIRTH

The major characteristic of visual perception is that it is organised. We perceive objects, people, and events that move and change in a coherent fashion; we do not perceive a world of fleeting, unconnected retinal images. There is clear experimental evidence that many types of visual organisation are present at, or soon after, birth, and these are discussed here.

The visual constancies

As objects move, they change in orientation, or slant, relative to an observer, but despite these changes we see the object as the same shape: This phenomenon is known as shape constancy. Size constancy refers to the fact that we perceive an object as being the same size despite changes to its distance, and hence changes to its retinal size. There is evidence for the presence of both of these constancies at birth (Slater & Morison, 1985; Slater, Mattock, & Brown, 1990).

Slater and Morison describe two experiments on shape constancy. In the first, using a preferential-looking procedure, newborns' preferences for one stimulus, an outline black square, were found to change in a consistent fashion with changes in slant: as the orientation of the square shifted consistently away from the fronto-parallel plane it became progressively less preferred than a paired stimulus (an outline trapezium) that remained in the frontal plane. This is evidence that the changes to the stimulus slant were clearly detected by the infants. In the second experiment newborn infants (an average of 2 days old) were desensitised to changes in the slant of either a square or a trapezium during familiarisation trials. On subsequent test trials they were able to recognise the familiar shape (they looked more at a new shape) even though it was shown at a different slant from any shown earlier. This indicates that the "old" shape was perceived as familiar despite the different slants it was seen in on the familiarisation trials, that is, shape constancy is present soon after birth.

In their experiment on size constancy (Slater et al., 1990) newborn infants were shown a single object, a cube, at different distances from the eyes on familiarisation trials. On subsequent test trials the infants looked more (i.e. gave a novelty preference) at a different-sized cube than at the same-sized one, even though the paired cubes were at different distances in order to make their retinal sizes the same.

The findings from these studies demonstrate that newborn infants are sensitive to changes in objects' slant and distance, but that they also have the ability to perceive objective, real shape and size: that is, shape and size constancy are organising features of perception that are present at birth.

Form perception and stimulus compounds

The terms "figure", "shape", "form", and "pattern" are often used inter-changeably, so it is worth mentioning that most theories of form perception have been concerned with static, achromatic, two- or three-dimensional figures that can stand as figures in a figure–ground relationship, and it is newborn infants' detection of, and response to, these types of stimuli that are considered here.

It would be impossible for a functional visual system *not* to respond to at least some variations in stimulus shape, and we know from visual preference studies, mentioned earlier, that newborn babies make a variety of such discriminations along dimensions such as slant, size, two- and three-dimensions, orientation. The findings from studies using habituation and familiarisation procedures add to this list of discriminations that infants are able to make. For example, in an early study by Slater et al. (1983 cited in Slater, 1995) newborn infants were habituated to a simple geometric form and on subsequent test trials they dishabituated (i.e. looked more at, or gave a novelty preference) to a different shape.

The findings from such studies can be difficult to interpret. The problem is the following: when newborn babies discriminate between, say, a triangle and a circle, it is possible that they might be making the discrimination on the basis of differences in the orientation of the lines that make up the stimuli, rather than seeing the triangle and circle as whole figures. Certainly, newborn infants easily discriminate between stimuli that differ in orientation alone (Atkinson et al., 1988; Slater, Morison, & Somers, 1988). An experiment by Cohen and Younger (1984) illustrates the problem and suggests that there may be an age difference in the way in which simple shapes are perceived in early infancy. The habituation and test stimuli they used are shown in Fig. 4.1. Each infant was habituated to one of the angles, and was then presented with the four test stimuli, which varied along the dimensions of angle, size, and orientation: test stimulus (1), $A_F O_F$ is the same as the familiar stimulus; (2), $A_F O_N$ differs in the orientation of the lines that make up the angle, but the angle is the same; (3), $A_N O_F$ differs in angle, but the orientation of the lines is the same as the familiar; (4), $A_N O_N$ differs in both orientation and angle. Cohen and Younger tested infants 6 and 14 weeks old and both groups responded identically, and predictably, to two of the test stimuli: neither recovered attention to the familiar stimulus (test stimulus 1); both recovered attention to test stimulus (4). However, an interesting age difference was found in recovery of attention to test stimuli (2) and (3): 6-week-olds recovered attention to

Habituation   **Test**

A_FO_F A_FO_N A_NO_F A_NO_N

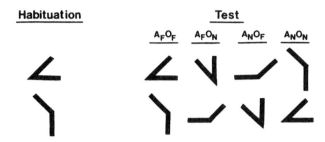

FIG. 4.1.   Habituation and test stimuli used by Cohen and Younger (1984). Half their infants were presented the stimuli shown on the top line, half the ones shown on the bottom line. Key: A, angle; O, orientation; F, familiar; N, novel. © Ablex Publishing Corporation reprinted with permission.

(2), the orientation change, but not to (3); 4-month-olds did the opposite and recovered to a change in angle (3), but not to a change in orientation (2).

These findings demonstrate that 4-month-old infants are able to perceive angular relationships, and hence have some degree of form perception, but suggest that form perception in infants 6 weeks old and younger might be dominated by attention to lower-order variables of stimulation such as orientation. However, an experiment by Slater, Mettock, Brown, and Bremner (1991a, Experiment 2) used these stimuli and found that, with different conditions of testing, newborn infants *can* process the relationship between two line segments, that is, the angle, independently of its orientation. In this experiment, each infant was given six familiarisation trials with one stimulus (either the acute 45° or obtuse 135° angle) but on each of these trials it was shown in a different orientation: thus, if newborn infants were detecting an invariant property of the stimulus across the familiarisation trials it could not be orientation. After this familiarisation period the infants were given test trials with the two angles, with each in a different orientation than any shown earlier, and they reliably looked longer at the novel angle.

All visual stimuli contain separate features that occur together at the same spatial location, and that the mature perceiver "binds together" as a whole. With such an ability we see, for example, the stimulus compounds of a blue cross and a red square, whereas without it we would see blue, cross, red, and square as separate, unrelated properties. An experiment by Slater, Mattock, Brown, Burnham, and Young (1991b) was designed to test whether newborn infants have the ability to remember simple stimulus compounds. The babies were familiarised, on successive trials, to two separate stimuli. For half the infants these were a green diagonal (GD) stripe and a red vertical (RV) stripe; the other babies were familiarised to

GV and RD. For the first group of infants there are two novel compounds of these elements, GV and RD; for the second group the novel compounds are GD and RV. On test trials the infants were shown one of the familiar compounds paired with one of the novel ones, and all of the 14 babies looked longer at the novel compound, the average novelty preference being 76% of the looking time. Note that these novelty preferences could not have resulted if the infants had processed only the separate properties of the familiarised stimuli, because the novel compounds consisted of stimulus properties (colour and orientation) that they had seen before. Thus, the findings are clear evidence that newborn infants can process and remember simple stimulus compounds.

Overview

The evidence presented here suggests that the newborn infant enters the world with several means with which to begin to perceive a coherent and stable visual world. Size and shape constancy are present at birth, and it appears that some rudimentary degree of form perception is also present. The findings of Cohen and Younger (1984) suggest that the ways in which infants parse the visual world change across early infancy; however, those of Slater et al. (1991a) suggest that some of these limitations can be overcome, even by newborn infants. The finding that newborn infants perceive stimulus compounds rather than isolated, separate parts is further evidence of some degree of form perception at birth.

INNATE REPRESENTATIONS AND EARLY LEARNING: THE CASE OF FACE PERCEPTION

The experiments described in the preceding section contribute to the view that several organisational principles are innately provided to newborn infants that help them to parse the visual world and that help them to create order out of what would otherwise be visual chaos. It has been suggested that in addition to these inborn abilities newborn infants have innate representational abilities, and it is also apparent that they engage in very rapid learning about the visual world. Evidence relating to these topics is discussed here, with particular reference to infants' perception of faces.

The human face is one of the most complex visual stimuli encountered by the human infant. It moves, is three-dimensional, has areas of both high and low contrast, and contains features that can appear both in changing (perhaps with changes of expression), and invariant (the positions of eyes, mouth, nose, hair, etc.) relationships. In addition, individual faces are all unique and differ from one another often in subtle ways. A major task confronting the newborn infant, therefore, is to make sense of "faces in general" and also to distinguish between different people's faces. We know that a considerable period of learning is required in order to achieve some degree of competence in these areas (see Chapters 8 and 9). However, it is clear that the newborn infant has something of a "head start" as shown both by rapid learning about faces and by the likelihood of an innately provided representation of the human face.

Early learning about faces

It is not surprising to find that the visual information detected by newborn infants is poor (Chapter 1 gives a detailed account of visual development), but Hainline and Abramov (1992, p. 40) point out that "while infants may not, indeed, see as well as adults do, they normally see well enough to function effectively in their role as infants". For newborn infants the visual stimuli that are likely to be of most relevance are people who interact with them and are therefore likely to be close to them. Figure 4.2 gives an indication of how a face might look to newborn infants at a distance of about a foot from their eyes, and how she would look to us. Although the image is degraded and unfocused for the newborn, enough information is potentially available for the infant to learn to recognise the mother's face and to discriminate her from others. Indeed, it seems that newborns quickly learn about, and show a preference for, their mother's face (Bushnell, Sai, & Mullin, 1989; Field, Cohen, Garcia, & Greenberg, 1984; Walton, Bower, & Bower, 1992).

We do not know precisely what aspects of the face newborn (and older) infants use in making these discriminations. De Schonen, Gil de Diaz, and Mathivet (1986) found that 4-month and older infants were able to recog-

FIG. 4.2.   A face as it might appear to us, and to a newborn infant.

nise their mother's face even when her hair/face separation line and outer head contour were covered with a scarf, suggesting that they were able to process, and to use, the internal facial features and their configuration in order to discriminate between faces. Pascalis et al. (1995) replicated and extended de Schonen et al.'s study with newborn (4-day-old) infants. They confirmed earlier findings in that their infants (Experiment 1) reliably discriminated and preferred their mother's face when all the facial information was present. However, when mother and stranger wore scarves around their heads (Experiment 2) they were no longer able to make the discrimination. This suggests that there might be an age difference in infants' processing of faces: by 4 months of age infants process both external and internal facial features: "However, it seems that what (newborns) have learned has to do with the external features of the face rather than the inner features" (Pascalis et al., 1995, p. 84).

An alternative interpretation of Pascalis et al.'s findings is that newborn infants process *both* internal and external facial features, and that removing one of these sets of features disrupts recognition. Certainly, there is considerable evidence that newborn infants *do* detect and learn about internal facial features. Walton and Bower (1993) reported that newborn infants who were shown four faces for a total looking time of less than one minute extracted a facial prototype, or averaged version, of the four in that they subsequently looked more at a composite of the previously seen faces than at a composite of four faces that had not been seen earlier: it would be difficult for the newborns to make these discriminations without attending to the internal features of the faces. A similar finding was reported for 6-month-olds by Langlois et al., 1995, and in both studies the composites were produced by pixel-averaging the features of the exemplar faces.

In a more recent study (Walton, Armstrong, & Bower, in press) newborn infants (averaging just over 1 day from birth) were first shown a female face while they were sucking on a pacifier. The babies controlled the presentation of the face in that it continued to be shown only if they continued to suck. This was the initial training, or familiarisation period, following which the newborns were presented with the same face transformed, or a different female face that had undergone the same transformation. The three facial transformations shown (in three separate experiments) were: (1) a photonegative transformation; (2) a size change (the transformed face was smaller than the original); (3) rotation in the third dimension (the training face was facing straight ahead and the transformed one was half profile). Newborns succeeded with all three transformations, in that they sucked more to see the transformed familiar face.

These preferences for a "familiar" composite of faces (Walton & Bower,

1993), and for the "familiar" transformation (Walton et al., in press) are further evidence that learning about faces, and the formation of a representation of faces, can be extremely rapid in the newborn period, and that what is learned is robust in that it holds across transformations of the original.

Is there an innate representation of the human face?

Several lines of evidence converge to suggest that newborn infants come into the world with some innately specified representation of faces. Goren, Sarty, and Wu (1975) reported that their newborn subjects, who averaged 9 *minutes* from birth at the time of testing, and had never seen a human face, turned their heads more to follow (i.e. track) a two-dimensional schematic face-like pattern than either of two patterns consisting of the same facial features in different arrangements. A replication of Goren et al.'s study was reported by Johnson and Morton (1991): the stimuli they used were three of those used by Goren et al., and are shown in Fig. 4.3. Johnson and Morton use these findings and other evidence to argue for the existence of an innate face-detecting device they call "Conspec" (short for conspecifics), which "perhaps comprises just three dark patches in a triangle, corresponding to eyes and mouth" (Pascalis et al., 1995, p. 80), and which serves to direct the newborn infant's visual attention to faces.

Imitation

Other evidence suggests that the hypothesised innate facial representation might be more detailed than simply a template that matches three dots. In particular it has been demonstrated that newborn (and older) infants will imitate a variety of facial gestures they see an adult model performing. This was first discovered by one of Piaget's students, Maratos (1973), who reported to him that if she stuck out her tongue to a young baby, the baby would respond by sticking its tongue out at her. (This goes against Piaget's views on imitation – according to his theory it should only emerge from the second year from birth.) When Piaget was appraised of his student's findings he apparently sucked contemplatively on his pipe for a few moments and then commented "how rude".

One of the first published reports of imitation by newborn and older infants was by Meltzoff and Moore (1977), and there are now many reports of such imitation (e.g. Field et al., 1982; Meltzoff & Moore, 1984, 1992, 1994, 1997). Reissland (1988) reported imitation of two facial gestures – lips widening and lips pursing – in infants who averaged only 30min from birth. Reissland was the experimenter and her face was the first face the babies saw, and the successful imitation is clear evidence that the capacity

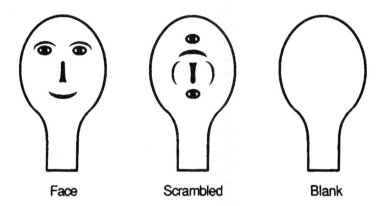

FIG. 4.3. The three stimuli used by Johnson and Morton (1991) in their replication of Goren et al. (1975): newborn infants tracked the Face in preference to Scrambled and Blank. © Blackwell Publishers reprinted with permission.

to imitate is present at birth. Meltzoff (1995) suggests that "newborns begin life with some grasp of people" (p. 43) and that their ability to recognise when their facial behaviour is being copied implies that "there is some representation of their own bodies" (p. 53).

Infants can see the adult's face, but of course they cannot see their own. This means that in some way they have to match their own, unseen but felt, facial movements with the seen, but unfelt, facial movements of the adult. Meltzoff and Moore (1997) propose that they do this by a process of "active intermodal matching" (AIM). The *active* component of this process is well illustrated by Meltzoff and Moore (1994), in which 6-week-olds saw an adult stick his tongue out of the corner of his mouth. The infants' first attempts at imitating this gesture were usually inaccurate, consisting of tongue protrusion but not to the corner of their mouths. The infants often displayed what Meltzoff and Moore term a "creative error", in that they would stick out their tongues while simultaneously turning their heads to one side. Over time the infants corrected their imitative behaviour until it gradually matched the adult target (see Fig. 4.4).

A fundamental question is "What is the motive for imitation in the newborn?" No man, and no baby, is an island, and one suggestion is that babies are born with a deep-seated need to communicate (Kugiumutzakis, 1993). A complementary interpretation is offered by Meltzoff and Moore (1992, 1994), who claim that imitation is an act of social cognition that serves to help the infant identify, understand, and recognise people: "infants use the nonverbal behavior of people as an identifier of who they

FIG. 4.4. Three infants imitating a large tongue-protrusion-to-the-side gesture. Meltzoff and Moore (1994) found that 6-week-old infants imitated this novel gesture by correcting their behaviour so that it gradually matched the adult target. This correction process is thought to be important for understanding the mechanism underlying early imitation, because it suggests that infants monitor their own tongue protrusion via proprioceptive feedback. Such correction is compatible with Meltzoff and Moore's AIM model of imitation, suggesting that early imitation is accompanied by "active intermodal matching". (Photos from Meltzoff & Moore, 1997).

(the people) are and use imitation as a means of verifying this identity" (1992, p. 479).

Infants prefer attractive faces

Samuels and Ewy (1985) showed pairs of black-and-white same-gender faces to 3- and 6-month-old infants. The slides were constructed such that the two faces in each pair were approximately matched for brightness and contrast, but differed in attractiveness as rated by adults: each pair consisted of one attractive and one unattractive face. Both age groups looked longest at the attractive faces for all 12 of the pairs shown. This finding has been replicated and extended by others, and the "attractiveness effect" seems to be robust in that it is found for stimulus faces that are infant, adult, male, female, and of two races (African-American and Caucasian) (Langlois et al., 1987, 1991); babies also preferred attractive to symmetrical faces when these two dimensions were varied independently (Samuels, Butterworth, Roberts, & Graupner, 1994).

A frequently expressed interpretation of the attractiveness effect is in terms of prototype formation and a cognitive averaging process. The origins of this interpretation can be traced back more than a hundred years. In the last century Charles Darwin received a letter from Mr A.L. Austin in New Zealand (Galton, 1907, p. 227). The letter read:

Although a perfect stranger to you, and living on the reverse side of the globe, I have taken the liberty of writing to you on a small discovery I have made in binocular vision in the stereoscope. I find by taking two ordinary carte-de-visite photos of two different persons' faces, the portraits being about the same sizes, and looking about the same direction, and placing them in a stereoscope, the faces blend into one in a most remarkable manner, producing in the case of some ladies' portraits, in every instance, a *decided improvement* in beauty.

Darwin passed the discovery to his half cousin, Francis Galton, who confirmed the effect. Galton went further and was the first scientist to average faces, which he did photographically by underexposing each individual picture. In recent times such averaging can be done by computer, and the resulting "average" or prototypical face is typically seen as more attractive than the individual faces that combine to produce it. For this reason, averageness has been claimed to be an important ingredient of attractiveness (Langlois & Roggman, 1990). According to this interpretation, therefore, attractive faces are seen as more "face-like" because they match more closely the prototype that infants have formed from their experience of seeing faces: thus, "Infants may prefer attractive or prototypical faces because prototypes are easier to classify as a face" (Langlois & Roggman, 1990, p. 119).

Recently, Slater, von der Schulenburg et al. (1998) have shown that even newborn babies, in the age range 14–151 hours from birth, prefer to look at attractive faces. It is possible that newborn infants' preferences for attractive faces result from an innate representation of faces that infants bring into the world with them: Langlois and Roggman (1990) discuss the possibility of an innate account for attractiveness preferences. Alternately, as mentioned earlier, we know that infants learn about faces soon after birth and it is possible that the newborns' preference for attractive faces is a preference for an image similar to a composite of the faces they have seen in the few hours from birth prior to testing.

Overview

It seems now to be reasonably well agreed that "there does seem to be *some* representational bias ... that the neonate brings to the learning situation for faces" (Karmiloff-Smith, 1996, p. 10). This representational bias might simply be a tendency to attend to stimuli that possess three blobs in the location of eyes and mouth ("Conspec"), or it might be something more elaborate: it is possible that evolution has provided the infant with a more detailed blueprint of the human face. The latter possibility is suggested by newborn infants' ability to imitate the facial gestures produced by the first face they have ever seen (Reissland, 1988), and also, perhaps, by newborn infants' preferences for attractive faces.

This representational bias ensures that newborn infants have a predisposition to attend to faces, and it is clear that soon after birth they learn to distinguish between individual faces, form prototypes of faces they have seen only briefly, recognise faces across transformations, and learn to "match the target" of an adult's facial gesture. Such remarkable early learning might result from an innately endowed face-specific learning mechanism, or it might be a product of a more general pattern-processing system that assists the infant in learning about complex visual stimuli. At present we cannot distinguish between these possibilities, but the literature on face perception soon after birth is a clear indication that "At birth visual processing starts with a vengeance" (Karmiloff-Smith, 1996, p. 10).

VISUAL ORGANISATION IN THE EARLY MONTHS

Many organisational principles contribute to the perceived coherence and stability of the visual world. As discussed earlier, shape and size constancy are present at birth, as is some degree of form perception. Other types of visual organisation have been found in young infants, and by way of illustration two of these are discussed here: subjective contours and Gestalt principles.

Subjective contours

Subjective contours are contours that are perceived "in the absence of any physical gradient of change in the display". Such contours were described in detail by Kanizsa (1979) and the Kanizsa square is shown in Fig. 4.5A: the adult perceiver usually "completes" the contours of the figure, despite the fact that the contours are physically absent. Convincing evidence that 3- and 4-month-old infants perceive subjective contours was provided by Ghim (1990). In one of Ghim's experiments the infants were familiarised to a pattern containing either a subjective contour indicating a square (A in Fig. 4.5) or to an arrangement of the elements that does not produce a subjective contour (i.e. B in Fig. 4.5). Following the familiarisation period the infants familiarised to the subjective contour discriminated it from a nonsubjective contour, whereas those in the latter group were unable to discriminate between the familiarised stimulus and a different nonsubjective contour pattern. These findings lead Ghim to conclude that " ... the difference between patterns with and without subjective contours is greater than the difference between patterns without subjective contours" (1990, p. 225). Ghim describes other experiments that lead to the conclusion that the infants were perceiving the complete form when viewing the subjective contour patterns.

Gestalt organisational principles

One of the main contributions of the Gestalt psychologists was to describe a number of ways in which visual perception is organised: Gordon and Slater describe some of these in Chapter 3. Quinn, Burke, and Rush (1993) report evidence that 3-month-old infants group patterns according to the Gestalt principle of similarity. Two of the stimuli they used are shown in Fig. 4.6. Adults reliably group the elements of such stimuli on the basis of lightness similarity and represent the figure on the left as a set of rows, and the other as a set of columns. Three-month-olds do the same, in that those habituated to the columns pattern generalise to vertical lines and prefer (perceive as novel) horizontal lines, whereas those habituated to the rows prefer the novel vertical lines.

Quinn, Brown, and Streppa (1997) describe two experiments, both using an habituation–novelty testing procedure, to determine if 3- and 4-month-old infants can organise visual patterns according to the Gestalt principles of good continuation and closure. The stimuli they used are shown in Fig. 4.7. In their first experiment infants were familiarised to the square and teardrop pattern (Fig. 4.7a) and were then tested with either the square or the teardrop (Fig. 4.7b) paired with the 4 (Fig. 4.7c). On the test trials the infants preferred to look at the number 4 in preference to either the square or the teardrop. This preference indicates that they perceived the number 4 as novel, and the square and teardrop as familiar: that is, they had parsed the familiarised figure into the two separate shapes of a square and a teardrop in the same way that adults do. In Quinn et al.'s second experiment they found that infants who were habituated to an intersecting square and circle parsed them into these coherent shapes on the basis of good continuation.

Overview

Only a sample has been given of the many articles that demonstrate that young infants organise the world in a similar manner to that of adult perceivers. But the newborn and young infant's world is very different from ours: "It must certainly lack associations, meaning and familiarity . . .: [they] see everything, but nothing makes sense" (Gordon, 1997, pp. 82–83). In the next section some of the ways in which perception is affected and changed by experience and learning in infancy are discussed.

THE ROLES OF EXPERIENCE AND LEARNING

We have already seen some of the ways in which learning affects and changes the world of the newborn infant, especially in learning about faces. As infants develop, and indeed throughout life, their experiences

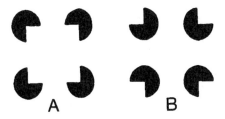

FIG. 4.5.   Pattern A (a Kanizsa square) produces subjective contours and is seen as a square. Pattern B contains the same four elements but does not produce subjective contours.

change their perception of the world. Some of the changes occurring in early infancy are discussed here, under the headings of *intermodal perception, biomechanical motion*, and *perception of object segregation*.

Intermodal perception

Most of the objects and events that we experience are intermodal in that they provide information to more than one sensory modality. Such intermodal information can be broadly categorised into two types of relation, amodal and arbitrary. Amodal perception is where two (or more) senses provided information that is equivalent in one or more respects, and many types of amodal perception have been demonstrated in early infancy. Newborn infants reliably turn their heads and eyes in the direction of a sound source, indicating that spatial location is given by both visual and auditory information (Butterworth, 1983; Muir & Clifton, 1985; Wertheimer, 1961). One-month-olds demonstrate cross-modal matching by recognising a visual shape (a pacifier) that had previously been experienced tactually by sucking, indicating that the shape is coded both tactually and visually (Meltzoff & Borton, 1979). By 4 months infants are sensitive to temporal synchrony specified intermodally in that they detect the common rhythm and duration of tones and flashing lights (Lewkowicz, 1986). Four-month-olds also detect and match appropriately the sounds made either by a single unitary element or by a cluster of smaller elements (Bahrick, 1987, 1988). Thus, there is evidence that infants, from birth, perceive a wide range of invariant amodal relations.

It is quite likely that the ability to detect amodal relations is innately given to the infant, and hence, minimal learning is required in their detection. However, many of the intermodal relationships that we perceive appear to be quite arbitrary. For example, there is no information specifying a priori that a particular voice has to be associated with a particular face, that a particular animal makes a certain sound, or that an object makes a certain sound on making contact with a certain surface. Research

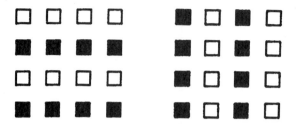

FIG. 4.6. Stimuli used by Quinn, Burke, and Rush (1993). Three-month-olds group by similarity and perceive the pattern on the left as rows, and that on the right as columns. © Ablex Publishing Corporation reprinted with permission.

suggests that many arbitrary intermodal relations are learned in infancy: Spelke and Owsley (1979) found that 3½-month-olds had learned to associate the sound of their mother's voice with the sight of her face, and Hernandez-Reif, Cigales, and Lundy (1994) reported that 6-month-olds learned the face–voice pairings of same-sex female strangers; Reardon and Bushnell (1988) reported that 7-month-olds were able to learn the association between the colour of a container and the taste of the food it contained.

There is evidence that newborn babies are also able to learn arbitrary intermodal relations. Slater et al. (1997) familiarised two-day-old infants, on successive trials, to two visual-auditory stimuli. One visual-auditory combination ("Red-mum") was a red vertical line, and when presented it was accompanied by the sound "mum" spoken in a male voice at a rate of once per second; the other combination ("Green-teat") was a green diagonal line accompanied by the sound "teat" in a female voice. One important characteristic of the familiarisation trials is that the sound was only presented when the infant was judged to be looking at the visual stimulus, meaning that the infants were provided with amodal information in that there was temporal synchrony of onset and offset of both stimuli. On the post-familiarisation test trials the infants were presented with one familiar combination (either "Red-mum" or "Green-teat"), which was alternately presented with a novel combination ("Red-teat" or "Green-mum"). On the test trials the infants gave a strong preference for the novel combination, giving a clear demonstration that newborn infants can learn arbitrary visual-auditory combinations. Note that these novelty preferences could not have resulted if the newborns had processed the separate properties of the stimuli presented on the familiarisation trials separately, because the novel pairings consisted of visual and auditory stimuli that had been presented earlier.

Many intermodal events give both amodal and arbitrary information.

STIMULUS   POSSIBLE ORGANISATIONS

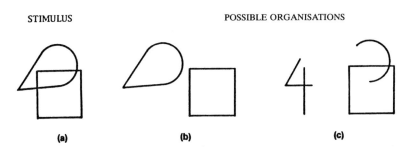

(a)   (b)   (c)

FIG. 4.7.   Patterns used by Quinn, Brown and Streppa (1997). Following familiarisation to pattern (a), tests revealed that the infants parsed the pattern into a square and a teardrop (b) rather than into the "less-good" patterns shown in (c). © Ablex Publishing Corporation reprinted with permission.

For instance, when a person speaks the synchrony of voice and mouth provides amodal information, whereas the pairing of the face and the sound of the voice is arbitrary. In several publications Bahrick (i.e. 1987, 1988, 1992; Bahrick & Pickens, 1994) has provided strong evidence that learning about *arbitrary* intermodal relations is greatly assisted if there is accompanying *amodal* information: "detection of amodal invariants precedes and guides learning about arbitrary object–sound relations by directing infants' attention to appropriate object–sound pairings and then promoting sustained attention and further differentiation" (Bahrick & Pickens, 1994, p. 226). In Slater et al.'s experiment amodal information was present, and it is likely that this facilitated the newborns' learning of the arbitrary intermodal relations. It is of interest to note that when the mother speaks to her infant the amodal information of temporal synchrony of voice and lips is quite likely to facilitate learning to associate her face and voice, and it seems likely that this learning occurs very soon after birth.

Biomechanical motion

Biomechanical motions are the motions that correspond to the movements of a person (or other biological organism) when the individual is walking or engaging in some other activity. Such motions are often depicted as point-light displays, which can be produced by filming a person in the dark who has points of light attached to the head and to the major joints (shoulder, elbows, wrists, hip, knees, and ankles). If observers are shown a single frame of the film (as in Fig. 4.8A) they are usually unaware that it represents a human form. However, if the film is in motion (depicted in Fig. 4.8B) then adults immediately detect the movement, and can make an impressive range of discriminations: they perceive the human form and can specify its actions (walking, running, skipping, dancing, etc.), and can also specify the gender from such displays (Bertenthal, 1993).

It has been found that infants as young as 3 months discriminate between "coherent" (Fig. 4.8B) and random (Fig. 4.8C) displays, and there is an intriguing age change between 3 and 5 months. Three-month-olds discriminate between an upright and upside-down point-light display of a person walking, as do older infants. However, 3-month-olds discriminate between an upside-down point-light walker and a random display, but 5- and 7-month-olds do not! (Bertenthal & Davis, 1988). Bertenthal and Davis explain this apparently paradoxical age difference in terms of the experience and accumulated knowledge of the older infants. By 5 months infants are familiar with people walking and they perceive the upright display as a human walker, whereas the upside-down and random displays are both unfamiliar. Adults, too, have difficulties with inverted point-light displays: they will typically report that an inverted display is several objects

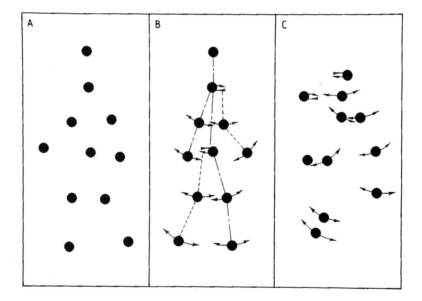

FIG. 4.8. Three possible point-light displays (derived from Bertenthal, 1993). A static display (A) is not usually seen as a human figure. When the display is in motion, as depicted in (B) (note that the broken lines connecting the points are for illustration only, and not seen by the observers), it is clearly seen as a person walking. When the point-light display moves in an incoherent, or random fashion (C), it tends to be perceived as a swarm of bees.

in motion, whereas the upright display is invariably seen as a moving person.

There are several constraints that distinguish biomechanical motion from other types of motion: for example, the foot can move back and forth and side to side relative to the knee, but is always a fixed distance from the knee. As yet, there are no reports of infants younger than 3 months being tested with these displays, suggesting that "It is therefore quite reasonable to propose that [detection of] these constraints are part of the intrinsic organization of the visual system" (Bertenthal, 1993, p. 209).

A reasonable interpretation of these findings is that younger infants detect the constraints inherent in biomechanical point-light displays, but they do not endow such displays with meaning: they thus discriminate between biomechanical and other displays on the basis of *perceptual* information. Older infants, however, imbue such displays with meaning, and interpret them as human walkers: thus, by 5 months knowledge of human motion, or *conceptual* information, constrains the interpretation of point-light displays of human walkers. The age at which perception interacts with knowledge will depend on the ways infants interact with, and learn about, their perceived world. To illustrate this point Bertenthal cites a study by Fox and McDaniels (1982), who found that 6-month-olds discriminated a point-light display of moving hands from an incoherent display, but younger infants did not. Visually directed reaching appears around 5 months of age, so the 6-month-olds would have had sufficient familiarity with their hands to allow the displays to be discriminated on the basis of familiarity.

Perception of object segregation

The visual world that we experience is immensely complex, consisting of many entities whose surfaces present a potentially bewildering array of changes, including overlapping textures, contrasts, colours, and contours. Sometimes these changes are found within a single object. For example, many animals have stripes, spots, changes to colouring, etc.; people wear different-coloured clothing, and there are natural colour and contrast changes, perhaps from hair to forehead, from eyes to face, and so on, but these changes of course are all part of the same person. Sometimes similar appearance is found for different objects, as when two or more similar objects are perceived. Thus, there is no simple rule that specifies that an abrupt or gradual change in appearance indicates one or more objects.

This means that the segregation of surfaces into objects is an important problem confronting the infant, and many of the rules that specify one or more objects have to be learned from experience. The infant's problems are well illustrated by Piaget (1954, pp. 177–178) who observed his son Laurent (aged 6 months 22 days) when reaching for objects:

> Laurent tries to grasp a box of matches. When he is at the point of reaching it I place it on a book; he immediately withdraws his hand, then grasps the book itself. He remains puzzled until the box slides and thanks to this accident he dissociates it from its support.

Piaget confirmed this observation with other small objects (pencil, pen-knife, eraser, watch, etc.) placed either on a notebook or on the palm of his hand, with the same result. His reasonable interpretation of these observations is that when the one object was on top of, and therefore touching, the other, Laurent did not realise that the two objects were separate, or independent of each other, despite their differences in shape and colour. As time passed Laurent gradually improved in his ability to segregate objects, but it was not until he was 10 months old that he "immediately grasps matchboxes, erasers, etc., placed on a notebook or my hand; he therefore readily dissociates the object from the support" (p. 178).

The young infant's limitations have been confirmed by others. Spelke and her colleagues (e.g. Kestenbaum, Termine, & Spelke, 1987; Spelke, Breinlinger, Jacobson, & Phillips, 1993) have found that 3-month-olds interpret displays in which two objects are adjacent and touching as being a single unit, even though the objects may be very different in their features. In an experiment reported by Needham and Baillargeon (in press) 4½-month-olds were familiarised with a stationary display consisting of a yellow cylinder lying next to, and touching, a blue box: this display is shown on the left of Fig. 4.9. Following this the infants saw two test events (Fig. 4.9). In both events a gloved hand came into view, grasped the cylinder, and moved it to one side, but in one, the *move-apart* condition, the box remained where it was, but in the other, the *move-together* condition, the box moved with the cylinder. The rationale underlying these manipulations is that if the infants perceived the cylinder and box as being two separate objects they would be surprised when presented with the move-together test condition, but if they understood them to be a single object they would be surprised at the move-apart condition. Infants typically will look longer at an event they find surprising, and the expectation therefore is that they would look longer at the test event that was inconsistent with their interpretation of the cylinder-and-box display.

In a separate experiment Needham and Baillargeon (1997) reported that 8-month-olds looked reliably longer in the move-together condition, indicating that they were using the featural differences between the cyl-

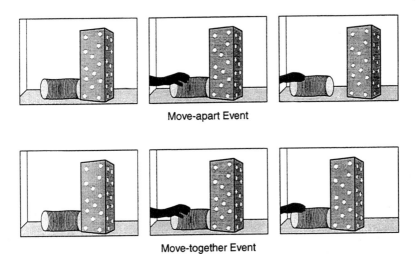

FIG. 4.9. The displays used by Needham and Baillargeon (in press). Following familiarisation to the cylinder and box display on the left, infants were shown either the *move-apart*
event (above), or the *move-together* event (below). Needham and Baillargeon found that
brief periods of familiarisation with either the cylinder or the box on its own were sufficient
to indicate to 4½-month-olds that the cylinder and box display consisted of two objects.
© Ablex Publishing Corporation reprinted with permission.

inder and box (differences in colour, pattern, and shape) to infer that they
were two separate objects. However, the 4½-month-olds in the present
experiment looked about equally at the two test events, suggesting that
they were uncertain whether the cylinder and box were one or two separate
units. In subsequent experiments Needham and Baillargeon found that if
the infants saw either the box alone for as little as 5 seconds, or the
cylinder alone for 15 seconds, these brief exposures were sufficient to
indicate to the infants that the cylinder-and-box display consisted of two
objects. That is, on the test trials the infants now reliably looked longer at
the move-together event, indicating that they were surprised when the two
objects moved as one.

The developmental story seems to be as follows. In the first few months
from birth infants consistently apply the rule "adjacency = a single unit/
object"; by 4½ months infants are uncertain, and experience plays a critical
role in assisting them to parse the events they encounter; by 8 or 10
months the rule "different features = different objects" seems to be applied
consistently, and has presumably been learned, or acquired, as a result of
experience.

CONCLUSIONS

The newborn baby enters the world visually naive, but possessed of a number of means with which to begin the business of making sense of the visually perceived world. Initial exploration of the visual world is guided by a few simple rules, which ensure that visual inspection is actively driven. Although visual acuity and other abilities are poor at birth and for the next few months, infants "normally see well enough to function effectively in their role as infants" (Hainline & Abramov, 1992, p. 40). Thus, objects that are near to the infant are most likely to have an impact on their lives, and these are seen reasonably clearly, even at birth. In addition to the "rules" that guide visual exploration, newborn infants perceive a coherent and organised visual world: they have size and shape constancy, some degree of form perception, and they perceive stimulus compounds rather than separate stimulus elements.

Newborn babies have, literally, a head-start in that it is now clear that they have some innate representational bias to attend to human faces, and perhaps some innate knowledge of the face. These conclusions result from studies of newborn infants' tracking of face-like patterns, and their ability to imitate adult facial gestures. Perhaps, too, the newborn's preference for looking at attractive faces might be guided by an innate facial representation that matches the attractive faces. The nature of infants' innate facial representation is not well understood, and is an intriguing area for future research.

Other types of visual organisation are found in early infancy, including perception of subjective contours, and organising visual patterns according to Gestalt principles such as similarity and good continuation. It is possible that these, and other, aspects of visual organisation are present at birth; but at present we do not have information from newborn infants.

It is reasonable to claim that the newborn and young infant are "competent" in that they perceive the world in an organised manner. Thus, their world is not the "blooming, buzzing confusion" described by William James (1890, p. 488); but it is clearly not the same as ours. At birth "visual processing begins with a vengeance" (Karmiloff-Smith, 1996, p. 10), and this processing can be seen in the rapidity with which newborn infants learn about faces, and about other types of stimuli and events.

As infants develop their perception of the world changes. For example, they initially perceive point-light displays of biomechanical motion *perceptually* as movements that display certain constraints, and later *conceptually* as the movements of people. A major task confronting the infant is to understand the world of objects. One aspect of this development that was illustrated here is the developing understanding of how shapes, patterns, colours, textures, and surfaces segregate into separate objects. Not surprisingly, many types of visual organisation take time to develop, and important aspects of this development are considered in the following chapters.

REFERENCES

Atkinson, J., Hood, B., Wattam-Bell, J., Anker, S., & Tricklebank, J. (1988). Development of orientation discrimination in infancy. *Perception*, **17**, 587–595.

Bahrick, L.E. (1987). Infants' intermodal perception of two levels of temporal structure in natural events. *Infant Behavior and Development*, **10**, 387–416.

Bahrick, L.E. (1988). Intermodal learning in infancy: learning on the basis of two kinds of invariant relations in audible and visible events. *Child Development*, **59**, 197–209.

Bahrick, L.E. (1992). Infants' perceptual differentiation of amodal and modality-specific audio-visual relations. *Journal of Experimental Child Psychology*, **53**, 197–209.

Bahrick, L.E., & Pickens, J.N. (1994). Amodal relations: the basis for intermodal perception and learning in infancy. In D.J. Lewkowicz & R. Lickliter (Eds.), *The development of intersensory perception: Comparative perspectives* (pp. 205–233). Hillsdale, NJ: Erlbaum.

Bertenthal, B.I. (1993). Infants' perception of biomechanical motions: Intrinsic image and knowledge-based constraints. In C. Granrud (Ed.), *Visual perception and cognition in infancy*. Hillsdale, N.J.: Lawrence Erlbaum Associates Inc.

Bertenthal, B.I., & Davis, P. (1988). *Dynamical pattern analysis predicts recognition and discrimination of biomechanical motions*. Paper presented at the annual meeting of the Psychonomic Society, Chicago, IL.

Bushnell, I.W.R., Sai, F., & Mullin, J.T. (1989). Neonatal recognition of the mother's face. *British Journal of Developmental Psychology*, **7**, 3–15.

Butterworth, G. (1983). Structure of the mind in human infancy. In L.P. Lipsitt & C.K. Rovee-Collier (Eds.), *Advances in infancy research*, **2**, 1–29. Norwood, NJ: Ablex.

Cohen, L., & Younger, B.A. (1984). Infant perception of angular relations. *Infant Behavior and Development*, **7**, 37–47.

De Schonen, S., Gil de Diaz, M., & Mathivet, E. (1986). Hemispheric asymmetry in face processing in infancy. In H.D. Ellis, M.A. Jeeves, F. Newcombe, & A. Young (Eds.), *Aspects of face processing*. Dordrecht: Martinus Nijhoff Publishers.

Field, T.M., Cohen, D., Garcia, R., & Greenberg, R. (1984). Mother–stranger face discrimination by the newborn. *Infant Behavior and Development*, **7**, 19–25.

Field, T.M., Woodson, R.W., Greenberg, R., & Cohen, C. (1982). Discrimination and imitation of facial expressions by neonates. *Science*, **218**, 179–181.

Fox, R., & McDaniels, C. (1982). The perception of biomechanical motion by human infants. *Science*, **218**, 486–487.

Galton, F. (1907). *Inquiries in human faculty and its development*. London: J.M. Dent & Sons Ltd.

Ghim, H.-R. (1990). Evidence for perceptual organization in infants: Perception of subjective contours by young infants. *Infant Behavior and Development*, **13**, 221–248.

Gordon, I.E. (1997). *Theories of visual perception* (2nd edn.). New York: Wiley.

Goren, C.C., Sarty, M., & Wu, P.Y.K. (1975). Visual following and pattern discrimination of face-like stimuli by newborn infants. *Pediatrics*, **56**, 544–549.

Hainline, L., & Abramov, I. (1992). Assessing visual development: Is infant vision good enough? In C. Rovee-Collier & L.P. Lipsitt (Eds.), *Advances in infancy research* (Vol. 7, pp. 39–102). Norwood, NJ: Ablex.

Haith, M.M. (1980). *Rules that babies look by*. Hillsdale, NJ: Erlbaum.

Hernandez-Reif, M., Cigales, M., & Lundy, B. (1994). *Memory for arbitrary adult face–voice pairs at six months of age*. Paper presented at the International Conference on Infant Studies, 2–5 June, Paris, France.

James, W. (1890). *The principles of psychology* (Vol. 2). New York: Holt.

Johnson, M.H., & Morton, J. (1991). *Biology and cognitive development*. Oxford: Blackwell.

Kanizsa, G. (1979). *Organization in vision: essays on gestalt perception*. New York: Praeger.

Karmiloff-Smith, A. (1996). The connectionist infant: Would Piaget turn in his grave? *SRCD Newsletter* (Fall issue), 1–10.

Kestenbaum, R., Termine, N., & Spelke, E.S. (1987). Perception of objects and object boundaries by 3-month-olds. *British Journal of Developmental Psychology*, **5**, 367–383.

Kugiumutzakis, G. (1993). Intersubjective vocal imitation in early mother–infant interaction. In J. Nadel & L. Camioni (Eds.), *New perspectives in early communicative development* (pp. 23–47). London & New York: Routledge.

Langlois, J.H., Musselman, L.E., Rubenstein, A.J., Smoot, M.T., Hallam, M.J., & Oakes, L.M. (1995). *Infants average faces: a basis for attractiveness preferences*. Paper presented at the Society for Research into Child Development, Indianapolis, March.

Langlois, J.H., Ritter, J.M., Roggman, L.A., & Vaughn, L.S. (1991). Facial diversity and infant preferences for attractive faces. *Developmental Psychology*, **27**, 79–84.

Langlois, J.H. & Roggman, L.A. (1990). Attractive faces are only average. *Psychological Science*, **1**, 115–121.

Langlois, J.H., Roggman, L.A., Casey, R.J., Ritter, J.M., Rieser-Danner, L.A., & Jenkins, V.Y. (1987). Infant preferences for attractive faces: Rudiments of a stereotype? *Developmental Psychology*, **23**, 363–369.

Lewkowicz, D.J. (1986). Developmental changes in infants' bisensory response to synchronous durations. *Infant Behavior and Development*, **9**, 335–353.

Maratos, O. (1973). *The origin and development of imitation during the first 6 months of life*. Unpublished doctoral dissertation, University of Geneva, Switzerland.

Meltzoff, A.N. (1995). Infants' understanding of people and things: From body imitation to folk psychology. In J.L. Bermúdez, A. Marcel, & N. Eilan (Eds.), *The body and the self* (pp. 43–69). Cambridge, MA, and London: MIT Press.

Meltzoff, A.N., & Borton, R.W. (1979). Intermodal matching by human neonates. *Nature*, **282**, 403–404.

Meltzoff, A.N., & Moore, M.K. (1977). Imitation of facial and manual gestures by human neonates. *Science*, **198**, 75–78.

Meltzoff, A.N., & Moore, M.K. (1984). Newborn infants imitate adult gestures. *Child Development*, **54**, 702–709.

Meltzoff, A.N., & Moore, M.K. (1992). Early imitation within a functional framework: The importance of person identity, movement, and development. *Infant Behavior and Development*, **15**, 479–505.

Meltzoff, A.N., & Moore, M.K. (1994). Imitation, memory, and the representation of persons. *Infant Behavior and Development*, **17**, 83–99.

Meltzoff, A.N., & Moore, M.K. (1997). Explaining facial imitation: A theoretical model. *Early Development and Parenting*, **6**, 179–192.

Muir, D.W., & Clifton, R. (1985). Infants' orientation to the location of sound sources. In G. Gottlieb & N. Krasnegor (Eds.), *The measurement of audition and vision during the first year of life: A methodological overview*. (pp. 171–194) Norwood, NJ: Ablex.

Needham, A. & Baillargeon, R. (1997). Object segregation in 8-month-old infants. *Cognition*, **62**, 121–149.

Needham, A. & Baillargeon, R. (in press). Effects of prior experience on 4.5-month-old infants' object segregation. *Infant Behavior and Development*.

Pascalis, O., de Schonen, S., Morton, J., Deruelle, C., & Rabre-Grenet, M. (1995). Mother's face recognition by neonates: A replication and an extension. *Infant Behavior and Development*, **18**, 79–85.

Piaget, J. (1954). *The construction of reality in the child*. New York: Basic Books.

Quinn, P.C., Brown, C.R., & Streppa, M.L. (1997). Perceptual organization of complex visual configurations by young infants. *Infant Behavior and Development*, **20**, 35–46.

Quinn, P.C., Burke, S., & Rush, A. (1993). Part–whole perception in early infancy: Evidence for perceptual grouping produced by lightness similarity. *Infant Behavior and Development*, **16**, 19–42.

Reardon, P., & Bushnell, E.W. (1988). Infants' sensitivity to arbitrary pairings of color and taste. *Infant Behavior and Development*, **11**, 245–250.

Reissland, N. (1988). Neonatal imitation in the first hour of life: Observations in rural Nepal. *Developmental Psychology*, **24**, 464–469.

Samuels, C.A., Butterworth, G., Roberts, T., & Graupner, L. (1994). Babies prefer attractiveness to symmetry. *Perception*, **23**, 823–831.

Samuels, C.A., & Ewy, R. (1985). Aesthetic perception of faces during infancy. *British Journal of Developmental Psychology*, **3**, 221–228.

Slater, A. (1995). Visual perception and memory at birth. In C. Rovee-Collier & L.P. Lipsitt (Eds.), *Advances in infancy research* (Vol. 9, pp. 107–162). Norwood, NJ: Ablex.

Slater, A., Brown, E., & Badenoch, M. (1997). Intermodal perception at birth: Newborn infants' memory for arbitrary auditory–visual pairings. *Early Development and Parenting*, **6**, 99–104.

Slater, A., Mattock, A., & Brown, E. (1990). Size constancy at birth: Newborn infants' responses to retinal and real size. *Journal of Experimental Child Psychology*, **49**, 314–322.

Slater, A., Mattock, A., Brown, E., & Bremner, J.G. (1991a). Form perception at birth: Cohen and Younger (1984) revisited. *Journal of Experimental Child Psychology*, **51**, 395–405.

Slater, A., Mattock, A., Brown, E., Burnham, D., & Young, A.W. (1991b). Visual processing of stimulus compounds in newborn infants. *Perception*, **20**, 29–33.

Slater, A., & Morison, V. (1985). Shape constancy and slant perception at birth. *Perception*, **14**, 337–344.

Slater, A., Morison, V., & Somers, M. (1988). Orientation discrimination and cortical functioning in the human newborn. *Perception*, **17**, 597–602.

Slater, A., von der Schulenburg, C., Brown, E., Badenoch, M., Butterworth, G., Parsons, S., & Samuels, C. (1998). Newborn infants prefer attractive faces. *Infant Behavior and Development*, **21**, 345–354.

Spelke, E., Breinlinger, K., Jacobson, K., & Phillips, A (1993). Gestalt relations and object perception: A developmental study. *Perception*, **22**, 1483–1501.

Spelke, E.S., & Owsley, C.J. (1979). Intermodal exploration and knowledge in infancy. *Infant Behavior and Development*, **2**, 13–27.

Walton, G.E., Armstrong, E.S., & Bower, T.G.R. (in press). Faces as forms in the world of the newborn. *Infant Behavior and Development*.

Walton, G.E., & Bower, T.G.R. (1993). Newborns form "prototypes" in less than 1 minute. *Psychological Science*, **4**, 203–205.

Walton, G.E., Bower, N.J.A., & Bower, T.G.R., (1992). Recognition of familiar faces by newborns. *Infant Behavior and Development*, **15**, 265–269.

Wertheimer, M. (1961). Psychomotor coordination of auditory and visual space at birth. *Science*, **134**, 1692.

ACKNOWLEDGEMENTS

The author's research reported in this chapter was supported by the following grants from the Economic and Social Research Council: C00230028/ 2114/ 2278; RC00232466.

CHAPTER FIVE

Object and spatial categorisation in young infants: "What" and "where" in early visual perception

Paul C. Quinn

Washington and Jefferson College, Washington, PA, USA

INTRODUCTION: THE IMPORTANCE OF PERCEPTUAL CATEGORISATION

In his book *Neural darwinism*, Gerald Edelman (1987) observes that "One of the fundamental tasks of the nervous system is to carry on adaptive perceptual categorisation in an 'unlabeled' world – one in which the macroscopic order and arrangement of objects and events (and even their definition or discrimination) cannot be prefigured for an organism" (p. 7). The term *perceptual categorisation*, as used by Edelman, among others, refers to the process by which organisms recognise discriminably different objects and their relations as members of the same category based on some internalised representation of the category. As the Edelman quote suggests, perceptual categorisation is not a trivial problem, at least for the pre-linguistic infant, who must come to transform an undifferentiated flux of contours, luminance levels, and wavelengths into a set of objects distinct from their backgrounds, with membership in equivalence classes such as cat, table, animal, and furniture. In addition, the taxonomic, spatial, and dynamic relations that can exist between objects must be structured into categories such as global versus basic, above versus below, and causal versus incidental.

The importance of perceptual categorisation becomes clear when one considers the large number of instances belonging to each of the various categories found in the environment. If all of the perceptual representations formed for the multitude of objects and their relations encountered during a lifetime were independent of each other, the outcome would be mental disorganisation and intellectual chaos. Cognition and its development would be difficult, if not impossible, under such circumstances. Fortunately, human adults possess abilities to group distinct, but related, objects and their relations into meaningful classes such that each member can be responded to in an equivalent manner. The information-processing advantages of perceptual categorisation include organised storage of information in memory, efficient retrieval of this information, and the capability of responding equivalently to an indefinitely large number of exemplars from multiple categories (including many not previously experienced).

This chapter discusses the development of perceptual categorisation during the first 6 to 7 months of life. When and how categorical representations develop in infants and young children have been central and enduring issues in the study of perceptual and cognitive development (e.g. Bruner, Olver, & Greenfield, 1966; Carey, 1985; Keil, 1989; Mandler, 1988, 1992; Markman, 1989; Quinn & Eimas, 1986a, 1996b; Vygotsky, 1962). However, even with this considerable focus of research effort, there still is a notable lack of data concerning the manner in which the perceptually based categorical representations of infants give rise to the presumably more conceptual, knowledge-based representations of children and adults (although Karmiloff-Smith, 1992, Mandler, 1992, and Quinn & Eimas, 1997, provide recent perspectives on how this transitional problem might be solved). Nevertheless, a (perhaps implicit) belief shared by a number of investigators of early infant cognition is that insight into how early, perceptually driven categories develop into higher-level conceptual structures will require precise knowledge of the nature (e.g. exemplar-based vs. prototype-based), level (e.g. basic vs. global) and developmental determinants (e.g. experience vs. maturation) of the earliest perceptually based categories. In other words, the transition between perceptual and knowledge-based concepts is not likely to be understood unless the input – the content and organisation of the infant's mental structures – at the time the transition begins is known.

The bulk of this chapter will concentrate on the development of perceptual categorisation for *objects* (e.g. triangle, cat, mammal) and their *spatial relations* (e.g. above, below, left, right). Studying the development of categorisation in *both* of these domains may be important, given evidence that the two kinds of perceptual information have distinct cortical locations of neural processing (Ungerleider & Mishkin, 1982). Anatomical and physiological data support the idea that the neural system subserving the representation of spatial or "where" information (posterior parietal cortex) is separable from the system responsible for representing object-shape or "what" information (inferior temporal cortex) (Mishkin, Ungerleider, & Macko, 1983). There are also recent neuro-developmental findings indicating that the rate and pattern of development may differ between the two pathways (Distler, Bachevalier, Kennedy, Mishkin, & Ungerleider, 1996). In light of these differences between the "what" and "where" brain systems, the development of categorisation within both the object and spatial perceptual categorisation systems will be examined.

METHODOLOGY

Before turning to a selective review of the data on object and spatial categorisation, it is necessary to describe the *serial habituation–dishabituation* and *familiarisation–novelty preference* procedures that have been used to assess visual categorisation in young infants. Both procedures rely on the well-established preference that infants from birth onwards display for novel stimuli (Fantz, 1964; Slater, 1995), and are adaptations of procedures for testing simple discrimination and memory skills. The basic protocol for testing the infant's ability to visually recognise a familiar stimulus and differentiate it from a novel stimulus involves initial familiarisation with a single stimulus and subsequent preference testing with the familiar stimulus and a novel stimulus, presented either in succession in the serial habituation–dishabituation procedure (e.g. Cohen & Younger, 1984) or paired together in the familiarisation–novelty preference procedure (e.g. Quinn & Eimas, 1986b). In the case of the serial habituation–dishabituation procedure, continuation of habituation to the familiar stimulus and dishabituation to the novel stimulus (usually measured in looking time or some other response measure such as sucking or heart rate) that cannot be attributed to an a priori higher responsiveness to the novel stimulus implies both memory for the familiar stimulus and the ability to distinguish between it and the novel stimulus. In the case of the familiarisation–novelty preference procedure, a reliable preference for the novel over the familiar stimulus that cannot be attributed to an a priori preference (cf. Colombo, O'Brien, Mitchell, & Horowitz, 1986) is taken as evidence that the infant has formed a memory-based representation of the familiar stimulus and can use it to differentiate the novel stimulus. It should be noted that an a priori preference for the novel over the familiar stimulus (observed reliably among a group of infants) would obviate the need for either of the two procedures; the spontaneous preference would itself be evidence for discrimination.

Modifications of the two procedures have allowed investigators to examine whether infants can form representations of a *categorical* nature. In the *serial habituation–dishabituation* method of assessing categorisation (e.g. Cohen & Younger, 1983), infants are presented with a number of instances from a single category (usually from 4 to 12), one at a time, until they show evidence of habituation as indexed by a decline in looking time. Immediately following habituation, infants are shown in succession a novel instance from the familiar category and an instance from a novel category. If infants generalise habituation to the novel exemplar from the familiar category and dishabituate to the novel category instance, and these responses cannot be attributed to a failure to discriminate among the familiar category instances or to an a priori higher interest in the novel category instance, then it can be concluded that infants have formed a categorical representation of the familiar exemplars that can be used to recognise novel instances as members or nonmembers of the familiar category.

In the *familiarisation–novelty preference* method of testing for categorisation, infants are presented with a number of different pairs of instances from the same category during a familiarisation period. The instances comprising a given pair can simply be two identical copies of the same stimulus or, as has been the case in a number of the author's object categorisation studies, two nonidentical exemplars (see Fagan, 1978, for evidence that paired presentations of distinct exemplars during familiarisation enhance recognition memory). Infants are then administered a paired presentation of a novel instance of the familiar category and an instance from a novel category. If infants display a looking-time preference for the instance from the novel category that cannot be attributed to an inability to discriminate among the familiar category exemplars, or to an a priori preference, then it can be concluded that a categorical representation of the familiar category has been formed.

These concerns over the possibility that infants might have preferred (or dishabituated to) the novel category instance because of a failure to discriminate among the familiar category instances, or because of an a priori preference, deserve further comment. If infants were unable to discriminate among the familiar category members, then they would have experienced the familiar category members, even the one viewed on the test trials, as a *single* instance. Thus, what might have appeared as a preference for a novel over a familiar *category*, was simply a preference for a novel over a familiar *stimulus*, and what was designed as an investigation of *categorisation* was reduced to a study of *discrimination*. A conclusion that categorisation has occurred thus requires that members of the familiar category be shown to be discriminable from each other.

The question of within-category discrimination raises the further methodological issue of how to measure discrimination in a way that would provide the best evidence that infants discriminated between exemplars when they were presented during the familiarisation portion of the categorisation testing procedure. This issue arises because of the mismatch in experience that infants have with a particular exemplar during categorisation and discrimination testing. For example, in a number of studies to be discussed in this chapter, infants being tested in a categorisation task will have had the opportunity to look at a particular exemplar for only 15 seconds of the familiarisation period (usually just a single trial), but they will have had the opportunity to look at this same exemplar for 60 or 90 seconds of familiarisation (during 4 or 6 15-second trials) in the accompanying discrimination "control" task. One may therefore reasonably ask whether the standard test of discrimination provides an overly optimistic assessment of what infants are capable of discriminating during the categorisation procedure (cf. Sherman, 1985). In response to this problem, some investigators have recently begun to use a single-trial familiarisation procedure to test for within-category discrimination (and Behl-Chadha & Eimas, 1995, have provided evidence that the single- and multiple-trial procedures yield equivalent results).

The other issue that needs to be considered when interpreting a novel category preference is whether this preference would have been obtained even without presentation of the familiar category. Infants need not have formed a categorical representation of the familiar exemplars to display a preference for a novel category exemplar; they might simply have an intrinsic preference for the novel over the familiar category exemplar that would be present irrespective of whether or not the familiar exemplars had been presented. Thus, in order to confirm that a novel category preference is the result of having formed a categorical representation of the familiar exemplars, it is necessary to show, in an additional control experiment, that no consistent preference for the novel category exemplar emerges when it is presented with the familiar category exemplar during a set of paired preference trials with no prior familiarisation experience. Later in this chapter, a new method of assessing a priori preferences will be described and the role that such preferences may play in producing categorical representations will be reconsidered (cf. Eimas & Quinn, 1994).

PERCEPTUALLY BASED CATEGORICAL REPRESENTATIONS FOR OBJECTS

Form categorisation

In one of the earliest studies of object or form-based categorisation in young infants, Bomba and Siqueland (1983) used the familiarisation–novelty preference procedure to investigate whether infants could form category representations for dot patterns generated from diamond, square, and triangle prototypes. Examples of the patterns are shown in Fig. 5.1. Adults classify such patterns without difficulty and may do so by forming a prototype representation of the form information presented during initial category training (Posner & Keele, 1968). The prototype, which was not shown during training, was the most reliably and confidently recognised member of the category in tests of generalisation, suggesting that subjects may have been abstracting a central tendency to represent the category, rather than storing away individual instances.

The 3- and 4-month-olds in the Bomba and Siqueland study were familiarised with 6 to 12 instances from one form category (e.g. triangle-like forms) and then administered a preference test pairing the novel prototype of the familiar category (e.g. triangle) with a novel category prototype (e.g. diamond or square). The prototypes are shown on the far left of Fig. 5.1. Infants reliably preferred the novel category prototype, indicating that they (1) had formed a categorical representation of the familiarisation exemplars, (2) recognised the familiar category prototype as a familiar category member even though it had not been seen during familiarisation, and (3) viewed the novel category prototype as a non-instance of the familiar category.

Bomba and Siqueland next wished to determine whether the information underlying the categorical representation takes the form of individual exemplars or a prototype. That is, during the presentation of the familiar category exemplars, were infants simply storing the exemplars or were they averaging them together to form a prototype? To answer this question, Bomba and Siqueland conducted additional experiments that repeated the familiarisation protocol from their original categorisation experiment, but which paired a previously seen exemplar with the novel prototype of the familiar category during the preference test. The rationale is that if infants represent the category by storing individual exemplars, then the familiar exemplar should be perceived as familiar, and the previously unseen prototype should be perceived as novel and consequently

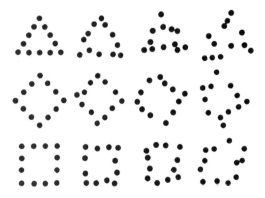

FIG. 5.1. Triangle, diamond, and square dot pattern prototypes and their corresponding distortions (from Bomba & Siqueland, 1983). Copyright © 1983 Academic Press, Inc. Reprinted with the permission of Academic Press, Inc.

preferred. Alternatively, if infants are representing the familiar category information in the form of a prototype (based on averaging the familiar exemplars together rather than including each as a distinct entity in the representation), then they should perceive the previously unseen prototype as familiar (paradoxically so) and regard the previously seen exemplar as novel and consequently prefer it.

Bomba and Siqueland found that under conditions of moderate memory demand (i.e. six familiarisation exemplars, no delay between familiarisation and test), no clear preference emerged for either stimulus. Given that infants did categorise in the initial experiment under the same familiarisation conditions, one possible explanation of the no-preference result is that infants may have been representing partial exemplar *and* prototype information, a result consistent with findings obtained with adults under similar conditions (Posner & Keele, 1968). Of course, no-preference results are always difficult to interpret and any explanation of these must be viewed with caution. However, under more demanding memory conditions (i.e. 12 familiarisation exemplars, 3min delay between familiarisation and test), a reliable preference for the previously seen exemplar emerged, suggesting that infants were abstracting and remembering a prototype rather than storing individual instances (cf. Posner & Keele, 1970; Strauss, 1979, also provided evidence of prototype abstraction in older infants with schematic face stimuli). This manner of organising category information in memory has the advantage of freeing a cognitive system from having to keep a record of the large amount of specific item information encountered during a lifetime (see, however, Nosofsky, 1991, for an exemplar-based representation that can account for some of the prototype effects observed with adults).

Quinn (1987) used the familiarisation–novelty preference procedure and form-category stimuli like those used by Bomba and Siqueland (1983) to examine conditions that might strengthen or weaken infants' formation of a prototype representation for shape-based information. In particular, Quinn wished to compare how infants would respond when they were presented with information from *one* form category (as in the Bomba and Siqueland investigation) with how they would respond when presented with instances from *two* categories (e.g. squares and triangles) during a single familiarisation session. Evidence obtained with adults suggested that categorical representations would be enhanced during multiple-category acquisition, perhaps because the learner registers both common *and* distinguishing features for each category (Homa & Chambliss, 1975). Alternatively, it seemed possible that the young infant's processing system might be unable to differentiate and compile two incoming streams of category information.

Quinn replicated the initial Bomba and Siqueland result that infants would reliably prefer a novel category prototype over a familiar category prototype after familiarisation with a set of six exemplars from a single category, but also observed that infants preferred a novel category prototype even more robustly when presented with six instances from each of two categories. It is important to note that this difference in the magnitude of the novel category preference cannot be attributed to simple amount of information presented during familiarisation (i.e. 6 vs. 12 exemplars). In a third condition in which infants were presented with 6 instances from a single form category along with one instance from each of 6 different form categories (see Fig. 5.2 for examples), the novel category prototype was not reliably preferred. The results of the two-category familiarisation condition indicate that information about how exemplars are similar to each other *and* how they are dissimilar to exemplars from a contrast category may contribute to the information underlying the categorical representation. The findings of the third condition suggest that there are limits to the advantages of experiencing contrasting category information in early infancy. It is likely that the additional information, which could not be incorporated into a single representation, simply overwhelmed the young infant's processing capacities.

Like Bomba and Siqueland (1983), Quinn (1987) was interested in the information underlying the categorical representations found in the one- and two-category familiarisation conditions. The one- and two-category familiarisation sequences were therefore administered to two additional groups of infants, but in this case, the groups were subsequently given the prototype test of Bomba and Siqueland: a familiar exemplar was paired with the previously unseen prototype. The findings were that infants in the single-category condition preferred the novel prototype, but infants in the two-category condition preferred the familiar exemplar. These data

FIG. 5.2. Distorted patterns from each of six different form categories (from Quinn, 1987). Copyright © Reprinted from *Cognition, 27*, Quinn, P.C., The categorical representation of visual pattern information by young infants, 145–179, 1987, with kind permission of Elsevier Science NL, Sara Burgerhartstraat 25, 1005 KV Amsterdam, The Netherlands.

indicate that infants familiarised with instances of a single category represented them as individual exemplars whereas infants familiarised with two categories represented each with a prototype. Differences in the amount of time a single exemplar was presented, and the levels of distortion used, may account for why Quinn found evidence of an exemplar-based representation under single-category familiarisation conditions, whereas Bomba and Siqueland observed a preference that was more ambiguous. Overall, the data are consistent with the idea that within certain limits, categorically structured information from *multiple sources* is in part what drives the infant to begin averaging instances to form a prototype representation.

Categorisation of animal species

Although the form categorisation studies have revealed important information about early category representations (see also Younger & Gotlieb, 1988), it can be argued that the stimulus materials used to construct the categories suffer from a lack of ecological realism. This limits progress in two important respects. First, it is not clear how well the categorisation routines of infants will work for naturally contrasting, multidimensional exemplars. Second, one cannot use artificial categories to study the problem of how the initial perceptually based categories formed by young infants develop into the more complex categories formed by children and adults, including superordinate categories and networks of categorical representations organised by higher levels of knowledge (e.g. naive theories of biology) (Carey, 1985; Murphy & Medin, 1985). In other words, only if one begins to study infants' formation of realistic categories, both natural and artefactual, can one begin to address the critical problem of how the knowledge-based representations of children and adults develop from the initial substrate of perceptually based categorical representations that are available to young infants.

Carey (1985) and Keil (1989) have begun to describe how newly acquired knowledge begins to determine reorganisations in conceptual structures between the ages of 4 and 10 years. Although this work has provided a number of interesting and provocative insights into conceptual development, it leaves open the means by which the initial representations of infancy begin the process of change. As was written some years ago, one strategy that will help to bridge this gap in our knowledge of early category development will be research that continues " ... to examine the processes of categorisation in early infancy, but with greater effort devoted to uncovering higher levels of conceptual competence in young infants. Such a strategy, if successful, should narrow the apparent gap between conceptual knowledge of infants and adults and thereby make the processes of transition less opaque" (Quinn & Eimas, 1986a, p. 357). This type of research, focusing on the formation of realistic categories, both natural and artefactual, has begun in the author's laboratory and that of others, and it is to a selective review of it that the chapter now turns.

Development of basic-level categories   In the summer of 1987, Peter Eimas and I began planning a series of studies to investigate when and how infants become able to form categorical representations for individual animal species, and for animals more generally. At the time we began this work, the prevailing view of conceptual knowledge in adults was that it was organised hierarchically into superordinate, basic, and subordinate levels of inclusiveness (e.g. Rosch, Mervis, Gray, Johnson, & Boyes-Braem, 1976). This view suggests that most adults possess a superordinate concept for animals that includes basic-level representations for dogs and birds, which are further divided into subordinate representations for boxers and collies and cardinals and blue jays. Initial developmental research suggested that basic-level representations were the first to be acquired and that only over time did children begin to group together related basic-level categories to form a superordinate representation (Daehler, Lonardo, & Bukatko, 1979; Horton & Markman, 1980; Mervis & Crisafi, 1982; but see Mandler & Bauer, 1988).

In the infant perception literature at this time, there were only a handful of studies that examined infants' categorisation of realistic stimuli. Generally, these investigations confirmed the results of the form category studies in showing that infants can form categorical representations for groups of stimuli that exclude exemplars of perceptually neighbouring categories. For example, Cohen and Caputo (1978) used the serial habituation–dishabituation procedure to show that 12-month-old infants could form a category for dogs that excluded an antelope. Colombo, O'Brien, Mitchell, Roberts, and Horowitz (1987) employed the familiarisation–novelty preference procedure and found that 6-month-old infants who were familiarised with black and white drawings of different birds displayed a preference for a novel horse over a novel bird, evidence of a categorical representation for birds that excluded horses (Roberts, 1988, reported comparable results with 9-month-old infants). These data provided some evidence that basic-level representations might be in place as early as 6 months of age. But the findings were tentative – there were only a few studies, two of which used black-on-white schematic drawings of the categories. Also, the Colombo et al. study used only three birds for the familiar category and one new bird and one new horse for the test. Thus, the nature of the stimuli, as well as their small number, provided only a weak approximation of the demands placed on the infant by the large number of multidimensional stimuli representing the variety of categories found in the natural environment.

With these concerns in mind we began our studies by examining what we believed at the time to be a necessary prerequisite for superordinate category formation, namely, the formation of individuated categorical representations for related basic-level categories belonging to the same superordinate structure. In particular, we investigated the formation of separate categorical representations for dogs, cats, and birds chosen from the superordinate category "animal". The stimuli were realistic colour photographs of the animals, representing numerous breeds, and depicted in various orientations. There were 18 exemplars chosen to represent each category and they were selected to be as nearly the same size as possible, in order to be sure that the infant would use cues other than size as bases for categorisation (e.g. facial, limb, torso, or global shape information). Black and white examples of the stimuli are shown in Fig. 5.3.

We first wished to examine whether any basic-level differentiation within a superordinate was possible, so an experiment was designed to determine whether infants could form distinct representations for cats and dogs, each of which excluded instances of birds (Quinn, Eimas, & Rosenkrantz, 1993). Infants were familiarised with 12 instances of cats or dogs and then tested with a novel exemplar from the familiar category paired with a bird. All familiarisation and test stimuli were randomly selected and different for each infant. Infants in both groups preferred the birds, a preference that control experiments revealed was not the result of an a priori preference, or an inability to discriminate within the familiar categories. Young infants were thus able to form categorical representations for cats and dogs, each of which excluded instances of birds. The findings support the conclusion that at least some differentiation within a superordinate category is possible in early infancy.

There are a number of possible bases by which infants could differentiate cats or dogs from birds including texture (fur vs. feather), number of legs (two vs. four), and facial features (nose vs. beak). Therefore, in the

FIG. 5.3. Black-and-white examples of the cat, dog, and bird categories investigated by Quinn, Eimas, and Rosenkrantz (1993) (from Quinn & Eimas, 1996b). Copyright © Reprinted with the permission of Ablex Publishing Corporation.

next experiment, we investigated whether infants could make the presumably more difficult distinction between the perceptually similar cats and dogs. These species possess comparably shaped torsos, the same basic facial features, the same number of legs, and similar colouring and body texture. As in the first experiment, one group of infants was familiarised with cats and a second was presented with dogs. Both groups were tested with novel cat–novel dog pairings. Infants familiarised with cats preferred dogs, but interestingly, infants presented with dogs looked equivalently at the test stimuli. These asymmetrical results indicate that infants had formed a categorical representation for cats that excluded dogs, but that infants had more difficulty establishing a representation for dogs that excluded cats. After establishing that the asymmetry did not result from a spontaneous preference for the dog stimuli, we surmised that the surprising outcome might be due to what appeared to us as a greater variability of the dog exemplars relative to the instances of cats. This observation was confirmed by adult typicality ratings of the stimuli – the variation of the typicality ratings obtained for the set of dog stimuli was found to be reliably greater than that obtained for the cat stimuli. When infants were then familiarised with a subset of dogs that matched the cats in their variability (using the adult typicality ratings as the index of variability), and tested with novel cat–novel dog pairings, a clear preference for the cats emerged. The combined results provide evidence that 3- and 4-month-old infants are able to form separate representations for dogs and cats, each of which excludes instances of the other. Moreover, the findings suggest that infants can form rather narrowly tuned representations for perceptually similar basic-level categories chosen from the same superordinate category.

In a second set of experiments, we attempted to increase the generality of our findings of basic-level differentiation within a superordinate category, and also sought to determine more precisely the exclusivity (i.e. range of extension) of these representations (Eimas & Quinn, 1994). Our interest in the exclusivity issue was sparked by the arguments of Mervis (1987), who suggested that early categorical representations may be formed at a *child-basic* level. A child-basic representation may have a broader range of extension that its adult counterpart. For example, an early representation for domestic cats may exclude birds and dogs, but it may include tigers and lions. By this account, development consists of further differentiation to arrive at the adult basic-level representation and grouping of basic-level representations to form a superordinate representation.

To test the degree of exclusivity of the early categorical representations of 3- to 4-month-olds, we familiarised one group of infants with domestic cats and then administered a series of preference tests, each one pairing a novel domestic cat with either a horse, a tiger, or a female lion (i.e. lacking the distinguishing male mane); a second group of infants was familiarised with horses and tested with a domestic cat, a giraffe, and a zebra, each paired with a novel horse. As was true in the Quinn et al. (1993) study, the familiarisation and test exemplars were randomly chosen and different for each infant. Black-and-white examples of these stimuli are shown in Fig. 5.4. We suspected that cats and horses might be differentiated from each other because of their differences in overall shape. We also believed that the salient body markings of the zebras and giraffes might allow them to be distinguished from horses, and that the conspicuous nature of the tiger stripes would allow them to be differentiated from domestic cats; these expectations were based on the importance of texture for stimuli with eyes that has been reported in the early naming literature (Jones, Smith, & Landau, 1991). Our prediction for the categorical representation of domestic cats was that it might include female lions because of the considerable perceptual overlap between the two categories.

The findings were in accord with expectations. Infants presented with horses looked more at domestic cats, giraffes, and zebras, whereas infants familiarised with domestic cats preferred horses and tigers, but not female lions. The results suggested that the categorical representation for horses included novel horses, but was differentiated enough to exclude cats, zebras, and giraffes; the categorical representation for domestic cats excluded horses and tigers, but included novel domestic cats and female lions. Thus, at 3 to 4 months of age, there is evidence for categories that have at least a child-basic level of exclusivity. It should be noted that we do not wish to claim that the categorical representation for horses is at an adult-basic level of exclusivity. Had we used test trial stimuli that had a higher degree of perceptual overlap with horses (e.g. deer or elk), then we might have uncovered child-basic representations for horses as well as domestic cats.

Is the development of exclusivity driven by maturation or experience?
One question that arose from the finding that 3- to 4-month-old infants include female lions in their categorical representation for domestic cats was as follows: How does the representation of domestic cats reach an adult-basic level of exclusivity? It could be that experience or maturation or some combination of the two are responsible for the development of categorical exclusivity. Our first line of inquiry into these possibilities was to identify when during development the categorical representation for domestic cats attains an adult-basic level of exclusivity (Eimas & Quinn, 1994). A group of 6- to 7-month-olds was familiarised with domestic cats and tested with tigers and female lions, both paired with novel cats. Infants looked more at the tigers and female lions, thereby providing evidence

FIG. 5.4.   Representative exemplars (shown in black and white) of the categories used in the experiments of Eimas and Quinn (1994b) (from Quinn & Eimas, 1996). Copyright © Reprinted with the permission of Ablex Publishing Corporation.

that by 6 to 7 months of age, the categorical representation for domestic cats excludes both tigers and female lions. However, we have more recently obtained evidence that even 3- and 4-month-old infants can form separate categorical representations for domestic cats and female lions if they are administered a complex familiarisation procedure that includes an initial presentation of a number of cat–cat pairs followed by presentations of cat–lion pairs along with cat–cat reminders (Eimas, Quinn, & Cowan, 1994). It would seem then that even young infants can differentiate between two perceptually very similar categories provided that they are given experience with exemplars from both (cf. Quinn, 1987).

Development of global categories   We next began to investigate the beginnings of global structures – to determine when basic-level representations start to cohere into a more superordinate-like representation. In particular, we attempted to determine if 3- and 4-month-old infants could form a global representation for "mammal" or "4-legged animal" under which basic-level representations for individual species could be grouped (Behl-Chadha, 1996; Behl-Chadha, Eimas, & Quinn, 1995). In one experiment, infants were familiarised with two examples (coloured photographs) from each of eight basic-level categories of mammals (e.g. deer, domestic cats, elephants, horses, rabbits, squirrels, tigers, and zebras). Black-and-white examples are shown in Fig. 5.5. Subsequent test trials involved three types of comparisons in which a novel instance from a novel mammal category, different for each type of comparison, was paired with (1) a novel example

FIG. 5.5.   Black-and-white examples of the "mammal" stimuli used by Behl-Chadha, Eimas, and Quinn (1995).

of a familiar mammal category, (2) a nonmammalian animal (bird or fish), and (3) a piece of furniture (e.g. chair, table). Black-and-white examples of the contrast categories are shown in Fig. 5.6.

The results indicated that infants formed a categorical representation of mammals: birds, fish, and furniture were preferred to novel mammal category instances, whereas novel mammal category instances were not preferred over novel exemplars of familiar mammal categories. These findings are of considerable theoretical importance in that they cast doubt on the idea that more global representations are necessarily conceptually based (cf. Mandler & McDonough, 1993). The age of the subjects and the nature of the stimuli (static pictorial instances of the categories) make it unlikely that conceptual knowledge about the "kind of thing something is" was relied on to perform successfully in the global categorisation task. The study therefore supports the position that both basic and global levels of representation may have a perceptual basis.

The role of a priori preferences reconsidered   In a number of early investigations of infant categorisation, a particular set of exemplars was shown to *each* infant participating in the familiarisation phase of the categorisation experiment. These infants were then tested with a novel exemplar from the familiar category and an exemplar from a novel category; the two stimuli shown were the *same* for *each* subject. This manner of assessing categorisation requires that the preference for the novel category exemplar be shown not to be explainable by an a priori preference. A control

FIG. 5.6.   Black-and-white examples of the categories contrasting with mammals during the preference test trials of Behl-Chadha, Eimas, and Quinn (1995).

experiment in which a separate group of infants is presented with the two test stimuli, but without prior familiarisation experience, becomes necessary. If infants in the control experiment do not prefer the novel category exemplar, then it can be concluded that the preference that occurred following familiarisation was due to the formation of a categorical representation of the familiar exemplars.

The animal categorisation experiments stand in contrast to a number of the early categorisation studies in that each infant was presented with a different, randomly selected set of familiar stimuli and then tested with different, randomly selected novel stimuli from the familiar and novel categories. Such a protocol for examining categorisation requires a different test for spontaneous preferences, namely, one in which each infant is presented with different, randomly selected pairs of pictures from the two categories across a series of trials. In this type of *category preference test* we have found that 3- and 4-month-olds show spontaneous preferences for tigers over domestic cats, for domestic cats over horses, and for mammals over birds (Behl-Chadha et al., 1995; Eimas & Quinn, 1994). Such preferences provide evidence of systematic differentiation of the exemplars of these categories.

Some of the category preferences may have their basis in a preference for a salient perceptual attribute possessed by members of one of the two categories, for example, the stripes of the tigers. The origins of other category preferences are not as clear. For example, it is more difficult to identify a specific perceptual feature that would account for why domestic cats are preferred to horses, or why mammals are preferred to birds. Subtle and at this time undetermined part and/or shape cues may be the basis for this second type of preference. Whatever the explanation, it would seem that spontaneous preferences, once thought to be potential confounds in traditional assessments of categorisation in infants, can now be more constructively regarded as possible facilitators of early category formation. It would be informative to investigate whether these preferences are innately specified, and if categories that are aided in their formation by such preferences are present earlier, or are more easily acquired, than categories not marked by preferred perceptual properties.

What are the bases for infants' categorical representations at the basic and global levels? Another important issue raised by our results concerns the attributes or properties young infants may use to form categorical representations at basic and global levels of inclusiveness. Consider the basic level first. The critical question is this: On what bases are infants forming a categorical representation for domestic cats that excludes birds, dogs, horses, tigers, and female lions, and for horses that excludes domestic cats, giraffes, and zebras? As noted earlier, there is little doubt that the distinguishing cues are perceptual, rather than conceptual, and some would appear to be quite salient. For example, birds can be distinguished from domestic cats on the basis of the number of legs, overall shape, and differences in facial features. Also, giraffes and zebras can be excluded from the categorical representation for horses because of distinctive body markings.

Of greater interest, however, is that a number of the categories, including dogs, domestic cats, and female lions have no clear, perceptually based, category-defining attributes. These species are of roughly comparable size and possess fur, four legs, a tail, a body torso perpendicularly aligned with the leg base, and a set of facial features. In these cases, then, the cues that permit categorical differentiation are not readily apparent. We reasoned that infants might use one of two kinds of information to make such distinctions. First, infants might detect subtle differences in overall shape or correlated attribute information (e.g. the co-occurrence of a particular kind of body, face, and tail observed among a category of animals), given evidence that they use this information to form at least some perceptually based categorical representations (Bomba & Siqueland, 1983; Younger, 1985). Second, infants might use more narrowly defined part information centred about the face, given that such information is apparently used by infants to recognise members of their own species and specific humans such as the primary caregiver (Johnson & Morton, 1991).

To examine the role that body/shape and face/head information might play in producing categorical distinctions between perceptually similar animal species, we compared young infants' use of face versus body information to form a categorical representation for domestic cats that excludes dogs (Quinn & Eimas, 1996a). Three- and 4-month-old infants were randomly assigned to one of three experimental conditions: Whole Animal, Face Only, or Body Only. In the Whole Animal group, infants were presented with cats and tested with novel cat–novel dog pairings. The Face Only and Body Only groups were familiarised and tested with the same animals as the Whole Animal group, but with their bodies (Face Only group) and faces (Body Only group) occluded, respectively. A black-and-white version of a representative instance of each category as it appeared in the three experimental conditions is displayed in Fig. 5.7.

Whole animal condition   Face only condition   Body only condition

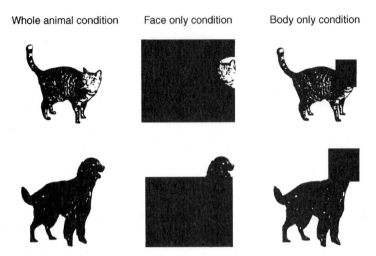

FIG. 5.7. Black-and-white examples of the stimuli presented to the three experimental groups of Quinn and Eimas (1996a) (from Quinn & Eimas, 1996a). Copyright © 1996 Academic Press, Inc. Reprinted with the permission of Academic Press, Inc.

The results showed that infants preferred the novel dog stimuli in the Whole Animal group (replicating Quinn et al., 1993) and Face Only group, but not in the Body Only group. Control experiments revealed that these preferences could not be attributed to spontaneous preferences, nor to an inability to discriminate among the familiar stimuli. Additional experimentation showed that the ability to use head and face information generalised to enlarged cat and dog heads presented in isolation, and that the cues for this categorical representation lay in the internal facial region (encompassing the eyes, nose, and mouth), and along the external contour of the head. Taken together, the findings indicate that information from the face and head region provides young infants with a necessary and sufficient basis to form a categorical representation for domestic cats that excludes dogs (Johnson & Morton, 1991, describe a mechanism by which such face-based differentiation might occur).

The findings of the body versus face study have implications for accounts of the information contained in categorical representations at the basic level. Arguments have been advanced that basic-level categories are distinguished from one another on the basis of overall shape (Marr, 1982) or a set of correlated attributes (Rosch et al., 1976). However, the data just described indicate that information used by young infants to form basic-level animal categories does not consist of perceptual attributes extracted from various bodily regions of the exemplars. Rather, it seems that information from a very specific region – the head and face – defines these categories (cf. Murphy, 1991). It may be that young infants generate their first categories by anchoring the representations to one or another conspicuous perceptual property and that only over time do these representations come to incorporate additional attributes (and their correlations) from the entire organism (cf. Younger, 1990).

Just as we are interested in determining the perceptual information that enables infants to form categorical representations at the basic level, we are similarly interested in examining the information that is the basis for a global representation of mammals. As already discussed, infants are almost certainly using perceptually based attributes and their relations (e.g. pattern of correlation) that can be observed among the mammals. What is an intriguing possibility is that the information that differentiates mammals and furniture (e.g. faces, fur, tails) may turn out to be more discriminable than that which can be used to separate dogs and female lions from domestic cats. If this idea is correct, then the ability to form a global categorical representation for mammals may precede the ability to form basic-level categorical representations for individual mammal species (see Mandler, Bauer, & McDonough, 1991, and Mandler & McDonough, 1993, for reports of global-to-basic categorical development, but with what were presumed to be conceptually based representations for animals in older infants). Interestingly, a group of connectionist networks that the author has recently developed to account for the data on early perceptual categorisation also make the "global-to-basic" developmental prediction (Quinn & Johnson, 1996, 1997); however, the hypothesis awaits confirmation with infant research participants that are younger than 3 to 4 months.

Summary The results of the animal categorisation studies have provided a systematic, consistent, and theoretically relevant set of findings regarding the formation of basic and global categorical representations in young infants. First, infants 3 to 4 months of age can form perceptually based representations for basic-level categories from the superordinate animal category. Evidence was obtained for categorical representations for domestic cats and horses, each of which excluded a number of other animal species. Second, infants can form a more global categorical representation for mammals that includes instances from novel mammal categories, but excludes birds, fish, and furniture. Third, some of the categorical differentiations are apparently aided by spontaneous preferences for instances of one category over exemplars of another (e.g. tigers over domestic cats, mammals over birds). Such preferences are likely to be based on preferred perceptual properties and we believe it reasonable to speculate that categories marked by such properties may be more easily acquired, and possibly present earlier in development, than categories not marked by such features. Fourth, we have begun to specify the perceptual information that allows infants to form categorical representations for animal species at the basic level. Three- and 4-month-old infants rely on information from the head and face region to form a categorical representation for domestic cats that excludes dogs. Clearly, then, this research has revealed that young infants possess quite sophisticated abilities to group object-based stimuli into categories that correspond to many of the groupings used by older children and adults. The chapter will now proceed to a discussion of the abilities of infants to organise physical space into categories defined by the positional arrangement of these objects – abilities that many believe are mediated by a different brain system.

CATEGORICAL REPRESENTATIONS FOR SPATIAL RELATIONS

Whereas there is a reasonably sized and growing data base concerning infants' abilities to form categorical representations for classes of objects, less has been written about infants' abilities to form categorical representations of the spatial relations of these objects. The ability to categorically represent spatial relations such as above, below, left, right, between, inside, and outside should allow infants "to experience objects in coherent spatial layouts rather than as spatially unrelated entities residing in disconnected locations" (Quinn, 1994, p. 59). Early spatial relations categories may also yield conceptual primitives that support lexical learning of spatial terms (Choi & Bowerman, 1991; Clark, 1973; Slobin, 1985), formation of cognitive maps (Newcombe & Liben, 1982), processing of spatial information from maps (Landau, 1986), visual recognition of objects and words (Biederman, 1987; Caramazza & Hillis, 1990), and reasoning about more complex spatial relations and events including support, collision, and containment (Baillargeon, 1993). Clearly, spatial knowledge of a categorical nature has considerable value for the development of a variety of human cognitive and linguistic abilities (Jackendoff & Landau, 1991; Landau & Jackendoff, 1993).

Categorical representations for above and below

One study that attempted to trace the developmental origins of the ability to represent spatial information was that of Antell and Caron (1985), who familiarised newborn infants with a display containing two shapes, square and cross, that maintained an invariant spatial arrangement (square above cross), despite changes in the absolute location of the shapes in the display. On testing, the neonates generalised their habituation to the same spatial arrangement in a new location, but dishabituated to a rearrangement of the shapes (cross above square), suggesting that even the youngest infants process and respond to simple spatial relations.

Quinn (1994) sought to extend the findings of Antell and Caron (1985) by investigating whether 3-month-old infants are able to form categorical representations for the above and below spatial relations of a dot and horizontal reference bar. The design of this study can be seen in Fig. 5.8 and Fig. 5.9. As is shown on the left side of panels (a) and (b) in Fig. 5.8, infants in a "dot above bar" group were familiarised with four exemplars, each depicting a single dot in a different position above a horizontal bar. For half of the infants in the group, each of the dots appeared in the above-left quadrant of the stimulus display (a); for the other half, the dots were shown in the above-right quadrant of the display (b). The infants were then tested with two novel exemplars, one in which the dot had been shifted to the right (a) or left (b) of the familiar exemplars, whereas in the other, the dot appeared below the reference bar.

If infants form a categorical representation for the dot appearing in the various locations above the bar, then the novel "dot above bar" exemplar should be perceived as familiar whereas the "dot below bar" exemplar should be viewed as novel and consequently preferred. If, alternatively, infants do not form a categorical representation of the "above" relation between the dot and the bar, and represent only information about the dot or the bar, or represent information about the dot and bar independently of each other (cf. Cohen & Younger, 1984), then one would not expect a consistent preference for either test exemplar. Panels (a) and (b) in Fig. 5.9 reveal how the same procedure and rationale was used to test whether infants in a "Dot Below Bar" group would form a comparable categorical

Familiar Stimuli   Test Stimuli

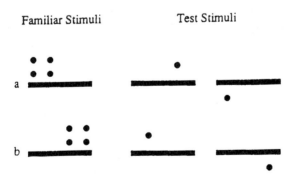

FIG. 5.8. Familiarisation stimuli (a composite of the four exemplars) and test stimuli used to test formation of the categorical representation "dot above bar" (from Quinn, 1994). Copyright © 1994 Reprinted with the permission of The Society For Research in Child Development, Inc.

Familiar Stimuli   Test Stimuli

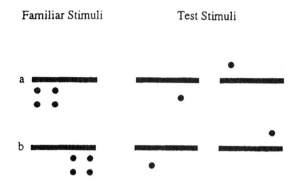

FIG. 5.9.   Familiarisation stimuli (a composite of the four exemplars) and test stimuli used to test formation of the categorical representation "dot below bar" (from Quinn, 1994). Copyright © 1994 Reprinted with the permission of The Society For Research in Child Development, Inc.

representation for the dot appearing in different positions beneath the reference bar.

Infants in both conditions preferred the exemplar from the novel spatial category, indicating that they had formed categorical representations for the above and below relations of the dot and the horizontal bar. A subsequent control experiment supported this conclusion by showing that infants could discriminate the position changes that occurred during familiarisation. It should also be noted that the novel category preferences could not be attributed to simple generalisation based on distance information as the dot appearing on the opposite side of the bar was the same distance away from the familiarisation positions as the dot in the novel location on the same side of the bar.

One still needs to rule out two additional alternative interpretations of the preference results from the Quinn (1994) "above and below" study. First, it could be that vertical (up–down) changes in the location of the dot are more salient (and responded to more robustly) than horizontal (left–right) changes. Second, it could have been the case that infants were encoding the dot locations categorically, but in relation to an *internal* horizontal midline, rather than the externally available bar (Huttenlocher, Newcombe, & Sandberg, 1994). Fortunately, the force of these interpretations can be assessed in a control condition in which the categorisation experiment was repeated with stimuli that presented the dot in the various locations, but without the horizontal reference bar. If infants were to perform in this control experiment as they did in the original above–below categorisation experiment, then both alternative explanations would receive support; if, however, infants looked equally at the test stimuli in the absence of the bar, then the categorical representation explanation would be considerably strengthened. Infants in the no-bar control did not display a preference for either test stimulus, thereby upholding the conclusion that infants had formed categorical representations of the dot's above and below relations with the horizontal bar in the original categorisation experiment.

Categorical representations for left and right

With the evidence indicating that young infants possess the ability to categorically represent at least some spatial relations, Behl-Chadha and Eimas (1995) proceeded to investigate the formation of categorical representations for left and right. The familiarisation-test format was similar to that employed by Antell and Caron (1985) with the exception that complex stimuli were used and presented in a left–right arrangement. Three- and 4-month-olds were familiarised with stimulus displays depicting discriminably different horse–zebra pairs presented in a constant left–right relation. Across the familiarisation trials, the individual exemplars of the pairs, the horses and zebras, varied in size, orientation of stance (i.e. head to the left or right), and absolute location in the stimulus display. Infants were then tested with two horse–zebra pairs that were novel in size and location; one pair maintained the familiar left–right relation, the other was presented in a novel right–left relation. Infants reliably preferred the novel right–left relation, a result that provides additional evidence confirming that young infants can form categorical representations for spatial relations, in this case, for the left–right relations of two complex objects. Moreover, the results suggest that the later difficulties with left–right discrimination exhibited by both children and adults (e.g. Corballis & Beale, 1976) may have more to do with abstract cognitive encoding strategies or verbal labelling than with initial perceptual encoding (Braine & Fisher, 1988; Braine, Plastow, & Greene, 1987; Quinn & Bomba, 1986; Quinn, Siqueland, & Bomba, 1985; Sholl & Egeth, 1981).

The effect of object variation

One question left unanswered by the Antell & Caron (1985), Quinn (1994), and Behl-Chadha & Eimas (1995) investigations concerns the degree of abstraction of the spatial representations being formed. Each of the studies showed that young infants are capable of representing spatial relations involving only two objects (i.e. cross and square, dot and bar, horse and zebra). However, children and adults, in activities such as object recognition, word recognition, and map learning, encounter many different objects, object parts, and features in various spatial relations, but are able to maintain their spatial concepts despite the variation in the entities depicting the relations. That is, children and adults are able to represent the equivalence of a particular spatial relation across contexts, despite changes in the specific locations or identities of the objects depicting that relation. Even earlier in development, toddlers between the ages of 17 and 20 months are beginning to acquire a lexicon of spatial terms with which to communicate and reason about spatial relations presented in a variety of arrangements (Choi & Bowerman, 1991). It is therefore not clear whether the abilities of young infants to categorise spatial relations are functionally equivalent to those possessed by toddlers, children, and adults.

Quinn, Cummins, Kase, Martin, and Weissman (1996) investigated whether young infants can form more abstract categorical representations for above and below that are independent of the objects used to signal these relations. To begin this series of experiments, Quinn et al. (1996) first attempted to replicate the Quinn (1994) findings with 3- and 4-month-old infants and similar stimuli. The stimuli, shown in Fig. 5.10, displayed a diamond in different above and below positions relative to a horizontal bar, which was in this case composed of a row of individual square elements. The infants performed as they did in the Quinn (1994) study. Those familiarised with instances from the *above* category preferred the *below* exemplars during the preference test, and those initially presented with *below* instances preferred the *above* exemplars during testing.

This replication made it possible for Quinn et al. to investigate the effect of object variation on infants' abilities to form categorical representations for above and below that are independent of the specific objects depicted in the above and below relations. Infants were familiarised as in the first experiment, but in this case with four distinct shapes (randomly selected from among seven shapes – an arrow, a diamond, a dollar sign, a dot, the letter E, a plus sign, and a triangle – shown to be discriminably different in a control experiment) appearing above or below the bar. Infants were also tested for preference as they were in the initial experiment, but with the change that a novel shape in the familiar spatial relation was paired with same shape in the novel spatial relation. If the infants form categorical representations for above and below despite variation in the forms depicting these relations, then they should perform as they did in the initial experiment and prefer the novel spatial relation. However, if the infants do not form categorical representations for above and below, possibly because the object variation recruits infants' attention away from the spatial nature of the task (cf. Vecera & Farah, 1994), then one would not predict a preference for either test stimulus, as both contain the same novel object. Unlike the infants in the initial experiment, the infants in this experiment did not show a preference for the novel spatial category test stimulus. This result indicates that the categorical representations for above and below formed by 3- to 4-month-olds in the first experiment,

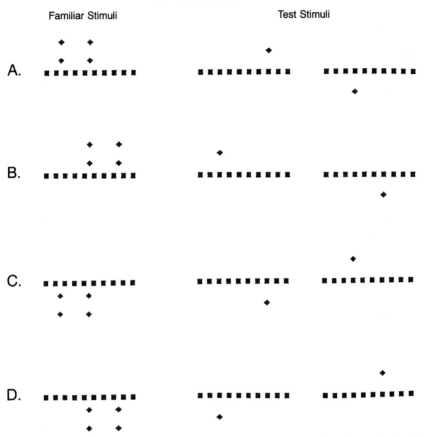

FIG. 5.10.   Familiarisation stimuli (a composite of the four exemplars) and test stimuli used to test for categorical representations of above and below by Quinn, Cummins, Kase, Martin, and Weissman (1996) (from Quinn et al., 1996). Copyright © 1996 by the American Psychological Association. Reprinted with permission.

and in Quinn (1994), were rather specific and limited to the two objects depicting the relations, i.e. the dot or diamond and the reference bar (see, Cohen & Oakes, 1993, for similar findings with older infants observing *causal* relations).

In a final experiment, Quinn et al. (1996) attempted to determine the age at which infants come to categorically represent abstract spatial relations that are independent of the particular objects used to display these relations. This experiment was therefore a replication of the *object variation* version of the above–below categorisation task, but conducted with 6- to 7-month-olds. This age group was selected because some of the object categorisation studies described earlier had shown age-related changes in performance between 4 and 6 months of life (e.g. Eimas & Quinn, 1994). The older infants in this last experiment displayed reliable preferences for the novel spatial category, indicating that they were able to categorically represent above and below relations independently of the particular objects used to display these relations. The overall pattern of results is thus consistent with the suggestion that categorical representations are initially quite concrete and specific (e.g. only one object can be spatially related to a second object) and with experience or maturation or both become more abstract and general (e.g. a number of different objects can be spatially related to each other within the same representation).

GLOBAL INFLUENCES ON THE DEVELOPMENT OF OBJECT AND SPATIAL CATEGORISATION

Although the findings on object and spatial categorisation discussed thus far have increased our understanding of early category formation, a complete account of development within a domain requires both a description of the developmental course and a specification of the factors affecting the process of change. The forces governing development within any domain have most typically been discussed in terms of biological maturation and environmental experience. Whereas some have argued that environmental and biological forces are largely inseparable (e.g. Gottlieb, 1992), the position taken here is that experience and maturation can often be distinguished by the primacy of their influence on development in various domains, and that important conclusions can be derived from such distinctions.

Mash, Quinn, and Dobson (1993, 1994; Mash, Quinn, Dobson, & Narter, in press) have been investigating the developmental determinants of object and spatial categorisation using an experimental design that involves comparison of performance between full-term infants and two age-matched groups of premature infants. One group of preterm infants, the *postnatals*, was matched with the full-terms on the basis of postnatal experience (that is, matched for age from birth), whereas the other group of preterm infants, the *postterms*, was matched to the full-terms by maturational status (matched for age from conception).

The full-term infants in the Mash et al. studies were tested at 3.5 months, an age at which categorisation of objects and specific spatial relations would be expected based on the findings already discussed. The preterm infants were on average 2 months premature (but healthy in all other respects – those with ophthalmological or more general health problems were excluded from the sample), so that the *postnatals* (matched for experience) were 3.5 months from birth at testing, and the *postterms* (matched for maturational status) were 5.5 months from birth at testing. Our reasoning was that if the early development of perceptual categorisation is determined by biological maturation, then the full-terms and *postterms* should perform equivalently, and both should outperform the *postnatals*. If, however, development is determined primarily by environmental experience, then one would expect the *postterms* to outperform the full-terms and *postnatals*. A third possibility is that prematurity, *per se*, may exert a limiting influence on the development of perceptual categorisation. In that case, the full-terms would be expected to outperform both the *postterms* and *postnatals*.

Mash et al. obtained evidence for two different developmental patterns, one associated with spatial categorisation, the other with object categorisation. In an above–below spatial categorisation task that was identical to the diamond–horizontal bar task used by Quinn et al. (1996), both full-terms and *postterms* displayed reliable novel category preferences; however, *postnatal* infants performed at chance. This pattern of preferences indicates that biological maturation is a more potent determinant of spatial categorisation than is the accumulation of environmental experience.

In contrast, in a cat–dog object categorisation task similar to that used by Quinn et al. (1993), full-term infants performed at an above-chance level, but neither group of premature infants performed differently from chance. One could argue that the poor performance of the premature infants reflected the difficulty of the cat–dog categorisation task; however, an additional group of postterm infants also failed to perform at an above-chance level on a cat–bird categorisation task. This pattern of performance thus suggests that preterm birth exerts a limiting effect on the abilities of infants to perform object categorisation tasks successfully.

How can we interpet the different developmental outcomes on the spatial and object categorisation tasks? One possibility is that the object categorisation task, perhaps because of the complexity of the natural object stimuli that varied along a number of dimensions, was simply more difficult (i.e. more computationally demanding) than the spatial categorisation task (cf. Rueckl, Cave, & Kosslyn, 1989). Although such an explanation cannot be ruled out entirely, it is weakened by the finding that the premature infants had difficulty with a relatively "high-contrast" categorical distinction such as cat–bird.

There is also evidence that the object/spatial performance difference is not specific either to categorisation tasks or to the particular stimuli and procedures used in these experiments, but is simply one manifestation of a more general spatial/object difference that has been reported by others. For example, Bower (1982) has argued that infants less than 5 months of age are more likely to use spatial location information than object feature information as a criterion for object identity (see also Xu & Carey, 1996). In addition, Baillargeon (1995) has reported less robust memory for object features compared with object location in "possible–impossible event" tasks assessing the development of physical knowledge conducted with slightly older infants in the age range between 5.5 and 9.5 months (see also Narter & Rosser, 1996). Also, Harman, Posner, Rothbart, and Thomas-Thrapp (1994), based on results obtained with infants participating in an "inhibition of return" task, have discussed the possibility that novelty preference for location information may develop earlier than that for object identity information. Furthermore, Colombo, Mitchell, Coldren, and Atwater (1990) report evidence for a *location* over *object* identity advantage in 3-month-olds participating in a contingency learning procedure. The findings of inferior performance for object feature information relative to spatial location information in several different experimental paradigms thus provide evidence for a phenomenon of a more general nature.

It seems likely that performance on the object and spatial categorisation tasks may be subserved by two different, brain-based systems of processing and representation, which may themselves have different rates or patterns of development. As mentioned briefly in the introduction to this chapter, Mishkin et al. (1983) reviewed evidence indicating that the visual processing of object properties and spatial relations in monkeys is carried out in two anatomically distinct systems (see also Wilson, O'Scalaidhe, & Goldman-Rakic, 1993). Processing of object or "what" features including colour, texture, and shape is mediated by a pathway linking primary visual cortex to inferior temporal cortex. Processing of spatial relations or "where" information occurs in a pathway connecting primary visual cortex to posterior parietal cortex. Evidence from humans with brain lesions (Newcombe, Ratcliff, & Damasio, 1987) and from recent brain imaging studies (Ungerleider & Haxby, 1994) suggests the presence of analogous "what" and "where" pathways in humans.

If the object and spatial categorisation tasks tap the "what" and "where" pathways, respectively, then the different patterns of group performance may reflect differences in the rates or patterns of development of the two cortical systems. Consistent with this suggestion are recent findings indicating that the occipito-parietal (spatial or "where") pathway in monkeys reaches full maturity at 3 months of age, whereas the occipito-temporal (object or "what") pathway does not reach an adult level of maturity until 4 months of age (Distler et al., 1996; see also, Bachevalier, Hagger, & Mishkin, 1991). Also relevant are data indicating that temporal brain regions are subject to damage in preterm infants (Paneth, Rudelli, Kazam, & Monte, 1994; see also Fuller, Guthrie, & Alvord, 1983). That temporal regions display such plasticity and susceptibility to the effects of differential experience is consistent with their more protracted period of maturation. Thus, the findings that the spatial information pathway develops more rapidly than the object features pathway (and may be more immutable to experience) may help to explain why a group of age-adjusted 3.5-month-old infants (i.e. the *postterms*) were capable of forming categorical representations for spatial relations, but not objects (and might also account for the other reported advantages for spatial over object processing during early development).

Additional experimentation that involves administering object and spatial categorisation tasks (and possibly other tasks of the sorts mentioned) to full-term infants less than 3 to 4 months of age will clearly be needed to confirm this "rate and pattern of development" explanation of the observed differences between object and spatial processing. Research with older infants will also be needed to examine the full time course of development of object and spatial processing, as Baillargeon's (1995) findings suggest that the spatial advantage continues (at least until 9.5 months), whereas results obtained from "inhibition of return" and contingency learning tasks indicate that object processing may "catch" and eventually surpass spatial processing by 6 months of age (Colombo et al., 1990; Harman et al., 1994).

Further studies that will be helpful in this regard will be those that attempt to determine what particular characteristics of parietal and temporal brain regions mediate the observed performance difference between object and spatial processing. For example, Maunsell (1995), using microelectrode recording techniques on behaving monkeys, has reported that memory-related activity of neurons in parietal cortex that code location information is greater than that of neurons in temporal cortex that code for object attributes such as shape or colour. How such differences in the duration of neuronal responsiveness by different regions of cortex to different aspects of a visual scene (i.e. objects vs. their spatial relations) arise developmentally is not known at this time and will be important to determine in subsequent investigations.

Finally, it should be noted that the attempt to relate performance in the object and spatial categorisation tasks to the "what" and "where" brain systems, directly and cleanly, is not without problems. For example, some authors have contended that object recognition necessarily involves processing of spatial relations between object parts (e.g. Bhatt & Rovee-Collier, 1996; Biederman, 1987; Treisman, 1988; but see Cave & Kosslyn, 1993, and Hayward & Tarr, 1995). This claim has led to the suggestion that the "what" system may in fact process spatial information (Bhatt & Rovee-Collier, 1996). Other authors have argued that one needs to distinguish between different kinds of spatial processing such as *coarse where* versus *fine where* (Atkinson & Braddick, 1989), and *within-object spatial coding* versus *between-object spatial coding* (Humphreys & Riddoch, 1995).

Such arguments have given rise to the proposal that different components of the "where" system may process different kinds of spatial information; in particular, the occipito-parietal brain region has been hypothesised to process spatial relations between objects, whereas the fronto-parietal area may be involved in processing spatial relations between attributes within an object (Humphreys & Riddoch, 1995). Thus, while the simple story of linking development of object and spatial processing with development of temporal and parietal brain regions may be appealing, a full accounting for the development of all aspects of object and spatial processing will most likely turn out to be more complex.

OVERVIEW

This chapter has provided a selective review of the evidence on object and spatial categorisation in early infancy. The findings indicate that even young infants possess remarkable abilities for parsing a variety of entities and their relations into equivalence classes such as cat, mammal, and the spatial relation "above". Although development may not proceed identically in the object and spatial domains, the overall pattern of data has provided the groundwork for a continuity-based view of early category development that has been outlined elsewhere (Eimas, 1994; Quinn, 1993; 1994; Quinn & Eimas, 1996b, 1997). For example, in the domain of objects, animals in particular, the emerging representations for individual animal species, and animals more generally, could presumably serve as the initial structures for a developing naive (proto)theory of biology (cf. Carey, 1985; Keil, 1989; Murphy & Medin, 1985). In the domain of spatial relations, early categorical representations for above, below, left, and right may yield the functional units (e.g. primitives) necessary for the acquisition of a spatial lexicon and for the construction of more complex representations of larger-scale spaces. Continuing investigations of the representations of young infants that utilise a *convergent measure* research strategy will be needed to further substantiate this continuity-based view of early category development. Laboratories that use a combination of behavioural, electrophysiological (i.e. high-density event-related potential, ERP) and connectionist modelling methodologies may be in the best position to provide evidence that is relevant to the question of how representations for category information are initially formed and elaborated during early development (Johnson, 1994).

REFERENCES

Antell, S.E.G., & Caron, A.J. (1985). Neonatal perception of spatial relationships. *Infant Behavior and Development*, **8**, 15–23.

Atkinson, J., & Braddick, O.J. (1989). "Where" and "what" in visual search. *Perception*, **18**, 181–189.

Bachevalier, J., Haggar, C., & Mishkin, M. (1991). Functional maturation of the occipito-temporal pathway in infant rhesus monkeys. In N.A. Lassen, D.H. Ingvar, M.E. Raichle, & L. Friberg (Eds.), *Brain work and mental activity*. Copenhagen: Munksgaard.

Baillargeon, R. (1993). The object concept revisited: New directions in the investigation of infants' physical knowledge. In C.E. Granrud (Ed.), *Visual perception and cognition in infancy. Carnegie Mellon symposium on cognition* (Vol. 23, pp. 263–315). Hillsdale, NJ: Erlbaum.

Baillargeon, R. (1995). A model of physical reasoning in infancy. In C. Rovee-Collier & L.P. Lipsitt (Eds.), *Advances in infancy research* (Vol. 9, pp. 305–371). Norwood, NJ: Ablex.

Behl-Chadha, G. (1996). Basic-level and superordinate-like categorical representations in early infancy. *Cognition, 60,* 105–141.

Behl-Chadha, G., & Eimas, P.D. (1995). Infant categorization of left-right spatial relations. *British Journal of Developmental Psychology, 13,* 69–79.

Behl-Chadha, G., Eimas, P.D., & Quinn, P.C. (1995, March). *Perceptually-driven superordinate categorization by young infants.* Paper presented at the meeting of the Society for Research in Child Development, Indianapolis, IN.

Bhatt, R.S., & Rovee-Collier, C. (1996). Infants' forgetting of correlated attributes and object recognition. *Child Development, 67,* 172–187.

Biederman, I. (1987). Recognition-by-components: A theory of human image understanding. *Psychological Review, 94,* 115–147.

Bomba, P.C., & Siqueland, E.R. (1983). The nature and structure of infant form categories. *Journal of Experimental Child Psychology, 35,* 294–328.

Bower, T.G.R. (1982). *Development in infancy* (2nd edn.). San Francisco, CA: Freeman.

Braine, L.G., & Fisher, C.B. (1988). Context effects in left-right shape discrimination. *Developmental Psychology, 24,* 183–189.

Braine, L.G., Plastow, E., & Greene, S.L. (1987). Judgments of shape orientation: A matter of contrasts. *Perception and Psychophysics, 41,* 335–344.

Bruner, J.S., Olver, R.R., & Greenfield, P. (1966). *Studies in cognitive growth*. New York: Wiley.

Caramazza, A., & Hillis, A.E. (1990). Levels of representation, co-ordinate frames, and unilateral neglect. *Cognitive Neuropsychology, 7,* 391–445.

Carey, S. (1985). *Conceptual change in childhood*. Cambridge, MA: MIT Press.

Cave, C.B., & Kosslyn, S.M. (1993). The role of parts and spatial relations in object identification. *Perception, 22,* 229–248.

Choi, S., & Bowerman, M. (1991). Learning to express motion events in English and Korean: The influence of language-specific lexicalization patterns. *Cognition, 41,* 83–121.

Clark, H.H. (1973). Space, time, semantics, and the child. In T.E. Moore (Ed.), *Cognitive development and the acquisition of language* (pp. 65–110). New York: Academic Press.

Cohen, L.B., & Caputo, N.F. (1978, May). *Instructing infants to respond to perceptual categories.* Paper presented at the meeting of the Midwestern Psychological Association, Chicago, IL.

Cohen, L.B., & Oakes, L.M. (1993). How infants perceive a simple causal event. *Developmental Psychology, 29,* 421–433.

Cohen, L.B., & Younger, B.A. (1983). Perceptual categorization in the infant. In E. Scholnick (Ed.), *New trends in conceptual representation: Challenges to Piaget's theory?* (pp. 197–220). Hillsdale, NJ: Erlbaum.

Cohen, L.B., & Younger, B.A. (1984). Infant perception of angular relations. *Infant Behavior and Development, 7,* 37–47.

Colombo, J., Mitchell, D.W., Coldren, J.T., & Atwater, J.D. (1990). Discrimination learning during the first year: stimulus and positional cues. *Journal of Experimental Psychology: Learning, Memory, and Cognition, 16,* 98–109.

Colombo, J., O'Brien, M., Mitchell, D.W., & Horowitz, F.D. (1986). Stimulus salience and relational processing. *Infant Behavior and Development*, **9**, 377–380.

Colombo, J., O'Brien, M., Mitchell, D.W., Roberts, K., & Horowitz, F.D. (1987). A lower boundary for category formation in preverbal infants. *Journal of Child Language*, **14**, 383–385.

Corballis, M.C., & Beale, I.L. (1976). *The psychology of left and right*. Hillsdale, NJ: Erlbaum.

Daehler, M.W., Lonardo, R., & Bukatko, D. (1979). Matching and equivalence judgments in very young children. *Child Development*, **50**, 170–179.

Distler, C., Bachevalier, J., Kennedy, C., Mishkin, M., & Ungerleider, L.G. (1996). Functional development of the cortico-cortical pathway for motion analysis in the macaque monkey: A C-2 deoxyglucose study. *Cerebral cortex*, **6**, 184–195.

Edelman, G.M. (1987). *Neural darwinism*. New York: Basic Books.

Eimas, P.D. (1994). Categorization in early infancy and the continuity of development. *Cognition*, **50**, 83–93.

Eimas, P.D., & Quinn, P.C. (1994). Studies on the formation of perceptually based basic-level categories in young infants. *Child Development*, **65**, 903–917.

Eimas, P.D., Quinn, P.C., & Cowan, P. (1994). Development of exclusivity in perceptually based categories of young infants. *Journal of Experimental Child Psychology*, **58**, 418–431.

Fagan, J.F. (1978). Facilitation of infants' recognition memory. *Child Development*, **49**, 1066–1075.

Fantz, R.L. (1964). Visual experience in infants: Decreased attention to familiar patterns relative to novel ones. *Science*, **164**, 668–670.

Fuller, P.W., Guthrie, R.D., & Alvord, E.C. (1983). A proposed neuropathological basis for learning disabilities in children born prematurely. *Developmental Medicine and Child Neurology*, **25**, 214–231.

Gottlieb, G. (1992). *Individual development and evolution: The genesis of novel behavior*. New York: Oxford University Press.

Harman, C., Posner, M.I., Rothbart, M.K., & Thomas-Thrapp, L. (1994). Development of orienting to objects and locations in human infants. *Canadian Journal of Psychology*, **48**, 301–318.

Hayward, W.G., & Tarr, M.J. (1995, November). *When does object recognition use outline shape?* Poster presented at the meeting of the Psychonomics Society, Los Angeles, CA.

Homa, D., & Chambliss, D. (1975). The relative contributions of common and distinctive information on the abstraction from ill-defined categories. *Journal of Experimental Psychology: Human Learning and Memory*, **3**, 375–385.

Horton, M.S., & Markman, E.M. (1980). Developmental differences in the acquisition of basic and superordinate categories. *Child Development*, **51**, 708–719.

Humphreys, G.W., & Riddoch, M.J. (1995). Separate coding of space within and between perceptual objects: Evidence from unilateral visual neglect. *Cognitive Neuropsychology*, **12**, 283–311.

Huttenlocher, J., Newcombe, N. & Sandberg, E.H. (1994). The coding of spatial location in young children. *Cognitive Psychology*, **27**, 115–147.

Jackendoff, R., & Landau, B. (1991). Spatial language and spatial cognition. In D.J. Napoli & J.A. Kegl (Eds.), *Bridges between psychology and linguistics: A Swarthmore Festschrift for Lila Gleitman*. Hillsdale, NJ: Erlbaum.

Johnson, M.H. (1994). Brain and cognitive development in infancy. *Current Opinion in Neurobiology*, **4**, 218–225.

Johnson, M.H., & Morton, J. (1991). *Biology and cognitive development*. Cambridge, MA: Blackwell.

Jones, S.S., Smith, L.B., & Landau, B. (1991). Object properties and knowledge in early lexical learning. *Child Development*, **62**, 499–516.

Karmiloff-Smith, A. (1992). *Beyond modularity.* Cambridge, MA: MIT Press.

Keil, F.C. (1989). *Concepts, kinds and cognitive development.* Cambridge, MA: MIT Press.

Landau, B. (1986). Early map use as an unlearned ability. *Cognition, 22,* 201–223.

Landau, B., & Jackendoff, R. (1993). "What" and "Where" in spatial language and spatial cognition. *Behavioral and Brain Sciences, 16,* 217–238.

Mandler, J.M. (1988). How to build a baby: On the development of an accessible representational system. *Cognitive Development, 3,* 113–136.

Mandler, J.M. (1992). How to build a baby: II. Conceptual primitives. *Psychological Review, 99,* 587–604.

Mandler, J.M., & Bauer, P.J. (1988). The cradle of categorization: Is the basic level basic? *Cognitive Development, 3,* 247–264.

Mandler, J.M., Bauer, P., & McDonough, L. (1991). Separating the sheep from the goats: Differentiating global categories. *Cognitive Psychology, 23,* 263–298.

Mandler, J.M., & McDonough, L. (1993). Concept formation in infancy. *Cognitive Development, 8,* 291–318.

Markman, E.M. (1989). *Categorization and naming in children.* Cambridge, MA: MIT Press.

Marr, D. (1982). *Vision.* San Francisco, CA: Freeman.

Mash, C., Quinn, P.C., & Dobson, V. (1993, March). *Determinants of early categorization: Maturational status, environmental experience, and premature birth.* Paper presented at the meeting of the Society for Research in Child Development, New Orleans, LA.

Mash, C., Quinn, P.C., & Dobson, V. (1994, April). *Relative effects of preterm birth, environmental experience, and maturational status on the early categorization of spatial relations.* Paper presented at the Conference on Human Development, Pittsburgh, PA.

Mash, C., Quinn, P.C., Dobson, V., & Narter, D.B. (in press). Global influences on the development of spatial and object perceptual categorization abilities: Evidence from preterm infants. *Developmental Science.*

Maunsell, J.H.R. (1995). The brain's visual world: Representation of visual targets in cerebral cortex. *Science, 270,* 764–769.

Mervis, C.B. (1987). Child-basic object categories and early development. In U. Neisser (Ed.), *Concepts and conceptual development* (pp. 201–233). Cambridge: Cambridge University Press.

Mervis, C.B., & Crisafi, M.A. (1982). Order of acquisition of subordinate, basic, and superordinate categories. *Child Development, 53,* 258–266.

Mishkin, M., Ungerleider, L.G., & Macko, K.A. (1983). Object vision and spatial vision: Two cortical pathways. *Trends in Neuroscience, 6,* 414–417.

Murphy, G.L. (1991). Parts in object concepts: Experiments with artificial categories. *Memory and Cognition, 19,* 423–438.

Murphy, G.L., & Medin, D.L. (1985). The role of theories in conceptual coherence. *Psychological Review, 92,* 289–316.

Narter, D.B., & Rosser, R.A. (1996, April). *Infants' memory for the features of hidden objects: Size as an early marker of object identity.* Paper presented at the International Conference on Infant Studies, Providence, RI.

Newcombe, F., Ratcliff, G., & Damasio, H. (1987). Dissociable visual and spatial impairments following right posterior cerebral lesions: Clinical, neuropsychological, and anatomical evidence. *Neuropsychologia, 25,* 149–161.

Newcombe, N., & Liben, L.S. (1982). Barrier effects in the cognitive maps of children and adults. *Journal of Experimental Child Psychology, 34,* 46–58.

Nosofsky, R.L. (1991). Tests of an exemplar model for relating perceptual classification and recognition memory. *Journal of Experimental Psychology: Human Perception and Performance, 17,* 3–27.

Paneth, N., Rudelli, R., Kazam, E., & Monte, W. (1994). *Brain damage in the preterm infant: Clinics in Developmental Medicine, No.* **131**. London: MacKeith Press.

Posner, M.I., & Keele, S.W. (1968). On the genesis of abstract ideas. *Journal of Experimental Psychology,* **77**, 353–363.

Posner, M.I., & Keele, S.W. (1970). Retention of abstract ideas. *Journal of Experimental Psychology,* **83**, 304–308.

Quinn, P.C. (1987). The categorical representation of visual pattern information by young infants. *Cognition,* **27**, 145–179.

Quinn, P.C. (1993, April). *Perceptual beginnings of conceptual categories.* Paper presented at the Early Cognition and Transition to Language Conference, University of Texas at Austin.

Quinn, P.C. (1994). The categorization of above and below spatial relations by young infants. *Child Development,* **65**, 58–69.

Quinn, P.C., & Bomba, P.C. (1986). Evidence for a general category of oblique orientations in four-month-old infants. *Journal of Experimental Child Psychology,* **42**, 345–354.

Quinn, P.C., Cummins, M., Kase, J., Martin, E., & Weissman, S. (1996). Development of categorical representations for above and below spatial relations in 3- to 7-month-old infants. *Developmental Psychology,* **32**, 642–650.

Quinn, P.C., & Eimas, P.D. (1986a). On categorization in early infancy. *Merrill-Palmer Quarterly,* **32**, 331–363.

Quinn, P.C., & Eimas, P.D. (1986b). Pattern-line effects and units of visual processing in infants. *Infant Behavior and Development,* **9**, 57–70.

Quinn, P.C., & Eimas, P.D. (1996a). Perceptual cues that permit categorical differentiation of natural animal species by infants. *Journal of Experimental Child Psychology,* **63**, 189–211.

Quinn, P.C., & Eimas, P.D. (1996b). Perceptual organization and categorization in young infants. In C. Rovee-Collier & L.P. Lipsitt (Eds.), *Advances in infancy research* (Vol. 10, pp. 1–36). Norwood, NJ: Ablex.

Quinn, P.C., & Eimas, P.D. (1997). A reexamination of the perceptual-to-conceptual shift in mental representations. *Review of General Psychology,* **1**, 271–287.

Quinn, P.C., Eimas, P.D., & Rosenkrantz, S.L. (1993). Evidence for representations of perceptually similar natural categories by 3-month-old and 4-month-old infants. *Perception,* **22**, 463–475.

Quinn, P.C., & Johnson, M.H. (1996). The emergence of perceptual category representations during early development: A connectionist analysis. In G.W. Cottrell (Ed.), *Proceedings of the Eighteenth Annual Conference of the Cognitive Science Society.* Mahwah, NJ: Erlbaum.

Quinn, P.C., & Johnson, M.H. (1997). The emergence of perceptual category representations in young infants: A connectionist analysis. *Journal of Experimental Child Psychology,* **66**, 236–263.

Quinn, P.C., Siqueland, E.R., & Bomba, P.C. (1985). Delayed recognition memory for orientation by human infants. *Journal of Experimental Child Psychology,* **40**, 293–303.

Roberts, K. (1988). Retrieval of a basic level category in pre-linguistic infants. *Developmental Psychology,* **24**, 21–27.

Rosch, E., Mervis, C.B., Gray, W.D., Johnson, D.M., & Boyes-Braem, P. (1976). Basic objects in natural categories. *Cognitive Psychology,* **7**, 573–605.

Rueckl, J.G., Cave, K.R., & Kosslyn, S.M. (1989). Why are "what" and "where" processed by separate cortical systems? A computational investigation. *Journal of Cognitive Neuroscience,* **1**, 171–186.

Sherman, T.L. (1985). Categorization skills in infants. *Child Development,* **56**, 1561–1573.

Sholl, M.J., & Egeth, H.E. (1981). Right-left confusion in the adult: A verbal labeling effect. *Memory and Cognition*, **9**, 339–350.

Slater, A.M. (1995). Visual perception and memory at birth. In C. Rovee-Collier & L.P. Lipsitt (Eds.), *Advances in infancy research* (Vol. 9, pp. 107–162). Norwood, NJ: Ablex.

Slobin, D.I. (1985). Cross-linguistic evidence for the language making capacity. In D.I. Slobin (Ed.), *The cross-linguistic study of language acquisition: Vol. 2. Theoretical issues* (pp. 1157–1256). Hillsdale, NJ: Erlbaum.

Strauss, M.S. (1979). Abstraction of prototypical information in adults and 10-month-old infants. *Journal of Experimental Psychology: Human Learning and Memory*, **5**, 618–632.

Treisman, A. (1988). Features and objects: The Fourteenth Bartlett Memorial Lecture. *Quarterly Journal of Experimental Psychology*, **40**, 201–237.

Ungerleider, L.G., & Haxby, J.V. (1994). "What" and "where" in the human brain. *Current Opinion in Neurobiology*, **4**, 157–165.

Ungerleider, L.G., & Mishkin, M. (1982). Two cortical visual systems. In D.J. Ingle, M.A. Goodale, & R.J.W. Mansfield, *The analysis of visual behavior* (pp. 549–586). Cambridge, MA: MIT Press.

Vecera, S.P., & Farah, M.J. (1994). Does visual attention select objects or locations? *Journal of Experimental Psychology: General*, **123**, 146–160.

Vygotsky, L.S. (1962). *Thought and language* (E. Hanfmann & G. Vacar, Trans.). Cambridge, MA: MIT Press.

Wilson, F.A.W., Scalaidhe, S.P.O., & Goldman-Rakic, P.S. (1993). Dissociation of object and spatial processing domains in primate prefrontal cortex. *Science*, **260**, 1955–1958.

Xu, F., & Carey, S. (1996). Infants' metaphysics: The case of numerical identity. *Cognitive Psychology*, **30**, 111–153.

Younger, B.A. (1985). The segregation of items into categories by ten-month-old infants. *Child Development*, **56**, 1574–1583.

Younger, B.A. (1990). Infants' detection of correlations among feature categories. *Child Development*, **61**, 614–620.

Younger, B.A., & Gotlieb, S. (1988). Development of categorization skills: Changes in the nature or structure of infant form categories? *Developmental Psychology*, **24**, 611–619.

ACKNOWLEDGEMENTS

Preparation of this chapter was supported by grant HD28606 from the National Institute of Child Health and Human Development and fellowships from the Human Frontier Science Program and the British Academy. I am grateful to Mark Johnson and the Medical Research Council, Cognitive Development Unit, London, UK, for hosting me during the preparation period. I also thank Alan M. Slater for his comments on an earlier draft.

CHAPTER SIX

The development of infant causal perception

Leslie B. Cohen, Geoffrey Amsel, Melissa A. Redford, and
Marianella Casasola
University of Texas at Austin, TX, USA

INTRODUCTION

Some degree of causal understanding permeates almost everything we do
and think. Whether it is in our social relationships, political actions, legal
decisions, scientific understanding, or even our basic survival, we are almost
incapable of *not* inferring cause and effect. How does this conception of
causality begin and what would our world be like if we had no notion
of causality?

Lightman considers this latter possibility in a humorous book of essays
about physical reality called *Einstein's dreams* (1993, p. 3):

> Consider a world in which cause and effect are erratic. Sometimes the first
> precedes the second, sometimes the second the first. Or perhaps cause lies
> forever in the past while effect in the future, but future and past are entwined.
>
> In this acausal world, scientists are helpless. Their predictions become
> postdictions. Their equations become justifications, their logic, illogic. Scien-
> tists turn reckless and mutter-like gamblers who cannot stop betting.
> Scientists are buffoons, not because they are rational but because the cosmos
> is irrational. Or perhaps it is not because the cosmos is irrational but because
> they are rational. Who can say which, in an acausal world?

Is this the world of the infant or does the infant come predisposed to
perceive or understand simple causal relationships?[1] In this chapter we
attempt to answer this question. For the past several years a few infant

laboratories, including our own, have been exploring infants' reactions to one type of causal event, a situation in which one inanimate object moves across a screen until it hits a second inanimate object that then moves the remaining way across the screen. This relatively simple and prototypic example of physical causality, referred to by Michotte (1963) as a "direct launching", is uniformly perceived by adults to be causal. By comparing the reactions of infants of different ages to direct launchings versus other similar events, we, and others, have been exploring the origin and development of infants' perception of causality.

Much of that evidence will be covered in this chapter. But the chapter is intended to be more than just a summary of our research and the research of others. We shall also mention a number of different theoretical views about the origins of infants' causal perception. Some of these views should be considered more philosophical than psychological and may be primarily of historical relevance. Other more contemporary views, a modular approach and an information-processing approach, are more directly related to current psychological and developmental issues. When possible, we will attempt to evaluate these views based on how consistent each view is with the available evidence.

We shall pay particular attention to modular explanations. To some of those with nativist leanings, evidence that young infants can respond to simple events on the basis of causality seems sufficient to demonstrate the existence of an organised, self-contained perceptual module for causality. In part because of inconsistencies in use of the term "module" (Carey, 1995), it may be impossible either to prove or disprove such a position. But certainly any explanation of infant causal perception should require more than just the demonstration that at some age infants can respond in terms of the causality of an event. The nativist-modular position, especially when taken to its extreme, reduces to a patently circular form of argument. Throughout this chapter, our central thesis will be that this type of modular account of causality perception is premature and actually contrary to the experimental evidence as a whole. It is our position that, regardless of one's overarching philosophical position, causality theories, to be useful, must be amenable to falsification, and relevant experiments must be amenable to replication.

Our evaluation of the evidence indicates that the nativistic concept of causality perception is problematic at best, and probably counter-productive. First, we have found that there appear to be developmental precursors to the perception of causality. By around 6 months of age some evidence of causal perception exists. Younger infants, those under $5\frac{1}{2}$ months of age, do not respond to causal events in the same way as those over 6 months of age. Instead, they appear to respond on the basis of simpler, perceptual characteristics of the event. Yet these perceptual characteristics may become ingredients in infants' later perception of causality. Second, we have discovered two quite different and compelling examples of older infants, at 10 to 12 months of age, who, under one set of circumstances, do respond in terms of causality, but under other very similar circumstances respond in terms of simpler perceptual differences rather than causality. According to our understanding of a modular approach, the infants should be responding the same way under both sets of circumstances. Finally, additional evidence from infants between 10 and 14 months of age demonstrates a close link between the perception of causality and certain aspects of language comprehension and semantics. Although this link between perception (or perhaps cognition) and language is not precluded by the notion of a causal module, it certainly does not receive sufficient emphasis by an approach that assumes the perception of causality is an autonomous, self-contained entity.

A WORKING DEFINITION OF CAUSALITY

As already indicated, the experiments we shall be discussing in this chapter typically employ stimulus events in which one inanimate object either collides with a second inanimate object, at which point the first object stops and the latter object moves (a direct launching event), or a similar event, but one in which a spatial gap or temporal delay is inserted at the point of object contact. For adults it is clear, at least, that the first event promotes the "illusion of causality" (Michotte, 1963), whereas the gap and delay events are both perceived as not being causal. These prototypical events trace their origins at least as far back as Hume (1777/1993), who offered the example of one billiard ball striking another as the simplest example of a sequence of events giving rise to the inference of "causation". In the next section, we discuss Hume's philosophy of causality in more detail, but for now the point is simply that when we talk about infants' perception of causality in this chapter, we are talking about their tendency, at least at some point in development, to distinguish between or to organise these sorts of stimulus events on the basis of causality, rather than on some other basis. Thus, for our purposes, an infant who treats the gap event and the delay event as more or less the same, but who treats the direct launching event as quite different from either the gap event or the delay event, is responding on the basis of causality.

HISTORICAL VIEWS AND DISTINCTIONS

More than any other investigator, Leslie (1984, 1986) has emphasised the similarity between infants' perception of simple causal events and adults' perception of those same events as reported by Michotte (1963). In addition to establishing a simple working definition of causality, it is essential that, for the most part, we limit our discussion conceptually to what Leslie referred to as "mechanical causality" (Leslie, 1995) and Piaget (1954) referred to as "physical causality". The limitation is crucial because, as discussed later, a distinct body of psychological literature and philosophical discourse has grown up around two distinct types of cause and effect relationships. Although the literature on this subject is vast, we will limit most of our discussion in this section to Hume and Piaget, the two major figures against whom Leslie seems to direct most of his criticism.

The mechanical causality referred to by Leslie is the sort of causality that pertains to the relation between two or more objects external to the observer. Hume's billiard ball collision is perhaps the best example. A distinct, but perhaps not totally separable, type of causality pertains to the relation between the observer as agent and other objects as recipients of action from the observer. Perhaps the best examples of this type come from Piaget, who stressed the young child's interactions with his environment, and his or her growing awareness of "psychological causality", i.e. the notion that the child is volitionally bringing about consequences in an external world.

The notion of causality as an inductive inference, derived originally from our own sense of power over our own limbs and organs, can be seen explicitly in Piaget (1954), who distinguished among various stages of causal understanding. The earliest stage is characterised by a combination of what Piaget called causal efficacy and phenomenological causality. At this stage the infant has no understanding of the concept of object or of self, and cannot have any meaningful understanding of psychological or physical causality. Even in the next stage of development of causal understanding, in which, Piaget proposed, the infant begins to have some dim sense of his power over his world, Piaget was emphatic that the child still has no understanding about the true nature of this power. The infant merely has some vague "magical" sense of his power to bring about pleasurable results. Later in development, however, as the infant learns to distinguish between himself and his environment, and to understand about the permanence of objects, the infant begins to differentiate between different sorts of cause and effect relationships. Finally, in the second year the infant comes to understand as distinct concepts psychological or internal causality, or knowledge about power over one's actions, and physical or external causality, or knowledge about the physical relationships between external objects.

Like Piaget, Leslie (1995) also made a distinction between mechanical (physical) and actional (psychological) properties of causality. Unlike Piaget, however, Leslie (1995) assumed that mechanical and actional causality are based on different mechanisms, a theory of body, ToBY (based on the notion of force) and a theory of mind mechanism, ToMM. Furthermore, he assumed that both ToBY and ToMM serve as bases for development rather than being products of development. These theories seem to be more descriptive than explanatory, with little or no indication from Leslie about how they might arise in the first place.

More than two centuries ago, in *An enquiry concerning human understanding* (1777/1993), Hume wrestled with the meaning of causality and where it originates. Indeed, he stated at the outset: "There are no ideas, which occur in metaphysics, more obscure and uncertain than those of *power, force, energy,* or *necessary connexion*..." (p. 40, emphasis in original). In the course of his analysis of causality, Hume entertained and rejected several arguments to the effect that we need not have repeated experience with physical objects in order to derive the notion of cause and effect in the external world. One of the arguments Hume rejected was that the idea of physical causality could be derived logically as an a priori truth by reasoning about the power we have to move our own bodies. Piaget later adopted the position that knowledge of causality in both the physical and psychological domains is derived from our prior experience of power over our own bodies. From Hume's philosophical perspective, however, there was no fundamental difference between the origin of psychological and physical causality. The power of a causal agent over a causal recipient in both cases was, for Hume, "unknown and inconceivable" (p. 44). The idea of power, or a "necessary connexion among events arises from a number of similar instances, which occur, of the constant conjunction of these events; nor can the idea ever be suggested by any one of these instances, surveyed in all possible lights and positions. ... [A]fter a repetition of similar instances, the mind is carried by habit, upon the appearance of one event, to expect its usual attendant" (p. 50). Thus, for Hume, the idea of cause and effect, in both its psychological and physical manifestations, was based on experience. It was not an innate predisposition of the mind.

Whether one agrees or disagrees with the emphasis Hume placed on repeated experience, the significance of the distinction between physical and psychological causality remains controversial. This chapter is not an attempt to resolve that controversy. We shall restrict our discussion primarily to issues related to the development of physical causality, while at the same time being fully aware that Leslie's recent views do include aspects of causality beyond physical causality, and that Piaget may well have been prescient in speculating that awareness of physical causality may be dependent on the earlier development of a more self-centred version of the phenomenon.

But returning to the earlier comment that Hume's and Piaget's writings on causality take the brunt of the criticism from Leslie and others, what exactly do modern-day modular theorists find objectionable about the basic tenet, expressed in different ways by both Hume and Piaget, that an understanding of causality develops over time? Leslie argued that, "Hume was wrong to conclude that our idea of causal relation must therefore be based on statistical association" (Leslie, 1995), or, in other words, learned over time. Yet in earlier writings Leslie was not just amenable, but emphatic about a distinction between the operation of a causal module in infancy, and an understanding of causality later in development (Leslie, 1988). He went so far as to call the output of the proposed causality module COSE, in order to make it clear that its output was not the same as an understanding of the concept of causality. In more recent writings, Leslie (1995) says that Hume was wrong about inference because infants do not need to learn about basic cause and effect. They come equipped with a "submodule" whose job it is to detect mechanical interactions in which force is transmitted (Leslie, 1995). Has Leslie backed away from his earlier distinction between COSE and an understanding of causality? Is he now assuming that an understanding as well as a perception of causality is part of some innate module?

Putting aside the issue of a distinction between COSE and cause, Leslie's idea of a causal module is borrowed explicitly from Marr (1982), who urged researchers in vision to adopt the computer science concept of a module in order to break down the dauntingly complex study of vision into more tractable pieces. Marr argued that if one can identify a process within vision, such as stereopsis, that appears to be relatively autonomous, hard-wired, and impervious to the influence of general knowledge, then it makes sense to approach the study of stereopsis as a separate problem. Marr was willing to call a process within vision a module only after experiments showed convincingly that it truly met these independence requirements. Marr also made it very clear that calling something such as stereopsis a module was merely the first step in attempting to understand the purpose and function of stereopsis: calling stereopsis a module was not a substitute for attempting to understand how stereopsis works. In keeping with Marr's rather strong admonitions in this regard, we respectfully question whether Leslie's proposal for a causality "module" is premature, and whether it comports with Marr's belief that calling something a module merely narrows the hypothesis space for formulating potential explanations.[2] We agree wholeheartedly with Marr's general proposition that processes typically must be isolated before they can be studied successfully, but we disagree with Leslie if he is arguing that calling something a causal module tells us very much about how the perception of causality works.

As a consequence of causality perception being characterised as the result of an innate module, there is no room in Leslie's formulation for causality perception to develop in stages. Accordingly, if anything relevant to causality develops, it must be causal *understanding* rather than causal *perception*. Is Leslie placing causal perception and causal understanding in separate compartments, and arguing that anything that changes after birth must be related to causal understanding? If so, then would a developmental progression in infants' treatment of causal and noncausal events count as evidence against a module, or just as evidence for the development of causal understanding?

The remainder of this chapter is about what infants actually do when confronted with the sorts of events described earlier in the working definition of causality. In the course of discussing these experiments, we hope to show that the arguments between Leslie, on the one hand, and Hume or Piaget, on the other, are not just quibbles over words. Instead, they are getting at significant questions about the relevance of development. As we shall show, the evidence strongly suggests that whether one calls it causal perception or an understanding of physical causality, infants' reactions to causal and noncausal events are not static over age; they change dramatically during the first year of life and beyond.

EVIDENCE FROM OCCLUDED EVENTS

As already discussed, in his most recent writings Leslie (1995) advances the strong view that causality is not a concept whose contours and complexities develop; on the contrary, it is a core cognitive property that must be in place at the outset in order for development to proceed. Causality, according to Leslie and other nativists, therefore is not something to study developmentally: it is a *non sequitur* to study the development of something that does not change. One simply needs to confirm its presence in young infants to verify that it is available as a building block for further development. In keeping with this position, experiments by Ball, Leslie, and others have attempted to demonstrate the presence of causality in infants during the first year of life.

In an unpublished experiment, which may have been the first to advance explicitly the notion of an innate causal module operating in infancy, Ball (1973) presented infants across a wide age range (9 to 122 weeks) with a three-dimensional stimulus display in which a red block moved horizontally from right to left and passed behind an occluding screen. Half-exposed at the left edge of the screen, a white block was poised in the path of the red block. At the moment that the red block reached the right edge of the white block behind the screen, the white block was put into motion in a manner suggesting, at least to an adult observer, that the red block had caused the white block to move. Subjects were shown this "screen event" ten times. After being familiarised with the event, half of the subjects were placed in the contact condition. They were shown 10 more presentations of the same sequence, from an adult perspective, but with the screen absent throughout. In other words, they were shown the red block actually contacting the white block, and then the white block moving to the left in response to this contact. The other half of the subjects, who were assigned to the noncontact condition, were shown the red block stopping 3cm short of the white block; then, after a 100msec delay, the white block nevertheless moved off to the left in the identical manner as in the contact condition.

There are numerous problems with the Ball experiment, including an extremely small sample size and a wide range of subject ages, a failure to produce habituation, an improper control group, and numerous marginal or statistically insignificant results that were overinterpreted.[3] Nevertheless, Ball's central finding was that infants in the noncontact condition appeared to show an increase in looking time compared to their performance during the familiarisation trials, whereas in the contact condition, no such increase was apparent. Ball interpreted this pattern of results as support for the notion that infants come into the world with at least some limited form of causal perception. His argument was that subjects were treating the noncontact event as novel, and therefore looking at it longer than at the familiarisation event, because the familiarisation event was perceived as causal, whereas the noncontact event was not. Ironically, Ball also suggested that the older subjects in his experiment appeared to be showing *less* of a tendency to look longer in the noncontact condition. He offered no explanation for why this might be so, and one wonders how such a result, if replicable, could be squared with Ball's conclusion that the younger infants were perceiving the various events in the adult-like way proposed by Michotte (1963), i.e. in terms of some automatic system that perceives causality.

Three recent studies raise additional questions about Ball's conclusions. In one report, Van de Walle, Woodward, and Phillips (1994) claim to have replicated Ball's results with 6-month-old infants. They tested a reasonable number of subjects and did make certain that habituation had occurred prior to the test phase, both improvements over the original Ball study. They also included a control group that was habituated to two stationary blocks, one on either side of the occluder. Unfortunately, their only significant effect seems to be in this control group, and one could reach the reasonable conclusion from their data that infants who had been habituated to objects that are initially separated from one another, will look longer at a test event when the objects touch one another.

Oakes (1992) also reported an attempt to replicate Ball's study, in this case with 10-month-old infants. She not only habituated one group of infants to a causal, direct launching event as Van de Walle et al. (1994) had done; she also habituated a second group to a delayed launching event, and a third group to a no collision event. As we have mentioned earlier, these latter two events are considered to be noncausal by adults. As an occluder was used, the defining moment for each type of event was hidden. The only perceptible difference between the events was the time interval between the disappearance of the first ball behind the occluder and the subsequent appearance of the second ball from the occluder. These times were 0.75sec for the direct launching event, 0.0sec for the no collision event, and 1.5sec for the delayed launching event. Each group was then tested with all three types of events, for the first time shown in full view, without the occluder, as Ball had done. Oakes found that unlike adult subjects, who had no trouble distinguishing occluded causal from occluded noncausal events, all three groups of infants treated their occluded habituation events as causal. All three looked longer at both noncausal events in the test than at the causal event. Thus, although the 10-month-old infants seemed to be responding on the basis of the causality, they were overgeneralising that causality to events that were not actually causal, and were certainly not responding in the same way as adults.

Finally, Lucksinger, Cohen, and Madole (1992) also presented infants with causal and noncausal events behind an occluder. Their procedure closely followed that of Baillargeon (1986). In the portion of the experiment most relevant to the present discussion, 6- and 10-month-old infants were habituated to a car that ran across a track, went behind one side of an occluder, and then reappeared at the other side of the occluder. During test trials, a second, distinctly *different* car was placed either on the track or behind the track, and then this part of the event was obscured by the occluder. As in the habituation phase, the first car traveled across the track and went behind the occluder, but now the second car reappeared from the other side. This event would be possible – a causal event, in fact – if the second car had been placed *on* the track, but it would be impossible, or at least improbable, and non-causal if the second car had been placed *behind* the track.

Based on Baillargeon's previous work, the prediction was that if infants were inferring the causality of the event (i.e. that the first car should have hit and pushed the second car) then they would look longer at the impossible event than at the possible event. Ten-month-olds performed as predicted, but 6-month-olds looked equally long at the two events. As in the previously mentioned studies, this experiment examined infants' ability to infer causality from a launching event in which the critical contact between objects was obscured by an occluder. Reviewing all of these studies in which an occluder was used to investigate infants' reactions to causality, the inevitable conclusion is that although clear evidence of causal perception or understanding can be found at 10 months of age, the evidence is inconsistent, at best, at younger ages.[4]

Such a conclusion would be compatible with a Piagetian point of view, because by 10 months of age, infants should be able to infer an object's existence even when it is hidden behind an occluder. That inference must be a necessary ingredient in any subsequent inference about a causal or noncausal relationship between two hidden objects. Perhaps more to the point of the present discussion, the conclusion would also be compatible with a "causal module" view such as the one proposed by Leslie (1986). In order for Leslie's automatic, perceptual module to be activated, it would need to receive the appropriate input. That input, namely the spatial contiguity and temporal continuity that occurs when the first object collides with the second object, is precisely what is obscured by the occluder. In fact, it is not apparent why occlusion should be employed in experiments examining causal perception. It would appear that simpler, more direct evidence of infants' causal perception can be obtained by allowing infants to see the collision, or lack of collision, between the two objects.

EVIDENCE FROM VISIBLE EVENTS

Several experiments have now been reported in which the entire events shown to infants were visible. In general, these experiments compared infants' responding to a causal event and one or more non-causal events. Figure 6.1 illustrates the four types of events used in these causal perception studies: a *direct launching event*, in which one object collides with a second object that then moves immediately following the collision; a *delayed launching* event, in which a short time interval (e.g. 1sec) elapses before the second object begins to move; a *no collision* event, in which the first object never reaches the second object and a spatial gap (e.g. 5cm) exists when the second object begins to move; and a *no collision plus delay* event, in which both the gap and the delay are present.

The logic behind most of these studies was to pit responding on the basis of causality against responding at a lower, perceptual level. The upper portion of Fig. 6.2 represents schematically the psychological space if infants are responding to these events solely in terms of their independent spatial and temporal characteristics. Some might believe that the appropriate measure of psychological distance would be a city block metric. Others might argue for a Euclidean distance approach. According to a city block metric, the difference between the delayed launching and the no collision would be obtained by summing lines $a + b$ in the upper portion of the figure, whereas the difference between the delayed launching and the direct launching would be only a. On the other hand, according to a Euclidean distance approach, the difference between the delayed launching and no collision would be c, but it would still be only a between the delayed launching and the direct launching. Thus, using

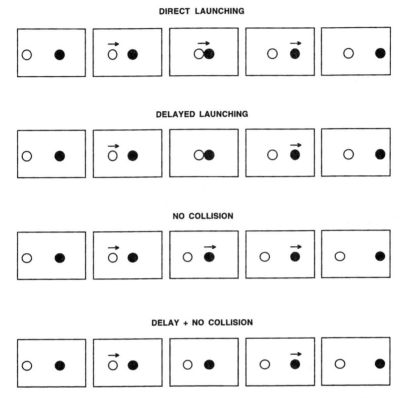

FIG. 6.1. Schematic examples of causal and noncausal events, adapted from Leslie and Keeble (1987). The open circle represents a green ball, the closed circle a red ball.

either a city block metric or a Euclidean distance approach, and assuming that *a* and *b* are greater than zero, the independent features view would predict that a delayed launching event would be a greater psychological distance and should differ more from a no collision event (from which it differs both spatially and temporally) than from a direct launching event (from which it differs only temporally).

In contrast, the lower portion of Fig. 6.2 represents the case psychologically if infants are responding to these events solely on the basis of causality. The direct launching would be the only causal event. As a result, it should be perceived as qualitatively different from the other three noncausal events. On the other hand, these other three events should be perceived as equivalent. Two objects move sequentially in each event, but the objects are moving independently; in none of the events is the first object causing the movement of the second object.

In a series of experiments, Leslie (1984) tested 6½-month-old infants on their ability to discriminate the events shown in Fig. 6.2. His results clearly showed evidence of responding on the basis of causality, but that was not the whole story. He also found evidence of responding on the basis of independent features. These mixed results led Leslie to propose a one-dimensional "spatiotemporal continuity gradient" incorporating both types of responding. Presumably, Leslie's infants were responding in terms of this gradient rather than solely in terms of causality. However, such a mixed bag of responding raises a number of questions about the modularity of causal perception. For example, if infants' responding is based (in part) on a causal module, why is it also based (in part) on an incompatible perceptual system in which the spatial and temporal features are independent? If, as Leslie (1995) proposes, this causal module (or perhaps this "spatiotemporal continuity gradient") is a core property that can serve as the basis for later development, but is not the product of previous

INDEPENDENT FEATURES MODEL

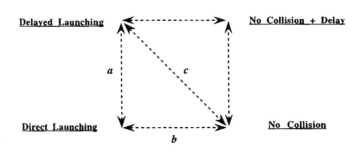

CAUSALITY MODEL

FIG. 6.2. Two models of infant perception of causal events: The Independent Features Model assumes infants are responding solely on the basis of spatial and temporal characteristics of the events. The Causality Model assumes those features are integrated into the perception of causality. (Adapted from Oakes & Cohen, 1994.)

development, then would one expect little if any developmental change in the gradient, or only in the modular part of the gradient? In short, it is unclear what, if any, predictions would flow from Leslie's model about developmental changes in infants' responses to simple causal events.

In contrast, Cohen (1994, 1998) and Oakes and Cohen (1994) have argued on the basis of their information processing view that infants' perception of independent spatial and temporal features is a developmental precursor to later causal perception. According to this view, one should find developmentally a decrease in responding in terms of independent features and an increase in responding in terms of causality. In fact, Oakes and Cohen (1994) also argued that the two types of responding found by Leslie (1984) in his $6\frac{1}{2}$-month-old infants, which Leslie assumed to be part of the same "spatiotemporal continuity gradient", may actually have resulted from summing over two types of infants: less advanced infants, who were still perceiving the events in terms of independent features, and more advanced infants, who had made the transition to causal perception.

Two recent studies lend support to this information-processing view. In one experiment reported by Oakes (1994), 7-month-old infants (approximately two weeks older than those Leslie had tested) were presented with simple events involving moving red and blue balls. Infants were habituated to either a causal direct launching, a noncausal delayed launching, or a noncausal no collision event. The infants were then tested on all three events. Oakes found significant evidence of responding on the basis of causality, but no significant evidence for responding on the basis of independent features.

In a very recent study conducted in our laboratory, Cohen and Amsel (1997), the Oakes procedure was used once again, this time with $6\frac{1}{4}$-month-old infants – infants just 1 to 2 weeks younger than Leslie's. The events involved moving red and green circles. The results, shown in Fig. 6.3, closely replicated those of Leslie. At this age, just as in Leslie's experiment, there was significant evidence not only of responding in terms of causality, but also in terms of the independent features.

Figure 6.3 presents the test data for infants habituated to the causal (direct launching), delay (delayed launching), and gap (no collision) events. As would be expected from either a causal or independent features view, infants habituated to the causal event dishabituated to both delay and gap events in the test. Infants habituated to delay or gap events dishabituated more to the causal event than to the other noncasual event (gap event or delay event, respectively). This pattern is precisely what would be predicted by a causal perception view. If infants are responding in terms of causality, they should dishabituate more when the meaning of the event changes from noncausal to causal, than when it remains noncausal.

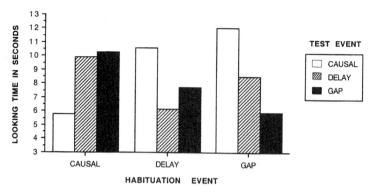

FIG. 6.3.   Responses of 6¼-month-old infants in the test to direct launching (CAUSAL), delayed launching (DELAY), and no collision (GAP) events. All events used simple red and green circles as objects.

However, clear evidence was also found for responding in terms of independent features. When infants who were habituated to one noncausal event (delay or gap) were tested on the other noncausal event (gap or delay) they also dishabituated significantly. Thus, the experiment replicated Leslie (1984) by providing reliable evidence of responding in terms of independent features as well as causality.

If one compares all three experiments, Cohen and Amsel at 6¼ months, Leslie at 6½ months, and Oakes at 7 months, a developmental trend appears showing evidence of causal perception at all three ages, but also showing a systematic decrease in independent feature perception from 6 to 7 months of age. This is just the trend predicted by the information-processing view.

We also had the opportunity to examine individual infants' performance in the Cohen and Amsel (1997) experiment. You will recall that Oakes and Cohen (1994) had argued that Leslie's results may have resulted from two subgroups of infants, one subgroup responding in terms of causality, and the other subgroup responding to independent features. In fact, Oakes and Cohen had shown that the two subgroup view predicted Leslie's results as well as his continuity gradient view. Accordingly, we examined the individual data for the 24 infants in Cohen and Amsel's (1997) study who had been habituated to a noncausal event. We were looking to see if these infants uniformly looked longer at the causal event than at the novel noncausal event (as predicted by the continuity gradient) or if some infants looked longer at the novel noncausal event than at the causal event (as predicted by the independent features view). Ten of the 24 infants looked at least 2sec longer at the causal test event than at the other noncausal test event, but 6 of the infants looked at least 2sec longer at the other noncausal event than at the causal event. Thus, some tentative evidence, at least, has been found for the existence of two subgroups rather than for one group responding to some overall "spatiotemporal continuity gradient".

What obviously is needed to resolve the developmental issue is evidence from yet younger infants. Will these infants respond even more in terms of independent spatial and temporal features, or perhaps in terms of even simpler perceptual characteristics? And what will happen to their perception of causality? Will it continue to be evident at younger ages, or will it be preceded by simpler, noncausal modes of responding?

EVIDENCE FROM YOUNGER INFANTS

The causality experiments recently completed in our laboratory (Cohen and Amsel, 1997) tested infants not only at $6\frac{1}{4}$ months – about the same age as those tested by Leslie and Keeble (1987) – but also at 4 months and $5\frac{1}{2}$ months. Our results, which are shown in Fig. 6.4, challenge Leslie's position that causality perception is largely innate and hard-wired. Instead, the data indicate a developmental progression involving at least two distinct modes of processing prior to anything resembling processing in terms of causality. Ironically, it is the more primitive of these two modes that may be getting misconstrued as a form of built-in causality perception. Infants were presented with the same events $6\frac{1}{4}$-month-olds had seen. Separate groups were habituated to a direct launching, or a delayed launching, or a no collision (gap) event. They were all then tested on all three events. The 4-month-old subjects displayed a pattern of posthabituation looking times that was dramatically different from the $6\frac{1}{4}$-month pattern described earlier. The key feature of looking behaviour at 4 months, which is apparent from the white bars in the top graph of Fig. 6.4, is that regardless of whether infants were habituated to the causal event or one of the noncausal events, they looked longer at the causal event during the test phase. Based on the logic of habituation, if infants are perceiving the events in terms of causality, then infants habituated to the causal event should be exhibiting exactly the opposite pattern of looking times. They should remain habituated to the causal test event, but dishabituate to either of the noncausal events. It is not clear why infants at 4 months showed such persistence in preferring to look at the causal event sequence, regardless of habituation. Lecuyer & Bourcier (1994) has reported the same overall preference for the causal event at 4 months when the objects were more realistic and complex than the red and green circles we had used.

One possible explanation for this result is that the causal event was preferred at 4 months of age, not because of any conceptual distinction

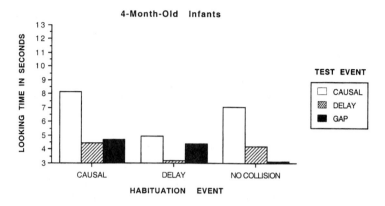

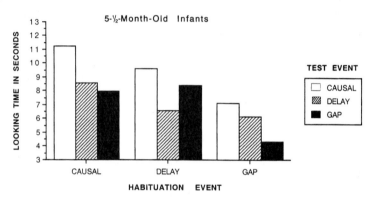

FIG. 6.4.   Responses of 4- and 5½-month-old infants in the test to direct launching (CAUSAL), delayed launching (DELAY), and no collision (GAP) events. All events used simple red and green circles as objects.

between it and the noncausal sequences, but simply because infants at this age were entrained by the uninterrupted, smooth movement of the two balls in the causal event. An analysis of the first four habituation trials shows that even prior to habituation, infants looked significantly longer at the causal event than at either of the two noncausal events. Obviously, much more work would have to be done to support a formal entrainment hypothesis, but it is offered here merely as one possible, albeit speculative, explanation for the tendency of infants at 4 months to prefer the "causal" event regardless of any habituation-induced novelty preference.

At 5½ months, again contrary to what Leslie and Keeble (1987) would have predicted, there still was no causality effect. Indeed, infants habituated to the causal event still looked longer at the causal test event than at either of the noncausal test events. Again, this result is exactly the opposite of what a proponent of innate modularity would predict in an habituation experiment, and exactly the opposite of the result we obtained in the identical experiment at $6\frac{1}{4}$ months. Thus, even at $5\frac{1}{2}$ months, infants still seem to be processing the causal event in terms of something other than causality.

The other crucial development at $5\frac{1}{2}$ months can be seen clearly in the bottom graph of Fig. 6.4. Infants habituated to either the delay or the gap event dishabituated significantly to the other noncausal event, i.e. to whichever noncausal event they were not exposed to during habituation. This effect is not hard to interpret if the events are considered in terms of their independent spatial and temporal features, instead of in terms of causality. Infants habituated to the gap event, for example, are seeing a spatial gap and continuous motion during habituation. In the delayed test event, they see two changes: no spatial gap, and discontinuous motion, whereas in the causal event, they see only one change: no spatial gap. Thus, the dishabituation the $5\frac{1}{2}$-month olds exhibited to the other noncausal event would be predicted by an independent features view. In fact, although infants at $6\frac{1}{4}$ months were beginning to show a pattern of results for the first time suggesting sensitivity to causality, it will be recalled that even these older infants were still showing a pattern of test responses indicating some sensitivity to the independent spatial and temporal features of the stimulus events. As indicated in Fig. 6.3, infants at $6\frac{1}{4}$ months, who were habituated to one of the noncausal events, still showed significant dishabituation to the other noncausal event.

Responding primarily in terms of something as simple as entrainment at one age, more in terms of spatial and temporal features at a later age, and then more in terms of causality at a still later age is problematic from an innate modularity perspective, but it makes perfect sense from a more traditional developmental perspective. Furthermore, the data support the developmental progression. Not only are the three distinct modes of processing visible in the three age groups studied in our laboratory, but remnants of the prior, simpler modes of processing are visible in the later age groups as well. In the data from $5\frac{1}{2}$-month-olds, it is clear that superimposed on the processing of independent attributes is a remnant of something like entrainment to the causal event. Similarly, at $6\frac{1}{4}$ months, evidence for this entrainment has disappeared, but superimposed on what appears to be causal processing is a remnant of processing based on independent features. Finally, at 7 months of age, causal processing remains, but processing based on independent features has decreased or disappeared. This simultaneous waxing and waning of more and less advanced forms of processing, respectively, is the hallmark of a more constructivist, information-processing perspective on development.

Furthermore, the evidence also seems consistent with, at least, some aspects of Michotte's (1963) view of causal perception in adults. For Michotte, a direct launching presents the perceptual system with a conflict. Continuity of motion is perceived but so are two distinct events, movement by the first object and movement by the second object. Michotte argued that the perceptual system resolves this conflict by perceiving the direct launching as causal. We are not certain whether Michotte's explanation of causal perception is totally correct. But assuming for the moment that it is, our results with 4-month-olds indicate their sensitivity to continuity of motion, and our results with $5\frac{1}{2}$-month-olds indicate their sensitivity to distinct events with different moving objects. Thus, the data supporting our information processing view of causality development are consistent with Michotte's conception of causality perception in adults. Although Michotte did not emphasise developmental mechanisms, and may have even been a nativist (see Ball, 1973), he did assume that the perception of causal events required both the perception of continuity of motion and the perception of two distinct moving objects. We are simply proposing that the perceptions of these two aspects of an event develop independently at first, and then combine at some later age to form the perception of causality.

EVIDENCE FROM OLDER INFANTS

Research presented thus far indicates a clear, three-step developmental progression in infants' perception of causality. It also indicates that infants can achieve causal perception of simple launching events by 6 or 7 months of age. Although evidence of developmental precursors to causal perception tends to undermine certain innatist, modular views such as those of Ball (1973), Leslie (1986), or Fodor (1983), it does not necessarily undermine all modular views. Karmiloff-Smith (1992), for example, draws a reasonable distinction between the notion of "pre-specified modules" and the process of "modularisation", by which she means that self-contained, encapsulated modules may be the products of development rather than be present full-blown at the outset. We are generally sympathetic towards Karmiloff-Smith's approach, and the evidence we have presented so far could be considered consistent with it. In fact, if we were to end the chapter at this point, it would be tempting to conclude that we had found evidence for the "modularisation" of infant causal perception at 7 months of age.

But modularisation implies encapsulation of whatever is being modularised. Just because, under some circumstances, 6- or 7-month-olds can respond on the basis of causality, it does not necessarily mean that 6- or 7-month-olds have developed, and are using, a self-contained, encapsulated module to perceive that causality. Presumably being self-contained, or encapsulated, refers to the fact that the module should be sensitive to certain relevant information, but impervious to irrelevant background information. But what should count as relevant and irrelevant information for a causal module? We have already noted that, at least according to Michotte, the relevant information should be the spatial and temporal relations between two objects that produce the perception of continuous movement, on the one hand, and the perception of two moving objects on the other. This conflicting information should be sufficient to trigger this causal module and produce the automatic perception of causality.

What should count as an example of irrelevant information? Michotte (1963) provides some guidance here as well. In his discussion of the direct launching event he says, "From all this we may conclude *that the causal impression which appears in the Launching Effect is independent in principle* (if we disregard the possibility of gradual differences) *of the phenomenal aspect of the objects*" (p. 85, italics included in original article). In other words, according to Michotte, in a simple launching event the nature of the objects should be irrelevant to the perception of causality.

Almost without exception, the research we have reviewed thus far has shown infants events that included only uniform, extremely simple objects such as red and green blocks or red and blue circles. Would the same results obtain if, instead, more realistic, complex objects were used in these events? We believe modularists ought to predict that the type of object should not make any difference. As long as movement of the objects produced the appropriate spatial and temporal information, infants should perceive the event as causal. Thus, even with complex objects, the module should trigger the perception of causality in 6- or 7-month-old infants.

In contrast, the information-processing view proposed by Oakes and Cohen (1994) would predict that the complexity of the objects could make quite a difference. According to this view, before infants can perceive a causal relationship between any two objects, they must discern that the moving stimuli being presented in the event are, in fact, distinctly different objects. With simple objects, such as green and blue blocks, even 6- or 7-month-old infants should have little difficulty making this distinction. But with more complex or realistic objects, integration of each of the objects' structural features into unified percepts of particular objects should be quite difficult for 6- or 7-month-olds. Thus, even though infants may be capable of perceiving a causal relationship between two simple objects at a relatively young age, they should be considerably older before they can perceive the same type of causal relationship between two complex objects.

As we have noted, in this chapter we have concentrated on studies using simple objects, but several additional studies have examined infant causal perception when the events included more complex objects. In general, the evidence from these studies is unambiguous. Infants have to be quite a bit older than 6 or 7 months of age before they can perceive the causality of these events. In one study that already has been mentioned, Lucksinger et al. (1992) found, using an occluded object task with drawings of a toy car and a toy truck, that 6-month-olds did not respond on the basis of causality, but 10-month-olds did. Of course, from the present point of view, a comparison of the Lucksinger results with those of others, such as Leslie's (1984) or Cohen and Amsel's (1997), that reported 6-month-olds could respond to visible events on the basis of causality, confounds the complexity level of the objects with the presence versus absence of occlusion. It would be more appropriate to compare two studies that differed from one another only in object complexity.

A study reported by Oakes and Cohen (1990) meets that criterion. They examined 6- and 10-month-old infants, using exactly the same design as Cohen and Amsel (1997), but with objects that were realistic toy vehicles. Examples of these type of vehicles are shown in Fig. 6.5A. Infants were habituated to a direct launching, a delayed launching, or a no collision event, and then tested on all three types of events. Clear evidence of causal perception was found at 10 months, but no evidence at all of causal perception was found at 6 months. Oakes and Cohen (1990) also showed that the 6-month-olds were not totally overwhelmed by the sight of realistic toys. The 6-month-olds did dishabituate when novel toys replaced the familiar toys. Apparently, at that age, they just did not notice the critical spatial or temporal differences between the causal and noncausal events.

The failure of 6-month-olds to respond in terms of causality when realistic objects are used could be considered an embarrassment to a modular view, but it certainly should not be considered a fatal flaw of that view. One might simply counter that although the toys may not have overwhelmed the infants completely, they may well have distracted the infants from other aspects of the events. One might even argue that the 6-month-olds were attending to certain interesting attributes of these toys, and not even processing them as unified and distinct objects. Although this latter argument might well be the explanation for the failure of the 6-month-olds, accepting it would be tantamount to accepting the information-processing view. A more definitive test of the modular view will be described.

As Leslie (1995) has noted, a more critical test would be to find an instance in which infants show sensitivity to the spatial and temporal characteristics of the event, but not to the causality of the event. We have already presented such evidence with 5½-month-old infants; however, by

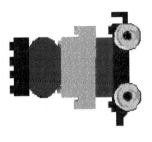

FIG. 6.5.   Types of complex objects used in causal perception studies. The upper portion of the figure provides examples of actual toys. The lower portion of the figure provides examples of experimenter-designed Lego toys.

some accounts that would not be the most telling evidence, as the infants have not yet developed their causal module. A more definitive test would be to show that infants who, under some circumstances, do respond to the causality of an event, under other circumstances respond to the spatial and temporal characteristics of the event, but not to the causality.

Cohen and Oakes (1993) provided that evidence. In their first experiment, they described what was basically a replication of the Oakes and Cohen (1990) study with 10-month-old infants, but with one small change. Once again different groups of infants were habituated to a direct launching, a delayed launching, or a no collision event. However, instead of using a single toy vehicle as the agent and a second toy vehicle as the patient, as Oakes and Cohen (1990) had done, each infant saw five different pairs of vehicles during habituation. Thus, although the infants were receiving consistent spatial and temporal information, the objects producing that spatial and temporal information changed from trial to trial. Fig. 6.6 shows, for comparison purposes, the test data from the original Oakes and Cohen (1990) study and below it the test data from this Cohen and Oakes (1993) multiple-object study. As one can see from the figure, the main difference between the two studies occurred with those infants who were habituated to a noncausal event. In Oakes and Cohen (1990) the infants dishabituated most to the causal event, a finding consistent with a causal perception view. In Cohen and Oakes (1993), on the other hand, the infants dishabituated most to the other noncausal event. This finding, which is consistent with an independent features view, indicates that the 10-month-old infants in the multiple-object study *were* sensitive to the spatial and temporal characteristics of the event, but nevertheless not to the causality of the event. In other words, under circumstances in which infants saw multiple objects, the requisite spatial and temporal characteristics were processed, but apparently no causal module was activated. To us, this result appears to be in direct contradiction to what would be predicted from a modular view of causal perception.

But the interpretation of Cohen and Oakes' (1993) first experiment goes beyond just demonstrating the inadequacy of a modular approach. From a more positive point of view, it also demonstrates that the specific objects involved in an event were included in the infants' percept of that event. In other words, 10-month-old infants who see a direct launching repeatedly with the same two objects, A and B, are not perceiving that somehow in the abstract, "causality is going on", or that, "this is a causal event". They are perceiving a causal event that involves objects A and B. Furthermore, Experiments 2 and 3 by Cohen and Oakes (1993) indicated the infants were actually parsing the events. They appeared to be able to group the type of action (causal or noncausal) with the particular object used as agent (A), but not with the object that served as patient (B).

The idea that infants may be doing more than perceiving causality, that they may also be distinguishing between agent and patient, is important to Leslie's (1995) theoretical position. He has argued that infants perceive or understand the concept of "agency", and that a study that demonstrates infants can distinguish between the roles of agent and patient would be the clearest evidence that the infants are actually perceiving causality. Therefore, we shall turn next to studies examining infants' ability to distinguish between agent and patient.

EVIDENCE ON THE AGENT–PATIENT DISTINCTION

Thus far, we have been discussing experiments employing one sort of logic. Infants are either exposed to one of two noncausal events or to a causal event during habituation, and then tested on all three events. Leslie (1995), however, has proposed that the most definitive test for causal perception would be to familiarise infants to events that are either causal or noncausal, and then to test their reaction when the familiarisation event is shown in reverse. He argued that if infants are sensitive to causality, then those in the causal condition should show greater dishabituation than those in the noncausal condition. This would be the prediction because reversal of a causal sequence reverses the action roles of the agent and patient, whereas in a noncausal sequence, the two objects do not have different roles, so a reversal would not create a significant change in those roles.

We disagree with Leslie that reversal experiments are necessarily a better test of causal perception than the sort of experiments we have described in the preceding sections. It certainly could be the case, for example, that infants come to appreciate the causality of an event prior to the time that they key in on the specific roles of the agent and patient. Nevertheless, Leslie's idea of reversing action roles is intriguing, and if infants do respond more to role reversals in a causal event than in a noncausal event, it almost certainly would indicate that the infants possess some degree of causal perception.

Golinkoff reported some of the earliest research on infants' reactions to action role reversals. In one experiment Golinkoff (1975), showed 14- to 24-month-old infants a man pushing a woman from left to right across the screen, (M→W). Infants subsequently watched a direction of action which entailed a role reversal, (M←W), more than just a direction of action reversal alone, (W←M). In another experiment Golinkoff and Kerr (1978) habituated 15- to 18-month-old infants either to a film of one man pushing a second man or to a film of a man pushing a chair. In both types of events the direction of action was varied from trial to trial during habituation. She found that infants dishabituated in the test when either event was reversed.

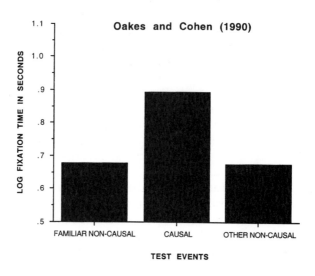

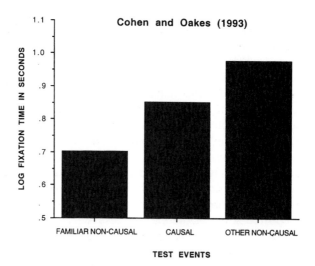

FIG. 6.6. Comparision of 10-month-old infants' performance in a standard causal perception task (Oakes & Cohen, 1990) versus a task in which the objects change from trial to trial (Cohen & Oakes, 1993). Log fixation times were used in Oakes and Cohen (1990) to normalise the data. For comparison purposes, therefore, log fixation times are also presented for Cohen and Oakes (1993).

Although both studies indicated that infants above 14 or 15 months of age notice something about the reversal of action roles, unfortunately one cannot conclude from either study that infants had a true understanding of agent–patient relationships because the studies did not include a noncausal condition in which the conceptual roles remained the same in spite of the action reversal.

Leslie and Keeble (1987) did include the required noncausal control condition. They reasoned that if young infants do, in fact, perceive causality they should respond to the reversal of a causal event more than to the reversal of a noncausal event because only in the causal event would there be a reversal of the role of agent. They habituated infants, ranging in age from 24 to 32 weeks, to a direct launching event or to a noncausal, delay event in which a 0.5sec delay occurred between time of contact of the objects and movement of the second object. As Leslie had done in earlier studies, the objects used in the events were a green and a red block. During habituation these objects moved from one side of the screen to the other (either left or right). For the critical test event the film was reversed so that the order of the objects in the events as well as the side of the screen from which the first object originated were reversed. Leslie and Keeble reasoned that in the noncausal event, a reversal would not be particularly interesting because the two blocks had not changed roles. In the causal event, however, a reversal of the film also reversed the causal roles of the red and green blocks. The agent now became the patient, and vice versa. They hypothesised, therefore, that infants in the causal group should dishabituate far more than those in the noncausal group. That is exactly what they found. Their infants showed greater dishabituation for reversal of the causal sequence than for reversal of the noncausal sequence. Thus Leslie and Keeble (1987) provide rather convincing evidence that at approximately 6½ to 7 months of age, infants do, under some conditions, notice when the agent and patient in a causal sequence are reversed. It remains to be seen whether, as Leslie (1995) argued, this result also provides evidence for an active causal module at 6½ months.

Redford and Cohen (1996) were specifically interested in the age at which infants acquire some understanding of agent and patient and what infants might perceive or understand prior to that age. As in Leslie and Keeble (1987), one group of infants was habituated to a direct launching event in which one object "pushed" another object. Unlike Leslie and Keeble, however, a second group received a no collision event, rather than a delay event, in which an 8cm spatial gap was inserted into the direct launching event. During habituation the event sometimes proceeded from left to right and other times from right to left. In the test the infants were shown both the familiar event and a novel event in which the two objects were switched. Thus, in the novel test event, the order of the objects was reversed from what had been presented in habituation, but the direction of movement was not. Also, the objects were much more complex than in Leslie and Keeble (1987). They were scanned-in colour photographs of stylised Lego toys. Examples of these toys are shown in Fig. 6.5B. Because the objects were more complex and because Oakes and Cohen (1990) had demonstrated that younger infants may be distracted to some extent by complex stimuli, the infants tested in Redford and Cohen (1996) were 10 and 14 months of age.

It was predicted that if infants had the concepts of agent and patient, they should dishabituate to the reversal of the causal event, in which one object (the agent) "pushes" another object (the patient), but not to the reversal of the noncausal, no collision event, in which the objects move independently and therefore could both be considered agents. If, on the other hand, the infants were discriminating between familiar and test events on a simpler perceptual basis, such that the first object (and/or last object) to have moved changed from habituation to test, without taking into account changes in the agent/patient action roles of objects, then they should dishabituate equally to both test events.

The results are shown separately for 10- and 14-month-olds in Fig. 6.7. The developmental shift between these two ages should be apparent. The 10-month-old infants dishabituated as much or more to a switch of objects in the noncausal, no collision condition as they did to a switch in the causal condition. This pattern of responses indicates that the 10-month-olds were processing the switch at a simpler, perceptual level, or at least not in terms of the action roles of agent and patient. The 14-month-olds, in contrast, dishabituated only to a switch in the causal, direct launching, condition. The fact that at 14 months of age the infants responded only when the switch entailed a reversal of roles suggests that by this age the infants did recognise that a causal event involves an action relationship between objects such that one object, an agent, "does" something to another object, a patient.

One may be tempted to argue that the reason 10-month-old infants in the present study responded at only a perceptual level was that they, like the 6-month-olds in Oakes and Cohen (1990), were overwhelmed by the complexity of the objects in the events. After all, the 7-month-olds in the Leslie and Keeble (1987) study appeared to respond to a role reversal when the stimuli were simple red and green blocks. However, this argument does not appear to be valid for the 10-month-old infants in the present experiment. For one thing, Oakes and Cohen (1990) also reported that by 10 months of age, infants were able to process the causality of an event that involved complex objects. For another, the 10-month-old infants in the Redford and Cohen (1996) study were paying attention to the change in the location and/or the relationship between the objects. But

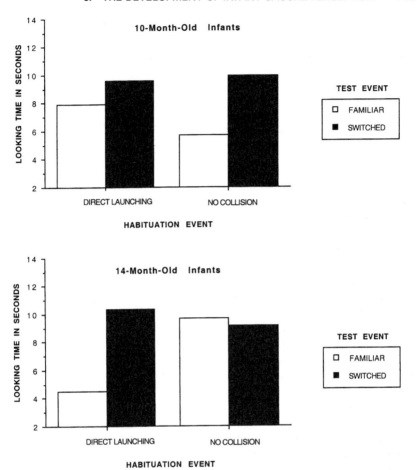

FIG. 6.7. Responses of 10- and 14-month-old infants in the test to familiar events versus events in which the first and second objects were switched.

the fact that they discriminated the switch in the order of the objects during the test events of both causal and noncausal conditions indicates that whatever aspects of the event the 10-month-olds were attending to, it was not the action roles of agent and patient.

What then does the research on infants' understanding of agents and patients reveal about infants' use of some encapsulated perceptual module for causality? The conclusion appears to be quite straightforward and quite similar to what was reported in the preceding sections of this chapter. If the objects are very simple, such as red and green blocks, then there is clear evidence that infants as young as 7 months perceive or understand the different roles of agent and patient. However, if the objects are more realistic or complex, there also is clear evidence that infants do not perceive these roles until 14 months of age. Furthermore, they fail to do so at 10 months even though they apparently have processed the requisite spatial, temporal, and object information. Thus, once again we seem to have evidence that tends to counter the notion of a perceptual module for causality.

MEETING FODOR'S CONDITIONS

Fodor (1985) asserted that three conditions must be met to provide a legitimate counter-instance to the modularity of a perceptual system. We question Fodor's tactic of putting the burden on those who would *disprove* modularity, and there may be disagreement over the necessity of all three of Fodor's conditions; nevertheless, it seems worthwhile to consider them in the present context.

The first condition is that background information should exert an influence that is exogenous from the point of view of the module. Clearly, the complexity of the objects represents just such background information. From a Michottean (1963) point of view, at least, as we noted earlier, the phenomenal nature of the objects is explicitly stated to be exogenous to the perception of causality. Nevertheless, as we have shown in this chapter, the nature of the objects appears to play a central role in whether infants of a particular age do or do not perceive an event in terms of causality.

The second of Fodor's conditions is that the effect of the background must be distinctively perceptual. Of course, this condition depends on what is meant by perceptual. But if proponents of a causal module believe that responding on the basis of causality is perceptual, then certainly responding on a more primitive basis in terms of the same elements that are supposed to be the required inputs to the causal module should be perceptual.

Fodor's final condition is that the system should be one that functions in normal circumstances and not some backup mechanism that operates only when the stimulus is too degraded for the module. One might be able to use this condition to argue against the Oakes and Cohen (1990) result that 6-month-olds do not process causality or spatial and temporal information when the stimuli are complex. As we noted earlier, their result represents weak evidence, at best, against a modular view. For example, one could argue that the complexity of the stimuli so distracted the 6-month-old infants that their perception of the remaining aspects of the event became degraded. The same argument, however, would not apply to the Cohen and Oakes (1993) multiple object study, nor to the Redford and Cohen (1996) agent–patient study. In both cases, the relevant input information for the proposed module was available, yet in neither was the proposed module activated.

Thus, to the extent that one can ever disprove the existence of a module, we believe we have done so with respect to the causal module proposed by Leslie (1986) to explain infants' perception of causality. We have shown developmental changes in the acquisition of causal perception, and significant effects of object complexity that are much more compatible with a developmental information-processing view (e.g. Cohen, 1988, 1991; Oakes & Cohen, 1994) than with an innate modular view. For example, according to the three-step developmental sequence proposed by Oakes and Cohen (1994), infants must first come to process objects as independent entities. Next, they should come to relate objects with their actions, and be able process simple relations between objects, such as spatial contiguity or temporal continuity. Finally, they should be able to use these relations to perceive or make inferences about the causality of an event. Based on the results reported in this section of this chapter, we would also propose a fourth step. Once infants do perceive or understand the causality of simple events, they then should be in a position to distinguish between different action roles, specifically the roles of agent and patient.

One still could assume that at some age the perception of the causality of simple events becomes modularised in the manner Karmiloff-Smith (1992) suggests. Certainly Michotte (1963) has shown the automaticity of such a perceptual system in adults. However, to assume some innate causal module, present in early infancy, seems to us to be counter-productive. Not only does it fail to explain the developmental pattern we have reported, but by assuming that causal perception is a self-contained or autonomous module, investigators are directed away from exploring important links between the perceptual or cognitive development of such a core concept as causality and development in other domains. In the final section of this chapter, we shall speculate on one of these links, on the possible connection between the acquisition of causality and the acquisition of related concepts in the language domain.

EXTENSIONS TO LANGUAGE

So far in this chapter we have outlined a developmental progression in the understanding of causality that is consistent with a constructivist-information-processing view of cognitive development. This progression proceeds from a perception of the individual elements of an event, such as the objects and the spatial and temporal relations between objects, to a more general conceptualisation of the whole event as either causal or noncausal. In addition to processing an event as either causal or noncausal, older infants also begin to recognise meaningful roles for the objects in these events. The transition from distinguishing that an event is causal or noncausal to formulating meaningful categories for the elements of the event, such as agent and patient, can be considered an important step in the elusive transition from perceptual analysis to conceptual represen- tation, or as Mandler (1992) refers to it, the transition from perceptual analysis to image schemata. However, as we have reported elsewhere in this chapter, processing the event on a causal and/or a meaningful level depends on the information-processing load placed on the infant. For example, if complex objects are introduced into the event, or the use of multiple objects transforms the task from a single event into a category problem, infants who may have been able to perceive causality under simpler conditions can no longer do so, and attention is shifted back to the individual elements of the event.[5] But even when infants are able to perform a conceptual analysis of the causality of an event with complex objects at 10 or 14 months of age, it is important to note that our evidence so far indicates that the analysis is still tied to the particular objects seen in the event. An additional step is still required to form an abstract conceptual representation or an image schema independent of the specific objects producing that representation. It is attractive to contemplate such an abstract redescription, and we are continuing to investigate when it may occur; but, as of now, we have no good evidence for one.

As previously noted, a nativist-modular perspective would not predict the type of developmental progression we have found, nor would it predict that infants may be distracted from perceiving causality if they are challenged with assimilating additional, complex information. At the end of the preceding section, therefore, we concluded that the nativist-modular view was not supported by the evidence. But we also noted that there is yet an additional reason to question the value of a nativist-modular approach. Because a nativist-modular approach conceives of causality as an auton- omous, self-contained mechanism, exploration of parallels and possible connections between different cognitive domains is de-emphasised. Yet, with reference to causality, one significant avenue for exploration is the parallel between cognitive development of causality and that of language development. Of the research already presented in this chapter, the most obvious parallel between causality and language is the development of concepts for the action roles played by objects in a causal event and the development of the linguistic notions of "agent" and "patient".

A number of researchers have posited some type of correspondence between semantic roles and general cognitive concepts. And some believe that the general cognitive concepts are a prerequisite to language learning (e.g. Bates, 1979; Mandler, 1992; Tomasello & Farrar 1984). If it can be shown that certain concepts that form part of the *perception* of causality are acquired prior to their presumably related *linguistic* concepts, then some indirect support may be provided for the connection posited by those researchers who perceive a cognitive basis for language acquisition. Redford and Cohen (1996), for example, have already demonstrated that the cognitive concepts of "agent" and "patient" are available between 10 and 14 months of age, even with complex objects. But we know from research on child language that the related linguistic concepts are not used until later, at around 24 months or the beginning of the two-word stage (e.g. Bloom, 1973; Brown, 1973).

The fact that the acquisition of the cognitive concepts of agent and patient precedes their use in language suggests to us that the observed parallel between the domains might actually be the manifestation of a connection between cognition and language whereby concepts must first be acquired in the general cognitive domain before they are acquired and expressed in the linguistic domain. We are, however, aware of the likelihood that a number of other steps must intervene between when an infant is first able to conceptualise action roles like agent and patient and when the infant acquires the corresponding linguistic concepts. For example, our work demonstrates that 14-month-old infants respond in terms of agent and patient, but as we mentioned previously, we have not demonstrated that these infants have concepts that extend beyond the particular physical event in which they occur. Note, however, that even though the infants' incomplete concepts of agent and patient are not fully comparable with the linguistic concepts of agent and patient, these fledgling concepts may still serve as the cognitive basis for those linguistic concepts.

In light of the obvious complexities associated with the transition from cognition to language, our purpose here is just to present some initial evidence for possible cognitive bases of language acquisition, not to theorise in detail about the exact progression from cognition to language. We have already shown that infants are sensitive to action roles of agent and patient well before they demonstrate a linguistic understanding of these concepts. Next, we shall examine another aspect of high-level perception or cognition of causality and how it may relate to language. That aspect is infants' ability to distinguish between perceptually similar, yet meaningfully distinctive types of causal action.

The ability to understand different types of causal actions represents a complex and advanced form of causal understanding because infants must not only perceive the existence of a causal relation between the objects, but must also note the type of causal relation that is occurring. In an experiment that examined this more advanced causal understanding, Cohen, Bradley, and Casasola (1995) presented 10- and 14-month-old infants with two different types of causal actions between inanimate objects. Infants were habituated to either a pushing or a pulling event, and were subsequently tested on both events, as well as on a totally novel event. In each event, a Lego toy rolled part of the way across a television screen and stopped. A toy can, with a picture of a cow on it, then dropped from the top of the screen either directly in front of or directly behind the Lego toy, which proceeded to either push or pull the can across the screen. The direction of movement varied from trial to trial so that discrimination of the two events could only occur on the basis of the action relation between the objects. In order to heighten infants' attention to the events and to facilitate any possible discrimination, instrumental music accompanied the actions.

The Cohen et al. (1995) experiment yielded results that were consistent with a developmental progression in the perception of causality. These results are shown in Fig. 6.8. As can be seen from the upper portion of Fig. 6.8, at 10 months of age infants provided no evidence of being able to discriminate between the pushing and pulling events. They did not look longer at the unfamiliar event (pushing if they had been habituated to pulling, or vice versa) than at the familiar event. The 10-month-olds, however, paid attention to *some* aspects of the events as they looked longer at a totally novel control event than at either the pushing or the pulling event.

On the other hand, as can be seen from the lower portion of Fig. 6.8, 14-month-old infants looked longer when the action changed from pushing to pulling or vice versa. These results indicate that the ability to discriminate between two perceptually similar causal events, solely on the basis of the type of relation between the objects, develops between 10 and 14 months of age. Thus, discriminating pushing from pulling appears to be a more sophisticated ability than just perceiving causality, as 10-month-old infants can discriminate causal from non-causal events, whereas 14-, but not 10-month-old infants, can discriminate between two different causal events.

How might the ability to discriminate between different types of causal events be related to language? One possibility is that infants recruit their pre-linguistic understanding of causality during language learning. Many transitive verbs (i.e. verbs that take a direct object, such as "hit", "push", and "pull") encode simple causal relations between two objects. The ability to perceive and discriminate between a wide range of physical causal events should aid in the acquisition of the related linguistic terms. Consequently, one component that should be needed for the eventual attainment of the syntactic category of verbs could well be a cognitive understanding of the different causal relations between objects. The study by Cohen et al. (1995) demonstrates that 14-month-old infants comprehend the causal actions of pushing and pulling, although the production of the verbs "push" and "pull" may not appear until a much later age. In

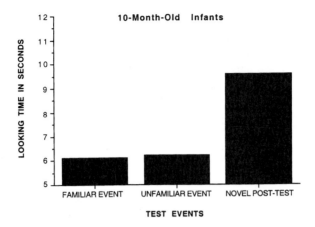

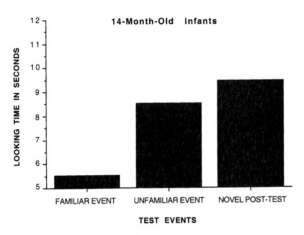

FIG. 6.8.   Responses of 10- and 14-month old infants in the test to a familiar event (either pushing or pulling), an unfamiliar event (either pulling or pushing), and a totally novel event. The same music is playing in the background during each event.

the section that follows, research is presented that examines whether 14-month-old infants can also learn to comprehend language labels for specific causal events.

In a series of studies by Casasola and Cohen (1996), the relationship between the understanding of a causal event and the ability to associate and thus comprehend a linguistic label for those events was investigated. In these experiments, the same pushing and pulling events from the Cohen et al. (1995) study were presented, but nonsense language labels replaced the instrumental music, and a modified habituation procedure, known as the "switch design", was adopted (see Cohen, 1998). Infants were habituated in alternation to two events. In one event, repeated presentations of a nonsense label, "neem", were paired with the initiation and for the duration of a pushing action, and in the alternate event, a second nonsense label, "lif", was paired with a pulling action. After habituation, infants were tested with one event that maintained the familiar pairing between the action and language label presented during habituation (e.g. push + "neem") and a second event that included a "switch" in the action-word combination (e.g. push + "lif"). The results indicated that the 14-month-old infants did not dishabituate to the event that presented the new combination of word and action. Evidently they had not formed an association between the word and type of event. These results are intriguing particularly because Lloyd, Cohen, Werker, Foster, and Swanson (1994), using the same procedure and same nonsense language labels, found that 14-month-olds could form an association between a word and a single moving object. What then is the reason that 14-month-old infants have so much more difficulty forming an association between word and type of action?

In an effort to find out, Casasola and Cohen (1996) next examined 14-month-old infants' ability to discriminate a change in just the nonsense label or a change in just the action: 14-month-old infants were habituated to a single event, either pushing or pulling paired with a nonsense label (either "neem" or "lif"). Following habituation, infants in the *constant action* group were tested with a change in the nonsense label while the action remained the same as in habituation. Infants in the *constant label* condition were tested with a change only in the action (e.g. from pushing to pulling) while the label remained the same as in habituation.

In light of the Cohen et al. (1995) findings, that when music was playing in the background infants this age could discriminate pushing from pulling, the results from this second Casasola and Cohen (1996) experiment revealed an interesting and unexpected pattern. These results are presented in Fig. 6.9. First, as shown in the upper portion of the figure, infants who observed a change in the nonsense label in the test did dishabituate, indicating that they did notice the change in the word. However, as shown in the lower portion of the figure, infants in the constant label condition, who observed a change in action while the label remained constant, did not dishabituate to the change in action.

Because 14-month-old infants in the Cohen et al. study had previously discriminated between the pushing and pulling events when these actions had been presented with instrumental music, it was surprising that the 14-months-old infants in the constant label condition of Casasola and Cohen (1996) did not dishabituate to the change in action.

These experiments revealed that 14-month-old infants have considerable difficulty learning the association between a particular novel language

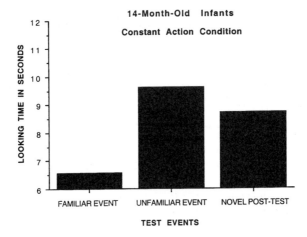

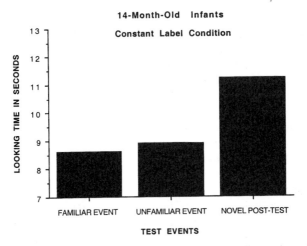

FIG. 6.9. Responses of 14-month-old infants to familiar, unfamiliar, and novel test events. In the upper portion of the figure, the unfamiliar event retains the same action (pushing or pulling) as in habituation, but the verbal label ("neem" or "lif") changes from habituation to test. In the lower portion of the figure the unfamiliar event retains the same verbal label, but the action changes from habituation to test.

label and a particular causal action. For some reason, not only are the labels not associated with causal actions, their mere presence seems to disrupt the infants' ability to discriminate between the two actions.

This difference in infants' ability to discriminate two causal events in the presence of music versus the presence of nonsense language labels might be explained in a number of ways. Tomasello and Kruger (1992) have noted that children are more likely to attach verbs to actions when the label is presented either before or after the completed action, but are least likely to do so when the label is presented simultaneously with the action. According to these researchers, the simultaneous presentation of word and action most likely creates an attentional overload as children must attend both to a novel label and the action. Perhaps, in Casasola and Cohen (1996) the presence of language labels presented too great a cognitive load on infants who had to process the linguistic terms and the causal relations simultaneously. As a consequence, infants in the current experiment should have been able to attend either to the language labels alone or to the causal events alone, but not to both. This explanation is consistent with the present results but it does not explain why the infants did attend just to the language labels in the presence of a single action, but did not attend just to the actions in the presence of a single label.

As a second alternative, the presence of linguistic constraints may have biased infants to associate the language labels with the individual objects in the event as opposed to the type of causal action (Markman, 1991). Constraints such as the whole-object and taxonomic constraints are believed by some to bias children to interpret a novel label as referring to an object in its entirety and lead children to reject relations between objects or actions as possible referents. Thus, the presence of a novel label during the causal events may have led infants to direct their attention away from the type of causal relation occurring between the objects and toward focusing on the individual objects in the events. In addition to explaining why infants could not associate a language label with a type of action, a whole-object constraint would explain why Lloyd et al. (1994), who used the same procedure as Casasola and Cohen (1996), found that infants could associate a language label with a particular object.

A third possibility stems from our more general information-processing viewpoint. It does not necessarily preclude the other explanations mentioned. As noted earlier, increasing the amount of information to which the infant must attend causes the infant to process that information at a lower developmental level (Cohen, 1991). For example, we have already reported that 10-month-old infants can respond on the basis of the causality in an event, but only if the objects in the event remain constant. If the objects change from trial to trial, the infants "drop down" to processing spatial and temporal perceptual characteristics (Cohen & Oakes, 1993). In light of the differential effects of cognitive load on the information-processing capabilities of infants at different developmental stages, a possible reason that 14-month-old infants are able to associate labels with particular objects, but not with particular causal actions, is that action discrimination is a higher-level task for infants at this age than is object discrimination. Action discrimination subsumes object discrimination and requires other additional steps as well. Infants must perceive the objects and their movements, the causal relation between the objects, and finally the type of causal relation that is occurring. Further support for this view is that, on a perceptual or cognitive level, the ability to discriminate individual objects as unique "wholes" emerges at a younger age, at about 5 to 7 months (Cohen, 1988), than does the ability to discriminate between different types of actions of an object, at about 14 months (Casasola & Cohen, 1996). Attaching a particular label adds an additional cognitive load. Therefore, infants at 14 months of age may be able to associate a language label with an object, but not with an action because of the additional processing required with actions.

The finding that infants are able to associate language labels with objects before they can associate labels with actions implies a developmental progression in the acquisition of language that is intimately tied to cognitive development. A number of researchers have explicitly addressed this probable tie between cognitive development and language development by showing that specific words, which encode specific concepts, emerge only once a child understands the concept (e.g. Gopnik 1988; Gopnik & Meltzoff 1985, McCune-Nicolich 1981; Tomasello & Farrar, 1984, 1986). Gopnik (1984), for example, has shown that the relational word "gone" emerges in the one-word stage once the infant demonstrates an advanced understanding of object permanence. With respect to the developmental progression in the acquisition of infant causal perception, we would propose the following parallels to the progression in the acquisition of certain key aspects of language.

An early step in the development of an understanding of causality is the conceptualisation of individual elements such as the objects and the spatial and temporal relationships between objects. This step parallels the first major stage in language production, the one-word stage, in which infants use nouns and relational words, but not verbs (Smiley & Huttenlocher, 1995). Conceptualisation of objects should be a prerequisite for object naming (Gentner 1982; Markman 1991) and conceptualisation of spatial and temporal relations should be a prerequisite for linguistic encoding of these and other relations with relational words such as "up" and "more" (Tomasello & Farrar, 1986).

A next step in understanding causality is the conceptualisation of the event as causal or noncausal. This step from processing the spatial and temporal characteristics of objects to processing the concept that one object is causing (or not causing) another object to move might parallel the shift proposed by Gopnik and Meltzoff (1985) from the pragmatic use of relational words to the more conceptual use of these words. Pragmatic uses of relational words indicate that the infant understands the relationship between the use of the relational word and the action, but not the abstract concept. Not until later in the first-word stage does the infant begin using certain relational words in contexts that demonstrate a conceptual understanding of these words. The conceptual understanding of relational words is a less sophisticated conceptual understanding of dynamic events than the conceptual understanding of verbs (Smiley & Huttenlocher, 1992), and therefore nicely parallels the initial perception of gaps and delays between objects before acquiring the conceptual understanding (i.e. the causality) implied by those gaps and delays.

A later step in the development of infant causal perception is the one in which infants begin to formulate meaningful categories of objects' roles (e.g. agent and patient) and the types of actions (e.g. pushing and pulling) in the event. This step may parallel the second major stage in language production – when words are combined – where it is thought that grammatical concepts are first demonstrated (e.g. Bloom 1973; Brown, 1973). For example, when infants begin to combine words they are said to demonstrate linguistic equivalents of concepts such as agent and patient, and of verbs such as push and pull (Bloom 1973; Brown 1973; Smiley & Huttenlocher, 1992).

The parallel in the progression of causal understanding and linguistic use set forth in this section is, admittedly, highly speculative and undoubtedly overly simplistic. It suffers, in particular, from leaving any direct causal links between cognition and language implicit and unspecified. Nevertheless, we feel that it is important to search for these types of parallels in order to help guide research that could make explicit causal connections between the general domains of cognition and language. An explicit theory of the causal connections between cognition and language could provide the beginnings of an explanatory account for how humans acquire the abstract representational structure that is language. Once again, a research programme that proceeds with the assumption that knowledge is innate and that the domains of knowledge are modular and encapsulated is not motivated to pursue such explanatory accounts for how knowledge develops, or to examine parallel processes and wonder whether one process can inform us about another.

GENERAL CONCLUSION

Throughout this chapter we have argued for a developmental view as opposed to a nativist-modular view of infants' perception of causal events. We believe the evidence we have presented supports our position. It indicates that infants under 6 months of age process these events in a very different way from those over 6 months of age. The evidence also indicates that even when infants show the first signs of causal perception, that perception is quite limited. It is limited to events with simple objects, and it is tied to the specific objects that serve as agent and patient. It seems to us to be rather arbitrary whether one wishes to assert that infants' processing first passes from the perceptual realm to the conceptual realm when the infants first respond to the causality of an event produced by simple objects, or when they can do it with complex as well as simple objects, or when they can clearly distinguish between agent and patient, or when they can clearly distinguish between different types of causal events, or when they can first understand that an event is causal, or involves pushing or pulling, independent of the objects producing that event. Labelling one or more of these achievements as "cognitive" seems less important to us than specifying the entire developmental progression.

We are particularly intrigued by the fact that although infant causal perception may be thought of as a specific domain, or subdomain, if not a module, the development of causal perception seems to demonstrate some of the same general information-processing principles that are hallmarks of the development of other domains of infant perception or cognition. For example, at each stage development appears to be constructive, taking elements or features that are independent at one stage and integrating them to form some higher-order unit or element at the next stage. In this way, at each succeeding stage, infants appear to be capable of processing and assimilating more information than in the preceding stage. Furthermore, if infants are faced with an information load that is above their current level of processing, they will tend to "drop down" and process the information at a less conceptually or perceptually sophisticated level. In the past these principles have been used to describe the development of infant form perception, object perception, and categorisation (Cohen, 1988, 1991, 1998). We believe we have shown in this chapter that the same "constructivist-information-processing" framework applies to the development of infants' perception of causality.

We have also made an initial attempt to connect both our research on infant causal perception and our more general framework with processes that occur in the development of language. We have also emphasised that a research programme, theoretically motivated by a nativist-modular position, would not attempt to make such connections across domains.

Finally, although this chapter has dealt exclusively with infant causal perception, we hope that what we have learned will be applicable to other areas (or domains) within infant perception and cognition as well. Perhaps there is one general lesson to be learned from the research described in this chapter. It is that just because under certain circumstances, and at some age, infants perform in what appears to be a relatively sophisticated cognitive manner, one should not necessarily assume that the infants have at their disposal some pre-specified, fully formed, innate module, immune to development, change, or improvement. On the contrary, what we have shown in infant causal perception, and what we hope researchers will discover when investigating other areas of infant perception and cognition, is that these areas (or as some call them, "domains") develop in significant ways throughout infancy. Although there may well be specific constraints on how each domain develops, there undoubtedly will also be critically important, nonspecific information-processing principles that apply across domains. It is these principles that guide development in general and tie specific domains together.

NOTES

1. We shall not draw a particularly sharp distinction in this chapter between infants' perception and their understanding of causality. Some possible differences between the two will be discussed at various points in the chapter, but we realise that for many, including ourselves, a sharp distinction between perception and cognition may be difficult to defend.
2. This reference to Marr is even more problematic in light of the fact that Marr's work on vision was decidedly not developmental. It would be irrelevant to Marr's theorising about the adult visual system whether the modules he identified for analysis were innate or the product of early development. In fact, we know that many of Marr's visual modules, such as stereopsis, are not functional early in development (e.g. Yonas & Granrud, 1995).
3. Spelke, Phillips, and Woodward (1995) noted that when they re-analysed Ball's data for infants under 7 months of age, the preference for the inconsistent (noncausal) test event was significant relative to baseline. We too re-analysed Ball's data. The appropriate comparison would be the difference in preferences, relative to their baselines, of inconsistent (noncausal) versus consistent (causal) test events. This difference did not approach significance for the subjects as a whole, nor for the subgroup under 7 months of age.
4. Spelke, et al. (1995, p. 51) state that " . . . a comparison across different studies reveals a convergence between infants' reactions to events involving visible objects and infants' reactions to events involving hidden objects." Based on the evidence we have cited, we disagree with their conclusion. As we shall indicate later, we believe infants respond to the causality of visible objects at a considerably younger age than they respond to the causality of hidden objects.
5. A similar "regression" to a simpler level when there is an overload of information has been noted by Cohen (1991) in his discussion of infants' ability to organise perceptual features into objects and to form categories of objects.

REFERENCES

Baillargeon, R. (1986). Representing the existence and the location of hidden objects: Object permanence in 6- and 8-month-old infants. *Cognition, 23*, 21–41.

Ball, W.A. (1973). *The perception of causality in the infant.* Report No. 37, Developmental Program, Department of Psychology, University of Michigan.

Bates, E. (1979). *The emergence of symbols: Cognition and communication in infancy.* New York: Academic Press.

Bloom, L. (1973). *One word at a time.* The Hague: Mouton.

Brown, R. (1973). *A first language: The early stages.* Cambridge, MA: Harvard University Press.

Carey, S. (1995). On the origin of causal understanding. In D. Sperber, D. Premack, & A.J. Premack (Eds.), *Causal cognition* (pp. 268–302). Oxford: Clarendon Press.

Casasola, M., & Cohen, L.B. (1996, April). *The influence of language labels on infants' ability to discriminate between pushing and pulling.* Poster presented at the International Conference of Infant Studies, Providence, RI.

Cohen, L.B. (1988). An information processing approach to infant cognitive development. In L. Weiskrantz (Ed.), *Thought without language* (pp. 211–228). Oxford: Oxford University Press.

Cohen, L.B. (1991). Infant attention: An information processing approach. In M.J. Weiss & P.R. Zelazo (Eds.), *Newborn attention: Biological constraints and the influence of experience* (pp. 1–21). Norwood, NJ: Ablex.

Cohen, L.B. (1994, June). *How infants perceive the causality of physical events.* Symposium paper presented at the biennial meeting of the International Conference on Infant Studies, Paris.

Cohen, L.B. (1998). An information-processing approach to infant perception and cognition. F. Simion & G. Butterworth (Eds.), *Development of sensory, motor, and cognitive capacities in early infancy. From sensation to cognition* (pp. 277–300). Hove, UK: Psychology Press.

Cohen, L.B., & Amsel, G. (1997, April). *Precursors to infants' perception of causality.* Poster presented at the meeting of the Society for Research in Child Development, Washington, DC.

Cohen, L.B., Bradley, K.L., & Casasola, M. (1995, May). *Infants' ability to discriminate between pushing and pulling.* Poster presented at the meeting of the Society for Research in Child Development, Indianapolis, IN.

Cohen, L.B., & Oakes, L.M. (1993). How infants perceive simple causality. *Developmental Psychology, 29,* 421–433.

Fodor, J.A. (1983). *The modularity of mind.* Cambridge, MA: MIT Press.

Fodor, J.A. (1985). Precis of the modularity of mind. *Behavioral and Brain Sciences, 8,* 73–77.

Gentner, D. (1982). Why nouns are learned before verbs. In S. Kuczaj (Ed.), *Language development. Vol. 2: Language, cognition and culture* (pp. 301–334). Hillsdale, NJ: Erlbaum.

Golinkoff, R.M. (1975). Semantic development in infants: The concept of agent and recipient. *Merrill-Palmer Quarterly, 21,* 181–193.

Golinkoff, R.M., & Kerr, J.L. (1978). Infants' perception of semantically defined action role changes in filmed events. *Merrill-Palmer Quarterly, 24,* 53–61.

Gopnik, A. (1984). The acquisition of "gone" and the development of the object concept. *Journal of Child Language, 11,* 273–292.

Gopnik, A. (1988). Three types of early words: The emergence of social words, names and cognitive-relational words in the one-word stage and their relation to cognitive development. *First Language, 8,* 49–70.

Gopnik, A., & Meltzoff, A.N. (1985). From people, to plans, to objects. *Journal of Pragmatics, 9,* 495–512.

Hume, D. (1777/1993). *An enquiry concerning human understanding.* Indianapolis, IN: Hackett.

Karmiloff-Smith, A. (1992). *Beyond modularity: A developmental perspective on cognitive science.* Cambridge, MA: MIT Press.

Lecuyer, R., & Bourcier, A. (1994). *Causal and non-causal relations between collision events and their detection by 3-month-old infants.* Symposium paper presented at the biennial meeting of the International Conference on Infant Studies, Paris.

Leslie, A.M. (1984). Spatiotemporal continuity and the perception of causality in infants. *Perception, 13,* 287–305.

Leslie, A.M. (1986). Getting development off the ground. Modularity and the infant's perception of causality. In P. v. Geert (Ed.), *Theory building in developmental psychology,* (pp. 406–437). Amsterdam: North Holland.

Leslie, A.M. (1988). The necessity of illusion: Perception and thought in infancy. In L. Weiskrantz (Ed.), *Thought without language* (pp. 185–210). Oxford: Oxford Science Publications.

Leslie, A.M. (1995). A theory of agency. In D. Sperber, D. Premack, & A.J. Premack (Eds.), *Causal cognition* (pp. 121–141). Oxford: Clarendon Press.

Leslie, A.M., & Keeble, S. (1987). Do six-month-olds perceive causality? *Cognition, 25,* 265–288.

Lightman, A. (1983). *Einstein's dreams.* New York: Pantheon Books.

Lloyd, V.L., Cohen, L.B., Werker, J.F., Foster, R., & Swanson, C.S. (1994, June). *Gender and motion: Important factors in infants' ability to learn word-object associations.* Poster presented at the biennial meeting of the International Conference on Infant Studies, Paris.

Lucksinger, K.L., Cohen, L.B., & Madole, K.L. (1992, May). *What infants infer about hidden objects and events.* Poster presented at International Conference on Infant Studies, Miami, FL.

Mandler, J.M. (1992). How to build a baby: II. Conceptual primitives. *Psychological Review, 99,* 587–604.

Markman, E.M. (1991). *The whole object, taxonomic, and mutual exclusivity assumptions as initial constraints on word meanings.* Cambridge: Cambridge University Press.

Marr, D. (1982). *Vision.* San Francisco, CA: Freeman.

McCune-Nicolich, L. (1981). The cognitive bases of relational words in the single word period. *Journal of Child Language, 8,* 15–34.

Michotte, A. (1963). *The perception of causality.* New York: Basic Books.

Oakes, L.M. (1992, May). *The role of continuity cues in infant causal perception.* Poster presented at International Conference on Infant Studies, Miami, FL.

Oakes, L.M. (1994). Development of infants' use of continuity cues in their perception of causality. *Developmental Psychology, 30,* 869–879.

Oakes, L.M., & Cohen, L.B. (1990). Infant perception of a causal event. *Cognitive Development, 5,* 193–207.

Oakes, L.M. & Cohen, L.B. (1994). Infant causal perception. In C. Rovee-Collier & L.P. Lipsitt (Eds.), *Advances in infancy research* (Vol. 9, pp. 1–54). Norwood, NJ: Ablex.

Piaget, J. (1954). *The construction of reality in the child.* New York: Basic Books.

Redford, M.A., & Cohen, L.B. (1996, April). *Infants' conceptual understanding of agent and patient.* Poster presented at the International Conference on Infant Studies, Providence, RI.

Smiley, P., & Huttenlocher, J. (1995). Conceptual development and the child's early words for events, objects, and persons. In M. Tomasello & W.E. Merriman (Eds.), *Beyond names for things: Young children's acquisition of verbs* (pp. 21–60). Hillsdale, NJ: Erlbaum.

Spelke, E.S., Phillips, A., & Woodward, A.L. (1995). Infants' knowledge of object motion and human action. In D. Sperber, D. Premack, & A.J. Premack (Eds.), *Causal cognition* (pp. 44–78). Oxford: Clarendon Press.

Tomasello, M., & Farrar, M.J. (1984). Cognitive bases of lexical development: Object permanence and relational words. *Journal of Child Language, 11,* 477–493.

Tomasello, M., & Farrar, M.J. (1986). Object permanence and relational words: a lexical training study. *Journal of Child Language, 13,* 495–505.

Tomasello, M., & Kruger, A.C. (1992). Joint attention on actions: Acquiring verbs in ostensive and non-ostensive contexts. *Journal of Child Language, 19,* 311–333.

Van de Walle, G., Woodward, A.L., & Phillips, A. (1994). *Infants' inferences about contact relations in a causal event.* Poster presented at the biennial meeting of the International Conference on Infant Studies, Paris, France.

Yonas, A., & Granrud, C.E. (1995). The development of sensitivity to kinetic, binocular and pictorial depth information in human infants. In D. Ingle, M. Jeannerod, & D. Lee (Eds.), *Brain mechanisms and spatial vision* (pp. 113–145). Dordrecht, The Netherlands: Nijhoff.

ACKNOWLEDGEMENTS

Preparation of the chapter and much of the research reported in it were supported by Grant HD-23397 to the first author from the National Institute of Child Health and Human Development.

CHAPTER SEVEN

Object perception and object knowledge in young infants: A view from studies of visual development

Scott P. Johnson
Lancaster University, UK

INTRODUCTION: OBJECT PERCEPTION AND OBJECT KNOWLEDGE IN EVERYDAY LIFE

Imagine you are sitting at a desk whose top is cluttered with various objects, such as papers, books, a computer and keyboard, and other such items. Among the clutter you spy two long, thin, yellow surfaces, whose edges are aligned, protruding from beneath a piece of paper. Without much difficulty, you are able to interpret these surfaces as belonging to a single object, in this case a partly occluded pencil. Not only can you *perceive* this object, but you *know* quite a bit about it. For example, you know that one end can be used to produce marks on paper – writing, drawing, and the like. You know what the pencil is composed of, and you might recall where you obtained the pencil.

But there is much more that you know, including general object knowledge that is not limited to this pencil. For example, you know that if you were to pick up the pencil and drop it, it would fall to the nearest surface below. You know that if you were to toss the pencil towards the bin, it might land in or near the bin, and would follow a predictable trajectory on the way to its resting place. You know that if you were to cover the pencil completely with the paper, the pencil would still be there, in the place you left it, were you to later search for it. You know that it is a solid object, and could not pass through the space occupied by another object.

Consider thus the extent of your knowledge of this pencil. Not only do you know about this particular item, with which you have had some experience, but you hold similar beliefs about almost every object you see every day, and countless other objects you have seen, will see in the future, or can imagine. Your everyday existence as you know it would scarcely be possible without this knowledge, because without it, the world and the results of your actions in the world would not be predictable.

Complete object knowledge comprises several supporting skills, some perceptual, some cognitive, and others rather more difficult to categorise. Perceptual skills include visual acuity (the ability to resolve detail), and the ability to distinguish the boundaries, colours, luminance levels, and textures of surrounding surfaces. Depth perception is necessary to discriminate surfaces against the background. The ability to track moving objects in the environment is important as well, because motion often is an important cue for segregation of visible surfaces. All of these skills rely on efficient visual scanning, the ability to *foveate* objects of interest (i.e. to focus the object's image on the fovea, the centre of the retina at the back of the eye, where visual acuity is generally highest).

Cognitive skills are also required for complete object knowledge, such as knowledge of objects' *physical* properties: unity, location, size, inertia, continuity across time and space, cohesion, gravity, and support, among others. For example, it is often necessary to "fill in" partly occluded portions of objects. This involves extension of the visible edges behind the occluder across a discontinuity in surface boundaries. An object's location and size must be recalled in order to recognise it as the same object on later encounters. The ability to keep in mind that an object maintains a lawful trajectory while moving, even when the trajectory is unseen, contributes to this recognition as well. Knowledge of cohesion underlies understanding solidity and the fact that an object cannot pass through the space occupied by another object.

Other skills seem both perceptual and cognitive, such as the *object constancies*: an object is recognised even though it is seen from a variety of angles (shape constancy), and from a variety of distances (size constancy). For example, the cover of a book would appear perfectly rectangular only if seen straight on – more often, its retinal image is that of a trapezium. The trapezium may be seen in a variety of shapes and sizes, but the "meaning" remains invariant: the cover of the book. Finally, *object identity* (or identity constancy) is the recognition that the object does not change into a new object when it moves, becomes temporarily occluded, or is encountered again after looking away. Object identity also dictates that an object moves to another location only on a continuous path – if an object similar in appearance turns up elsewhere in the visual array, it must be a distinct object. Clearly, many skills are involved in the simple act of recognising your pencil, and these skills are used countless times in your daily activities.

THE DEVELOPMENT OF OBJECT KNOWLEDGE: PIAGET'S THEORY

How did you come to this state of knowledge about the world and the objects in it? Did you learn about objects when you were a young infant, by handling, examining, and manipulating them? Alternatively, does most object knowledge come from being taught, via language? Or is object knowledge accessible simply by *looking* – are object properties perceived directly, without cognitive input? Or is object knowledge present at birth, as part of our genetic endowment?

If you have spent much time around young infants older than 5 or 6 months (when coordinated reaching for objects emerges in most infants), you might conclude that the first of these possibilities provides the best account of the development of object knowledge. After infants develop reaching and grasping skills, they often grab any small object they can, visually inspect it, bang it on the nearest hard surface, shake it, put it in their mouth, drop it, and so on. These are excellent ways of exploring object properties.

Infants' use of manual skills to learn about objects was the focus of the first comprehensive theory to address the question of development of object knowledge, that of Jean Piaget (1952; 1954). Piaget was a keen observer of infants and children (including his own), meticulously recording their responses to everyday situations and tasks he devised. Although Piaget wrote extensively about many aspects of development, I will discuss here only a small part of his theory, concerning *object permanence*, or the *object concept*. According to Piaget (1954), object permanence encompasses the knowledge that objects continue to exist, and that they maintain their physical and spatial properties, when no longer in sight or manual contact. On the basis of infants' responses to hiding tasks, he outlined a progression of stages through which infants pass on their way to full object permanence.

In stages 1 and 2 (birth to about 4 months), infants who watch as an interesting object is covered act as if the occluded object no longer exists: they show no surprise at the object's disappearance, nor do they attempt to look for the object. In stage 3 (about 4 to 8 months), infants will retrieve an object from behind an occluder if they are in current manual contact, but will not search otherwise. In stage 4 (about 8 to 12 months), infants will search under an occluder, even without manual contact on occlusion. Thus they demonstrate knowledge that the occluded object still exists.

However, this does not yet constitute object permanence, for infants at stage 4 often make a very interesting search error when confronted with *two* occluders. If an object is repeatedly hidden at one location (location A), the infant is allowed to search and retrieve the object, and then the object is hidden at a second location (location B) *as the infant watches*, he or she will often direct the search at A again! This outcome seems surprising – after all, the infant watched as the object was being hidden at B – why would he or she then search at A? Piaget (1954) accounts for this "A-not-B" error (also called the stage 4 error) by arguing that stage 4 infants do not maintain an objective mental representation of the object. Rather, for the infant, reaching at a particular location results in an interesting outcome (the desired object). Thus the object is represented by the infant in terms of his or her actions, not as separate from them. (The A-not-B error has inspired a very large number of studies. For an excellent summary and theoretical account, see Wellman, Cross, & Bartsch, 1987.) By stage 5 (about 12 to 18 months), infants overcome the tendency to search at A incorrectly if they watch the object being hidden at B. However, if the object is transferred *invisibly* to B, for example in the hider's hand, stage 5 infants often err in search. By stage 6 (about 18 to 24 months), infants demonstrate full object permanence, because they search all possible locations – thus indicating that they know the object has to be somewhere. This constitutes the advent of representational abilities, which would encompass many of our common-sense notions of the pencil's properties described above.

For Piaget (1954), then, evidence of infants' object knowledge was provided by effective search for an object that was hidden and then displaced. Even before manual search abilities emerge, however, there is ample evidence (some of which is reviewed later) that infants have already acquired much object knowledge. The viewpoint espoused in this chapter is that visual skills are the foundation for much of humans' object perception and object knowledge. It is true that search patterns can be informative, as Piaget suggested, but it may be that manual search is not always the best index of an infant's cognitive abilities (Baillargeon, Graber, DeVos, & Black, 1990). It is also true that other perceptual and cognitive domains contribute in very important ways to our understanding of the world (such as our facility at using language as a communicative tool). However, humans are an inherently visual species, and much information we take in about our environment is visual. Fortunately for those of us interested in the development of object perception and object knowledge, the past three decades have seen tremendous advances in the use of methodologies that exploit infants' visual preferences. Researchers have obtained a fair measure of what it is that infants at various ages attend to, what they find interesting, what they may or may not be able to distinguish, and the like, and from there infer some of the cognitive activities that must underlie these preferences. Many of these methodologies are described later.

The next part of the chapter will follow a chronological sequence. First I briefly describe fundamental visual skills and their development from birth, and then outline what is currently believed to be the state of object knowledge in different age groups. After this summary of the research, a brief consideration of theoretical viewpoints since Piaget will be presented.

VISUAL SKILLS IN THE NEONATE: THE FOUNDATIONS OF OBJECT PERCEPTION AND OBJECT KNOWLEDGE

At first glance (and perhaps even with repeated glances!), the neonate, or newborn infant, seems hopelessly disorganised. Sleeping, waking, and feeding may not follow any discernible pattern for months to come. At times, the neonate may seem completely unresponsive to visual or auditory stimuli. He or she may thrash about, or cry, or stare into space for no apparent reason. Young humans require adult care for many months before they are able to perform even simple tasks, such as feeding themselves. In this way, humans are an *altricial* species, as opposed to other species that are better described as *precocial* (for example, hatchling sea turtles receive no care, and on hatching must rush to the ocean and begin life on their own).

There is currently much controversy about whether very young infants' perceptual and cognitive abilities are also best described as altricial. For example, one view posits that neonates' visual abilities are limited by lack of cortical functioning (Atkinson, 1984; Johnson, 1990), or more precisely, that there are only "islands" of cortical functioning at birth. (Cortical functioning refers to the cortex, the largest part of the human brain. The cortex is responsible for humans' reasoning, planning, and linguistic abilities, and many visual skills.) Without full functioning of the cortex, object knowledge obviously would be restricted. However, the results of a variety of studies suggest that neonates do respond to some object properties.

Neonates' visual limitations

Chapter 1 in this volume provides an excellent overview of the development of fundamental visual skills. At the risk of being redundant, a few points bear repeating in the context of the present chapter.

Foveation consists of directing one's gaze to items of interest in the visual array. Foveation is most readily accomplished in humans via eye movements, although head and body movements also contribute. Even a neonate seems to foveate small objects, if he or she is motivated and the object is not too difficult to see (i.e. it can be distinguished against the background and it is close to the eyes).

However, there are limitations in very young infants' abilities to success-fully produce certain eye movements. For example, until 8 to 10 weeks of age, infants rarely engage in smooth pursuit, or the tracking of a slowly moving small target (Aslin, 1981). Very young infants also appear to be limited in their ability to effectively scan stationary patterns (Bronson, 1990, 1991), often producing "inefficient" patterns (e.g. fixating away from edges, or fixating only small portions of a visual stimulus). A third way in which very young infants' scanning abilities improve is via control over *reflexive* eye movements, optokinetic nystagmus (OKN) and the vestibulo-ocular reflex (VOR) (see Chapter 1). A combination of OKN, VOR, and smooth pursuit is responsible for adults' ability to move around the world while effortlessly maintaining fixation on targets of choice, say moving or stationary objects (Aslin & Johnson, 1996). Aslin and Johnson (1994; 1996) found that at 2 and 4 months of age, infants were proficient at suppressing both OKN and VOR in response to small, (presumably) interesting targets. However, 1-month-olds displayed little suppression of OKN (and some VOR suppression), although both OKN and VOR were observed in this age group. These findings imply that very young infants lack the ability to maintain effective fixation on objects as they themselves are moved around the environment, and perhaps even when stationary.

Although foveation has been observed even in the youngest infants, this does not necessarily imply that when neonates foveate, they see what adults see. Neonates are limited in visual acuity, contrast sensitivity, and colour perception. That is, they are less able to discriminate fine detail in visual patterns, and they are less able to discriminate differences in luminance contrast (i.e. shades of grey) and colours, than are older infants and adults (see Chapter 1).

Thus neonates seem to be limited in many visual skills (although attempts at foveation have been noted at birth). How would this affect object perception? If scanning is limited, whether scanning of stationary targets, or moving targets, or under conditions of self-motion, then oppor-tunities for visual abstraction of object properties are also necessarily limited, especially if accompanied by deficits in acuity and contrast sensi-tivity. If neonates learn about object properties primarily by visual inspection, visual limitations might have detrimental effects on this process. Scanning limitations are largely overcome by the fourth month of life; other limitations improve more slowly. Whether the development of object knowledge is concomitantly limited in very young infants as a result is presently unknown, but seems likely.

Neonates' visual abilities

After presenting this rather bleak portrait of neonates' perceptual capabilities, I now turn to a variety of studies presenting a contrasting picture. These studies describe organisation of eye movements, memory abilities, visual preferences, and face recognition, all in infants no more than a few days old. Many of the abilities revealed by these studies are difficult to reconcile with the notion that vision is severely compromised in neonates, and these discrepancies remain unresolved. (The debate continues!)

Using corneal reflection, Haith (1980) recorded eye movements of neonates under a variety of conditions, and found that much of their visual behaviour could be captured by the following "rules," or innate tendencies. Rule 1: If awake and alert and light not too bright, open eyes. Rule 2: If in darkness, maintain a controlled, detailed search. Rule 3: If in light with no form, search for edges by relatively broad, jerky sweeps of the field. Rule 4: If an edge is found, terminate the broad scan and stay in the vicinity of that edge (Haith, 1980, p. 96). It seems that even though vision may be compromised in neonates, they often seem motivated to look at their surroundings.

Neonates display the capacity for memory (Slater, Morison, & Rose, 1982). If a neonate is repeatedly shown the same stimulus, looking duration typically is high initially but declines after several trials. If a novel stimulus is then presented, looking duration often increases again. This pattern of attention has been interpreted to reflect decrement of interest (*habituation*) and subsequent recovery of interest (*dishabituation*). Thus the habituation stimulus is held in memory while viewed repeatedly, and subsequently compared to the novel (*test*) stimulus. The mismatch between the remembered and novel stimuli leads to renewed interest. This method is widely used to investigate perceptual and cognitive development in infants, including older infants, as we will see. (Care is taken to ensure that posthabituation recovery is not due to inherent biases or preferences. Controls were employed in the studies presented later to address this issue, but will not be discussed.)

Neonates show "natural", or unlearned, visual preferences. That is, neonates seem to prefer some stimuli over others when stimuli are presented side by side. Based on evidence from dozens of studies, Slater (1995) outlined nine specific preferences: patterned over nonpatterned stimuli, curvature over straight edges, moving over stationary stimuli (and certain types of motion are preferred over others), three-dimensional over two-dimensional stimuli, horizontal over vertical gratings, upright over slanting stimuli (when the stimulus slants away from view), high over low contrast, certain sizes over others, and faces over similar, "nonface" stimuli. Attempts have been made to explain these innate preferences with a single principle, such as the contrast sensitivity function (Banks & Salapatek, 1981), with some, but not universal, success (see Slater, 1995, for discussion).

One surprising recent finding is the innate preference for faces over other stimuli. Figure 7.1 depicts stimuli that have been shown to neonates (Johnson, Dziurawiec, Ellis, & Morton, 1991). The infants were seated on an experimenter's lap, who held each stimulus at midline about 18–25 cm from the infant's eyes, and then moved it side to side until the infant no longer tracked it. The infants tracked the face-like stimulus farther than any of the others, indicating the ability to discriminate the stimuli, as well as the innate preference for faces.

Neonates have also been found to learn individual faces very rapidly, distinguishing real faces from one another. The most likely candidate for a readily learned face is, of course, the mother, and mother's face is learned within days after birth (Bushnell, Sai, & Mullin, 1989). In this preferential-looking study, 4-day-old neonates consistently looked longer at their mother's face than at a female stranger, who was similar to the mother in terms of hair colour and skin tone. Apparently, this recognition is not dependent solely on facial features. The effect disappears if the women's hairlines are covered with a scarf (Pascalis, de Schonen, Morton, Deruelle, & Fabre-Grenet, 1995). Thus attention to outer contours seems to contribute to neonates' face recognition abilities.

OBJECT PERCEPTION AND OBJECT KNOWLEDGE IN THE NEONATE

We have seen evidence for both limitations and compentencies in neonates' visual abilities. My goal in presenting these studies has been to offer the reader some appreciation of the challenges faced by the neonate, who

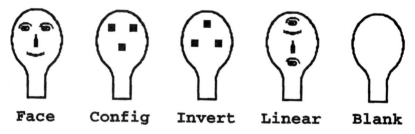

Face   Config   Invert   Linear   Blank

FIG. 7.1. Stimuli presented to neonates in a face perception experiment. The neonates seemed to prefer the "face" stimulus, laterally tracking it farther than any of the others. Note the similarity between the face and some of the others, in terms of feature type ("linear") and placement of "blobs" ("config"). Apparently neonates are sensitive to both features *and* their placement. (Adapted from Johnson et al., 1990).

is born not only with no visual experience, but with poor vision with which to try to make sense of the world! Nevertheless, there is clear evidence that some visual skills are present at birth. Do these skills extend to object perception, and perhaps object knowledge?

There have been few studies of object perception and object knowledge with neonates, and these studies provide mixed evidence for such abilities. The question is whether infants experience the visual array as a mosaic of shapes, or as composed of objects that are independent, bounded entities, located at different distances from the observer. To my knowledge, there have been no published studies of neonates' knowledge of objects' physical properties, except perception of object unity, described later.

Neonates have been found to demonstrate both size and shape constancy. In a study of size constancy, Slater, Mattock, and Brown (1990) presented neonates with cubes at different distances using a *familiarisation* method (similar to habituation, but with a fixed trial duration). Each infant viewed either a small cube or a large cube during familiarisation. Thus each infant was exposed to the same-sized object at different distances. After familiarisation, the infants were shown both cubes side-by-side, the small cube nearer and the large cube farther, so that their retinal images were identically sized (Fig. 7.2). The infants looked longer at the cube they were not familiarised with (consistent with the novelty preferences commonly observed in habituation studies). This indicates that the neonates differentiated the two cube sizes despite the similarities of the retinal sizes, and abstracted the familiar cube's real size over changes in distance.

In a study of shape constancy, Slater and Morison (1985) adopted a similar method. Neonates were presented with a single shape during familiarisation, either a trapezium or a square, shown at a different slant during each trial. Each infant thus viewed the same shape in different orientations. After familiarisation, the infants saw both stimuli side-by-side, the novel stimulus in the frontal plane, and the familiar stimulus in a new orientation. The infants looked longer at the stimulus they had not seen during familiarisation, indicating that they abstracted the *real* shape of the stimulus seen during familiarisation as it was rotated in three dimensions.

Studies of identity constancy have yielded less straightforward results, perhaps because identity constancy itself incorporates several aspects of object knowledge. Slater, Morison, Town, and Rose (1985) habituated neonates to either a stationary cross or a stationary triangle, and subsequently showed both of these stimuli side-by-side, both moving back and forth. The novel stimulus was consistently preferred, indicating recognition of the familiar stimulus despite the change from being stationary to motion. However, in another experiment, neonates failed to make the same discrimination when the objects rotated. These findings, together

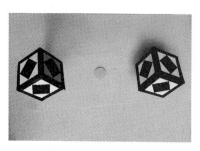 

(A)   **(B)**

FIG. 7.2. (A) Two cubes, as they appeared to neonates, in a size constancy study. Note that the retinal images of the cubes are identical in size. (B) A neonate being tested in the size constancy study. (Reprinted from Slater, Mattock & Brown, 1990, by permission).

with other studies described later, suggest that object identity may be present in rudimentary form at birth but undergoes development throughout the first year.

Neonates seem to have difficulty accurately perceiving occlusion. In a study of perception of partly occluded objects, Slater et al., (1990) habituated neonates to a display consisting of a rod, moving back and forth, whose centre was occluded by a box (Fig. 7.3). After habituation, the infants viewed two test displays with no occluder, one a complete rod, and the other a broken rod (i.e. with a gap in the location previously covered by the box). The infants consistently looked longer at the complete rod, indicating that the rod parts in the habituation display were perceived as disjoint. That is, the complete rod was experienced by the neonates as novel, and the broken as familiar (recall that infants typically prefer a novel stimulus after habituation). Thus neonates apparently do not perceive partly occluded objects as consisting of both visible and nonvisible portions. Rather, they seem to respond only to what they see directly. This finding was recently replicated with displays that were quite rich in visual cues, such as a large depth difference between the rod, box, and background, small occluder size, and textured (i.e. patterned) background, all designed to heighten the contrast between the objects and thus facilitate perception of object unity. The neonates did not seem to take advantage of the extra visual information in the displays, still preferring the complete rod after habituation (Slater, Johnson, Brown, & Badenoch, 1996; Slater, Johnson, Kellman, & Spelke, 1994).

Returning to our earlier question, do neonates display evidence of object knowledge? The answer depends on how one defines object knowledge. One standard of object knowledge is distinguishing *proximal* from *distal* stimuli. The proximal stimulus is the stimulus itself – in this case, the pattern of light falling on the retina. The distal stimulus consists of what is represented by the pattern of stimulation – in this case, the object itself. Neonates distinguish proximal from distal stimuli when they demonstrate size and shape constancy: the object is perceived accurately, despite changes in its retinal image.

Another standard of object knowledge is going beyond what is immediately perceptible, using *inference* to assess the proximal stimulus. Neonates have not been found to infer hidden portions of objects, as we saw in their apparent failure to perceive object unity. Thus, there is only mixed empirical support for object knowledge in the youngest humans. (Of course, it is possible that more mature levels of object knowledge are present in neonates, but were not revealed by the studies presented earlier.)

Object knowledge develops rapidly over the first year of life. Although neonates may be limited in object perception and object knowledge by deficits in visual skills, such skills emerge so quickly that it seems unlikely that older infants are limited in the same way. Thus, in the ensuing discussions of older infants, we will consider visual skills as being sufficiently developed so as to not hinder the emergence or expression of object knowledge. Differences between age groups may lie, rather, in attention to visual information, interpretation of visual information, and/or knowledge of the physical properties of objects.

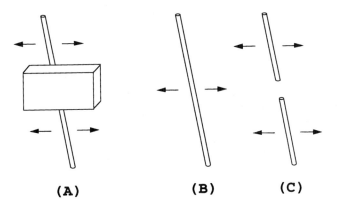

(A)   (B)   (C)

FIG. 7.3. (A) Rod-and-box display shown to infants to test perception of object unity. The rod parts undergo common motion behind the box. Adults report that the rod parts seem to be connected, forming a partly occluded surface. (B) Complete rod test display. (C) Broken rod test display. Both test displays move in like manner to the rod parts in the first display. See text for details. (Adapted from Kellman & Spelke, 1983.)

OBJECT PERCEPTION AND OBJECT KNOWLEDGE IN THE 2- TO 3-MONTH-OLD

The 3-month-old is a very different person than he or she was at birth. In many infants, the period from 2 to 3 months of age sees the advent of such milestones as more regular patterns of sleep, wakefulness and attentiveness, improvements in neurological control of volitional movements and posture, and social interaction and smiling (see Prechtl, 1984). There is also evidence that object knowledge is elaborated during this time.

Two-month-olds, unlike neonates, have been shown to perceive the unity of partly occluded objects. This implies inferential skills, and perception of occlusion and depth. In an habituation study, Johnson and Aslin (1995) presented rod-and-box displays to 2-month-olds, and followed with complete and broken rod test displays (Fig. 7.4A). In contrast to neonates, the 2-month-olds consistently looked longer at the broken rod, suggesting that they had received the impression of a complete rod behind the box in the habituation display. (Interestingly, there was no actual depth in these displays, which were computer-generated, presented on a two-dimensional television screen.)

Perception of object unity undergoes considerable development after 2 months, and seems somewhat tenuous at this age. In another object unity study with 2-month-olds, Johnson and Náñez (1995, Experiment 2) used a larger occluder relative to that employed by Johnson and Aslin (1995), and found no consistent preference for either the broken or the complete rod (Fig. 7.4B). Thus unity apparently is not perceived when less of the rod's surface can be seen, suggesting that 2-month-olds' attentional skills are limited: increased occluder size may make it more difficult to note, for

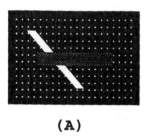 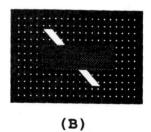

(A)   **(B)**

FIG. 7.4. Rod-and-box displays used to test perception of object unity in 2-month-olds. In both (A) and (B), the rod parts underwent common motion. After habituation, the infants were shown complete and broken rod test displays. Consistent preference for the broken rod occurred only after habituation to (A), suggesting that seeing more of the rod's surface facilitates perception of object unity in this young age group. (Adapted (A) from Johnson & Aslin 1995, and (B) from Johnson & Náñez, 1995).

example, that the two rod parts' edges are aligned, that the rod surfaces move together, and so on. As we will see, the object unity task has been used with older infants to further explore young infants' object perception.

Although 2-month-olds seem to perceive objects in depth, it is presently unknown how this is accomplished. Do they attend to the common motion of the rods' surfaces to determine segregation and depth ordering? Do they analyse differences between surfaces, in terms of colour, texture, and boundaries? Studies described later suggest the answer to the first question is yes. A study by Kestenbaum, Termine, and Spelke (1987) suggests the answer to the second question is no. Kestenbaum et al. presented 3-month-olds with displays consisting of two objects arranged in depth. From the infant's vantage point, the smaller object was closer and its boundaries were contained within the boundaries of the larger object (Fig.7.5). Each object was covered with a different patterned texture. The infants saw these objects either separated or adjacent in depth. After habituation, the infants viewed test displays with the same two objects in novel arrangements. In one test display, both objects were displaced closer to the infant ("two forward"); in the other test display, only the nearer object was displaced ("one forward"). Kestenbaum et al. (1987) reasoned that if the infants segregated the objects in the habituation display by analysing differences in surface textures or boundaries, then the infants who saw either the separated or adjacent arrangement would look longer at the

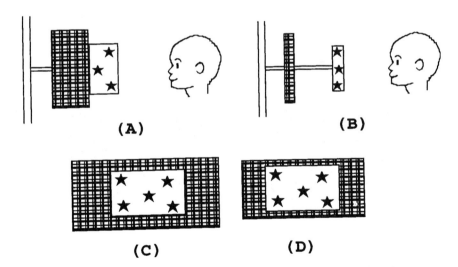

FIG. 7.5. Schematic depictions of the objects shown to 3-month-olds in a study of object segregation. (A) Side view of the adjacent objects display. (B) Side view of the separated objects display. After habituation, the infants viewed (C) the two forward and (D) one forward displays. See text for details. (Adapted from Kestenbaum et al., 1987.)

one forward test display, because of its novel arrangement. However, only the infants who were habituated to the separated arrangement looked longer at the one forward display. This suggests that the infants did not use colour, texture, and size differences to segregate the objects in the habituation display (as adults would). Rather, they only perceived the objects as separate entities when there was an actual depth difference. This study provides corroborative evidence that very young infants perceive objects in depth, but are limited in their capacity to do so.

There is also evidence that 2- to 3-month-olds demonstrate some knowledge of objects' physical properties. Spelke, Breinlinger, Macomber, and Jacobson (1992, Experiment 3) investigated 2.5-month-olds' knowledge of continuity and solidity, which are constraints on object motions. These constraints dictate that objects in motion move on an unobstructed path, and will not pass through the space occupied by another object. The infants were habituated to events in which a ball rolled behind a screen (Fig. 7.6). The test events were similar, except a barrier was placed in the object's path. The ball either stopped at the barrier (the "consistent" event), or appeared to have rolled beyond it (the "inconsistent" event), after the ball was revealed. The infants looked longer at the inconsistent event, suggesting that they found this event unusual, perhaps because it violated their expectations of continuity and solidity.

What, then, is the state of the infants' object perception and object knowledge by the time he or she is 3 months of age? Even though few studies are available of infants this young, they provide evidence indicating much progress since birth. Whereas the neonate appears to have only rudimentary object knowledge, the 3-month-old has been found to perceive depth relations and occlusion. This is a major advance on the way to experiencing the visual array as consisting of more than meets the eye (no pun intended!). Moreover, infants at this young age are beginning to appreciate objects' physical properties.

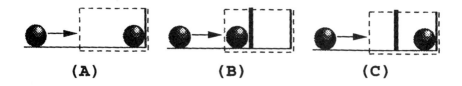

(A)   **(B)**   **(C)**

FIG. 7.6.   Schematic depictions of events shown to 2.5-month-olds in a study of knowledge of object continuity and solidity. (A) Habituation event. (B) Consistent test event. (C) Inconsistent test event. The infants looked longer at (C), suggesting sensitivity to continuity and solidity. (Adapted from Spelke et al., 1992.)

OBJECT PERCEPTION AND OBJECT KNOWLEDGE IN THE 4- TO 6-MONTH-OLD

I have described fundamental changes from birth through 3 months of age. Studies to be discussed in this section report continuing developments in infants' abilities to segregate visible surfaces. Perhaps most notable, however, is the wealth of evidence concerning knowledge of objects' physical properties after 4 months of age, including awareness of the existence, location, and size of occluded objects, as well as object support and object identity.

Studies of infants' perception of object unity were originally undertaken to explore the visual cues used by 4-month-olds in determining whether two surfaces are joined behind an occluder (Kellman & Spelke, 1983; Kellman, Spelke, & Short, 1986). A reliable preference for the broken rod occurred only when the two surfaces, above and below the box, moved together (either back and forth, up and down, or backwards and forwards in depth). However, when the displays were stationary, or when the box moved with the rod surfaces or by itself, there was no consistent preference for either test display (Fig.7.7).

Kellman and Spelke (1983; see also Kellman, 1993) interpreted these

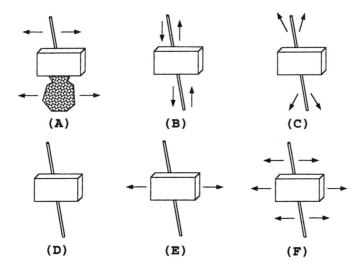

FIG. 7.7. Displays shown to 4-month-olds in studies of perception of object unity. The infants demonstrated preferences for the broken object after habituation to (A), (B), or (C), as well as the display depicted in Fig. 7.3A, but there was no preference after habituation to (D), (E), or (F). Thus, common motion of the surfaces above and below the occluder seems to be an important cue to perception of unity. (Adapted from Kellman & Spelke, 1983, and Kellman et al., 1986).

results by proposing that common motion of the occluded surfaces is the primary cue supporting young infants' perception of object unity. Johnson and Aslin (1996) explored the possibility that other cues also contributed. Four-month-olds were habituated to two-dimensional rod-and-box displays in which there was no background texture, or in which texture was present but the rod edges were either aligned or misaligned (Fig. 7.8). There was a reliable posthabituation preference for the *broken* rod when the edges were aligned and texture was present, and a preference for the *complete* rod when the edges were misaligned so that they would not connect behind the box, if the edges were to be extended. These results suggest that a complete rod was perceived behind the box in the former case, and two disjoint rod parts in the latter case. No preference was observed in the other two cases. Note that common motion was present in all these displays. Thus, edge orientation and background texture seem to be important cues in determining unity (edge orientation may even override common motion).

Recall that Piaget proposed that not until 8 to 12 months of age do infants maintain awareness of an occluded object's continued existence, as revealed by their patterns of search for a previously seen object. Baillar-

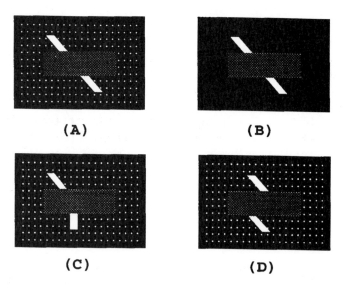

(A)   **(B)**

(C)   **(D)**

FIG. 7.8. Two-dimensional, computer-generated displays shown to 4-month-olds in studies of perception of object unity. The rod parts underwent common motion in all four displays. There was a preference for the broken rod after habituation to (A), no preference after habituation to (B) and (C), and a preference for the complete rod after habituation to (D). Thus, edge orientation and background texture seem important cues to perception of unity, in addition to motion. (Adapted from Johnson & Náñez, 1995, and Johnson & Aslin, 1996.)

geon and colleagues have reported a series of studies demonstrating this level of object knowledge, and more, in infants as young as 4 months of age. One of Baillargeon's most important findings involves her claim that 4-month-olds have object permanence (Baillargeon, 1987). Infants were habituated to a screen that rotated through 180° (Fig. 7.9). During test, a box was placed behind the screen, so that when the screen rotated back again, it should have stopped rotating at the point where it contacts the box. The experimenters surreptitiously removed the box on some trials, however, and the infants looked longer at this event than an event in which the screen stopped rotating where the box was located, perhaps because the former event was unexpected. Because the box was completely occluded by the screen, this finding suggests that the infants represented the box's continued existence and location, and understood that the screen could not move through the space occupied by the box.

Baillargeon and DeVos (1991) reported evidence that 3.5-month-olds represent the size of a hidden object. Infants were habituated to two events presented in alternation, both involving a toy carrot moving left and right, periodically becoming occluded behind a screen in front of its path. The carrot was either tall or short. After habituation, the infants viewed two test events in alternation, similar to the habituation event. In both events, there was a window at the top of the screen. One of the events was "impossible": the tall carrot was not visible in the window as it travelled behind the screen. In the "possible" event, the short carrot was not visible in the window either, but this was not impossible because it was too short to reach the window. The infants looked reliably longer at the impossible event. This suggests that the infants represented not only the hidden object's continued existence, but its height as well.

Young infants have been found to demonstrate awareness of support relations between objects. Needham and Baillargeon (1993) showed 4.5-month-old events in which a hand brought a box into view, and withdrew,

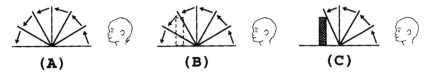

(A)   **(B)**   **(C)**

FIG. 7.9.   Schematic depictions of events shown to 4-month-olds in a study of knowledge of objects' existence and location after becoming occluded. (A) Habituation event, a screen that rotated through 180°. After habituation to (A), a box was placed behind the screen as the infants watched, and then the screen rotated again. (B) Impossible event: the screen could not rotate through the place where the object was located. (C) Possible event: the screen stopped rotating as it contacted the object. The infants looked longer at (B) than (C), suggesting that they represented the hidden object's existence and location. (Adapted from Baillargeon, 1987.)

leaving the box. The box was deposited either on top of a second box, or seemingly in mid-air without support, an impossible event (produced with the aid of support from behind, unseen by the infant). The infants consistently looked longer at the impossible event, suggesting that they expected the box to fall if unsupported.

The final study to be discussed in this section concerns object identity. Recall that object identity incorporates understanding that an object remains the same entity if it changes location or becomes temporarily occluded. It follows that an object that is similar in appearance, but located in a different part of the visual field, is a separate object, if the original object did not move on a continuous path to the new object's location. Evidence for infants' understanding of the first and second aspects of object identity was described earlier (Slater et al., 1985; Baillargeon, 1987). Evidence for the third aspect of object identity was reported by Spelke and Kestenbaum (1986, cited in Spelke, 1988). Four-month-olds were habituated to one of two events with two vertically oriented occluders. In the continuous event, a single object moved back and forth behind the occluders (Fig. 7.10). In the discontinuous event, two objects moved out successively from behind the screens, one at a time. To adults, the first event gives rise to the impression of a single object in motion. The second event appears to adults to contain two objects – the first object remains occluded as the second emerges. After habituation, the infants viewed test events with either one or two objects (no occluders). The infants who had been habituated to the discontinuous event looked reliably longer at the one-object event, indicating that they received the impression of two objects, one of which was always occluded. Infants who viewed the continuous event did the opposite. This suggests that infants who saw the continuous event inferred that only one object moved behind the occluders, whereas infants who saw the discontinuous event inferred that two objects were involved. (Evidence is presented later suggesting that object identity undergoes further development throughout the first year.)

OBJECT PERCEPTION AND OBJECT KNOWLEDGE IN THE 7- TO 12-MONTH-OLD

The major accomplishments during the last half of the infant's first year consist mainly of embellishments of perceptual and cognitive skills that have already been attained, as revealed by studies of older infants' perception of object unity, knowledge of support and gravity, and object identity.

Recall that the 4-month-olds observed by Kellman and Spelke (1983) did not seem to perceive object unity unless the partly occluded surfaces underwent common motion behind a stationary occluder. Craton (1996) reported that at 6.5 months of age, infants perceived object unity in

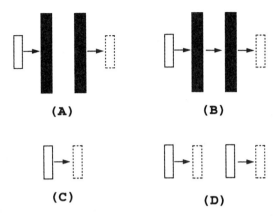

FIG. 7.10. Schematic depictions of displays from a study on 4-month-olds' perception of object identity. Infants were habituated to either (A) the discontinuous event, or (B) the continuous event. After habituation, infants in both groups saw (C) a one-object event or (D) a two-object event. Infants who viewed (A) subsequently looked longer at (C), whereas infants who viewed (B) subsequently looked longer at (D). Thus, the infants appeared to represent either two objects or one object in the habituation events, respectively. (Adapted from Spelke, 1988.)

stationary displays. This finding obtained after habituating 5.5-, 6.5-, and 8-month-olds to partly occluded rectangle displays, followed by test displays consisting of broken and complete rectangles. The younger infants displayed no preference, but the older infants preferred the broken rectangle.

Craton (1996) also investigated infants' perception of the *form* of the hidden region. Infants aged 5.5, 7, and 8 months were presented with a stationary partial occlusion display until habituation. Test displays consisted of a connected rectangle and a cross (Fig. 7.11). The latter test display would be unexpected if the infants perceived the whole rectangular shape with a *boundary interpolation* process, by which the boundaries of the visible regions were perceptually extended behind the occluder (Kellman & Shipley, 1991). Only the 8-month-olds preferred the cross, suggesting that they found the cross novel and the rectangle familiar. Thus infants between 2 and 8 months perceive the unity, but not necessarily the form, of partly occluded objects, whereas 8-month-olds perceive both unity and form.

Recall that 4.5-month-olds were found to be sensitive to violations of support relations (Needham & Baillargeon, 1993). Baillargeon and Hanko-Summers (1990) investigated the conditions under which older infants would respond to adequate and inadequate support. Infants between 7.5 and 9.5 months were shown displays consisting of three boxes, arranged such that one box was in contact with two boxes below (Fig. 7.12). Each

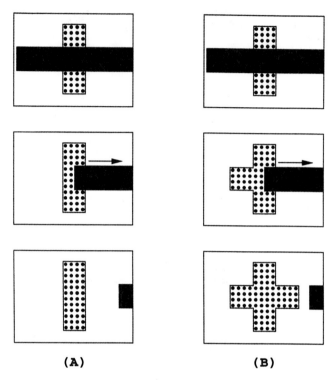

FIG. 7.11. Schematic depictions of test events in a study of infants' perception of the form of a partly occluded object. (A) Rectangle. (B) Cross. After habituation to the occluded object, 8-month-olds, but not younger infants, looked longer at the cross than at the rectangle, suggesting that not until 8 months of age do infants perceive the form of partly occluded objects. (Adapted from Craton, 1996.)

infant saw two events: in the possible event, one of the lower boxes was moved, but the top box maintained adequate support, and thus should not be expected to fall. In the impossible event, the other lower box was moved, such that there was only a small amount of contact remaining with the top box. The infants looked longer at the impossible event, suggesting that they expected the top box to fall without adequate support. However, in another experiment, infants did not distinguish between possible and impossible events that differed in the balance of the top object. Thus infants' understanding of support relations undergoes development after 9.5 months of age.

Infants' sensitivity to gravity was investigated by Kim and Spelke (1992), who habituated 5- and 7-month-olds to one of two events, in which a ball rolled either down or up an inclined plane ("speeding up" or "slowing down" conditions, respectively). When the ball rolled down, it accelerated,

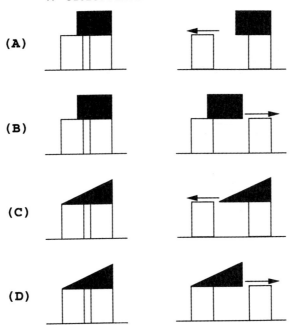

FIG. 7.12. Schematic depictions of events used to investigate 7.5- and 9.5-month-olds' understanding of support relations. (A) Habituation event (left) and possible test event (there is sufficient contact for the top object to remain supported). (B) Habituation event (left) and impossible test event (there is insufficient contact for the top object to remain supported). Infants looked longer at the impossible test event, suggesting sensitivity to amount of contact as information for support. (C) Habituation event (left) and possible test event (the top object would remain balanced and thus supported). (D) Habituation event (left) and impossible test event (the top object is off balance and thus should fall). There was no preference for either test event, suggesting that the infants did not attend to balance in reasoning about the top object's support. Note that the amount of contact in events (C) and (D) is equivalent. (Adapted from Baillargeon and Hanko-Summers, 1990.)

and when it rolled up, it decelerated (adults report these changes in speed appear natural). The infants were then presented with test events in which the incline changed (from down to up, or from up to down), and both acceleration and deceleration of the ball were shown, in alternation. Only the 7-month-olds responded during test by looking longer at the unnatural event, even though the speed of the ball in that event was familiar. Thus 7-month-olds, but not 5-month-olds, seemed to understand that an object rolling down a hill accelerates, whereas an object rolling up a hill decelerates.

The final study to be discussed concerns object identity. Xu and Carey (1996) provide evidence that full object identity is not attained until 12 months of age. Ten- and 12-month-old infants were familiarised with events in which two distinct objects were repeatedly brought out from behind a screen, one at a time (Fig. 7.13). To adults, this gave the impression of two objects behind the screen. After familiarisation, the infants were shown one- and two-object displays in alternation (no screen). In previous experiments, Xu and Carey had noted a strong *baseline* preference for two objects versus one object – that is, infants find two objects more interesting than one, regardless of any familiarisation period. If the infants expected two objects to be involved in the familiarisation event, they should look longer at the one-object test event. However, because of the strong baseline preference for two objects, it might be more likely that this novelty preference would be manifested by an equivalent preference for both displays (i.e. the baseline and novelty preferences would "pull" the infants' interest in different directions, cancelling each other). The 10-month-olds showed a preference for two objects during test, no different from baseline. The 12-month-olds, on the other hand, showed an equivalent preference for the one- and two-object test displays, suggesting that the one-object display was novel (although the two-object display was still rather interesting).

This intriguing finding indicates that when 10-month-old infants view two distinct objects appearing at different times from behind an occluder, they do not seem to form an impression of two objects – rather, they appear satisfied thinking there may be only one object! Xu and Carey (1996) account for this result by suggesting that although 10-month-olds have a concept of *object*, they do not seem to have a concept of individual objects (*sortals*) that can be distinguished on the basis of appearance. This finding is especially interesting in light of the fact that even neonates can distinguish objects based on appearance – that is, they will habituate to one object and dishabituate to another. However, this does not necessarily mean that objects are thought of as stable in appearance, an important aspect of object identity.

CAVEATS: THE PROBLEMS OF REPLICABILITY AND DISAGREEMENT BETWEEN STUDIES

I have highlighted the results of dozens of studies in the preceding sections of this chapter. (This list of studies is far from exhaustive. For example, I have omitted studies of infants' perception of number and causality, and categorisation abilities.) On the basis of these findings, today's commonly accepted view is that in his or her first year the infant is highly competent in the perception and knowledge of the world and its objects. This view is not universally accepted, but it is supported by the majority of the evidence. In this section, I discuss problems that are faced in interpretations

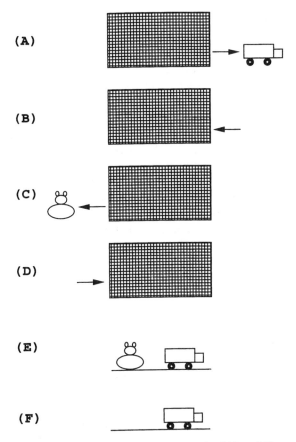

FIG. 7.13.   Schematic depictions of events used in a study of 10- and 12-month-olds' object identity. (A), (B), (C), and (D) consisted of two distinct toys repeatedly brought out from behind a screen, and returned. (E) and (F): two- and one-object displays, respectively. See text for details. (Adapted from Xu & Carey, 1996.)

of some of the data presented earlier, in terms of failures to replicate reported results, and disagreements between outcomes of studies.

Good scientific studies have three characteristics: they are objective, they are based on measurable phenomena, and they are replicable. The last point is especially important in a relatively new field of endeavour, such as the study of infants' perceptual and cognitive abilities. (Systematic studies of infant visual perception only began about 35 years ago; see Fantz, 1961.) Many of the findings described earlier have been replicated under various conditions. However, others have not been as replicable.

An example of a phenomenon that has been widely replicated is infants' perception of object unity. Since the publishing of Kellman and Spelke's original studies in 1983, there have been over a half-dozen reports of similar findings, by investigators in different laboratories, using somewhat diverse techniques (e.g. real objects vs. computer-generated displays) with infants at various ages. Such a pattern of consistent results suggests that perception of object unity is a reasonably robust phenomenon, and argues persuasively that it is representative of infants' "true" abilities.

A phenomenon that has not been as widely replicated is the surprise infants demonstrate when one object seems to pass through the space occupied by another object. Baillargeon has reported several instances of replications of the rotating screen study (e.g. Baillargeon, 1987). However, other investigators have found this effect difficult to replicate. For example, Cohen (1995) cites an instance in which 8-month-olds did not seem surprised by a computer-generated event in which a ball appeared to roll straight through a solid wall! The point here is not to call into question the results of any study or series of studies, but rather to impart a sense of healthy scepticism, and to underscore the importance of the generalisability of an effect to its acceptance.

A problem related to replicability is sets of studies that produce conflicting results. For example, Needham and Baillargeon (1993) reported that 4.5-month-olds looked longer at an event in which a hand deposited a box seemingly in mid-air, compared to when the box rested on a surface. In an investigation of infants' understanding of object continuity, Spelke et al. (1992, Experiment 4) showed 4-month-olds an event in which a ball dropped behind a screen, and was later revealed to be resting on the floor, or seemingly floating in mid-air (it was supported from behind). In contrast to what would be expected on the basis of Needham and Baillargeon's result, the infants did not look longer at the impossible event. Needham and Baillargeon suggest that perhaps the infants observed by Spelke et al. did not show surprise at the lack of support because they were somehow able to infer the presence of hidden support. At minimum, these conflicting results suggest that this level of object knowledge is fragile in its early form.

The problem of disagreement is not limited to these two studies. In many cases, studies of a newly discovered phenomenon will produce conflicting results. This is often due to methodological issues, as it may be in the example given earlier. But it also suggests, again, that it is wise to maintain a sceptical attitude.

THEORETICAL ACCOUNTS OF THE DEVELOPMENT OF OBJECT KNOWLEDGE

I have contrasted Piaget's theory with an account of burgeoning visual skills, thereby implying that much learning about the world must necessarily take place by observing objects and events over the first year of life.

I think this is accurate, but this view is not yet well specified, and it should not be considered a proper theory of the development of object perception and object knowledge. The two most well-known theories of these phenomena are those of Elizabeth Spelke and Renee Baillargeon. These researchers take contrasting views of early cognitive development.

Spelke (1994; Spelke & Van de Walle, 1993) proposes that a system of "core principles" guides infants' perception and knowledge of objects from birth. These principles arise from an intuitive, innate theory of objects and their physical properties. Spelke's view discounts distinctions between perception and knowledge in infants, stressing instead that understanding the world is based on intuitions of objects as obeying certain constraints, the principles of *cohesion, contact,* and *continuity.* For example, perception of object unity, on this account, arises from the tendency to assign visible surfaces to the same object, if the surfaces undergo common motion and lead behind an occluder (the principle of contact: surfaces move together if and only if they are in contact). Spelke adds that early knowledge encompasses fundamental environmental constraints, the highly reliable ways in which objects behave. Because our ancestors evolved under these same constraints, natural selection may have endowed humans with innate knowledge that captures their essence.

Support for Spelke's view comes from parallels between infants' and adults' physical knowledge. For example, adults do not expect an object to travel from one place to another without following a continuous path between places (the principle of continuity). We have seen that 4-month-olds seem to have the same expectation (Spelke, 1988). However, adults often have difficulty with appropriate expectations of object inertia, a constraint dictating that moving objects travel on straight paths until they come to rest. Kaiser, McCloskey, and Proffitt (1986), for instance, found that many adults expect a ball that rolls out of a curved tube to continue following a curved trajectory. Likewise, infants' understanding of inertia seems less well-developed than other kinds of physical knowledge. Spelke, Katz, Purcell, Ehrlich, and Breinlinger (1994) reported that sensitivity to inertia appears to emerge quite gradually. Even at 10 months of age, infants did not seem to reliably expect a moving object to come to rest in a predictable spot behind an occluder.

In contrast to Spelke, Baillargeon (1994) depicts the development of object perception and object knowledge in terms of innate mechanisms that guide learning. When infants first learn about a new physical phenomenon, they form a preliminary, "all-or-none" *initial concept* that captures the essence of the phenomenon but few of its details. Added experience leads to the identification of relevant *variables* with which the initial concept is elaborated. For example, infants initially expect unsupported objects to fall, unless there is some contact with another surface

(Needham & Baillargeon, 1993). This initial concept may arise from the many experiences infants have watching objects drop, experiences that are ubiquitous and available from birth. With further experience, such as manual exploration, and placement of objects on surfaces, infants may realise that the amount of contact is important in predicting whether an object will fall. Thus *amount of contact* becomes a relevant variable in understanding of support relations. We have seen that 7.5- to 9.5-month-olds are sensitive to amount of contact as important in support relations (Baillargeon & Hanko-Summers, 1990), but do not seem to realise that *balance* is also involved, a variable that may require even more experience to be identified.

Evidence for Baillargeon's (1994) view comes from patterns of learning of a variety of other physical phenomena, such as collision and "unveiling" (revealing an object under a cloth cover). At 2.5 months of age, infants demonstrate understanding that a wheeled toy should roll when hit by another object. However, it is not until after 5.5 months of age that infants seem to make judgements about how far the toy should roll, based on the size of the object that strikes it. At 9.5 months of age, infants seem to understand that a protuberance under a cloth cover signifies an object underneath, but not until 12.5 months do they judge the hidden object's size based on the size of the protuberance.

Note that both Spelke and Baillargeon postulate innate skills that contribute to object perception and object knowledge, Spelke in the form of concepts and Baillargeon in the form of mechanisms for learning. That is, the infant *brings something to the task* of knowing the world. Knowledge does not arise from nothing – the infant is not considered a "blank slate". For Spelke, development is a process of enrichment of initial conceptions. For Baillargeon, development is a process of applying learning mechanisms to available data. Both theories are highly attractive and intriguing, and each can account for a proportion of the data presented here.

Nevertheless, each theory has its problems. For example, Spelke's (1994) postulated core principles fail to account for the development of perception of object unity. Recall that the contact principle dictates that surfaces that move together must be connected. We have seen that neonates do not seem to perceive object unity in displays with rod parts undergoing common motion (Slater et al., 1996). Moreover, 4-month-olds do not perceive unity in displays in which the rod parts are misaligned (Johnson & Aslin, 1996). Spelke's theory also has difficulty explaining why *gravity* is not a core principle. This is a fundamental constraint on object behaviour, but infants do not seem sensitive to gravity until after 5 months of age (Spelke et al., 1994).

Baillargeon's (1994) theory of innate learning mechanisms does not adequately capture innate perceptual abilities, such as size and shape constancy (Slater et al., 1990; Slater & Morison, 1985), nor can it provide an account of neonates' preference for faces (Johnson et al., 1991). (In fairness, it should be noted that Baillargeon limits her theory to infants' physical knowledge.) It is clear that both theories provide important ways of looking at infants' perceptual and conceptual skills, and although both successfully capture some aspects of the development of these abilities, neither furnishes a complete account on its own.

CONCLUSIONS

The studies presented in this chapter portray infants as limited in many aspects of object perception and object knowledge but highly competent in others, and certainly capable of rapid learning about objects and their properties. It seems as if the most rapid period of development of these skills is in the first few weeks of life. For example, consider the emergence of perception of object unity. Neonates apparently only respond to what they see directly, not inferring the unity of the rod parts even in displays rich in visual cues. Within 2 months, this ability has emerged. How does this happen? (This question may seem reminiscent of the questions I asked earlier in the chapter.)

The precise mechanisms of visual learning remain a mystery. Are cognitive abilities limited by poor visual skills? That is, does suboptimal vision prevent infants from effectively sampling the visual array, thus depriving them of the opportunity to abstract information about objects? Or are visual skills limited by poor cognitive abilities? That is, does inefficient attention prevent infants from attending to the most informative aspects of the environment? It may be that these questions themselves are ill-founded. They are certainly based on my view that visual learning is of primary importance to humans. Other researchers might disagree. My goal with this discussion is not to answer all the questions, but rather to leave you with a sense of wonder about how it is that you perceive and know so much, and how that came to be.

REFERENCES

Aslin, R.N. (1981). Development of smooth pursuit in human infants. In D.F. Fisher, R.A. Monty, & J.W. Senders (Eds.), *Eye movements: Cognition and visual perception* (pp. 31–51). Hillsdale, NJ: Erlbaum.

Aslin, R.N., & Johnson, S.P. (1994, May). *Suppression of VOR by human infants*. Poster presented at the Association for Research in Vision and Ophthalmology conference, Sarasota, FL.

Aslin, R.N., & Johnson, S.P. (1996). Suppression of the optokinetic reflex in human infants: Implications for stable fixation and shifts of attention. *Infant Behavior and Development*, **19**, 235–242.

Atkinson, J. (1984). Human visual development over the first six months of life: A review and a hypothesis. *Human Neurobiology*, **3**, 61–74.

Baillargeon, R. (1987). Object permanence in 3½ and 4½-month-old infants. *Developmental Psychology*, **23**, 655–664.

Baillargeon, R. (1994). How do infants learn about the physical world? *Current Directions in Psychological Science*, **3**, 133–140.

Baillargeon, R., & DeVos, J. (1991). Object permanence in young infants: Further evidence. *Child Development*, **62**, 1227–1246.

Baillargeon, R., Graber, M., DeVos, J., & Black, J. (1990). Why do infants fail to search for hidden objects? *Cognition*, **36**, 255–284.

Baillargeon, R., & Hanko-Summers, S. (1990). Is the top object adequately supported by the bottom object? Young infants' understanding of support relations. *Cognitive Development*, **5**, 29–53.

Banks, M.S., & Salapatek, P. (1981). Infant pattern vision: A new approach based on the contrast sensitivity function. *Journal of Experimental Child Psychology*, **31**, 1–45.

Bronson, G.W. (1990). Changes in infants' visual scanning across the 2- to 14-week age period. *Journal of Experimental Child Psychology*, **49**, 101–125.

Bronson, G.W. (1991). Infant differences in rate of visual encoding. *Child Development*, **62**, 44–54.

Bushnell, I.W.R., Sai, F., & Mullin, J.T. (1989). Neonatal recognition of the mother's face. *British Journal of Developmental Psychology*, **7**, 3–15.

Cohen, L.B. (1995, March). *How solid is infants' understanding of solidity?* Paper presented at the Society for Research in Child Development conference, Indianapolis, IN.

Craton, L.G. (1996). The development of perceptual completion abilities: Infants' perception of stationary, partially occluded objects. *Child Development*, **67**, 890–904.

Fantz, R.L. (1961). A method for studying depth perception in infants under six months of age. *Psychological Record*, **11**, 27–32.

Haith, M.M. (1980). *Rules that babies look by*. Hillsdale, NJ: Erlbaum.

Johnson, M.H. (1990). Cortical maturation and the development of visual attention in early infancy. *Journal of Cognitive Neuroscience*, **2**, 81–95.

Johnson, M.H., Dziurawiec, S., Ellis, H., & Morton, J. (1991). Newborns' preferential tracking of face-like stimuli and its subsequent decline. *Cognition*, **40**, 1–19.

Johnson, S.P., and Aslin, R.N. (1995). Perception of object unity in 2-month-old infants. *Developmental Psychology*, **31**, 739–745.

Johnson, S.P., & Aslin, R.N. (1996). Perception of object unity in young infants: The roles of motion, depth, and orientation. *Cognitive Development*, **11**, 161–180.

Johnson, S.P., & Náñez, J.E. (1995). Young infants' perception of object unity in two-dimensional displays. *Infant Behavior and Development*, **18**, 133–143.

Kaiser, M.K., McCloskey, M., & Proffitt, D.R. (1986). Development of intuitive theories of motion: Curvilinear motion in the absence of external forces. *Developmental Psychology*, **22**, 67–71.

Kellman, P.J. (1993). Kinematic foundations of visual perception. In C. Granrud (Ed.), *Visual perception and cognition in infancy* (pp. 121–173). Hillsdale, NJ: Erlbaum.

Kellman, P.J., & Shipley, T.F. (1991). A theory of visual interpolation in object perception. *Cognitive Psychology*, **23**, 141–221.

Kellman, P.J., & Spelke, E.S. (1983). Perception of partly occluded objects in infancy. *Cognitive Psychology*, **15**, 483–524.

Kellman, P.J., Spelke, E.S., & Short, K.R. (1986). Infant perception of object unity from translatory motion in depth and vertical translation. *Child Development*, **57**, 72–86.

Kestenbaum, R., Termine, N., & Spelke, E.S. (1987). Perception of objects and object boundaries by 3-month-old infants. *British Journal of Developmental Psychology*, **5**, 367–383.

Kim, I.K., & Spelke, E.S. (1992). Infants' sensitivity to effects of gravity on visible object motion. *Journal of Experimental Psychology: Human Perception and Performance,* **18,** 385–393.

Needham, A., & Baillargeon, R. (1993). Intuitions about support in 4.5-month-old infants. *Cognition,* **47,** 121–148.

Pascalis, O., de Schonen, S., Morton, J., Deruelle, C., & Fabre-Grenet, M. (1995). Mother's face recognition by neonates: A replication and an extension. *Infant Behavior and Development,* **18,** 79–85.

Piaget, J. (1952). *The origins of intelligence in children.* New York: International Universities Press.

Piaget, J. (1954). *The construction of reality in the child.* New York: Basic Books.

Prechtl, H.F.R. (Ed.) (1984). *Continuity of neural functions from prenatal to postnatal life.* Oxford: Blackwell.

Slater, A. (1995). Visual perception and memory at birth. In C. Rovee-Collier and L. Lipsitt (Eds.), *Advances in infancy research* (Vol. 9, pp. 107–162). Norwood, NJ: Ablex.

Slater, A., Johnson, S.P., Brown, E., & Badenoch, M. (1996). Newborn infants' perception of partly occluded objects. *Infant Behavior and Development,* **19,** 145–148.

Slater, A., Johnson, S.P., Kellman, P.J., & Spelke, E.S. (1994). The role of three-dimensional depth cues in infants' perception of partly occluded objects. *Early Development and Parenting,* **3,** 187–191.

Slater, A., Mattock, A., & Brown, E. (1990). Size constancy at birth: Newborn infants' responses to retinal and real size. *Journal of Experimental Child Psychology,* **49,** 314–322.

Slater, A., & Morison, V. (1985). Shape constancy and slant perception at birth. *Perception,* **14,** 337–344.

Slater, A., Morison, V., & Rose, D. (1982). Visual memory at birth. *British Journal of Psychology,* **73,** 519–525.

Slater, A., Morison, V., Somers, M., Mattock, A., Brown, E., and Taylor, D. (1990). Newborn and older infants' perception of partly occluded objects. *Infant Behavior and Development,* **13,** 33–49.

Slater, A., Morison, V., Town, C., & Rose, D. (1985). Movement perception and identity constancy in the new-born baby. *British Journal of Developmental Psychology,* **3,** 211–220.

Spelke, E.S. (1988). Where perceiving ends and thinking begins: The apprehension of objects in infancy. In A. Yonas (Ed.), *Perceptual development in infancy* (pp. 197–234). Minnesota Symposium, Vol. 20. Hillsdale, NJ: Erlbaum.

Spelke, E.S. (1994). Initial knowledge: Six suggestions. *Cognition,* **50,** 431–445.

Spelke, E.S., Breinlinger, K., Macomber, J., & Jacobson, K. (1992). Origins of knowledge. *Psychological Review,* **19,** 605–632.

Spelke, E.S., Katz, G., Purcell, S.E., Ehrlich, S.M., & Breinlinger, K. (1994). Early knowledge of object motion: Continuity and inertia. *Cognition,* **51,** 131–176.

Spelke, E.S., & Van de Walle, G.A. (1993). Perceiving and reasoning about objects: Insights from infants. In N. Eilan, R. McCarthy, & B. Brewer (Eds.), *Spatial representation: Problems in philosophy and psychology* (pp. 132–161). Oxford: Blackwell.

Wellman, H.M., Cross, D., & Bartsch, K. (1987). Infant search and object permanence: A meta-analysis of the A-not-B error. *Monographs of the Society for Research in Child Development,* **51**(3), Serial No. 214.

Xu, F., & Carey, S. (1996). Infants' metaphysics: The case of numerical identity. *Cognitive Psychology,* **30,** 111–153.

Perception of social stimuli

Introduction

The chapters in Part II are primarily concerned with the development of infants' knowledge about the physical world – spatial awareness, categorisation, causality, and the world of objects. One extremely important aspect of perception, of course, is perception of social stimuli, that is people, and this is the focus of the chapters in Part III.

In Chapter 8 Muir and Nadel describe many of the ways in which infants engage in dynamic social interactions with others, where the others are one or two adults, or peers with no adults present. Infants discriminate between objects and people from an early age. For example (and related to Chapter 6), 7-month-olds expect an object that moves to have been set in motion by another object (or person) colliding with it, or pushing it; people, on the other hand, do not require an external force to be applied to them to begin moving. Muir and Nadel propose that this perception of agency that is attributed to people is probably operating as early as 2 months of age when infants are engaged in face-to-face interactions with others: at this age infants become upset if the adult reacts noncontingently, perhaps by the mother presenting a "still-face", with a neutral, fixed expression.

Muir and Nadel explore the effects of several variables on infants' responses in an interacting situation. These include changes in eye-direction (looking at, or away from the infant), upright versus inverted faces, happy or sad facial expression (of the adult!), voice (presence or not, and synchronised or not with the lips), and interacting or not (i.e. the still-face effect). In order to allow these manipulations to be made, the adult's face is usually shown on a monitor placed in front of the infant.

They make two general points. An important methodological point is that when the interacting adult's social stimuli change, conventional measures of the amount of visual attention displayed by the infant may be entirely insensitive to the change. However, and in marked contrast, all of the changes affect the amount of smiling by the infant: the largest impact is when the adult stops interacting (the still-face effect), and when the adult face is shown inverted, which presumably makes it difficult for the infant to read the adult's facial expression. The second point they stress is that infant social perception cannot be fully described by nonsocial test procedures, such as visual habituation and preferential-looking paradigms, as such procedures, of course, are usually insensitive to the dynamic nature of social interactions.

Facial expressions are an important way of communicating emotions: if we can recognise facial emotion we are then in a position to detect another person's emotional state or reactions, and we have cues to how to respond and behave in social situations. Clearly, in order to begin to understand the meaning of different facial expressions, infants must be able to discriminate between them. De Haan and Nelson, in Chapter 9, discuss the development of infants' perceptual categories of emotion. They begin their review by describing the development of infants' ability to discriminate different facial emotions. Some emotional expressions (i.e. happy, sad, surprise) appear to be discriminated soon after birth, whereas others are discriminated later: for instance, 6-month-olds show no evidence of discriminating joy from anger or interest.

De Haan and Nelson then turn to the development of the ability to categorise emotional expressions, that is, to recognise that discriminably different exemplars of the same emotion, or group of emotions, are similar. Even by 10 months infants often have difficulty in recognising an expression when nonprototypical exemplars are shown. They then discuss ways in which facial expressions may be encoded by infants: whether infants attend to specific facial features in detecting expressions; whether they respond on the basis of configurations of features (holistic) rather than individual features.

A major conclusion is that there is currently insufficient evidence either to confirm or to disconfirm the hypothesis that facial expressions are somehow "special" relative to other stimuli, or that there are special-purpose neural processors (or modules) designed for recognising facial expressions.

The two chapters in this section present an interesting contrast. In de Haan and Nelson's chapter the main evidence comes from studies in which visual preferences, habituation–dishabituation, and familiarisation-test procedures are used. Muir and Nadel focus on studies in which infants are engaged in dynamic interactions. As they point out, converging evidence from the different types of procedures reveal that infants react to a variety of social stimuli, and discriminate different emotional expressions from early infancy. Clearly, the different procedures combine to tell the developmental story. The aim for the future is to integrate the evidence from different procedures to provide a comprehensive picture of the development of infant social perception.

CHAPTER EIGHT

Infant social perception

Darwin W. Muir
Queen's University, Kingston, Ontario, Canada

Jacqueline Nadel
Laboratoire de Psycho-Biologie du Développement, EPHE-CNRS, Paris, France

INTRODUCTION

Long ago, Wallon (1934, 1938) put forward an overview of ways to study ontogenesis that stressed the value of taking into account simultaneously the two facets of development: emerging properties and disappearing features. Although there is little disagreement that human development can best be conceptualised in this manner, as a dynamic system that integrates both emerging and fading behaviours as a function of age, currently little use is being made of this consensual statement.

Within Wallon's framework, transitory adaptations are critical for mapping epigenesis as they highlight the basic, rather than vestigial, functions of momentary adaptive means (Nadel, 1994). The study of transitory adaptations helps us to recognise that distinct behaviours may fulfil the same adaptive function during different developmental periods, and that similar behaviours may have different meanings according to the developmental level (Nadel 1980, 1984). Behaviours change, or change their function and meaning, over the course of ontogenesis. This stresses the heterotypic aspect of the developmental process. One example that illustrates a change in meaning is the infant's waving behaviour. Blurton-Jones and Leach (1972) note that "waving" is used to indicate the child's approach before one year of age, and signals his/her departure after one year of age. A second example is a perceptual response that changes radically during the first year of life – the auditory localisation response.

At birth, infants turn repeatedly toward off-centred sound sources, including voices and nonanimate rattle sounds, in an almost obligatory fashion. At around 1 month of age they stop turning towards sounds, and at around 4 months of age they again turn reliably to sounds. After 5 months of age, the auditory localisation response habituates rapidly without visual reinforcement (see review by Muir, Clifton, & Clarkson, 1989). A third example illustrates a disappearing function of a behaviour. Imitation serves two functions in young children, a cognitive function of exploring and understanding events (for instance, how to open a new box), and a social-communicative function of interpersonal exchange (Uzgiris, 1981). After 2 years of age, however, the communicative function declines and the use of imitation as a means of communication disappears with language mastery after 3 years of age (Nadel & Fontaine, 1989). These observations need to be considered when designing experimental paradigms, as well as in selecting relevant parameters in the study of social perception. Both the nature of the stimuli and the method of evaluating the infant's competence have to be changed according to the agenda of the evolving capacities and goals of the baby.

An important consideration derived from Wallon's (1934) view is that relevant situations must be constructed so that children will spontaneously select the responses that they construe to be the most efficient means to achieve their goals. In Chapter 9 de Haan and Nelson provide an excellent review of the perception of faces in pictures, based primarily on the visual habituation literature. Habituation procedures are very effective tools for studying infant perception; they tell us when babies can discriminate among stimuli, and when they generalise in categorical perception studies. However, we have argued that infant competence in social perception is optimally revealed by placing them in a social context (e.g. Gusella, Muir, & Tronick, 1988; Muir, Hains, & Symons, 1994a). A relatively natural context should exploit the infants' functional resources to perform optimally since their goal is explicit. As Butterworth (1986, p. 6) notes:

> ... early infant perception is most efficient in the complex dynamic case. The apparently simple, static, two-dimensional visual stimulus is actually atypical of the spatiotemporal world to which the infant is biologically pre-adapted. The static case actually required an analysis akin to that involved in explaining picture perception. Perception in the baby is not pre-adapted for comprehending pictures. Rather it is based on events and encounters of adaptive significance from whatever modality the information is derived. It is from this dynamic spatio-temporal perspective on perception that exciting insights have come which hold such promise for further study of the perceptual world of the young baby ...

A case for using face-to-face interactions

Observations in naturalistic settings should be the ideal method for examining infant social capacities, but they are difficult contexts to study as they include many uncontrolled variables. Furthermore, naturalistic observations do not guarantee ecological validity, as systematic observations introduce noise in the ecological system being observed. The abilities of very young infants to make social discrimination responses, to respond to and imitate adult emotional and gestural expressions, and to sense the contingent aspects of adult stimulation have to be clearly demonstrated with careful experimental observations that permit one to distinguish description from interpretation.

It has been our observation that only a few paradigms have documented social perception using face-to-face interactions between the baby and either one or more adults, or peers with no adults present. In this chapter, we will review the evidence for the development of social perception during infancy with a focus on studies that employ dynamic, contingent displays of people in relatively complex contexts to provide a portrait of the infant's early competence in social perception. We will begin by defining dynamic social, as opposed to object, perception. Some theorists who study object–person differentiation have derived a set of rules that they hypothesise infants use when they respond to objects (visual attention; instrumental acts) as opposed to people (social interactions; communicative acts) in their environment. For example, Premack and Premack (1995) proposed that infants perceive people as perceptual events that are self-propelled and goal-directed objects. Spelke, Phillips, and Woodward (1995, p. 60) elaborated the following description of the infant's concept of humans: "Three aspects of human interactions that are accessible in principle to young infants are contingency (humans react to one another), reciprocity (humans respond in kind to one another's actions), and communication (humans supply one another with information)." Spelke et al. provided evidence that infants perceive object motion using three principles, including the "Principle of Contact". To illustrate the contact principle, they employed a habituation procedure to show that infants expect an object that moves to have been set in motion by another object (or person) pushing it; people, on the other hand, did not require an external force to be applied for them to begin moving. Spelke et al. demonstrated that this perception of agency is present by 7 months of age.

We propose that the perception of agency is probably operating in infants as early as 2 months of age when face-to-face interaction procedures are used. This is an effective context for infants to display their social-perceptual competence. Although newborns may have some competency in social perception, it is not always easy to generate reciprocal responding during the first few weeks of life. We will argue that there is a developmental course for the establishment of social perception, beginning with some primitive abilities during the newborn period, followed by new developments during the first 1–2 months after birth. By 3 months of age, infants readily engage in face-to-face interactions, but do not seem to process adult responses to other objects and people in their environment. They seem to be fixed on dyadic interactions, responding to one object or person at a time. By 6 to 9 months of age, infants focus more on novel objects in their environment, using the adults to obtain information about third parties. Around this age, imitation both becomes reciprocal during face–voice interactions, and is used to interact in a social manner with objects. This has been referred to as the onset of social referencing. We propose that the social referencing concept is valid, but too simple. As discussed near the end of the chapter, as infants age, their social referencing behaviour becomes increasingly complex. For example, during social engagements they begin to imitate each other's actions with various objects in the environment; this behaviour is triggered when they are provided with identical objects (Eckerman, 1993; Nadel & Peze, 1993; Nadel-Brulfert & Baudonnière, 1982). We will conclude by arguing that much of our current understanding of infant social perception has been paradigm-bound – e.g. based on visual habituation procedures. New paradigms for studying social perception provide converging evidence that infants use "social perception" to establish a base for cognitive development.

NEWBORN SOCIAL PERCEPTION

Even newborns may have a rudimentary form of social perception. At this age, infants readily orient to auditory, visual, and tactile stimulation (see Muir, Humphrey, & Humphrey, 1994b review). Indeed, Blass, Ganchrow, and Steiner (1984) demonstrated that newborns rapidly form expectancies. Blass et al. established the expectancy for food by preceding its delivery to one side of the mouth with a stroke on the newborn's forehead, using a modified classical conditioning procedure. Infants began to anticipate the food reward by turning and making sucking responses as soon as they were touched, thereby demonstrating associative learning. More important in the present context, almost all infants cried when the food reward was withheld during extinction – their response to a violation of expectancy.

As noted earlier, neonates are very sensitive to dynamic auditory stimulation. They readily turn towards the location of a voice. Furthermore, they prefer one voice over another – they will change their sucking pattern to produce their mother's voice over that of a stranger (e.g. DeCasper &

Fifer, 1980). This latter finding indicates that babies have been processing auditory input during the foetal period (foetal auditory perception is reviewed in Chapter 10).

Newborns have very poor visual acuity (Banks & Ginsberg, 1985) and lack patterned visual experience during the foetal period. Thus, one would expect their ability to perceive faces to be very limited (see also Chapter 4). However, immediately after birth neonates will visually track a schematic face further than the same elements in scrambled configurations (e.g. Johnson & Morton, 1991). Newborns also appear to establish a memory for repeated presentations of a picture of a face (habituation–novelty test) that lasts for several minutes (Pascalis & de Schonen, 1994). By 4 days of age, when they are presented with their mother's face next to a stranger's face, neonates look longer at their mothers (Bushnell, Sai, & Mullin, 1989; Field, Cohen, Garcia, & Greenberg, 1984). However, this apparent maternal face preference may not have been based on the internal features of the face. When Pascalis, de Schonen, Morton, Deruelle, and Fabre-Grenet (1995) obscured the hairline by having mothers and strangers wear head scarves, the preference for the mother's face disappeared. Pascalis et al. concluded that newborns appear to learn the outer rather than inner features of the face.

Newborns do attend to internal features of the face that move. Researchers have shown that newborns as young as 20 minutes (Kugiumutzakis, 1985; Reissland, 1988) or 42 minutes (Meltzoff & Moore, 1983) of age can successfully imitate facial expressions, provided they see facial movement (Vinter, 1986). Newborns have been reported to imitate not only tongue protrusion, but a large range of gestures including mouth opening (Heimann & Schaller, 1985; Legerstee, 1991), lip pursing, eye blinking (e.g. Kugiumutzakis, in press), head movements, cheek movements (Fontaine, 1984), and hand gestures (Meltzoff & Moore, 1989). It has also been reported that they will imitate vocal sounds such as /m/, /a/, and /ang/ as early as 40 minutes after birth (Kugiumutzakis, 1993). Finally, Field and co-workers report that neonates will imitate happy, sad, and surprise facial emotional expressions (e.g. Field et al., 1983).

The neonatal imitation phenomena cannot be a product of learning, given the babies' brief experience with adult caretakers. Also, it appears to be more than a rote, automatic mechanism, because it appears to be effortful (e.g. the preparatory movements of the tongue inside the buccal cavity, or the improvements of vocal matching) and includes corrections of "mistakes" as reported by several authors (Heimann, 1989; Kugiumutzakis, in press; Maratos, 1973; Meltzoff & Moore, 1983). More likely, imitation by newborns is an innate capacity in the human species. Such early imitative abilities question the connection between perception and the control of action, in so far as newborns see a model and spontaneously produce an action based on this perception. Is this capacity different from other examples of perceptual–motor coupling like catching moving objects (von Hofsten, 1983), or avoiding looming objects (Bower, Broughton & Moore, 1970)? Meltzoff has argued that imitation is distinctive because it reveals an "interpersonal" coupling. According to Meltzoff and Moore (in press) infants are regulating their actions in order to bring them in line with a dynamically changing, animate display, rather than with an inanimate visual framework. Meltzoff and Moore also emphasise that even newborns are able to imitate a person or action that has disappeared from view; these imitative acts are not coupled with current perception. In the "observation-only" design developed by Meltzoff (1985), infants are shown a target act but not allowed to respond immediately (e.g. they observe a model's tongue protrusion while sucking on a pacifier that prevents any imitative response). Even newborns will produce an imitation (tongue protrusion) while looking at the model's stationary face when the pacifier is removed a few minutes later.

We now have convincing evidence that newborns can discriminate one face/hairline or voice from another (at least the mother's from a stranger's face/voice) and various internal features of dynamic faces; however, the basis for such discriminations has not been established. We do not know if newborns are processing the face as a Gestalt, using configural (relational) properties, or are simply responding to a difference in local features (e.g. two dots in the upper visual field). Furthermore, many of the face-discrimination effects we have described are weak. It is generally the case that many neonates fail the discrimination test, or only show a very small preference, as a group. This visual performance contrasts with the newborn's easily elicited orientation to off-centred sound sources (e.g. Muir & Field, 1979) and their capacity rapidly to form expectancies based on associative learning (e.g. Blass et al., 1984) . The infants' competence in social perception at such an early age may be hard to reveal because of their limited behavioural repertoire of brief visual attention and crying. Perhaps more powerful procedures, like Blass's, which establish a "social expectancy" and then violate that expectancy, will reveal new social competencies during the newborn period.

SOCIAL AWAKENING BETWEEN 1 AND 2 MONTHS OF AGE

A dramatic shift in perceptual responses to both auditory and visual stimuli occurs between 1 and 2 months of age. For example, a number of studies have shown that infants stop turning towards off-centred sounds around 5 to 6 weeks of age (e.g. Muir et al., 1989), which contrasts with the almost perfect performance displayed during the newborn period. At the same time 1- to 2-month-olds display long fixation times to visual patterns (e.g. Stechler & Latz, 1966). Humphrey (reported in Muir et al., 1994b) compared the behaviour of 2- and 4-month-olds on auditory localisation and visual fixation tasks in the same test session. The auditory stimulus was a recorded rattle sound presented 90 degrees to the left and right of midline which lasted for 20 seconds or until the infant made a head-turn greater than 45 degrees. The visual task consisted of presenting a central red-and-black bullseye pattern for a 2-minute inspection period. The 2-month-olds rarely turned towards the sound source (23% correct) and seemed to be captured by the visual target (fixating the bullseye for 90% of the inspection period; first fixation lasting M = 14sec). This contrasts with the performance of 3- to 4-month-olds who turned towards the sound sources on 90% of the trials and were less captured by the bullseye (looking at it for only 25% of the period; first fixation lasting M = 4sec). This developmental peak in visual capture suggests that when an intermodal spatial conflict occurs, infants of this age experience visual dominance that causes them to ignore sound location. However, this visual dominance explanation does not completely account for the decline in auditory localisation responses because, when visual interference was eliminated by presenting sounds in the dark, 1- to 2-month-olds still failed to turn towards the sounds (Muir, Abraham, Forbes, & Harris, 1979).

The rapid growth in sustained visual attention over the first few months of life may reflect neural maturation. For example, Johnson, Posner, and Rothbart (1991) hypothesised that the prolonged fixation in infants of this age may occur because the neural pathways that inhibit activity in the superior colliculus (which plays an important role in eye movements) mature. By 3–4 months of age, the pathway coming from the frontal eye fields to the colliculus, which controls anticipatory eye movements, develops, which allows the infant to disengage visual fixation. A similar maturation of inhibitory processes for orienting the head towards sounds may explain the temporary loss of sound localisation responses at 1–2 months of age and the recovery of the response at 3–4 months of age (a detailed theoretical discussion is given in Muir et al., 1994b).

During the first few months of life, infants become increasingly interested in looking at faces (e.g. Fantz, 1961) and display a shift in the pattern of scanning a face. Haith and his colleagues (e.g. Haith & Campos, 1977) found that 1-month-olds scanned the edge of live faces (both mother's and stranger's) more than the central features such as the eyes – a finding that may be related to the neonatal preference for mother's hairstyle. Two- to 3-month-olds fixated on the eyes and mouth more than the outer contour of the face and looked longer at talking than at silent moving faces.

Onset of social smiling

Coincident with the loss of auditory localisation responses and an increasing interest in adult faces is the onset of a major social releaser for adults – infant smiling. Social smiling has been defined as the smiling that is elicited primarily by a human face (e.g. Gewirtz, 1965; Wolff, 1987) and voice (Wolff, 1987). Although some smiling in newborns does occur (e.g. Brazelton, 1980), it is rare (e.g. Ellsworth, 1987) and usually is seen at the onset of sleep, during the rapid eye movement phase (Wolff, Gunnoe, & Cohen, 1985). Also, as noted earlier, Field et al. (1983) reported newborn imitation of adult happiness. However, during the first few weeks of life, infants have not been found to smile more at social than nonsocial stimuli (e.g. voices versus rattles; faces vs. abstract patterns [e.g. Freedman, 1974; Wolff, 1963]).

Although social smiling may be rare in the newborn period, by the end of the first month of life infants begin to smile when they are stimulated, especially by an adult's face and voice (the classic studies are by Freedman, 1974; Spitz & Wolf, 1946; Wolff, 1987). For example, Wolff (1987) reported longitudinal observations of 22 infants' responses to the voice alone versus the silent face. He found that the frequency of smiling to a human voice rapidly increased between 2 and 6 weeks of age, declined rapidly during the second month, and almost disappeared by the third month of life. At its peak, the human voice was more effective at eliciting smiles than nonhuman sounds (bells and whistles) and silent faces, suggesting that it is a social smile. Smiling elicited by an adult's silent, smiling face (nodding or stationary) was slower to develop. It began around 5 weeks of age, and rapidly increased in frequency during the second month of life. Others have noted that social smiling peaks at around 3 to 4 months of age (e.g. Gewirtz, 1965; Legerstee, Pomerleau, Malcuit, & Feider, 1987) and then declines, perhaps reflecting the onset of stranger wariness. The interaction between the developmental functions for smiling to the voice and to the face are illustrated in Fig. 8.1.

Given that both visual attention and expressions of affect (smiling and upset) are such potent social cues for adults, it seems reasonable to include both dependent measures in studies of social perception once they become functional.

The onset of sensitivity to contingent social stimulation

Social interaction theorists (e.g. Lewis & Goldberg, 1969; Stern, 1985; Trevarthen, 1974; Tronick, 1989) proposed that very early in life infants not only discriminate between adult facial and vocal expressions, but understand and respond to the "social message" during face-to-face inter-

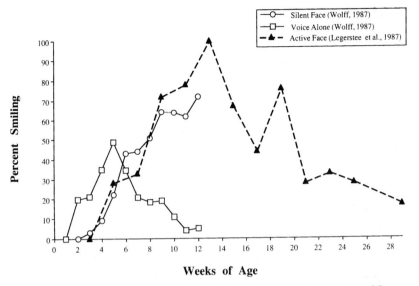

FIG. 8.1. The development of social smiling depicted by merging data abstracted from two sources. Wolff's Fig. 14 (1987, p. 119) shows the percent frequency of smiling by infants presented with a stranger's voice alone (open squares connected by solid lines) and a stranger's smiling, nodding face (open circles connected by solid lines), when they were tested weekly from 1 to 12 weeks of age. Legerstee et al.'s (1987) mean proportion smiling data for an active stranger's face were taken from her Table 1 (p. 88). To compare the two sets of data, Legerstee et al.'s data are given as the percentage of smiling relative to the maximum smiling score they obtained for 13-week-olds.

actions. Given that infants during the newborn period readily form an expectancy for associations between various stimuli, it follows that they should form an expectancy for certain adult behaviours, based on many hours of social interaction with caretakers. Tronick (1989) suggests that infant–adult interactions are bidirectional; that is, the partners are engaged in goal-directed exchanges, mutually regulating each other's emotional state in a coordinated, reciprocal manner. The "infant smiles and vocalisations (and looks) are contingent on specific maternal affective turn-taking signals ... adults make similar modifications" (Tronick, 1989, p. 115). Based on expectancy theory, Muir et al. (1994a) argued that the social perception processor is optimally engaged in a social interaction context. If this is the case, then one might expect that very young infants should be extremely sensitive to perturbations in the contingent aspects of adult social behaviour.

A good example of an infant's powerful response to a violation in expectancy is the still-face effect (Tronick, Als, Adamson, Wise, & Brazelton, 1978). It is produced by presenting infants with three brief (1–2min) periods: (1) the mother responds to the baby in a playful manner, smiling, vocalising, and touching; (2) she poses a still-face with a neutral expression and no touch; and (3) she interacts normally again. During the still-face period, relative to the normal interaction periods (or no-change controls), infant smiling drops, gaze aversion increases, and some infants become upset. This occurs in infants as young as 2 months of age (e.g. Lamb, Morrison, & Malkin, 1987). The still-face effect represents the ultimate noncontingent mother, given her total lack of social stimulation. However, infant upset might be generated by a variety of changes in her behaviour, including the loss of auditory, visual, or tactile stimulation as well as contingent stimulation.

Murray and Trevarthen (1985) developed a new procedure to isolate the importance of contingent social stimulation by mothers of infants in their second month of life (referred to as the Double Video or TV Inter-action Paradigm). They filmed five mothers and their infants while they interacted by viewing each other on TV monitors over a closed-circuit video system. Thirty seconds later, they replayed to the baby a sample of the mother's behaviour which had appeared on the baby's TV monitor during the previous contingent interaction period. In the replay condition, the mother's social stimulation does not correlate with the infant's responses. If the infant's behaviour changes, one can infer that the violation of contingency is a major parameter of social expectancies. Murray and Trevarthen reported that the infants between 6 and 12 weeks of age immediately became upset and looked away during the TV replay period. These negative responses were presumed to be the infants' reaction to the violation of their expectancy for contingent maternal stimulation. Another possibility noted by Hains and Muir (1996a) is that the increase in infant upset was simply due to an increase in fussiness with the passage of time, a common observation in infant–adult interaction studies (e.g. Gusella et al., 1988). Nadel (1996) suggested that the break between the two sequences could provoke a difference in social context that may explain the behavioural change. In any case, Murray and Trevarthen's results were obtained with a very small sample of babies of different ages, with repeated measures on the same infants.

Nadel and colleagues (Nadel, 1996; Nadel et al., 1997) modified Murray and Trevarthen's procedure by giving infants a continuous presentation of dynamic maternal behaviour for about 3 minutes, during which the shift from the live to a replay condition occurred without a break in maternal stimulation. The apparatus they used for their Double Video procedure is illustrated in Fig. 8.2. During the initial live period (Live 1) Nadel carefully selected a segment of the maternal behaviour to record for replay (Replay), which ensured that both mother and infant were engaged in highly contingent interactions. Then Nadel waited about 30 seconds before inserting the Replay segment, which was followed by a second live period (Live 2). Nadel's results for 10 9-week-olds, shown in Fig. 8.3, are in overall agreement with Murray and Trevarthen's, despite her procedural modifications, which should have made it more difficult for the infants to perceive the violation of contingency. Compared to Live 1, two positive and independent indexes decreased significantly during Replay: *gaze to mother*, which fell from 57% to 38% of time, and *smiling*, which fell from 14% to 3%, whereas two negative and independent indexes increased significantly during Replay: *frowning*, which increased from 7% to 24% of time, and *mouth closed*, which increased from 8% to 22%. Finally, fussiness cannot be invoked to explain the negative responses to the Replay, since out of the 10 babies, 7 recovered both *gaze to mother* and *smiling* during the Live 2 condition.

In summary, several results drawn from experiments that employed a social context, such as the *still-face* and *double video* paradigms, suggest that during the second month of life, infants are very sensitive to the contingent nature of social stimulation given by their mothers. However, we do not know if this sensitivity generalises to strangers, or which aspects of the adult's behaviour are the active agents. For example, are these infants responding to the adults' vocal or facial communicative signals, or both? Indeed, we do not even know if this contingency response can be generated by any "interactive" dynamic object. These issues are addressed in the next section, in studies of older infants.

SOCIAL DISCRIMINATION: SOCIAL SIGNALS DRIVING AFFECT AND ATTENTION OF 3- TO 6-MONTH-OLDS

In this section, we will focus primarily on studies in which either dynamic or contingent presentations of adult behaviour are used to establish the important components of adult stimulation that drive infant social behaviour. We recognise the importance of noninteractive procedures, such as preferential looking and visual habituation paradigms, but argue that they do not provide a complete story (see reviews in Chapters 4 and 9, and discussions by Gusella et al., 1988, and Muir & Hains, 1993). The general conclusion extracted from the visual habituation literature is that infants begin to discriminate between adult facial expressions of happy, sad, angry, neutral, and fear by 4 to 5 months of age, and match vocal and visual expressions of adult affect between 5 and 7 months of age (e.g. Walker-Andrews, 1997). However, it is difficult to interpret the order effects and null results obtained by some researchers and to rule out the possibility that these discriminations are based on the infant's response to

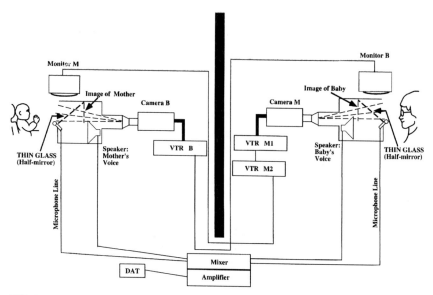

FIG. 8.2.   The design of Nadel et al.'s (1997) double video apparatus. The infant and adult viewed each other on video monitors that were reflected from half-silvered mirrors to guarantee that eye-contact was perceived by both partners during face-to-face interactions. This DAT system also allowed Nadel et al. to switch from a contingent interaction to a replay of the mother's behaviour recorded during the previous period (the noncontingent display) with no obvious (at least to adults) break in her behaviour.

a local feature, such as toothiness, rather than the defining features of the emotion, *per se.*

As mentioned earlier, a dramatic response is produced in the still-face procedure. By 2 months of age, infants appear to expect contingent social stimulation from their mothers. We used the same basic procedure of first engaging infants in a face-to-face interaction and then manipulating the adult's response during the second period to identify the infant's sensitivity to various components of the adult's behaviour (e.g. which components elicited and maintained infant social responses – looking and smiling). First, Gusella et al. (1988) established that the still-face effect was robust and could be generated experimentally (using either in-person interactions or a TV interaction procedure similar to Murray and Trevarthen's, 1985). The experimental procedure for the TV interactions is illustrated in Fig. 8.4. The general procedure for most of the interaction studies discussed in this section consisted of infants receiving three brief (1–2 min) periods of interaction in an ABA design. A was always a normal, face-to-face inter-action between an adult and the infant, whereas B was some perturbation in the adult's behaviour. Complete cessation of adult interaction was the

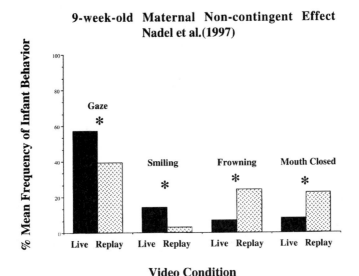

FIG. 8.3. The percent average frequency of infant behaviour from Nadel et al. (1997), which illustrates a significant (denoted by the asterisk) drop in gaze and smiling and an increase in frowning and mouth closing when the mother's behaviour was switched from contingent to a replay of her interactions during a preceding period.

most extreme perturbation – producing the still-face effect. Also, most studies included a no-change control group (AAA). Although a number of infant responses have been measured, the most useful and reliable measures appear to be frequency and duration of looking (visual attention) and smiling (positive affect).

A typical still-face effect, obtained from groups as small as $n = 6$, is shown in Fig. 8.5I,A for duration of looking and Fig. 8.5II,A for smiling (the smiling schematic face over Dynamic = normal interaction, compared with the neutral schematic face over the Static condition = still-face). As can be seen in the figure, infant attention dropped by about 50% and smiling all but disappeared (dropping from about 17% to 3%) during the still-face period, relative to normal periods (or period 2 in no-change controls, not shown). It should be noted that we found few age effects in 3- to 6-month-olds, so the age variable in various studies has been collapsed in Fig. 8.5. Finally, although about 50% of infants become upset in the still-face procedure, few infants actively protest in the manipulations described later, so in most cases negative responses are not discussed.

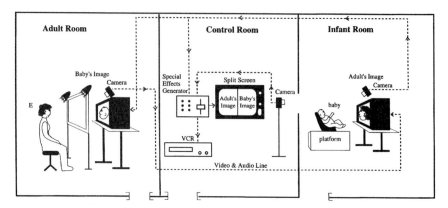

FIG. 8.4. The design of Gusella et al.'s (1988) TV interaction apparatus (abstracted from Cao et al., 1992). It should be noted that the camera in the adult's room recording the adult's behaviour was placed on top of the TV monitor that displayed the infant's behaviour at a distance of approximately 2 metres from the adult. This minimised the vertical displacement of the adult's eyes from the camera. Hains and Symons (see Hains & Muir, 1996b) found that, from the infant's perspective, adults only were seen as making eye-contact when they looked at the infant's face in the centre of the TV monitor; when they made eye-contact with the camera lens, they were seen as looking up.

Person perception: categorical perception of people and objects

As noted in the introduction, whereas objects tend to be inert, people are self-propelled, goal-directed (exhibiting "agency"; Premack & Premack, 1995), and are expected to respond reciprocally during face-to-face inter-actions (Spelke et al., 1995). Thus, one would predict that the still-face effect should be generated by people, not objects. Also, if infants had a generalised expectancy that people would interact with them reciprocally with positive affective emotional displays, then a similar still-face effect should be generated by strangers. This was important to establish because mothers could not carry out more subtle perturbations (e.g. averting their eyes, acting sad, etc.) consistently during face-to-face interactions and therefore practised adults were required.

Ellsworth, Muir, and Hains (1993) addressed these issues by having either a mother or a stranger sit in front of an infant and carry out the still-face procedure. Each infant also underwent a second "SF" procedure (order counterbalanced), this time replacing the adult with a hand-puppet having internal features similar to a scrambled abstract face (see Fig. 8.5). The puppet was moved (along with the internal features) in accompaniment with synthesised tones (to replace the voice) in a contingent manner as the hidden puppeteer attempted to interact with the infant as though

I. Visual Attention

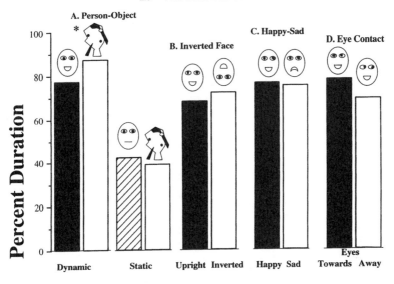

II. Smiling

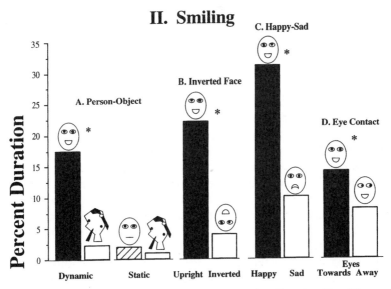

FIG. 8.5. A composite figure comparing the visual attention (I) and smiling (II) recorded during normal periods of interaction (all black bars) with the same behaviour, in grey and white bars, recorded when infants are presented with dynamic/static objects (A), inverted faces (B), sad facial expressions (C), and breaks in eye-contact (D). The data were collapsed across age and TV versus live interaction procedures and in all studies the adults were also vocalising during the interactions (see text for details). The asterisk indicates a significant difference between infant attention and smiling during normal versus perturbation periods.

261

she were using her face and voice. The results are shown in Fig. 8.5I,A and 8.5II,A. Infants looked slightly longer at the novel puppet (Object) than the person during the interaction (Dynamic) periods, and slightly less at the puppet than the person when they both were stationary (Static). Although the first of these differences in visual attention was significant, it was not large. A much more dramatic difference in infant smiling was found. Substantial smiling was generated by interacting adults, but it was almost nonexistent in the presence of the interacting object, similar to the amount elicited during the Static periods for both people (still-face) and objects. Finally, as expected, there were no mother–stranger differences.

One possibility for why infants fail to smile at interacting objects is that their smiles are reserved for their engagements with people. Their social smiles may be elicited by mutual affect regulation (Tronick, 1989), by imitation (e.g. Field, Goldstein, Nitza, & Porter, 1986) or as part of a released response generated by adult facial expressions (Caron, Caron, Roberts, & Brooks, 1997). Finally, although Ellsworth et al. (1993) may have been the first researchers to attempt to match many of the characteristics of the person and object (e.g. novelty, distance, contingency, accompanying sounds), their results are consistent with those of others who compared infant responses to various kinds of dynamic objects and people (e.g. Brazelton, Koslowski, & Main, 1974; Klin & Jennings, 1979; Legerstee et al., 1987).

Role of adult facial expressions in driving infant social responses

Ellsworth et al. (1993) established that the modulation of infant positive affect in the still-face effect was governed by people, not just any contingently interacting object. Next, an attempt was made to isolate the critical features of adult stimulation that regulated infant affect and attention. Gusella et al. (1988) began this task by using the TV interaction procedure to isolate the face and voice, using the ABA design. They had mothers and infants interact over TV and then either switched off the mother's voice during the second period (silent, interacting face condition) or replayed a pre-recording of the mother's still face while leaving the sound on (still-face, interacting voice condition). These perturbations with no-change control and standard still-face groups were compared. When the second-period performance was compared, infants in the silent, interacting face group showed a slight drop in smiling when the voice was turned off and little loss of attention. Their performance was very similar to the no-change control group. By contrast, when the mother's voice remained contingent but she was still-faced, infants performed like the still-face group. Gusella et al. concluded that infant interactive behaviour was driven primarily by the mothers' facial expressions. The following studies reinforce this conclusion with more direct manipulations of adult facial expressions.

Inverted face effect   In the adult face-perception literature, it is well known that inverting the picture of a face makes recognising emotional expressions more difficult (e.g. Thompson, 1980). One theory is that configural properties of emotional expressions are rapidly processed in a holistic manner in upright faces, but when the face is inverted its components are processed as separate elements (see Suzuki & Cavanagh, 1995; Tanaka & Farah, 1993). Watson and colleagues (Hayes & Watson, 1981; Watson, 1966; Watson, Hayes, Vietze, & Becker, 1979) showed that infants also are affected by facial orientation. They reported that 3-month-olds but not 2- or 5-month-olds smiled more to upright than inverted faces. Watson and colleagues pioneered work on the facial inversion effect, but their use of complex, within-subject designs with multiple periods including both stationary and dynamic – but non-contingent – talking and silent faces, may have contributed to the relatively small and inconsistent effects of facial inversion across age. Our objective was to manipulate facial orientation while keeping all other variables constant to determine if this would produce a still-face or object–person effect.

Roman (1986) used the TV interaction procedure and an ABA design, inverting the mother's face in the second period. When she compared the inverted face group with a no-change control group, she found that 5-month-olds' attention was maintained but they stopped smiling when the mother's face was inverted. This was replicated by Rach-Longman (see Muir & Hains, 1993; Muir & Rach-Longman, 1989) in a series of studies with mothers and female strangers as interactors using both live and TV interaction procedures. In all cases, the results were consistent. As illustrated in Fig. 8.5I,B, infants looked at the upright and inverted faces for the same amount of time, but they rarely smiled when the face was inverted (Fig. 8.5II,B). Furthermore, there was no difference in the performance of infants between 3 and 6 months of age. This failure to replicate Watson's age effect may be due to procedural differences, especially our use of the interaction procedure. Finally, Rach-Longman constructed an orientation tuning curve by varying the orientation of an adult stranger's face in 45 degree steps around a perimeter (in this study, order of facial orientation was counterbalanced). Her 5-month-olds' attention remained constant across all orientations, but smiling dropped relative to the upright face by about 50% for the 45 degree face and reached a constant low level for the face rotated by 90 through 180 degrees.

Muir and Hains (1993) offered several explanations for the inverted face effect. The results support the predictions derived from the adult literature reviewed earlier – infants may have found the facial expression difficult to interpret. However, the pattern of results for the inverted face effect is strikingly similar to that for the object–person effect. When one switched from an upright face to an object or inverted face, infant attention was relatively unaffected, while smiling dropped substantially (shown in Fig. 8.5I and 5II, A vs. B). Thus, infants may have perceived the inverted face as an interesting object and stopped interacting. Another possibility is that infants stopped smiling because of the conflict between the affective expressions displayed in the inverted mouth (looking sad) and the happy voice; however, this is unlikely, given that the same effect has been obtained with silent, interacting faces (Cao, Hains, & Muir, 1992). Finally, we cannot rule out the possibility that the face in a novel orientation switched the infants from an interactive behavioural mode to a cognitive-analytic one that captured the infants' attention and suppressed their social responses.

Differentiating emotional expressions: Happy versus sad

A more direct test of infant sensitivity to adult facial expressions was conducted by D'Entremont. In still-face studies, the adult maintains a positive affective expression while interacting with the infant in the normal periods; by contrast, the still-face expression is always neutral. Infants may have been reacting in the still-face period to the loss of *contingent stimulation*, or to the change in the adult's emotional expression. D'Entremont and Muir (1997) examined the effect of the still-face expression by having a female stranger pose either neutral, sad, or happy still faces during the perturbation period. They found a typical still-face effect irrespective of the adult's facial expression, although there was slightly, but significantly, more smiling to the smiling still-face. Thus, while a static smiling face can elicit some smiling from infants, contingent interactions appear to be a much more effective elicitor of infant positive affect.

A number of researchers have shown that infants are negatively affected when the adult appears depressed during face-to-face interactions. For example, both Cohn and Tronick (1982) and Field et al. (1988) compared infants' responses when mothers acted happy versus "depressed". More negative infant responses (e.g. protest, gaze aversion) were observed during the depressed periods. However, the effect of specific adult emotional expressions on young infants is unknown. Termine and Izard (1988) did manipulate adult emotional expressions during face-to-face interactions with matching amounts of either happy or sad expressions. They reported that 9-month-olds looked longer and expressed more joy when the mother expressed joy, and showed more sadness and anger when she expressed sadness. In an attempt to determine younger infants' sensitivity to shifts in contingent emotional expressions, D'Entremont (1995) conducted a series of studies. In an ABA design, a practised stranger interacted using happy expressions during A and matching amounts of sad expressions during B. Her results are summarised in Fig. 8.5I,C and II,C. Compared to a no-change control group, infants remained equally attentive to both emotional displays, but their smiling was significantly reduced, by around 60% across several studies, during the sad period. D'Entremont also conducted a longitudinal study to establish the age of onset for this differential response to adult emotional expressions. She tested infants monthly from 1 to 5 months of age and found that infant visual attention was not affected by shifting to a sad expression at any age. By contrast, differential smiling to happy versus sad expressions emerged at 3 months of age.

D'Entremont's studies provide strong evidence that young infants are very sensitive to shifts in adult facial expressions of some emotions during face-to-face interactions when the dependent measures include positive affect.

The role of eye contact

Eye contact is an important part of adult communications (e.g. Goffman, 1963). It signals to one adult that the message contained in another person's verbal and nonverbal behaviour is intended for them. As noted by Wolff (1987), although we do not have "decisive objective criteria for measuring when two pairs of eyes are actually in contact, . . . the subjective experience is always powerful and unmistakable" (p. 212). Stern (1974) theorised that during infant–adult interactions eye contact serves as a cue for initiating and terminating social interactions. Wolff (1963) suggested that the ability to make eye contact develops around 1 month of age and is important for the development of smiling. Several researchers have shown that infants are particularly interested in eyes by 2 months of age (e.g. Maurer & Salapataek, 1976). Caron, Caron, Caldwell, and Weiss (1973), using an habituation procedure, found that the eyes were more salient than the mouth area for 3-month-olds. Vecera and Johnson (1995) showed that 4- but not 2-month-olds could discriminate direction of eye gaze in schematic faces using a preferential looking procedure; however, frontal eye gaze was not favoured. Despite this, Samuels (1985) reported that 3-month-olds preferred a moving over a stationary face but appeared to be insensitive to adult eye-direction.

Only a few studies have manipulated adult eye-direction in dynamic or contingently interacting adult faces, and the results have been somewhat mixed. Bloom (1974) used adult social responses to reinforce infant vocalisation and found that as long as the eyes were present, their direction was unimportant. This contrasts with the findings of Caron, Caron, Roberts, and Brooks (1997). They showed 3-, 5-, and 7-month-olds videorecordings of an adult female displaying positive expressions under various eye–head direction conditions: the adult's eyes were frontal, averted, closed, and averted along with the head. Caron et al. measured both attention and smiling and found an age effect. When they compared frontal and averted eye conditions, their 5-month-olds, but not 3- and 7-month-olds, smiled slightly more when the adult's gaze was frontal, whereas visual attention was similar for these conditions at all 3 ages. However, the youngest infants did show less gaze and smiling when the eyes were closed or the head was averted. Finally, Lasky and Klein (1979) used a partial interaction procedure. They had an adult stranger interact with the infant while making eye contact, and display social behaviour while looking away at a baby picture above the infant's head. Their 5-month-olds looked longer, and some smiled more, in the eye-contact condition. However, both contingency and eye-direction may have varied between conditions.

Hains and Muir (1996b) conducted two studies in which adult eye-direction was varied while contingency was kept constant. They had adults engage in face-to-face interactions with 3- to 6-month-olds for four 1min periods in an ABAC design. Adults made eye contact in A, and during B and C looked away at a TV monitor of the infant's face which allowed them to keep interacting contingently. The TV monitor was displaced 40 degrees from the front in the study that used the TV interaction procedure, and 20 degrees in the study where interactions were live. There were no age effects and the results were consistent across studies. As summarised in Fig. 8.5I,D and II,D, infants showed a slight (nonsignificant) reduction in looking and a significant reduction in smiling (about 40%) at the adult when her eyes were averted.

Using the ABAC versus no-change control (AAAA) design and the live procedure, Symons, Hains, and Muir (in press) tested the limits of this eye-direction effect. They presented 3- to 5-month-olds with an adult stranger who made eye contact during the A periods and shifted her gaze during B and C periods to the infant's right and left ears, respectively (horizontal displacement) or to the forehead and chin (vertical displacement), resulting in an adult eye deviation of approximately 5 degrees. Infants again showed a decline in smiling each time the adult looked at the ears, compared to no-change controls who showed little change in looking and smiling over time. Moreover, infants appeared to be insensitive to the vertical deviations in adult eye-direction. This lack of response to small shifts in vertical eye gaze makes sense given that we make these shifts normally during conversations, i.e. looking at the person's mouth.

The role of the voice

An excellent literature review of infant responses to adult vocal expressions of emotions can be found in Walker-Andrews (1997), and will not be reiterated here. Instead, we will consider the functional role of adult vocal stimulation during face-to-face interaction, but will begin by highlighting a few important results from the noninteraction literature. First, at a very young age, infants use vocal information to focus their attention in ambiguous situations. For example, Burnham et al. (1993) report that 1-month-olds discriminate between dynamic displays of mother's and stranger's faces only if speech accompanies the presentation. Caron, Caron, and MacLean (1988) found that 4- to 7-month-olds' ability to discriminate among emotional expressions in pre-recorded facial displays is facilitated by an accompanying vocal track. In an extensive series of studies, Walker-Andrews (1997, see summary) presented pre-recorded faces expressing different emotional expressions simultaneously on two adjacent TV monitors (e.g. happy vs. sad or angry), accompanied by a single vocal track that matched one expression. Her 4-month-olds looked longer at only the happy face when it was sound-matched, whereas 5- and 7-month-olds increased fixation to any facial expression that was sound-matched. These results could have been based on the infants' preference for synchrony between lip movements and vocal stimulation. However, Walker-Andrews' older infants also showed face–voice matching when the sound track was delayed relative to the face. Finally, Walker-Andrews reported that the auditory–visual matching disappeared when the faces were inverted – consistent with the inversion effect described earlier and suggesting that the infants were actually reading the emotions expressed in the adult's face.

Cao, Hains, and Muir (1996) used a version of Walker-Andrews' procedure to manipulate independently face–voice synchrony versus affect in infants between 4 and 7 months of age. Cao et al. videorecorded an adult expressing either happy or sad emotional expressions. Different affective expressions produce different intensities of vocal intonation and facial movements. They controlled for this confound by contrasting one videorecorded expression (e.g. happy) with the same recording modified by inverting the mouth area and blending it into the face. The two identical videorecordings, except for the inverted mouth in one, making it look "sad", were played on adjacent TV monitors, out of temporal synchrony. A single voice track matched either the normal happy face or the face with the inverted mouth. A different pattern of visual attention was found as a function of age. In both the conflict and matching face–voice conditions, 4-month-olds appeared to "tune out" by adopting a strong side bias and they showed no visual preference. Five-month-olds looked longer at the happy face when it was voice-matched, whereas 7-month-olds only preferred the novel (inverted mouth) face when it was voice-matched. These results complement Walker-Andrew's (1997) findings and, taken together, suggest that infants can discriminate between certain affective vocal emotional expressions by 4 months of age and can use the adult's voice to guide their visual analysis of faces in different ways as they grow older.

Infants also display differential affect to static faces as a function of vocal stimulation. As noted earlier, Wolff (1987) found that more infant smiling could be generated by an adult's voice than the face at the beginning of the second month after birth, but smiling to the voice declined rapidly while that to the face increased with age. However, the adult voice can generate some positive affect in older infants. For example, Fernald (1993) presented 5-month-olds with pre-recorded adult approval and prohibition vocalisations sequentially, each from a different loudspeaker located behind a picture of a female face with a neutral expression. After infants oriented to the sound source, they could terminate the adult voice by looking away. Fernald reports that infants from English-speaking homes had *slightly* higher positive affect scores while listening to approvals than prohibitions, and *slightly* higher negative affect scores when listening to prohibitions. The same differential effects for approvals and prohibitions were generated in these infants by adults speaking German and Italian (non-native languages). Although Fernald found no *looking preference* for English approvals, her infants did look slightly longer at approvals in foreign speech.

Fernald's results suggest that infant affect and attention can be influenced by the adult's voice; thus, one might expect an even greater response to perturbations in the voice during face-to-face interactions between young infants and adults. However, as noted earlier, Gusella et al. (1988) found that in TV interactions the still-face effect was not influenced by the presence of the voice. Thus, adults were allowed to talk to the infants in all of the interaction studies reviewed so far, and the perturbation effects were large and reliable. For example, although the adult's voice did not change when her face was inverted, infant smiling dropped substantially. However, the conclusion that the voice is irrelevant must be qualified. A glance at Fig. 8.5B shows that the adult's inverted face did elicit some smiling and it should be noted that this figure summarises results collapsing across TV and live interaction studies. In fact, overall, more smiling has been generated during live interactions (e.g. Hains & Muir, 1996a). In two studies using the live interaction procedure to boost smiling, Cao et al. (1992) demonstrated that significantly less smiling was directed toward a silent (about 3%) than a talking inverted face (11%), which was the same as that directed towards the talking face when it was obscured by a white circular mask with a central red dot.

D'Entremont (1995; D'Entremont & Muir, 1996) conducted a series of studies comparing infant responses generated by happy and sad interacting faces with and without vocal accompaniment. In one experiment, she used the ABA (happy-sad-happy versus no-change controls) design described earlier; in A the happy face was talking, and in B the happy or sad face was either talking or silent. In another study, she presented all three periods in silence; in this case the duration of the interaction periods was only 30sec because infants were found to fuss after about 90sec of no-voice happy interactions. D'Entremont discovered that infant visual attention was not affected by any of the manipulations and that by 3 months of age infants smiled more at happy than at sad faces, whether the voice was present or absent. D'Entremont also had adults interact vocally with 5-month-olds in three 1min periods (happy-sad-happy voices) with their faces obscured by the mask described earlier. Her infants smiled during approximately 20% of the first period, replicating Cao et al.'s (1992) results that the adult's voice without a visible face can elicit positive affect. However, there were no significant differences between the experimental and no-change control groups on any behaviour, and no change in response when the sad voice changed back to a happy voice in the third period. D'Entremont's results are consistent with those of several intermodal habituation studies with noncontingent face–voice stimuli. For example, Lewkowicz (1996) habituated 4-, 6- and 8-month-olds to a dynamic face–voice combination, followed by a change in the face, voice, or both. In three experiments, his 4-month-olds failed to dishabituate to a change in the voice alone, although they dishabituated approximately the same amount to changes in the face alone and the face plus voice. The older age groups dishabituated to changes in the face and face plus voice in all three experiments, and to the voice alone condition in only one experiment. Walker-Andrews and Lennon (1991) tested 5-month-olds' ability to respond to a change in vocal expressions (e.g. from happy to angry) either with facial accompaniment or without (a checkerboard was shown). Infant attention was re-established only when the vocal change was accompanied by a face.

In general, the adult's facial expressions appear to be the major driving force during social interactions with infants younger than 6 months of age. Although the adult's voice can elicit positive affect on its own, and may help to keep infants engaged in lengthy face-to-face interactions, it seems to be neither a sufficient nor necessary condition for enabling the infant to differentiate between happy and sad adult emotions during contingent interactions. However, there is one auditory perturbation in the adult's behaviour that does upset young infants during face-to-face interactions –

replacing the voice with a nonhuman sound. In Experiment 2, in the object-person differentiation study discussed earlier, Ellsworth et al. (1993) tested 3-month-olds' responses to interactive puppets with different abstract or face-like features versus a live, human face. The objective was to isolate variations in visual patterned stimulation, and because the voice did not influence the still-face effect, both the puppet's and the adult's face were accompanied by synthesised melodic sounds timed to replace the voice. Infants smiled only at the interacting face, but their smiling was approximately 50% lower than that generated in Experiment 1, when the face was accompanied by the voice. D'Entremont (1997) re-examined Ellsworth et al.'s videorecords and discovered that only 25% of smiles occurred during the synthesiser sequences and, of those, 69% ended within 1 second after synthesiser onset. The synthesiser appeared to turn off infant smiling and Ellsworth may have responded to infants' displeasure by only presenting brief episodes of synthesised sounds. D'Entremont tried to repeat Ellsworth's procedure using 5-month-olds, taking care to match every mimed word with a synthesised tone. She only tested a few infants because they immediately became upset! Next, she engaged infants in face-to-face interactions, silently miming words, and each time the infant smiled, she either continued to mime, or briefly accompanied each mimed word with either a synthesised tone or her voice. Infants smiled about three times longer to the face + voice than to the face + synthesiser or silence. Thus, it appears that the violation of infant expectancy that an adult's face should be accompanied by either a voice or silence disrupts infant social behaviour, whereas vocal accompaniments may help to maintain infant social responding to the adult's face and be rewarding.

Adult contingency revisited

Based on Murray and Trevarthen's (1985) report, it was assumed that maintaining adult contingent interactions was necessary to engage infants optimally in social perception tasks, and Nadel's (in press) recent replication supports this assumption. However, the maternal noncontingency effect may decline with age. Gusella et al. (1988), in the discussion section of their paper on the Still-Face Effect, reported on a TV-replay study similar to Murray and Trevarthen's, which was designed to demonstrate the importance of adult contingency in the regulation of older infants' affect and attention. They had mothers interact with their 5-month-olds for three 1.5min periods over TV using the ABA versus AAA design. Mothers were always contingent in A, while B consisted of a replay of the mother's behaviour during first period. Gusella et al. found no differences in smiling or visual attention for the experimental and control groups. This null result was replicated by Cathy Mann (see Hains & Muir, 1996a;

Muir & Hains, 1993). Hains and Muir (1996a) explained this failure to find a *maternal* noncontingency effect in older infants by noting the variety of experiences infants presumably have when mothers do not behave contingently, at least for brief periods. The brief maternal TV-replay experience may not have been a major violation of the older infants' expectations for maternal stimulation. These infants may even have perceived the mother's videoreplay as novel and interesting, given Watson's (1985) evidence that infants seem to enjoy some imperfect contingencies.

Recently, Marian, Neisser, and Rochat (1996) also failed to find a negative maternal noncontingency effect with older infants. They attempted to replicate exactly Murray and Trevarthen's (1985) experiment with 3-month-olds, and they included a control for changes over time. One group received three 1min periods consisting of a live-replay-live sequence and another group received a live-live-replay sequence. Marian et al. compared the two groups' replay and live sequences, which counterbalanced the order, and found no differences in the duration of infant attention or frowning and slightly more smiling during the replay period. They concluded that Murray and Trevarthen's results may have been due to an order effect rather than the lack of maternal contingent responding, and that manipulating contingency in TV interactions is not an effective way to demonstrate infant sensitivity to maternal contingency.

Marian et al.'s conclusions may be premature for two reasons. First, their 3-month-olds may not have been properly engaged in a social interaction during their brief, standardised, initial interaction period by the time the replay condition was introduced – producing a floor effect on some dependent measures. Their 12-week-olds looked at the mothers about 75% of the time, but only smiled at them 1% to 5 % of the time. This very low rate of smiling, although agreeing with that obtained by Murray and Trevarthen, is much lower than that reported by Nadel et al. (1997) for 2-month-olds, who smiled 14% of the time, and that typically found in the TV interaction studies with 4- to 5-month-olds, who smile between 10% and 20% of the time.

Second, while Hains and Muir (1996a) failed to find a replay effect for mothers, when infants were tested with strangers a large non-contingency effect was obtained. Hains and Muir presented 4- to 6-month-olds with practised strangers in three conditions: a live interaction, a TV interaction, and a TV-replay of the stranger's interaction with another infant. Order varied across groups. Figure 8.6, which summarises the major results for the TV conditions, shows that contingent TV interactions generated typically high levels of visual attention and smiling. By contrast, when the TV-replay period was introduced, visual attention dropped by about 30% and smiling was virtually eliminated. The only group displaying some smiling during the TV-replay period received that condition first, and the latency

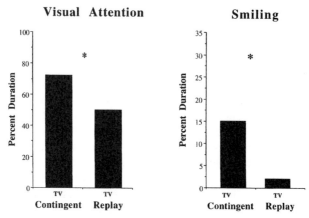

FIG. 8.6.   A summary of Hains and Muir's (1996a) smiling and visual attention results for contingent TV interactions and replays of strangers' interactive behaviour. The asterisk indicates a significant difference between the contingent and replay periods.

to initiate smiling was almost twice as long as that in the contingent TV condition.

These results suggest that by 3 to 5 months of age infants have formed a generalised expectancy that strangers will initially engage them in reciprocal interactions. When a stranger fails to do so this might constitute a substantial violation of the infant's social expectancy – much greater than that generated by brief episodes of maternal noncontingency (for a more detailed consideration of early social contingency sensitivity see Nadel, in press, and Muir and Hains, in press). Unfortunately, the noncontingency age effect we have described is based on cross-sectional data. What is needed is a longitudinal study that tracks the infant's sensitivity to contingent social stimulation throughout the first 5 months of life.

A decline in imitation?

It is now clear that certain behaviours decline with age (e.g. the loss of auditory localisation responses, social response to adult voices, and the maternal noncontingency effect), but other instances of declines in behaviour may reflect procedural artifacts. For example, initial studies on the developmental course of infant imitation of facial gestures suggested that infants also lose their ability to imitate around 2 months of age (Meltzoff & Moore, 1992). However, later research demonstrated that 2- to 3-month-olds do imitate both facial gestures and vocal sounds (e.g.

Field et al., 1986; Kugiumutzakis, 1985; Meltzoff & Moore, 1992) when they are tested under proper conditions. The drop in imitation responses observed by some researchers in 2- to 3-month-olds may be due to the onset of social expectancies about what adults typically do during face-to-face interactions with infants. Unlike newborns, 2-month-olds may find an adult model's repetitive tongue protrusion or mouth-opening, while making eye contact, a violation of social expectancies.

Meltzoff & Moore (1992) reported that the older infants (2- to 3-month-olds) only displayed imitation after they greeted the adults "when they first saw them, trying out motor routines as if to engage in a nonverbal interchange" (p. 499). After the social initiation, the infants were able to imitate, suggesting that a violation of social expectancies can mask underlying competence in certain cases. The results of an experiment on deferred imitation by Meltzoff & Moore (1994) also may be explained in the light of social expectancies. At 6 weeks, babies were found to perform deferred imitation after a 24-hour delay. In the "observation-only" condition, infants were shown a gesture on one day and returned the next day to see the adult pose a passive-face. Infants looked at the adult and then imitated the facial expression from the preceding day, indicating the presence of long-term memory. Meltzoff and Moore proposed that infants were probing the adult during the second meeting, using imitative behaviours they had exchanged during the previous interaction in order to establish the adult's identity.

Summary

In this section we have reviewed a number of studies that indicate infants are very responsive to various perturbations in adult behaviour during social interactions. In contrast to the literature on face perception derived from habituation and visual preference studies, infants as young as 3 months of age react strongly to shifts in facial orientation and emotional expressions and breaks in eye contact. In many cases their reactions to these perturbations were apparent only when infant positive affect was considered, suggesting that this response is part of a dyadic social engagement mechanism, whereas visual attention may be driven by either cognitive or social processing of events. Finally, although contingent maternal stimulation may not be necessary to elicit social responses from older infants, the maintenance of contingent stimulation does seem to be important if strangers are the agents for testing infant social perception (although Caron et al. 1997 would disagree). In any case, the context of social exchange appears to play a more important role in studies of infant social perception as the infant's behavioural repertoire and social expectancies increase with age.

THE ONSET OF THE TRIADIC SYSTEM

In the last section, we will briefly discuss two phenomena that emerge as the young infant's social perception expands from dyadic interactions to include more elements in the social interactions toward the end of the first year of life. Infants begin to engage in joint visual attention and social imitation activities. Both phenomena involve a minimum of three components (i.e. classically two people and an object) and both involve face-to-face interactions.

Joint attention studies

Around 6 months of age, babies appear to enter a new stage of social perception. They begin to include in their interactions with adults references to other people and objects in their environment. First, they engage in acts of *joint visual attention*, defined by Butterworth and Cochran (1980) as the ability to follow another person's gaze, and a few months later infants begin to direct the adult's attention towards objects the infants are interested in by pointing to them. In both cases the infants are expanding their activities and learning about objects and people in their environment based partially on the information provided during face-to-face interactions with their caretakers.

It should be noted that a primitive type of "joint attention response" has been elicited from infants younger than 6 months of age. Scaife and Bruner (1975) had an interacting adult break eye contact and look at a distant target outside of the infant's field of view. They reported that by 12 months of age all infants followed the adult's line of sight; but even a few 2-month-olds (30%) turned their heads in the same direction as the adult on at least one of two trials. However, a possible problem with this study is that the younger infants' performance might have included chance responses. Recently, D'Entremont, Hains, and Muir (1997) used a very effective procedure to demonstrate 3- to 6-month-olds' sensitivity to shifts in the *direction* of an adult's gaze during face-to-face interactions. Their adult interacted with the infant, periodically breaking eye contact to turn towards and talk briefly to one of two lion hand-puppets placed on either side of her shoulders (well within the infant's field of view) several times in each direction. They found no age effects and 73% of the infants' first eye-turns were in the same direction as the adult's head–eye turns.

These young infants may not be engaged in *active joint attention* at all. Although 3-month-olds may glance in the direction of the adult's shift in head/eye position, this does not indicate their awareness that the perceptual state of the other person provides information about that person's object of gaze, or which target, among several on the same side, the adults are referencing. Butterworth and Jarrett (1991) emphasise that joint attention is a reciprocal phenomenon and, along with Corkum and Moore (1994), they have demonstrated that the development of *sustained* joint visual attention is a gradual process beginning around 6 months of age, which does not mature until 12 to 18 months of age. According to Schaffer (1984), it is more often the mother's readiness to share the infant's interest that accounts for active joint attention before 1 year of age. Usually infants begin at around the same time to produce protodeclarative pointing gestures (Bates, Benigni, Bretherton, Camaioni, & Volterra, 1979). These joint attention activities are important in promoting language, as they generally are embedded in a verbal context by the adult, who frequently names or makes comments about the objects of mutual interest during the interaction.

Whereas joint attention activity normally expands the infant's social perception, this does not appear to be the case with autistic children. Indeed, numerous studies (e.g. Mundy, Sigman, & Kasari, 1993) account for a specific deficit of joint attention in autistic disorders. Some theorists, including Baron-Cohen (1995), propose that before being able to "read" the minds of others, young infants are able to detect an adult's eye-direction and, later on, begin to use joint attention activities with an adult to obtain information about what the adult is thinking about the object of joint regard. Baron-Cohen et al. (1996) have shown that it is possible to give an early diagnosis of autism (by 18 months of age) by detecting deficits in shared attention. This supports the hypothetical connection between shared attention and mindreading, and links perceptual discrimination, social competence, and metacognitive development.

During the second year of life, many exchanges between the infant and the adult are triadic, with both participants involved in declarative behaviours, sharing attention *à propos* a third object. In fact, Jacobson (1981) observed that infants older than 15 months would engage in relatively lengthy, complex joint attention activities consisting of a series of exchanges with a partner and an object. Presumably, this reflects cognitive advances in their ability to attend to and explore the properties of multiple targets of interest. Recently, a new paradigm has been developed by Tremblay-Leveau and Nadel (1996) to assess infant sensitivity to perturbations in an adult's behaviour when another infant, rather than an object, is present. Their *exclusion paradigm* involved two toddlers of the same age, an adult experimenter, and a variety of objects such as a scarf, a bottle, and a teddy bear. After engaging the two toddlers in triadic interactions, the adult momentarily excluded one from the ongoing interaction by communicating exclusively with the other child. This procedure can be thought of an extension of the still-face procedure into a triadic interaction context. Infant reactions when they are excluded demonstrate their mastery of attention monitoring and social engagements. First they perceived their exclusion and then they attempted to overcome it by trying to engage the adult and other child in a new activity. This complex, adaptive social activity was apparent in infants as young as 11 months, under competitive conditions in a complex, multiparticipant context. This is an earlier age than that previously reported by Bakeman and Adamson (1984), who observed 6- to 18-month-olds playing in their homes with their mother and a peer. They found that coordinated joint engagement did not exceed 10% of observation time until 15 months of age. They also reported lower rates of joint engagement when infants were with peers instead of mothers. This is in striking contrast to the precocious capacities observed with the exclusion paradigm (Tremblay-Leveau & Nadel, 1995, 1996).

Imitation and joint attention

Imitation of facial expressions was identified earlier as one of the infant's initial social responses. As infants age, imitation becomes a major component of topic sharing during social interactions. The important difference between the tongue-protrusion-matching seen in neonates and the immediate social imitation observed in older infants is that for older infants imitation is part of a social interchange that involves peers interacting with objects. Uzgiris (1981) noted that as infants grow older, imitations are more likely to appear if actions involving concrete objects are modelled.

An analysis of Wallon's view led Nadel (1980) to propose that synchronous imitation may be the main pre-verbal system of interaction. To test this hypothesis, Nadel and colleagues filmed 18- to 42-month-old dyads or triads of familiar peers meeting without an adult presence in an experimental setting. The children were placed in a room with 2 or 3 identical sets of 10 attractive objects, so that each child could choose an object either for its intrinsic attractiveness or because a partner chose it. Most of the objects, such as umbrellas, cowboy hats or sunglasses, allowed bodily modelling. Nadel-Brulfert and Baudonnière (1982) showed that choosing the identical object was the most frequent and long-lasting behaviour in 2-year-old triads. When they held identical items, the children imitated each other's bodily postures and activities. This result led to the conclusion that the amount of time identical objects were held was a good index of imitative sequences. This measure also revealed that imitation was the most predominant means for long-lasting interactions before the age of 3. These results were replicated with an adult present (Mertan, Nadel, & Leveau, 1993).

To establish the importance of having two sets of identical objects present in order to elicit social imitation, Nadel & Fontaine (1989) filmed 2½- and 3½-year-olds in two different settings. One setting contained two identical sets of 10 objects, enabling synchronous imitation to develop, the other contained a single set of 20 different objects, equally attractive. The social behaviours of the 2½-year-olds but not 3½-year-olds were far more numerous, long-lasting, and positive in the double-object setting. This suggests that identical objects must be used to enable displays of imitation during social interactions. Nadel, Guérini, and Rivet (in press) argue that young children can more easily share a topic about an object by focusing their attention on identical items they are holding. This kind of joint attention may be a scaffolding for long-lasting joint activity, and imitative activities with identical objects may be the simplest way for children to share their interest with each other.

Finally, it is important to note that the 3½-year-olds' social behaviours were not affected by having single versus double sets of objects; imitative behaviours were no longer their predominant means of communication (Nadel, 1986; Nadel & Fontaine, 1989). Thus, immediate imitation appears to have a transitory function in social communications that vanishes at the end of infancy, as pre-verbal communication is replaced by verbal interactions.

GENERAL SUMMARY AND CONCLUSIONS

In this chapter, we followed Wallon's (1934) theme in order to characterise the development of infant social perception as being composed of emerging and declining social responses to various types of social stimuli. We described the existence of several U-shaped functions, including those for auditory localisation and imitation responses. Both responses are present at birth and appear to decline during the second month of life, and reappear in a different form at a later age. Their decline is coincident with the onset of a very significant social response for adults, smiling, which is elicited in a selective manner first by human voices. Smiling to vocal stimulation declines as infants begin to smile more at faces. The power of the voice for eliciting sustained smiling may not recover until much later in infancy, if at all. During the second month of life, infants also become upset when their mothers present noncontingent social stimulation during face-to-face interactions (as in the TV-replay studies). The noncontingent TV-replay response to mothers also appears to decline by 3 to 5 months of age, but strangers are expected to respond contingently during face-to-face interactions.

At 3 to 5 months of age, infants become very responsive to social stimulation. They recover their interest in the spatial location of sounds and readily engage in reciprocal social exchanges during face-to-face interactions with adults. When various perturbations in adult facial displays are introduced during face-to-face interactions, such as replacing the face with an interacting object, posing a still-face, inverting the face, changing the facial expression of emotion, and breaking eye contact, infants react by altering their social responses.

A glance at Fig. 8.5 illustrates a second theme that we have tried to emphasise throughout the chapter. In the figure, the effects of various perturbations in adult social stimulation on infant visual attention and smiling are compared. When the adult's social stimuli are altered, in many cases the visual attention measure does not reveal the infant's sensitivity to the manipulation. Except for slightly greater visual attention devoted to a novel, interacting audiovisual object (the puppet with abstract features and melodic sounds), and the large drop in attention when the adult posed a still face, none of the other perturbations significantly affected the infant's interest. By contrast, all of the manipulations affected smiling to some degree. Clearly, the largest impact occurred when adults stopped inter-acting (the still-face effect) or when the face was inverted, presumably making it difficult for the infant to read the adult's facial expression. When the adults shifted from happy to sad emotional expressions, the drop in infant positive affect was muted, and when the adult continued to display happy emotions but broke eye contact, infant smiling was reduced the least. Thus, although infants clearly discriminated all of these shifts in adult social stimuli, they reacted more strongly to some than to others. A theoretical model is needed to explain this apparent hierarchy.

The role of the adult's vocal behaviour during face-to-face interactions is less clear. The presence of the voice seems to boost smiling in some cases, but its presence is not necessary for infants to engage in reciprocal interactions and respond to the perturbations described. The most signifi-cant reaction occurred when a nonhuman sound replaced the adult's voice during face-to-face interactions and infants became upset.

A final point we tried to stress in the chapter is that infant social perception cannot be fully described by nonsocial test procedures (e.g. visual habituation and preferential-looking paradigms). This is because the infants may not be fully engaged in the test unless they are tested in a social context. When the test procedure becomes more interactive, infants may become more responsive. A number of examples given in the chapter illustrate this point. For example, infant imitation can be recovered at two months of age when the adult models display several facial gestures, perhaps simulating an interactive game. The face-to-face interaction pro-cedure shows that infants discriminate between happy and sad dynamic facial expressions by 3 months of age. And when the adult also responds to objects during the interaction, infants of this age briefly follow the direction of the adult's shift in attention.

As infants grow older and their social context expands, their behaviour becomes increasingly complex. During the latter part of the first year of life, they shift their attention from one person to another person, or to an object of mutual interest, in joint attention paradigms. New interaction procedures (e.g. the exclusion paradigm) reveal that social imitation shifts from simple reactions to another person's facial expressions to imitations of another person's actions with objects. Toddlers will engage in imitative acts when playing with peers, but only when identical objects are available. Finally, by 11 months of age, infants will react when they are excluded from social interactions with an adult and another child, indicating that they continually monitor the attention of the people during social engagements. Their social response to this situation is to attempt to rejoin the three-way interaction by introducing a new topic for joint attention.

To conclude, converging evidence from visual habituation, preferential looking, and social interaction procedures has revealed that infants react to a variety of social stimuli early in infancy. Our future task is to integrate the evidence derived from different procedures to provide a comprehensive picture of the development of infant social perception.

REFERENCES

Bakeman, R., & Adamson, L.B. (1984). Coordinating attention to people and objects in mother-infant and peer-infant interaction. *Child Development*, **55**, 1278–1289.

Banks, M., & Ginsberg, A.P. (1985). Infant visual preferences: A review and new theoretical treatment. In H.W. Reese (Eds), *Advances in child development and behavior* (pp. 207–246). New York: Academic Press.

Baron-Cohen, S. (1995). *Mind blindness: An essay on autism and Theory of Mind*. Cambridge, MA: MIT Press.

Baron-Cohen, S., Cox, A., Baird, G., Sweettenham, J., et al. (1996). Psychological markers in the detection of autism in infancy in a large population. *British Journal of Psychiatry*, **168**(2), 158–163.

Bates, E., Benigni, L., Bretherton, I., Camaioni, L., & Volterra, V. (1979). *The emergence of symbols*. New York: Academic Press.

Blass, E.M., Ganchrow, J.R., & Steiner, J.E. (1984). Classical conditioning in newborn humans 2–48 hours of age. *Infant Behavior and Development*, **7**(2), 223–235.

Bloom, K. (1974). Eye contact as a setting event for infant learning. *Journal of Experimental Child Psychology*, **17**, 250–263.

Blurton-Jones, N., & Leach, G. (1972). Behaviour of children and their mothers at separation and greeting. In N. Blurton-Jones (Ed.), *Ethological studies of child behaviour*. Cambridge: Cambridge University Press.

Bower, T.G.R., Broughton, J.M., & Moore, M.K. (1970). The coordination of visual and tactual input in infants. *Perception and Psychophysics*, **8**, 51–53.

Brazelton, T.B. (1980). Neonatal assessment. In S.I. Greenspan & G.H. Pollack (Eds.), *The course of life: Psychoanalytic contributions toward understanding personality development*. Bethesda, MD: NIMH Press.

Brazelton, T.B., Koslowski, B., & Main, W. (1974). The origins of reciprocity: The early mother-infant interaction. In M. Lewis & L.A. Rosenblum (Eds.), *The effect of the infant on its caregiver* (pp. 49–76). New York: Wiley.

Burnham, D., Taplin, J., et al. (1993). Maturation of precedence-effect thresholds: Full-term and preterm infants. *Infant Behavior and Development*, **16**(2), 213–232.

Bushnell, I.W.R., Sai, F., & Mullin, J.T. (1989). Neonatal recognition of the mother's face. *British Journal of Developmental Psychology*, **7**, 3–15.

Butterworth, G.E. (1986, May). Events and encounters in infant perception. *The New Psychologist*: Annual Journal of the Open University Psychological Society.

Butterworth, G., & Cochran, E. (1980). Towards a mechanism of joint visual attention in human infancy. In L. Weiskrantz (Ed.), *Thought without language* (pp. 5–25). Oxford: Oxford University Press.

Butterworth, G., & Jarrett, N. (1991). What minds have in common is space: Spatial mechanisms serving joint visual attention in infancy. Special issue: Perspectives on the child's theory of mind: I. *British Journal of Developmental Psychology*, **9**(1), 55–72.

Cao, Y., Hains, S., & Muir, D. (1992). Isolating the effect of adult vocal and facial stimulation during interactions with 4- to 6-month-olds. *Infant Behavior and Development*, **15** (Special ICIS Issue), 334.

Cao, Y., Hains, S.M.J., & Muir, D.W. (1996). Infant preferential looking: Face-voice synchrony versus affect. *Infant Behavior and Development*, **19** (Special ICIS Issue), 371.

Caron, A.J., Caron, R.F., Caldwell, R.A., & Weiss, S.J. (1973). Infant perception of the structural properties of the face. *Developmental Psychology*, **9**, 385–399.

Caron, A.J., Caron, R.F., & MacLean, D.J. (1988). Infant discrimination of naturalistic emotional expressions: The role of face and voice. *Child Development*, **59**, 604–616.

Caron, A.J., Caron, R., Roberts, J., & Brooks, R. (1997). Infant sensitivity to deviations in dynamic facial–vocal displays: The role of eye regard. *Developmental Psychology*, **33**, 802–813.

Cohn, J.F., & Tronick, E.Z. (1982). Communicative rules and sequential structure of infant behaviour during normal and depressed interaction. In E.Z. Tronick (Ed.), *Social interchange in infancy: Affect, cognition, and communication* (pp. 59–77). Baltimore, MD: University Park Press.

Corkum, V., & Moore, L. (1994). Development of joint visual attention in infants. In C. Moore & P.J. Dunham (Eds.), *Joint attention: Its origins and role in development* (pp. 61–83). Hillsdale, NJ: Erlbaum.

D'Entremont, B. (1995). *One- to six-month-olds' attention and affective responding to adults' happy and sad expressions: The role of face and voice*. Doctoral Dissertation, Queen's University, Kingston, Canada.

D'Entremont, B. (1997, April). *A study of 5-month-olds' responding to vocal expressions versus synthesised tones during social interactions*. At Biennial Meeting of the Society for Research in Child Development, Washington, DC.

D'Entremont, B., Hains, S.M.J., & Muir, D.W. (1997). A demonstration of gaze-following in 3- to 6-month-olds. *Infant Behavior and Development*, **20**, 569–572.

D'Entremont, B., & Muir, D. (1996). The development of infants' responding during contingent social interactions. *Infant Behavior and Development*, **19** (Special ICIS Issue), 420.

D'Entremont, B., & Muir, D. (1997). Five-month-olds' attention and affective responses to still-faced emotional expressions. *Infant Behavior and Development*, **20**, 563–568.

DeCasper, A.J., & Fifer, W.P. (1980). Of human bonding: Newborns prefer their mothers' voices. *Science*, **208**, 1174–1176.

Eckerman, C. (1993). Imitation and toddlers' achievement of co-ordinated action with others. In J. Nadel & L. Camaioni (Eds.), *New perspectives in early communicative development* (pp. 116–138). London: Routledge.

Ellsworth, C.P. (1987). *Person-object differentiation by young infants: The importance of affect measures in evaluation of social competence*. Doctoral dissertation, Queen's University, Kingston, Canada.

Ellsworth, C.P., Muir, D.W., & Hains, S.M. (1993). Social competence and person-object differentiation: An analysis of the still-face effect. *Developmental Psychology*, **29**(1), 63–73.

Fantz, R.L. (1961). The origin of form perception. *Scientific American*, **204**, 66–72.

Fernald, A. (1993). Approval and disapproval: Infant responsiveness to vocal affect in familiar and unfamiliar languages. *Child Development*, **64**, 657–674.

Field, T.M., Cohen, D., Garcia, R., & Greenberg, R. (1984). Mother-stranger face discrimination by the newborn. *Infant Behavior and Development*, **7**(1), 19–25.

Field, T., Goldstein, S., Nitza, V.-L., & Porter, K. (1986). Changes in imitative behavior during early infancy. *Infant Behavior and Development*, **9**(4), 415–421.

Field, T.M., Healy, B., Goldstein, S., Perry, S., Bendell, D., Schanberg, S., Zimmerman, E.A., & Kuhn, C. (1988). Infants of depressed mothers show "depressed" behavior even with nondepressed adults. *Child Development*, **59**, 1569–1579.

Field, T.M., Woodson, R., Cohen, D., Greenberg, R., Garcia, R., & Collins, E. (1983). Discrimination and imitation of facial expressions by term and preterm neonates. *Infant Behavior and Development*, **6**(4), 485–489.

Fontaine, R. (1984). Imitative skills between birth and six months. *Infant Behavior and Development*, **7**, 323–333.

Freedman, D. (1974). *Human infancy: An evolutionary perspective*. Hillsdale, NJ: Erlbaum.

Gewirtz, J.L. (1965). The course of infant smiling on four child-rearing environments in Israel. In B.M. Foss (Ed.), *Determinants of infant behaviour* (pp. 205–260). London: Methuen.

Goffman, E. (1963). *Behavior in public places*. New York: Free Press of Glencoe.

Gusella, J.L., Muir, D., & Tronick, E.A. (1988). The effect of manipulating maternal behavior during an interaction on three- and six-month-olds' affect and attention. *Child Development*, **59**(4), 1111–1124.

Hains, S.M.J., & Muir, D.W. (1996a). Effects of stimulus contingency in infant-adult interactions. *Infant Behavior and Development*, **19**(1), 49–61.

Hains, S.M.J., & Muir, D.W. (1996b). Infant sensitivity to adult eye-direction. *Child Development*, 1996, **67**, 1940–1951.

Haith, M.N., & Campos, J.J. (1977). Human infancy. *Annual Review of Psychology*, **28**, 251–294.

Hayes, L.A., & Watson, J.S. (1981). Facial orientation of parents and elicited smiling by infants. *Infant Behavior and Development*, **4**, 333–340.

Heimann, M. (1989). Imitation under de forsta levnadsmanaderna: Vad vi vet och inte vet. / Imitation during the first months of life: What we know and what we don't know. *Nordisk Psykologi*, **41**(3), 193–203.

Heimann, M., & Schaller, J. (1985). Imitative reactions among 14–21 day old infants. *Infant Mental Health Journal*, **6**(1), 31–39.

Jacobson, J.L. (1981). The role of inanimate objects in early peer interaction. *Child Development*, **52**, 618–626.

Johnson, M.H., & Morton, J. (1991). *Biology and cognitive development*. Cambridge: Blackwell.

Johnson, M.H., Posner, M.I., & Rothbart, M.K. (1991). Components of visual orienting in early infancy: Contingency learning, anticipatory looking, and disengaging. *Journal of Cognitive Neuroscience*, **3**, 335–344.

Klin, R.P., & Jennings, K.D. (1979). Responses to social and inanimate stimuli in early infancy. *The Journal of Genetic Psychology*, **135**, 3–9.

Kugiumutzakis, J. (1985). Development of imitation during the first six months of life. *Uppsala Psychological Reports*, No.377. Uppsala, Sweden: Uppsala University.

Kugiumutzakis, G. (1993). Intersubjective vocal imitation in early mother-infant interaction.

In J. Nadel & L. Camaioni (Eds.), *New perspectives in early communicative development.* (pp. 23–47) London: Routledge.

Kugiumutzakis, G. (in press). Genesis and development of early infant mimesis to facial and vocal model. In J. Nadel & G. Butterworth (Eds.), *Imitation in infancy* Cambridge: Cambridge University Press.

Lamb, M.E., Morrison, D.C., & Malkin, C.M. (1987). The development of infant social expectations in face-to-face interactions: A longtitudinal study. *Merrill-Palmer Quarterly,* **33**, 241–254.

Laskey, R.E., & Klein, R.E. (1979). The reactions of five-month-olds to eye contact of the mother and of stranger. *Merrill-Palmer Quarterly,* **25**, 163–170.

Legerstee, M. (1991). The role of person and object in eliciting early imitation. *Journal of Experimental Child Psychology,* **51**(3), 423–433.

Legerstee, M., Pomerleau, A., Malcuit, G., & Feider, H. (1987). The development of infants' responses to people and a doll: Implications for research in communication. *Infant Behavior and Development,* **10**(1), 81–95.

Lewis, M., & Goldberg, S. (1969). Perceptual-cognitive development in infancy: A generalized expectancy model as a function of mother-infant interaction. *Merrill-Palmer Quarterly,* **15**, 745–751.

Lewkowicz, D.J. (1996). Infants' response to the audible and visible properties of the human face. I: Role of lexical/syntactic content, temporal synchrony, gender, and manner of speech. *Developmental Psychology,* **32**, 347–366.

Maratos, O. (1973, April). *The origin and development of imitation in the first six months of the life.* At British Psycological Society Annual Meeting, Liverpool, UK.

Marian, V., Neisser, U., & Rochat, P. (1996). Infants' sensitivity to interpersonal contingency: An attempt to replicate Murray and Trevarthen. *Infant Behavior and Development,* **19**, (Special ICIS Issue), 602.

Maurer, D., & Salapataek, P. (1976). Developmental changes in the scanning of faces by young infants. *Child Development,* **47**, 523–527.

Meltzoff, A.N. (1985). Immediate and deferred imitation in fourteen- and twenty-four-month-old infants. *Child Development,* **56**, 62–72.

Meltzoff, A.N., & Moore, M. (1983). Newborn infants imitate adult facial gestures. *Child Development,* **54**, 702–709.

Meltzoff, A.N., & Moore, M.K. (1989). Imitation in newborn infants: Exploring the range of gestures imitated and the underlying mechanisms. *Developmental Psychology,* **25**, 954–962.

Meltzoff, A.N., & Moore, M.K. (1992). Early imitation within a functional framework: The importance of person identity, movement, and development. *Infant Behavior and Development,* **15**(4), 479–505.

Meltzoff, A.N., & Moore, M.K. (1994). Imitation, memory, and the representation of persons. *Infant Behavior and Development,* **17**(1), 83–99.

Meltzoff, A., & Moore, M.K. (in press). Persons and representation: Why infant imitation is important for theories of human development. In J. Nadel & G. Butterworth (Eds.), *Imitation in infancy.* Cambridge: Cambridge University Press.

Mertan, B., Nadel, J., & Leveau, H. (1993). The effect of an adult presence on communicative behaviour among children. In J. Nadel & L. Camaioni (Eds.), *New perspectives in early communicative development* (pp. 190–201). London: Routledge.

Muir, D., Abraham, W., Forbes, B., & Harris, L. (1979). The ontogenesis of an auditory localisation response from birth to four months of age. *Canadian Journal of Psychology,* **33**, 320–333.

Muir, D.W., Clifton, R.K., & Clarkson, M.G. (1989). The development of a human auditory localisation response: A U-shaped function. Special issue: Infant perceptual development. *Canadian Journal of Psychology*, **43**(2), 199–216.

Muir, D., & Field, J. (1979). Newborn infants orient to sounds. *Child Development*, **50**, 431–436.

Muir, D.W., & Hains, S.M.J. (1993). Infant sensitivity to perturbations in adult facial, vocal, tactile, and contingent stimulation during face-to-face interactions. In B. de Boysson-Bardies et al. (Eds.), *Developmental neurocognition: Speech and face processing in the first year of life* (pp. 171–185). Dordrecht, The Netherlands: Kluwer.

Muir, D., & Hains, S.M.J. (in press). Young infants' perception of adult intentionality: Adult contingency and eye-direction. In P. Rochat (Ed.), *Early social cognition*. Mahwah, NJ: Erlbaum.

Muir, D.W., Hains, S.M.J., & Symons, L.A. (1994a). Baby and me: Infants need minds to read. *Cahiers de Psychologie Cognitive*, **13**(5), 669–682.

Muir, D.W., Humphrey, D.E., & Humphrey, G.K. (1994b). Pattern and space perception in young infants. Special issue: Invariance, recognition, and perception. In honour of Peter C. Dodwell. *Spatial Vision*, **8**(1), 141–165.

Muir, D.W., & Rach-Longman, L.K. (1989). Once more with expression: On de Schonen and Mathivet's (1989) model for the development of face perception in human infants. *Cahiers de Psychologie Cognitive*, **9**(1), 103–109.

Mundy, P., Sigman, M., & Kasari, C. (1993). The theory of mind and joint attention in autism. In S. Baron-Cohen, H. Tager-Flusberg, & D. Cohen (Eds.), *Understanding other minds: Perspectives from autism*. Oxford: Oxford University Press.

Murray, L., & Trevarthen, C. (1985). Emotional regulation of interaction between two-month-olds and their mothers. In T.M. Field & N.A. Fox (Eds.), *Social perception in infants* (pp. 101–125). Norwood, NJ: Ablex.

Nadel, J. (1980). *Wallon aujourd'hui [Wallon nowadays]*. Paris: Scarabee.

Nadel, J. (1984). *La fonction sociale de l'imitation directe: Tome 1: Les bases du fonctionalisme de Wallon [Social function of imitation. Vol. 1: Bases of Wallon's functionalism]*. Unpublished doctoral dissertation, Université de Paris X-Nanterre.

Nadel, J. (1986). *Imitation et communication entre jeunes enfants*. Paris: Presses Universitaires de France.

Nadel, J. (1994). The development of communication: Wallon's framework and influence. In A. Vyt, H. Bloch, & M. Bornstein (Eds.), *Early child development in the French tradition* (pp. 177–189). Hillsdale, NJ: Lawrence Erlbaum.

Nadel, J. (1996). *Does the capacity for imitation contribute to the foundation of language in early infancy?* At European Research Conference: The Development of Sensory Function, Barcelona, Spain.

Nadel, J. (in press). Early interpersonal timing and the perception of social contingencies. In P. Rochat (Ed.), *Early social cognition*. Mahwah, NJ: Erlbaum.

Nadel, J., & Fontaine, A.M. (1989). Communicating by imitation: A developmental and comparative approach to transitory social competence. In B. Schneider et al. (Eds.), *Social competence in developmental perspective*. Dordrecht: Kluwer.

Nadel, J., Guérini, C., & Rivet, C. (in press). Developmental changes in imitation as an evolving format for communication among typical young children and children with autism. In J. Nadel & G. Butterworth (Eds.), *Imitation in infancy*. Cambridge: Cambridge University Press.

Nadel, J., Marcelli, D., Pezé, A, Kervella, C., & Reserbat-Plantey, D. (1997, April). Contingent interaction in French 2-month-olds with their mother. At *Society for Research in Child Development*, Washington, DC:

Nadel, J., & Pezé, A. (1993). What makes immediate imitation communicative in toddlers and autistic children? In J. Nadel & L. Camaioni (Eds.), *New perspectives in early communicative development* (pp. 139–156). London and New York: Routledge.

Nadel-Brulfert, J., & Baudonnière, P.M. (1982). The social function of reciprocal imitation in 2-year-old peers. *International Journal of Behavioral Development*, **5**, 95–109.

Pascalis, O., & de Schonen, S. (1994). Recognition memory in 3–4-day-old human infants. *NeuroReport*, **5**, 1721–1724.

Pascalis, O., de Schonen, S., Morton, J., Deruelle, C., & Fabre-Grenet, M. (1995). Mother's face recognition by neonates: A replication and extension. *Infant Behavior and Development*, **18**, 79–85.

Premack, D., & Premack, A.J. (1995). Intention as psychological cause. In D. Sperber, D. Premack, & A.J. Premack (Eds.), *Causal cognition: A multidisciplinary debate*. Oxford: Clarendon Press.

Reissland, N. (1988). Neonatal imitation in the first hour of life: Observations in rural Nepal. *Developmental Psychology*, **24**, 464–469.

Roman, J. (1986). *Six-month-olds' responses to an inverted image of their mother's face during social interactions.* Unpublished honours thesis, Queen's University, Kingston, Canada.

Samuels, C.A. (1985). Attention to eye contact opportunity and facial motion by three-month-old infants. *Journal of Experimental Child Psychology*, **40**, 141–166.

Scaife, M., & Bruner, J.S. (1975). The capacity for joint attention in the infant. *Nature*, **253**, 265–266.

Schaffer, R. (1984). *The child's entry into a social world*. New York: Basic Books.

Spelke, E.S., Phillips, A., & Woodward, A.L. (1995). Infants' knowledge of object motion and human action. In D. Sperber, D. Premack, & A.J. Premack (Eds.), *Causal cognition: A multidisciplinary debate* (pp. 45–78). Oxford: Clarendon Press.

Spitz, R., & Wolf, K. (1946). The smiling response: A contribution to the ontogenesis of social relations. *Genetic Psychology Monographs*, **34**, 57–125.

Stechler, G., & Latz, E. (1966). Some observations on attention and arousal in the human infant. *Journal of the American Academy of Child Psychology*, **5**, 517–525.

Stern, D. (1985). *The interpersonal world of the infant*. New York: Basic Books.

Stern, D.N. (1974). Mother and infant at play: The dyadic interaction involving facial, vocal, and gaze behaviours. In M. Lewis & L.A. Rosenblum (Eds.), *The effect of the infant on its caregiver* (pp. 187–213). New York: Wiley.

Suzuki, S., & Cavanagh, P. (1995). Facial organization blocks access to low-level features: An object inferiority effect. *Journal of Experimental Psychology*, **21**, 901–913.

Symons, L., Hains, S.M.J., & Muir, D.W. (in press). Look at me: 5-month-old infants' sensitivity to very small deviations in eye gaze during social interactions. *Infant Behavior and Development*.

Tanaka, J.W., & Farah, M.J. (1993). Parts and wholes in face recognition. *Quarterly Journal of Experimental Psychology*, **46**, 225–245.

Termine, N.T., & Izzard, C.E. (1988). Infants' responses to their mothers' expressions of joy and sadness. *Developmental Psychology*, **24**, 223–229.

Thompson, P. (1980). Margaret Thatcher: A new illusion. *Perception*, **9**, 483–484.

Tremblay-Leveau, H., & Nadel, J. (1995). Young children's communicative skills in triads. *International Journal of Behavioral Development*, **18**, 227–242.

Tremblay-Leveau, H., & Nadel, J. (1996). Exclusion in triads: Can it serve "meta-communicative" knowledge in 11- and 23-month-old children? *British Journal of Developmental Psychology*, **14**, 145–158.

Trevarthen, C. (1974). Conversations with a 2-month-old. *New Scientist*, **May**, 230–235.

Tronick, E.Z. (1989). Emotions and emotional communication in infants. Special Issue: Children and their development: Knowledge base, research agenda, and social policy application. *American Psychologist*, **44**(2), 112–119.

Tronick, E., Als, H., Adamson, L., Wise, S., & Brazelton, T.B. (1978). The infants' response to entrapment between contradictory messages in face-to-face interactions. *Journal of the American Academy of Child Psychiatry*, **17**, 1–13.

Uzgiris, I.C. (1981). Two functions of imitation during infancy. *International Journal of Behavioral Development*, **4**, 1–12.

Vecera, S.P., & Johnson, M.H. (1995). Gaze detection and the cortical processing of faces: Evidence from infants and adults. *Visual Cognition*, **2**, 59–87.

Vinter, A. (1986). The role of movement in eliciting early imitations. *Child Development*, **57**, 66–71.

Von Hofsten, C. (1983). Catching skills in infancy. *Journal of Experimental Psychology: Human Perception and Performance*, **9**, 75–85.

Walker-Andrews, A.S. (1997). Infants' perception of expressive behaviours: Differentiation of multimodal information. *Psychological Bulletin*, **121**, 437–456.

Walker-Andrews, A.S., & Lennon, E.M. (1991). Infants' discrimination of vocal expressions: Contributions of auditory and visual information. *Infant Behavior and Development*, **14**, 131–142.

Wallon, H. (1934). *Les origines du caractère chez l'enfant*. Paris: Presses Universitaires de France.

Wallon, H. (1938). *La vie mentale*. Paris: Larousse.

Watson, J.S. (1966). Perception of object orientation in infants. *Merrill-Palmer Quarterly*, **12**, 73–94.

Watson, J.S. (1985). Contingency perception in early social development. In T. Field & N. Fox (Eds.), *Social perception in infants*. (pp. 156–176). Norwood, NJ: Ablex.

Watson, J.S., Hayes, L.A., Vietze, P., & Becker, J. (1979). Discriminating infant smiling to orientations of talking faces of mother and stranger. *Journal of Child Psychology*, **28**, 92–99.

Wolff, P.H. (1987). *The development of behavioral states and the expression of emotions in early infancy: New proposals for investigation*. Chicago: University of Chicago Press.

Wolff, P.H., Gunnoe, C., & Cohen, C. (1985). Neuromotor maturation and psychological performance: A developmental study. *Developmental Medicine and Child Neurology*, **27**(3), 344–354.

Wolff, P.M. (1963). Observations on the early development of smiling. In B.M. Foss (Ed.), *Determinants of infant behaviour*. London: Methuen.

ACKNOWLEDGEMENTS

We gratefully acknowledge the contributions of Anna Pezé to some of the research reported in this chapter. We also thank Larry Symons and Alan Slater for their editorial comments on drafts of this manuscript and Christine Hains for her work on the reference section. Finally, we wish to thank Henriette Bloch for sponsoring D. Muir's visit to the Laboratoire de Psycho-Biologie du Developpement in Paris in the autumn of 1996, which initiated this collaborative effort, the EPHE-CNRS for their generous support, and The Natural Sciences and Engineering Research Council of Canada for supporting Muir's research.

CHAPTER NINE

Discrimination and categorisation of facial expressions of emotion during infancy

Michelle de Haan
MRC Cognitive Development Unit, London, UK

Charles A. Nelson
University of Minnesota, MN, USA

INTRODUCTION

Facial expressions are an important way to communicate emotions (Izard, 1991). Recognising facial emotion permits us to detect another person's emotional state or reactions and can provide cues on how to respond and behave in social situations. Facial expressions are probably an especially important form of communication for infants who cannot yet use language to perceive and express emotion. For example, an infant's recognition of a happy expression displayed by a caregiver could facilitate the expression of happiness in the infant, which could contribute to the development of the attachment relationship (Bowlby, 1969). Thus, some investigators have argued that it may be adaptive for infants to be able to recognise expressions early in life (Darwin, 1896; Nelson, 1987). A selective adaptation for recognising facial expressions may have resulted in the creation of specialised neural systems that subserve this ability and require little experience to develop (Nelson, 1987; Nelson & de Haan, 1997). One piece of evidence cited in support of this hypothesis is that infants are able to discriminate among different types of facial expressions (e.g. happy, fearful, etc.) very early in life.

However, the mere observation that infants are able to discriminate among expressions early in life does not necessarily imply that recognition of expressions relies on a specialised neurocognitive system. It is possible that infants can discriminate among other types of visual stimuli at an equally early age. If so, this would argue against the view that a specialised neural system underlies infants' ability to recognise facial expressions. Another possibility is that there is a more general-purpose visual recognition system that emerges early in life and mediates discrimination of several different types of patterned information. The goal of this chapter is to review the development of emotion recognition in the context of determining whether there is evidence that this ability develops differently – either with respect to timing or processes – than the ability to recognise nonaffective visual stimuli.

In order to understand the meaning of different facial expressions, infants must be able to tell the difference between them. Our discussion of the development of emotion recognition will be limited to the development of perceptual categories of expressions and will not include the development of the ability to understand the meaning of these expressions, though this is clearly also an important aspect of recognising expressions. Presumably, infants' perceptual categories form the basis of their conceptual categories (a point also argued by Quinn in Chapter 5). For example, if there were some "prewiring " that made it easier for infants to learn perceptual categories for expression than other stimuli, this in turn could facilitate the emergence of their conceptual understanding of these categories.

We begin our review by describing the development of the infant's ability to discriminate different facial expressions. We then compare this ability to results from selected experiments on the discrimination of other visual stimuli to determine whether the timing of the emergence of these abilities is unique for facial expressions. We then turn to the development of infants' ability to categorise different facial expressions, raising similar questions to those concerning discrimination. From this review we will conclude that there is little evidence to suggest that infants' discrimination and categorisation of expressions occurs earlier than for other stimulus materials. However, future studies in which facial expressions and other stimuli are more directly compared may reveal a different pattern. Next, we discuss the way in which facial expressions may be encoded by infants and whether this differs from the way in which other visual stimuli are encoded. Again, we will conclude that there is little evidence of differences, but that future studies in which facial expressions and other stimuli are more directly compared may reveal a different pattern. Finally, we discuss implications of these conclusions for understanding the development of the ability to recognise facial expressions of emotion.

DISCRIMINATION OF FACIAL EXPRESSIONS

How is it studied?

Discrimination refers to the ability to perceive the difference between two or more stimuli. The ability to discriminate among visual stimuli can be studied in infants using visual preference and familiarisation-test or habituation–dishabituation procedures. In the visual preference procedure, infants view two or more stimuli and their length of looking to each is noted. Longer looking at one stimulus than another is taken as evidence of discrimination between the two. This method may be especially sensitive to infants' spontaneous reactions to the expressions, and thus can help to determine whether, for example, there are certain expressions that capture infants' attention more than others. However, if infants do not look longer at one expression than another it is not possible to know whether this is because they could not discriminate between them or because they simply were not motivated to look longer at one than the other.

The familiarisation-test and habituation–dishabituation procedures are similar to the visual preference procedure except that infants are first familiarised (i.e. shown a stimulus until a fixed amount of actual time or looking time has elapsed) or habituated (i.e shown a stimulus until looking time has decreased below a criterion) to one of the stimuli. Longer looking to a novel stimulus compared to the familiar one following habituation or familiarisation is taken as evidence of discrimination. These procedures allow a more direct assessment of discrimination. If infants do not look longer at the novel than the familiar expression, this can be taken as presumptive evidence that they cannot discriminate between them. However, a disadvantage of this procedure is that infants' looking times can be influenced by factors other than experimental familiarity. These reactions may either enhance or conflict with experimental familiarity so that evidence of discrimination may not be observed. For example, if infants have a pre-experimental preference for one expression, they may continue to look longer at it than a novel expression even following habituation.

When does it emerge?

Infants may be able to discriminate between expressions by 36 hours of age (Field, Cohen, Garcia, & Collins, 1983; Field, Woodson, Greenberg, & Cohen, 1982). In these two studies infants were presented with a happy, sad, or surprised expression posed by a live female model until they looked for less than two seconds, and then saw the other two expressions presented in the same way. Infants' looking times increased when the expression changed, suggesting that they were able to discriminate among the expressions. However, there was no comparison group tested with the same procedure but without a change in expression to show that the changes in looking time were due to the change in expression. This is a concern because looking times on the trials used to determine whether habituation has occurred are by definition constrained (i.e. looking times must be low), while the following trials are not (i.e. looking times can be high or low). As a result, the looking times to novel and familiar stimuli may be differentially affected by regression to the mean. Regression to the mean refers to the fact that scores at the extreme ends of a distribution tend to move closer to the mean with repeated testing. Looking times on criterion trials are extreme scores, therefore looking times may increase on the next trial simply due to chance. If only the novel stimulus is presented following habituation, only the novel stimulus will be affected by this tendency. This could have caused the appearance of increased looking to the new expression when in fact the differences were due to chance alone.

Studies with older infants provide stronger evidence of discrimination, as the confound of regression to the mean was controlled for by testing control groups that did not see a change in expression following habituation (Young-Browne, Rosenfeld, & Horowitz, 1977); by showing both novel and familiar stimuli following habituation (Barerra & Maurer, 1981; McGrath, 1983; Nelson, Morse, & Leavitt, 1979; Schwartz, Izard, & Ansul, 1985); or by assessing only visual preferences without habituation (LaBarbera, Izard, Vietze, & Parisi, 1976; Oster & Ewy, 1980). The results of these studies show that 3-month-olds tested using a habituation–dishabituation procedure can discriminate happy from surprised faces (Young-Browne et al., 1977) and smiling faces from frowning faces (Barrera & Maurer, 1981), but they do not consistently discriminate sad faces from surprised faces and show no evidence of discriminating sad faces from happy faces (Young-Browne et al., 1977). In addition, 3- to 6-month-olds can discriminate among happy, surprised, and angry expressions in a familiarisation-test procedure. By 4 months of age, infants in a visual preference test look longer at joyful expressions than angry or neutral ones (LaBarbera et al., 1976) and look longer at happy faces with toothy smiles than sad faces (Oster & Ewy, 1980) but look equally long at angry and neutral expressions (LaBarbera et al., 1976) or happy faces with closed mouths when paired with sad faces (Oster & Ewy, 1980). Five-month-olds can discriminate between sad and fearful faces and can discriminate both of these expressions and an interest expression from angry, but only if they are first habituated to angry and then tested with fear, sad or interest, and not if they are shown the expressions in the reverse order. At the same age infants show no evidence of discriminating joy from anger or interest (Schwartz et al., 1985), and at 6 months they show no evidence of discriminating surprised from fearful expressions (Nelson & Horowitz, 1980). At 7 months infants look longer at fearful than happy faces in a visual preference test (Nelson & Dolgin, 1985) and can discriminate happy from fearful faces in a habituation–dishabituation test, but only if they first habituate to happy and not if they first habituate to fear (Nelson et al., 1979).

By the first few months of life infants can also discriminate among different exemplars of the same expression. For example, 3-month-olds can discriminate among smiling faces that vary in intensity (Kuchuk, Vibbert, & Bornstein, 1986), 4-month-olds can discriminate between mild and intense examples of fearful faces (Nelson & Ludemann, 1986) and 7-month-olds can discriminate between mild and intense exemplars of happy and fearful faces (Ludemann & Nelson, 1987).

The results of these studies suggest that within the first half-year of life infants are able to discriminate at least some of the features that to adults denote different expressions. With one exception (Schwartz et al., 1985), the results of several studies are in agreement that during the first few months of life infants are able to discriminate happy from surprised and angry expressions (see Table 9.1), but happy may be harder to discriminate from sad expressions. Discrimination between other expressions has been less extensively studied, and the results appear to be affected by the order of presentation of the expressions. This may be because factors other than experimental familiarity are more important determinants of infants' visual attention for these particular expressions and/or for that particular age range (5–7 months).

Do expressions differ from other stimuli?

Even newborns are able to discriminate among some types of visual stimuli in visual preference and habituation–dishabituation tests. For example, newborns look longer at high-contrast than low-contrast stimuli (Morison & Slater, 1985) and look longer at three-dimensional than two-dimensional stimuli (Slater, Rose, & Morison, 1983) Following habituation, newborns can discriminate between lines of different orientations (Slater, 1989) and between a triangle, square, circle and cross (Slater, Morison & Rose, 1983). However, newborns typically require more time than older infants to habituate to the same pattern and are unable to perform some of the same discriminations as older infants (for discussion, see Bornstein, 1985; Olson & Sherman, 1983).

Newborns can also discriminate among different facial identities, suggesting that facial expression is not the only complex visual information in a face that can be discriminated shortly after birth. Newborns look longer at the mother's face than at a stranger's face shortly after birth (Bushnell, Sai, & Mullin, 1989; Field, Cohen, Garcia, & Greenberg, 1984; Pascalis, de Schonen, Morton, Deruelle, & Fabre-Grenet, 1995). However, this discrimination may be based on the external features and contour of the face rather than the internal features involved in expressions (Pascalis et al., 1995).

Thus, it does not seem that the ability to discriminate among expressions emerges earlier than the ability to discriminate among nonaffective stimuli

TABLE 9.1

A summary of the results of studies of infants' discrimination of expressions during the first year of life

Expression pair	Age	Method	Discrimination?	Authors
Happy-surprised	Newborn	Habituation	Yes	Field et al., 1982 Field et al., 1983
	3 months	Habituation	Yes	Young-Brown et al., 1977
	3–6 months	Familiarisation	Yes	McGrath, 1983
Happy-Sad	Newborn	Habituation	Yes	Field et al., 1982 Field et al., 1983
	3 months	Habituation	No	Young-Browne et al., 1977
	4 months	Preference	Yes, if toothy smile No, if nontoothy smile	Oster & Ewy, 1980
Happy-Angry	3 months	Habituation	Yes	Barrera & Maurer, 1981
	3–6 months	Familiarisation	Yes	McGrath, 1983
	4 months	Preference	Yes	LaBarbera et al., 1976
	6 months			
	5 months	Familiarisation	No	Schwartz et al., 1985
Happy-Fearful	7 month	Habituation	Yes, if habituate to happy and test fearful No, if habituate to fearful and test happy	Nelson et al., 1979
	7 months	Preference	Yes	Nelson & Dolgin, 1985

Expression pair	Age	Method	Discrimination?	Authors
Sad-Surprised	Newborn	Habituation	Yes	Field et al., 1982
				Field et al., 1983
	3 months	Habituation	Sometimes	Young-Browne et al, 1977
Sad-Fearful	5 months	Familiarization	Yes	Schwartz et al., 1985
Angry-Sad	5 months	Familiarization	Yes-If habituate to angry and test sad	Schwartz et al., 1985
			No-If habituate to sad and test angry	
Angry-Fearful	5 months	Familiarization	Yes-If habituate to angry and test fearful	Schwartz et al., 1985
			No-If habituate to fearful and test angry	
Angry-Surprised	3-6 months	Familiarization	Yes	McGrath, 1983
Fearful-Surprised	6 months	Familiarization	Yes	Nelson & Horowitz, 1980

or even other information about the face. If the observation that newborns may be able to discriminate between facial expressions (e.g. Field et al., 1982, 1983) can be replicated with appropriate controls, this might suggest that infants are able to perceive emotion in the internal features of the face before they can perceive identity in these features. It also is not entirely clear whether infants can discriminate among patterns that are as complex as expressions at an equally early age. Many of the other patterns used with newborns were simpler; thus it is possible that infants are able to discriminate between facial expressions at an early age but not between equally complex nonaffective stimuli.

CATEGORISATION OF FACIAL EXPRESSIONS

How is it studied?

Categorisation refers to the ability to respond in a similar manner to members of a group of noticeably different stimuli. Infants' abilities to categorise visual stimuli are usually assessed using variants of the familiarisation-test and habituation–dishabituation procedures. Instead of presenting only one example of the category during the familiarisation or habituation phase, multiple exemplars are presented. Infants are then tested with a new exemplar of the familiar category and an exemplar from a new category. If infants have formed a category, their looking should increase to the exemplar of the new category, but not to the exemplar of the familiar category. In order to conclude that infants have actually formed a perceptual category, it is important to show that they are able to discriminate between the exemplars of the familiar category. This rules out the possibility that infants' looking times remain low for the new exemplar of the familiar category because they did not notice it was different from those seen previously (i.e. failure to discriminate), rather than because they recognised the similarity between the new and old exemplars despite the noticeable differences (i.e. categorisation).

Studying infants' categorisation of expressions provides information that cannot be learned from studying only discrimination. Simple discrimination between expressions does not tell whether (a) infants' responses would generalise beyond the model tested or (b) infants were discriminating local pattern information (e.g. upturned vs. downturned mouth, or even some other features less relevant to the expression) or were responding based on an invariant configuration of features making up an expression. If infants are able to recognise that an expression is the same even when it is posed by several models, it suggests that their responses are not limited to a particular model's face and are unlikely to be based only on local differences in pattern information.

When does it emerge?

In an early test of infants' categorisation of expressions, Nelson et al. (1979) familiarised 7-month-olds to two different models posing happy expressions, and then showed infants a new model posing a happy expression and a fearful one. Infants looked longer at the fearful expression than the happy one, suggesting that they recognised the happy expression as familiar despite the change in model and were able to discriminate this expression from the fearful one. Infants were able to discriminate between the different happy and fearful faces; thus these results cannot be due to failure to discriminate. Unfortunately, because of the familiarisation procedure used, it was not possible to compare whether looking times to the happy face during the test trials were increased relative to looking at the end of familiarisation. If the looking times to the happy face did increase relative to levels at the end of familiarisation, it would suggest that infants had not categorised happy.

In contrast to these results, infants at this age did not show evidence of discrimination if they were first familiarised to different models posing fearful expression (Nelson et al., 1979). Subsequent studies replicated and extended this pattern. For example, 7-month-olds showed categorisation of happy following habituation to happy faces posed by (a) multiple male or female models (Nelson & Dolgin, 1985), and (b) female models that varied in how intensely the expressions were depicted (Ludemann & Nelson, 1988a). However, it was consistently observed that 6- to 7-month-olds showed no evidence of categorising fear or surprise when habituated to multiple models posing these expressions and then tested with happy (Caron, Caron, & Myers, 1982; Nelson & Dolgin, 1985; Ludemann & Nelson, 1988a). One interpretation of these findings is that infants' pre-experimental familiarity with the expressions affects their looking times. For infants, happy may be a more familiar expression than fear or surprise. It is possible that when infants view a more familiar expression during familiarisation or habituation they are able to categorise it and discriminate it from a more novel expression. However, if infants view a less familiar expression during habituation they may have difficulty categorising it and discriminating it from another expression (Ludemann & Nelson, 1988a). However, 4-month-old infants are able to form categories for both happy and fearful faces regardless of the order of presentation of the expressions (Ludemann & Nelson, 1988b). If infants' pre-experimental familiarity with expressions is responsible for the order effects, then they should be present at earlier ages as well. Thus, the results with 4-month-olds suggest that pre-experimental familiarity is not the cause, or at least not the only cause, of these effects.

Infants' abilities to categorise some other expressions have also been tested. Four- to 6-month-old infants are able to categorise fear and anger, but only show evidence of categorising surprise if they are tested with anger and not when tested with fear (Serrano, Iglesias & Loeches, 1992). In another study, 4- to 9-month-olds showed evidence of categorising happy, angry, and neutral expressions (Serrano, Iglesias, & Loeches, 1995), although these results contradict those of a previous study using the same types of expressions (Phillips, Wagner, Fells, & Lynch, 1990). In the studies showing evidence of categorisation (Serrano et al., 1992, 1995), investigators did not test whether infants could discriminate among the exemplars within a category; thus the results could have occurred because infants failed to discriminate between the different examples of the same expression and not because they were able to categorise them.

Even by 7 months of age, infants' ability to categorise expressions may be limited. They appear to have difficulty grouping different expressions into the broader categories of positive and negative expressions. For example, in one study 7- and 10-month-olds were habituated to either a variety of models posing various prototypical positive expressions (e.g. happy) or a variety of models posing mixed or blended expressions collectively labelled by adults as representing "positive " affect (Ludemann, 1991). Following habituation, infants were tested with either novel models portraying positive expressions or novel models portraying negative expressions (angry and fear). Ten-month-olds, but not 7-month-olds, could recognise the familiar expression and discriminate it from the novel one following habituation to prototypical positive expressions. In contrast, neither age group showed evidence of categorisation following habituation to blended positive expressions. These results suggest that it is not until 10 months that infants are able to categorise expressions as positive or negative. Even by this age, infants' knowledge of facial expressions may be bounded by prototypes, as infants did not recognise the expression when nonprototypical exemplars were used.

Do expressions differ from other stimuli?

It appears to be difficult for newborns to form categories from viewing two-dimensional stimuli. In one study newborns and 3- to 5-month-olds were familiarised to six different exemplars of the same shape, and then tested with a new exemplar of the same shape and a different shape (Slater & Morison, 1987, cited in Slater, 1989). The older infants looked longer at the different shape, whereas the newborns did not. This suggests that infants a few months old, but not newborns, can form categories. This may be because newborns base their discriminations on lower-order variables such as orientation or contrast, rather than higher-order variables such as overall form (Slater, 1989). In other words, it may be harder to form a category if infants are paying attention to isolated features that may not be related to category membership.

Infants do seem to be able to form perceptual categories of nonaffective complex visual stimuli by 2–4 months of age. For example, in one study (Quinn, Eimas, & Rosencrantz, 1993) infants were familiarised to the category cats or dogs by showing six 15-second trials in which pairs of two different exemplars of the same categories were shown. They were tested with a new exemplar of the familiar category and a novel category – bird. Infants' looking increased for the birds but not for the exemplar of the familiar category. Importantly, control experiments showed that this was not because infants could not discriminate between different exemplars of dogs or cats. By this age infants can also form a category horse and discriminate it from cat, giraffe, and zebra, and form the category cat and discriminate it from horse and tiger, though not female lion (Eimas & Quinn, 1994). These results show that infants can form categorical representations based on seeing pictures of perceptually complex natural kinds. They can remember this information over at least a 5–15 minute delay (Roberts, 1988; Sherman, 1985). Thus, even newly formed perceptual categories can be made available at a later time by pre-linguistic infants and this could be used as a guide at the onset of learning object words. This observation strengthens the idea that perceptual categories may play a facilitative role in learning of object words and/or conceptual categories. However, it would seem important to establish whether infants can also remember information over longer periods of time, as this would more closely parallel language learning in the natural environment.

The results of several studies of infants' categorisation of faces (not expressions) and patterns of dots suggest that infants form prototypes based on perceptual categories (Bomba & Siqueland, 1983; Strauss, 1979; Younger, 1985). For adults, the nature of the prototypical representation that is formed seems to depend on features of the task and stimuli. When the features that vary between categories are easily discriminable or are attended to more because of task instructions, adults tend to form a modal representation (i.e. a representation consisting of the most frequently occurring feature values). In contrast, when the features are very similar or less attended to, adults tend to form an average representation (i.e. a representation consisting of the average across exemplars of the feature values). In the one study to test whether infants show similar responses, 10-month-olds appeared to form average representations both when the features were easier and harder to discriminate (Strauss, 1979). One possibility is that infants are unable to form modal representations. However, this interpretation seems unlikely because in other studies in which infants were shown fewer exemplars they did show evidence of having formed a modal prototype (Sherman, 1985). Another possibility is that, for infants, even in the easy condition the different feature values seemed similar to the infants and thus they formed an average prototype.

There are several factors that appear to help infants form a perceptual category. For example, 3- to 4-month-olds' preference for a novel category of dot patterns over a novel example from the familiar category tends to be stronger if they were exposed to two categories rather than only one during familiarisation (Quinn, 1987). Thus, exposure to more than one category during habituation may enhance categorisation. This may be because a prototype not only has the greatest number of attributes in common with members of a category, but also has the least number of attributes in common with contrasting categories. Thus, to know what features are valid for defining category membership, it helps to have some experience with categories that contrast with the target category.

A number of factors may also hinder the formation of a category. One factor is the presence a non-structured set of stimuli along with a set that forms a category. For example, when 3- to 4-month-olds are shown shapes that do not form a category intermixed with exemplars of a single-shape category, they do not show evidence of categorisation (Quinn, 1987). Another factor that can hinder formation of a category is showing poor exemplars (i.e. nonprototypical). For example, 9-month-olds can form the category birds if shown prototypical exemplars but not if given poor ones (Roberts & Horowitz, 1986).

The results of studies with nonaffective stimuli suggest that a number of factors can influence whether infants form a perceptual category and the nature of the representation. At least under some circumstances, infants appear to be able to form prototypic representations of non-affective stimuli. Infants' representations of facial expressions may also be in the form of prototypes, although this has not been directly tested. The observation that 10-month-olds can discriminate positive expressions from negative expressions only when shown prototypical examples is consistent with this hypothesis (Ludemann, 1991). If infants are forming prototypic representations of expressions, it is possible that, as for nonaffective stimuli, the nature of the familiarisation affects the nature of the represent-ation. For example, if a salient, easily discriminable feature is present (e.g. "toothiness") it is possible infants are more likely to form a modal proto-type based on that feature, particularly if relatively few different models are presented. In contrast, if such a feature is not present they may be more likely to form an average representation possibly based on more features.

Infants' preferences for certain types of stimuli may also influence perceptual categorisation. Preferences that involve many and perhaps all members could provide the basis for early segregation of objects in the visual environment in a coherent manner and in this way could facilitate acquisition of perceptual categories. For example, 10-month-olds prefer cats to horses (Eimas & Quinn, 1994) and in a categorisation task they show a larger and more reliable novelty preference for cats after habituation to horses than for horses after habituation to cats.

The studies of the development of categorisation of nonaffective stimuli also demonstrate that infants' pre-existing preferences for certain stimuli may influence their responses in categorisation tests. For example, they can cause order effects if the infants prefer to look at exemplars of a certain category even if they are not a novel category. It is possible that these preferences facilitate the acquisition of categories in the real world if, for example, they help infants to notice the similarities among the members of the category. Another possibility is that these preferences emerge at the times when infants are forming categories or developing some new understanding of the category in the real world. For both affective and nonaffective stimuli, both the preferences and order effects are not necessarily stable over age. It may be that as they are learning about these categories, their interest level or reactions to members of the category change.

Infants can form categories based on experience during the experiment, even if they have had little prior experience with the category. For example, 9-month-olds formed the category bird even though mothers' reports suggest that infants of this age have little if any knowledge of this category outside of the experimental context (Roberts, 1988). Function (what things can do or what can be done with them) may be an important factor for guiding the formation of conceptual categories. In contrast, the results of these studies suggest that form information is sufficient for developing a perceptual category. Function information is not necessary though it is possible that it would facilitate formation of the category. It is possible that function plays an especially important role in the development of recognition of expressions. For example, infants may begin to recognise and discriminate between certain expressions when these expressions become more "functional " in the sense of being adaptive for the infant to respond to them (Izard, 1991). For example, it may be that recognition of an expression such as happy is adaptive even very early in life, as the infant can respond with positive affect, which in return can promote the development of the infant–caregiver relationship. For other expressions, such as fear or anger, it may be useful only later for the infant to recognise the expression – for example, as the infant starts to be able to locomote and is able to respond to such expressions by moving from the dangerous situation.

In summary, the results of these studies suggest that infants are able to form categories of nonaffective visual stimuli at least as early as for facial expressions. However, as infants younger than 3–4 months have not been tested for categorisation of expressions it is possible that differences would also be observed at these earlier ages.

HOW ARE EXPRESSIONS ENCODED?

If there is a neural system that is specialised for processing facial expressions, it is possible that it develops at the same rate as a more general-purpose processing system but that the way it processes expressions is different. Little is known about the way in which infants encode and represent facial expressions. In this section, we will discuss several factors that appear to contribute to adults' recognition of expressions and whether they also appear to be involved in infants' recognition of expressions.

Features

For adults, certain features of the face may contribute more to an expression than others. For example, happiness and surprise are more easily recognised by attending to the mouth than to the eye and/or brow regions; sadness and fear are more easily recognised from the eye/brow region; anger is sometimes more easily recognised from the mouth and at other times the eye/brow; and surprise is equally recognisable from both these areas (Boucher & Ekman, 1975; Plutchik, 1962; Stoddart, 1987). It is possible that certain regions of the face are also more important than others for infants' recognition of expressions.

Some investigators have suggested that infants in studies of expression recognition may be responding only on the basis of certain salient features that may or may not be relevant to the expressions. For example, in one study infants discriminated happiness from anger only when teeth were displayed in the happy expression and not in the angry expression (Caron, Caron, & Myers, 1985). Even when infants were shown toothy and non-toothy exemplars of the same expression during familiarisation, so that the presence or absence of the teeth was not consistently related to an expression category, they showed no evidence of categorising happy and angry (Phillips et al., 1990). However, others have shown that infants can still discriminate and categorise expressions even when the presence of teeth does not differ between them (Kestenbaum & Nelson, 1990; Ludemann & Nelson, 1988a; Schwartz et al., 1985). These results do suggest that a salient feature of the face may attract infants' attention even if it is not relevant to the expression, and in that case may detract their attention from expression-relevant features.

There is some evidence to suggest that certain features of the face that are relevant to expressions are also more salient than others. Nelson and Horowitz (1980) familiarised 6-month-olds to a surprised face and then tested them with that face and either (a) the same surprised face but with eyes changed to show fear, or (b) the same surprised face but with the mouth changed to show fear, or (c) a fearful face. Infants showed evidence of discrimination only between the surprised face and the surprised face with fearful eyes. This suggests that the eye region may be more important than the mouth region for discriminating surprised and fearful faces.

Thus, it seems that salient features of the face can attract infants' attention but that this is not unique to features of the face that denote expression. However, this is a relatively unstudied area and thus it is possible that further study would reveal differences. It does seem that even for other visual stimuli, certain "features" of the stimuli may be more important than others. For example, the face may be more important than the body for infants' categorisation of animals. It is also likely that which features are important is partly determined by the nature of the particular stimuli used in the experiment – e.g. the features that vary most, etc. may differ for different sets of stimuli.

Holistic/Configural Processing

Another possible way in which the processing of expressions may differ from other stimuli is that it relies more heavily on perceiving configurations of features (i.e. all the features that make up the expression and the relations among them). In adults, this has been studied most extensively in the context of assessing hemispheric differences in the recognition of emotion. One way in which this is studied is using the divided visual field procedure. Here stimuli are presented to the right or left of the centre of gaze. Because of the nature of the neural projections from the retina to the primary visual cortex, information about stimuli presented to the left of the centre of gaze (left visual field; LVF) will reach the right hemisphere before the left, whereas information presented to the right of the centre of gaze (right visual field; RVF) will reach the left hemisphere before the right. Facial expressions are usually detected more quickly and accurately in the LVF than the RVF, so the LVF/right hemisphere is said to have an "advantage " for processing that type of stimulus (e.g. Ley & Strauss, 1986). This advantage may occur because the right hemisphere is better at processing configural information important for recognising expressions and/or because the right hemisphere is better at recognising emotion in general (e.g. for other types of emotional material, such as a voice, as well).

Few studies have examined the development of hemispheric differences in cognitive abilities during infancy and none have specifically tested with facial expressions (for discussion of the neural basis of the development of face recognition generally, see Nelson & de Haan, 1997). Studies of hemispheric differences in infant memory and perception can also be done using a split visual field procedure if latency to move the eyes to the peripherally presented patterns is used as the dependent measure. Studies with 4- to 9-month-olds suggest that, although both the right and left hemispheres may be able to process information about the specific nature of the components of a pattern, the right hemisphere may be better at detecting the arrangement of the features (Deruelle & de Schonen, 1991, 1995). Thus, there may be different modes of visual pattern processing in the two hemispheres that are present early in life. However, it is not known how these might contribute to expression recognition as it has not been studied in this context.

Orientation

Perception of facial expressions may rely more on perceiving the faces in the correct orientation than does perception of other visual stimuli. Several investigators have noted that inverting a face affects infants' perception of its expression, as well as other facial information (e.g. attractiveness; see Chapter 4). For example, infants can discriminate happy expressions from angry and fearful ones even if the faces are upside down, but can categorise them only if the faces are upright (Kestenbaum & Nelson, 1990). This may be because discrimination is based more on isolated features that are equally easily perceivable in upright and inverted faces but categorisation is based more on emotionally relevant orientation-specific information (Kestenbaum & Nelson, 1990). Infants also need more time to encode inverted expressions than upright ones (McGrath, 1983).

To study further the effect of inversion on infants' processing of faces, we (de Haan & Nelson, 1996) examined infants' looking time and event-related potential (ERP) responses to happy and fearful faces. We first asked whether infants' visual preferences would be affected by inversion. If so, this might suggest that the preferences are based on emotionally relevant orientation-specific information rather than information about isolated features that may or may not be relevant to the expression. Second, we examined event-related potentials (ERPs) invoked by infants' viewing emotions to assess whether the neural activity occurring while infants view faces is affected by inversion.

Seven-month-old infants participated in a two-part test. In the first part, infants' visual preferences for happy and fearful faces (taken from the Ekman collection; see Ekman, 1976) were measured with four infant-controlled trials. Each face was presented once in the first two trials with the order counterbalanced across infants. The second two trials were the reverse of the first two. Half of the infants saw the faces upright ($n = 14$) and half saw them inverted ($n = 14$).

Infants looked longer at upright fearful faces than upright happy faces, replicating previous reports (Nelson & Dolgin, 1985). However, when the faces were inverted they looked equally long at both expressions. As shown in Fig. 9.1, the difference in responding between the two faces when presented upright compared to inverted is due mostly to decreased looking at inverted compared to upright fearful faces – the responses to happy faces changed less. This suggests that visual recognition of and/or responses to fearful expressions, in contrast to happy ones, depend more on features that are difficult to perceive upside-down.

In the second part of the study event-related potentials were recorded while the same infants watched pictures of a happy face and a fearful face. (ERPs represent the electrical activity generated by the brain in response to the presentation of a discrete stimulus, when some aspect of that stimulus must be processed at the cognitive – versus sensory – level.) Each infant saw faces in the same orientation seen during the preference test. Brain activity was recorded using silver–silver chlorided electrodes referenced to linked ears. The ERP test consisted of 70 trials. Each trial began with a 100msec period during which baseline activity was recorded, fol-

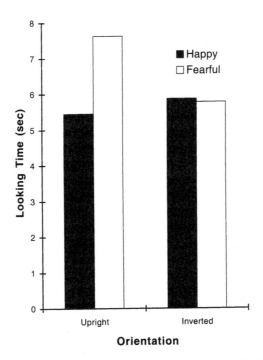

FIG. 9.1. – Distribution of looking times when viewing happy (black bars) and fearful (white bars) faces in both upright (left side) and inverted (right side) orientations.

lowed by a 500msec exposure to the face, after which brain activity continued to be recorded for another 1200msec. The inter-trial interval varied randomly between 500msec and 1200msec. Across the 70 trials, the two expressions were presented randomly and with equal probability.

As seen in Fig. 9.2, a middle-latency (400–800msec) negative component was elicited for both happy and fearful faces in both upright and inverted orientations. This component was larger for upright (dashed lines) than inverted faces (solid lines) and this difference was especially prominent for the fearful faces (graphs to the left). Comparison of the response to upright fearful faces shows that the negative component is larger for the fearful faces (dashed line, graphs to the left) than for the happy faces (dashed line, graphs to the right). This negative component is thought to be related to infants' visual preferences for expressions (Nelson & de Haan, 1996). The pattern in this study is consistent with this: inversion affected both the negative component and the looking times more for fearful than happy faces and the negative component was larger and looking times longer for upright fearful than happy faces.

Following the negative component, positive activity occurred that was especially prominent at posterior electrodes. This component may represent infants' encoding/updating of a representation (Nelson, 1994). Thus, one interpretation of this pattern is that inverted expressions are more difficult to encode. Another related possibility is that, because infants' looking times were shorter to inverted than to upright expressions during the preference test, they had formed a less complete representation of the inverted faces that required more updating when they were subsequently re-exposed to the faces during ERP recordings.

Together, these results suggest that the orientation of a face does affect how infants respond to it (also see Fagan, 1972). However, as less is known about how inversion affects infants' recognition of other stimuli it is difficult to say whether or not these effects are unique to expressions.

SUMMARY AND CONCLUSIONS

The goal of this review was to discuss the development of recognition of facial expressions in the context of the development of visual recognition in general. The results of studies of infants' perception of facial expressions is that infants can discriminate between at least some expressions by 3–4 months of age and can form categories of expressions by 7 months of age. There is little evidence from available studies to show that the development of infants' recognition of expressions differs from the development of visual recognition in general. However, in many cases the critical tests of this hypothesis (e.g. testing infants at the same age and with the same procedure but differing stimulus content) have not been performed. It

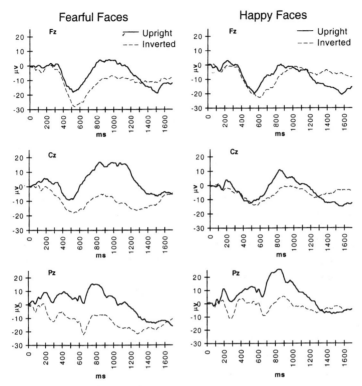

FIG. 9.2. – Grand average ERP responses to upright (solid lines) and inverted (dashed lines) happy (right side) and fearful (left side) faces. Each face was presented for 500msec. The data displayed are from the midline parietal (Pz), central (Cz), and frontal (Fz) scalp locations.

also is possible that any differences do not emerge until later in infancy or childhood. There may be a more general-purpose system operating early in life that differentiates/specialises with further brain development and/or visual experience. Most of the studies during infancy have focused on the first half-year of life; it may be that the "specialisation" of the processes involved in recognition of facial expressions does not occur until the second year or later.

It is also possible that the methods available to study the neural basis of visual recognition are not sensitive enough or are not appropriate to detect differences in the neural circuits that underlie infants' (and adults') recognition of expressions compared to other stimuli. For example, a limitation of many ERP methods is that the relatively small number of electrodes used makes it difficult to determine and/or isolate the neural generators responsible for the scalp-recorded ERP. As a result, it may not be possible to distinguish those neural networks that are involved in the recognition of facial expressions from those involved in recognition of other objects or events.

Another factor to consider is that, even within the domain of facial expressions, the development of recognition of different expressions may depend on different factors. For example, it may be that recognition of the happy expression, but not other expressions, is adaptive early in life. In this case, there may be a special system designed for detecting happy expressions whereas a more general-purpose visual recognition system is used for learning to recognise other expressions. Another possibility is that a special system designed for detecting expressions may become more "fine-tuned" to happy than other expressions if happy is a more common expression than others early in life. One way to test this hypothesis would be to examine recognition of expressions by infants raised in environments where happy may not be the most salient or frequent expression (e.g. infants being raised by a depressed caretaker).

The emotional nature of expressions in and of itself may contribute to how infants encode and recognise expressions. For example, if expressions are more often seen in a context where the infant is also experiencing an emotion, then this may affect how this information is learned compared to stimuli that typically are seen in a more emotionally neutral context.

Overall, the evidence available to date is consistent with the view that infants are sensitive to subtle differences in the features of the face that denote expression; that within the first half-year of life they are able to discriminate a wide range of expressions; and that by the end of the first year of life they are also able to categorise a number of different expressions. However, there is currently insufficient evidence to confirm or disconfirm the hypothesis that facial expressions are somehow "special" relative to other visual stimuli, or that there are special-purpose neural processors designed for recognising facial expressions. However, with further advances in the domains of both perceptual development and cognitive neuroscience definitive answers to these puzzles may be forth-coming.

REFERENCES

Barrera, M.E., & Maurer, D. (1981). The perception of facial expressions by the three-month-old. *Child Development, 52,* 203–206.

Bomba, P.C., & Siqueland, E.R. (1983). The nature and structure of infant form categories. *Journal of Experimental Psychology, 35,* 294–328.

Bornstein, M H. (1985). Habituation as a measure of visual information processing in human infants: Summary, systematisation, and synthesis. In G. Gottlieb & N.A. Krasnegor (Eds.), *The measurement of audition and vision in the first year of postnatal life: A methodological overview* (pp. 253–300). Norwood, NJ: Ablex.

Boucher, J.D., & Ekman, P. (1975). Facial areas and emotional information. *Journal of Communication*, **25**, 21–29.

Bowlby, J. (1969). *Attachment and loss Vol. 1: Attachment*. New York: Basic Books.

Bushnell, I.W.R., Sai, F., & Mullin, J.T. (1989). Neonatal recognition of the mother's face. *British Journal of Developmental Psychology*, **7**, 3–15.

Caron, R.F., Caron, A.J., & Myers, R.S. (1982). Abstraction of invariant face expressions in infancy. *Child Development*, **53**, 1008–1015.

Caron, R.F., Caron, A.J., & Myers, R.S. (1985). Do infants see emotional expressions in static faces? *Child Development*, **56**, 1552–1560.

Darwin, C. (1896). *The expressions of the emotions in man and animals*. New York: Appleton.

de Haan, M., & Nelson, C.A. (1996). *Inversion affects infants' event-related potential and looking time responses to facial expressions of emotion*. Poster presented at the meeting of the International Conference on Infant Studies, Providence, RI.

Deruelle, C., & de Schonen, S. (1991). Hemispheric asymmetries in visual pattern processing in infancy. *Brain and Cognition*, **16**, 151–179.

Deruelle, C., & de Schonen, S. (1995). Pattern processing in infancy: Hemispheric differences in the processing of shape and location of visual components. *Infant Behavior and Development*, **18**, 123–132.

Eimas, P.D., & Quinn, P.C. (1994). Studies on the formation of perceptually based basic-level categories in young infants. *Child Development*, **65**, 903–917.

Ekman, P. (1976). *Pictures of facial affect*. Palo Alto, CA: Consulting Psychologists Press.

Fagan, J.F. (1972). Infants' recognition memory for faces. *Journal of Experimental Child Psychology*, **14**, 453–476.

Fagan, J.F. (1976). Infants' recognition of invariant features of faces. *Child Development*, **47**, 627–638.

Field, T.M., Cohen, D., Garcia, R., & Collins, R. (1983). Discrimination and imitation of facial expressions by term and preterm neonates. *Infant Behavior and Development*, **6**, 485–489.

Field, T.M., Cohen, D., Garcia, R., & Greenberg, R. (1984). Mother-stranger discrimination by the newborn. *Infant Behavior and Development*, **7**, 19–25.

Field, T.M., Woodson, R.W., Greenberg, R., & Cohen, C. (1982). Discrimination and imitation of facial expressions by neonates. *Science*, **218**, 179–181.

Izard, C.E. (1991). *The psychology of emotions*. London: Plenum.

Kestenbaum, R., & Nelson, C.A. (1990). The recognition and categorisation of upright and inverted emotional expressions by 7-month-old infants. *Infant Behavior and Development*, **13**, 497–511.

Kuchuk, A., Vibbert, M., & Bornstein, M.H. (1986). The perception of smiling and its experiential correlates in 3-month-olds. *Child Development*, **57**, 1054–1061.

LaBarbera, J.D., Izard, C.E., Vietze, P., & Parisi, S.A. (1976). Four- and six-month-old infants' visual response to joy, anger and neutral expressions. *Child Development*, **47**, 535–538.

Ley, R.G., & Strauss, E. (1986). Hemispheric asymmetries in the perception of facial expressions by normals. In R. Bruyer (Ed.), *The neuropsychology of face perception and facial expression* (pp. 269–281). Hillsdale, NJ: Erlbaum.

Ludemann, P.M. (1991). Generalised discrimination of positive facial expressions by seven- and ten-month-old infants. *Child Development*, **62**, 55–67.

Ludemann, P.M., & Nelson, C.A. (1987, April). *Categorisation and discrimination of positive and negative facial expressions*. Paper presented at the biennial meeting of the Society for Research in Child Development, Baltimore, MD.

Ludemann, P., & Nelson, C.A. (1988a). The categorical representation of facial expressions by 7-month-old infants. *Developmental Psychology*, **24**, 492–501.

Ludemann, P.M., & Nelson, C.A. (1988b, April). *Generalised discrimination of positive and negative facial expressions*. Paper presented at the International Conference on Infant Studies, Washington, DC.

McGrath, S.K. (1983, April). *Infants' recognition of facial expressions*. Paper presented at the meeting to the Society for Research in Child Development, Detroit, MI.

Morison, V., & Slater, A.M. (1985). Contrast and spatial frequency components in new-born visual preferences. *Perception, 14*, 345–348.

Nelson, C.A. (1987). The recognition of facial expressions in the first two years of life: Mechanisms of development. *Child Development, 58*, 889–909.

Nelson, C.A. (1994). Neural correlates of recognition memory in the first postnatal year of life. In G. Dawson & K. Fischer (Eds.), *Human behavior and the developing brain* (pp. 269–313). New York: Guilford Press.

Nelson, C.A., & de Haan, M. (1996). Neural correlates of infants' visual responsiveness to facial expressions of emotion. *Developmental Psychobiology, 29*, 577–595.

Nelson, C.A., & de Haan, M. (1997). A neurobehavioral approach to the recognition of facial expressions in infancy. In J.A. Russell (Ed.), *The psychology of facial expression*. Cambridge, MA: Cambridge University Press.

Nelson, C.A., & Dolgin, K. (1985). The generalised discrimination of facial expressions by 7-month-old infants. *Child Development, 56*, 58–61.

Nelson, C.A., & Horowitz, F.D. (1980). *A note on infants' perception of facial expressions from partial features of the face*. Unpublished manuscript.

Nelson, C.A., & Ludemann, P.M. (1986, May). *The discrimination of intensity changes of emotion by 4- and 7-month-old infants*. Paper presented at the Midwest Psychological Association, Chicago, IL.

Nelson, C.A., Morse, P.A., & Leavitt, L.A. (1979). Recognition of facial expressions by seven-month-old infants. *Child Development, 50*, 1239–1242.

Olson, G.M., & Sherman, T. (1983). Attention, learning and memory in infants. In M.M. Haith & J.J. Campos (Eds.), P.H. Mussen, Series Editor, *Handbook of Child Psychology*, (Vol. 2, pp. 1001–1080). New York: Wiley

Oster, H., & Ewy, R. (1980). *Discrimination of sad vs. happy faces by 4-month-olds: When is a smile seen as a smile?* Unpublished manuscript, University of Pennsylvania.

Pascalis, O., de Schonen, S., Morton, J., Deruelle, C., & Fabre-Grenet, M. (1995). Mother's face recognition in neonates: A replication and an extension. *Infant Behavior and Development, 18*, 79–86.

Phillips, R.D., Wagner, S.H., Fells, C.A., & Lynch, M. (1990). Do infants recognise emotion in facial expressions? Categorical and "metaphorical" evidence. *Infant Behavior and Development, 13*, 71–81.

Plutchik, R. (1962). *The emotions: Facts, theories, and a new model*. New York: Random House.

Quinn, P.C. (1987). The categorical representation of visual pattern information in young infants. *Cognition, 27*, 145–179.

Quinn, P.C., Eimas, P.D., & Rosencrantz, S.L. (1993). Evidence for representations of perceptually similar natural categories by 3-month-old and 4-month-old infants. *Perception, 22*, 463–475.

Roberts, K. (1988). Retrieval of basic-level category in prelinguistic infants. *Developmental Psychology, 24*, 21–27.

Roberts, K., & Horowitz, F.D. (1986). Basic level categorisation in seven- and nine-month-old infants. *Journal of Child Language, 13*, 191–208.

Schwartz, G., Izard, C., & Ansul, S. (1985). The 5-month-olds' ability to discriminate facial expressions of emotions. *Infant Behavior and Development, 8*, 65–77.

Serrano, J.M., Iglesias, J., & Leoches, A. (1992). Visual discrimination and recognition of facial expressions of anger, fear and surprise in four- to six-month-olds infants. *Developmental Psychobiology*, **25**, 411–425.

Serrano, J.M., Iglesias, J., & Leoches, A. (1995). Infants' responses to adult static facial expressions. *Infant Behavior and Development*, **18**, 477–482.

Sherman, T. (1985). Categorisation skills in infants. *Child Development*, **56**, 1561–1573.

Slater, A.M. (1989). Visual memory and perception in early infancy. In A. Slater & G. Bremner (Eds.), *Infant development* (pp. 43–71). Hove, UK: Lawrence Erlbaum Associates Ltd.

Slater, A.M., Morison, V., & Rose, D. (1983). Perception of shape by the new-born baby. *British Journal of Developmental Psychology*, **1**, 135–142.

Slater, A.M., Rose, D., & Morison, V. (1983). New-born infants' perception of similarities and differences between two- and three-dimensional stimuli. *British Journal of Developmental Psychology*, **2**, 287–294.

Stoddart, R.M. (1987). *Do the eyes have it: preschoolers' skills in decoding the distinctive feature of emotions*. Paper presented at the biennial meeting of the Society for Research in Child Development, Baltimore, MD.

Strauss, M.S. (1979). Abstraction of prototypical information by adults and 10-month-old infants. *Journal of Experimental Psychology: Human Learning and Memory*, **5**, 618–632.

Young-Browne, G., Rosenfeld, H.M., & Horowitz, F.D. (1977). Infant discrimination of facial expressions. *Child Development*, **48**, 555–562.

Younger, B.A. (1985). The segregation of items into categories by ten-month-old infants. *Child Development*, **56**, 1574–1583.

PART IV

Perception of speech

Introduction

The development of infants' understanding of speech is one of the most intriguing and compelling stories in contemporary psychology. It has a shorter history than the development of visual perception, almost certainly because it was more difficult to find procedures that would access infants' abilities. Lecanuet, in Chapter 10, reviews the body of evidence concerning foetal responsiveness to auditory stimulation, and especially speech sounds. Acoustical analyses of the foetal environment have shown that the womb is a relatively quiet place, and that various maternal noises, especially the heart beat, can be heard, and also external sounds such as the mother's voice: the mother's voice is normally transmitted more clearly than other external voices. A variety of evidence – electrical, neurochemical, and behavioural – demonstrates that the foetal auditory system is functional from about 22–24 weeks gestational age, and its abilities improve during the last trimester of pregnancy.

Lecanuet describes his own and others' research, which has shown that the foetus responds to many sounds, such as music, and also to speech. The foetus is also actively learning about auditory stimuli, as shown by habituation studies. Measures of foetal habituation to sounds are relevant to the diagnosis of potential neural effects, and a number of risk factors significantly affect habituation patterns. For example, foetuses whose mothers have recently smoked are likely to have abnormal habituation rates (they usually take longer) compared to times when their mothers have not smoked; the foetuses of mothers who smoke require a greater intensity of stimulation to evoke a response to auditory stimulation. Generally, foetuses who are known to be at risk of developmental delay (such as Down syndrome), and the foetuses of drug-addicted mothers, habituate more slowly than control foetuses.

Lecanuet suggests that despite the peculiar condition in which audition operates, the foetus receives a great deal of information both from his/her mother and from the outer world. Indeed, there is also evidence that deprivation of sound in the foetal period actually delays the development of the auditory system: sounds reaching the foetal ear contribute to the structural and functional shaping of the auditory pathway.

Towards the end of gestation the foetus is able to make a number of important speech-relevant acoustic discriminations. The foetus discriminates between phonetic contrasts, and between male and female voices, and it is probable that foetal learning affects subsequent preferences for auditory stimuli. Thus, newborn infants have been shown to display a variety of preferences for auditory stimuli, when such preferences are measured by contingent sucking procedures. These preferences include: the mother's voice rather than a female stranger's; a story the mother had read out loud during the 6 weeks before birth; the mother singing a lullaby to which the infants had been exposed prenatally. Foetal and newborn learning about speech is even so advanced that 2-day-olds prefer their native language to an unfamiliar one!

Although newborn infants enter the world with some knowledge of speech and other sounds, clearly there is an enormous amount of development yet to take place. They have much to learn about the sound patterns of the native language they will later master, and recent studies have shown that experience in a particular language environment begins to affect speech perception capacities even in the first year of life.

In Chapter 11 Jusczyk, Houston, and Goodman summarise what is known about basic speech perception capacities of young infants. They begin with an account of early speech-perception capacities. Research into these capacities began in earnest when Peter Eimas and his colleagues demonstrated that 1- and 4-month-old infants could discriminate subtle phonetic contrasts. Their infants discriminated between the sounds /ba/ and /pa/, and they also showed categorical perception in that they treated different /ba/ sounds as the same, and different from /pa/ sounds.

Subsequently, researchers began to explore infants' capacities by investigating a variety of different phonetic contrasts, some involving consonants, others involving vowels. The picture that emerges from these investigations is that at least some speech contrasts are discriminated without any previous exposure to them: as an example, one- to four-month-old Kikuyu infants discriminate between /ba/ and /pa/, despite the fact that this distinction is not one that is made in their native language. Infants also have been found to respond categorically to speech sounds in a variety of ways. For example, infants as young as 2 months can discriminate "bug" from "dug" even when the words are spoken by different speakers of both genders.

The role of experience appears to be in fine-tuning infants' early perceptual categories to those used in the native language. Several researchers have found that young infants have the ability to discriminate phonetic contrasts that are not made in their native language, but that sensitivity to these non-native contrasts often declines in later infancy. As an example, younger Japanese infants discriminate between the English [r]–[l] contrast, but 10–12-month-olds do not – as they become older the infants become "native listeners".

Words in fluent speech are seldom, if ever, clearly demarcated from each other with pauses. A formidable task confronting the infant, therefore, is to determine what the important units are in the speech stream. In the final sections of the chapter Jusczyk et al. explore this, the most recent aspect of speech perception to be investigated with infants. The story that is told is one of infants as dynamic detectives, devising, exploring, and testing a whole range of hypotheses concerning the ways in which speech segments into words and other units such as phrases and clauses. Because the world's languages differ widely in their prosodic, allophonic, and phonotactic properties, infants devise strategies that are specific to the kinds of native language input that they are exposed to.

Breakthroughs in the methodologies used to test infants have made it possible to explore their perceptual capacities, and of course the infancy researcher is critically dependent on there being a technique, method, or procedure that can be used or modified to address particular research questions. In order to explore infants' speech perception indirect measures of auditory attention and abilities have to be used, and in Chapter 12 Werker, Shi, Desjardins, Pegg, Polka, and Patterson describe three of the methods that are used in laboratories around the world. The first method they describe is the conditioned head-turn procedure. This is an extremely versatile procedure, and with modification can be used to test all ages, from infants to adults. In the infant version of the procedure the infant learns to turn his/her head to a sound or to a change in sound. This conditioning procedure may sound simple, but in practice it is not!

The second procedure they discuss is visual habituation. This was first used in the 1970s, when researchers discovered that infants will look longer at a visual display when they are listening to an interesting auditory stimulus. As interest in the sounds decreases visual fixation also decreases, and in some variations of the procedure presentation of the sounds is made contingent on the infant's looking. Visual fixation should increase when a novel auditory stimulus is presented, and in this way speech-sound discrimination can be measured.

The third method they discuss is the high-amplitude sucking procedure (HAS). Sucking is one of the few motor activities over which the young infant has good control, and fortunately it can be conditioned easily, even from birth. Using HAS the infant sucks on a pacifier and presentation of auditory stimulation is contingently related to sucking activity: usually strong sucking (above a particular baseline) is reinforced by an auditory and/or a visual stimulus, and habituation/dishabituation of sucking intensity gives a measure of auditory discrimination.

Werker et al. discuss the strengths and limitations, and recent variations, of each procedure. However, the chapter is much more than a description of methods, as one of their primary aims is to highlight the link between the research question of interest and the selection and modification of the appropriate method to address that question. Finding a match between theory, research questions, and methodology is a major task confronting infancy researchers, and this chapter is a splendid example of how this is done.

CHAPTER TEN

Foetal responses to auditory and speech stimuli

Jean-Pierre Lecanuet
*Institut de Psychologie, Université René Descartes,
Paris, France*

INTRODUCTION

It is reported in the Indian legendary text of the Mahābhârata (Busnel 1991) that while he was in his mother's womb Abhimangu listened to a story told by his father Ananda about a long and hard fight he had won. The legend says Abhimangu's mother fell asleep during this story, thus preventing him from hearing the end. Twenty years later, Abhimangu was involved in a fight. He was on the verge of winning with the help of the memory of his father's tricks – up to a moment similar to the one where – during the telling – his mother had fallen asleep. Having missed the remainder of his father's fight, he was killed by an unexpected blow.

In this legend the foetus is not only able to hear external sounds (via the mother's ears, which is not always the case in such stories) but also to remember very precisely what he had heard a long time ago. This last characteristic of foetal memories – as well as the massive effect of foetal experience on subsequent behaviour – is more frequently mentioned in prenatal tales found in sacred texts like the New Testament or the Talmud. The approach of foetal behaviour and foetal sensory abilities through popular tales, legends, has long been the only source of information about this period of life. It was partly based on maternal experiences of foetal startles to loud sounds.

In a scientific context, Preyer (1882) first suggested that the human foetus might be exposed to sensory stimulation. Prior to that time, modern obstetricians considered the foetus to be sensorially isolated from the outer world. The isolation was thought to protect the foetus from external influences and it was assumed that this was beneficial to the foetus' development. It is only in the 1920s and 1930s that obstetricians began systematically to investigate foetal responsiveness to sounds. Since then, research on foetal audition, supported by the development of ultrasound techniques that allow the observation of the foetal behaviour, has widely developed.

This chapter aims to review the body of experimental evidence stemming from various sources on the topic of foetal response to auditory stimulation, and especially to speech sound. In the first section, the acoustical structure of the foetal environment is described, with an emphasis on the most recent acoustical analyses. It is shown that the uterus is not only a place where maternal noises, and particularly the heart beat sounds, can be heard, but that various external sounds, including speech sounds (maternal and external) can be recorded. Data obtained from animal studies, mostly performed on sheep, bring, as in other areas, data that cannot be obtained from human studies. The second section describes the peripheral maturation of the auditory system and defines the possible time of onset of its functioning. The third section presents evidence obtained at various levels of prenatal auditory functioning. Attempts at defining foetal auditory competencies such as researches from our laboratory indicating that speech-related discriminative abilities are present in the near-term foetus will be reported. The conclusion will evoke the consequences of prenatal functioning of the auditory system in the pre- and postnatal periods.

POTENTIAL SOURCES OF STIMULATION IN THE FOETAL MILIEU

The foetal sound environment

Microphones covered with rubber membranes were used to perform the first series of human intra-abdominal recordings. They were inserted in the vagina or the cervix nearest to the uterus in either pregnant (Bench, 1968; Murooka, Koie, & Suda, 1976; Walker, Grimwade, & Wood, 1971) or non-pregnant women (Busnel, 1979; Tanaka & Arayama, 1969; Walker et al., 1971). In other studies they were placed inside the amniotic cavity, after rupture of the membranes, during or after delivery (Henshall, 1972; Johansson, Wedenberg, & Westin, 1964; Murooka et al., 1976; Walker et al., 1971). Except for the acoustic band analysis of Murooka et al. (1976) and Busnel (1979), only global measures were performed in these studies. On the whole, they described a very noisy womb (72 to 96dB Sound Pressure Levels (SPL), ref.: 20µPa) with only very loud external low-frequency sounds being transmitted to the amniotic fluid. The important background noise was interpreted as originating from the maternal cardiovascular system. However, some authors recorded significantly lower sound pressure levels (SPLs between 30 and 50dB) in nonpregnant women or after delivery (Bench, 1968; Murooka et al., 1976).

MATERNAL BACKGROUND NOISE

The more recent recordings using hydrophones adapted to fluid impedance and narrow-band analysis have indicated, in contrast to the findings from the initial studies, that the womb is a relatively quiet place. When the mother is in a calm environment and when there are no abdominal gurgles that clearly emerge with high SPLs from the background noise, the mean SPLs are comparable to those usually encountered externally (Benzaquen, Gagnon, Hunse & Foreman, 1990; Gerhardt, 1989; Graham et al., 1991; Querleu, et al., 1988). The recorded intra-uterine background noise is a composite of (a) electronic noises from the hydrophone and amplifiers, (b) ambient external noises, and (c) various biological maternal and foetal noises (respiratory, movements, gastro-intestinal, cardiovascular, laryngeal); it is principally composed of low frequencies under 500–700Hz. Pressure level shows a regular and significant decrease as frequency rises. Frequency band analyses have demonstrated that the important global pressure levels previously obtained were due to infra-sounds (Benzaquen et al., 1990, and Gagnon, Benzaquen, & Hunse, 1992, measured 85–97dB at 12.5Hz) and/or very low frequencies below 50–60Hz (Benzaquen et al., 1990; Querleu et al., 1989) for which human absolute auditory thresholds are very high. Peters et al. (1991) clearly showed that this high energy peak represents very low frequency vibrations originating from the buildings in which the recordings were performed.

Low-pitched pulsations recorded at frequencies above 50–60Hz and under 500–700Hz, and interpreted as vascular sounds, were identified either as the maternal heart beat (Murooka et al., 1976; Querleu, Renard, & Versyp, 1981; Walker et al., 1971), the umbilical artery (Graham et al., 1991), the uterine artery (Bench, 1968), or utero-placental blood flow (Querleu et al., 1988, 1989; Benzaquen et al., 1990). All the recent data suggest that vascular sounds, occasionally present in the recordings, are not always present at the same sound pressure level everywhere inside the human amniotic cavity. For instance, during delivery, Benzaquen et al. (1990) were able to record maternal cardiovascular sounds at the foetal neck level in only 2 out of 10 mothers and never during uterine contractions. This was interpreted to mean that the sounds were of utero-placental not maternal origin. When these pulsating noises could be recorded, their emergence from the background noise was of only 19dB SPL at 100Hz and 2dB SPL at 650Hz.

Power spectrum analysis showed that when considering intra-uterine components at or above 100Hz, various values were found as a result of different transducers (best sensitivity in the low or in the high frequencies) and recording sites. Querleu et al. (1981, 1988), after several series of recordings with different transducers far from or close to the placenta, measured mean SPLs from 65 to 28dB SPL, the lowest value being obtained far from the placenta with only 20dB SPL at 500Hz and no more than 10dB SPL at and above 700Hz; an overall 25dB SPL emergence of the maternal heart beat was found. The authors suggested that noises from the placenta probably have a higher masking effect than cardiac noise. Gagnon et al. (1992), using another type of hydrophone located in a pocket of fluid near the foetal neck and, therefore, far from the placenta, measured 60dB SPL at 100Hz with less than 40dB above 200Hz. Thus, it now seems clear that the contribution of vascular sounds to the recorded background noise depends on the location of the transducer.

IN UTERO ATTENUATION OF AUDITORY STIMULI

The most recent band analysis on the attenuation of airborne broad- and narrow-band noises and pure tones when emitted in close vicinity (less than 2 metres from the maternal abdomen) showed that there were variations in the *in utero* SPL in both the human (Nyman et al., 1991; Richards, Abrams, Gerdhardt, & McCann, 1992) and the ewe (Vince et al. 1982, 1985; Gerhardt 1989; Lecanuet, Gautheron, Locatelli, Schaal, Jacquet, and Burnel, in press). Some appeared systematic and related to the distance between the source and the transducer when the location of the transducer was changed *in utero*. Richards et al. (1991) and Lecanuet et al. (in press) found that the intra-uterine noise level in pregnant ewes decreased as the distance from the sound source increased, although Nyman et al. (1991) were unable to confirm this relationship in human subjects; Peters et al. (1993b) recently drew iso pressure lines inside the uterus of a dead ewe filled with fluid and demonstrated that the attenuation of frequencies over 1000Hz increased from the outside to the centre of the cavity, suggesting a "wrapping around" effect. Other sources of variation are less clearly defined.

Major results, most of them obtained on sheep, can be summarised as follows:

1. The pressure levels of sounds at long wavelength low frequencies (<300Hz), were generally comparable *in* and *ex utero*: *in utero* measurements showed some variability, with several dB SPL attenuation or enhancement (at 50 and 63Hz in the sheep for Peters et al. 1993a) depending on the research teams. When the wavelength of the frequency was longer than the diameter of an object reached by this frequency the

entire volume of the object might be set in motion by this frequency without sound absorption.

2. According to Peters et al. (1993a) *in utero* pressure loss in the ewe was moderate between 400 and 1000Hz and grew by 6.5dB/octave on average between 1000 and 8000Hz, thus peaking at 20dB. Lecanuet et al. (manuscript in press) found that this pressure loss started around 300–500Hz, depending on the distance between the hydrophone and the abdominal skin of the ewe. In the human, Querleu et al. (1988) reported a similar pressure drop of 20dB developed at a rate of 6dB/octave, and Richards et al. (1992) recorded a maximum attenuation of 10dB at 4000Hz. In all recent studies and in both species, maximum attenuation never exceeded 30–35dB SPL up to 10kHz.

3. A shift tendency has been found in the ewe at higher frequencies, the *in utero* pressure increasing and becoming even higher than *ex utero* pressure, a phenomenon already seen in the measurements of Vince et al. (1982). Peters et al. (1993a) observed this reversal from 12,500Hz onwards, and because they used ⅓-octave band noise stimuli, they found it linear. Using sweeping pure tones Lecanuet et al. (in press) have found such increases as low as 4000Hz, the frequency values depending again on the depth of the hydrophone in the sheep. These increases appeared as a series of pressure peaks of resonance and anti-resonance probably due to standing waves caused by reflection of the short waves on the internal walls of the uterus.

DIFFERENTIATION OF SPEECH FROM THE BACKGROUND NOISE

Data on voice differentiation and attenuation *in utero* agree with the results presented earlier. Recent acoustical recordings revealed that the maternal voice as well as external speech located near the mother clearly emerged from the uterine background noise components over 100Hz. Recordings performed by Busnel (1979) and Querleu et al. (1988, with an SPL level of 60dB) have shown that both the mother's and others' speech: (a) was muffled and significantly attenuated in the high-frequency components, (b) had well-preserved prosodic characteristics, and (c) was somewhat intelligible, as some phonemes (up to 30% in Querleu et al., 1988), and words could be recognised by adults when the recordings were performed far from the placenta. This was also true of external voices recorded from the pregnant ewe by Vince et al. (1982, 1985) and Gerhardt (1989). In a recent work Griffiths et al. (1994) found that phonemes emitted by a male voice and recorded in a pregnant ewe had a mean intelligibility score of 55% (61% at 85dB, 47% at 75dB and 41% at 65dB) whereas they had only a 34% mean score when emitted by a female voice. Compared to external recordings the intelligibility scores were respectively reduced by 29% and 50%. Analysis of VCV (vowel-consonant-vowel) stimuli transmission showed that voicing information was better transmitted *in utero* than information related to articulatory "place" or "manner", and that it was less preserved for a female than for a male speaker. *In utero* speech, in certain recording conditions, might even be clearly intelligible in the human (Benzaquen et al., 1990; Smith, Satt, Phelan, & Paul, 1990) or the ewe (Lecanuet et al., in press, at 90dB SPL).

Human studies of *in utero* speech transmission performed with a hydrophone near the foetal head during delivery have all shown that there is a significantly better transmission of the maternal voice than of the external voice. Querleu et al. (1988) and Benzaquen et al. (1990) measured an overall 20dB SPL attenuation of external voices, with no significant difference between male and female voices. In contrast, there is only an 8dB SPL attenuation of the maternal voice. Richards et al. (1992) recorded the maternal voice, which had an external 72dB SPL level, 5dB SPL louder *in utero* than *ex utero*. External voices emitted at 90dB SPL suffered almost no attenuation at all: 2dB for male voices and 3dB for female voices; this represents a mean difference of only 8dB between the maternal voice and external ones in this experiment; comparable, therefore, to the 12dB difference reported in Querleu's study (1988). It is of interest to note that results related to *in utero* maternal bleats in the pregnant ewe are similar. Gerhardt (1989) recorded no attenuation in their components up to 300Hz, and Vince et al. (1985) noted several dB SPL enhancement of these frequencies inside the uterus compared to simultaneous *ex-utero* recordings; pressure loss started only at around 1700Hz.

The higher *in utero* sound pressure level of the maternal voice compared to the sound pressure level of externally presented voices spoken at the same level can be readily explained by the particular mode of transmission *in utero* via two different pathways. On the one hand, the maternal voice is airborne and is transmitted like any other close external sound and may thus suffer from the same acoustic modifications. On the other hand, the maternal voice is internally transmitted via body tissues and bones. Petitjean's (1989) study confirmed the excellent bone conduction of the fundamental frequency and higher harmonics through the spine and the pelvic arch.

Sound isolation of the foetus

Transmission of external pressures to the foetal ear is controlled by two factors that compose the isolation from the sound environment: (1) the attenuation due to the transmission to the amniotic cavity and (2) the transformation of the *in utero* pressures into cochlear displacements. Whereas, as demonstrated earlier, the first factor has been quite extensively described, the proportion of the *in utero* pressures that reaches the foetal internal ear remains unknown. This proportion depends on the transduction mode at foetal head level; it is either directly made through the external and middle-ear fluids or via bone conduction in the foetal head. For the moment the pathways taken by acoustic pressures have not been defined.

Gerhardt et al. (1992) attempted to define the isolation of the foetal sheep cochlea – i.e. the attenuation plus the biological transduction – by comparing the external pressure levels necessary to elicit identical cochlear potentials before and after delivery. Values of this isolation grew from 11dB at 125Hz to 45dB at 2000Hz. Abrams, Gerhardt, and Peters (1995) concluded that the foetal ear is not protected from low-frequency (<125Hz) signals, an important finding in view of the fact that low-frequency signals are coded in the foetus by cochlear cells that will later code for high frequencies, and thus need to be protected in order to prevent future auditory deficits. Rubel and Ryals (1983) showed that the cochlear tonotopy (i.e. the spatial distribution of frequency sensitivity in the cochlea) changes during maturation.

ONTOGENY OF THE AUDITORY SYSTEM

In the inner ear, the cochlea develops from the otocyst, a structure appearing around the 28th gestational day. It starts to curl by the 6th week, reaches its full morphological development – measuring 3mm and curled into $2\frac{1}{2}$ turns – by the 10th week, and its final adult size by the 20th week. The organ of Corti, which bears the auditory receptors, develops within the cochlea from the 8th week onwards. The first auditory cells (inner hair cells) and the three rows of outer hair cells can be seen as differentiated types of cells by the 11th week. None of them are functional at this age, nor by the 14th week when the cell positioning on the basilar membrane has reached its final stage (Pujol, 1993).

According to Pujol and Uziel (1986), who base their inference on the parallelism in chronology of cochlear development in humans and in every studied mammal, the human cochlea seems functional by the 18–20th week, while histological studies have shown that the auditory receptors are not completely mature at this time. The first cochlear potentials can be recorded in all animal studies at the same developmental stage. In the human foetus it is by the 20th week that the efferent innervation of the outer hair cells takes place, mature synapses being found between the 24th and 28th week (Pujol, Lavigne-Rebillard, & Uziel, 1991). Maturation of the inner ear probably ends during the 8th month with the organisation of afferent and efferent synaptic connections.

At the onset of cochlear functioning, auditory competencies, which have been characterised in animal studies, are poor. Electrophysiological responses can only be recorded for medium frequencies (1000–2000Hz, depending on the species). Auditory thresholds are high (around 100dB); there is no frequency discrimination and no temporal coding. However, these abilities improve rapidly, and by stages: auditory thresholds decrease, temporal coding begins, frequency sensitivity widens first in the low-frequency range, followed by the high ones, and finally response selectivity of auditory nerve units sharpens. The first cochlear potentials are evoked by mid-frequencies, although the base of the cochlea, which usually codes high frequencies when mature, is the first cochlear zone to develop (see Rubel & Ryals, 1983).

It has been thought that residual embryonic mesenchyma and amniotic fluid, still present in the external and middle-ear at birth, may impair *in utero* middle-ear functioning. However, the anatomical studies of McLellan et al. (1964) and the tympanometric studies of Keith (1975) showed that they do not induce ear-drum and ossicles stiffness. Nevertheless, it can be assumed that the middle-ear is not necessary for foetal audition, as it is adapted to the amplification of acoustic stimuli in aerial life. Without this amplification, clinical studies show that there is an average loss of 30dB from the aerial environment of the outer ear to the liquid environment of the cochlea. *In utero*, because the outer and middle-ear are filled with amniotic fluid, and because liquids, tissues, and bones have close conducting properties, the acoustic energy inside the uterine cavity can reach the cochlear receptors with negligible energy loss, thus suppressing the need for an amplifying system. Middle-ear transmission might still be possible; however, as pointed out by Rubel (1985), its prenatal functioning is necessarily different from its postnatal one.

EVIDENCE OF FOETAL AUDITORY FUNCTIONING

Electrophysiological and neurochemical demonstrations of prenatal auditory functioning have been obtained in several mammalian species. In the human, cardiac and motor responses to certain vibro-acoustic and acoustic stimulation have been studied, and some evoked potential measurements have been taken during labour.

Auditory evoked potentials

Foetal brainstem and cortical auditory evoked potentials have been extensively studied *in utero* in the chronically implanted guinea-pig (Scibetta & Rosen, 1969) and sheep (Woods & Plessinger, 1989). These potentials display the same characteristics and the same developmental course as those recorded *ex utero*. In the human, they have been recorded with electrodes placed on the foetus's scalp during labour (Barden, Peltzman, & Graham, 1968; Scibetta, Rosen, Hochberg, & Chick, 1971; Staley, Iragui, &

Spitz, 1990). In the premature baby, short-, middle- and late-latency evoked auditory responses have also been extensively examined. All three may be recorded, but are not consistently detectable at 24–25 weeks gestational age (GA). Detectability of major components progressively increases with age, and is stable by 30–32 weeks (Krumholz, Felix, Goldstain, & McKenzie, 1985; Pasman, Näätanen, & Alho, 1991; Starr, Amlie, Martin, & Sanders, 1977). Brainstem responses are consistent and reproducible, but, as previously inferred from animal studies, with very high thresholds (100dB SPL) at 25 weeks. Thresholds gradually decrease with development, and by 35 weeks GA are no more than 10–20dB Hearing Level different from the threshold of adults. The five principal components showing neural activation from the cochlear nerve to the inferior colliculus are then regularly obtained but are still immature with regard to peak and inter-peak latencies and amplitudes.

Neuro-chemical responses – Local cerebral (14-C) 2-deoxyglucose uptake (2-DG)

This method, which allows investigating foetal brain activity *in utero* through cerebral glucose utilisation (energy metabolism), has been used in two animal models, the foetal guinea-pig (Horner, Servières, & Granier-Deferre, 1987; Servières, Horner, & Granier-Deferre, 1986) and the foetal sheep (Abrams, Peters, Gerhardt, & Burchfield, 1993). Pure tones in guinea-pigs and vibro-acoustic stimulation in sheep induce a marked increase in 2-DG uptake in auditory structures: in the brainstem in the guinea-pig, and in all auditory structures, including the auditory cortex, in the foetal sheep. In the guinea-pig, frequency-specific auditory labelling has been obtained to loud, external free-field pure tones up to 20kHz. The location of the labelling in the cochlear nucleus and in the inferior colliculus is a function of the frequency of the tones. The tonotopic organisation of the structures has thus been evidenced *in utero*.

Behavioural studies

When obstetricians began to investigate foetal responsiveness, guided by the observations made by many pregnant women that their babies moved when a very loud noise occurred, they analysed foetal responses to "naturalistic" stimuli like warning horns (Fleischer, 1955; Peiper, 1925) and wood claps (Forbes & Forbes, 1927; Ray, 1932; Spelt, 1948).

ADMINISTRATION MODE AND STRUCTURE OF STIMULATION

In the 1950s experimenters started utilising carefully defined acoustic stimulation, like pure tones and band noises, emitted through loudspeakers located at various distances from the maternal abdomen. Later, this *air-*

borne mode of stimulation was abandoned in favour of stimulation applied directly on the mother, near the foetal head, so as to avoid or minimise sound pressure loss. Two procedures were used:

1. Stimulation was directly transmitted to the maternal abdomen by an oscillatory source (*vibro-acoustic mode*) usually a bone vibrator, a tuning fork, an electric toothbrush, or an Electro-Acoustic Larynx (EAL). The EALs, which were adopted in the 1980s, delivered broad-band noises at a fundamental frequency of 87Hz with multiple harmonics up to 20,000Hz (Gagnon et al., 1986a; Gagnon 1989). The surface of the instrument also vibrated at all frequencies between 10Hz and 15,000Hz. Intrauterine pressure estimations during EAL application have ranged from 95dB (Birnholz & Benacerraf, 1983) to 139dB (Gerhardt et al., 1988). Gagnon et al. (1992) measured an average pressure during active labour of 95dB SPL, which can be as high as 125dB.

2. Stimulation was *air-coupled*, and in most cases the loudspeaker (usually part of headphones) was isolated from the mother's abdomen with a rubber or foam ring.

Vibro-acoustic devices are designed to propagate sound pressure more efficiently through tissues and fluids than through air. Impedance mismatches are therefore avoided. However, such devices may activate nonauditory structures: foetal cutaneous receptors, which mature very early (Hooker, 1952), and also possibly the sacculus. The latter, which is part of the vestibular system, matures two weeks earlier than the auditory apparatus (Pujol & Sans, 1986) and is known to be activated by loud low-frequencies in various species including the human one (Cazals, Aran, & Erre, 1983; Ribaric, Bleeker, & Wit, 1991). The air-coupled procedure is likely to result in important alteration of stimulus if the loudspeaker is applied directly to the mother's abdomen. The partial blockade of the loudspeaker membrane causes low-frequency distortion and high-frequency amplification. In contrast, when the loudspeaker is coupled with a rubber or a foam ring, it is the low frequencies that are more likely to be amplified. Therefore, the conditions produced by these two procedures are very different from the conditions of foetal auditory activation by external everyday sounds. This is probably why, in the 1980s, investigators came back to the use of airborne stimulation by placing loudspeakers at various distances from the maternal abdomen (1m to 10cm) (Granier-Deferre et al., 1983, 1985; Kisilevsky, Muir, & Low, 1989; Kisilevsky & Muir, 1991; Lecanuet et al., 1986, 1988; Querleu et al., 1981, 1989).

Since foetal studies began, various types of stimuli have been emitted via the different administration modes – airborne, air-coupled or vibrato-acoustic: pure tones, various bandwidth frequency noises, high-pass filtered or unfiltered pink or white noises, and the EAL stimulation.

Even though the SPLs measured at different *ex* or *in utero* sites varied across a wide range (from 65 to 125dB SPL), most studies, for reasons such as the ones mentioned earlier, were performed at or above 100dB SPL.

NATURE OF FOETAL RESPONSES

It has been repeatedly mentioned before that the most obvious sign of foetal audition, perceived by any third trimester pregnant woman, was a foetal startle. Thus, the first systematic observations were concerned with the recording of *motor responses* and the concomitant *heart rate changes*.

Motor responses Since the earliest observations, motor responses were classified either as isolated, strong, and sudden – startle responses – or as a sustained increase in foetal activity. Inhibition of ongoing movements (Bouché, 1981; Fleischer, 1955; Tanaka & Arayama, 1969; Vecchietti & Bouché, 1976) and habituation to the stimulus (cessation or a decrement of responses after repetition of stimulation) were also described very early (Sontag & Wallace, 1934), and regularly observed in many subsequent studies (Bench & Mittler, 1967, Dwornicka, Jasienska, Smorlarz, & Wawryk, 1964; Johansson et al., 1964; Ogawa, 1955).

In order to detect foetal startles, Peiper and other early investigators had to rely either on visual or tactile estimation of foetal movement or on mothers' perception of movement. More recently, studies have demonstrated that mothers' perception of movement is only partially reliable (Kisilevsky, Killen, Muir, & Low, 1991). Researchers attempted objective recordings of maternal abdominal wall modifications due to foetal movement, independently of those evoked by mothers' breathing. Different systems using pressure transducers (Ray, 1932; Sontag & Wallace, 1934, 1936) or piezo-electric accelerometers (Goupil et al., 1975) were built to record the abdominal changes more precisely.

Analysis of foetal motor responses entered a golden age with the development of real-time ultrasound scanning systems in the 1970s. A great number of studies produced startle response estimations by looking at a transverse view of the foetal trunk and lower limbs. This was either (1) performed on-line by the ultrasonographist, who knew (and this might bias the observation) whether the foetus received a "true" or a sham stimulation, and/or by a second observer who looked at the ultrasound image on a video screen placed in a room adjacent to the test room, or (2) defined a posteriori by several independent observers on "blind" reading of videotaped trials.

Latency of a specific movement has not often been computed. Experimenters usually looked for the occurrence of any movement before a previously fixed delay. Of course mean or median latency depends on this delay. When this delay lasted several minutes, as in the case of the nonstress test, latencies for global movements ranging from 6 to 92sec were recorded (average latency was 64sec when foetuses were in a quiet sleep state and 24sec in an active sleep state) (Weiner, Serr, & Shalev, 1989). With a few seconds' delay, recorded latencies ranged between 1 and 2sec (Birnholz & Benacerraf, 1983; Kuhlman, Burns, Depp, & Sabbagha, 1988; Querleu et al., 1981), or were less than 5sec (Kisilevsky et al. 1989; Divon et al. 1985). Hepper and Shahidullah (1992) found an average latency of 0.34sec (evoked by a pure-tone 250Hz stimulation given between 80 and 100dB), a value close to the ones recorded in the newborn studies. Comparison between maternal perception of response movements and ultrasonographically detected response movements showed that between 23 and 29 weeks the mothers "feel" approximately 50% of these movements (the rate of ultrasonographically detected movements increases from 22% to 94% during this period) (Kisilevsky et al., 1991). Over this age, mothers detect 95% of the movements induced by over 103dB stimuli according to Yao et al. (1990). Local components of the startle response have also been ultrasonographically analysed: head rotations and/or retroflexions, extension/flexion and/or abductions of upper and lower limbs, hand or mouth opening (Bouché, 1981; Divon et al., 1985; Visser et al., 1989). Tongue protrusions, cheek movements and hand-to-face movements, the simultaneously spontaneous occurrence of which is rare, have been reported by Kuhlman et al. (1988). It should be noted that in the very first study performed using a vibro-acoustic stimulus, Birnholz and Benacerraf (1983), observed the eye-blink response, a motor activity that is less than easy to detect on the ultrasound imaging. This response, the most sensitive component of the startle response, has an average latency of 0.031sec (Yamada 1984) from 33 weeks to normal term in the premature baby. It occurs *in utero* in conjunction with cheek and forehead contraction with an average latency of 0.5sec. Using an electronic analysis procedure of ultrasonographic B and M imaging modes, Ishige, Numaka, and Muntjewerff (1990) computed eye-blink and eyeball rotations latencies. From 29 weeks on their average latency was 0.099sec.

Looking at leg movements evoked during a 5sec airborne 105–110dB broad band noise, Granier-Deferre et al. (1985) and Lecanuet et al. (1986, 1988) defined three types of fast movements: (1) a leg flexion or extension, followed or not by a return to the initial location, (2) a double flexion at hip and knee levels – (1) and (2) were usually followed by a leg or body translation and rotation – and (3) leg movements induced by a global body displacement. Median latencies ranged from 0.73 to 2sec depending on the acoustical structure of the noise. These values are far greater than the acoustic startle latencies recorded in the newborn: from 0.16 to 0.67sec (Irwin, 1932; Monod & Garma, 1971; Peiper, 1925; Steinschneider, Lipton, & Richmond, 1966; Weir, 1979). However, it is difficult to assess this parameter precisely because the leg was sometimes moving out of the frame; these leg movements lasted on average 1.25sec (range 0.34–3.1sec), whatever the foetal state.

Some very intense acoustical stimuli (>110dB) and most vibroacoustic stimuli induce a long-lasting (up to 30min according to Gelman et al., 1982) increase in the number of movements compared to the pre-stimulation period. This increase usually reflects a change in foetal state, a point that is developed later.

Heart rate changes   Mostly phasic heart rate (HR) accelerations, but also sustained HR modifications, such as tachycardia, or a change in HR variability, were described as cardiac responses. Some authors studied both motor and cardiac responses and showed that motor response rates were lower than cardiac acceleration rates (Grimwade et al., 1971; Tanaka & Arayama, 1969).

Most studies on foetal audition have used loud stimuli. Two factors influenced the design of these studies. First, due to the idea that the foetus was sensorially isolated and to observations of pregnant women that their babies moved when a very loud noise occurred, it was believed that last-trimester foetuses probably perceived only sudden, very loud sounds. Second, the major clinical concerns, which were antenatal detection of deafness and diagnosis of foetal well-being, required the use of acoustic stimuli that were easy to deliver and were known to elicit startle responses (sudden, strong motor responses), easily recognisable in daily medical practice. Thus, we will first review major results from the startling stimulation studies and then describe the promising data obtained with less intense, nonstartling stimuli.

STARTLING STIMULATION

Ontogeny of responses   Using *pure tones* stimulation, motor responses were first detected in vibro-acoustic and air-coupled studies at 27–28 weeks (Shenhar, Da Silva, & Eliachor, 1982; Vecchietti & Bouché, 1976) or at around 7 months (Gelman et al., 1982; Tanaka & Arayama 1969). Cardiac accelerative changes were described as early as 5–6 months (Ogawa, 1955), 26 weeks (Wedenberg, 1965), 27 weeks (Vecchietti & Bouché, 1976), 28 weeks (Shenhar et al., 1982), or 30 weeks (Tanaka & Arayama, 1969). Because of the important experimental design differences, no precise conclusion can be drawn concerning the ontogeny of foetal responses to pure tones. However, a gradual increase in responsiveness was observed with gestational age for both motor responses (Sontag & Wallace, 1935; Tanaka & Arayama 1969; Vechietti & Bouché, 1976), and cardiac accelerative changes (Jensen, 1984b; Tanaka & Arayama, 1969; Vecchietti & Bouché, 1976; Wedenberg, 1965). According to Sontag and Wallace (1936), cardiac accelerations display larger amplitudes as foetuses get older. By 8 months, motor response and accelerative change rates found in most studies were between 70% and 90% (Fleischer, 1955; Sontag & Wallace, 1935; Tanaka & Arayama, 1969; Vecchietti & Bouché, 1976; Wedenberg, 1965). These discrepancies may be explained by differences in response-detection procedures and also because of stimulus characteristics. However, no systematic studies have been conducted to analyse the effect of frequency, intensity or duration of stimulation on the proportion and characteristics of early foetal responses to pure tones.

Vibro-acoustic studies using *broad-band noises* and EALs have shown that motor responses, i.e. reliable stimulus-driven movements, were evoked in some foetuses as early as 24 weeks GA (Birnholz & Benacerraf, 1983; Crade & Lovett, 1988; Leader, Baillie, Martin, & Vermeulen, 1982a), and in all subjects at 26 weeks (Kisilevsky et al., 1992), 28 weeks (Birnholz & Benacerraf, 1983; Groome et al., 1991; Kuhlman et al., 1988; Querleu et al., 1981) and 30 weeks GA (Crade & Lovett, 1988; Divon et al., 1985; Druzin et al., 1989; Leader et al., 1982a). According to Leader et al. (1982a) only 7% of foetuses responded by 23–24 weeks, whereas this rose to 89% by 27–28 weeks. The onset of the response occurred earlier in females than in males: 75% of the females responded by 25–26 weeks, compared to only 33% of the males. All females responded by the 28th week, whereas only 80% of the males responded at this age. The authors relate these findings to established neurophysiological data that female infants mature earlier than males (Singer, Westphal, & Niswandu, 1968).

It should however be noted that, using a 110dB broad-band noise in an air-coupled situation, Shahidullah and Hepper (1993) recorded a slow latency diffuse motor response as early as 20 weeks GA. By 25 weeks the response was an immediate startle-type response. According to the authors, the development of outer hair cells, or some other maturational process occurring within the auditory system, may contribute to this change in responsiveness.

Two classes of HR responses   Administration of a 5sec EAL stimulation induces *first* an HR acceleration *followed* by a delayed response, which consists of an increase in the number of HR accelerations between 10 and 20min. Concerning the maturation of the first HR response, its developmental time course, compared to motor responses, was delayed by 2–3 weeks – similarly for pure tone responses (Gagnon et al., 1987c; Druzin, Edersheim, Hutson, & Bond, 1989; Kisilevsky et al., 1992). The latter study did not find reliable cardiac accelerations before 29 weeks. The pattern of this type of response was found to be discontinuous "with a rather abrupt change from no response to a relatively mature response between 29 and 31 weeks". The authors mention that at 26–28 weeks, 9/12 subjects showed an average HR deceleration of 2.6bpm instead of the expected HR acceleration. Several maturational explanations are considered and it is noted that this result suggests an independent control of HR and movement response (the somato-cardiac effect of the concomitant movement should evoke an HR acceleration). According to Gagnon et al. (1987c), the initial HR acceleration shows an increase in its amplitude between 28 and 30 weeks, as well as the appearance of an inverse relationship between the prestimulus baseline and this amplitude. The authors consider that the rapidity of this response (<10sec) indicates that it is provoked by direct stimulation of the autonomic nervous system, which is functionally mature at 30 weeks, and not a response mediated through catecholamine release by the adrenal medulla. The delayed response is present only after 33 weeks GA. It is an increase in the number and incidence of gross foetal body movements between 10 and 20min following a 5sec stimulation, and this delayed response could persist up to 1h in some foetuses. In approximately 15% of term foetuses there is a profound tachycardia lasting up to 90min (Gagnon et al., 1987a,b; Visser et al., 1989), "which does not correspond to any typical foetal heart rate (FHR) pattern observed under resting conditions". In addition, foetal movements and breathing patterns are also severely altered after 33 weeks. Term foetuses breathe less and more irregularly following stimulation. Petrikovsky, Schifrin, and Diana (1993) observed that foetal swallowing rate increased from 17% to 42% after a vibro-acoustic stimulation (VAS). The same stimulation induced sustained foetal panting (127breath/min one day, 119 the next day) in a 30 weeks at-risk foetus (Sherer et al., 1991).

As mentioned earlier, these modifications reflect a change in foetal state provoked by the stimulation. According to Visser et al. (1989) a small number of foetuses of healthy pregnant women at term showed a switch from "quiet" sleep to "active" sleep or else "active" wakefulness (respectively 1F, 2F and 4F foetal behavioural states defined according to Nijhuis, Prechti, Martin, and Bots, 1982) following stimulation with the EAL. Under normal conditions, the human foetus experiences spontaneous transitions from "quiet" sleep to "active" sleep, and then to "active" wakefulness.

Effects of stimulus characteristics, foetal behavioural state and risk status
In near-term foetuses (35–41 weeks GA), as in newborns, responses evoked with loud vibro-acoustic or airborne stimuli (over 105dB SPL) are modulated by the characteristics of both the stimulus and the foetal state.

Effects of stimulus characteristics (1) Acoustical structure: The three groups of recent airborne studies mentioned earlier demonstrated that broad-band noise given at the same SPL, 110dB, elicited much higher rates of accelerative changes and motor responses than pure tones or narrow-band noises. This is in contrast to the air-coupled and direct vibratory conditions, where high proportions of responses were obtained with pure tones. A probable explanation is that the SPLs reaching the amniotic fluid are much greater in the latter condition.

(2) Pressure level: As mentioned before, most studies were performed with loud stimuli (over 100dB SPL) that induced – more or less reliably – an HR acceleration usually accompanied by a motor response. In the airborne mode of stimulation Kisilevsky et al. (1989) found that the threshold intensity for a reliable HR acceleration is somewhere between 100dB and 105dB. Lecanuet et al. (1988) found that when controlling foetal state, relatively high percentages of HR accelerative responses were elicited with octave-band noises presented at 100dB in a high-variability HR state: 50% at 2000Hz and 55% at 5000Hz, with an average amplitude of 18bpm for the two frequencies.

Whatever the stimulation mode, when the acoustic pressure level of the stimulus was enhanced, motor and cardiac response rates increased, as did acceleration amplitudes (Jensen & Flottorp, 1982; Kisilevsky et al., 1989; Yao et al., 1990). A 5dB SPL difference was sufficient to modify foetal responsiveness (Kisilevsky et al. 1989). This general increase was observed independently of foetal behavioural state. However, both cardiac and motor responsiveness were greater in high HR variability (active sleep) than in low variability (quiet sleep) (Schmidt et al., 1985; Lecanuet et al., 1986).

(3) Frequency/pitch: Contradictory results have been obtained in studies using pure tones (in air-coupled and vibratory modes of stimulation), response rate being higher for high-frequency stimulations than for low-frequency ones or vice versa. With broad-band noises given in the airborne mode of stimulation, higher-pitched sounds induced more responses than lower ones (Lecanuet et al., 1988). Low frequencies, such as a 500Hz-centred noise, induced very few motor responses. When motor reactions were induced, mean amplitude of FHR accelerations was higher (22bpm; ranging from 6 to 48bpm) than when there were no concomitant foetal movements (12.5bpm), thus reflecting a somato-cardiac effect.

Effects of foetal behavioural state   Since the publication by Nijhuis et al. (1982), four behavioural states have been described in the near-term foetus: "active" and "quiet" sleep, and "active" and "quiet" wakefulness. In "active" sleep, both cardiac and motor responsiveness to acoustical stimulation are greater; cardiac accelerations have higher amplitudes and are more often accompanied with a motor response than during "quiet" sleep (Lecanuet et al., 1986, 1988; Schmidt et al., 1985). Schmidt et al. (1985) also found a greater reactiveness in quiet and active wakefulness compared to sleep states. We have seen that when acoustic stimuli were above 110dB SPL, or VAS were given, response ratios appeared to be no longer modulated by state; and that when administered in quiet sleep these stimulations induced an immediate change to active sleep or wakefulness with movement, thus suggesting some disturbing or even stressful effect.

Effect of risk status   Kisilevsky, Muir, and Low (1990), studying 32–34 weeks foetuses whose mothers were hospitalised threatened by preterm delivery, found that when stimulated with a moderately strong vibro-acoustic signal foetuses showed a delay in the latency of the HR acceleration response and weaker magnitude of this response (average over 1sec intervals) than nonhospitalised agemates. As the size of the hospitalised group was similar to that found in a 29–31 weeks nonhospitalised group the authors suggest that hospitalised foetuses have a less mature response than nonhospitalised ones.

After the introduction of antepartum FHR testing, several investigators using a variety of acoustic stimuli (Davey et al., 1984; Grimwade et al., 1971; Jensen, 1984a; Pereira-Luz et al., 1980; Querleu et al., 1984; Read & Miller, 1977) have suggested the use of FHR response to external acoustic stimulation as an indicator of foetal health and metabolic status. Clinical use of foetal acoustic stimulation (FAS) started with the introduction of vibroacoustic stimulation with the EAL (Smith et al., 1986). According to Gagnon (1995), the sensitivity of FAS or VAS used antenatally to predict intrapartum foetal distress or low 5min Apgar score has been less than 60% and the positive predictive value less than 20%. These observations suggested that VAS may have evoked reactivity in foetuses with early compromise, and raised concerns about using VAS to discriminate between the healthy and unhealthy foetuses. In the only randomised controlled trial of VAS for antepartum monitoring (Smith et al., 1986), no difference in outcomes was observed between the use of VAS for a high-risk group and a control group, both followed with standard antepartum FHR monitoring. Clark, Sohey, and Jolley (1989) tested 2628 women with singleton high-risk pregnancies. Currently available data obtained from these two studies suggest that the risk of intra-uterine foetal death in the presence of an FHR response to foetal vibro-acoustic stimulation is probably not higher than following a spontaneously reactive nonstress test (1.6 per 1000).

NONSTARTLING AIRBORNE STIMULATION
Sounds emitted between 85 and 100dB SPL *ex utero* do not induce startle responses or cardiac accelerations, but evoke moderate heart rate deceleration, unaccompanied by movement. For example, Lecanuet et al. (1988) found that a 500Hz octave-band noise emitted at 100dB elicited only

cardiac deceleration, and that the deceleration had the same amplitude in quiet and active sleep (–10bpm). This type of response had been anecdotally mentioned by many authors (Bernard & Sontag, 1947; Dwornicka et al., 1964; Goodlin & Schmidt, 1972; Goodlin & Lowe, 1974; Grimwade et al., 1971; Jensen, 1984a; Tanaka & Arayama, 1969; Vecchietti & Bouché, 1976). Some of the decelerative responses were described as part of biphasic cardiac responses. Pilot studies confirmed that (1) these cardiac decelerative responses could be reliably elicited in quiet sleep foetuses by various types of continuous or rhythmic airborne stimuli, emitted within this 85–100dB range *ex utero*, or to maternal speech; and that (2) these then quickly habituated to a repeated stimulus (given every 3–4sec). This made it feasible to examine the possibility of discriminative auditory capacities in the 36–40 weeks GA foetus. An habituation/dishabituation procedure derived from the study of Clarkson and Berg (1983) on speech discrimination in the awakened neonate was used.

In the first study (Lecanuet et al., 1987) foetuses that were exposed to a pair of syllables ([ba] and [bi], or [bi] and [ba]) uttered in French by a female speaker every 3.5sec, and emitted at the same pressure level (95dB), displayed a decelerative response. Reversing the order of the paired syllables after 16 presentations also reliably induced the same type of response. This response recovery suggested that the foetus discriminated between the two stimuli. However, this discrimination may have been made on the basis of an intensity difference between the [ba] and the [bi], as the equalisation of these syllables was done on the basis of the sound pressure level, not the hearing level.

In the next study (Lecanuet et al., 1992) a conservative data analysis procedure was developed that took into account each subject's pre-stimulus HR variability. This procedure defined for each subject (a) whether the stimulus presentation and the modification of its acoustic structure induced a HR change, (b) whether the direction of the HR change was accelerative or decelerative, and (c) what was the amplitude of this change. Results obtained with this procedure demonstrated (1) that near-term foetuses exposed to a short sentence "Dick a du bon thé" uttered by a male voice (minimum fundamental frequency, Fo, = 83Hz) or a female voice (minimum Fo = 165Hz) at the same hearing level (90–95dB SPL) and at 3.5sec intervals, reacted with a high proportion of decelerative responses (77% to the male voice, 66% to the female voice) within the first 10sec of stimulation, compared to a group of nonstimulated subjects. After HR returned to a stable pattern, the initial voice (male or female) was either replaced by the other voice or continued (in two control conditions). A majority (69%) of the experimental subjects displayed an HR deceleration to the change, whereas 43% of the control subjects displayed a weak amplitude acceleration (Lecanuet et al., 1993).

The presence of these significant novelty responses showed that near-term foetuses may perceive a difference between the voice characteristics of two speakers, at least when they are highly contrasted for Fo and timbre. These results, of course, cannot be generalised for all female and male voices or for all utterances. It should be emphasised that in this experiment FHR change occurred within the first seconds of exposure to the novel stimulus, thus suggesting that only a short speech sample was needed for the foetal auditory system to detect an acoustically relevant change in speaker. As the most obvious acoustic cues for the discrimination were fundamental frequency and timbre, near-term foetuses in quiet sleep may perform pitch discrimination, as was found during quiet sleep in the newborn by Alho et al. (1990) on analysis of the EEG.

Foetal responses to musical stimuli   Almost every pregnant woman has noticed that the baby she carries seems to react differentially according to the type of music emitted in the environment. Data described earlier suggest that various other factors than the type of music, i.e. its loudness, its pitch, and to a large extent, the behavioural state of the foetus, may control its reaction. Thus, the differential average increase of HR variability measured on a group of 20 subjects exposed to the air-coupled presentation of two distinct sequences of classical music by Olds (1985a) may partly be due to such effects. A global increase in the number of HR accelerations and movements can be expected in response to the presentation of any loud sequence of stimulus, a response observed by Olds to the emission of 5min of singing or piano music. An air-coupled presentation by Woodward (1992) of 15sec of a sample of a Bach organ Prelude given at 100dB induced a high percentage of HR acceleratory responses (93%) in a high variability state, much more than in a low variability state. Almost all of these responses started within 5sec of presentation of the stimulation.

Finally, the potential indirect effects of music on the foetus must be considered: those induced by the maternal response to this music. This is a very difficult task because the psychobiological impact of music on an adult depends not only on the style of the music but also on the personal history of this subject. Zimmer et al. (1982) gave a 25min sequence of music to future mothers via headphones (classical or pop music), and found that the foetuses of these mothers showed more body movements and less respiratory movements than during a silent period. This effect was more significant with the mother's favourite music. Conversely, no modification of foetal HR was found by Olds (1985b) during a presentation of music to the mother through headphones.

Foetal responses to maternal speech   It was mentioned earlier that, looking for stimuli inducing foetal HR deceleration, we noticed that maternal speech had this potentiality. Preliminary unpublished data suggested that this response was most frequently elicited in low HR variability state ("quiet" sleep), and when the mother spoke with a 70dB Leq level. Recent work by Masakovsky and Fifer (1992) demonstrated that near-term foetuses tested in "quiet" sleep state showed an HR decrease from baseline during the last 5sec of a 10sec episode of out-loud maternal speech. Silent or mother whispering episodes did not evoke a significant HR change.

RESPONSES TO PREVIOUSLY ENCOUNTERED STIMULATION: FOETAL LEARNING

Habituation

MOTOR AND CARDIAC RESPONSES IN NONPATHOLOGICAL FOETUSES
It has already been mentioned that since the pioneer studies experimenters have noticed that repetition at short intervals of a startling acoustic stimulus led to the disappearance of the startle response, thus suggesting an habituation to this stimulus. Due to their interest in foetal diagnosis of potential neural defects, a large number of studies aim to analyse foetal habituation to loud stimuli. Such studies have indicated that the number of stimulus presentations required to obtain habituation depends on (a) the type of observed response (motor or cardiac), (b) the defined habituation criteria (i.e. the number of trials inducing no response, and the use or not of a dishabituation stimulus), (c) the characteristics of the stimulus (spectral organisation and duration, inter-stimulus time interval) and (d) the foetal behavioural state.

With an *airborne auditory stimulation* given at – or lower than – 110dB SPL *ex utero*, local and/or global components of the startle response significantly decreased or disappeared after only 2–4 presentations (Fleischer, 1955; Goupil et al., 1975; Kisilevsky & Muir, 1991; Lecanuet et al., 1986; Peiper, 1925). As in the premature baby or the term newborn, the foetal cardiac response is slower to habituate than the motor response. Significant reduction or disappearance of this response is obtained after 2 to 7 presentations (Goodlin & Lowe, 1974; Kisilevsky & Muir 1991; Lecanuet et al., 1986). The amplitude of the cardiac acceleration also diminishes after a few repetitions of the stimuli (Bench et al., 1967; Bench & Mentz, 1978; Lecanuet et al., 1986). Using a classical habituation/dishabituation procedure, Kisilevsky and Muir (1991) have obtained a significant decrement of both cardiac accelerative and movement responses to a complex noise, given at 110dB SPL, followed by a recovery of these responses to a vibro-acoustic stimulus. Foetal state interferes with habituation, this process being faster during quiet sleep state than during active sleep state (Lecanuet et al., 1986). More recently, Hepper and Shahidullah (1992) found prenatal habituation of the motor response to sine wave signals with a frequency of either 250 or 500Hz and a sound pressure level individually defined for each foetus.

When applying *vibro-acoustic stimulation*, motor response rate decrement is much slower than with airborne auditory stimulation. It takes at least 6–40 presentations for the decrement to occur depending on foetal age, foetal condition, and habituation criteria (Birnholz & Benacerraf, 1983 [blink startle response]; Kuhlman et al., 1988; Leader et al., 1982a,b [10–50 trials]; Leader & Baillie, 1988; Madison et al., 1986 [16–18 trials]; Shalev et al., 1989, 1990). Among the 15 subjects tested on two successive days on their 36th week of gestation in the Leader et al. (1982a) study, 14 required fewer stimuli for habituation on day 2. Infants tested after intervals of 3–4 days showed no consistent habituation pattern. The authors concluded that this seems to indicate some evidence of foetal memory that lasts for 24h and not for 72h. They did not notice any effects of foetal state.

Motor habituation becomes easier to establish as gestational age increases: with a 12-stimulation habituation criterion 31-week-old foetuses needed on average 10.3 stimulations to habituate, and 40-week-old foetuses only 6.2 (Kuhlman et al., 1988). According to Groome et al. (1995) who replicated this study from 28 weeks onwards and coded the strength of motor responses, there was no change whatever the age of the subjects, but the decrease of the strength with stimulation was faster after 32 weeks than before this age.

Concerning HR responses Leader et al. (1984) tested habituation to three 5sec EAL stimulations. There was a significant decrease in the response, and in the mean time for the foetal heart rate to return to its baseline, between the first and second stimuli, as well as between the second and third stimuli. These results indicate that the use of VAS in this study did not induce the sustained and severe tachycardia (as well as the excessive movements) reported by Visser et al. (1989) and Gagnon et al. (1987c). Indeed, comparing the effect of the toothbrush used in their 1982 studies with the effect of a Corometrics acoustic stimulator and a sham stimulation, Leader, Fawcus, and Clark (1992) found that "although there were some changes in foetal state, these were short-lived, and foetuses who were regarded to have changed to state 4 reverted back to either state 1 or 2 before the next stimulus was due". The authors did not observe the atypical patterns nor the tachycardias described as frequent by Visser et al. (1989). The difference in findings between the studies is attributed to the intensity and frequency of the VAS. This, in our opinion, seems unlikely, as most VAS (not electric toothbrush) have similar large frequency spectrums and close mechanical devices. Although poorly plausible, the differences between results might be due the fact that (1) the VAS was not placed at the same location: both experimenters stimulate at foetal head level, but Gerhardt

(1989) found that intra-uterine pressure transmitted from a VAS falls rapidly as distance from the stimulation site increases; or (2) pressure exerted by the experimenters with the VAS was different. Leader (1995) supports his conclusion on the harmless effect of the VAS with the demonstration by Fisk et al. (1991) that this stimulation is not associated with a rise in adrenaline or noradrenaline, and the absence of postnatal effects of this stimulation on auditory functioning (Ohel et al., 1989) or on infant development (Nyman, Barr, & Westgren 1992).

Goldkrand and Litvak (1991) also demonstrated HR response habituation of 28–43 weeks GA foetuses to 20 stimulations given every minute with a VAS for 1sec each. Kisilevsky and Muir (1991) did not observe any statistically significant FHR accelerative response decline after eight VAS trials, but only a trend in that direction.

EFFECTS OF VARIOUS CONTEXTUAL EVENTS ON AUDITORY HABITUATION
Cigarette smoking and drugs Leader (1987) found that 7 out of 10 end of gestation foetuses, who were tested less than an hour and a half after their mother had a cigarette, had an abnormal habituation pattern (taking <9 or >50 stimulus presentations to habituate) compared to the one they showed 3–4 days before (habituating in the range of 10–50 stimulus presentations). Other subjects, whose mothers smoked 40 cigarettes a day, required 6 hours before foetal habituation returned to normal pattern. Hepper (1992) showed that foetuses whose mothers smoke required a greater intensity of stimulus to evoke a response compared to those whose mothers do not smoke.

In addition, Leader (1995) compared the evolution of the habituation rate of a group of more than 36 weeks GA foetuses of nonsmoking mothers tested three times (the second time 30min after the first, the third time 20min after the second), and the rate of a group of foetuses of smoking mothers who had refrained from smoking for 6h but had smoked two cigarettes at the end of the second trial. There was a progressive decrease in the number of stimuli required for habituation after the third trial in the nonsmokers group. The foetuses of smokers took significantly longer to habituate than those of the nonsmokers.

The same research group compared habituation rates on a control group (no-drug) and a group of more than 36 weeks GA foetuses whose mothers had taken 30mg of phenobarbitone every 8h for 3 days. While the two groups did not differ on an habituation test given on day 1, before the barbiturate ingestion, only 3 foetuses out of 9 in the drug group had a normal habituation pattern on a test given on days 4–5. When retested after stopping the sedatives, their habituation pattern had returned to normal. Kuhlman et al. (1988) found that drug-addicted mothers' foetuses habituate slower than those of mothers who do not take drugs.

Alteration in inspired maternal oxygen   Leader and Baillie (1988) analysed the effect on foetal habituation to their vibro-acoustic stimulus during the breathing by mother of only 12% oxygen during the test. This is equivalent to living at 13,000 feet above sea level, and reduces the maternal PAO_2 from 99mm Hg to 44mm Hg. The arterial saturation, however, only falls to 86%. Two counterbalanced experimental groups had the 12% oxygen breathing either on a first or on a second test (given the next day). In both cases only one foetus out of 8 and 10, respectively, showed a normal habituation pattern under this maternal breathing situation. However, when the foetuses were tested when their mothers did *not* have the restricted oxygen supply, 7 out of 8 showed a normal habituation pattern.

Foetal pathology   Of two cases of Down syndrome foetuses tested for habituation to pure tone stimuli by Hepper and Shahidullah (1992), one failed to habituate, and the other took longer to habituate than control subjects. The one that failed to show any change in its motor response latency died shortly after birth, although there was no detectable difference between the two antenatally.

In the VAS study by Leader et al. (1984), giving three stimulations and measuring HR change, at-risk foetuses (suspected of intra-uterine retardation or in other cases showing hypertension) not only had an initial response significantly smaller than optimal foetuses, but there was also no habituation of the response on trials two and three.

Conditioning

Two controversial attempts at establishing classic conditioning have been conducted (Ray, 1932, and Spelt, 1948). A nonstartling conditional stimulus (a low-frequency vibration) was repeatedly presented before an unconditional startling sound stimulus, until it was able to evoke this startle response. Apparently, such conditioning would have been erased and reinstated after a 3-week delay. More recently Feijoo (1981) claimed to have associated the musical theme of *Peter and the Wolf* by Prokofiev (given at 60dB SPL) with a state of deep maternal relaxation (presented as an unconditional stimulus inducing foetal movements), several times a week during the 6th, 7th and 8th pregnancy months. When tested in the 37th week, trained foetuses responded immediately with movements to the presentation of the musical theme, whereas nonexposed foetuses moved only 6–10min later. Backwards presentation of the sequence did not have any effect on trained subjects.

Effects of mere exposure

To maternal voice   Foetuses of 36 weeks GA showed no ability to discriminate between their mother's voice and a stranger's voice played to them via an air-coupled loudspeaker placed on the abdomen, but they did discriminate between their mother's voice when played to them through the loudspeaker and their mother's voice produced by her speaking, showing fewer movements in response to the direct speaking voice (Hepper, Scott, & Shahidullah, 1993). According to the authors, this latter discrimination may be due to the presence of internally transmitted components of speech that the foetus perceives when the mother is speaking, but that are not present when the tape recording of the mother's voice is played. It has also already been mentioned that, when measured at an equivalent external acoustic pressure, maternal voice was recorded with a higher *in utero* pressure than another female voice played out of a loudspeaker.

To a spoken sentence   Airborne presentation at 85dB to 37 weeks GA foetuses of a story repeatedly played twice a day during the previous month induced a transitory HR decelerative response, whereas another story spoken by the same female voice did not induce any significant change, thus suggesting a prenatal recognition of the familiar story (DeCasper, Lecanuet, Busnel, Granier-Deferre, & Maugeais, 1994). Since the two stories were spoken at the same external level, weaker than the level at which nonfamiliar sentences evoked HR decelerations in our pilot studies, we may assume that HR response threshold was lower for a familiar speech sequence than for an unfamiliar one.

CONCLUSION

The three groups of evidence reported have shown (a) in the normal environment of the human foetus, sound stimuli to which he/she may respond exist; (b) the foetal auditory system is functional after 22–24 weeks GA and can improve during the last trimester of gestation; and (c) electrical, neurochemical, and mostly behavioural responses to auditory stimuli have been described within the last 60 years. Findings indicate that, despite the peculiar condition in which foetal audition operates, the human prenate receives a great deal of information both from the mother and from the outer world. Several research hypotheses remain to be tested; but a large number of speech components – mostly, but not only, the prosodic ones – are transmitted to the amniotic milieu. Toward the end of gestation, the foetus is able to perform significant speech-relevant acoustic discriminations.

We have also seen that responsiveness of the foetus to auditory stimuli can be modified after repeated presentation (habituation), conditioning, and mere exposure to these stimuli. This leads to the question of the possible postnatal effects of prenatal sound exposure. Does prenatal learning affect postnatal behaviour? Are there other kinds of effects on the foetus, for example structural and functional effects?

Structural and functional effects

Such effects have been demonstrated on species in which the auditory function starts after birth (mouse, rat, gerbil, cat, guinea-pig); but one may legitimately infer they can be found in species in which the auditory function starts before birth. It has been shown that afferent input is necessary to establish and maintain a correct functioning of the auditory system, and partially to control sound integration in the brainstem. Bilateral auditory deprivation starting before or during the period of appearance of cochlear potentials causes the same anatomical alterations, but to a smaller extent, as a bilateral destruction of the cochlea: (1) a reduction in the number and size of the neurons in utero along the auditory relays of the brainstem acoustic pathway, (2) higher electrophysiological auditory thresholds, and (3) a reduction in the ability to discriminate complex rhythmic structures. Monaural deprivation causes neuronal and electrophysiological alterations affecting mostly ipsilateral structures dealing with binaural interactions. Several experiments have shown that sound deprivation would mainly induce a delay in the development of auditory sensitivity: impairment can be reversed if the deprivation does not extend to a critical period (review in Ruben & Rapin, 1980; Clopton, 1986; Conlee & Parks, 1981; Moore, 1985). Such deficits impair auditory spatial localisation (Clements & Kelly; 1978; Knudsen, Knudsen, & Esterly, 1982). On the other hand, prolonged exposure to selectively enriched sound environments – which do not induce any acoustic trauma – stimulates local dendritic growth (Smith, Gray, & Rubel, 1983), modifies the reactivity of central acoustic units (Clopton & Winfield, 1976; Sanes & Constantine-Paton, 1983), and seems to facilitate some discriminative auditory tasks. Thus, it can be hypothesised that sounds reaching the foetal ear might contribute to the structural and functional shaping of the auditory pathway.

Behavioural effects

Prenatal auditory experience may result in general and/or specific learning, the effects of which are evidenced in various postnatal situations. Familiar stimuli or classes of stimuli may – more or less selectively – soothe the crying newborn or elicit orienting responses during quiet states. Stimuli may lose their avoidance properties after the baby has been exposed to them during foetal life. More convincingly, familiar stimuli or classes of stimuli can be preferred to unfamiliar ones in choice test situations (e.g. nonnutritive high-amplitude sucking).

Soothing and orientation effects, long-term habituation to startling stimuli

Two classes of sound stimuli have been studied for their soothing and/or reinforcing effects:

Maternal heart beat and other endogenous sounds   Salk (1960, 1962) first found that newborn babies daily exposed to the sound of an adult heart beat emitted at 72bpm – a sound presumed to be familiar from the earliest foetal period – were soothed by this sound, slept sooner, and gained weight more rapidly than nonstimulated babies. Salk's work was followed by a series of investigations on the effects of maternal-generated internal noises. Initially, these studies were restricted to an examination of the soothing effect of maternal cardiac noises on the neonate. Results have not been conclusive, some describing a soothing effect that others did not confirm (Brackbill, 1970, 1973; Brackbill et al., 1966; Detterman, 1978; Kato et al., 1985; Murooka et al., 1976; Palmqvist, 1975; Roberts & Campbell, 1967; Smith & Steinchneider, 1975; Takemoto, 1964; Tulloch et al., 1964; Schmidt et al., 1980). This is probably due to differences in experimental design, such as the use of different types of stimuli, or different observation timings (short-term or long-term).

Murooka et al. (1976), comparing various stimuli, including recordings of the intra-uterine background noise (i.e. recorded close to the placenta and thus including loud maternal cardiovascular components), concluded that any noise having an acoustical structure close to that noise had a short-term pacifying effect. The pacifying effect of the intra-uterine noise has been confirmed by Kato et al. (1985), and by Asada et al. (1987), who recorded heart rate and respiration rate modification in crying babies. Yoshida et al. (1988) reported a similar effect on irritable babies, lasting at least for the first 7 postnatal days. Yoshida and Chiba (1989) showed that the intra-uterine noise emitted at 75dB lowered the Fo (fundamental frequency) of crying and elicited positive facial mimicry (for example motor components of smile). Using a non-nutritive sucking choice procedure, DeCasper and Sigafoos (1983) demonstrated that the heart beat sound used by Murooka had a reinforcing value for 3-day-old babies.

Speech sounds and musical episodes   It has been mentioned earlier that speech sounds, especially those emitted by the maternal voice, are not masked by the intra-uterine background noise. The prolonged exposure of the human foetus to such stimuli may thus have postnatal effects. Natural or synthetic speech sounds seem particularly attractive to the newborn, who shows transient decelerative responses to the onset of their presentation (Brazelton, Koslowski, & Main, 1974; Eisenberg, 1976), an effect that may, however, be induced by many other auditory low-pitched, moderately intense, stimuli (Hutt & Hutt, 1970; Turkewitz, Birch, & Cooper, 1972). Many studies conducted during the last 25 years have suggested that newborns process speech stimuli in a specific way different from the treatment of other auditory stimuli (see review in Aslin, Pisoni, & Jusczyk, 1983). This is usually seen as a consequence of an inherited human sensitivity to linguistic sounds (Chomsky, 1975) rather than as the effect of a prenatal exposure to speech sounds. However, these explanations are not mutually exclusive.

The particular attractiveness of *the mother's voice* for less-than-2-week-old neonates has been described by several authors (André-Thomas, 1966; Brazelton, 1978; Hammond, 1970; Wolff, 1969). The explanation accounting for this phenomenon could be postnatal association of this voice with positive reinforcers rather than prenatal learning. However, conflicting evidence will be presented. Concerning *musical sequence*, Feijoo (1981) in the delivery room, and Hepper (1988) on 4–5-day-old babies, observed that infants were significantly soothed and attentive to musical sequences that their mothers listened to daily during the last three months of pregnancy. Feijoo delivered the bassoon part of Prokofiev's *Peter and the Wolf*; in Hepper's study the target stimulation was the musical theme of the mothers' favourite British TV sitcom *Neighbours*.

One field of study concerns long-term habituation. Human and guinea-pig neonates are significantly less disturbed by a startling sound if they have been repeatedly exposed to it prenatally. As an illustration of this, the longer the prenatal exposure of human neonates – living in the Osaka airport neighbourhood – to aeroplane noises, the better they slept compared to babies whose mothers had lived in the area of the airport for shorter times during pregnancy (Ando & Hattori 1970, 1977).

Auditory preference

For the maternal voice Concerning maternal voice, studies performed with 2–4-day-old neonates, using a selective Inter Bursts (of sucks) Interval (IBI) duration reinforcement procedure of non-nutritive sucking, demonstrated that the mother's voice was not only attractive to newborns as already mentioned, but was also preferred to another female's voice (DeCasper & Fifer, 1980, and Fifer, 1981). The possibility of very fast postnatal acquisition was again argued. Spence and DeCasper (1987) then compared the sucking behaviour of experimental babies who had to choose between an airborne (nonfiltered) version and a low-pass filtered version (simulating sounds that were available before birth) of their mother's voices to the behaviour of control babies who had to choose between filtered and unfiltered versions of unfamiliar voices. Experimental babies showed no particular preference for either version of their mother's voice (the two being, maybe, equally reinforcing). But control babies preferred the unfiltered version of an unfamiliar voice. This difference in the between-group responsiveness to the low-pass voice sample was considered to be consistent with the hypothesis that prenatal experience with low-frequency characteristics of maternal voices influences early postnatal perception of maternal voices. Finally, Fifer and Moon (1989), and Moon and Fifer (1990), using a modified version of the "intra-uterine" mother's voice (either mixed or not with maternal cardiovascular sounds), found that newborns preferred an "intra-uterine" form of their mother's voice over an airborne version. In addition, DeCasper and Prescott (1984) found that 2-day-old babies did not prefer their father's voice to another male voice even after 4 to 10 hours of postnatal contact with their father; this postnatal contact was thus insufficient to induce a preference for this voice. Together, these results suggest that the absence of a preference for the father's voice is probably due to lesser prenatal experience with the father's voice than with the mother's voice.

Prenatal familiarisation with the maternal voice may explain why Hepper et al. (1993) found that newborns discriminate normally intoned speech from "motherese"-intoned speech (i.e. with exaggerated contours) only for the maternal voice. Subjects discriminated maternal voice from a strange female voice, however.

For a speech sequence   DeCasper and Spence (1986) showed (using the non-nutritive IBI contingent sucking procedure), that 2–3-day-old newborns preferred hearing a story their mother had read out loud during 6 weeks before birth to a story that they had never heard. As no difference was found during testing whether the story was read by the mother's voice or another woman's voice, prenatal learning of some acoustic features of the story, probably prosodic, is suggested.

For musical sequences   Using the non-nutritive sucking procedure, Panneton (1985) showed that newborns whose mothers had been singing a melody – using the syllable "la" instead of the words of the song – changed their pattern of sucking in order to turn on a recording of this melody more often than the recording of an unfamiliar melody; both melodies contained the same segmental information (i.e. the syllable "la") and the same individual notes, but the temporal order, duration and relative number of the notes were different in each melody. Using a different sucking procedure (i.e. prenatally presented music being contingent to a sucking pause (an IBI), and novel music being contingent to the onset of a burst of sucks in one test condition, and vice versa in another condition), Woodward (1992) tested newborns who had been exposed from 34 weeks GA onwards either to a sequence of classical music or to a sequence of jazz music (depending on the future mother's own preference). Using a conditioned sucking procedure she found a preference for the "familiar" music.

For a speech sequence sung by the mother In an experiment performed by Satt (1984) with the DeCasper's non-nutritive sucking test 3 days after birth, babies had to choose between two lullabies, both recorded by their mother. During the end of their foetal life they had been repeatedly exposed to one of the two lullabies, for which they now showed a preference.

For the maternal language In the following studies, the neonates had some postnatal experience with the maternal language before they were tested, and they were tested either for a specific preference for this language or for their capacity to discriminate between the maternal and another language. Using a non-nutritive sucking choice procedure, with both Spanish- and English-speaking women, Moon, Panneton-Cooper, and Fifer (1993) demonstrated that 2-day-old newborns preferred their mother's language to the unfamiliar language. In these studies the maternal or "native" language was not spoken by the mother, so that preference for the native language was not confounded with a preference for the mother's voice. Demonstration of a preference for the mother's language at such an early age favours an interpretation of the data of Mehler et al. (1986, 1988) in terms of prenatal familiarisation. In these last studies, 4-day-old babies discriminated between two languages (French/Russian or English/Italian), one of which was the mother's language. Moreover, babies born to French-speaking mothers showed a higher average sucking rate during the habituation phase of an experiment when the speech emitted during this period was French than when it was Russian, both languages being spoken by the same bilingual woman. Such a response persisted when babies were exposed to low-pass (<400Hz) filtered versions of the two languages, which kept only prosodic cues of the spoken sentences. In addition, babies born from mothers speaking neither French nor Russian were unable to discriminate between those two languages, as if the absence of any familiar prosodic cue rendered the perception of differences impossible. Thus, such data may reflect either prenatal familiarisation to a specific language, augmented by 3–4 days of postnatal exposure to this language, or fast learning processes occurring during this neonatal period.

REFERENCES

Abrams, R.M., Gerhardt, K.J., & Peters, A.J.M. (1995). Transmission of sound and vibration to the fetus. In J-P. Lecanuet, W.P. Fifer, N. Krasnegor, & W.P. Smotherman (Eds.), *Fetal development: a psychobiological perspective* (315–330). Hillsdale, NJ: Erlbaum.

Abrams, R.M., Peters, A.J.M., Gerhardt, K.J., & Burchfield, D.J. (1993). Vibroacoustic stimulation in fetal sheep: Effect on cerebral glucose utilization and behavioural state. *Journal of Developmental Physiology,* **19**, 171–177.

Alho, K., Sainio, K., Sajaniemi, N., Reinikainen, K., & R. Näätänen, R. (1990). Event-related brain potential of human newborns to pitch change of an acoustic stimulus. *Electroencephalography and Clinical Neurophysiology,* **77**, 151–155.

Ando, Y., & Hattori, H. (1970). Effects of intense noise during fetal life upon postnatal adaptability (Statistical study of the reactions of babies to aircraft noise). *Journal of the Acoustical Society of America,* **47**, 1128–1130.

Ando, Y., & Hattori, H. (1977). Effects of noise on sleep of babies. *Journal of the Acoustical Society of America,* **62**, 199–204.

André-Thomas, A.S. (1966). *Locomotion from prenatal life.* Spastic Society, London: Heinemann.

Asada, M., Minagawa, J., Yamada, T., Ohmichi, M., & Hasegawa, T. (1987). Neonates' response to music. *Obstetrics and Gynecology Proceedings,* **36**, 1749–1756.

Aslin, R.N., Pisoni, D.B., & Jusczyk P. (1983). Auditory development and speech perception in infancy. In M.M. Haith & J.J. Campos (Eds.), *Handbook of Child Psychology* (Vol. II, 527–687). New York: Wiley.

Barden, T.P., Peltzman, P., & Graham, J.T. (1968). Human fetal electroencephalographic response to intrauterine acoustic signals. *American Journal of Obstetrics and Gynecology,* **100**, 1128–1134.

Bench, R.J. (1968). Sound transmission to the human fetus through the maternal abdominal wall. *Journal of Genetic Psychology,* **113**, 1172–1174.

Bench, R.J., & Mentz, D.L. (1978). Neonatal auditory habituation and state change. *Quarterly Journal of Experimental Psychology,* **30**, 355–362.

Bench, R.J., & Mittler, P.J. (1967). Changes of heart rate in response to auditory stimulation in the human fetus. *Bulletin of the British Psychological Society,* **20**, 14a.

Benzaquen, S., Gagnon, R., Hunse, C., & Foreman, J. (1990). The intrauterine sound environment of the human fetus during labor. *American Journal of Obstetrics and Gynecology,* **163**, 484–490.

Bernard, J., & Sontag, L.W. (1947). Fetal reactivity to tonal stimulation, A preliminary report. *Journal of Genetic Psychology,* **70**, 205–210.

Birnholz, J.C., & Benacerraf, B.B. (1983). The development of the human fetal hearing. *Science* **222**, 516–518.

Bouché, M. (1981). Echotomographic evaluation of fetal sound stimulation. *Ultrasons,* **2**, 339–341.

Brackbill, Y. (1970). Acoustic variations and arousal level in infants. *Psychophysiology,* **6**, 517–526.

Brackbill, Y. (1973). Continuous stimulation reduces arousal level: stability of the effect over time. *Child Development,* **44**, 43–38.

Brackbill, Y., Adams, G., Crowell, D., & Gray, L. (1966). Arousal level in neonates and preschool children under continuous auditory stimulation. *Journal of Experimental Child Psychology,* **4**, 178–188.

Brazelton, T.B. (1978). The remarkable talents of the newborn. *Birth and the Family Journal,* **5**, 4–10.

Brazelton, T.B., Koslowski, B., & Main, M. (1974). The origins of reciprocity in mother-infant interaction. In M. Lewis & L.A. Rosenbloom (Eds.), *The effect of the infant on its caregiver*. New York: Wiley.

Busnel, M.-C. (1979). Mesures intravaginales du niveau et des distorsions acoustiques de bruits maternels. *Electrodiagnostic Therapy*, **16**, 142.

Busnel, M.-C. (1991). Le double combat. In M.-C. Busnel & E. Herbinet (Eds.), *L'Aube des sens*. Paris: Stock.

Cazals, Y., Aran, J.-M., & Erre, J.P. (1983). Intensity difference thresholds assessed with eighth nerve and auditory cortex potentials: compared values from cochlear and saccular responses. *Hearing Research*, **10**, 263–268.

Chomsky, N. (1975). *Reflections on language*. New York: Pantheon Books.

Clark, S.L., Sohey, P., & Jolley, K. (1989). Nonstress testing with acoustic stimulation and amniotic fluid measurement, 5973 tests without unexpected fetal death. *American Journal of Obstetrics and Gynecology*, **160**, 694–697.

Clarkson, M.G., & Berg, W.K. (1983). Cardiac orienting and vowel discrimination in newborns: Crucial stimulus parameters. *Child Development*, **54**, 162–171.

Clements, M., & Kelly, J.B. (1978). Auditory spatial responses of young guinea pigs (*Cavia porcellus*) during and after ear blocking. *Journal of Comparative and Physiological Psychology*, **92**, 34–44.

Clopton, B.M. (1986). Neural correlates of development and plasticity in the auditory, somatosensory and olfactory systems. In W.T. Greenough & J.M. Juraska (Eds.), *Developmental neuropsychobiology*. New York: Academic Press.

Clopton, B.M., & Winfield, J.A. (1976). Effect of early exposure to patterned sound on unit activity in rat inferior colliculus. *Journal of Neurophysiology*, **39**, 1081–1089.

Conlee, J.W., & Parks, T.N. (1981). Age and position dependent effects of monaural acoustic deprivation on nucleus magnocellularis of the chicken. *Journal of Comparative Neurology*, **202**, 373–374.

Crade, M., & Lovett, S. (1988). Fetal response to sound stimulation: Preliminary report exploring use of sound stimulation in routine obstetrical ultrasound examinations. *Journal of Ultrasound Medicine*, **7**, 499–503.

Davey, D.A., Dommisse, J., Macnab, M., & Dacre, D. (1984). The value of an auditory stimulation test in antenatal fetal cardiotocography. *European Journal of Obstetrics Gynecology and Reproductive Biology*, **18**, 273–277.

DeCasper, A.J., & Fifer, W.P. (1980). Of human bonding: newborns prefer their mother's voice. *Science*, **208**, 1174–1176.

DeCasper, A.J., Lecanuet, J.-P., Busnel, M.-C., Granier-Deferre, C., & Maugeais, R. (1994). Fetal reaction to recurrent maternal speech. *Infant Behavior and Development*, **17**, 159–164.

DeCasper, A.J., & Prescott, P.A. (1984). Human newborns' perception of male voices: preference, discrimination, and reinforcing value. *Developmental Psychobiology*, **17**, 481–491.

DeCasper, A.J., & Sigafoos, D. (1983). The intra-uterine heart beat: a potent reinforcer for newborns. *Infant Behavior and Development*, **6**, 19–25.

DeCasper, A.J., & Spence, M.J. (1986). Prenatal maternal speech influences newborn's perception of speech sounds. *Infant Behavior & Development*, **9**, 133–150.

Detterman, D.K. (1978). The effect of heart beat sound on neonatal crying. *Infant Behavior and Development*, **1**, 36–48.

Divon, M.Y., Platt, L.D., Cantrell, C.J., Smith, C.V., Yeh, S.Y., & Paul, R.H. (1985). Evoked fetal startle response: A possible intrauterine neurological examination. *American Journal of Obstetrics and Gynecology*, **153**, 454–456.

Druzin, M.L., Edersheim, T.G., Hutson, J.M., & Bond, A.L. (1989). The effect of vibroacoustic stimulation on the nonstress test at gestational ages of thirty-two weeks or less. *American Journal of Obstetrics and Gynecology*, **161**, 1476–1478.

Dwornicka, B., Jasienska, A., Smolarz, W., & Wawryk, R. (1964). Attempt of determining the fetal reaction to acoustic stimulation. *Acta Otolaryngolica*, **57**, 571–574.

Eisenberg, R.B. (1976). *Auditory competence in early life: The roots of communicative behavior*. Baltimore, MD: University Park Press.

Feijoo, J. (1981). Le foetus, Pierre et le Loup. In E. Herbinet, & M.-C. Busnel (Eds.), *L'Aube des Sens* (pp. 192–209). Paris: Stock.

Fifer, W.P. (1981). *Early attachment: maternal voice preference in one- and three-day-old infants*, PhD. dissertation, University of Greensboro, NC.

Fifer, W.P., Moon, C. (1989). Psychobiology of newborn auditory preferences. *Seminars in Perinatology*, **13**, 430–433.

Fisk, N.M., Nicolaidis, P.K., Arulkumaran, S., Weg, M.W., Tannirandorn, Y., Nicolini, U., Parkes, M.J., & Rodeck, C. (1991). Vibroacoustic stimulation is not associated with sudden catecholamine release. *Early Human Development*, **25**, 11–17.

Fleischer, K. (1955). Untersuchungen zur Entwicklung der Innenohrfunktion (Intra-uterine Kinderbewegungen nach Schallreizen). *Zeitschrift für Laryngologie und Rhinologie*, **3**, 733–740.

Forbes, H.S., & Forbes, H.B. (1927). Fetal sense reaction: hearing. *Journal of Comparative Physiological Psychology*, **7**, 353–355.

Gagnon, R. (1989). Stimulation of human fetuses with sound and vibration. *Seminars in Perinatology*, **13**, 393–402.

Gagnon, R. (1995). Developmental aspects of alterations in fetal behavioral states. In J.-P. Lecanuet, W.P. Fifer, N. Krasnegor, & W.P. Smotherman (Eds.), *Fetal Development: A Psychobiological Perspective* (pp. 129–148). Hillsdale, NJ: Erlbaum.

Gagnon, R., Patrick, J., Foreman, J., & West, R. (1986a). Stimulation of human fetuses with sound and vibration. *American Journal of Obstetrics and Gynecology*, **155**, 848–851.

Gagnon, R., Hunse, C., Carmichael, L., Fellows, F., & Patrick, J. (1986b). Effects of vibratory acoustic stimulation on human fetal breathing and gross fetal body movements near term. *American Journal of Obstetrics and Gynecology*, **155**, 1127–1130.

Gagnon, R., Hunse, C., Carmichael, L., Fellows, F., & Patrick, J. (1987a). External vibratory acoustic stimulation near term: fetal heart rate and heart rate variability responses. *American Journal of Obstetrics and Gynecology*, **156**, 323–327.

Gagnon, R., Hunse, C., Carmichael, L., Fellows, F., & Patrick, J. (1987b). Human fetal responses to vibratory acoustic stimulation from twenty-six weeks to term. *American Journal of Obstetrics and Gynecology*, **157**, 1375–1381.

Gagnon, R., Campbell, K., Hunse, C., & Patrick, K. (1987c). Patterns of human fetal heart rate accelerations from 26 weeks to term. *American Journal of Obstetrics and Gynecology*, **157**, 743–748.

Gagnon, R., Benzaquen, S., & Hunse, C. (1992). The fetal sound environment during vibroacoustic stimulation in labor: Effect on fetal heart rate response. *Obstetrics and Gynecology*, **79**, 950–955.

Gelman, S.R., Wood, S., Spellacy, W.N., & Abrams, R.M. (1982). Fetal movements in response to sound stimulation. *American Journal of Obstetrics and Gynecology*, **143**, 484–485.

Gerhardt, K.J. (1989). Characteristics of the fetal sheep sound environment. *Seminars in Perinatology*, **3**, 362–370.

Gerhardt, K.J., Abrams, R.M., Kovaz, B.M., Gomez, K.Z., & Conlon, M. (1988). Intrauterine noise levels in pregnant ewes produced by sound applied to the abdomen. *American Journal of Obstetrics and Gynecology*, **159**, 228–232.

Gerhardt, K.J., Otto, R., Abrams, R.M., Colle, J.J., Burchfield, D.J., & Peters, A.J.M. (1992).

Cochlear microphonics recorded from fetal and newborn sheep. *American Journal of Otolaryngology*, **13**, 226–223.

Goldkrand, J.W., & Litvack, B.L. (1991). Demonstration of fetal habituation and patterns of fetal heart rate response to vibroacoustic stimulation in normal and high-risk pregnancies. *Journal of Perinatology*, **11**, 25–29.

Goodlin, R.C., & Lowe, E.W. (1974). Multiphasic fetal monitoring: a preliminary evaluation. *American Journal of Obstetrics and Gynecology*, **119**, 341–357.

Goodlin, R.C., & Schmidt, W. (1972). Human fetal arousal levels as indicated by heart rate recordings. *American Journal of Obstetrics and Gynecology*, **114**, 613–621.

Goupil, F., Legrand, H., Breard, G., Le Houezec, R., & Sureau, C. (1975). Sismographie et réactivité foetale. *5e Journées Nationales de Médecine Périnatale* (pp. 262–266). Le Touquet.

Graham, E.M., Peters, A.J., Abrams, R.M., Gerhardt, K.J., & Burchfield, D.J. (1991). Intraabdominal sound levels during vibroacoustic stimulation. *American Journal of Obstetrics and Gynecology*, **164**, 1140–1144.

Granier-Deferre, C., Lecanuet, J.-P., Cohen, H., & Busnel, M.-C. (1983). Preliminary evidence on fetal auditory habituation. In G. Rossi (Ed.), *Noise as a public health problem* (pp. 561–572). Milan, Italy: Edizione Techniche a cura del centro Ricerche.

Granier-Deferre, C., Lecanuet, J.-P., Cohen, H., & Busnel, M.-C. (1985). Feasibility of prenatal hearing test. *Acta Otolaryngolica*, (Suppl.) **421**, 93–101.

Griffiths, S.J., Brown, W.S. Jr., Gerhardt, K.J., Abrams, R.M., & Morris, R.J. (1994). The perception of speech sounds recorded within the uterus of a pregnant sheep. *Journal of the Acoustical Society of America*, **96**, 2055–2063.

Grimwade, J.C., Walker, D.W., Bartlett, M., Gordon, S., & Wood, C. (1971). Human fetal heart rate change and movement in response to sound and vibration. *American Journal of Obstetrics and Gynecology*, **109**, 86–90.

Groome, L.J., Gotlieb, S.J., Neely, C.L., Waters, M.D., & Colwell, G.D. (1991). Development of the fetal response decrement. *American Journal of Obstetrics and Gynecology (SPO Abstracts)*, **164**, 361.

Groome, L.J., Singh, K.P., Burgard, S.L., Neely, C.L., & Deason, M.A. (1995). Motor responsivity during habituation testing of normal human fetuses. *Journal of Perinatal Medicine*, **23**, 159–166.

Hammond, J. (1970). Hearing and response in the newborn. *Developmental Medicine and Child Neurology*, **12**, 3–5.

Henshall, W.R. (1972). Intrauterine sound levels. *Journal of Obstetrics and Gynecology*, **112**, 577.

Hepper, P.G. (1988). Fetal "soap" addiction. *Lancet*, **1**, 1147–1148.

Hepper, P.G. (1992). An interface between psychology and medicine. The antenatal detection of handicap. In R. Kiimek (Ed.), *Pre- and perinatal psycho-medicine*. Cracow, Poland: DWN Dream.

Hepper, P.G., Scott, D., & Shahidullah, S. (1993). Newborn and fetal response to maternal voice. *Journal of Reproductive and Infant Psychology*, **11**, 147–153.

Hepper, P.G., & Shahidullah, S. (1992). Habituation in normal and Down's syndrome fetuses. *Quarterly Journal of Experimental Psychology*, **44B**, 305–317.

Hooker, D. (1952). *The prenatal origin of behavior*. Lawrence, KS: University of Kansas Press.

Horner, K., Servières, J., & Granier-Deferre, C. (1987). Deoxyglucose demonstration of *in utero* hearing in the guinea-pig fetus. *Hearing Research*, **26**, 327–333.

Hutt, S.J., & Hutt, C. (1970). *Direct observation and measurement of behavior*. Springfield, IL: C.C. Thomas.

Irwin, O.C. (1932). The latent time of the body startle in infants. *Child Development*, **3**, 104–107.

Ishige, T., Numata, T., & Muntjewerff, H. (1990). Human fetal response to acoustic stimulation. *Proceedings of the XIVth World Congress of Otorhinolaryngology, Head and Neck Surgery* (1059–1063), Madrid, 10–15 September. Amsterdam: Kugler & Ghedini Publications.

Jensen, O.H. (1984a). Fetal heart rate response to controlled sound stimuli during the third trimester of normal pregnancy. *Acta Obstetrica Gynecologica Scandinavica*, **63**, 193–197.

Jensen, O.H. (1984b). Accelerations of the human fetal heart rate at 38 to 40 weeks' gestational age. *American Journal of Obstetrics and Gynecology*, **149**, 918.

Jensen, O.H., & Flottorp, G. (1982). A method for controlled sound stimulation of the human fetus. *Scandinavian Audiology*, **11**, 145–150.

Johansson, B., Wedenberg, E., & Westin, B. (1964). Measurement of tone response by the human fetus. A preliminary report. *Acta Otolaryngologica*, **57**, 188–192.

Kato, Y., Tanaka, S., Tabata, T., & Takeda, S. (1985). The responses of neonates to intrauterine sound, with special reference to use for screening of hearing impairment. *Wakayama Medicine and Reproduction*, **28**, 9–14.

Keith, R.W. (1975). Middle-ear function in neonates. *Archives of Otolaryngology*, **101**, 376–379.

Kisilevsky, B.S. (1995). The influence of stimulus and subject variables on human fetal responses to sound and vibration. In J.P. Lecanuet, W.P. Fifer, N. Krasnegor, & W.P. Smotherman, (Eds.), *Fetal development: A psychobiological perspective* (pp. 263–278). Hillsdale, NJ: Erlbaum.

Kisilevsky, B.S, Killen, H., Muir, D.W., & Low, J.A. (1991). Maternal and ultrasound measurements of elicited fetal movements: A methodologic consideration. *Obstetrics and Gynecology*, **77**, 889–892.

Kisilevsky, B.S., & Muir, D.W. (1991). Human fetal and subsequent newborn responses to sound and vibration. *Infant Behavior and Development*, **14**, 1–26.

Kisilevsky, B.S., Muir, D.W., & Low, J.A. (1989). Human fetal response to sound as a function of stimulus intensity. *Obstetrics and Gynecology*, **73**, 971–976.

Kisilevsky, B.S., Muir, D.W., & Low, J.A. (1990). Maturation of responses elicited by a vibroacoustic stimulus in a group of high-risk fetuses. *Maternal–Child Nursing Journal*, **19**, 239–250.

Kisilevsky, B.S., Muir, D.W., & Low, J.A. (1992). Maturation of fetal heart rate and movement responses to vibroacoustic stimulation. *Child Development*, **63**, 1497–1508.

Knudsen, E.I., Knudsen, P.F., & Esterly, S.D. (1982). Early auditory experience modifies sound localization in barn owls. *Nature*, **295**, 238–240.

Krumholz, A., Felix, J.K., Goldstein, P.J., & McKenzie, E. (1985). Maturation of the brain-stem auditory evoked potential in premature infants. *Electroencephalography and Clinical Neurophysiology*, **62**, 124–134.

Kuhlman, K.A., Burns, K.A., Depp, R., & Sabbagha, R.E. (1988). Ultrasonic imaging of normal fetal response to external vibratory acoustic stimulation. *American Journal of Obstetrics and Gynecology*, **158**, 47–51.

Leader, L.R. (1987). The effects of cigarette smoking and maternal hypoxia on fetal habituation. In K. Maeda (Ed.), *The fetus as a patient* (pp. 83–88). Amsterdam: Elsevier.

Leader, L.R. (1995). The potential value of habituation in the prenate. In J.P. Lecanuet, W.P. Fifer, N. Krasnegor, & Smotherman W.P. (Eds.), *Fetal Development: A psychological perspective* (383–404). Hillsdale, NJ: Erlbaum.

Leader, L.R., & Baillie, P. (1988). The changes in fetal habituation patterns due to decrease in inspired maternal oxygen. *British Journal of Obstetrics and Gynaecology*, **95**, 664–668.

Leader, L.R., Baillie, P., Martin, B., & Vermeulen, E. (1982a). The assessment and significance of habituation to a repeated stimulus by the human fetus. *Early Human Development*, **7**, 211–283.

Leader, L.R., Baillie, P., Martin, B., Molteno, C., & Wynchank, S. (1984). Fetal responses to vibrotactile stimulation: A possible predictor of fetal and neonatal outcome. *Australian and New Zealand Journal of Obstetrics and Gynecology*, **24**, 251–256.

Leader, L.R., Baillie, P., Martin, B., & Vermeulen, E. (1982b). Fetal habituation in high risk pregnancies. *British Journal of Obstetrics and Gynaecology*, **89**, 441–446.

Leader, L.R., Fawcus, S., & Clark, I. (1992). *The effect of repeated vibroacoustic stimulation on fetal behavioural state.* Presented at the annual meeting of the Royal Australian College of Obstetricians and Gynaecologists, Melbourne.

Lecanuet, J.P., Granier-Deferre, C., Cohen, H., Le Houezec, R., & Busnel, M.-C. (1986). Fetal responses to acoustic stimulation depend on heart rate variability pattern, stimulus intensity and repetition. *Early Human Development*, **13**, 269–283.

Lecanuet, J.P., Granier-Deferre, C., DeCasper, A.J., Maugeais, R., Andrieu, A.J., & Busnel, M.-C. (1987). Perception et discrimination foetale de stimuli langagiers, mise en évidence à partir de la réactivité cardiaque. Résultats préliminaires. *Compte-Rendus de l'Académie des Sciences de Paris*, **305**, Série III, 161–164.

Lecanuet, J.P., Granier-Deferre, C., & Busnel, M.C. (1988). Fetal cardiac and motor responses to octave-band noises as a function of central frequency, intensity and heart rate variability. *Early Human Development*, **18**, 81–93.

Lecanuet, J.P., Granier-Deferre, C., Jacquet, A.Y., & Busnel, M.C. (1992). Decelerative cardiac responsiveness to acoustical stimulation in the near term foetus. *Quarterly Journal of Experimental Psychology*, **44b**, 279–303.

Lecanuet, J.P., Granier-Deferre, C., Jacquet, A.Y., Capponi, I., & Ledru, L. (1993). Prenatal discrimination of a male and a female voice uttering the same sentence. *Early Development and Parenting*, **2**, 217–228.

Lecanuet, J.P., Gautheron, B., Locatelli, C., Schaal, B., Jacquet, A.Y., & Busnel, M.-C. (in press). *In utero* sheep transmission of external sounds.

McLellan, M.S., Brown, R.J., Rondeau, H., Soughro, E., Johnson, R.A., & Hale, A.R. (1964). Embryonal connective tissue and exudate in ear. *American Journal of Obstetrics and Gynecology*, **108**, 164–170.

Madison, L.S., Adubato, S.A., Madison, J.K., Nelson, R.M., Anderson, J.C., Erickson, J., Kuss, L.M., & Goodlin, R.C. (1986). Fetal response decrement: True habituation? *Journal of Developmental and Behavioural Pediatry*, **7**, 14–20.

Masakovski, Y., & Fifer, W.P. (1992). The effects of maternal speech on fetal behaviour (Abstract). ICIS Meeting, Paris, 3–5 May, 810.

Mehler, J., Lamberz, G., Jusczyk, P., & Amiel-Tison, C. (1986). Discrimination de la langue maternelle par le nouveau-né. *Compte rendus de l'Académie des Sciences*, Paris, **303**, 637–640.

Mehler, J., Jusczyk, P., Lamberz, G., Halsted, N., Bertoncini, J., & Amiel-Tison, C. (1988). A precursor of language acquisition in young infants. *Cognition*, **29**, 143–178.

Monod, N., & Garma, L. (1971). Auditory responsivity in the human premature. *Biology of the Neonate*, **17**, 292–316.

Moon, C., & Fifer, W.P. (1990). Newborns prefer a prenatal version of mother's voice. *Infant Behavior and Development*, **13**, (special ICIS issue) 530.

Moon, C., Panneton-Cooper, R.P., & Fifer, W.P. (1993). Two-day-olds prefer their native language. *Infant Behavior and Development*, **16**, 495–500.

Moore, D.R. (1985). Postnatal development of the mammalian central auditory system and the neural consequences of auditory deprivation. *Acta Otolaryngolica*, **42**, (Suppl,) 9–30.

Murooka, H., Koie, Y., & Suda, D. (1976). Analyse des sons intrautérins et de leurs effets tranquillisants sur le nouveau-né. *Journal de Gynécologie Obstétrique et de Biologie de la Reproduction*, **5**, 367–376.

Nijhuis, J.G., Prechtl, H.F.R., Martin, C.B., & Bots, R.S.G.M. (1982). Are there behavioural states in the human fetus? *Early Human Development*, **6**, 177–195.

Nyman, M., Arulkumaran, S., Hsu, T.S., Ratnam, S.S., Till, O., & Westgren, M. (1991). Vibroacoustic stimulation and intrauterine sound pressure levels. *Obstetrics and Gynecology*, **78**, 803–806.

Nyman, M., Barr, M., & Westgren, M. (1992). A four-year follow-up of hearing and development in children exposed *in utero* to vibroacoustic stimulation. *British Journal of Obstetrics and Gynaecology*, **99**, 685–688.

Ogawa, G. (1955). The audiovisual sensories of fetus. *Journal of Obstetrics and Gynecology, Hokkaido*, **6**, 60–65.

Ohel, G., Horowitz, E., Linder, N., & Sohmer, H. (1989). Neonatal auditory acuity following *in utero* vibratory acoustic stimulation. *American Journal of Obstetrics and Gynecology*, **157**, 440–441.

Olds, C. (1985a). *A sound start in life*. Wickford, UK: Runwel Hospital.

Olds, C. (1985b). Fetal response to music. *Midwives Chronicle*, **98**, 202–203.

Palmqvist, H. (1975). The effect of heart beat sound stimulation on the weight development of newborn infant. *Child Development*, **46**, 292–295.

Panneton, R.K. (1985). *Prenatal auditory experience with melodies: Effects on postnatal auditory preferences in human newborns*. Unpublished doctoral dissertation, University of North Carolina at Greensboro.

Pasman, R.L., Näätanen, R., & Alho, K. (1991). Auditory evoked responses in prematures. *Infant Behavior and Development*, **14**, 129–135.

Peiper, A. (1925). Sinnesempfindungen des Kindes vor seiner Geburt. *Monatsschrift für Kinderheilkunde*, **29**, 236–241.

Pereira-Luz, N., Pereira-Lima, C., Hecker-Luz, S., & Feldens, V.L. (1980). Auditory evoked responses of the human fetus I. Behavior during progress of labor. *Acta Obstetrica Gynecologica Scandinavica*, **59**, 395–404.

Peters, A.J.M., Abrams, R.M., Gerhardt, K.J., & Burchfield, D.J. (1991). Vibration of the abdomen in non-pregnant sheep: Effect of dynamic force and surface area of vibrator. *Journal of Low Frequencey Noise and Vibration*, **10**, 92–99.

Peters, A.J.M., Abrams, R.M., Gerhardt, K.J., & Griffiths, S.K. (1993a). Transmission of airborne sounds from 50–20,000Hz into the abdomen of sheep. *Journal of Low Frequency Noise and Vibration*, **12**, 16–24.

Peters, A.J.M., Gerhardt, K.J., Abrams, R.M., & Longmate, J.A. (1993b). Three dimensional intraabdominal sound pressures in sheep produced by airborne stimuli. *American Journal of Obstetrics and Gynecology*, **169**, 1304–1315.

Petitjean, C. (1989). *Une condition de l'audition foetale: la conduction sonore osseuse. Conséquences cliniques et applications pratiques envisagées*. M.D. thesis, University of Besançon.

Petrikovsky, B.M., Schifrin, B., & Diana, L. (1993). The effect of fetal acoustic stimulation on fetal swallowing and amniotic fluid index. *Obstetrics and Gynecology*, **81**, 548–550.

Preyer, W. (1882). *Die Seele Des Kindes*. Leipzig: Fernau.

Pujol, R. (1993). Développement et plasticité du système auditif de l'enfant. *Communiquer*, **111**, 13–16.

Pujol, R., Lavigne-Rebillard, M., & Uziel, A. (1991). Development of the human cochlea. *Acta Otolaryngologica*, **482**, 7–12.

Pujol, R., & Sans, A. (1986). Synaptogenesis in the cochlear and vestibular receptors. In R.E. Aslin (Ed.), *Advances in neural and behavioral development* (Vol. 2). Norwood NJ: Ablex.

Pujol, R., & Uziel, A. (1986). Auditory development: Peripheral aspects. In P.F. Timiras & E. Meisami (Eds.), *Handbook of Human Biologic Development*. Boca Raton, C.R.C. Press.

Querleu, D., Boutteville, C., Renard, X., & Crépin, G. (1984). Evaluation diagnostigue de la soufrance foetale pendant la grossesse au moyen d'un test de stimulation sonore. *Journal of Gynecology, Obstetrics and Reproductive Biology*, 13, 789–796.

Querleu, D., Renard, X., Boutteville, C., & Crépin, G. (1989). Hearing by the human fetus? *Seminars in Perinatology*, 13, 430–433.

Querleu, D., Renard, X., & Versyp, F. (1981). Les perceptions auditives du foetus humain. *Médecine et Hygiène*, 39, 2101–2110.

Querleu, D., Renard, X., Versyp, F., Paris-Delrue, L., & Crépin, G. (1988). Fetal hearing. *European Journal of Obstetrics and Reproductive Biology*, 29, 191–212.

Ray, W.S. (1932). A preliminary study of fetal conditioning. *Child Development*, 3, 173–177.

Read, J.A., & Miller, F.C. (1977). Fetal heart rate acceleration in response to acoustic stimulation as a measure of fetal well-being. *American Journal of Obstetrics and Gynecology*, 129, 512–517.

Ribaric, K., Bleeker, J.D., & Wit, H.P. (1991). Perception of audio-frequency vibrations by profoundly deaf subjects after fenestration of the vestibular system. *Acta Otolaryngologica*, 112, 45–49.

Richards, D.S., Abrams, R.M., Gerhardt, K.J., & McCann, M.E. (1991). Effects of vibration frequency and tissue thickness on intrauterine sound levels in sheep. *American Journal of Obstetrics and Gynecology*, 165, 438–442.

Richards, D.S., Frentzen, B., Gerhardt, K.J., McCann, M.E., & Abrams, R.M. (1992). Sound levels in the human uterus. *Obstetrics and Gynecology*, 80, 86–190.

Roberts, B., & Campbell, D. (1967). Activity in newborns and the sound of a human heart. *Psychonomic Science*, 9, 339–340.

Rubel, E.W. (1985). Auditory system development. In G. Gottlieb & N. Krasnegor (Eds.), *Measurement of audition and vision in the first year of postnatal life: a methodological overview*, (53–90) Norwoord NJ: Ablex.

Rubel, E.W., & Ryals, B.M. (1983). Development of the place principle: Acoustical trauma. *Science*, 219, 512–514.

Ruben, R.J., & Rapin, I. (1980). Plasticity of the developing auditory system. *Annals of Oto-Rhino-Laryngology*, 89, 303–311.

Salk, L. (1960). The effects of the normal heart beat sound on the behavior of newborn infant: Implications for mental health. *World Mental Health*, 12, 1–8.

Salk, L. (1962). Mother's heart beat as an imprinting stimulus. *Transactions of the New York Academy of Sciences*, Ser. 2, 4, 753–763.

Satt, B.J. (1984). *An investigation into the acoustical induction of intra-uterine learning*. Ph.D. thesis. California School of Professional Psychology.

Sanes, D.H., & Constantine-Paton, M. (1983). Altered activity patterns during development reduce normal neural tuning. *Science*, 221, 1183–1185.

Schmidt, K., Rose, S.A., & Bridger, W.H. (1980). Effect of heart beat sound on the cardiac and behavioural responsiveness to tactual stimulation in sleeping preterm infants. *Developmental Psychobiology*, 3, 175–184.

Schmidt, W., Boos, R., Gniers, J., Auer, L., & Schulze, S. (1985). Fetal behavioural states and controlled sound stimulation. *Early Human Development*, 12, 145–153.

Scibetta, J.J., & Rosen, M.G. (1969). Response evoked by sound in the fetal guinea-pig. *Obstetrics and Gynecology*, 33, 830–836.

Scibetta, J.J., Rosen, M.G., Hochberg, C.J., & Chick, L. (1971). Human fetal brain response to sound during labor. *American Journal of Obstetrics and Gynecology*, 109, 82–85.

Servières, J., Horner, K., & Granier-Deferre, C. (1986). Mise en évidence de l'activité fonctionnelle du système auditif in utero du foetus de cobaye autoradiographie au (14C) 2-désoxyglucose. *Compte rendu de l'Académie des Sciences, Paris,* **302**, série III, 37–42.

Shahidullah, S., & Hepper, P.H. (1993). The developmental origins of fetal responsiveness to an acoustic stimulus. *Journal of Reproductive and Infant Psychology,* **11**, 135–142.

Shalev, E., Bennett, M.J., Megory, E., Wallace, R.M., & Zuckerman, B. (1989). Fetal habituation to repeated sound stimulation. *Israeli Journal of Medical Sciences,* **25**, 77–80.

Shalev, E., Weiner, E., & Serr, D.M. (1990). Fetal habituation to sound stimulus in various behavioural states. *Gynecological and Obstetrical Investigation,* **29**, 115–117.

Shenhar, B., Da Silva, N., & Eliachor, I. (1982). Fetal reactions to acoustic stimuli: A clinical trial. *XVIth International Congress of Audiology,* Helsinki.

Sherer, D.M., Abramowicz, J.S., D'Amico, M.L., Allen, T., & Woods, J.R. (1991). Fetal panting: Yet another response to the external vibratory acoustic stimulation test. *American Journal of Obstetrics and Gynecology,* **164**, 591–592.

Singer, J.E., Westphal, M., & Niswander, K.R. (1968). Sex differences in the incidence of neonatal abnormalities and abnormal performance in early childhood. *Child Development,* **39**, 103–112.

Smith, C.R., & Steinschneider, A. (1975). Differential effects of prenatal rhythmic stimulation on arousal states. *Child Development,* **46**, 574–578.

Smith, Z.D.J., Gray, L., & Rubel, E.W. (1983). Afferent influences on brain stem auditory nuclei of the chicken: nucleus laminaris dendritic length following monaural acoustic deprivation. *Journal of Comparative Neurology,* **220**, 199–205.

Smith, C.V., Nguyen, H.N., Phelan, J.P., & Paul, R.H. (1986). Intrapartum assessment of fetal well-being: A comparison of fetal acoustic stimulation with acid-base determination. *American Journal of Obstetrics and Gynecology,* **155**, 726–728.

Smith, C.V., Satt, B., Phelan, J.P., & Paul, R.H. (1990). Intrauterine sound levels: intrapartum asessment with an intrauterine microphone. *American Journal of Perinatology,* **7**, 312–315.

Sontag, L.W., & Wallace, R.F. (1936). Changes in the rate of the human fetal heart in response to vibratory stimuli. *American Journal of Disabled Children,* **51**, 583–589.

Spelt, D.K. (1948). The conditioning of the human fetus in utero. *Journal of Experimental Psychology,* **38**, 338–346.

Spence, M.J., & DeCasper, A.J. (1987). Prenatal experience with low frequency maternal voice sounds influences neonatal perception of maternal voice samples. *Infant Behavior and Development,* **10**, 133–142.

Staley, K., Iragui, V., & Spitz, M. (1990). The human fetal auditory evoked brainstem. *Electroencephalography and Clinical Neurophysiology,* **77**, 1–3.

Starr, A., Amlie, R.N., Martin, W.H., & Sanders, S. (1977). Development of auditory function in newborn infants revealed by auditory brainstem potentials. *Pediatrics,* **60**, 831–839.

Steinschneider, A., Lipton, E.L., & Richmond, J.B. (1966). Auditory sensitivity in the infant: effect of intensity on cardiac and motor responsivity. *Child Development,* **37**, 233–252.

Takemoto, Y. (1964). Sleep induction by heart beat rhythm. *Folia Psychiatrica Japonica,* **7** (*Suppl.*), 347–351.

Tanaka, Y., & Arayama, T. (1969). Fetal responses to acoustic stimuli. *Practical Oto-Rhino-Laryngology,* **31**, 269–273.

Tulloch, J.P., Brown, B.S., Jacobs H.L., Prugh, D.G., & Greene, W.A. (1964). Normal heart beat sound and behavior of newborn infants, a replication study. *Psychosomatic Medicine,* **26**, 661–670.

Turkewitz, G., Birch, H.G., & Cooper, K.K. (1972). Patterns of responses to different auditory stimuli in the human newborn. *Developmental Medicine and Child Neurology,* **14**, 487–491.

Vecchietti, G., & Bouché, M. (1976). La stimulazione acustica fetale: indagini preliminari sul significato delle reazioni evocate. *Attualità Ostetrica Ginecologica*, **22**, 367–378.

Vince, M.A., Armitage, S.E., Baldwin, B.A., Toner, Y., & Moore, B.C.J. (1982). The sound environment of the fetal sheep. *Behaviour*, **81**, 296–315.

Vince, M.A., Billing, A.E., Baldwin B.A., Toner J.N., & Weller, C. (1985). Maternal vocalisations and other sounds in the fetal lamb's sound environment. *Early Human Development*, **11**, 164–170.

Visser, G.H.A., Mulder, H.H., Wit, H.P., Mulder, E.J.H., & Prechtl, H.F.R. (1989). Vibro-acoustic stimulation of the human fetus: Effect on behavioural state organization. *Early Human Development*, **286**, 296–312.

Walker, D.W., Grimwade, J.C., & Wood, C. (1971). Intrauterine noise: a component of the fetal environment. *American Journal of Obstetrics and Gynecology*, **109**, 91–95.

Wedenberg, E. (1965). Prenatal test of hearing. *Acta Otolaryngology*, **206** (*Suppl.*), 27–30.

Weiner, E., Serr, D.M., & Shalev, E. (1989). Fetal motorical and heart response to sound stimulus in different behavioural states. *Gynecological and Obstetrical Investigations*, **28**, 141–143.

Weir, C. (1979). Auditory frequency sensitivity of human newborns: Some data with improved acoustic and behavioural controls. *Perception and Psychophysics*, **26**, 282–293.

Wolff, P.H. (1969). The natural history of crying and other vocalizations in early infancy. In B.M. Foss (Ed.), *Determinants of infant behavior* (Vol.4). London: Methuen.

Woods, J.R., & Plessinger, M.A. (1989). Fetal sensory sequencing: Application of evoked potentials in perinatal physiology. *Seminars in Perinatology*, **13**, 380–392.

Woodward, S.C. (1992). *The transmission of music into the human uterus and the response to music of the human fetus and neonate*, Ph.D. thesis, University of Cape Town.

Yamada, A. (1984). Blink reflex elicited by auditory stimulation: Clinical study in newborn infants. *Brain and Development*, **1**, 45–53.

Yao, Q.W., Jakobsson, J., Nyman, M., Rabaeus, H., Till, O., & Westgren, M. (1990). Fetal responses to different intensity levels of vibroacoustic stimulations. *Obstetrics and Gynecology*, **75**, 206–209.

Yoshida, A., & Chiba, Y. (1989). Neonate's vocal and facial expression and their changes during experimental playbacks of intra-uterine sounds. *Journal of Ethology*, **7**, 153–156.

Yoshida, A., Horio, H., Makikawa, Y., Chiba, Y., Asada, M., Hasegawa, T., Minami, T., & Itoigawa, N. (1988). Developmental changes in neonates' response to intra-uterine sounds. *Abstracts of IX Biennal Meetings of International Society for the Study of Behavioural Development* (303).

Zimmer, E.Z., Divon, M.Y., Vilensky, A., Sarna, Z., Peretz, B.A., & Paldi, E. (1982). Maternal exposure to music and fetal activity. *European Journal of Obstetrics, Gynecology and Reproductive Biology*, **13**, 209–213.

ACKNOWLEDGEMENTS

Parts of the materials presented in this chapter have been adapted from previous publications written in cooperation with Dr C. Granier-Deferre and Dr M.-C. Busnel. The author wishes to express his gratitude to these persons and to Mrs A.-Y. Jacquet for her great help in the preparation of the references.

CHAPTER ELEVEN

Speech perception during the first year

Peter W. Jusczyk and Derek Houston
Johns Hopkins University, Baltimore, USA

Mara Goodman
State University of New York at Buffalo, USA

INTRODUCTION

It was not so long ago that many researchers wondered how infants ever learned to discriminate the speech sounds that they heard in their environments. In other words, infants were not envisioned to have any particular sorts of capacities, even auditory ones, that would help make sense of language input. Thus, prior to any studies of infant speech perception, the general view was that infants learned to discriminate speech sounds, at least in part, by listening to the perceptual consequences of their own speech productions in babbling, and trying to match these to speech sounds they heard produced by others around them.

When breakthroughs in the methodology used to test infants made it possible to explore their perceptual capacities, it was discovered that infants do discriminate speech sounds long before they begin to produce them. Moreover, each new investigation seemed to provide further evidence of some additional phonetic contrast that infants could discriminate. Thus, the pendulum began to swing in the opposite direction – away from the view that infants are naive listeners and toward the view that all the basic speech perception capacities are in place soon after birth. In view of the mounting evidence of infants' speech perception capacities, one might have been led to believe that learning plays little role in the development of these capacities. However, on further reflection, it is clear that the sound structures of different languages vary considerably from one another. Thus, infants have much to learn about the sound patterns of the native language that they are trying to master. Furthermore, new studies began to find evidence that experience in a particular language environment begins to affect speech perception capacities even in the first year of life. One consequence of the latter studies has been to rekindle interest in how the development of speech perception capacities is affected by linguistic input. In addition, the greater knowledge available regarding the nature of infants' speech perception capacities and their development has put investigators in a better position to understand the role of these capacities in language acquisition.

This chapter summarises what is known about the basic speech perception capacities of young infants, focusing particularly on their abilities to discriminate speech sounds and to cope with variability present in the speech signal. Information about the way linguistic experience affects these capacities is also considered. In particular, findings concerning changes in phonetic perception are examined. The final sections of the chapter explore an aspect of speech perception that has only been recently addressed in studies with infants. Namely, how and when do infants begin to segment fluent speech into linguistically relevant units, such as clauses, phrases, and words?

EARLY SPEECH PERCEPTION CAPACITIES

An essential step in acquiring a language is to be able to distinguish one word from another. This not only requires that learners be able to discriminate significant differences in the sound patterns of words, but also that they are able to ignore the acoustic variation that occurs when different talkers produce the same word. Many of the studies with infants between birth and 6 months of age have focused on the first of these issues – namely, infants' capacities to discriminate one sound pattern from another. However, there have also been a number of investigations that have examined infants' abilities to deal with the variability present in utterances of the same words or syllables. This section reviews what is known about both kinds of abilities in young infants.

Discriminative capacities of young infants

Infant speech perception studies began in earnest when Eimas and his colleagues (Eimas, Siqueland, Jusczyk & Vigorito, 1971) tested 1- and 4-month-old English-learning infants' ability to discriminate [ba] from [pa]. The phonetic contrast that Eimas and his colleagues chose was a subtle one because these two syllables differ only in a single phonetic feature – voicing. Because the vocal cords are vibrating as the lips are released when [b] is produced, it is said to be voiced. By comparison, the vocal cords do not start vibrating until some time after the lips are released when [p] is produced, so it is referred to as voiceless. In other respects, the two sounds are identical. However, the timing of vocal cord vibration with respect to the release from lip closure is not exact. Hence, the timing of these two gestures varies from one occasion to another. Yet, adult listeners tend to be oblivious to slight variations in timing among different productions of [b]s (or among different productions of [p]s). But adults are very sensitive to these sorts of timing variations at the boundary region that separates [b]s from [p]s. In this respect, their perception of the voicing contrast between [b] and [p] is said to be categorical. That is, the changes in timing do not result in a gradual diminishment of the [b]-like qualities of a syllable to more [p]-like qualities. Instead, the change from [b] to [p] is abrupt. Prior to Eimas et al.'s investigation there was some question as to whether categorical perception was a learned ability or not.

Eimas et al. tested 1- and 4-month-olds on both between-category (e.g. [ba] vs. [pa]) and within-category (e.g. [ba$_1$] vs. [ba$_2$]) contrasts. Their results indicated that infants discriminated the former, but not the latter. Thus, not only can infants as young as 1 month discriminate a voicing contrast between two syllables, but like adults their discrimination of such contrasts appears to be categorical. Given the early age at which infants demonstrated these abilities, Eimas et al. speculated that infants might be innately endowed with specialised speech perception capacities.

Eimas et al.'s findings spawned a great deal of interest about the extent of infants' speech perception capacities and the mechanisms underlying these. Subsequently, researchers began to explore the extent of infants' capacities by investigating a variety of different phonetic contrasts – some involving consonants, others involving vowels. Questions about underlying mechanisms were addressed in a variety of ways. To explore the role of experience in speech discrimination, some studies presented infants with non-native speech contrasts. To examine whether specialised processing mechanisms underlie infants' abilities, several different approaches were employed. Some investigators examined possible similarities and differences in how infants perceived speech and nonspeech contrasts, whereas other researchers contrasted how humans and non-human animals perceive the same sounds.

Discrimination of consonantal contrasts   A number of the early studies focused on how infants perceive contrasts that relate to differences in place of articulation. For sounds such as [b] and [p], the point at which the vocal tract is closed is at the lips. By comparison, for sounds such as [d] and [t], the closure occurs at the (alveolar) ridge just behind the upper teeth, whereas for [g] and [k], the point of closure is farther back, at the palate. Thus, voiced stop consonants like [b], [d], and [g] contrast only in place of articulation. Using a heart rate dishabituation measure, Moffitt (1971) found that 5-month-olds discriminated a contrast between [ba] and [ga]. Morse (1972) found similar results for 2-month-olds when he used a high-amplitude sucking procedure. Both of these investigations provided evidence that infants can at least discriminate contrasts involving place of articulation differences. Eimas (1974) went a step further by demonstrating that 2- to 3-month-olds discriminated a similar contrast, [bae] versus [dae], in a categorical manner, as do adult English speakers. Finally, Bertoncini, Bijeljac-Babic, Blumstein, and Mehler (1987) found that even French newborns are able to discriminate these kinds of place of articulation contrasts. This last finding suggests that the mechanisms required for discriminating such contrasts are in place at birth.

Young infants' sensitivity to place of articulation distinctions involving other kinds of speech sound categories has also been investigated. Holmberg, Morgan, and Kuhl (1977) reported that 6-month-olds can discriminate a contrast between [fa] and [θa]. Levitt, Jusczyk, Murray, and Carden (1988) found that 2-month-olds also discriminated this same contrast, as well as a related one between [va] and [ða]. There is also evidence that 2-month-olds can also discriminate place of articulation contrasts involving [ma] and [na] (Eimas & Miller, 1980b), and [wa] and [ja] (Jusczyk, Copan, & Thompson, 1978).

Another important feature that distinguishes different speech sound classes has to do with the manner of articulation. Sounds such as [b], [d], and [g] are articulated in such a way that the vocal tract is completely shut off at some point. Other sounds are articulated in a different manner. For fricative sounds, such as [f] and [s], the vocal tract is not completely shut, but rather there is an intermittent closure at some point of constriction. For the glides [w] and [j], the vocal tract is not closed but only narrowed. Nasal sounds such as [n] and [m] are produced by opening the velum, which allows the nasal cavity to resonate. When the liquids [r] and [l] are produced, different parts of the tongue contact the roof of the mouth, but the tongue does not completely close the vocal tract. A number of studies have examined how infants perceive differences involving manner of articulation. Eimas (1975a) studied one such contrast that often shows up late in speech production by language learners (and is often difficult for non-native speakers of English), namely, the distinction [ra] versus [la]. Nevertheless, Eimas found that 2-month-olds from American homes discriminated this contrast categorically, just as native English-speaking adults do.

An investigation by Hillenbrand, Minifie, and Edwards (1979) first showed that 6 to 8 month-olds are sensitive to the manner of articulation contrast that distinguishes [ba] from [wa]. Subsequent research by Eimas and Miller (1980a; Miller & Eimas, 1983) found that 2-month-olds demonstrably discriminate this contrast categorically. Eimas and Miller (1980b) also investigated 2- to 4-month-olds' perception of a different manner of articulation distinction, namely, the oral/nasal contrast between [ba] and [ma]. Although the infants proved able to discriminate this contrast, they also gave evidence of discriminating within-category distinctions involving stimuli from this test series. Hence, perception of the oral/nasal distinction does not appear to be categorical for young infants.

Discrimination of vowel contrasts   Although much of the research on the early speech perception capacities of infants has been on consonantal contrasts, information is also available regarding the perception of certain vowel contrasts. Trehub (1973) first demonstrated that 1- to 4-month-olds can discriminate contrasts such as [a]-[i] and [i]-[u]. Kuhl and Miller (1982) replicated and extended Trehub's findings for the [a]-[i] pair by showing that infants could still discriminate this pair even when there was irrelevant variation in the pitch contour of the vowel tokens.

Other investigations have explored the ability of infants to detect more subtle distinctions between vowels. Swoboda, Morse, and Leavitt (1976) investigated 2-month-olds' perception of the contrast [i] versus [ɪ]. Not only did the infants discriminate this contrast, but they were also able to discriminate within-category vowel contrasts from the same series. Hence, just like adults (Fry, Abramson, Eimas, & Liberman, 1962; Pisoni, 1973; Stevens, Liberman, Studdert-Kennedy, & Ohman, 1969), the infants' discrimination of different vowel tokens was continuous, rather than categorical. In a study with English-learning 6-month-olds, Kuhl (1983) found evidence for discrimination of another difficult vowel contrast, [a] versus [ɔ]. Finally, Polka and Werker (1994) tested English-learning infants on a pair of vowel contrasts that do not occur in their native language. Specifically, they found that 4- to 6-month-olds, although not older English-learning infants, discriminate two German vowel contrasts: [Y]-[U] (a lax high front-rounded vs. a lax high back-rounded vowel) and [y:]-[u:] (a tense high front-rounded vs. a tense high back-rounded vowel).

There has also been at least one report of a failure by infants to discriminate a particular vowel contrast. Lacerda (1992) found that although Swedish infants were able to discriminate a native-language contrast between [a] and [ʌ], they did not detect a similar contrast between [a] and [ɑ]. He speculates that vowel contrasts dependent on first formant differences (e.g. [a] vs. [ʌ]) may be perceptually more salient for infants than ones that depend on second formant differences (e.g. [a] vs. [ɑ]). He notes that contrasts of the first type are more commonly used than the latter ones in the world's languages. It will be interesting to see whether this pattern holds when a wider variety of vowel contrasts of both types are investigated.

Discrimination of non-native language contrasts Soon after the first reports of infants' capacities to discriminate speech contrasts, there was considerable interest in the extent to which these capacities were directly mediated by specific language experience. Consequently, several investigations were conducted to determine whether young infants could discriminate contrasts that do not occur in their language-learning environment. In one such investigation, Streeter (1976) explored the perception of the voicing contrast, [ba]-[pa], by Kikuyu infants. This voiced/voiceless distinction is not one that occurs in Kikuyu, even though the language does have a prevoiced/voiceless distinction. Despite their lack of experience with this particular voicing contrast, 1- to 4-month-old Kikuyu infants were able to discriminate [ba] from [pa]. Lasky, Syrdal-Lasky, and Klein (1975) reported a similar finding for 4½- to 6-month-old Guatemalan infants who were raised in Spanish-speaking environments. In this case, Spanish does have a voicing contrast, although it differs considerably from that of English (Lisker & Abramson, 1970; Williams, 1977). Nevertheless, the infants only gave evidence of discriminating the contrast that corresponded to the English [ba]-[pa] distinction. Thus, some realignment of infants' perceptual categories (Aslin & Pisoni, 1980) may be necessary for discriminating the Spanish voicing contrast. In addition to these studies of how infants from non-English speaking homes perceive the English voicing distinction, there have also been investigations of how English-learners perceive non-native language prevoiced/voiced distinctions. Studies by Eimas (1975b) and by Aslin, Pisoni, Hennessy, and Perey (1981) reported some evidence of discrimination of the prevoiced/voiced distinction by infants from English-speaking homes. However, sensitivity to prevoiced/voiced distinctions was considerably weaker than for voiced/voiceless distinctions. Taken together, what these findings on voicing contrasts suggest is that infants have some inherent ability to make these kinds of distinctions. However, experiential factors do appear to contribute to the establishment of the specific perceptual boundaries that are used in a particular language.

In addition to voicing contrasts, other kinds of non-native phonetic distinctions have also been explored in studies with infants. Trehub (1976) reported that 1- to 4-month-old infants from English-speaking homes were able to discriminate an oral/nasal vowel contrast, [pa] versus [pã], (found in languages such as French and Polish), and a Czech consonantal contrast, [řa] versus [za]. Werker and Tees (1984) demonstrated that 6-month-old English-learners are able to discriminate a retroflex/dental place of articulation contrast from Hindi and a glottalised velar/uvular contrast from Nthlakapmx. Best and her colleagues have also obtained evidence of English-learning infants' abilities to discriminate contrasts found in African languages, such as a lateral versus medial click contrast from Zulu

(Best, McRoberts, & Sithole, 1988) and a place of articulation distinction between ejectives from Ethiopian (Best, 1991). Finally, Tsushima and his colleagues (Tsushima et al., 1994) have shown that at 6–8 months Japanese infants are able to discriminate the English [r] versus [l] and [w] versus [y] contrasts.

The picture that emerges from these investigations of infants' perception of non-native contrasts is that at least some speech contrasts are discriminated without any previous exposure to them. The role of experience appears to be in fine-tuning infants' early perceptual categories to those used in the native language that they are acquiring.

The nature of infant speech perception capacities   In addition to mapping out the extent of infants' abilities to discriminate speech contrasts, researchers in this area have been interested in determining whether the underlying capacities are general ones or highly specialised ones dedicated to processing speech. Two different approaches have been employed to address this issue. First, a number of investigations have focused on the extent to which non-human animals display the same range of abilities for processing speech. The rationale here is that strong parallels in the way that humans and non-humans perceive speech support the view that the mechanisms are general ones, rather than speech-specific ones. The second approach to identify the nature of the underlying mechanisms has been to compare how infants process both speech and nonspeech signals. The extent to which infants exhibit the same patterns of categorisation and discrimination for nonspeech sounds as for speech sounds is taken as evidence for or against the view that the underlying mechanisms are general rather than specific to speech processing.

The first suggestion that nonhuman mammals may display similar speech processing abilities to humans came from a study with chinchillas by Kuhl and Miller (Kuhl, 1981; Kuhl & Miller, 1975; Kuhl & Miller, 1978). They found that chinchillas display categorical-like discrimination functions for several different speech contrasts, and that these functions correspond closely to ones produced by human adults. Moreover, in a study with Japanese quail, Kluender, Diehl, and Killeen (1987) trained these birds to categorise speech sounds according to the place of articulation contrasts used by English-speakers. In addition, investigations carried out with nonhuman primates have yielded findings in accordance with those obtained for human listeners. For example, Kuhl and Padden (1982, 1983) reported that macaque monkeys processed voicing and place-of-articulation contrasts in manner similar to human listeners. Other investigations with primates have also provided evidence that monkeys discriminate speech contrasts, although not always in ways that match those of human listeners. For example, Waters and Wilson (1976) noted that although rhesus monkeys perceived voicing contrasts categorically, unlike humans their boundaries were affected by the nature of the initial training stimuli. Similarly, Sinnott, Beecher, Moody, and Stebbins (1976) found that although macaques discriminated place of articulation differences, they required much larger stimulus differences to detect these than do human listeners. Finally, Kuhl (1991) has reported that although human listeners demonstrate a "perceptual magnet effect" for certain vowel contrasts, this same effect is not evident in monkeys' responses to the same stimuli.

The first attempt to compare infants' perception of speech and nonspeech signals came in an investigation by Eimas (1974, 1975a). He tested 2- to 3-month-olds on stimuli from a [bae]-[dae] continuum. Some of the infants were tested with speech contrasts from this series. These infants discriminated the stimulus pairs categorically (i.e. they detected differences between the stimuli from the different phonemic categories, but not ones from within the same phonemic category). The rest of the infants were tested on nonspeech contrasts that were produced by using the isolated second formant transitions ("chirps") from the [bae]-[dae] continuum. Hence, the critical acoustic differences among the nonspeech stimuli were similar to those in the speech series. The infants were able to discriminate these differences for the nonspeech stimuli. However, they discriminated within-category pairs as well as between-category pairs. Hence, unlike the case for the speech sounds, their discrimination of these stimuli was not categorical. Eimas interpreted these findings as support for the existence of specialised speech-processing mechanisms. However, it should be noted that the speech and nonspeech sounds in this case differed considerably in their durations and overall complexity.

Other investigations of nonspeech processing in infants have used stimulus series that were constructed as analogues of English voicing contrasts. Research by Pisoni (1977) with English-speaking adult subjects raised the possibility that general auditory mechanisms responsible for detecting temporal-order differences underlie the perception of voicing contrasts. Specifically, Pisoni found that adults listening to a series of two-component tones grouped these into three different categories corresponding to the prevoiced, voiced, and voiceless categories in speech. Jusczyk, Pisoni, Walley, and Murray (1980) tested 2-month-olds on stimuli from the same nonspeech series and found that the infants discriminated these stimuli categorically. A subsequent investigation by Jusczyk, Rosner, Reed, and Kennedy (1989) directly compared 2-month-olds' discrimination of voicing differences for speech sounds with their discrimination of temporal order differences in nonspeech sounds. The locus of category boundaries for the speech and nonspeech stimuli corresponded closely, leading Jusczyk et al. to conclude that the same general auditory processing mechanisms may underlie the perception of both types of stimuli.

Another area in which possible parallels in speech and nonspeech processing have been explored relates to the mechanisms that compensate for changes in speaking rates. Eimas and Miller (1980a; Miller & Eimas, 1983) first demonstrated that infants are sensitive to changes in syllable duration that correspond to changes in speaking rates, and that their perceptual categorisation of stimuli from a [ba]-[wa] series shifts to accommodate perceived changes in speaking rates. Eimas and Miller interpreted this as due to the existence of specialised speech-processing mechanisms. However, in a subsequent investigation, Jusczyk, Pisoni, Reed, Fernald, and Myers (1983) found that 2-month-olds exhibited similar responses to durational changes in nonspeech sinewave stimuli. Thus this finding raises the possibility that the same mechanism is operating in both the speech and nonspeech cases.

In conclusion, some interesting parallels have been observed in the way that human and nonhuman listeners perceive speech contrasts, and in the way that human infants perceive speech and nonspeech contrasts. However, the range of cases examined thus far has been relatively limited. Thus it is premature to draw any firm conclusions as to whether specialised processing mechanisms exist for speech perception.

Coping with variability in speech

Fluent speaker/hearers of a language are able to compensate for a wide range of acoustic differences in how words are produced by different talkers, or even the same talker on different occasions. This skill is often referred to as *perceptual normalisation* (Bladon, Henton, & Pickering, 1984; Rand, 1971; Verbrugge, Strange, Shankweiler, & Edman, 1976). Without this ability, listeners would have difficulty in determining when different talkers are using the same words – every acoustic difference could be interpreted as conveying a difference in meaning.

As noted earlier, Eimas and Miller (1980a; Miller & Eimas, 1983) demonstrated that 2- to 3-month-old infants are apparently able to cope with one type of variability in the speech signal, namely, changes in speaking rate. This is important because some of the cues that distinguish different speech contrasts such as [ba] versus [wa] depend on the rate of change of spectral information (in this case, the initial formant transitions). Short, rapidly changing formant transitions are associated with the production of [ba], whereas more gradually changing formant transitions occur in the production of [wa]. However, adults' judgements of whether a given change is rapid or gradual have been shown to depend on speaking rate

(Miller & Liberman, 1979) and, as Eimas and Miller showed, this holds true for infants as well.

The most widely studied source of variability in the speech signal is that owing to differences among talkers. The first investigation to explore how infants cope with this source of variability was by Kuhl (1979, 1983). In an earlier investigation with 1- to 4-month-olds (Kuhl, 1976; Kuhl & Miller, 1982), she found that infants were able to ignore irrelevant variations in pitch contours of syllables to detect a vowel change from [a] to [i]. In her subsequent study (Kuhl, 1979), she tested 6-month-olds on a much wider range of stimulus variability, involving not only pitch changes, but also differences among talkers. She used the operant head-turning procedure to train infants to discriminate a contrast between [a] and [i] when both talker's voice and pitch contour were held constant. When the infants showed they could discriminate this contrast, they were then tested for their ability to maintain the discrimination when pitch and talker's voice were varied gradually over a series of training stages. In the final stage, tokens of each vowel produced by three different talkers using two different pitch contours were used. Still, the infants continued to successfully detect the vowel contrast. In a follow-up study, Kuhl (1983) tested 6-month-olds on a more difficult vowel contrast, [a] versus [ɔ]. This contrast is particularly difficult because productions of these two vowels by different talkers often result in considerable acoustic overlap. Thus, what counts as an [ɔ] for one talker may be an [a] for another talker. Although the infants had more difficulty with variability for this vowel contrast than the previous one, they still gave evidence of detecting the [a]/[ɔ] contrast even with the maximum degree of variability present. Thus, by 6 months of age, infants clearly do possess some ability to deal with the kind of variability attributable to different talkers.

Subsequently, Jusczyk, Pisoni, and Mullennix (1992) found that infants as young as 2 months display some capacity for handling talker variability. Jusczyk et al. tested infants with tokens of the words "bug" and "dug" produced by 6 male and 6 female talkers. During the preshift phase of the high amplitude sucking procedure (HAS), one group heard all 12 tokens of one of the two words, and in the postshift phase they heard the tokens of the other word. Infants detected the postshift change from one word to the other despite the talker variability. In fact, the postshift performance of this group did not differ significantly from one who had been exposed to only a single token of each word produced by the same talker. As with Kuhl's studies with 6-month-olds, these results show that 2-month-olds can detect a stop consonant difference in the face of talker variability. Thus, the rudiments of perceptual normalisation seem to be present at a very early point in infancy.

One interesting aspect of Jusczyk et al.'s investigation was the demonstration that handling talker variability does have costs associated with it for infants' speech processing capacities. Just as studies have shown that talker variability can affect adult listeners' retention of speech (Martin, Mullennix, Pisoni, & Summers, 1989), Jusczyk et al. found that infants' memories for speech information were also affected by talker variability. Thus, when a 2-minute delay period was introduced between the preshift and postshift phase of the HAS procedure, infants who heard only a single token of each word produced by the same talker continued to discriminate the contrast between "bug" and "dug". By comparison, infants who heard all 12 tokens of the words produced by different talkers did not show evidence of discrimination following the delay. Evidently, talker variability affected the infants' retention of the speech sounds. Moreover, this effect held even for variability among tokens produced by a single talker. Overall, the results show that although 2-month-olds can cope with variability in speech, their processing resources available for the encoding and retrieval of speech information are likely to be affected.

PERCEPTUAL CAPACITIES AND LANGUAGE ACQUISITION

With a complement of basic perceptual capacities that allow them to begin to analyse the speech signal and to discriminate and categorise individual sounds, infants are well-positioned to face the remaining challenges of language acquisition. The task ahead remains daunting, including the correct segmentation and storage of sound patterns, linking these to their intended referents, learning how words are related in syntactic units, etc. Yet the young language learner accomplishes these tasks in a surprisingly consistent and timely fashion, regardless of the specific nature of the input. Although different natural languages have varying structural features and different organisations, learners do ultimately adapt successfully to the form of the speech input that they receive. In this section, we examine how the nature of the input affects infants' basic speech perception capacities. We also consider the role that speech perception capacities play in acquiring language – not only in segmenting speech into grammatically relevant units, but also in helping infants to identify and learn words.

How input affects perceptual capacities

Because languages can potentially vary along so many different dimensions, it is not plausible that infants are innately endowed with a set of categories that correspond directly to those in their native language. The basic perceptual capacities with which the infant approaches language acquisition must be flexible enough to encompass the full range of potential speech sounds and patterns that could occur in any natural language. This immediately suggests that any initial perceptual capacities that infants have must undergo some changes during development in response to the specific linguistic input. As noted earlier, Guatemalan infants' initial voicing categories appear to be closer to those used in English than to those in Spanish, the native language that they are acquiring (Lasky et al., 1975). Moreover, young Japanese infants show a capacity for discriminating [r] from [l] that is lacking among many adult speakers of Japanese (Miyawaki et al., 1975). Thus, during the course of language acquisition, two different tendencies are evident. The first is a finer tuning to the kinds of sound patterns and distinctions that occur in the native language. The second is a diminution of sensitivity to patterns that do not typically appear in native language utterances. Research on the role of experience in speech perception began with studies investigating when infants begin to show declines in sensitivity to non-native contrasts. We will consider these first, and then examine what is known about the other process – learning about the sound structure of the native language.

Developmental changes in sensitivity to non-native contrasts   Interest in the issue of when sensitivity to non-native contrasts begins to decline began after an investigation by Werker, Gilbert, Humphrey, and Tees (1981) indicated that although 7-month-old infants from English-speaking homes were able to perceive certain Hindi consonantal contrasts, English-speaking adults from the same environments could not. In a follow-up study, Werker and Tees (1983) attempted to delineate better the developmental time course of this decline. They tested a number of different age groups between 4 years and adulthood. However, even the youngest age group, 4-year-olds, showed a loss in sensitivity to these non-native contrasts. Werker and Tees then began to take seriously the possibility that the decline in sensitivity to non-native contrasts might occur much earlier, during the first year. Subsequently, Werker and Tees (1984) tested infants from English-speaking homes at three ages, 6–8 months, 8–10 months, and 10–12 months, on English ([ba]-[da]), Hindi ([ʈa]-[ta]), and Nthlakapmx ([k'i]-[q'i]) contrasts. They found that whereas 6- to 8-month-olds successfully discriminated all the contrasts, older infants experienced more difficulty. Namely, by 8–10 months, only a portion of the infants were able to make the discriminations, and by 10–12 months, hardly any infants successfully discriminated the non-English contrasts. The same pattern of results held when Werker and Tees tested a group of infants from English-speaking homes in a longitudinal study. That the decline had to do with lack of experience with these particular non-native contrasts was confirmed when several Hindi- and Nthlakapmx-learning infants were tested. These infants showed no decline in their sensitivity to the contrasts appropriate to their native language, even at 12 months of age. Another investigation by Werker and Lalonde (1988) with English-learning infants used different, synthetically produced, Hindi contrasts. The outcome was the same – a decline in sensitivity by English-learning infants between 6 and 12 months of age. Taken together, these studies suggest, in the absence of specific experience with these contrasts, sensitivity to them declines during the latter half of the first year.

Although the data from Werker's initial studies suggest a systematic decrease in sensitivity to non-native contrasts, the real story is somewhat more complex. First, some types of contrasts appear to decline sooner than others. Second, declines in sensitivity are not apparent for certain types of non-native contrasts. Let us consider the first type of case. When Polka and Werker (1994) tested English-learning infants on two different German vowel contrasts [ʏ] versus [ʊ] and [y] versus [u], they found that neither 10- to 12-month-olds, nor 6- to 8-month-olds successfully discriminated these contrasts. However, the same contrasts were discriminated by a group of English-learning 4- to 6-month-olds. Hence, the decline in sensitivity to these non-native vowel contrasts occurs at an earlier point in development than does the decline in sensitivity to the non-native consonantal contrasts that Werker and her colleagues had previously studied.

Next consider the issue of whether declines in sensitivity occur for all non-native contrasts. Best, McRoberts, and Sithole (Best et al., 1988) studied the perception of a lateral versus medial click contrast from Zulu – a type of contrast that does not exist in English. They found that infants of varying ages from English-speaking homes (6–8, 8–10, 10–12, and 12–14 months old), as well as English-speaking adults, were all able to discriminate this contrast. The fact that even English-speaking adults did not have any trouble with the contrast indicates that there is no decline in sensitivity for it. In subsequent investigations, Best (1991, 1995) has found evidence of declines in sensitivity to some types of contrasts, but not to others. On the one hand, English-learning infants showed no decline in their ability to discriminate an Ethiopian place of articulation distinction between ejective consonants (Best, 1991). On the other hand, English-learning 10- to 12-month-olds do show declines in sensitivity to a Zulu lateral fricative voicing distinction (Best, 1991) and to Zulu plosive versus implosive contrasts and aspirated versus ejective contrasts (Best, 1995). Similarly, Tsushima and his colleagues (1994) report that Japanese-learning 10- to 12-month-olds no longer discriminate the English [r]-[l] contrast.

What accounts for whether sensitivity to a particular non-native contrast is likely to decline during the course of language acquisition? The most detailed account is offered by Best (1993, 1995) in her Perceptual Assimilation Model. The model assumes that whenever non-native contrasts map onto two different native contrasts or to no native language categories, they will not undergo any decline in discriminability. By comparison, those non-native distinctions that map to a single native-language phonemic category will be most apt to undergo a decline in discriminability. The Perceptual Assimilation Model accounts for many of the previous results. However, there are some findings from Best's own investigations (Best, 1995) that do not quite fit the predictions of the model. Thus, there may be other factors that enter into whether a non-native contrast is apt to decline or not.

Developmental changes in sensitivity to native-language sound categories
In addition to focusing on the decline of perceptual sensitivity to non-native consonants, investigators have worked to document changes in sensitivity to native-language sound categories. For example, Kuhl and co-workers (Grieser & Kuhl, 1989; Kuhl, 1991, 1993; Kuhl, Williams, Lacerda, Stevens, & Lindblom, 1992) have suggested that native-language input may affect the nature of infants' vowel categories by 6 months of age. Kuhl claims that vowel categories are organised around prototypical instances from native-language input. Grieser and Kuhl (1989) exposed American 6-month-olds to either a prototypical instance or an atypical instance of the English vowel [i]. They found that infants were more likely to generalise to a greater range of instances from the [i] category after exposure to the prototypical instance of [i]. Kuhl (1991) refers to this as a "perceptual magnet effect". She argues that the prototypical instances from the category act as magnets by shortening the perceptual distances from the centre to the edges of the category (Lively & Pisoni, 1993; Sussman & Lauckner-Morano, 1995). Kuhl (1993) has implicated the perceptual magnet effect as a factor in the decline in sensitivity that infants show for non-native vowel contrasts. More specifically, she suggests that acquired experience with a range of native-language tokens helps to organise infants' vowel space and to reflect the categories that are used in the language. Her own investigation (Kuhl et al., 1992) demonstrated that American and Swedish infants displayed perceptual magnet effects only for vowel contrasts in their own native language. Thus, Swedish infants show perceptual magnet effects for the Swedish [y], but not for the English [i], whereas American infants showed the reverse pattern. It is significant that the age Kuhl identifies as the time at which vowel categories are formed is the same as the age at which Polka and Werker (1994) note the beginning of a decline in sensitivity to non-native vowel contrasts.

Sensitivity to the organisation of native-language sound patterns develops in other ways as well. Some of these, including sensitivity to the prosodic and phonotactic properties of the native language, will be discussed in the next section of this chapter. For the moment, we focus on how the infant discovers the internal organisation of units such as syllables and words. Throughout the history of infant speech-perception research, there has been considerable discussion about the kinds of units that infants pull out of the speech stream. One suggestion that has received considerable empirical support is that, at least in the early stages of development, the syllable serves as the natural processing unit for infants. For example, Bertoncini and Mehler (1981) found that 2-month-olds were better able to discriminate pairs of stimuli that conform to a syllabic ([pæt] versus [tæp]) pattern as opposed to a nonsyllabic ([pst] versus [tsp]) pattern in a language. Bijeljac-Babic, Bertoncini, and Mehler (1993) found that newborn infants are sensitive to the number of syllables in an utterance, but not to the number of phonetic segments. Moreover, it has been demonstrated that 2-month-olds benefit from syllabic organisation in remembering speech information (Jusczyk, Jusczyk, Kennedy, Schomberg, & Koenig, 1995). In the latter case, 2-month-olds exposed to a series of bisyllabic utterances showed better retention of these utterances when they contained a common syllable than when they had no syllables in common. In a comparable investigation involving syllables that either shared or did not share common phonetic segments, 2-month-olds did not show any advantage for the syllables sharing a common phonetic segment (Jusczyk, Kennedy, & Jusczyk, 1995). Hence, there is considerable evidence that syllables are important processing units for young infants.

During the latter half of the first year, there are some indications that infants may be learning about the internal organisation of syllables. For instance, Hillenbrand (1983) trained 6-month-olds on a contrast between the oral stop, [ba], and the nasal, [ma]. In subsequent training stages, he added new syllables to each category (e.g. [da] and [na]) and found that the infants successfully generalised to new instances of the stop and nasal categories. Hillenbrand (1984) also reported that 6-month-olds were more apt to learn a rule based on a place of articulation distinction among nasals ([m] vs. [n]) than one that arbitrarily grouped the same syllables. One interpretation of these findings is that infants are beginning to perceive similarities between portions of syllables – perhaps even segments or features.

Further support for this view comes from a series of recent studies by Jusczyk and his colleagues (Bauman, Goodman, & Jusczyk, 1995; Goodman, Jusczyk, & Bauman, in press; Jusczyk, Bauman, & Goodman, submitted). They used the Headturn Preference Procedure to present 9-month-olds with lists of monosyllabic cvc items. On half of the lists, the items shared some common element (such as an initial consonant). On the other half of the lists, the items were unrelated (i.e. there was no element in common to all of the items). They found that when the items on the lists either shared their initial consonant (e.g. "foat", "feev", "fas", etc.) or their initial consonant and vowel (e.g. "bife", "bime", "bige", etc.), the infants listened significantly longer to these than to the unrelated lists. However, when the items on the lists merely shared the same vowel (e.g. "med", "jek", "pesh", etc.) or the same vowel and final consonant (e.g. "bod", "lod", "yod", etc.), the infants did not listen any longer to these lists than to the unrelated ones. Thus, these results suggest that although English-learning 9-month-olds are attending to some similarities among syllables, some types of similarity are more salient than others. In particular, the 9-month-olds appear to be more sensitive to similarities involving the onsets of syllables. Moreover, the results of a follow-up study (Bauman et al., 1995) suggests that this pattern holds for English-learners at 14 and 18 months of age. Thus, even for 18-month-olds, Goodman et al. found no indication that these infants were attending to similarities involving the offsets (rimes) of syllables.

There are several possible explanations why 9-month-olds may have shown this asymmetry in the kinds of similarities that they attended to. One possibility is that this sequence is peculiar to learning English. For example, English does not make widespread use of similarities in the ends of words to mark the way in which words are grouped within an utterance. Languages with well-developed case-marking systems, like Spanish, may be more likely to have words within a particular syntactic grouping agree in terms of their endings. Another possibility is that the asymmetry is actually language-universal rather than language-specific. An account along these lines is that the attention to onsets of words is a consequence of developing a lexicon, wherein distinctions and similarities among the onsets of words may be, at least initially, more important for infants to encode in order to avoid confusions among lexical items. Regardless of its source, the tendency for infants to attend to similarities involving onsets of syllables could signal that they are beginning to develop subsyllabic representations of speech. A potential developmental change may be occurring with respect to the kind of features that draw infants' attention. Although younger infants may attend more to similarities and differences involving entire syllables, older infants may begin to attend to relations among parts of syllables.

Segmenting speech

One of the critical tasks for any language learner is to determine what the important units are in the speech stream. Although fluent speakers (and especially fluent readers) of a language may have the sense that the boundaries of individual words and phrases are clearly separated in the speech stream, this is far from true. An experience listening to speakers of an unfamiliar foreign language converse for even a short time is usually enough to remind the average listener that it is often hard to tell where one word ends and another begins. Words in fluent speech are seldom, if ever, clearly demarcated from one another with pauses, a fact that renders automatic recognition of words by machines so difficult. The task for pre-linguistic infants is apparently not much easier. Not only do they not know very many words, but they have little information about how these are typically sequenced in native-language utterances. Yet despite these potential obstacles, the average 18-month-old seems well on the way to learning words and putting them together. In this section, we focus on how infants learn about the way information is typically packaged in speech and how they begin to segment words from fluent speech.

Using prosody to help locate grammatical units   How and when infants learn the way that prosodic information is structured in the native language is interesting in its own right. However, interest in this aspect of language acquisition has been heightened by the possibility that prosody provides cues to the syntactic organisation of the language. Analyses of fluent speech suggest that boundaries between important grammatical units such as clauses and phrases are often marked by changes in variables related to prosody, such as changes in pitch contour, increases in syllable duration, and pausing (Beckman & Edwards, 1990; Cooper & Paccia-Cooper, 1980; Grosjean & Gee, 1987; Nakatani & Dukes, 1977; Price, Ostendorf, Shattuck-Hufnagel & Fong, 1991). Adult listeners are sensitive to such prosodic markers and appear to use them in understanding speech (Collier & t'Hart, 1975; Lehiste, Olive & Streeter, 1976; Price et al., 1991; Scott & Cutler, 1984). These data have led to speculation that learners use prosody to determine the location of linguistically relevant units, such as clauses and phrases (Gleitman & Wanner, 1982; Hirsh-Pasek et al., 1987; Morgan, 1986; Morgan & Demuth, 1996; Peters, 1983). At the very least prosodic markers might be helpful by allowing learners to break speech up into smaller chunks for further analysis.

Hirsh-Pasek et al. (1987) first investigated whether infants respond to prosodic marking of clausal units in fluent speech. They collected speech samples of a mother talking to her 18-month-old infant. They chose passages that were 15 to 20sec long and modified these by inserting 1sec pauses in the passages in one of two ways. Either the pauses were inserted in the boundary between two successive clauses (coincident versions) or between two words within each clause (noncoincident versions). Hirsh-Pasek et al. hypothesised that if infants are sensitive to prosodic marking of clausal units, they might listen longer to the versions with pauses coinciding with the clause boundaries than to those versions with the noncoincident pauses. Groups of 6- and 9-month-old infants, tested using the head-turn preference procedure, both showed significant listening preferences for the coincident versions. Hirsh-Pasek et al. concluded that sensitivity to prosodic markers of clausal units is present in infants as young as 6 months.

The kinds of prosodic changes observed at clause boundaries in English are also known to occur in many other languages (Cruttenden, 1986). Consequently, American infants' responsiveness to these prosodic changes may not relate to learning about English *per se*, but to some more general ability for processing the input. Indeed, it is conceivable that infants might not need to learn about the particulars of prosodic structure in order to detect clausal units in their native language. However, this does not apply to subclausal units because the organisation of units within clauses differs considerably from language to language. In languages like English, where word order is used to indicate important grammatical relations, some prosodic marking of information that occurs together within the same phrase is likely. However, case languages such as Serbian use affixes to mark grammatical relations and allow much freedom in ordering words within a clause. Two words within the same phrase could be separated by words from other phrases. Any prosodic marking of phrasal units in Serbian is bound to be very different from that in English. Thus, infants must discover the existence of any prosodic marking of subclausal units in their native language.

Jusczyk et al. (1992) investigated whether American infants are sensitive to prosodic marking of major phrasal units (subject phrase; predicate phrase) in English. The stimuli were analogous to the ones with the clausal units, only this time pauses were inserted either between two phrasal groups (coincident versions) or within a phrasal group (noncoincident versions). At 6 months of age, the infants showed no clear preferences for the coincident versions. However, by 9 months, infants displayed significantly longer listening times for the coincident versions. Therefore, in contrast to the case for clausal units, sensitivity to prosodic markers of phrasal units in English does not appear to develop until between 6 and 9 months of age. Jusczyk et al. speculated that more familiarity with native-language sound structures may be necessary before infants can detect prosodic marking of phrasal units.

Even if the infant can detect the prosodic organisation of speech input, it is not always possible to derive the syntactic organisation from the prosody. Indeed, mismatches in the prosodic and syntactic phrasing may occur even in simple sentences directed to language-learners. Consider the following two sentences.

1. Johnny read the book.
2. He read the book.

In (1), the talker is likely to produce prosodic boundary cues after the subject NP, "Johnny". However, in (2), even two-year-old talkers (Gerken, 1991, 1994) either produce no prosodic boundary cues or produce them between the verb and the object NP, "the book". This is because a weakly stressed pronoun subject tends to be phonologically joined (or "cliticised") to a following stressed verb – i.e. the subject and verb form a prosodic unit. Hence, there is no prosodic marking of the syntactic boundary between the subject and the predicate phrases.

How do infants respond to utterances in which prosodic and syntactic boundaries mismatch? Only a small percentage of the spontaneous speech samples (about 15%) used by Jusczyk et al. actually contained potential mismatches of the sort found in (2). For this reason, Gerken, Jusczyk, and Mandel (1994) created new materials to compare infants' responses to sentences with pronoun subjects, as in (2), to those to sentences with nouns as subjects, as in (1). Nine-month-olds who heard the sentences with noun subjects behaved exactly like the infants in the Jusczyk et al. study – namely, they listened significantly longer to samples in which pauses were inserted between the subject and verb phrases than to ones in which pauses were inserted between the verb and object NP phrases. By comparison, infants who listened to the sentences with pronoun subjects did not show a significant preference for either type of segmentation. In a follow-up experiment, Gerken et al. used sentences in which there was likely to be a prosodic boundary between a pronoun subject and the verb – namely, sentences with inversions between a pronoun and an auxiliary, i.e. Yes–No questions. In such sentences, the pronoun and auxiliary tend to form a clitic group that is separate from the verb. For these sentences, 9-month-olds listened significantly longer to versions with pauses between the subject and verb phrases. Hence, what these results show is that infants are primarily responding to prosodic units in the speech stream. Whenever such units coincide with syntactic units, infants may be able to gain some information about the grammatical organisation of their native language. Even when the correlation between prosodic and syntactic units is less than perfect, they are likely to be left with well-formed phrase fragments that may be helpful in learning about syntactic constituents (Fisher & Tokura, 1996).

Given that infants demonstrate some sensitivity to potential prosodic markers of syntactic units, when might they actually begin using this information in segmenting speech? One possibility is that prosody might provide infants with an organisation for encoding and remembering speech information. Early psycholinguistic studies with adult subjects demonstrated that their memory for information in speech is better when it is linked within a clause or phrase (Marks & Miller, 1964; Miller & Isard, 1963; Suci, 1967). Mandel, Jusczyk, and Kemler Nelson (1994) asked whether the same advantage for good prosodic organisation would also hold true for 2-month-olds' memory for speech. They used the HAS procedure to determine whether words that are prosodically linked within a clause are better remembered by infants than words produced as individual items from a list. Half of the infants heard stimuli that were produced as complete sentences; the other half heard the same sequences of words, but these were taken from long lists of words spoken in isolation. The overall durations of both types of materials were matched. During the preshift phase, infants repeatedly heard either a single sentence or list sequence (e.g. "The cat raced white mice"). Following habituation to this stimulus, the preshift phase ended and was followed by a 2-minute silent interval. In the postshift phase, the infants heard either the same stimulus as during the preshift phase, one which differed by one word (e.g. "The cat chased white mice"), or one that differed by two words (e.g. "The rat chased white mice"). The results indicated that performance was significantly better for the sentences than for the lists. A follow-up experiment replicated and extended these findings by showing that 2-month-olds' memories for information within a sentence is better than for the same information in fragments of two adjoining sentences. More recently, Mandel, Kemler Nelson, and Jusczyk (1996) demonstrated that infants better preserve information about the serial order of words when they occur within the same well-formed prosodic unit.

Thus, even 2-month-olds benefit from the organisation provided by sentential prosody. Not only are infants sensitive to prosodic markers in the speech stream, but these markers may also play a role in what infants remember about utterances.

Finding words in fluent speech   Infants can segment words from fluent speech either by matching the input to stored representations in the lexicon or by knowing enough about the characteristics of words in their language to predict which sound sequences are words. For words to be stored in the lexicon prior to their segmentation, they would need to be learned in isolation. Caregivers may indeed repeat some words in isolation to their infants, and these could become stored in the lexicon. However, researchers have come to realise that caregivers, even when instructed to teach words, almost always place them in sentential contexts (Morgan, 1996; Woodward & Aslin, 1990). If infants must rely on rare occurrences of isolated word utterances before they can recognise a sequence of sounds as a word, then the task of making sound–meaning correspondences should be even more difficult than it already seems (Clark, 1973, 1983; Markman, 1991; Quine, 1960). However, the paucity of input with respect to isolated words does not seem to pose a serious problem to the infant acquiring language. Increasing evidence supports the possibility that sensitivity to language-specific properties of speech allows infants to recognise general characteristics of words that they can identify in fluent speech. Sensitivity to the phonetics, phonotactics (how sounds can be ordered within words), and prosody of words in a language could help place infants in position to segment fluent speech by using the knowledge of word characteristics to segment the input into pieces likely to be words.

Listeners can gain some insights about the structure of words in a given language by paying attention to the frequency with which a particular sound or a sequence of sounds occurs. Consequently, part of predicting possible words in fluent speech involves being able to ascertain if a sequence of sounds are sounds that have occurred often in their language. Several studies indicate that by 9 months, infants are sensitive to the sounds and the typical orderings of sounds occurring in the speech around them. Much of the evidence comes from cross-linguistic studies that test infants' ability to discriminate languages differing in specific ways. For example, Jusczyk, Friederici, Wessels, Svenkerud, and Jusczyk (1993) used Dutch and English because the two languages have a similar prosody. Because prosodic characteristics were similar for the two languages, these investigators were able to explore infants' sensitivity to language-specific phonetic and phonotactic characteristics of words. They presented Dutch and American infants with lists of Dutch and English words. Nine-month-olds, but not 6-month-olds, showed a significant listening preference for the lists in their own language. Language-discrimination studies with newborns and 2-month-olds (Mehler et al., 1988) have shown that infants can use prosodic information to recognise utterances from their native language. Nine months is the earliest age that infants have been found to discriminate languages based on nonprosodic features of the input.

The ability to recognise sequences of sounds as being native or nonnative is important not only for discriminating languages in a multilingual environment, but also because it reflects a more general tendency to notice the distribution of sounds in a language. For speech segmentation, the frequency in which sounds occur together is crucial because it provides an indication of where a word might begin and end. An atypical cluster of sounds is more likely to indicate a word boundary than a cohesive unit. For instance, although Polish allows words to begin with two successive stop consonants ("dba", "kto", etc.), this kind of sequence cannot occur within an English syllable. Rather, a sequence such as "db" in fluent speech is most likely across a boundary between two words, such as "red box".

By 9 months of age, infants demonstrate some sensitivity to sound clusters in speech. Friederici and Wessels (1993) found that Dutch infants were sensitive to whether or not the onsets or offsets of lists of words were permissible phonotactic sequences for words in their native language. In another investigation, Jusczyk, Luce, and Charles-Luce (1994) showed that American 9-month-olds listened longer to syllables containing high-frequency English phonotactic sequences (e.g. "mim", "gen") than to ones that included permissible, but much more infrequently occurring, sequences (e.g. "rawch", "wooth"). Hence, the 9-month-olds appear to be tracking the way in which sounds are sequenced and learning something about the frequency with which certain sound patterns co-occur.

Noticing the co-occurrences of specific sounds in the input could facilitate speech segmentation, not only by providing clues to possible word boundaries, but also by building up representations of speech in memory. When sounds occur together often, the listener may infer that the sounds belong together. The recognition of the frequent sound sequences will allow them to be better represented in memory because each occurrence will further stabilise the unit in memory, allowing for a detailed analysis of its characteristics. The infant may not intend to store sound sequences in memory. However, by merely attending to speech, the infant will come across sequences that belong together as words more often than sequences that do not, simply because the former sequences occur more often than the latter.

Another important source of information that listeners can potentially use in segmenting words from speech is prosody. Although much research on prosody has focused on infants' sensitivity to prosodic information at the sentential, clausal, and phrasal levels, it is only recently that some attention has shifted to the word level. For example, Jusczyk et al. (1993) also explored whether infants can discriminate native-language words from those of a non-native language, Norwegian, whose words have a characteristic prosody that differs considerably from English. American 6-month-olds not only discriminated these words, but also discriminated low-pass filtered versions of them. The latter result suggests that the infants were responding to the prosodic, rather than the phonetic, characteristics of the words.

Other investigations of prosody have focused on infants' sensitivity to the predominant stress patterns of words in their native language. Interest in this area has been stimulated by the observations of Cutler and her colleagues, who noted that a high proportion of English content words in conversational speech begin with a strong syllable (Cutler, 1990; Cutler & Carter, 1987; Cutler & Norris, 1988). Because content words so frequently begin with strong syllables (e.g. "gentle", "falter", "vestibule", "alligator"), Cutler and her colleagues have suggested that English listeners may follow a strategy (the "metrical segmentation strategy") in which they identify each strong syllable as marking a new word onset.

Converging evidence from several research groups strongly suggests that English-learning infants have picked up information about the predominant stress pattern of English words. For example, an experiment by

Jusczyk, Cutler, and Redanz (1993) showed that American 9-month-olds, but not 6-month-olds, attended longer to English bisyllabic words that followed a strong/weak stress pattern (e.g. "pliant", "donor") than weak/strong (e.g. "abut", "condone"). Also, Echols, Crowhurst, and Childers (1997) demonstrated that 9-month-olds showed a preference for strong/weak over weak/strong patterns. They presented infants with trisyllables with the stress falling on the middle syllable and a pause occurring either before or after the stressed syllable. The infants preferred prestress over poststress pauses, indicating that they considered the strong/weak units to be more natural than the weak/strong.

If English-learning infants expect words in fluent speech to begin with a strong syllable, then they may be able to use this information in speech segmentation. A series of studies by Jusczyk, Newsome, and Houston (manuscript in preparation) explored this possibility. In earlier work, Jusczyk and Aslin (1995) had devised a new paradigm to study the word segmentation abilities of young infants. They tested 7½-month-olds in a headturn preference procedure that involves two phases. During the familiarisation phase, two monosyllabic words (e.g. "cup" and "dog") were repeated in isolation until the infant reached a looking-time criterion. During the test phase, a series of four passages were presented. Each passage contained a target word once in each of six sentences. For two of the passages the target words were the same words presented in the familiarisation phase and were thus called "familiar passages". The other two "unfamiliar" passages each contained a word that was repeated in each sentence (e.g. "bike" or "feet"), but the repeated word was not one of the ones presented during the familiarisation phase. The infants' looking times to the familiar passages were compared to the average looking times toward the "unfamiliar passages". Jusczyk and Aslin found that 7½-month-olds, but not 6-month-olds, listened significantly longer to the passages containing the words from the familiarisation period. Hence, Jusczyk and Aslin concluded that the infants were able to detect the presence of these words in the fluent speech passages.

The primary question that Jusczyk, Newsome, and Houston addressed was whether or not the stress pattern of target words would impact on the infants' ability to locate them in fluent speech. They tested 7½-month-olds using the word-detection paradigm and found that the infants listened significantly longer to the familiar than to the unfamiliar passages when the target words were ones with a strong/weak (i.e. "doctor", "candle", "hamlet", "kingdom") rather than weak/strong (i.e. "guitar", "device", "surprise", "beret") stress pattern. Further studies focusing on the weak/strong words revealed the source of the infants' difficulty in detecting these in fluent speech contexts. Consistent with the metrical segmentation strategy, when the weak/strong words occurred in fluent speech the infants appeared to notice only the strong syllables. Hence, infants who were familiarised with "tar" and "vice" actually listened longer to passages containing the words "guitar" and "device" than they did to ones containing "surprise" and "beret" (even though in the previous study infants familiarised with the whole words "guitar" and "device" did not detect these same words in the passages).

In comparison to their responses to weak/strong words, infants tended to treat the strong/weak words as cohesive trochaic units; they did not respond to just the strong syllables of words like "kingdom" and "doctor". This latter finding suggests that when infants noticed strong syllables in a context, they paid attention to any information that consistently followed these (as opposed to information that might consistently precede these as in the case of weak/strong words). In other words, when English is the input language, infants may adopt a heuristic of expecting strong syllables to begin words.

The notion that infants may pay attention to what follows strong syllables in fluent speech was tested further by Jusczyk et al. (manuscript in preparation), who investigated whether infants would apply the strategy even in situations that would lead to misparsings of the speech stream. New passages were created with the same weak/strong target words in which each weak/strong target word was consistently followed by a function word (e.g. "guitar is", "device to", etc.). Under these circumstances the infants treated the consistently following function words as part of the strong syllables of the weak/strong words. First, they no longer responded to just the strong syllables (e.g. "tar" and "vice") of the weak/strong words in these new contexts. Instead, they were more prone to cross word boundaries and to respond to strong/weak pseudowords formed from the strong syllable of the weak/strong word and its consistently following function word (e.g. "taris" and "viceto"). Thus, it appears that as an initial segmentation strategy, 7½-month-olds make a first pass at finding words by attending to strong syllables and whatever consistently follows them in the speech stream.

It is difficult to understand how infants could become aware of the typical stress pattern in their language before they are able to segment words from fluent speech. One possibility is that even though words may not be presented often enough in isolation for infants to learn them one at a time, they may be able to get an idea of a word's typical characteristics. Perhaps the very first words that infants often hear will make a big impact on what they will expect other speech units to have. Even though words are rarely spoken in isolation, it may be that some words like "baby", "mommy", "daddy", "doggie", "bottle" do occur relatively frequently in isolation. These particular words and others that are often repeated to infants are trochaic feet. Also, in English, many names often begin with strong syllables and those that do not often have nickname forms that begin with strong syllables. Names like Michelle and Elizabeth are changed to forms such as Shelly and Liz or Betty. Names and other frequently occurring word patterns directed towards infants may affect infants' expectations about typical native-language word patterns. Morgan (1996) proposes that a trochaic bias may develop in infants because, as they begin to hypothesise sound sequences as being meaningful, if they store a strong/weak bisyllable in memory, it is more likely to recur in the input than a weak/strong bisyllable.

Other investigations have also documented that around 9 months of age, there is a tendency for English-learners to respond to the rhythmic and phonotactic properties characteristic of the words in their language (Echols et al., 1997; Morgan & Saffran, 1995). For example, Morgan and his colleagues have examined the roles of distributional and rhythmic information and how infants might integrate them. Goodsitt, Morgan, and Kuhl (1993) showed that, without any rhythmic information, 7-month-olds are more likely to group sets of sounds together if they occur across a variety of contexts than if the context is fixed. Morgan and Saffran (1995) showed that 6-month-olds used only rhythmic cues, whereas 9-month-olds integrated both rhythmic and distributional information in their perception of the cohesiveness of bisyllables. However, distributional information only helped the 9-month-olds when the rhythmic information was held constantly strong/weak. When the rhythmic properties of the bisyllables were variable, transitional probabilities no longer aided in treating bisyllables as cohesive units.

By beginning to use information about the predominant stress patterns of words to segment the speech stream, infants may gain a foothold that allows them to make a more detailed analysis of the sound properties of words. Carving the input into smaller chunks may make it easier for infants to represent information about speech in memory. It might also permit further analyses of these chunks to pull out more information about native-language word structure. Studies of older infants have revealed sensitivities to the kinds of subtle characteristics of words that could improve infants' abilities to segment speech more accurately. Jusczyk et al. (manuscript in preparation) found 10½-month-olds are able to segment weak/strong words, such as "guitar" and "device", from fluent speech contexts. Moreover, these older infants did not appear to treat the consistently following function words as part of a unit with the strong syllables of weak/strong words.

One possible reason that 10½-month-olds no longer attach following function words to the strong syllables of weak/strong words is that they may have already learned something about the nature of function words. Morgan, Allopenna, and Shi (1996) suggest that infants may distinguish function words and content words by using intercorrelated acoustics cues. Morgan et al.'s analysis indicates that although the discriminating information between content and function words at the word, syllable, segmental, and acoustic/phonetic levels was not enough to accurately distinguish the categories, a multivariate analysis was able to classify syllables with up to 90% accuracy. Function words tend to have few and simple syllables with low amplitude and centralised vowels.

Another possible reason why 10½-month-olds can separate following function words from content words is that they are able to detect the kinds of phonotactic and allophonic cues that can help them to segment words more reliably. Myers et al. (1996) found that 10½-month-olds showed a preference for speech in which pauses were inserted between words rather than within them, but only when the speech was not low-pass filtered. The latter suggests that infants were using other sources of information than prosody to detect whether words were interrupted or not. Myers et al.'s analyses of their target words indicated the presence of strong phonotactic cues relating to word boundaries, even for the weak/strong words that they used. Allophonic cues can also serve as a source of information about potential word boundaries, because some allophones are more likely to occur at the beginning of words than in other positions (Church, 1987). For example, the similar items "nitrate" and "night rate" are distinguished by the allophones (or variants) of [t] and [r] that occur in these words. Specifically, the [t] and [r] in "night rate" are the kinds of segment that occur in the final and initial positions of words, respectively. This is not true of the allophones of [t] and [r] of "nitrate". Jusczyk, Hohne, and Bauman (1995) reported evidence that 10½-month-olds, but not 9-month-olds, are able to use allophonic cues to segment words from fluent speech. When tested using the word detection paradigm, 10½-month olds familiarised with a word such as "nitrate" listened significantly longer to a "nitrate" passage than they did to one containing "night rate". Infants familiarised with "night rate" showed the opposite pattern.

In summary, it appears that English-learning infants may initially rely on a prosodically based strategy to segment word-like units from fluent speech. This strategy allows them to detect the presence of certain kinds of words, those with the predominant strong/weak stress patterns of English words. However, exclusive reliance on this strategy would cause infants to miss words that begin with weak syllables and to mis-segment the speech signal in other ways as well. Nevertheless, the availability of smaller-sized units of input may in itself help the infant to discover other properties of English word structure (relating to phonotactic and allophonic features) that could be helpful in word segmentation. There is some evidence that English-learning infants may begin to use such cues at around 10½ months of age. Because languages differ widely in their prosodic, allophonic, and phonotactic properties, it is likely that learners devise strategies that are specific to the kinds of native-language input that they are exposed to. The kinds of cues that are most helpful to infants learning English will likely not be those that are most helpful to infants learning Turkish or Tagalog.

REFERENCES

Aslin, R.N., & Pisoni, D.B. (1980). Some developmental processes in speech perception. In G.H. Yeni-Komshian, J.F. Kavanagh, & C.A. Ferguson (Eds.), *Child phonology* (Vol. 2). New York: Academic Press.

Bauman, A., Goodman, M., & Jusczyk, P.W. (1995). *Infants' sensitivities to sound similarities within words*. Paper presented at the *20th Annual Boston University Conference on Language Development*, Boston, MA.

Beckman, M., & Edwards, J. (1990). Lengthening and shortenings and the nature of prosodic constituency. In J. Kingston & M.E. Beckman (Eds.), *Papers in laboratory phonology I: Between the grammar and physics of speech*, (pp. 152–178). Cambridge: Cambridge University Press.

Bertoncini, J., Bijeljac-Babic, R., Blumstein, S.E., & Mehler, J. (1987). Discrimination in neonates of very short CV's. *Journal of the Acoustical Society of America*, **82**, 31–37.

Bertoncini, J., & Mehler, J. (1981). Syllables as units in infant speech perception. *Infant Behavior and Development*, **4**, 247–260.

Best, C.T. (1991). *Phonetic influences on the perception of non-native speech contrasts by 6–8 and 10–12 month olds*. Paper presented at the *Biennial Meeting of the Society for Research in Child Development*, Seattle, WA.

Best, C.T. (1993). Emergence of language-specific constraints in perception of native and non-native speech: A window on early phonological development. In B. de Boysson-Bardies, S. de Schonen, P. Jusczyk, P. MacNeilage, & J. Morton (Eds.), *Developmental neurocognition: Speech and face processing in the first year of life*. (pp. 289–304). Dordrecht: Kluwer.

Best, C.T. (1995). Learning to perceive the sound patterns of English. In C. Rovee-Collier & L.P. Lipsitt (Eds.), *Advances in infancy research* (Vol. 9, pp. 217–304). Norwood, NJ: Ablex.

Best, C.T., McRoberts, G.W., & Sithole, N.M. (1988). Examination of perceptual re-organisation for nonnative speech contrasts: Zulu click discrimination by English-speaking adults and infants. *Journal of Experimental Psychology: Human Perception and Performance*, **14**, 345–360.

Bijeljac-Babic, R., Bertoncini, J., & Mehler, J. (1993). How do four-day-old infants categorize multisyllabic utterances? *Developmental Psychology*, **29**, 711–721.

Bladon, R.A., Henton, C.G., & Pickering, J.B. (1984). Towards an auditory theory of speaker normalisation. *Language and Communication*, **4**, 59–69.

Church, K. (1987). Phonological parsing and lexical retrieval. *Cognition*, **25**, 53–69.

Clark, E.V. (1973). What's in a word? On the child's acquisition of semantics in his first language. In T.E. Moore (Ed.), *Cognitive development and the acquisition of language* (pp. 65–110). New York: Academic Press.

Clark, E.V. (1983). Meanings and concepts. In J.H. Flavell & E.M. Markman (Eds.), *Cognitive development* (Vol. III). New York: Wiley.

Collier, R., & t'Hart, J. (1975). The role of intonation in speech perception. In A. Cohen & S.G. Nooteboom (Eds.), *Structure and process in speech perception* (pp. 107–121). Heidelberg: Springer Verlag.

Cooper, W.E., & Paccia-Cooper, J. (1980). *Syntax and speech.* Cambridge, MA: Harvard University Press.

Cruttenden, A. (1986). *Intonation.* Cambridge: Cambridge University Press.

Cutler, A. (1990). Exploiting prosodic probabilities in speech segmentation. In G.T.M. Altmann (Ed.), *Cognitive models of speech processing: psycholinguistic and computational perspectives* (pp. 105–121). Cambridge, MA: MIT Press.

Cutler, A., & Carter, D.M. (1987). The predominance of strong initial syllables in the English vocabulary. *Computer Speech and Language,* **2,** 133–142.

Cutler, A., & Norris, D.G. (1988). The role of strong syllables in segmentation for lexical access. *Journal of Experimental Psychology: Human Perception and Performance,* **14,** 113–121.

Echols, C.H., Crowhurst, M.J., & Childers, J.B. (1997). Perception of rhythmic units in speech by infants and adults. *Journal of Memory and Language,* **52,** 1135–1145.

Eimas, P.D. (1974). Auditory and linguistic processing of cues for place of articulation by infants. *Perception & Psychophysics,* **16,** 513–521.

Eimas, P.D. (1975a). Auditory and phonetic coding of the cues for speech: Discrimination of the [r-l] distinction by young infants. *Perception & Psychophysics,* **18,** 341–347.

Eimas, P.D. (1975b). Speech perception in early infancy. In L.B. Cohen & P. Salapatek (Eds.), *Infant perception: From sensation to cognition* (Vol. 2). New York: Academic Press.

Eimas, P.D., & Miller, J.L. (1980a). Contextual effects in infant speech perception. *Science,* **209,** 1140–1141.

Eimas, P.D., & Miller, J.L. (1980b). Discrimination of the information for manner of articulation. *Infant Behavior and Development,* **3,** 367–375.

Eimas, P.D., Siqueland, E.R., Jusczyk, P.W., & Vigorito, J. (1971). Speech perception in infants. *Science,* **171,** 303–306.

Fisher, C.L., & Tokura, H. (1996). Acoustic cues to grammatical structure in infant-directed speech: Cross-linguistic evidence. *Child Development,* **67,** 3192–3218.

Friederici, A.D., & Wessels, J.M.I. (1993). Phonotactic knowledge and its use in infant speech perception. *Perception & Psychophysics,* **54,** 287–295.

Fry, D.B., Abramson, A.S., Eimas, P.D., & Liberman, A.M. (1962). The identification and discrimination of synthetic vowels. *Language and Speech,* **5,** 171–189.

Gerken, L.A. (1991). The metrical basis for children's subjectless sentences. *Journal of Memory and Language,* **30,** 431–451.

Gerken, L.A. (1994). Young children's representation of prosodic phonology: evidence from English-speakers' weak syllable omissions. *Journal of Memory and Language,* **33,** 19–38.

Gerken, L.A., Jusczyk, P.W., & Mandel, D.R. (1994). When prosody fails to cue syntactic structure: Nine-month-olds' sensitivity to phonological vs syntactic phrases. *Cognition,* **51,** 237–265.

Gleitman, L., & Wanner, E. (1982). The state of the state of the art. In E. Wanner & L. Gleitman (Eds.), *Language acquisition: The state of the art* (pp. 3–48). Cambridge: Cambridge University Press.

Goodman, M.B., Jusczyk, P.W., & Bauman, A. (in press). Developmental changes in infants' sensitivity to internal syllable structure. In J. Pierrehumbert & M. Broe (Eds.), *Proceedings of Labphon V.* Cambridge: Cambridge University Press.

Goodsitt, J.V., Morgan, J.L., & Kuhl, P.K. (1993). Perceptual strategies in prelingual speech segmentation. *Journal of Child Language,* **20,** 229–252.

Grieser, D., & Kuhl, P.K. (1989). The categorisation of speech by infants: Support for speech-sound prototypes. *Developmental Psychology,* **25,** 577–588.

Grosjean, F., & Gee, J.P. (1987). Prosodic structure and spoken word recognition. *Cognition,* **25,** 135–155.

Hillenbrand, J. (1983). Perceptual organisation of speech sounds by infants. *Journal of Speech and Hearing Research*, **26**, 268–282.

Hillenbrand, J. (1984). Speech perception by infants: Categorisation based on nasal consonant place of articulation. *Journal of the Acoustical Society of America*, **75**, 1613–1622.

Hillenbrand, J.M., Minifie, F.D., & Edwards, T.J. (1979). Tempo of spectrum change as a cue in speech sound discrimination by infants. *Journal of Speech and Hearing Research*, **22**, 147–165.

Hirsh-Pasek, K., Kemler Nelson, D.G., Jusczyk, P.W., Wright Cassidy, K., Druss, B., & Kennedy, L. (1987). Clauses are perceptual units for young infants. *Cognition*, **26**, 269–286.

Holmberg, T.L., Morgan, K.A., & Kuhl, P.K. (1977). *Speech perception in early infancy: Discrimination of fricative consonants.* Paper presented at the *Meeting of the Acoustical Society of America*, Miami Beach, FL.

Jusczyk, P.W., Bauman, A., & Goodman, M. (submitted). Sensitivity to sound similarities in different utterances by 9-month-olds.

Jusczyk, P.W., Copan, H., & Thompson, E. (1978). Perception by two-month-olds of glide contrasts in multisyllabic utterances. *Perception & Psychophysics*, **24**, 515–520.

Jusczyk, P.W., Cutler, A., & Redanz, N. (1993). Preference for the predominant stress patterns of English words. *Child Development*, **64**, 675–687.

Jusczyk, P.W., Friederici, A.D., Wessels, J., Svenkerud, V.Y., & Jusczyk, A.M. (1993). Infants' sensitivity to the sound patterns of native language words. *Journal of Memory and Language*, **32**, 402–420.

Jusczyk, P.W., Hirsh-Pasek, K., Kemler Nelson, D.G., Kennedy, L., Woodward, A., & Piwoz, J. (1992). Perception of acoustic correlates of major phrasal units by young infants. *Cognitive Psychology*, **24**, 252–293.

Jusczyk, P.W., Hohne, E.A., & Bauman, A.L. (1995). *Infants' sensitivity to word juncture cues.* Paper presented at the *36th Annual Meeting of the Psychonomic Society*, Los Angeles, CA.

Jusczyk, P.W., Jusczyk, A.M., Kennedy, L.J., Schomberg, T., & Koenig, N. (1995). Young infants' retention of information about bisyllabic utterances. *Journal of Experimental Psychology: Human Perception and Performance*, **21**, 822–836.

Jusczyk, P.W., Kennedy, L.J., & Jusczyk, A.M. (1995). Young infants' retention of information about syllables. *Infant Behavior and Development*, **18**, 27–42.

Jusczyk, P.W., Luce, P.A., & Charles Luce, J. (1994). Infants' sensitivity to phonotactic patterns in the native language. *Journal of Memory and Language*, **33**, 630–645.

Jusczyk, P.W., Newsome, M., & Houston, D. (manuscript in preparation). The beginnings of word segmentation in English-learning infants.

Jusczyk, P.W., Pisoni, D.B., & Mullennix, J. (1992). Some consequences of stimulus variability on speech processing by 2-month-old infants. *Cognition*, **43**, 253–291.

Jusczyk, P.W., Pisoni, D.B., Reed, M., Fernald, A., & Myers, M. (1983). Infants' discrimination of the duration of a rapid spectrum change in nonspeech signals. *Science*, **222**, 175–177.

Jusczyk, P.W., Pisoni, D.B., Walley, A.C., & Murray, J. (1980). Discrimination of the relative onset of two-component tones by infants. *Journal of the Acoustical Society of America*, **67**, 262–270.

Jusczyk, P.W., Rosner, B.S., Reed, M., & Kennedy, L.J. (1989). Could temporal order differences underlie 2-month-olds' discrimination of English voicing contrasts? *Journal of the Acoustical Society of America*, **85**, 1741–1749.

Kluender, K.R., Diehl, R.L., & Killeen, P.R. (1987). Japanese quail can learn phonetic categories. *Science*, **237**, 1195–1197.

Kuhl, P.K. (1976). Speech perception in early infancy: the acquisiton of speech sound categories. In S.K. Hirsh, D.H. Eldridge, I.J. Hirsh, & S.R. Silverman (Eds.), *Hearing and*

Davis: Essays honoring Hallowell Davis (pp. 265–280). St Louis: Washington University Press.

Kuhl, P.K. (1979). Speech perception in early infancy: Perceptual constancy for spectrally dissimilar vowel categories. *Journal of the Acoustical Society of America, 66*, 1668–1679.

Kuhl, P.K. (1981). Discrimination of speech by nonhuman animals: Basic auditory sensitivities conducive to the perception of speech-sound categories. *Journal of the Acoustical Society of America, 70*, 340–349.

Kuhl, P.K. (1983). Perception of auditory equivalence classes for speech in early infancy. *Infant Behavior and Development, 6*, 263–285.

Kuhl, P.K. (1991). Human adults and human infants show a "perceptual magnet effect" for the prototypes of speech categories, monkeys do not. *Perception & Psychophysics, 50*, 93–107.

Kuhl, P.K. (1993). Innate predispositions and the effects of experience in speech perception: The native language magnet theory. In B. de Boysson-Bardies, S. de Schonen, P. Jusczyk, P. McNeilage, & J. Morton (Eds.), *Developmental neurocognition: Speech and face processing in the first year of life* (pp. 259–274). Dordrecht: Kluwer.

Kuhl, P.K., & Miller, J.D. (1975). Speech perception by the chinchilla: voiced-voiceless distinction in alveolar plosive consonants. *Science, 190*, 69–72.

Kuhl, P.K., & Miller, J.D. (1978). Speech perception by the chinchilla: Identification functions for synthetic VOT stimuli. *Journal of the Acoustical Society of America, 63*, 905–917.

Kuhl, P.K., & Miller, J.D. (1982). Discrimination of auditory target dimensions in the presence or absence of variation in a second dimension by infants. *Perception & Psychophysics, 31*, 279–292.

Kuhl, P.K., & Padden, D.M. (1982). Enhanced discriminability at the phonetic boundaries for the voicing feature in macaques. *Perception & Psychophysics, 32*, 542–550.

Kuhl, P.K., & Padden, D.M. (1983). Enhanced discriminability at the phonetic boundaries for the place feature in macaques. *Journal of the Acoustical Society of America, 73*, 1003–1010.

Kuhl, P.K., Williams, K.A., Lacerda, F., Stevens, K.N., & Lindblom, B. (1992). Linguistic experiences alter phonetic perception in infants by 6 months of age. *Science, 255*, 606–608.

Lacerda, F. (1992). *Does young infants' vowel perception favor high/low contrasts?* Paper presented at the *XXV International Congress of Psychology*, Brussels, Belgium.

Lasky, R.E., Syrdal-Lasky, A., & Klein, R.E. (1975). VOT discrimination by four to six and a half month old infants from Spanish environments. *Journal of Experimental Child Psychology, 20*, 215–225.

Lehiste, I., Olive, J.P., & Streeter, L. (1976). The role of duration in disambiguating syntactically ambiguous sentences. *Journal of the Acoustical Society of America, 60*, 1199–1202.

Levitt, A., Jusczyk, P.W., Murray, J., & Carden, G. (1988). The perception of place of articulation contrasts in voiced and voiceless fricatives by two-month-old infants. *Journal of Experimental Psychology: Human Perception and Performance, 14*, 361–368.

Lisker, L., & Abramson, A.S. (1970). The voicing dimension: Some experiments in comparative phonetics, *Proceedings of the Sixth International Congress of Phonetic Sciences*. Prague: Academia.

Lively, S., & Pisoni, D.B. (1993). An examination of the "perceptual magnet" effect. *Journal of the Acoustical Society of America, 93*, 2423.

Mandel, D.R., Jusczyk, P.W., & Kemler Nelson, D.G. (1994). Does sentential prosody help infants to organize and remember speech information? *Cognition, 53*, 155–180.

Mandel, D.R., Kemler Nelson, D.G., & Jusczyk, P.W. (1996). Infants remember the order of words in a spoken sentence. *Cognitive Development, 11*, 181–196.

Markman, E.M. (1991). The whole-object, taxonomic, and mutual exclusivity assumptions as initial constraints on word meanings. In S.A. Gelman & J.P. Byrnes (Eds.), *Perspectives on language and thought* (pp. 72–106). Cambridge: Cambridge University Press.

Marks, L., & Miller, G.A. (1964). The role of semantic and syntactic constraints in the memorisation of English sentences. *Journal of Verbal Learning and Verbal Behavior, 3*, 1–5.

Martin, C.S., Mullennix, J.W., Pisoni, D.B., & Summers, W.V. (1989). Effects of talker variability on recall of spoken word lists. *Journal of Experimental Psychology: Learning, Memory, and Cognition, 15*, 676–684.

Mehler, J., Jusczyk, P.W., Lambertz, G., Halsted, N., Bertoncini, J., & Amiel-Tison, C. (1988). A precursor of language acquisition in young infants. *Cognition, 29*, 144–178.

Miller, G.A., & Isard, S. (1963). Some perceptual consequences of linguistic rules. *Journal of Verbal Learning and Verbal Behavior, 2*, 217–228.

Miller, J.L., & Eimas, P.D. (1983). Studies on the categorisation of speech by infants. *Cognition, 13*, 135–165.

Miller, J.L., & Liberman, A.M. (1979). Some effects of later-occurring information on the perception of stop consonant and semivowel. *Perception & Psychophysics, 25*, 457–465.

Miyawaki, K., Strange, W., Verbrugge, R., Liberman, A.M., Jenkins, J.J., & Fujimura, O. (1975). An effect of linguistic experience: The discrimination of /r/ and /l/ by native speakers of Japanese and English. *Perception & Psychophysics, 18*, 331–340.

Moffitt, A.R. (1971). Consonant cue perception by twenty-to-twenty-four-week old infants. *Child Development, 42*, 717–731.

Morgan, J.L. (1986). *From simple input to complex grammar*. Cambridge, MA: MIT Press.

Morgan, J.L. (1996). A rhythmic bias in preverbal speech segmentation. *Journal of Memory and Language, 35*, 666–688.

Morgan, J.L., Allopenna, P., & Shi, R. (1996). Perceptual bases of rudimentary grammatical categories: Toward a broader conception of bootstrapping. In J.L. Morgan & K. Demuth (Eds.), *Signal to syntax* (pp. 263–283). Mahwah, NJ: Erlbaum.

Morgan, J.L., & Demuth, K. (Eds.) (1996). *Signal to syntax*. Mahwah, NJ: Erlbaum.

Morgan, J.L., & Saffran, J.R. (1995). Emerging integration of sequential and suprasegmental information in preverbal speech segmentation. *Child Development, 66*, 911–936.

Morse, P.A. (1972). The discrimination of speech and nonspeech stimuli in early infancy. *Journal of Experimental Child Psychology, 13*, 477–492.

Myers, J., Jusczyk, P.W., Kemler Nelson, D.G., Charles Luce, J., Woodward, A., & Hirsh-Pasek, K. (1996). Infants' sensitivity to word boundaries in fluent speech. *Journal of Child Language, 23*, 1–30.

Nakatani, L., & Dukes, K. (1977). Locus of segmental cues for word juncture. *Journal of the Acoustical Society of America, 62*, 714–719.

Peters, A. (1983). *The units of language acquisition*. Cambridge: Cambridge University Press.

Pisoni, D.B. (1973). Auditory and phonetic memory codes in the discrimination of consonants and vowels. *Perception & Psychophysics, 13*, 253–260.

Pisoni, D.B. (1977). Identification and discrimination of the relative onset of two component tones: Implications for voicing perception in stops. *Journal of the Acoustical Society of America, 61*, 1352–1361.

Polka, L., & Werker, J.F. (1994). Developmental changes in perception of non-native vowel contrasts. *Journal of Experimental Psychology: Human Perception and Performance, 20*, 421–435.

Price, P.J., Ostendorf, M., Shattuck-Hufnagel, S., & Fong, C. (1991). The use of prosody in syntactic disambiguation. *Journal of the Acoustical Society of America, 90*, 2956–2970.

Quine, W.V.O. (1960). *Word and object*. Cambridge, MA: MIT Press.

Rand, T.C. (1971). Vocal tract size normalisation in the perception of stop consonants. *Haskins Laboratories Status Report on Speech Research, 27*, 141–146.

Scott, D.R., & Cutler, A. (1984). Segmental phonology and the perception of syntactic structure. *Journal of Verbal Learning and Verbal Behavior*, **23**, 450–466.

Sinnott, J.M., Beecher, M.D., Moody, D.B., & Stebbins, W.C. (1976). Speech sound discrimination by monkeys and humans. *Journal of the Acoustical Society of America*, **60**, 687–695.

Stevens, K.N., Liberman, A.M., Studdert-Kennedy, M.G., & Ohman, S.E.G. (1969). Cross-language study of vowel perception. *Language and Speech*, **12**, 1–23.

Streeter, L.A. (1976). Language perception of 2-month old infants shows effects of both innate mechanisms and experience. *Nature*, **259**, 39–41.

Suci, G. (1967). The validity of pause as an index of units in language. *Journal of Verbal Learning and Verbal Behavior*, **6**, 26–32.

Sussman, J.E., & Lauckner-Morano, V.J. (1995). Further tests of the "perceptual magnet effect" in the perception of [i]: Identification and change/no change discrimination. *Journal of the Acoustical Society of America*, **97**, 539–552.

Swoboda, P., Morse, P.A., & Leavitt, L.A. (1976). Continuous vowel discrimination in normal and at-risk infants. *Child Development*, **47**, 459–465.

Trehub, S.E. (1973). Infants' sensitivity to vowel and tonal contrasts. *Developmental Psychology*, **9**, 91–96.

Trehub, S.E. (1976). The discrimination of foreign speech contrasts by infants and adults. *Child Development*, **47**, 466–472.

Tsushima, T., Takizawa, O., Sasaki, M., Siraki, S., Nishi, K., Kohno, M., Menyuk, P., & Best, C. (1994). *Discrimination of English /r-l/ and /w-y/ by Japanese infants at 6–12 months: Language-specific developmental changes in speech perception abilities*. Paper presented at the *International Conference on Spoken Language Processing*, Yokohama, Japan.

Verbrugge, R.R., Strange, W., Shankweiler, D.P., & Edman, T.R. (1976). What information enables a listener to map a talker's vowel space? *Journal of the Acoustical Society of America*, **60**, 198–212.

Waters, R.S., & Wilson, W.A. (1976). Speech perception by rhesus monkeys: The voicing distinction in synthesized labial and velar stop consonants. *Perception & Psychophysics*, **19**, 285–289.

Werker, J.F., Gilbert, J.H., Humphrey, K., & Tees, R.C. (1981). Developmental aspects of cross-language speech perception. *Child Development*, **52**, 349–355.

Werker, J.F., & Lalonde, C.E. (1988). Cross-language speech perception: Initial capabilities and developmental change. *Developmental Psychology*, **24**, 672–683.

Werker, J.F., & Tees, R.C. (1983). Developmental changes across childhood in the perception of non-native speech sounds. *Canadian Journal of Psychology*, **37**, 278–286.

Werker, J.F., & Tees, R.C. (1984). Cross-language speech perception: Evidence for perceptual reorganisation during the first year of life. *Infant Behavior and Development*, **7**, 49–63.

Williams, L. (1977). The voicing contrast in Spanish. *Journal of Phonetics*, **5**, 169–184.

Woodward, J.Z., & Aslin, R.N. (1990). *Segmentation cues in maternal speech to infants*. Paper presented at the *7th biennial meeting of the International Conference on Infant Studies*, Montreal, Quebec, Canada.

ACKNOWLEDGEMENTS

Preparation of this chapter was facilitated by a Research Grant to Peter W. Jusczyk from NICHD (#15795) and by support for Mara Goodman on a Training Grant from NIDCD (00035).

CHAPTER TWELVE

Three methods for testing infant speech perception

Janet F. Werker, Rushen Shi and Renee Desjardins
University of British Columbia, Vancouver, Canada

Judith E. Pegg
Centre for Community Child Health Research,
Vancouver, Canada

Linda Polka
School of Communication Sciences & Disorders, McGill
University, Montreal, Canada

Michelle Patterson
University of British Columbia, Vancouver, Canada

INTRODUCTION

There are many different procedures that can be used for testing speech perception capabilities in young infants. These include behavioural methods, psychophysiological methods, and methods that assess brain responses. The purpose of this chapter is to present and describe three different behavioural methods that we currently use for testing speech perception capabilities in infants. These methods are the conditioned head-turn (CHT) procedure, visual habituation (VH), and the high-amplitude sucking (HAS) procedure. These three measures are commonly used in many different labs around the world. By focusing on these methods, we hope to provide not just another description of particular methods, but also to highlight the link between the research question of interest and the selection of an appropriate method to answer that question. Our laboratory investigations have always been driven first and foremost by a particular research question. With this question in mind, we then seek a method that will best address that question. Finding a match between theory and methodology has even meant modifying existing procedures or developing new tasks.

THE CONDITIONED HEAD-TURN (CHT) PROCEDURE

The first procedure that was used in our laboratory was the CHT procedure. When the first author (JFW) began her research in the area of cross-language speech perception, the literature suggested that infants are born with the ability to discriminate the universal set of phonetic contrasts and that experience with a specific language serves to narrow infants' discriminatory capabilities. Although this suggestion was indeed provocative, it was based on research with infants using either high-amplitude sucking or heart rate deceleration techniques, and on research with adults using labelling tasks. It was possible, therefore, that the tasks used for testing infants were more sensitive than those used for testing adults and that it was a difference in methodology, rather than a difference in perceptual sensitivity between infants and adults, that had been revealed. A procedure was needed that could be adapted with only minor modifications for testing people from infancy through adulthood on their ability to discriminate native and non-native phonetic contrasts.

The CHT procedure is one of the most versatile procedures for testing people of different ages. It is based on the premise that a more accurate picture of sensory and perceptual capabilities will be obtained if we engage subjects in a task that is fun and rewards them for correct responses. In the infant version of this procedure, the infant learns to turn his/her head to a sound or to a change in sounds. The infant sits on the caregiver's lap across the table from an experimental assistant. To keep the infant interested, the assistant quietly shows the infant brightly coloured toys. An audio speaker and dark Plexiglas box are located to one side of the parent/infant. Speech stimuli are presented over the speaker. The infant is taught to turn his/her head in the direction of the Plexiglas box whenever she detects a change in a speech stimulus (or stimuli). When the baby makes a correct head-turn, the dark box is illuminated and animated toy animals are displayed. The assistant also smiles and praises the infant. Incorrect head-turns are not reinforced.

The CHT procedure is used most widely with infants between 5.5 and 18 months of age, but it is most ideal for infants between roughly 6 and 10 or 12 months of age. Between 6 and 10 months the infant is a "captive audience" and is not easily bored by the reinforcer. Beginning at roughly 11 months, some infants' mobility increases and they are less content to sit quietly on the parent's lap for long periods of time. These older infants can become bored with the visual reinforcer and thus appropriate social reinforcement becomes even more critical. Also, varying the visual reinforcer across the test session can help maintain interest in the task with these older infants.

As well as testing infants, the basic head-turn procedure can also be adapted to test children and adults. To test adults and older children (roughly 5 years and up), the head-turn response is generally replaced with a hand signal. Minimal instructions are given if direct comparison with infant data is of interest. With younger children (between roughly 2 and 5 years), the head-turn response can be replaced with a button or bar press. The visual reinforcer may be adequate to engage some young children in the task; however, success depends on age-appropriate social praise and encouragement provided by an assistant. In addition, a tangible reward (small toy or sticker) given after a block of trials may be needed to maintain cooperation in the task. These adjustments make the CHT procedure a useful tool for studying both infant perceptual abilities and developmental changes in these abilities across the life span.

Babies typically cannot be conditioned to perform reliable short-latency head-turns before they are about 5.5 months of age. However, there are behaviours that infants 5 months and younger display in response to sound, such as eye-widening, eyebrow movements, or a global pause in ongoing activity. Recent studies show that these behaviours, like the head-turn response, can also be conditioned (e.g. Olsho, Koch, Halpin, & Carter, 1987). To do so, the experimenter is trained to judge whether the baby has heard a change (experimental trials) or no change (control trials) by attending to any behaviour emitted by the baby. Although this modification to the procedure shows promise as a technique for assessing speech perception in very young infants, in our laboratory we have used the CHT procedure only with infants 5.5 months of age and older. As will be noted later, we have also used the several variations that can be used with toddlers, children, and adults.

Implementing the CHT procedure

The CHT procedure was originally developed from "peep show audiometry" designed by Dix and Hallpike (1947) and Suzuki and Ogiba (1960) for assessing auditory perception in children. In "peep show audiometry" children are reinforced with a live model for correctly detecting the presentation of a sound. In this way, auditory thresholds can be assessed. The procedure was subsequently modified by Eilers, Wilson, and Moore (1977) and later by Kuhl (1985) for assessing auditory and speech perception in infants (see also Polka, Jusczyk, & Rvachew, 1995).[1]

The CHT procedure is implemented slightly differently in almost every laboratory in which it is used. In our laboratory, the mother/infant pair and the experimental assistant (E1) are seated inside a sound-attenuated booth. A second experimenter (E2), situated outside the booth, operates the computer and observes the infant through either a one-way glass or a closed-circuit television (see Figs. 12.1 and 12.2).

The parent and E1 both wear headphones delivering music so they cannot hear the stimuli being presented to the infant. E2 presses a button whenever the infant is in a state of readiness (watching, but not totally engaged in the toys being shown by the assistant). The computer is programmed to select either an experimental trial (a change in the speech stimulus) or a control trial (no change in the stimulus). E2 monitors the infant's behaviour and pushes a button if a head-turn occurs. In our instrumentation of the procedure, this button press is recorded by the computer.

The procedure typically involves several stages. There is an initial *training stage* (designed to familiarise the infant with the reinforcer) wherein the visual reinforcer is activated immediately after the first presentation of a new stimulus. Following a specified criterion number of trials in this first stage (typically 3–8), the *conditioning stage* begins. During conditioning, every trial is a "change" trial. It is E2's job to gradually "condition" or "shape" the infant to turn toward the reinforcer. Thus, during the first few trials, E2 will turn the reinforcer on immediately following the presentation of a change trial; E2 then gradually increases the delay across trials to give the infant an opportunity to initiate a head-turn on his or her own. Once the infant has performed a criterion number

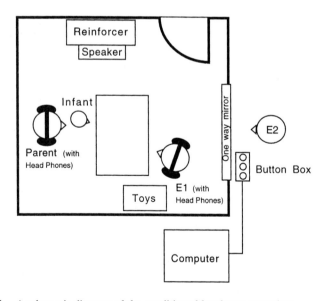

FIG. 12.1.   A schematic diagram of the conditioned head-turn procedure.

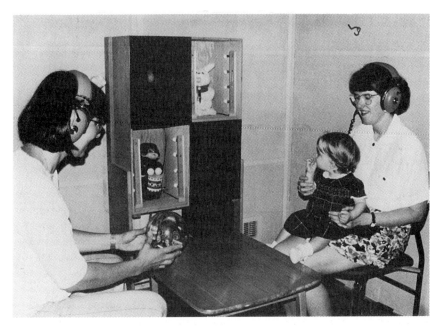

FIG. 12.2. Madeleine performing in the conditioned head-turn procedure.

of anticipatory head-turns (we require 3 in a row), the *testing phase* begins. During the testing phase, the computer randomly presents experimental and control trials. E2 does not know the trial type during any observation interval; his/her task is to monitor the infant's behaviour and push a button when the infant makes a head-turn. If that button-press has occurred within a criterion window (4–6 seconds, allowing the infant to hear 3 change stimuli), the reinforcer is activated and a "Hit" is recorded. If no head-turn occurs and thus no button press, there is no feedback and a "Miss" is recorded. "Correct Rejections" occur when an infant inhibits a head-turn during a control trial and "False Alarms" occur when the infant turns his/her head during a control trial.

The data can be analysed in many different ways. The dependent variable can be treated as continuous, allowing analysis of overall percent correct responses or simply percent correct head-turns to change trials. Using either of these dependent variables, *t*-tests or analysis of variance can be conducted to look for group differences. Single-group *t*-tests can also be used to ascertain whether the performance of any particular group of subjects is greater than chance. To correct for different response strategies among infants, hits can be compared to false alarms in a variety of ways; we typically compute an A′ that can be analysed using *t*-tests or

ANOVA. Alternatively, the dependent variable can be treated as discrete by setting a criterion performance level to ascertain whether individual infants can or cannot discriminate a particular stimulus set (we typically use 7 out of 8 continuous correct responses achieved at some point during a sequence of 25 test trials). The resulting categorical data can be analysed using techniques such as χ^2, analysis of proportions, or randomisation tests. Furthermore, the relationship between individual differences in speech perception and other developmental events can be investigated by entering criterion data into a regression or causal modelling analysis (see Lalonde & Werker, 1995 for an example).

As you might imagine, many infants really enjoy this procedure. Unlike other procedures where the infant is a passive observer, the infant is able to make things happen in the CHT procedure. Infants who are interested in participating quickly learn the association between the sound change and activation of the reinforcer. Some infants quickly lose interest in the reinforcer, but still seem to enjoy their ability to "make it come on" by turning their head at the right time. These infants swing their head around when the sound changes and immediately look back to E1 for a smile and praise. Other infants point in the direction of the toy animals while they turn their heads, and still others clap for themselves following successful head-turns! On the other hand, some of the infants we test are not at all interested in this game and refuse to participate (see the section on strengths and limitations). On occasion, we test an infant who finds the animated toy animals frightening rather than rewarding. For these infants, we keep a still toy animal in one compartment of the Plexiglas box. This animal is illuminated, but is not activated following correct head-turns.

Questions addressed using the CHT procedure

The conditioned head-turn procedure originated as a technique for conducting audiological assessment with infants and continues to serve as a standard technique for clinical evaluation of auditory acuity in infants and for psychophysical research in infant audition. The procedure has been adapted for assessing infants' perception of musical structure by Trehub and colleagues (Trehub, Bull, & Thorpe, 1984). As mentioned earlier, and of particular interest to us, this procedure has also allowed researchers to investigate infant speech perception. One such speech perception phenomenon involves *discrimination*, the ability to detect differences between speech stimuli (e.g. two different consonants or vowels). For example, to determine whether infants can discriminate syllables, a background (or referent) syllable is presented repeatedly to the infant (e.g. /da, da, da/); when the infant is in a ready state, the presented signal changes to a different syllable (e.g. /ta, ta, ta/). If the infant can hear the difference between the two syllables, he/she will learn to make a head-turn when the syllable changes.

We used the CHT procedure to examine experiential influences on non-native speech perception by comparing younger infants, older infants, children, and adults on their ability to discriminate non-native consonant or vowel distinctions. In our initial work (Werker, Gilbert, Humphrey & Tees, 1981), we compared English-learning infants of ages 6–8 months with both English- and Hindi-speaking adults on their ability to discriminate the following distinctions: (1) two consonant distinctions that are used in Hindi but not in English, and (2) one consonant distinction that is used in both languages. We found that the English-learning 6–8 month olds could discriminate native and non-native contrasts equally well, but that the English-speaking adults had difficulty with the non-English (i.e. Hindi) contrasts. We then used the button-press variation of the procedure to test English-learning children of 4, 8, and 12 years of age on the Hindi contrasts. We found that children of all three ages had difficulty with the Hindi distinctions; interestingly, the youngest children had the most difficulty of all. To ensure that the test was appropriate for 4-year-olds, we also included an English contrast; the 4-year-olds had no difficulty with this. We also tested Hindi-learning 4-year-olds and found they could discriminate the Hindi contrasts with ease. Finally, we tested children younger than 4 years of age. We began pilot-testing with children aged between 6 months and 4 years using the head-turn, button-press, and bar-pressing versions of the CHT procedure. We hypothesised that important changes are occurring within the first year of life and then focused on testing infants aged 6–8, 8–10, and 10–12 months, all with the CHT procedure. We found that 6- to 8-month-olds perform better than both 10- to 12-month-olds and adults on their ability to discriminate non-native phonetic distinctions (Werker & Tees, 1984). This finding of a developmental decline in sensitivity between 6–8 months and 10–12 months of age suggests that infants begin life with language-general speech perception capabilities and gradually focus selectively on the specific variation that characterises speech sounds in their native language. We have subsequently used the CHT procedure to replicate and extend this initial finding in a number of ways (see Pegg & Werker, 1997; Polka & Werker, 1994; Werker & Desjardins, 1994).

Another speech perception phenomenon investigated using this procedure involves *categorisation*, the ability to perceive exemplars from different categories as distinct and exemplars from the same category as similar. To determine if infants can group speech stimuli in the same manner as adults, we present infants with several different exemplars of one category as the background stimuli and, on change trials, we present several different exemplars of a new category. If infants treat the within-category variants as similar and the cross-category variants as different, they will only turn their heads on change trials. Several studies have clearly demonstrated that infants can discriminate speech sounds on the basis of category identity even when they are unable to discriminate the within-category variants. Such findings show that infants can form equivalence classes that match adult perceptual categories. For example, using syn-thesised speech, Kuhl (1983) showed that 6-month-olds can treat multiple exemplars of /i/ as similar to each other and different from a set of exemp-lars of /a/ even though each set consisted of different pitches (rising, falling) and voices (male, female, child) that were discriminable to these infants. In contrast, infants of this age failed to detect arbitrary categories that were constructed using the same stimuli. In a recent study, Bohn and Polka (1995) used the category change paradigm with modified natural syllables to explore the acoustic determinants of vowel identity in young infants.

Kuhl (Grieser & Kuhl, 1989; Kuhl, 1991) has used the CHT procedure in a slightly different way to examine the internal structure of phonetic categories. She has found that, for at least some synthesised stimulus sets, subjects show differences in their ability to discriminate instances from the same category depending on whether a "good" or a "bad" exemplar of the category is presented as the background (or referent). Adults are initially presented with several exemplars of a category and are asked to judge the quality of each exemplar on a numerical scale. Those exemplars judged as the best representatives of the category are considered "good" exemplars. Next, adults are tested in the head-turn procedure controlling for the order of presentation of two exemplars. Evidence of a "perceptual magnet effect" is provided when adults discriminate variations in the two exemplars of the vowel /i/ more easily when a "poor" instance of /i/ is presented as the referent than when a "good" instance of /i/ is used as the referent. The greater generalisation (i.e. poorer discrimination) associated with the "good" exemplar is taken as evidence that, within a vowel cate-gory, a "good" exemplar acts like a perceptual magnet to organise the phonetic category. Because infants showed the same pattern of discrimi-nation results as adults, it can be inferred that the phonetic category for this vowel is similarly structured for infants and for adults (Kuhl, Williams, Lacerde, Stevens, & Lindblom, 1992; see also Polka & Werker, 1994, and Polka & Bohn, 1996, for a related approach using natural speech).

Strengths and limitations of the procedure

A number of strengths contribute to the status of the conditioned head-turn procedure as a classic method for assessing perception of auditory information in infants. First, many procedures that are used to assess auditory perception in infants, such as the auditory brainstem response

(ABR), measure electrophysiological responses. Such measures are informative but, at present, provide a restricted view of auditory function. Furthermore, we cannot be confident that electrophysiological measures can be equated with functional hearing (see Hecox & Burkard, 1982, for a review). In contrast, the information gathered using the CHT procedure relies on behavioural responses from infants and can readily be accepted as a index of functional hearing.

It is imperative that the procedure be performed under conditions that control for test bias. Thus, it is essential that the parent and E1 both wear headphones delivering music so they cannot hear stimulus changes and potentially influence the infant to turn his/her head. It is also essential that E2 does not hear the stimuli and has no knowledge of whether a control or an experimental trial is occurring.

Secondly, a special feature of the CHT procedure is that, unlike many other behavioural procedures (e.g. habituation), the stimulus and the reinforcer are independent events. This means we can evaluate an infant's response to the test stimuli independently of his/her response to the reinforcer. Thus, we can more easily determine when the infant is having perceptual difficulty versus showing general disinterest or uncooperativeness. This is a tremendous advantage because it provides a way to design experiments that allow interpretation of the meaning of infants' failure to detect or discriminate auditory information.

A third important feature of the CHT procedure for both auditory assessment and perceptual research is that we can present multiple test trials to the same infant; this makes it possible to ascertain whether an individual infant can or cannot reliably detect or discriminate particular stimuli. Data on the perceptual abilities of individual infants contribute to the meaningfulness of the findings. Moreover, it allows the researcher to identify infants at risk for hearing loss or perceptual difficulties; it allows identification of potential developmental delays or aberrant patterns of development; it permits the implementation of a wide range of research designs; and it allows the researcher to study how performance on auditory or speech perception tasks varies with performance on other tasks or whether it predicts later emerging competencies (see, for example, Lalonde & Werker, 1995). Furthermore, with slight modifications it is possible to use the CHT procedure across the life span. The strengths outlined make the CHT procedure a useful instrument for both cross-sectional and longitudinal studies of perceptual development.

Despite the significant strengths of the CHT procedure, this methodology is not without its weaknesses. At present, three major limitations can be identified, each of which may be overcome with further developments of the procedure. First, this procedure, like other infant procedures, is characterised by variable attrition rates (varying from 5% to 50%).

Attrition rates can be kept to a minimum if the researcher ensures that the reinforcer and behavioural response are age-appropriate. Nevertheless, individual infants differ in the ease with which they can be condition in the task. Thus, it is critical that the team of researchers testing the infants (E1 and E2) be carefully trained and be able to modify the timing of trials and the intensity of the social feedback in response to the needs and interests of each individual infant. Attrition rates increase when infants are tested with background and target stimuli that are difficult to discriminate.

A second limitation concerns the type of stimuli that can be studied using this methodology. The CHT procedure has proved to be a superb method for studying the perception of relatively short speech patterns, such as syllables, single and multisyllabic words, short melodic patterns, or brief trains of noise. However, it is generally not the method of choice to investigate discrimination or categorisation of speech patterns of longer duration, such as intonational patterns, sentential stress patterns, or discourse samples.

Finally, there are some inherent restrictions in the interpretations that can be drawn from studies using the CHT procedure. Researchers have designed innovative experiments from which we can draw inferences about more sophisticated abilities such as categorisation; however, it is important to realise that we cannot directly conclude "what" the infant perceived in the test procedure. Therefore, whether the infant recognised or identified the target and background stimuli in the same way as the adult subject or whether the infant has attached a specific meaning to the stimuli is still debatable.

Newer variations on the procedure

Several laboratories have attempted to modify this procedure from a discrimination task into an identification task. The basic approach has been to attempt to teach infants or children to make two different responses to two different kinds of stimuli (e.g. Burnham, Earnshaw, & Quinn, 1987; Kubaska & Aslin, 1985; Murphy, Shea, & Aslin, 1989). For purposes of illustration, we will briefly present the *two-choice* version of the procedure used by Murphy et al. (1989) with 3-year-old children. In this variation, 3-year-olds are seated either alone or with a parent, again in a sound-attenuated room. An audio speaker is situated directly in front of and slightly above the child. Two television monitors are in the room, one 45° to the left and one 45° to the right of the audio speaker. Short video clips, rather than animated toy animals, are used as reinforcers. The child is taught to point to one television monitor when he/she hears one kind of stimulus (e.g. a particular vowel) and to the other television monitor when he/she hears a contrasting stimulus (e.g. a different vowel). (See also

Burnham, Earnshaw, & Clark, 1991, for a similar kind of procedure used with slightly older children.)

There have also been attempts to assess identification abilities in infants by extending two-choice procedures to children under 3 years of age. Infants are required to turn their head to one side in response to one particular sound and to the other side in response to a second sound. These attempts have met with mixed success and there is disagreement as to their validity with infants (see Burnham, Earnshaw, & Clark, 1986, for a discussion of some of the problems).

A modification of the CHT procedure that functions somewhat like an identification procedure but can be used successfully with infants is the *noise detection technique* (Morgan, 1994). The set-up for this procedure is identical to that used in the CHT procedure and the logic of progressing through shaping, conditioning, and testing phases is maintained. However, in this procedure, infants are taught to turn their head to one side whenever they detect a particular sound (e.g. a buzz or click) inserted into speech rather than whenever they detect a change in the sound stimulus. Correct head-turns are reinforced, again, typically with animated illuminated toy animals. Morgan used response latency as a dependent variable as well as correct head-turns. Unlike the two-choice procedure described earlier, with the noise detection technique infants need only learn to turn their head in one direction in response to a particular sound. The fact that they need not learn two distinct responses for two different kinds of sounds may account for the greater success with this procedure. It should be noted, however, that learning a single response to a single sound is more easily understood as simple conditioning than as an ability to identify or "label" a particular sound.

The noise detection technique allows researchers to investigate whether some stimuli or sequences are more coherent than others. The logic follows from the click detection methods used in adult sentence processing: that is, infants will more readily detect a click at a boundary (e.g. a clause or phrase or syllable boundary) than when a click is inserted within a perceptual grouping. This technique can thus expand the range of questions that can be investigated with the CHT procedure. For example, using Morgan's modification, Morgan and Saffran (1995) found developmental changes between 6 and 9 months of age in the contextual variables that influence click detection. This modification allows researchers to investigate the influences of sentential level prosody, phrasal structure, and other grouping properties on infant speech processing. If infants can be taught to detect clicks, they may also be able to be taught to monitor for particular syllables or words. Used in this way, the technique may be considered similar to an identification task in ascertaining not just when infants can hear a change, but when they notice a particular syllable or word.

Summary

In summary, the conditioned head-turn procedure is a very useful procedure for assessing infant perceptual capabilities and for comparing infant capabilities to those of children and adults. It can be used to assess basic auditory sensitivities, perception of music and rhythm, and perception of speech. It provides data on detection, discrimination, categorisation, and perceptual grouping. Because it can be implemented with subjects of very different ages, it can be used to study developmental change and, because it can provide data on individual subjects, it can also be used to assess individual differences. Using this technique we have greatly increased our understanding of infant speech perception. With ongoing refinements and exciting new variations of the basic technique we can expect the conditioned head-turn procedure to remain one of the essential tools for the perceptual researcher and clinical audiologist.

THE VISUAL HABITUATION (VH) PROCEDURE

The VH procedure has been used for nearly four decades to test many aspects of infant visual perception (Cohen, 1969; Cohen & Menten, 1981; Kagan & Moss, 1965). Considerable research has been directed toward testing and describing the conditions under which the VH procedure yields the most reliable and interpretable results (see Cohen & Menten, 1981, for a review), including studies investigating the benefits of different types of control conditions (e.g. Bertenthal, Haith, & Campos, 1983). VH has consistently been proved more sensitive than many other behavioural techniques for revealing infants' discrimination capabilities (e.g. Humphrey & Tees, 1980). Infants' ability to categorise stimuli can also be assessed using this method and performance in habituation tasks can be used as a predictor of information processing capacity. It has also been shown to yield reliable results with infants as young as 6 weeks of age (Ames et. al., 1978). Thus, VH is a well-understood procedure that can be used reliably across the infancy period to address a number of issues.

The VH procedure is based on the premise that infants prefer novelty and thus will visually attend to a display when it is new. When presented with the same display over repeated trials, infants will become familiar with the display and it will no longer be novel. Infants' looking time will then decline and the experimenter can infer that habituation has occurred. At this time, infants in the experimental group will be presented with a new display. If they can discriminate it from the old display (and if they find the change interesting), looking time should increase. To ensure that the recovery in looking time is not merely random variation, a control group is usually included where there is no new display.

It was not until 1974 (Horowitz, 1975; but see also Kagan & Moss, 1965) that the vh procedure was first adapted for assessing infant auditory and speech discrimination abilities. Horowitz (see also Haith, 1986) provided empirical evidence that infants will look longer at a visual display when they are listening to an interesting auditory stimulus. With the establishment of this fundamental principle, the vh procedure could be extended to be used to assess auditory discrimination. The logic for assessing auditory discrimination is identical to that used in tests of visual discrimination: infants are presented with an auditory stimulus accompanied by a visual display. Initially, they attend visually to the display when the auditory stimulus is presented. (As will be shown later, in infant-controlled versions of the procedure, presentation of the auditory stimulus is made contingent on visual fixation on the display.) Over repeated presentations of a single auditory stimulus (or category of auditory or speech sounds), the infant becomes familiar with the sounds and visual fixation decreases. If a novel auditory stimulus is then presented, and if the infant can discriminate the new auditory stimulus as distinct from the old one, visual fixation should again increase.

Implementing the vh procedure

In the vh procedure the infant is seated either in an infant-seat or on the caregiver's lap directly facing a television monitor or, in the case of very young infants, the infant is held over the caregiver's shoulder facing the monitor (Fig. 12.3). The illumination of the testing room is dim and there is little else in the testing room to interest the infant. A red flashing light, either above the monitor or as part of the display on the screen, is used to attract the infant's attention to the screen. Once the experimenter determines that the infant is looking at the screen, the trial begins. A trial consists of a visual reinforcer, such as a checkerboard or a bull's eye, on the screen plus an auditory stimulus (e.g. the syllable /da/ presented repeatedly). The auditory stimulus is referred to as the habituation or familiarisation stimulus. In the *fully infant-controlled* version of this procedure, as long as the infant continues to look at the visual reinforcer on the screen, the infant hears the familiarisation stimulus. When the infant looks away from the screen, the experimenter signals the computer to end the trial and the combined visual and auditory stimuli are turned off. At this point, the red light is turned on and the cycle begins again.

On subsequent trials, the infant is again presented with the identical visual and auditory stimuli. The procedure continues in this way until the average duration of the infant's looking to the visual reinforcer decreases to a preset criterion; for example, until the average of three sequential looks is less than 50% of the average of the initial three looks. When the

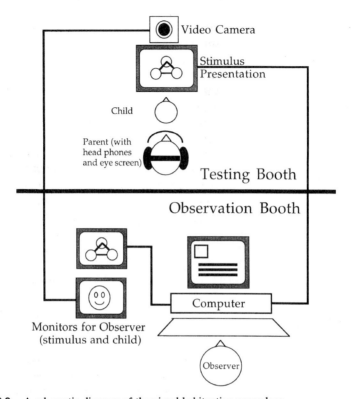

FIG. 12.3.   A schematic diagram of the visual habituation procedure.

habituation criterion has been met, a novel speech stimulus is presented on the next trial (e.g. the syllable /ta/ presented repeatedly). Parents and experimenters listen to masking music over headphones so that they cannot tell on which trial the novel speech stimulus occurs. As mentioned, following from the logic behind the habituation procedure, infants should show renewed interest (i.e. look longer) to the visual display if they discriminate the new sound, the dishabituation stimulus, from the old (familiarisation stimulus).

One way to analyse the data collected using the habituation procedure is to use repeated measures t-tests or analysis of variance to compare average looking time, across a group of infants, on the last few familiarisation trials (the criterion trials used to determine when habituation occurred) to the average looking time on the dishabituation trial(s). In some laboratories, infants are omitted from the analyses if they failed to reach the habituation criterion within a predetermined number of trials. If there is a significant increase in the duration of looking on the dishabituation trial relative to the preceding trials, then one can conclude that infants are able to discriminate the familiarisation and dishabituation stimuli.

A control condition in which infants are presented with the familiar stimulus in place of the novel stimulus on the dishabituation trial is an important component in the experimental design because infants may show spontaneous recovery of visual interest on the dishabituation trial – independent of the novelty of the speech stimulus. Data from the control group can be analysed in the same manner as the data from the experimental group. If infants in the control group fail to show a significant increase in looking time to the familiar stimulus on the dishabituation trial, then the researcher can feel confident that a significant increase in looking time to the dishabituation stimulus in the experimental group is due to the novelty of the speech stimulus and not due to spontaneous recovery.

It is also of interest to compare the mean looking time to the first few familiarisation trials during the habituation phase across different groups of infants. This may be useful in determining whether different familiarisation stimuli are equally interesting to the infants. Likewise, the mean looking time on the last few trials before the dishabituation trial can be compared across different conditions. Additionally, the number of trials required before the habituation criterion was met can be calculated as an index of how interested infants were in different familiarisation stimuli. Another way to compare across conditions is to measure the slope of the habituation curve; this method is useful for determining how quickly infants become familiar with different speech stimuli. Therefore, the VH procedure provides a rich source of data that can be analysed in various ways to provide different information.

Variations

Other than the aforementioned variations in seating arrangements, there are variations in the way the VH procedure is implemented. Earlier instantiations of the procedure typically involved two experimenters observing through peepholes to determine when the infant was looking at the screen. Typically, both experimenters had to indicate via a button-press that the infant was looking in order for a trial to begin. In this way a high degree of reliability could be obtained. This set-up is still used for testing very young infants whose eye movements are more difficult to track accurately (see Ames et al., 1978).

With older infants, current technology makes it possible to have only one observer watch the infant via a closed-circuit video camera, which relays the image to a monitor in an adjacent room. In this way, the experimenter is not required to be in the testing room and thus cannot inadvertently cue the infant; also, only one experimenter is required to run the procedure. A videorecording made at the time of testing allows for a second person to recode a portion of the sessions to establish the reliability of the experimenter. The availability of the videorecord also provides the opportunity to code other behaviours that occurred during testing, such as babbling or smiling.

It is also possible to modify the procedure in terms of length and number of trials. An experimenter may find it important that the infant hear on each trial the whole pattern or a discrete amount of the speech stream (e.g. an entire infant-directed utterance or list of words). To ensure that infants hear the whole segment, the experimenter would likely instantiate a *partially infant-controlled* version of the procedure. (A fully infant-controlled version was described earlier.) In this version, the trial would begin as usual when the infant looked at the screen but would continue until the end of the segment was reached regardless of whether the infant continued to look at the screen or looked away before the trial ended. Another variation is to pre-set the number of trials in which habituation must occur. For example, the researcher could set either a maximum or an absolute number of trials to be presented to all infants. An absolute number of trials ensures that all infants have the same amount of exposure to the familiarisation pattern before the dishabituation trial occurs. The data analyses can be carried out on all infants or only on those who showed a decrement in looking to a pre-set level within the allotted number of trials.

Yet another modification involves the presentation of two or more dishabituation trials in the same session with order of presentation counterbalanced across infants. In some instances, one of these trials may be the familiar stimulus (a control trial) and the other the novel stimulus. In other instances, there may be two trials of the same novel stimulus or two different novel stimuli. The data from this design can be treated as described earlier (i.e. testing for significant increases in looking time to each of the dishabituation stimuli relative to the last trials of the familiarisation stimulus) or the researcher can examine only the dishabituation trials to see if infants look significantly longer during the experimental trial than control trial. Although this modification has all the advantages of a within-subjects design, the obvious limitation is the need to include a sufficient number of infants in each group to adequately test for order effects. The type of speech stimulus used – a repeated single syllable, multisyllablic words, intonational patterns, discourse – and the research question will guide the experimenter's choice of modifications to the procedure.

Questions addressed using the VH procedure

We first implemented this procedure in our laboratory when we had equivocal results concerning *preference* for infant-directed over adult-directed speech in infants of 6–7 weeks of age (Pegg, Werker, & McLeod, 1992). We were concerned that perhaps infants were unable to show a preference for one type of speech over the other because they might not even be able to discriminate the two styles of speaking. Because it is known for its sensitivity in revealing fine discriminatory abilities, the VH procedure was selected to test infants' ability to discriminate infant-directed from adult-directed speech. Using the VH procedure, we obtained robust evidence that infants aged 6–7 weeks can discriminate these two speaking styles; this was evident from greater recovery of looking time for infants in the experimental conditions (change in speaking style between the familiarisation and test period) in comparison to infants in the control conditions (same speaking style in both the familiarisation and test phases). Furthermore, we obtained indirect evidence that 6- to 8 week-olds prefer infant-directed speech: infants who were familiarised to adult-directed speech showed greater recovery in the switch to infant-directed speech than did infants who were tested in the reverse direction (familiarised to infant-directed and then switched to adult-directed) (see Pegg et al., 1992).

The second time we decided to use the VH procedure was in a study of age-related changes in the perception of non-native vowel contrasts. Using the CHT procedure that we had used in previous studies of cross-language consonant perception, Polka and Werker (1994) found that only about half the English-learning infants aged 6 months could discriminate the two non-English (German) vowel contrasts of interest. Research by others (e.g. Kuhl et al., 1992) raised the possibility that infants might become tuned to the characteristics of native vowels at a younger age than is typically found for consonants. If this were true, then perhaps the reason only about half the English-learning 6-month-olds could discriminate the German vowels was because they were already losing their sensitivity to "universal" vowel categories. If this explanation is correct, the developmental progression for vowels would be identical to that for consonants, only occurring earlier – a movement from broad-based sensitivity to the universal set of vowel distinctions to a more limited sensitivity to only those vowel contrasts that are used in the native language. The alternative possibility is that vowels are perceived differently than consonants. In this case, the developmental progression of vowel perception might begin with a vowel space that has little or no organisation in the very young infant; therefore, experience with the native language would be required to establish phonetic categories. If the first explanation is correct, we would expect English-learning infants younger than 6 months to discriminate the

German vowels. If the second explanation is correct, we would expect infants younger than 6 months to perform even more poorly than the 6-month-olds on their discrimination of the German vowels.

To tease apart these hypotheses, we needed a reliable and sensitive procedure for assessing phonetic discrimination in infants younger than 6 months, but that could also be employed in identical form with 6-month-olds. We selected the VH procedure to test English-learning infants at both 4 and 6 months of age on their ability to discriminate both the German and an English vowel contrast. In this study, all infants were habituated to multiple instances from one category of vowels and were then given two test trials: the first test trial involved the presentation of vowels from the contrasting category, whereas the second test trial involved the presentation of vowels from the same category.

Using the VH procedure we found that English-learning 4-month-olds perform better than English-learning 6-month-olds on the two German vowel contrasts. These results are consistent with the first hypothesis discussed: infants are born with the ability to discriminate the universal set of vowel contrasts and experience with a particular language serves to reduce discrimination performance on non-native vowels. This finding parallels that shown for consonants, but just occurs at an earlier age (see Polka & Bohn, 1996, for additional data). Only by using a procedure that can be used in identical form with both 4- and 6-month-olds were we able to obtain and be confident with these findings.

Several other researchers have used VH to assess infant speech perception. It has been used to assess infants' ability to discriminate (Best, 1995; Best, McRoberts, & Sithole, 1988; Cohen, Diehl, Oakes, & Loehlin, 1992) and categorise (Eimas & Miller, 1992; Fowler, Best, & McRoberts, 1990; Miller & Eimas, 1996) syllables differing in single phonetic features. As it can also be used to assess perception of longer passages, it has also been used to assess discrimination of gender (Miller, 1983) and of passages of the native versus an unfamiliar language (Mehler et al., 1988).

Strengths and limitations of the procedure

The habituation procedure has many strengths. It is relatively easy to implement, experimenters can be trained quickly, and with the use of current technology only one experimenter is required at the testing session for all but very young infants.

Unlike the CHT procedure, the experimenter does not have to train or condition the infant to make a response when he/she notices a change in the stimulus. Rather, this procedure capitalises on infants' tendency to look at a visual stimulus in the presence of an interesting auditory stimulus. Because even very young infants exhibit this looking behaviour, this procedure can be used with infants throughout the first year of life. In her work, Best has used the habituation procedure to test toddlers and even adults (Best et al., 1988).

As well as being suited to use with many ages with only slight modifications in seating arrangements, this procedure is suitable for studying discrimination of a wide variety of speech stimuli. Like the CHT procedure, the habituation procedure can be used to study consonant or vowel discrimination, single or multisyllabic words, and other short patterns. The habituation procedure can also be used to study discrimination of longer patterns such as intonational contours, stress patterns, and different styles of speaking (e.g. infant-directed vs. adult-directed). Virtually any speech discrimination can be studied with small adaptations to the habituation procedure. With the combined advantages of use with a wide age-range and a large range of speech stimuli to be discriminated, the habituation procedure is a very practical and flexible tool for speech perception research.

As with most experimental methods, there are some weaknesses in the habituation procedure. Its chief limitation is that, unlike the CHT procedure, an individual infant's data cannot easily be examined independently from group data. Typically, the researcher only describes the discrimination behaviour of infants as a group. In many cases, this is sufficient. Where it is not sufficient, techniques have been developed to allow investigators to infer whether or not individual infants show discrimination (e.g. Werker & Lalonde, 1988). Researchers have examined the shape of the habituation function and the degree of preference for novelty as indices of individual differences. However, the VH procedure requires larger numbers of infants than does the CHT procedure to assess individual performance, and the statistical techniques used for comparing individual infants are not fully agreed on by the research community.

As with other infant procedures, attrition rates may be high in the VH procedure, especially for young infants whose states change quickly and for toddlers who might find it hard to stay on their parents' lap for the duration of testing. However, when the number of trials and/or habituation criterion as well as the interest value of the stimuli are carefully matched to the infant's developmental level, the attrition rate can be substantially lowered.

One difficulty associated with the VH procedure is the interpretation of negative findings. In the CHT procedure, infants are reinforced for responding correctly to a change in the stimulus with a display of toy animals and praise. In the VH procedure, the novelty of the new stimulus itself is the only reward. This raises the possibility that infants may notice that the discrimination stimulus differs from the familiarisation stimulus, but may not be motivated to "show" the experimenter because the infant does not find the novel stimulus sufficiently different or attractive to warrant a longer look at the visual target. Despite these criticisms, the literature suggests that the VH procedure is sensitive and flexible enough to test many questions of interest; and, indeed, this procedure has generated a great deal of exciting research.

Newer variations of the procedure

Recently the habituation procedure has been adapted in our laboratory (Desjardins & Werker, 1995, 1996) and in other laboratories (e.g. Burnham & Dodd, 1996; Rosenblum, Schmuckler, & Johnson, 1997) for the study of audiovisual speech perception in infants. Many existing studies of bimodal speech perception in infants have asked whether or not infants can match the heard stimulus to the proper articulatory movements. To answer this question, researchers use a preference technique wherein infants are shown two visual displays of a person articulating a syllable while an acoustic syllable that matches one of the two displays is presented over a central speaker. Looking behaviour is coded to see if infants look preferentially to the side that matches the audible syllable (see Kuhl & Meltzoff, 1982).

Although the preferential-looking technique examines infants' ability to *match* the correct visual display with the presented sound, this method does not address whether or not infants integrate the audible and visual components of speech into a single, coherent percept. Previous research has revealed a fascinating phenomenon with both children and adults whereby the actual percept "heard" can be significantly altered by watching a speaker's mouth movements. For example, hearing the syllable /ba/ while watching a speaker mouth the syllable /da/ results in reports of a "heard" /ga/ (e.g. McGurk & MacDonald, 1976; Summerfield, 1979). Thus, what we "hear" is not determined solely by acoustic stimuli but is also affected by visual information. Speech perception appears to be a bimodal phenomenon.

To assess whether infants are similarly influenced by attending to a speaker's lip movements, a procedure other than a visual preference paradigm was required. The required procedure would have to allow comparison of the percept infants experience when one visible articulation is paired with an audible signal to their percept when a different visible articulation is paired to that same audible signal. Researchers in three different laboratories simultaneously converged on variations in the VH procedure to address this problem (Burnham et al., in press; Desjardins & Werker, submitted; Rosenblum et al., 1997).

In our modification of the VH procedure to assess the question of visual influence on speech perception in infants, we familiarised infants to a synchronised presentation of a woman's face and voice articulating the syllable /bi/ (for one group of infants) or /vi/ (for a second group of infants). On reaching the habituation criterion, both groups of infants were given a dishabituation (test) trial of a mismatched audiovisual syllable, an auditory /bi/ paired with a visual /vi/. We found that female infants familiarised to an audiovisual /bi/ showed renewed visual interest to the audio /bi/-visual /vi/, but infants familiarised to an audiovisual /vi/ did not renew interest (Desjardins & Werker, 1996). We also included a control group of infants who were presented with the familiarisation stimulus on the dishabituation trial. As expected, this group of infants did not show renewed visual interest on the dishabituation trial. The results suggest that female 4-month-olds, like adults, perceive the audio /bi/-visual /vi/ as /vi/ – that is, their percept is captured by the visual /vi/; however, this effect was not found with male 4-month-olds.

Using a slightly different design, Rosenblum et al. (1997) habituated infants to only the lower half of the speaker's face; these authors have also shown that young infants' perception of speech is influenced by attending to the visible articulation. Using multiple trials, Burnham & Dodd (1996) are examining which audio and visual cues infants find most distinguishing. These recent endeavours support a growing body of literature that suggests that infant speech perception is very much influenced by both audio and visual aspects of speech.

The VH procedure can also be extended to examine other aspects of speech and language processing. For example, several members of our laboratory have been collaborating with Les Cohen (co-author of Chapter 6) to modify the VH procedure to investigate infants' early word-learning (Werker, Cohen, Lloyd, Casasola, & Stager, in press). In this modification of the VH procedure, we habituate infants to words paired with objects and test infants on their ability to detect a switch in word–object pairings. Although very young infants can rapidly learn the characteristics of either the words or the objects in the procedure, it is not until about 14 months of age that infants show reliable evidence of linking the word to the object. In summary, the VH procedure is a very versatile procedure that has been extensively used in many different applications to address infants' ability to process speech.

THE HIGH-AMPLITUDE SUCKING (HAS) PROCEDURE

The focus of most of our laboratory research is on understanding the kinds of speech perception abilities young infants are born with and how these abilities change as a function of being exposed to and learning a particular language. To address this issue fully, it is essential to begin testing infants at as young an age as possible. Even though newborn infants have had exposure to at least some characteristics of the native language while still in the womb (Chapter 10), a procedure that would allow us to test neonates would enable us to understand more fully how initial biases and perceptual experience work together to prepare an infant to acquire the native language. The techniques we typically use to test older infants rely on behavioural responses; thus we wanted to select a technique for testing newborns that would also rely on behavioural responses. Therefore, two years ago we established an HAS laboratory at Vancouver's largest maternity hospital.[2]

Sucking is one of the few activities over which young infants have good motor control. Infants are born with a sucking reflex and in the first months of life they suck not only for food but, as any observant parent knows, they also suck on virtually any object they can get in their mouth! Fortunately, sucking behaviour can be easily conditioned; therefore, the HAS technique is an ideal way to measure newborns' perceptual abilities. This technique was used by Siqueland and DeLucia (1969), who used visual reinforcement to condition infants' sucking. In their experiments, strength of sucking directly controlled the brightness of a visual display, and they showed that 4-month-olds can learn the contingency between sucking and presentation of a light.

In 1971, Eimas, Siqueland, Jusczyk, and Vigorito adapted the HAS procedure to assess 1- to 4-month-old infants on their ability to discriminate /ba/ versus /pa/ stimuli. Although adult listeners can easily distinguish between /ba/ and /pa/, they typically fail to discriminate within-category acoustic variations of /ba/ or /pa/ (Lisker & Abramson, 1970). To assess whether infants show this same pattern of "categorical perception", Eimas et al. presented infants in the experimental group with a between-category shift (e.g. /ba$_4$/-/pa$_1$/) and presented infants in the control group with a within-category shift (e.g. /ba$_1$/-/ba$_4$/). Stimuli were synthetically prepared such that the voice onset time differences between the pre-shift and shift tokens were equal for both between-category and within-category conditions. Results showed that infants increased their sucking rate after the between-category /ba$_4$/-/pa$_1$/ shift but not after the within-category shifts for either /ba/ or /pa/; therefore, it appears that, like adults, infants perceive speech in a categorical manner (categorical perception in infants is discussed in Chapter 5). This study, and later ones, demonstrate that the HAS procedure can be profitably used to describe discrimination abilities in very young infants.

Implementing the HAS procedure

In the standard HAS procedure, the infant is placed in a reclining seat, with a loudspeaker and, in some cases, a picture screen located on the ceiling above the infant. The room is dimly lit to discourage distractions. A pacifier is placed in the baby's mouth and is gently held there throughout the experiment, either by some kind of mechanical device (we attach the pacifier to the end of a goose-neck microphone stand) or by an experimenter.[3] The pacifier is connected to a pressure transducer via a plastic tube. The pressure transducer sends electric signals of various strengths, proportional to the strengths of sucks, to a computer. The sucks reaching or exceeding a pre-set level of sucking activate the auditory and visual reinforcers. Many currently used HAS procedures take into account each individual infant's sucking strength when determining the criterion level of sucking, rather than using one predetermined level for all infants. To determine an individual infant's sucking strength, the infant sucks in silence for one or two minutes prior to presentation of the stimulus and the computer calculates the level of high-amplitude sucking for that infant.[4] Subsequently, strong sucks are reinforced by an auditory and/or a visual stimulus. The number of high-amplitude sucks are recorded by the computer.

To assess infants' speech discrimination ability, several modifications were made to the original procedure. In our HAS lab, high-amplitude sucks are reinforced with presentation of an auditory stimulus (or category of auditory stimuli). One stimulus or category is presented in the *habituation phase*. Following achievement of a habituation criterion, the *shift (or test) phase* occurs. For infants in the experimental group, a different stimulus (or set of stimuli) is presented; for infants in the Control Group, the same stimulus is presented. As with the VH procedure, if infants in the experimental group detect the change in stimulus, the sucking rate is expected to increase at the beginning of the Shift Phase; since infants in the Control Group receive the same stimulus, no change in sucking rate is expected.

The criterion for reaching habituation varies from laboratory to laboratory.[5] A common criterion is a 25% decline in sucking rate for two consecutive minutes in comparison to the immediately preceding two minutes. To compensate for the great variability in sucking responses in the initial minutes of speech presentation, habituation criterion calculations often only start from the third minute. Once the habituation criterion is reached, the procedure automatically switches to the shift phase, which lasts four minutes.

When using the HAS procedure, data analysis is usually similar to that with the VH procedure. The number of high-amplitude sucks during the final habituation window (e.g. the final 2 minutes if the window size is 2 minutes) is compared to the number of high-amplitude sucks during either the first 2 minutes or the full 4 minutes of the post-shift phase. Here, as in the VH procedure, it is imperative that there be both an experimental group, where a change in speech sound or category is presented in the post-shift phase, and a control group, where the same stimuli or category continues to be presented. It is also important to examine initial sucking rate across the groups to ensure that there are no systematic differences. Finally, researchers often compare the sucking rate during the initial 2 minutes and the final 2 minutes of the habituation period to ensure that habituation has occurred.

Age variations

The HAS paradigm is suitable for testing infants from birth to almost 1 month, and from 2 to 4 months. The procedure does not work well with 1-month-olds because infants at this age, for some reason, show little interest in sucking.

There is strong evidence that 2- to 4-month-olds are indeed able to learn the contingency between high-amplitude sucks and the presentation of stimuli (e.g. Siqueland & DeLucia, 1969; Trehub & Chang, 1977; Williams & Golenski, 1978). The sucking rate reliably increases when high-amplitude sucks are linked to the presentation of a stimulus. However, whether younger infants can learn this contingency is somewhat controversial (Floccia, Christophe, & Bertoncini, 1997). Newborn infants do suck in response to interesting stimuli and do reduce their sucking rate after repeated trials, but it is still unclear whether newborns can learn that stimulus presentation is linked to their sucking behaviour. In light of this recent finding, the question of whether or not data collected from newborns are directly comparable to data collected from older infants needs to be reconsidered.

Questions addressed using the HAS procedure

Since the pioneering study by Eimas et al. (1971), the HAS paradigm has been adopted in a number of speech laboratories across North America and Europe. Extensive studies have examined infants' ability to discriminate phonetic contrasts as well as their initial representations of speech (see Kuhl, 1987). The HAS procedure has shown that young infants are capable of discriminating a wide range of speech contrasts based on one phonetic feature distinction such as voice-onset time and place of articulation. Not only are young infants able to discriminate contrasts that occur in their native language environment, but they can also discriminate contrasts that do not appear in their native language (Eimas, 1975; Trehub, 1976). Thus, it was research using the HAS procedure that first led to the hypothesis that infants are born with an innate capacity for distinguishing phonetic contrasts in any human language.

The HAS procedure has been adapted to assess whether infants are capable of more sophisticated types of categorisation. As mentioned earlier, the CHT procedure has shown that 6-month-olds perceive multiple exemplars of a single vowel category. Categorisation can be assessed using the HAS procedure by presenting the infant with multiple stimuli during the habituation phase that share a common characteristic but contain irrelevant variations. During the shift phase, new stimuli with only one key characteristic changed are presented. If the sucking rate increases for the switch stimuli, it might be inferred that the infants have identified the key characteristic and used this information to treat the habituation stimuli as a distinct set.

Using this categorisation variation of the HAS procedure, Bijeljac-Babic, Bertoncini, and Mehler (1993) tested whether neonates are able to discriminate multisyllabic sequences based on the number of syllables. Infants were presented with phonetically variable 2-syllable sequences during the habituation phase followed by phonetically variable 3-syllable sequences during the shift phase. The 4-day-olds treated both the 2- and 3-syllable sequences as two separate sets. However, infants were not able to categorise stimuli based on the number of *phonemes*. Consistent with this finding, Bertoncini, Floccia, Nazzi, and Mehler (1995) have recently shown that neonates cannot categorise stimuli based on the number of morae (a subsyllabic timing unit used in Japanese). Taken together, these studies suggest that the syllable may be a privileged timing unit.

In addition to assessing infants' discrimination and categorisation abilities, the HAS procedure has also been used to study infants' ability to store and remember phonetic information. In an innovative study, Jusczyk, Pisoni, and Mullenix (1992) showed that 2-month-olds can discriminate words such as "bug" versus "dug" even when several different talkers are used, if the infants are tested immediately. However, when exactly the same stimuli are used with a 2-minute delay inserted between the familiarisation and the shift phases, 2-month-olds fail this discrimination task.

We began using the HAS procedure to study infants' sensitivity to syllable form. In English, some syllables receive more stress than others. For example, in the word "printer", the initial syllable carries the strongest stress, whereas in the word "computer" it is the middle syllable that is primarily stressed. In French, all syllables are more evenly stressed. Considerable research shows that English- and French-speaking adults listen differently to words; adults primarily use the cues to syllable structure (e.g. intensity, duration, and the quality of the vowel) that are predominant in their native language (Cutler, Mehler, Norris, & Sgui, 1986). It is likely that all of these cues are available to the foetus. Therefore, in a collaborative study with Josiane Bertoncini, we are testing whether newborns are sensitive to the language-specific cues that specify syllable form. Is one instantiation of syllable form more "natural" than another, or are newborns able to process any of the syllable forms that are used across the world's languages? To address these questions, we are testing newborns in an HAS procedure in our Vancouver laboratory. We also plan to conduct this set of studies in Paris with French-learning infants in order to test whether or not newborns' speech preferences reflect innate biases or prenatal experience.

Strengths and limitations of the procedure

The main advantage of the HAS procedure is that it allows us to study perceptual processes of infants as young as a few hours old. By testing such young infants, we can learn what kinds of perceptual biases the infant brings to postnatal life. Cross-cultural extensions help us to understand which perceptual biases have a strong biological basis, which are influenced by prenatal experience, and which are developed through gradual exposure to the language input after birth.

Unlike the more passive physiological measures such as heart rate or ERPs, sucking is a behaviour that can be actively controlled by the infant. Thus, sucking patterns provide information about what infants' sensory systems can detect and, perhaps more interestingly, which differences in sounds are of significance to the infant.

One of the major limitations of the HAS procedure is the high subject drop-out rate. In order for the HAS procedure to be successful, infants must pay attention to the task; infants who are fussy or sleepy have difficulty completing the task. This is problematic when studying newborns, whose states change quickly; it is not unusual for the drop-out rate to be over 50%. A high drop-out rate may skew the results toward overestimating infant abilities, as the infants who stay alert may be different from those who do not (Williams & Golenski, 1979).

Newer variations of the procedure

Since the original Eimas et al. (1971) study, many modifications have been made to the HAS procedure. Two variations will be described here. Spring and Dale (1977) presented infants with a single stimulus (e.g. AAA) during the habituation phase. As in the standard procedure, the control group received the same stimulus in the test phase (e.g. AAA); however, infants in the experimental group were presented with the old stimulus alternating with a new stimulus (e.g. ABABAB).

In another variation of the HAS procedure, Cowan, Suomi & Morse (1982) presented infants in the experimental group with two different stimuli in alternating minutes for a set period of time. Infants in the control group were presented with the same stimulus over and over again. It was expected that the shape of the habituation curve would be quite different for infants in the experimental group compared to infants in the control group. That is, in the experimental group, the sucking rate should increase or stay constant whereas it should decline or stay constant for infants in the control group. This modification has the advantage of reducing the drop-out rate; this is partly because total testing time is reduced to between 9 and 11 minutes, whereas in the standard procedure some infants take up to 15 minutes to habituate before the 2–4 minutes of post-shift trials are even administered.

In a recent study, Sansavini, Bertoncini, and Giovanelli (1997) successfully used the Cowan et al. (1982) alternating procedure to show that Italian newborns are more sensitive to the strong–weak syllable pattern than to some of the other stress patterns used across the world's languages. In our own work we have found that the standard procedure works well when there are multiple instances of a category; however, when testing for discrimination of one single stimulus from another, the alternating variation of the procedure is more successful.

Summary

The HAS procedure is an effective behavioural technique for assessing speech perception in newborns. As relative neophytes to this procedure, we readily admit to the difficulty in learning just how to work with newborns. We can also attest to the very high drop-out rate that occurs if infants are not in a quiet, alert state. Once these conditions are met, however, the HAS procedure is a highly sensitive and reliable tool for assessing competencies and biases across the first 4 months of life.

SUMMARY AND CONCLUSIONS

Although they are not yet able to speak, young infants have a remarkable ability to perceive various aspects of speech. In order to discover exactly what capabilities the infant is born with and develops during the first year of life, researchers must be very innovative when designing experiments. Young infants have a relatively restricted behavioural repertoire; however, infants do make use of a universal nonverbal language of behaviours (e.g. head-turning, looking, sucking). Researchers have designed experimental procedures that allow precise control of desired variables as well as undesirable effects that may falsify interpretations. Three of the most widely used behavioural techniques in the field of infant speech perception are discussed in this chapter: the conditioned head-turn, visual habituation, and high-amplitude sucking procedures.

All three of these methods are based on two well-established phenomena: first, infants have a spontaneous tendency to be interested in novel stimuli; and, secondly, infants are able to learn the contingency between a behavioural response and a new event or new stimulus.

Researchers have exploited these phenomena to ask very precise questions about infant abilities. The HAS procedure, employed with newborns and very young infants, measures the duration and volume of sucking behaviour while presenting the infant with various auditory stimuli. It is based on the premise that infants can learn to increase their sucking intensity in order to hear a sound of interest, and will let that intensity decrease again when the sound is no longer of interest. The CHT procedure trains infants to turn their head when a change occurs in the auditory stimulus; infants are rewarded for correct, but not incorrect, head-turns. Again, it is based on infants' ability to learn the association between a correct head-turn and a reward. The VH procedure presents a visual stimulus (with or without concurrent auditory stimulation) repeatedly until the infant is no longer interested and looks away; a new stimulus is then presented to see if the infant's attention will be engaged once more. In many versions of the VH procedure, the infant learns to control presentation of the stimulus by looking at the visual display. Thus, both a learning component and a preference for novelty form the foundation of this procedure.

Together, these procedures have produced, and continue to produce, exciting findings regarding infant speech perception abilities. These procedures can complement each other because each works best with a different age group and measures different behaviours. The HAS procedure works best with newborns up until about 4 months of age; the VH procedure is most effective with infants 2 months of age and older; the CHT procedure works best with infants between 6 and 12 months of age. Converging evidence from studies using these procedures has allowed us to be quite confident in describing infant speech perception. For example, we now know that infants can discriminate virtually all the phonemic contrasts relevant to all of the world's languages and appear to shift from a language-general to a language-specific strategy within the first year of life; we know that infants can discriminate and categorise speech sounds in a manner similar to adults soon after birth; and we know that infants' perception of speech is influenced by both auditory and visual aspects of the speech signal.

The decision regarding which procedure to employ depends on careful consideration of the research question. The types of issues that must be considered include the age of the infants you wish to study, the independent and dependent variables of interest, the nature of the control group, and the nature of the stimuli. All of these issues stem from the research question. In other words, the linkage between theory and methodology is never haphazard.

In conclusion, with these procedures, and their growing numbers of innovative variations, we are well equipped to tackle the questions that continue to puzzle and challenge us. Mysteries abound in the area of infant speech perception, but the future promises to be an exciting one.

NOTES

1. In the clinical context the procedure is often referred to as VRISD (visually reinforced infant speech discrimination).
2. The HAS laboratory at BC Women's Hospital is part of a collaborative project with J. Bertoncini and J. Mehler of the CNRS in Paris. Our set-up is identical in all respects to their HAS lab in Paris. J. Bertoncini visited UBC twice to train us in HAS procedures.
3. If an experimenter holds the pacifier, it is essential to implement controls to ensure that he/she cannot hear the stimuli that are being presented to the infant and that he/she is completely blind to the experimental condition.
4. There is great deal of variation in the high-amplitude sucking criterion. Some researchers only include the top 33% of an individual infant's sucks, whereas others include as much as 80% of all sucks (Eilers, 1977). The purpose for selecting an appropriate criterion is to reduce individual variability and to allow the infant to learn the contingency.
5. The habituation criterion usually ranges from 20% (Eimas et al., 1971) to 33% (Jusczyk, 1977) decline in sucking rate.

REFERENCES

Ames, E.W., Hunter, M.A., Black, A., Lithgow, P.A., & Newman, F.M. (1978). Problems of observer agreement in the infant control procedure. *Developmental Psychology*, **14**, 507–511.

Bertenthal, B.I., Haith, M.M., & Campos, J.J. (1983). The partial-lag design: A method for controlling spontaneous regression in the infant-control habituation paradigm. *Infant Behavior and Development*, **6**, 331–338.

Bertoncini, J., Floccia, C., Nazzi, T., & Mehler, J. (1995). Morae and syllables: Rhythmical basis of speech representations in neonates. *Language and Speech*, **38**(4), 311–329.

Best, C.T. (1995). Learning to perceive the sound pattern of English. In C. Rovee-Collier & L.P. Lipsitt (Eds.), *Advances in infancy research* (Vol. 9). Norwood, NJ: Ablex.

Best, C.T., McRoberts, G.W., & Sithole, N.M. (1988). Examination of perceptual reorganiz-ation for nonnative speech contrasts: Zulu click discrimination by English-speaking adults and infants. *Journal of Experimental Psychology*, **14**(3), 345–360.

Bijeljac-Babic, R., Bertoncini, J., & Mehler, J. (1993). How do 4-day-old infants categorize multisyllabic utterances? *Developmental Psychology*, **29**(4), 711–721.

Bohn, O.-S., & Polka, L. (1995). What defines vowel identity in prelingual infants? *Proceed-ings of the International Congress of Phonetic Sciences* (Vol. 1, pp. 130–133). Stockholm, Sweden.

Burnham, D. (1998). Language specificity in the development of auditory-visual speech perception. In R. Campbell, B. Dodd, & D. Burnham (Eds.), *Hearing by eye II: Advances in the psychology of speechreading and auditory-visual speech*. Hove: Psychology Press.

Burnham, D., & Dodd, B. (1996). Auditory–visual speech perception as a direct process: The McGurk effect in infants and across languages. In D. Stark & M. Hennecke (Eds.), *Speech reading by humans and machines*. New York: Springer-Verlag.

Burnham, D.K., Earnshaw, L.J., & Clark, J.E. (1986). Categorical identification of phonemic and non-phonemic bilabial stops by infants, children, and adults. *Speech and Language Research Centre Working Papers*, **4**.

Burnham, D.K., Earnshaw, L.J., & Clark, J.E. (1991). Development of categorical identifi-cation of native and non-native bilabial stops: infants, children and adults. *Journal of Child Language*, **18**, 231–260.

Burnham, D.K., Earnshaw, L.J., & Quinn, M.C. (1987). The development of the categorical identification of speech. In B.E. McKenzie & R.H. Day (Eds.), *Perceptual development in early infancy: Problems and issues*. Hillsdale, NJ: Erlbaum.

Cohen, L.B. (1969). Observing responses, visual preferences, and habituation to visual stimuli in infants. *Journal of Experimental Child Psychology*, **7**, 419–433.

Cohen, L.B., Diehl, R.L., Oakes, L.M., & Loehlin, J.C. (1992). Infant perception of /aba/ versus /apa/: Building a quantitative model of infant categorical discrimination. *Developmental Psychology*, **28**, 261–272.

Cohen, L.B., & Menten, T.G. (1981). The rise and fall of infant habituation. *Infant Behavior and Development*, **4**, 269–280.

Cowan, N., Suomi, K., & Morse, P.P. (1982). Echoic storage in infant perception. *Child Development*, **53**, 984–990.

Cutler, A., Mehler, J., Norris, D., & Sgui, J. (1986). The syllable's differing role in segmentation of French and English. *Journal of Memory and Language*, **25**, 385–400.

Desjardins, R.N., & Werker, J.F. (1995, 29 June–2 July). *4-month-old infants notice both auditory and visual components of speech*. Poster presented at the Seventh Annual Convention of the American Psychological Society, New York.

Desjardins, R.N., & Werker, J.F. (1996, 18–21 April). *4-month-old female infants are influenced by visible speech*. Poster presented at the Xth Biennial International Conference on Infant Studies, Providence, RI.

Desjardins, R.N., & Werker, J.F. (submitted). The interaction of heard and seen speech is not mandatory for infants.

Dix, M.R., & Hallpike, C.S. (1947). The peep-shows. New technique for pure-tone audiometry in young children. *British Medical Journal*, **2**, 719.

Eilers, R.E. (1977). Context sensitive perception of naturally produced stop and fricative consonants by infants. *Journal of the Acoustical Society of America*, **61**, 1321–1336.

Eilers, R.E., Wilson, W.R., & Moore, J.M. (1977). Developmental changes in speech discrimination in infancy. *Journal of Speech Hearing Research*, **20**, 766–780.

Eimas, P.D. (1975). Auditory and phonetic coding of the cues for speech: Discrimination of the [r-l] distinction by young infants. *Perception and Psychophysics*, **18**, 341–347.

Eimas, P.D., & Miller, J.L. (1992). Organization in the perception of speech by young infants. *Psychological Science*, **3**(6), 340–345.

Eimas, P.D., Siqueland, E.R., Jusczyk, P., & Vigorito, V. (1971). Speech perception in infants. *Science*, **171**, 303–306.

Floccia, C., Christophe, A., & Bertoncini, J. (1997). High-amplitude sucking and newborns: The quest for underlying mechanisms. *Journal of Experimental Child Psychology*, **64**, 175–198.

Fowler, C.A., Best, C.T., & McRoberts, G.W. (1990). Young infants' perception of liquid coarticulatory influences on following stop consonants. *Perception and Psychophysics*, **6**, 559–570.

Grieser, P., & Kuhl, P.K. (1989). Categorization of speech by infants: Support for speech-sound prototypes. *Developmental Psychology*, **25**, 577–588.

Haith, M.M. (1986). Sensory and perceptual processes in early infancy. *Journal of Pediatrics*, **109**, 158–171.

Hecox, K., & Burkard, R. (1982). Developmental dependencies of the human brainstem auditory evoked response. *Annals of the New York Academy of Sciences*, **388**, 538–556.

Horowitz, F.D. (1975). Infant attention and discrimination: Methodological and substantive issues. *Monographs of the Society for Research in Child Development*, **39** (Serial no. 158).

Humphrey, K., & Tees, R.C. (1980). Auditory-visual coordination in infancy: Some limitations of the preference methodology. *Bulletin of the Psychonomic Society*, **16**(3), 213–216.

Jusczyk, P.W. (1977). Perception of syllable-final stop consonants by two-month-old infants. *Perception and Psychophysics*, **21**, 450–454.

Jusczyk, P.W., Pisoni, D.B., & Mullenix, J.W. (1992). Some consequences of stimulus variability on speech processing by 2-month-old infants. *Cognition*, **43**, 253–291.

Kagan, J., & Moss, M. (1965). Studies of attention in the human infant. *Merril-Palmer Quarterly*, **11**, 95–127.

Kubaska, C.A., & Aslin, R.N. (1985). Categorization and normalization of vowels by 3-year-old children. *Perception and Psychophysics*, **37**, 355–362.

Kuhl, P.K. (1983). Perception of auditory equivalence classes for speech by infants. *Infant Behavior and Development*, **6**, 263–285.

Kuhl, P.K. (1985). Methods in the study of infant speech perception. In G. Gottlieb & N.A. Krasnegor (Eds.), *Measurement of audition and vision in the first year of postnatal life: A methodological overview*. Norwood, NJ: Ablex.

Kuhl, P.K. (1987). Perception of speech and sound in early infancy. In P. Salapatek & L. Cohen (Eds.), *Handbook of Infant Perception* (Vol. 2, pp. 275–382). New York: Academic Press.

Kuhl, P.K. (1991). Human adults and human infants show a "perceptual magnet effect" for the prototypes of speech categories, monkeys do not. *Perception and Psychophysics*, **50**, 93–107.

Kuhl, P.K., & Meltzoff, A.N. (1982). The bimodal perception of speech in infancy. *Science*, **218**, 1138–1141.

Kuhl, P.K., Williams, K.A., Lacerda, F., Stevens, K.N., & Lindblom, B. (1992). Linguistic experience alters phonetic perception in infants by 6 months of age. *Science*, **255**, 606–608.

Lalonde, C.E., & Werker, J.F. (1995). Cognitive influences on cross-language speech perception in infancy. *Infant Behavior and Development*, **18**, 459–476.

Lisker, L., & Abramson, A.S. (1970). The voicing dimension: Some experiments in comparative phonetics. In *Proceedings of the Sixth International Congress of Phonetic Sciences*, Prague, 1967. Prague: Academia.

McGurk, H., & MacDonald, J. (1976). Hearing lips and seeing voices. *Nature*, **264**, 746–748.

Mehler, J.L., Jusczyk, P.W., Lambertz, G., Halstead, N., Bertoncini, J., & Amiel-Tison, C. (1988). A precursor of language acquisition in young infants. *Cognition*, **29**, 143–178.

Miller, C.L. (1983). Developmental changes in male/female voice classification by infants. *Infant Behaviour and Development*, **6**, 313–330.

Miller, J.L., & Eimas, P.D. (1996). Internal structure of voicing categories in early infancy. *Perception and Psychophysics*, **58**, 1157–1167.

Morgan, J.L. (1994). Converging measures of speech segmentation in preverbal infants. *Infant Behavior and Development*, **17**, 389–403.

Morgan, J.L., & Saffran, J.R. (1995). Emerging integration of sequential and suprasegmental information in preverbal speech segmentation. *Child Development*, **66**(4), 911–936.

Murphy, W.D., Shea, S.L., & Aslin, R.N. (1989). Identification of vowels in "vowelless" syllables by 3-year-olds. *Perception and Psychophysics*, **46**, 375–383.

Olsho, L.W., Koch, E.G., Halpin, C.F., & Carter, E.A. (1987). An observer-based psycho-acoustic procedure for use with young infants. *Developmental Psychology*, **23**, 627–640.

Pegg. J.E., & Werker, J.F. (1997). Adult and infant perception of an English phonetic distinction. *Journal of the Acoustical Society of America*, **102**, 3742–3753.

Pegg, J.E., Werker, J.F., & McLeod, P.J. (1992). Preference for infant-directed over adult-directed speech: Evidence from 7-week-old infants. *Infant Behavior and Development*, **15**, 325–345.

Polka, L., & Bohn, O.-S. (1996). A cross-language comparison of vowel perception in English-learning and German-learning infants. *Journal of the Acoustical Society of America*, **100**, 577–592.

Polka, L., Jusczyk, P.W., & Rvachew, S. (1995). Methods for studying speech perception in infants and children. In W. Strange (Ed.), *Speech perception and linguistic experience: Theoretical and methodological issues in cross-language speech research*. Timonium, MD: York Press.

Polka, L., & Werker, J.F. (1994). Developmental changes in perception of non-native vowel contrasts. *Journal of Experimental Psychology: Human Perception and Performance*, **20**, 421–435.

Rosenblum, L.D., Schmuckler, M.A., & Johnson, J.A. (1997). The McGurk effect in infants. *Perception and Psychophysics*, **59**, 347–357.

Sansavini, A., Bertoncini, J., & Giovanelli, G. (1997). Newborns discriminate the rhythm of multisyllabic stressed words. *Developmental Psychology*, **33**, 3–11.

Siqueland, E.R., & DeLucia, C.A. (1969). Visual reinforcement of non-nutritive sucking in human infants. *Science*, **20**, 224–232.

Spring, D.R., & Dale, P.S. (1977). Discrimination of linguistic stress in early infancy. *Journal of Speech and Hearing Research*, **20**, 224–232.

Summerfield, Q. (1979). Use of visual information for phonetic perception. *Phonetica*, **36**, 314–331.

Suzuki, Y., & Ogiba, Y. (1960). A technique of pure tone audiometry for children under three years of age: Conditioned orientation reflex (C.O.R.) audiometry. *Revue de Laryngologie*, 3–43.

Trehub, S.E. (1976). The discrimination of foreign speech contrasts by infants and adults. *Child Development*, **47**, 466–472.

Trehub, S.E., Bull, D., & Thorpe, L.A. (1984). Infants' perception of melodies: The role of melodic contour. *Child Development*, **55**, 821–830.

Trehub, S.E., & Chang, H. (1977). Speech as reinforcing stimulation for infants. *Developmental Psychology*, **13**, 170–171.

Werker, J.F., Cohen, L., Lloyd, V.L., Casasola, M., & Stager, C.L. (in press). Acquisition of word-object associations by 14-month-old infants. *Developmental Psychology*.

Werker, J.F., & Desjardins, R.N. (1994). Listening to speech in the first year of life. *Current Directions in Psychological Science*, **4**(3), 76–81.

Werker, J.F., Gilbert, J.H., Humphrey, K., & Tees, R.C. (1981). Developmental aspects of cross-language speech perception. *Child Development*, **52**, 349–355.

Werker, J.F., & Lalonde, C.E. (1988). Cross-language speech perception: Initial capabilities and developmental change. *Developmental Psychology*, **24**(5), 672–683.

Werker, J.F., & Tees, R.C. (1984). Cross-language speech perception: Evidence for perceptual reorganization during the first year of life. *Infant Behavior and Development*, **7**, 49–63.

Williams, L., & Golenski, J. (1978). Infant speech sound discrimination: The effects of contingent versus noncontingent stimulus presentation. *Child Development*, **49**, 213–217.

Williams, L., & Golenski, J. (1979). Infant behavioural state and speech sound discrimination. *Child Development*, **50**, 1243–1246.

ACKNOWLEDGEMENTS

This work was supported in part by grants from the Natural Science and Engineering Research Council of Canada to J.F. Werker (OGP0001103) and to L. Polka (OGP0105397). The first portion of this chapter is modified from a paper by Werker, Polka, and Pegg (1997). The conditioned head-turn procedure as a method for testing infant speech perception. *Development and Parenting*, **6**(2), 1–8.

Author Index

Subject Index